Sylvia Mieszkowski, Sigrid Nieberle (Hg.)
Unlaute

Musik und Klangkultur

Sylvia Mieszkowski, Sigrid Nieberle (Hg.)
unter Mitarbeit von Innokentij Kreknin

Unlaute
Noise / Geräusch in Kultur, Medien und Wissenschaften seit 1900

[transcript]

Ermöglicht durch die VolkswagenStiftung, Hannover,
und die Dr. German Schweiger-Stiftung, Erlangen.

Bibliografische Information der Deutschen Nationalbibliothek
Die Deutsche Nationalbibliothek verzeichnet diese Publikation in der Deutschen Nationalbibliografie; detaillierte bibliografische Daten sind im Internet über http://dnb.d-nb.de abrufbar.

© 2017 transcript Verlag, Bielefeld

Die Verwertung der Texte und Bilder ist ohne Zustimmung des Verlages urheberrechtswidrig und strafbar. Das gilt auch für Vervielfältigungen, Übersetzungen, Mikroverfilmungen und für die Verarbeitung mit elektronischen Systemen.

Umschlaggestaltung: Kordula Röckenhaus, Bielefeld
Umschlagabbildung: »Pharao's Dance« von Martin Klimas, 2011,
 © Martin Klimas (www.martin-klimas.de)
Satz: Dr. Innokentij Kreknin
Printed in Germany
Print-ISBN 978-3-8376-2534-9
PDF-ISBN 978-3-8394-2534-3

Gedruckt auf alterungsbeständigem Papier mit chlorfrei gebleichtem Zellstoff.
Besuchen Sie uns im Internet: *http://www.transcript-verlag.de*
Bitte fordern Sie unser Gesamtverzeichnis und andere Broschüren an unter:
info@transcript-verlag.de

Inhalt

I Einleitung

»No purposes. Sounds.«
Periodische Klänge und nicht-periodische Geräusche aus
kulturwissenschaftlicher Perspektive
Sylvia Mieszkowski und Sigrid Nieberle | 11

II Epistem und Geräusch

Das Rauschen bei Foucault
Marion Schmaus | 37

Multiplicities: Noise, Sound and Silence
Ben Byrne | 51

Wie kommen Geräusche in die Sprache?
Wort und Geräusch aus linguistischer Perspektive
Christine Ganslmayer | 73

Der Dreck in der Stimme – eine Spurensuche
Uta von Kameke-Frischling | 103

III Technologien und Bedeutsamkeit von Geräuschen

»Automobile gehen über mich hin.«
Urbane Dispositive akustischer Innervation um 1900
Daniel Morat | 127

Fragrant Steam
Anthony Moore | 149

**Audio Technology and Extraneous Noises –
All Past and No Present?**
George Brock-Nannestad | 161

On the overheard
Brandon LaBelle | 179

IV NOISE OF THE ART: GERÄUSCH UND LITERARISCHER TEXT

**Noise, Whirling Sounds and Narrative Dizziness in
M. P. Shiel's *The House of Sounds***
Sylvia Mieszkowski | 193

»Ur-Geräusch«
Rilkes Betrachtungen eines Unmusikalischen
Thomas Martinec | 219

Noise and Voice
Female Performers in George Meredith, George Eliot and Isak Dinesen
Barbara Straumann | 239

Viel Lärm um *Noise*
Die Aktualität von Shakespeares Caliban
Ina Schabert | 261

V MEDIENEINSATZ: GERÄUSCHE IN VIRTUELLEN WELTEN

Sounds and Vision
Geräusche in Jacques Tatis *Les vacances de Monsieur Hulot* und
David Lynchs *Eraserhead*
Kay Kirchmann | 279

Rauschen im Fernsehen
Kommunikation mit Astronauten
Sven Grampp | 301

»Der Mund entsteht mit dem Schrei.«
Zur Inszenierung der Stimme in Heiner Goebbels' Hörstücken
nach Texten von Heiner Müller
Matthias Warstat | 325

Das Getöse der Wall Street
Die Inszenierung des Börsenhandels als *noise*
Sabine Friedrich | 339

Environmental Audio Programming
Geräusch und Klang in virtuellen Welten
Bettina Schlüter | 363

AUTORINNEN UND AUTOREN | 375

I Einleitung

»No purposes. Sounds.«[1]
Periodische Klänge und nicht-periodische Geräusche aus kulturwissenschaftlicher Perspektive

Sylvia Mieszkowski und Sigrid Nieberle

If a noise annoys you ...

TRANSMEDIATION: »PHARAO'S DANCE«

Das Foto »Pharao's Dance« von Martin Klimas auf dem Buchumschlag entstand aus der Transmediation des gleichnamigen »Pharao's Dance« von Miles Davis, dem ersten Stück auf dem Album *Bitches Brew* aus dem Jahr 1969/70. Seine Betrachtung provoziert die Nähe von Laut, Struktur, Bild und Diskurs und eignet sich deshalb in idealer Weise, um in ein Thema hineinzufinden, das nicht nur medientheoretische und wahrnehmungspsychologische Fragen aufwirft, sondern zugleich an den Rändern der Synästhetik verortet ist und auf der Grenze zwischen Bedeutungslosigkeit und Bedeutungsgenerierung operiert. Zeichen in ihren Strukturen wecken Aufmerksamkeit und wollen gedeutet werden, sofern ihre Bedeutung nicht in ihrer Unstrukturiertheit selbst liegt.

Martin Klimas ist ein deutscher Hochgeschwindigkeitsfotograf, der sich mit der Frage beschäftigt: »What does sound look like?«[2] Mit seinen »Sonic Sculptures« greift er ein kreatives Prinzip auf, das die Akustiklehre des 19. Jahrhunderts hervorbrachte. Ernst Florens Friedrich Chladni beschrieb 1797 in seinen *Entdeckungen über die Theorie des Klanges* als erster das Phänomen, dass sich aufgestreuter Sand mit Hilfe der Eigenfrequenz von dünnen Metallplatten in visuell eindrucksvollen Mustern organisieren lässt, wenn man sie mit einem Geigenbogen anstreicht. Dieses Verfahren wurde Ende des 19. Jahrhunderts von Henry Holbrook Curtis weiterentwickelt. Anstatt Sand auf

---
1 | Cage: Experimental Music: Doctrine (1955), S. 17.
2 | Bosmann: Painting With Sound; http://www.martin-klimas.de/de/news.html (30.9.16).

dünne Metallplatten zu streuen, spannte er eine Membran über einen Hohlkörper. Die auf der Membran entstandenen Grafiken konnte er bereits fotografisch archivieren. Mit diesem Verfahren war Curtis in der Lage, periodische Eigenfrequenzen nicht nur für Chladnis Metallplatten, sondern Töne aus jeglichem Instrument oder der menschlichen Stimme synästhetisch zu visualisieren.[3]

Der Arzt und Naturforscher Hans Jenny führte die Forschungen in der Tradition von Chladni und Curtis insofern fort, als er Wellenphänomene für vielfältige Visualisierungsmethoden von Klängen nutzte und als Wissenschaft der Kymatik (Cymatics) zu systematisieren versuchte;[4] mit seinen Arbeiten inspirierte er später den Fotografen Martin Klimas. Dessen »Sonic Sculptures« entstehen, indem er eine Membran über eine Lautsprecherbox spannt und eine Farbzusammenstellung auf die Membran aufbringt, bevor ein Musikstück daraus erklingt. Die Farben folgen der von der Musik ausgelösten Membranschwingung, wenn sie von den Impulsen der Schallwellen hochgeschleudert werden.[5] Mehr als 1.000 Bilder benötigt Klimas, bis die Schwingungen verschiedener Musikstücke in entsprechende Farbskulpturen gebannt sind.

Das Foto »Pharao's Dance« setzt die Zeit aus: Laokoonianisch friert es den Augenblick einer auralen Gegenwart ein, die keine Bedeutungszuschreibung erlaubt, wie sie sonst den Gesetzmäßigkeiten sonischer Rezeption folgt.[6] Erst der vorhergehende oder nachfolgende Laut/Ton stiftet die Bedeutung zum fraglichen Klang, der gedeutet sein will. Steht der Faktor Zeit nicht in gewohnter Weise zur Verfügung, hilft der Diskurs aus: Der Titel »Pharao's Dance« weckt Assoziationen, lässt womöglich Kenner des Stückes innerlich aufhorchen und provoziert die schriftbildliche Interpretation eines vielleicht noch niemals Gehörten. Wenn dieses Foto von Klimas nun 2014 wiederum für die Gestaltung eines Albums von Miles Davis verwendet wird,[7] greift es seinerseits in die Rezeption der Musik und ihrer klanglichen Zusammenhänge ein. Es entsteht eine veritable synästhetische, transmediale und interstrukturelle Deutungsspirale.

Weder aus der Ansicht des Bildes »Pharao's Dance« noch aus dem Wissen über seine Verfertigung lässt sich schlussfolgern, dass es sich bei Miles Davis' Musik um eine Anhäufung unstrukturierter Laute handelt. Vielmehr

---

3 | Vgl. http://www.tonograph.com/ (30.9.16) für eine digitalisierte Illustration im Netz.
4 | Jenny: Kymatik. Wellenphänomene und Schwingungen.
5 | Vgl. das Video »Martin Klimas Making of«, https://vimeo.com/90840430 (30.9.16).
6 | Vgl. Ernst: Im Medium erklingt die Zeit.
7 | Miles At The Fillmore: Miles Davis 1970: The Bootleg Series Vol. 3, 4 CDs, veröffentlicht 2014. Die CDs enthalten veröffentlichte Gigs aus dem »Fillmore East« in New York und bisher unveröffentlichte Mitschnitte aus dem »Fillmore« in San Francisco aus dem Jahr 1970.

suggeriert die visuelle Transformation eines den Regelmäßigkeiten und Regelbrüchen des Jazz bzw. JazzRock (Fusion) unterliegenden Stücks, dass ein prekäres Verhältnis von Struktur und Unstrukturiertheit gegeben ist, das wiederum aus den auralen Ereignissen und deren spezifischer Transmediation entstanden sein muss. Was als Ursache der spontanen Eruption der Farbe zu vermuten ist, erschließt sich gerade nicht durch eine strukturelle Homologiebildung, wie sie die Chladni'schen Klangfiguren noch nahelegten. Dennoch vermittelt das Foto sowohl ästhetische als auch epistemologische Aspekte, weil es mit Farbe und Form auch Aspekte aus der Forschungsgeschichte der Akustik aufruft. Das große Potential dieser ereignishaften Skulpturenfotografie kann im physiologischen Reiz auraler Anschauungsformen liegen, die ihrerseits von den Möglichkeiten synästhetischer Transmediationen abhängig sind: Wie über Sound und seine Strukturen sprechen und schreiben? Wie darstellen und ausstellen? Wie verstehen und reflektieren?

SOUND STUDIES UND AUDITIVE STUDIEN

Nach Unlauten zu forschen, gehört zu den Erkenntnisinteressen der Sound Studies, die sich der kulturwissenschaftlichen Erforschung von Schall widmen. Zu den Unlauten zählen wir Laute, die mit Negationen bezeichnet werden (*un-strukturiert, un-sinnig, un-intendiert, un-schön, un-passend* etc. pp.), so dass Hörgewohnheiten und kulturelle Konventionen demzufolge auf der anderen Seite von kultureller Sinnstiftung und Funktionalität stehen – und zwar so lange, bis sie wahrgenommen und mit Bedeutung belegt werden. In interdisziplinärer und intermedialer Perspektivierung gilt es deshalb zunächst, zu einer qualitativen und quantitativen Ausdifferenzierung von Schall, Geräuschen, Lärm, Tönen in musikalischen Grenzbereichen zu gelangen, um deren kommunikative und soziale Bedingungen, Funktionen und Auswirkungen zu beschreiben.

Der Erforschung dieser damit aufgerufenen ästhetischen, sozialen und semiotischen Dimensionen widmen sich in den letzten Jahren verstärkt Forscherinnen und Forscher aus kultur- und geisteswissenschaftlichen Disziplinen. Hierzu ist es nötig, auditive und visuelle mit diskursiven Forschungsansätzen zu verbinden. Während der letzten fünfzehn Jahre hat sich in der angloamerikanischen Forschung das Fach der Sound Studies etablieren können, das seither auch in größeren Zusammenhängen reüssiert und sich immer weiter ausdifferenziert. Von einem Boom der US-amerikanischen Forschung zu auditiven Kulturen zu sprechen, erscheint nicht übertrieben. Wichtige Meilensteine für die Institutionalisierung und breite Rezeption dieses Forschungsansatzes sind die Gründung der ESSA (European Sound Studies Association) sowie Publikationen wie Veit Erlmanns *Reason and*

Resonance: A History of Modern Aurality (2010), *The Sound Studies Reader* von Routlegde, den Jonathan Sterne herausgab (2012), das von Karin Bijsterveld und Trevor Pinch herausgegebene *Oxford Handbook of Sound Studies* aus dem selben Jahr und jüngst der von Jens Gerrit Papenburg und Holger Schulze herausgegebene Band *Sound as Popular Culture. A Research Companion* der MIT-Press (2016).[8] Rasch konnten eindrückliche Analysen das Forschungsdesiderat verdeutlichen, etwa die Frage, warum das von Potenz und Status kündende Motorengeräusch seit den 1920er Jahren einen wichtigen Verkaufsfaktor für die Autoindustrie liefert, während andere Bauteile der Fahrzeuge und aerodynamische Einflüsse möglichst keine störenden Geräusche verursachen sollen: »[...] engineers had begun stressing that mechanical friction and noise were two sides of the same coin and that noise reduction implied greater motor efficiency and longer engine lifespan.«[9] Das Beispiel zeigt zugleich, wie stark die Wahrnehmung und – in diesem Fall empfindlich unterschiedliche – Bewertung von Geräuschen vom Kontext ihrer jeweiligen Rezeption abhängen.

Mit dem Etikett der Sound Studies sind inzwischen auch in der deutschsprachigen Forschung zahlreiche kulturwissenschaftliche Studien entstanden, die sich sowohl der Theorie als auch der historisch und kulturell variablen Praxis von Klangproduktion, -rezeption und -interpretation widmen.[10] Damit haben auch die etablierte Musikwissenschaft und Musikliteraturforschung entscheidende Impulse zur interdisziplinären und internationalen Erweiterung und Vernetzung erhalten,[11] liegen einem traditionellen Verständnis von Musik doch traditionell die Abwertung von Lärm und Geräusch als ästhetisches Qualitätskritierium zugrunde.[12] Es ist davon auszugehen,

---

8 | Weitere wichtige Monographien und Anthologien zu Soundscapes und Hörkulturen sind: Bijsterveld: Mechanical Sound; Bull: Sound Moves; Bull und Back (Hg.): The Auditory Culture Reader; Dolar: A Voice and Nothing More; Connor: Dumbstruck; Goodman: Sonic Warfare; Hendy: Noise; Kahn: Noise Water Meat; LaBelle: Acoustic Territories; Nancy: Listening; O'Callaghan: Sounds; Smith: The Acoustic World of Early Modern England; Smith (Hg.): Hearing History; Smith: Listening to Nineteenth-Century America; Thompson: The Soundscape of Modernity; Sterne: The Audible Past; Voegelin: Listening to Noise and Silence; Weheliye: Phonographies.

9 | Bijsterveld und Cleophas: Selling Sound, S. 104; vgl. umfassender Bisterveld et al.: Sound and Safe.

10 | Ernst und Mungen (Hg.): Sound und Performance; Meyer (Hg.): ə'ku:stik tə:n; Schulze (Hg.): Sound Studies.

11 | Vgl. Schlüter: Musikwissenschaft als Sound Studies; Hongler et al. (Hg.): Geräusch – das Andere der Musik. Beispielhaft für eine Einzelanalyse vgl. Heinz: Urban Opera (2013).

12 | Noch ganz diesem Verständnis zeigt sich der Ansatz des Musikkritikers bei *The New Yorker*, Alex Ross, verpflichtet, der mit seiner Musikgeschichte des 20. Jahrhunderts

dass die bereits erhöhte Aufmerksamkeit in den kultur- und geisteswissenschaftlichen Fächern ein hohes und noch nicht einmal ansatzweise ausgeschöpftes Analysepotential für kulturelle Prozesse generiert. Erste Ansätze zur Bedeutung der menschlichen Stimme über ihre sprachliche und gesangliche Funktion hinaus liegen vor.[13] Trotz vereinzelter Publikationen[14] wird das Spektrum von Geräuschen, sein Zeichenvorrat und dessen Semantisierung im deutschsprachigen Raum erst noch zur vollen Entfaltung für die Kulturanalyse gebracht werden müssen.[15] Die fächerübergreifende Diskussion, die über die bekannten philologisch oder intermedial orientierten Arbeitsansätze hinausgeht, steht darin zweifellos noch sehr am Anfang.

Unlaute: Noise / Geräusch

Für die Konzeption des vorliegenden Bandes war die starke thematische Konzentration auf eine bestimmte Art von Schall entscheidend, weil die Beiträge von Geräuschen ausgehen, die sich ästhetisch, epistemisch und semiotisch ex negativo beschreiben lassen. Ausgehend von jener, noch näher zu erläuternden Unterscheidung zwischen periodischen Klängen und nicht-periodischen Geräuschen, die Hermann Helmholtz 1863 in seiner *Lehre von den Tonempfindungen* getroffen hat, greifen wir die herkömmliche Opposition zwischen Nutz- und Störschall auf, um sie kritisch zu hinterfragen. Auch jüngere Forschungsbeiträge der Sound Studies unterscheiden noch insofern zwischen gewollten und unwillkürlichen Lauten, als sie die Interferenz, den Knall, das Rauschen und Summen als un-sinnige Opposition zu einer semantisch motivierten Sinnstiftung sprachlicher oder musikalischer Art einstufen.[16] Indessen sind unstrukturierte Laute historischer und kultureller Kontingenz unterworfen, bringen ihrerseits Emergenz hervor und bilden einen reichen Zeichenvorrat aus, der neben den akustischen Kriterien auf sein rezeptives und ästhetisches Potential befragt werden sollte.[17] In räumlicher wie identitätsspezifischer und ästhetischer Hinsicht bieten Unlaute den RezipientInnen sowohl Orientierung als auch Desorientierung im

---

unter dem Titel *The Rest is Noise* die kanonische Trennlinie trotz vielfältiger Überschreitungsphänomene explizit aufrechtzuerhalten versucht.

13 | Felderer (Hg.): Phonorama; Kittler, Macho und Weigel (Hg.): Zwischen Rauschen und Offenbarung; Kolesch und Krämer (Hg.): Stimme.
14 | Vgl. Geisel: Nur im Weltraum ist es wirklich still; Gess, Schreiner und Schulz (Hg.): Hörstürze; Herrmann (Hg.): Dichtung für die Ohren.
15 | Vgl. Daiber: Franz Kafka und der Lärm.
16 | Vgl. Keizer: The Unwanted Sound of Everything We Want.
17 | Vgl. Grimshaw und Garner: Sonic Virtuality.

Raum und sorgen für die Stabilisierung und zugleich die Destabilisierung der Wahrnehmung.

John Cage hat mehrfach auf die rezeptionsästhetisch unterschätzte Wirkung von *noise* und Geräuschen pointiert hingewiesen. Zum einen möchten Geräusche häufig nicht überhört werden: »Wherever we are, what we hear is mostly noise. When we ignore it, it disturbs us. When we listen to it, we find it fascinating.«[18] Zum anderen kommt es ganz auf die Hörenden an, denen ein Geräusch begegnet: »Which is more musical: a truck passing by a factory or a truck passing by a music school?«[19] Das bewusste Hin-Hören auf den unstrukturierten Laut wird bisher unerkannte Strukturen zutage treten lassen. Liegt dem häufig zitierten englischen Binnenreim *noise/annoys*[20] noch ein assonierendes Wortspiel und damit ein gewisses Harmoniesignal zugrunde, so zeigt sich die translative Begriffspaarung *Noise/Geräusch*, die wir für den Untertitel gewählt haben, bereits störungsanfälliger: Lediglich die Anmutung des assonierenden Diphtongs oi/äu erlaubt es, hier außerdem von einem un-reinen Reim und vokaler Dissonanz zu sprechen. In der Übersetzung beschreibender Sprache selbst also liegt das kaum zu überschätzende Potential produktiver Störgeräusche, was gleichermaßen für die transmedialen und synästhetischen Übertragungsprozesse in den Sound Studies gelten kann.

Wenn Wissenschaft – wie in der Aufklärung bereits herbeiphantasiert – eine Maschine wäre, dann könnte man an ihr auch die Geräusche schätzen lernen, die in anderen Kontexten negiert werden. Das unter dem Akronym E.A.T. firmierende Künstlerkollektiv »Experiments in Art and Technology« um Robert Rauschenberg, Billi Klüver und Robert Whitman, zu dem auch John Cage später beitrug, arbeitete mit Ansätzen, die technologische, mediale und ästhetische Aspekte neu konzipieren helfen sollten. Überaus inspirierend für die geräusch- und mechanikaffine Kunst des Kollektivs war anfangs eine Skulptur von Jean Tinguely mit dem Titel *Homage to New York*, die 1960 für großes Aufsehen sorgte, denn die riesige Geräuschmaschine vermochte sich mit einer Performance im Garten des Museum of Modern Art unter großem Getöse selbst zu zerstören. Diese eindrucksvolle Konstruktion wurde mit folgender Pressemitteilung beworben:

Recently Tinguely himself has devised machines which shatter the placid shells of Art's immaculate eggs, machines which at the drop of a coin scribble a moustache on the automatistic Muse of abstract expressionism, and (wipe that smile off your face) an apocalyptic far-out breakthrough which, it is said, clinks and clanks, tingels and

---

18 | Cage: The Future of Music: Credo (1937), S. 3.
19 | Cage: Composition as Process (1958), S. 41.
20 | Azar: Understanding and using English grammar, S. 236.

tangels, whirrs and buzzes, grinds and creaks, whistles and pops itself into a katabolic Götterdämmerung of junk and scrap.²¹

Allein die Pressemitteilung über eine Maschine, die mit Geräuschen arbeitet, stellt bereits eine onomatopoetische Leistung dar, die versucht, das Ereignis *sound* für künftige Ausstellungsbesucher zu vermitteln. Auch die unwillkürliche emotionale Reaktion der BesucherInnen – a specific smile on their faces? –, die Geräusche auslösen können, sowie die Aspekte der Archivierung und Mythisierung sind angesprochen. Der Text kündet von Lauten, die neugierig machen. Gerade solche Laute, die un-bekannt und un-erhört sind, können diese Neugierde wecken: sowohl in der Kunst als auch in der Forschung.

Gemeinsamer Ausgangspunkt aller Beiträge in diesem Band ist die Frage, inwieweit unstrukturierte Laute die Wahrnehmung der Umwelt, insbesondere öffentlicher sowie ästhetischer Räume und ihrer medialen Inszenierung, strukturieren helfen. Auch Überlegungen, auf welche Weise figurale und literale Bedeutungszuschreibungen mittels *noise*/Geräusch entstehen und welche epistemologischen Implikationen damit verknüpft sind, spielen generell eine wichtige Rolle für die Sound Studies. Besondere historiographische Bedeutung kommt der Fokussierung auf die Kultur- und Mediengeschichte seit dem ausgehenden 19. Jahrhundert zu. Seither brachten die technischen Möglichkeiten der Schallaufzeichnung spezifische mediale Dispositive und Archive hervor. Die analogen und später digitalen Möglichkeiten der Schallarchivierung und damit auch die technische Basis der Untersuchungsgegenstände vorausgesetzt, lässt sich von einer gemeinsamen Diskussionsgrundlage ausgehen, die sich über die Fächergrenzen hinweg als disparat und produktiv genug erwiesen hat. Sich erst in einem nächsten Schritt auch früheren Zeitabschnitten zu widmen und dabei auf Text- und Bildquellen zu konzentrieren, ist durchaus denkbar und wünschenswert.

KLANG VS. GERÄUSCH

Schall ist akustisch mess- und beschreibbar. Frequenz, Lautstärke, Dauer und Periodizität sind hierfür die wichtigsten Parameter. In seiner *Lehre von den Tonempfindungen als physiologische Grundlage für die Theorie der Musik* (1863) trifft Hermann Helmholtz die folgenreiche akustische Unterscheidung zwischen Geräuschen und musikalischen Klängen:

---

21 | Pressemitteilung Nr. 27, The Museum of Modern Art, 18.3.1960, MoMa, Archives; zitiert nach Battista: E. A. T. – The Spirit of Collaboration, S. 29.

> Das Sausen, Heulen und Zischen des Windes, das Plätschern des Wassers, das Rollen eines Wagens sind Beispiele der ersten Art, die Klänge sämmtlicher [sic] musikalischer Instrumente Beispiele der zweiten Art des Schalls.[22]

Zwar räumt Helmholtz ein, dass sich »Geräusche und Klänge in mannichfach wechselnden Verhältnissen [...] vermischen und durch Zwischenstufen ineinander übergehen« können, hält aber daran fest, dass »ihre Extreme [...] weit voneinander getrennt« seien.[23] Bereits in diesem Konzept scheint die Differenz zwischen musikalischen Klängen und unwillkürlichen, ›natürlichen‹ Lauten als Kontinuum organisiert zu sein. Spätestens seit der Erweiterung des Musikbegriffs durch die Avantgarde und der Einverleibung eben jenes von Helmholtz exemplarisch für alles Geräuschhafte benannten ›Zischens‹, ›Plätscherns‹ und ›Rollens‹ ins Klangliche, durch den *bruitisme* und die *musique concrète,* ist jedoch die kategorische Trennung von Geräuschen vs. Klang hinfällig geworden. Für die exakte Definition von Unlauten scheint die zweite Helmholtz'sche Definition zunächst hilfreicher zu sein:

> Die Empfindung eines Klanges wird durch schnelle periodische Bewegungen der tönenden Körper hervorgebracht, die eines Geräuschs durch nicht periodische Bewegungen.[24]

Genau jene Art von Schall, die hier anhand der nicht-periodischen Bewegung als Geräusch definiert wird, steht im Mittelpunkt der Analysen. Neben seinen physikalischen Charakteristika hat jedoch Schall, zumindest in der Art, wie er wahrgenommen wird, immer auch Komponenten, die historischen und kulturellen Kontingenzen unterliegen.[25]

EINE ÜBERFÄLLIGE AUFWERTUNG: NOISE / GERÄUSCH

Die Rede von Unlauten vermeidet gezielt den Begriff *Lärm,* weil ihm – mehr noch als dem *Geräusch* – eine negative Wertung innewohnt, die es grundsätzlich zu hinterfragen gilt. Voraussetzung für eine Unterscheidung von Klang und Geräusch ist das Ohr des hörenden Subjekts. Technologien, die Geräusche hörbar machen, bedürfen eines »geschulten Ohrs«, um sich als nützlich erweisen zu können.[26] Die Techniken der Auskultation oder der

---

22 | Helmholtz: Die Lehre von den Tonempfindungen, S. 14.
23 | Ebd.
24 | Ebd., S. 16, Sperrung i. Orig.
25 | Vgl. Kursell: Epistemologie des Hörens.
26 | Vgl. Schoon und Volmar: Das geschulte Ohr; Spehr (Hg.): Funktionale Klänge.

Wetterprognostik sind darauf ebenso angewiesen wie Kriegsführung und Fertigungstechniken.

Auch das englische *noise* ist nicht völlig frei von einer pejorativen semantischen Anreicherung. *Noise,* so konstatiert Peter Bailey, nimmt den niedrigsten Platz in der Hierarchie der Klänge ein:

> [to] echo Mary Douglas, on dirt as ›matter out of place‹, we might call noise ›sound out of place‹. In any hierarchy of sounds it comes bottom, the vertical opposite of the most articulate and intelligible of sounds, those of speech and language and their aesthetic translation into music. In the official record such expressions ›make sense,‹ whereas noise in nonsense.[27]

Die von Bailey auf den Punkt gebrachte (Ab-)Wertung des Lärms als Un-Sinn beruht hauptsächlich auf einer dichotomen Begrifflichkeit, die über eine vorgegebene semantische Opposition Bedeutung generiert. Das Gegenteil zu *noise* wären demzufolge *speech, language, music*. Anstatt ein solches Modell einfach zu übernehmen, gilt es das Geräusch aus dieser Dichotomie zu lösen und das ganze Spektrum von Unlauten zu berücksichtigen – etwa mit der Untersuchung unstrukturierter Laute *in* der Sprache und im Text[28] –, um deren Relation zu Sinnstiftung und Wissensproduktion neu zur Diskussion zu stellen. Damit wird der Zugang zu einer unvoreingenommenen Untersuchung kultureller Phänomene frei, der durch die bisherige Opposition von Lärm/Geräusch einerseits und Sprache/Musik andererseits verstellt war.

Seit der Industrialisierung, als mechanischer Lärm ungeahnte Ausmaße annehmen konnte, hat sich Lärm in urbanen und industriell geprägten Lebensräumen zur gesundheitlichen Gefahrenquelle entwickelt.[29] Hinzu kommt, dass die Möglichkeiten der Messtechniken ständig verfeinert wurden und damit zugleich die Tendenzen zur Objektivierung zunahmen. Die subjektiven Zumutbarkeiten von Geräuschimmissionen – hervorgerufen vom Schienen-, Auto- oder Flugverkehr und gemessen in konkreten Dezibelzahlen – gehören zu den umstrittensten Werten moderner Gesellschaften.[30] In zahlreichen Publikationen von und über Initiativen zum Lärmschutz wird ein Ausspruch des Mediziners und Mikrobiologen Robert Kochs kolportiert, der um 1910 gesagt haben soll: »Eines Tages wird der Mensch den Lärm

---

27 | Bailey: Breaking the Sound Barrier, S. 23f.
28 | Vgl. Mieszkowski: Resonant Alterities, S. 218-220.
29 | Vgl. Bijsterveld: Mechanical Sound; Thompson: The Soundscape of Modernity.
30 | Vgl. z.B. Umweltbundesamt: Auswahlbibliographie Lärmschutz. Informationsmaterialien und Linklisten zu Vorschriften, Initiativen und Lärmschutzverbänden auf nationaler und europäischer Ebene bietet der Umweltbund Leipzig e.V. an, http://www.machsleiser.de/infokiste/laermlinks (20.9.16).

ebenso unerbittlich bekämpfen müssen wie die Cholera und die Pest.«[31] Dieser Ausspruch ist ein eindrückliches Beispiel für die kontextabhängige negative Konnotation von Geräuschen, die als störend, beschwerlich und gesundheitsschädigend empfunden werden. Wenn Lärm allerdings wie eine Ansteckungsgefahr behandelt werden muss, dann stellt sich die Frage, wie Koch in einer hochtechnisierten Gesellschaft Lärmerreger minimieren und hierfür die Lärmträger isolieren wollte. Eine Impfung kommt kaum in Frage, es sei denn, das Ziel besteht lediglich darin, den Menschen gegen Lärm immun zu machen. Womöglich könnte man sich auch vor Ansteckung schützen, indem spezifische Filter und Schutzvorrichtungen verwendet werden, zum Beispiel heute in geräuschreduzierenden Kopfhörern (*noise-cancelling headphones*). Kochs Vergleich hinkt allemal.

Die vielzitierte Sentenz, die häufig als Mahnung und Autorisation gleichermaßen dient, ist jedoch selbst ein anschauliches Beispiel dafür, wie die Binarismen von Nutz- und Störschall sich gegenseitig unterlaufen. Denn der Ausspruch verbirgt auch die interessante autoreferentielle Finesse, dass Lärm etymologisch von den Waffen herrührt (ital. *all'arme:* zu den Waffen). Kochs Prognose eines unerbittlichen Kampfes gegen Lärm fügt dieser semantischen Sedimentierung eine weitere Schichtung hinzu. Gegen den militärischen Schlachtruf wird nun der virologische Appell gesetzt, was lediglich dafür sorgt, die dem Lärmdiskurs seit der Industrialisierung eingeschriebene und überaus destruktive Überbietungsdynamik voranzutreiben.[32]

Anstatt Lärm mit rhetorischen und lärmenden Mitteln immer weiter zu übertönen, kann man ihn auch, wie John Cage es zum Programm ausrief, in den Mittelpunkt der Aufmerksamkeit rücken und positiv besetzen. Als ästhetisches Programm mag dies einleuchten; als alltägliche Strategie betroffener Anwohner, die unter dem Fluglärm einer neu gebauten Startbahn in allernächster Nähe leiden, kann das Programm nur zynisch erscheinen. Jacques Attali hat an das Todespotential von Lärm erinnert: »Noise is a weapon and music, primordially, is the formation, domestication, and ritualization of that weapon as a simulacrum of ritual murder.«[33] Spätestens seit dem Bekanntwerden der Foltermethoden amerikanischer Militärs im Irakkrieg hat

---

31 | Zum Beispiel in Noppeney: Erkenntnisfortschritt und fehlende Umsetzung, S. 150 und 153.

32 | Für das 19. Jahrhundert typisch ist Johanna Kinkels Erzählung *Aus dem Tagebuch eines Komponisten* (1849), worin Lärm mit Musik bekämpft werden soll; vgl. Nieberle: FrauenMusikLiteratur, S. 134-145.

33 | Attali: The Political Economy of Music, S. 24.

der Popsong als vermeintlich harmloses Produkt der Unterhaltungsindustrie seine Unschuld verloren.³⁴

Aus diesem Grund sei auch an die zivilen Protestinitiativen erinnert, die Lärm als politisches Instrumentarium und Störsignal einsetzen, weil sie auf diese Weise die Bestrebungen des Staates, Lärm zu monopolisieren, unterlaufen.³⁵ Mit einer Serie von Casseroles-Aktionen protestierten BürgerInnen und Studierende im Mai 2012³⁶ in Montreal gegen die Anhebung der Studiengebühren an kanadischen Universitäten: Sie umgingen damit die Beschränkungen des Versammlungsrechts, weil individuell und im privaten Kontext, mit Töpfen und Pfannen erzeugter Lärm keine anmeldungspflichtige Demonstration darstellt. In Chile sind die sogenannten Cacerolazos bereits seit 1971 bekannt und haben sich seither in südamerikanischen Ländern als Protestform weiter etabliert.³⁷ Als der deutsche Bundespräsident Christian Wulff 2012 unter dem Druck staatsanwaltschaftlicher Ermittlungen vom Amt zurückgetreten war und ihm zu Ehren die Bundeswehr einen Großen Zapfenstreich abhielt, protestierten die Bürgerinnen und Bürger gegen Wulff ebenfalls mit Lärm: Sie schlugen Krach und bliesen darüber hinaus ohrenbetäubend auf Vuvuzelas, um die militärische Zeremonie mit einem Klangteppich aus widerständiger Zivilcourage zu unterlegen.³⁸

Indessen wurden die herkömmlich als Störung konnotierten Geräusche auch erkenntnistheoretisch aufgewertet, weil sie für kultur- und medienwissenschaftliche Analysen überaus produktiv sein können. So lässt sich in der Störung nicht nur die bedrohliche Zerstörung einer bestehenden Struktur erkennen, sondern auch ein initiativer Impuls »für die Entstehung neuer Ordnung«.³⁹ Mit Helmholtz gesprochen, überlagern sich in der Störung periodische und nicht-periodische Schallwellen; oder es werden periodische Schwingungsmuster von nicht-periodischen abgelöst. Klang wird dann zum Geräusch, wenn er in seiner Periodizität nicht wahrgenommen wird; Geräusche aber werden zum Lärm, wenn sie keinen Ort und keine Funktion haben. Der Kulturhistoriker Hillel Schwartz betont, welch reiches Forschungsfeld sich jenen öffnet, die sich diesem Phänomen der Negation widmen:

---

34 | Vgl. Grüny: Von der Sprache des Gefühls zum Mittel der Qual; Pieslak: Sound Targets. Vgl. auch Steve Goodman: Sonic Warfare.
35 | Vgl. Attali: The Political Economy of Music, S. 19.
36 | https://www.youtube.com/watch?v=4MdeH-pkLtg (30.9.16).
37 | Vgl. Andrada: Cacerolas y Plumas.
38 | Vgl. die auditiv unterschiedlich ausgestaltete Berichterstattung der TV-Sender n24: https://www.youtube.com/watch?v=WYe0-euBEPM (30.9.16) und Phoenix: https://www.youtube.com/watch?v=nNsi9feE9_Y (30.9.16).
39 | Vgl. Kümmel und Schüttpelz: Medientheorie der Störung / Störungstheorie der Medien, S. 9.

The everyday definition of noise is ›any unwanted sound‹. What an opening for a historian! By its very definition, noise is an issue less of tone or decibel than of social temperament, class background, and cultural desire, all historically conditioned.[40]

Es sind vor allem diese sozialen Faktoren und kulturellen Dimensionen der Unlaute, die mit der vermeintlichen Eigenschaft des Ungewollten und Unwillkürlichen belegt werden. Diese Zuschreibungen provozieren nachzufragen, welche und wessen Interessen sich in diesen Wertungen ausmachen lassen. Mit Hilfe solcher Überlegungen wird nicht zuletzt die Vielschichtigkeit von Unlauten als kulturelle bedeutungs- und identitätsstiftende, jedoch gleichermaßen destabilisierende Größe in der Moderne und Postmoderne zutage treten.

DIE BEITRÄGE IM ÜBERBLICK

Die Beiträge des Bandes nähern sich Unlauten aus den unterschiedlichen Perspektiven ihrer Fachdisziplinen, die geschichts-, literatur-, medien-, musik-, theaterwissenschaftlich oder philosophisch geprägt, aber darauf nicht beschränkt sind. Ein erster wissenschaftshistorischer Abschnitt kehrt die Produktivität von Unlauten in der Philosophie, Diskurstheorie, Sprachwissenschaft und Stimmbildung hervor, wenn man sich erst dem »Rauschen« im Diskurs oder dem »Dreck in der Stimme« zuwendet. Funktion und Bewertung von Geräuschen in Technik und Technikgeschichte diskutieren die Beiträge zu Soundscapes der Großstadt, zu Möglichkeiten der Schallarchivierung und zu Wahrnehmungsstrategien im öffentlichen Raum. Der Repräsentation von Unlauten und ihrer performativen Dimension widmen sich die beiden folgenden Kapitel zu Geräuschen im literarischen Text, in Film und Fernsehen, in der Performancekunst und in Computerspielen. In allen Beiträgen werden die problematischen Kategorien des Unwillkürlichen und Nicht-Periodischen besonders deutlich. Darüber hinaus sind ihnen epistemologische Überlegungen insofern gemeinsam, also sie danach fragen, inwiefern Lärm, Geräusche, Klänge, Laute an Wissensgenerierung beteiligt sind und inwieweit sie selbst in epistemischen Modellen Berücksichtigung finden.

MARION SCHMAUS' Beitrag zum »Rauschen bei Foucault« setzt bei der Relation zwischen Rauschen und Botschaft in Claude E. Shannons Kommunikationsmodell an. Weil in diesem Kontext das Störgeräusch die nicht-hermeneutische Ordnungsstruktur des Modells überhaupt erst hervorbringt, werden Kommunikation und Rauschen nicht nur gleich-ursprünglich

---

[40] | Schwartz: On Noise, S. 52. Vgl. auch Augoyard und Torgue (Hg.): Sonic Experience.

gedacht, sondern sie stehen auch gleichberechtigt nebeneinander. Diese Erkenntnis dient Schmaus als Basis der Auseinandersetzung mit einigen von Michel Foucaults Schriften aus den 1980er Jahren, die sich auf die Verortung der Metapher des Rauschens im Spannungsfeld von Diskurs und Gegendiskurs konzentrieren. Das traditionelle Modell versteht den kranken Körper als rauschenden Kanal, der das »Nichtschweigen der Organe«, das seinerseits von der Medizin hörbar gemacht und gedeutet werden muss, als Botschaft überträgt (Balint). Diesem Entwurf setzt Foucault einen nachrichtentechnisch inspirierten entgegen, demzufolge medizinische Codes das Rauschen des Körpers nicht hörbar machen, sondern zum Schweigen bringen. Das rhetorisch-emphatisch aufgeladene Rauschen wird so als das ›Andere‹ der Vernunft konturiert. Zeigt sich dieser Prozess vom Diskurs der Aufklärung dominiert, so wird dieses Andere durch die Etikettierung als ›Wahnsinn‹ systematisch zum Verstummen gebracht. Als Gegendiskurs fungiert die Literatur, die, weil sie auf nichts Anderes verweist als auf sich selbst, Rauschen und Diskurs aneinander annähert und auf diese Weise ihr subversives Potential, das im Sprechen im Angesicht der Macht besteht, entfaltet.

BEN BYRNES Argument in »Multiplicities: Sound, Noise and Silence« hat zur Prämisse, dass die Konzeptualisierung von Klang als ›Ding‹ (das als Gegenteil der Stille und im Kontrast zu Lärm verstanden wird) hoffnungslos in Essentialismen verstrickt und deswegen zu ersetzen ist. Byrnes Vorschlag besteht darin, Klang, Stille und Lärm stattdessen als sich gegenseitig konstituierende Vielfältigkeiten (mit physischen, wahrnehmungsspezifischen und begrifflichen Facetten) zu verstehen. John Cages *4'33'*, eine Performance des Fluxus-Künstlers Yasunao Tone auf dem UTS Music.Sound.Design-Symposium 2008 und eine Arbeit der Künstlergruppe Wandelweiser von 2012, die den Titel *Wandelweiser und so weiter* trägt, dienen ihm als Objekte einer Analyse, die mit Begriffen von Henri Bergson, Gilles Deleuze und Michel Serres operiert. So kann Byrne aufzeigen, dass Cage sich vor allem für die Vielfältigkeit des Klangs interessiert; wie es Tone gelingt, sein Publikum die Vielfältigkeit des Lärms erfahren zu lassen; und welche Fortschritte Wandelweiser dabei macht, die Vielfältigkeit der Stille zu erkunden.

CHRISTINE GANSLMAYERS Untersuchung der Frage »Wie kommen die Geräusche in die Sprache?« setzt sich aus linguistischer Perspektive mit der Codierung von Lauten in sprachlichen Zeichen auseinander, insbesondere mit der Beziehung zwischen Sprache und Umgebungsgeräuschen. Als Zeichenbenutzer verarbeiten Menschen Schall immer mit Hilfe von Schall. Da sprachliche Zeichen arbiträr und konventionalisiert sind, können geräuschbezeichnende sowie geräuschnachahmende sprachliche Zeichen nicht grundsätzlich als unstrukturiert gelten. Die Konzeptualisierung des Schallereignisses als Hörereignis setzt voraus, dass ein unbekanntes Geräusch in Beziehung zu erlernten Geräuschmustern gesetzt und dabei qualitativ bewertet wird. In diesem Zusammenhang stellt Ganslmayer die Frage, ob und inwieweit die Art und Weise, wie Geräusche sprachlich kodiert werden, Rückschlüsse auf unsere Einstellung zu Geräuschen zulässt. Die Analyse von onomatopoetischen Verben (in journalistischem Sprachgebrauch, Lyrik und Comic-Sprache), die sowohl phonologisch wie morphologisch untersucht werden, mündet im Postulat eines Zusammenhangs zwischen dem Fehlen von Klassifikationsmodellen und der auffälligen semantischen Vagheit im Bereich geräuschbezeichnender Lexeme.

Ausgehend von der klassischen Gesangspädagogik und der ihr inhärenten Verteilung der Definitionsmacht im Meister-Schüler-Prinzip untersucht UTA VON KAMEKE-FRISCHLING Geräuschanteile in der menschlichen Singstimme, ihre anatomischen Ursprünge und akustischen Aspekte, ihre Reduktion durch Gesangstechnik und jene historisch variierenden kulturellen Zuschreibungen, die sich an verschiedene Stimmgeräusche anlagern. Vielfach ist die Vorstellung vom »Dreck in der Stimme« anzutreffen, was der Beitrag im Titel aufnimmt und im Spannungsfeld zwischen theoretischem Musikwissen und tatsächlicher Gesangsperformanz untersucht. Ute von Kameke-Frischling sieht in Geräuschen ihr epistemisches und kreatives Potential. Unter dieser Voraussetzung diskutiert sie kritisch das Verhältnis von stimmlicher Tragfähigkeit und Geräuscharmut bzw. das von Geräusch als Ordnungsstörung und vermeintlicher Authentizität der Stimme. Die genrespezifische Ab- oder Umwertung unstrukturierter Laute und ihrer Produktion wird dabei als jener Punkt identifiziert, vom dem aus sich sowohl die Definition von Musikkultur als auch ein mit ihr kompatibles Körperverständnis operationalisieren lassen.

Sektion III des Bandes widmet sich »Technologien und Bedeutsamkeit von Geräuschen« und wird von DANIEL MORATS Beitrag »›Automobile gehen über mich hin.‹ Urbane Dispositive akustischer Innervation um 1900« eröffnet. Als Ausgangspunkt seiner Untersuchung, wie die moderne Großstadt als dynamisierter Hör- und Klangraum textuell repräsentiert wird, dient Morat der Begriff der »Innervation«, den Walter Benjamin in seinem Kunstwerkaufsatz einführt. Inspiriert durch Peter Baileys Übertragung der Benjamin'schen »Innervation« vom Bereich des Visuellen in den des Akustischen, diskutiert Morat den Zusammenhang von auditiver Reizstruktur und »gesteigertem Nervenleben« (Simmel). Die Untersuchung des Verhältnisses von Nervositäts- und Lärmdiskurs in zeitgenössischen Texten mündet in die These, dass urbane Diskurse akustischer Innervation über die Frage der neuropathologischen Qualität des Großstadtlärms beziehungsweise der krankhaften Nervosität der unter ihm Leidenden hinausgehen, indem sie neben Krankheit und Degeneration auch Aspekte der Kultivation und modernen Zivilisation kommunizieren.

ANTHONY MOORES zwischen Wissenschaft und verschriftlichter Performanz changierender Beitrag »Fragrant Steam« setzt sich mit einer von John Cages *Roaratorio* und James Joyces *Finnegans Wake* inspirierten Passage auseinander, die die Klanglichkeit der Sprache in den Vordergrund rückt. Moore zeigt zunächst, dass sich die vermeintliche Grenze, die »Rauschen« klar von »Information« zu trennen scheint, bei genauer Untersuchung auflöst, um im nächsten Schritt der These von der Allursprünglichkeit des Geräuschs nachzugehen, wobei er *noise* – sowohl akustisch als auch auf atomarer Ebene – als dynamisches System beschreibt. Die »raw mass of primal sound« diskutiert Moore in den Dimensionen der Simultaneität und der Dauer, wobei ihm Rainer Maria Rilkes Text über das »Ur-Geräusch« als Ausgangspunkt dient. Anschließend widmet sich der Beitrag dem Geräusche produzierenden Ohr – sowohl in seiner gesunden als auch in zweien seiner erkrankten Formen des nieder-frequenten Tinnitus und der auditiven Halluzination. Gefragt wird nach der idealen Position des individuellen Hörens als einem gleichsam intra-subjektiven *sweet spot*: dieser müsste eindringendes Hören begünstigen, das Raum lässt für ein »three-part voicing of the one, the other, and the both«.

In seinem Beitrag »Audio Technology and Extraneous Noises – All Past and No Present?« konzentriert GEORGE BROCK-NANNESTAD sich auf Geräusche, die bis vor relativ kurzer Zeit noch Teil jeder Rezeption von Tonaufnahmen waren, jüngst aber aus unserem Hör-Alltag verschwunden sind. Vor der Erfindung von Digitalisierungstechnologie waren Tonaufnahmen geradezu durch Geräusche charakterisiert, die entweder ein unvermeidliches Nebenprodukt des Aufnahmeprozesses waren oder während des Abspielens produziert wurden. Brock-Nannestad plädiert dafür, dass unsere Hörerfahrung eine wichtige Dimension einbüßt, wenn wir uns damit zufriedengeben, die Rolle von Geräuschen zu ignorieren. Um die ausdifferenzierte Diskussion von Hörpraktiken zu bereichern, evaluiert dieser medienhistorische Beitrag eine Reihe von spezifischen Geräuschen, die bei der Aufnahme und dem Abspielen von Tonaufnahmen auf unterschiedlichen Geräten (Phonograph, Grammophon, Pianola, Plattenwechsler, Musikautomat, Plattenspieler, Hi-Fi Installationen, Walkman) entstehen oder sich ihrer medialen Materialität verdanken (Zylinder, Schallplatte, Tonband, Schellack, Vinyl etc.). Diese kleine Geräuschgeschichte reicht bis in die Gegenwart, seitdem der als allzu ›rein‹ empfundene Klang der CD das Beimischen artifiziell produzierter Geräusche (›dither‹) notwendig macht, um dem Geschmack der Musikkonsumenten zu entsprechen.

BRANDON LABELLES Beitrag »On the overheard« führt *noise* als generatives Prinzip des Sozialen ein. Gegebenenfalls birgt diese Form des Geräuschs die Gefahr der Konfrontation – dann nämlich, wenn Schall das übersteigt, was historisch und kulturell als zumutbare Grenze verhandelt wurde; sie eröffnet jedoch zugleich die Chance, neue Möglichkeiten für zwischenmenschlich produzierte Klangkonfigurationen zu eröffnen. LaBelle ruft zu einer neuen Kunst des (Zu-)Hörens auf, die das Geräusch als Erfahrungsraum konzipiert und sich in drei Dimensionen entfaltet: der multiplen Akustiken, des Supplements und der Unterscheidungsproduktion. Insgesamt ergeben diese drei Dimensionen die Koordinaten der Interferenz, die ihrerseits als Einsatzpunkt für eine neue Form der Sozialität gelten muss. (Zu-)Hören als Belauschen (*overhearing*, das auch als *over-here-ing* verstanden werden muss) des ›Anderen‹ bringt aber auch das Potential der Irritation mit sich. Der Aufruf, neu und anders zuzuhören, zieht deswegen die Re-Lektüre von Irritation nach sich, die nicht als Beschneidung sondern als Chance, an das Andere anzuschließen, zu verstehen ist. Die Hoffnung des vorgestellten Konzepts der Interferenz besteht darin, Klang im Allgemeinen und Geräusch im Besonderen als Kategorie der Relationalität (mit dem sozial Anderen) fassen zu können, ohne ihre problematische Komponente einzuebnen.

SYLVIA MIESZKOWSKI untersucht in »Noise, Whirling Sounds and Narrative Dizziness in M. P. Shiel's *The House of Sounds*« ein autobiographisches Fragment vom Anfang des 20. Jahrhunderts und die letzte Fassung einer Kurzgeschichte des aus der Karibik stammenden Genreautors. Anhand einer phonemischen Lektüre des 1911 publizierten *The House of Sounds* werden narrative Techniken analysiert, die Zustände der Orientierungslosigkeit, der Instabilität und des Drehschwindels, denen der Protagonist auf der Handlungsebene ausgesetzt ist, auf der Erzählebene für den Leser reproduzieren. Das erzählerische Programm von Shiels ›strudelnder Sprache‹, so eine der Kernthesen, schlägt sich nieder in seiner Repräsentation von Geräusch im Text und in seiner Manipulation von Text als Geräusch. Schließlich inszeniert *The House of Sounds* Lärm als Quelle masochistischer Lust, während das krankhaft übersensible Ohr zum privilegierten Ort wird, an dem Wissen, das durch Wahrnehmung aus Geräusch gefiltert wurde, in Wahnsinn kippt. Auf der einen Seite verbindet die Kurzgeschichte – durch ihre Obsession mit Phänomenen der Degeneration – die Erzähltradition des *gothic* mit klassischen Texten der Dekadenz; auf der anderen Seite schlägt sie – über ihre Fokussierung auf Geräusche und Lärm – die Brücke bis knapp vor den Beginn der Moderne.

Wie bereits im Beitrag von Antony Moore, widmen sich auch die Ausführungen von THOMAS MARTINEC dem berühmten Text Rainer Maria Rilkes über das »Ur-Geräusch«. Martinecs erkennt in Rilkes Beschreibung eines skurrilen Experiments, in dem eine Phonographennadel an der Kreuznaht eines menschlichen Schädels entlanggeführt wird, einen poetologischen Impuls. Der 1919 publizierte Text lässt sich demzufolge als kritische Mahnung vor einem (allzu) unbekümmerten Brückenschlag zwischen Ton, Geräusch und Musik verstehen. Die zentrale Frage, wie diese Überlegungen zu bewerten seien, beantwortet Martinec damit, dass die im »Ur-Geräusch«-Text formulierte Poetologie (die das Geräusch als unsinnliche, stumme Rückseite der Musik fasst) nur aus Rilkes spezifischem Doppelstatus als Dilettant *und* Avantgardist zu erklären sei. Die eigentliche Bedeutung des »Ur-Geräusch«-Texts liege – aufgrund der Tatsache, dass Rilke sowohl das nötige technische Wissen (über Phonographen) als auch das musikalische Wissen fehlte – nicht in seinem theoretischen Potential, sondern in seiner Rolle als literarischer Komplexitätsgenerator. Dessen Inspiration verdanken sich letztlich die Formulierungen anderer, dann epistemologisch plausiblerer Theoretisierungen des Verhältnisses von Geräusch und Musik.

BARBARA STRAUMANNS Aufsatz mit dem Titel »Noise and Voice: Female Performers in George Meredith, George Eliot and Isak Dinesen« kreist um Präsenz und Relevanz der weiblichen Sing- oder Sprech-Stimme im öffentlichen Raum. Drei literarische Stichproben erkunden, wie die Performanz der *female voice* im Kontext von theatralen, politischen und religiösen Diskursen imaginiert und narrativ repräsentiert wird. An drei Figuren fiktiver Opernsängerinnen – Emilia/›Vittoria‹ aus George Merediths *Sandra Belloni* (1864) und *Vittoria* (1867), die Alcharisi aus George Eliots *Daniel Deronda* (1876) und Pellegrina Leoni aus Isak Dinesens *The Dreamers* (1934) – kann Straumann zeigen, dass ermächtigende *noise effects,* die auf der Ebene der Diegesis und der Narration operieren, politische und ästhetische Aspekte wirksam miteinander verkoppeln. Michail Bakhtins Begriff der Heteroglossie dient als Ankerpunkt für die Analyse metaphorischer ›Geräusche‹ im literarischen Text.

In ihrem Beitrag »Viel Lärm um *Noise:* Die Aktualität von Shakespeares Caliban« beschreibt INA SCHABERT die neue Popularität des hybriden Nicht-Helden aus *The Tempest* (1610) als Effekt zeitgenössischer Präferenz für Pluralität und Polysemie. Deren Signifikanten, die zunächst kontextlosen *noises* auf Calibans Insel, sind in eine Kulturgeschichte der Geräuschproduktion einzutragen, wo sie im Laufe der Shakespeare-Rezeption und der kulturellen Zitation in Malerei, Erzählliteratur, Musik und Eventkultur unterschiedliche Bewertungen erfahren haben. Während die Figuren des Stücks die Geräusche als unerklärbare Störung erfahren, bringt Shakespeares Text den Lärm strategisch und damit sinnhaft zum Einsatz, wobei Caliban zugleich über sein Verhältnis zu den *noises* charakterisiert wird. Die Interpretation dieses letzten Punktes erfährt im 20. Jahrhundert eine radikale Wendung. Unter dem Einfluss des Postkolonialismus und seiner Neudeutung Calibans als Personifikation einer afro-karibischen, oralen wie auralen Gegenkultur, treten – sowohl in Inszenierungen des *Tempest* als auch in intertextuellen Referenzen – die Sensibilität für Klänge, das Protestpotential der *noises* und ihre Rolle als Quelle alternativen Wissens in den Vordergrund.

Die abschließende Sektion »Medieneinsatz: Geräusche in virtuellen Welten« setzt mit einem filmwissenschaftlichen Beitrag von KAY KIRCHMANN ein. In »Sounds and Vision: Geräusche in Jacques Tatis *Les Vacances de*

Monsieur Hulot und David Lynchs *Eraserhead*« befasst er sich mit zwei Arbeiten, die die Filmästhetik der Moderne, die ganz im Zeichen des Zeit-Bildes steht, historisch rahmen. Das dezidiert moderne Element beider Filme, so Kirchmann, liegt dabei in der Entkoppelung der Ton- von der Bildquelle bei gleichzeitiger Enthierarchisierung des Bild-Ton-Verhältnisses. Im Rahmen der seriellen Erzähllogik von *Les Vacances de Monsieur Hulot* (1953) wird das Geräusch als »reine akustische Situation« im Sinne von Deleuze nobilitiert. Dabei tritt vor allem die Interdependenz zwischen Geräusch und Raum in den Vordergrund, während der Dialog, die traditionell wichtigste Tonsorte im Film, abgewertet und Sprache an sich als sinnentleert vorgeführt wird. Geräusche werden dabei von Tati bewusst vielfältig gestaltet und, was seine kausale Attribuierung wie räumliche Verortung angeht, absichtlich uneindeutig belassen. Wie Tati weist auch Lynch dem Geräusch die dominierende Rolle zu, wenn er in seinem, von surrealen Elementen durchzogenen Werk *Eraserhead* (1977) den Ton erfolgreich von der Tyrannei des Bildes befreit. Der Ton fungiert in seiner radikalisierten Autonomie als akustische Wucherung, die ihrerseits eine Vielfalt differenzzersetzender Bilder hervortreibt.

Weil sich die Medienwissenschaft aus der Umdeutung von Geräuschen als Ursprung aller Kommunikation entwickelt hat (McLuhan), ist *noise* aus Sicht dieser Disziplin ein grundsätzlich positives und ebenso produktives wie beobachtungsabhängiges Phänomen: Erst und gerade in der Störung, so die Prämisse, zeigt sich des Mediums Medialität. Als Einsatzpunkt seines Beitrags zu »Rauschen im Fernsehen. Kommunikation mit Astronauten« dient Sven Grampp der Hinweis auf die Störungsanfälligkeit eines aus dem All gesendeten Signals, das multiple Übertragungsprozesse durchläuft: von Schall in elektromagnetische Wellen, die große Distanz zu überwinden haben, zurück in Schall. Grampps primäre Untersuchungsobjekte sind verschiedene Übertragungen der Apollo-11-Mission im noch jungen Medium Fernsehen; dazu gehört auch der kulturelle Remix der ikonisch gewordenen Bilder dieses Ereignisses. Vier Punkte der Apollo-Übertragung werden als exemplarisch herausgegriffen: die den Willen zur Struktur unter Beweis stellende Selektion von Sinn aus Geräuschen; die gegenseitige Überlagerung verschiedener strukturierter Laute, die auf diese Weise Geräusche produzieren; die Entstrukturierung eigentlich strukturierter Laute; schließlich der Entzug strukturierter Laute durch die Leerstelle der mondschattenbedingten Übertragungspause.

In »›Der Mund entsteht mit dem Schrei‹: Zur Inszenierung der Stimme in Heiner Goebbels' Hörstücken nach Texten von Heiner Müller« postuliert der Theaterwissenschaftler Matthias Warstat die Zentralität des Geräuschs für die von Müller/Goebbels entwickelte Variante des Tragischen. Die dafür eingesetzten künstlerischen Verfahren im Hörstück *Die Befreiung des Prometheus* bestehen demnach in der Musikalisierung, Historisierung und Spaltung; gemeinsam ist ihnen das Prinzip der Unterbrechung. Als markante Elemente der Musikalisierung werden Wiederholung, Polyvokalität, Dekomposition der Satzstruktur und Unterbrechung durch verbale Störgeräusche herausgestellt. Die Gestaltung von Klangräumen durch Kunst erfolgt durch die historische Referenz auf die (Un-)Möglichkeit des Sprechens bei gleichzeitiger Verpflichtung zum Ausdruck. Bei Goebbels/Müller wird der Schrei so zur einzig adäquaten Form des Gesangs, und nur die lärmenden Übergangsräume zwischen Schweigen und Schreien bieten mögliche Strategien zur Überwindung der Sprache.

Für ihren Beitrag zum »Getöse der Wall-Street: Die Inszenierung des Börsenhandels als *noise*« konfrontiert SABINE FRIEDRICH Lärm als Instrument politischen Protests im Rahmen der *Occupy-Wall-Street*-Bewegung mit Federico García Lorcas Gedicht »Danza de la muerte« (Todestanz) aus der Sammlung *Poeta en Nueva York*, das die Erfahrung des Börsenkrachs von 1929 verarbeitet. In ihrer Analyse führt Friedrich vor, inwiefern die New Yorker Börse gleich in mehrfacher Hinsicht als Ort der ikonischen Verdichtung (post-)moderner *noises* gelten kann. An drei exemplarischen Filmen – Oliver Stones Klassiker *Wall Street* (1987), dessen Fortsetzung *Wall Street: Money Never Sleeps* (2010) und Jeffrey C. Chandors *Margin Call* (2011) – wird der Funktionswandel von Geräuschen in der Börse deutlich: Von der Glocke, die seit 1870 den Beginn und das Ende des Handelstages verkündet, über das Stimmengewirr der schreienden Händler und das Rauschen des Börsentickers zum *noise trader*, der seine Investmententscheidungen auf unzuverlässige Informationen stützt, findet das Störgeräusch immer neue Formen der Repräsentation. Auf Basis der systemtheoretischen Erkenntnis, dass das System seine eigene Umwelt als Rauschen definiert, diskutiert Friedrich, ob aus diesem Rauschen dann Information entstehen kann, sobald es dem System gelungen ist, sich die eigene Umwelt einzuverleiben.

BETTINA SCHLÜTER legt in ihrem Beitrag »Environmental Audio Programming: Geräusch und Klang in virtuellen Welten« vier Spuren aus, um zu erkunden, wie Unlaute im kulturell Imaginären zu unterschiedlichen Zeiten bewertet werden. Demzufolge gilt es vier unterschiedliche Modi der auditiven Aneignung des Raums zu unterscheiden: Der medienanthropologischen Programmierung der Menschen stehen die psychotechnische, die kulturelle und die digitale Programmierung gegenüber. Aus der medienanthropologischen Analyse des ›Wegs der Statue‹ in Condillacs »Abhandlung über die Empfindungen« (1754) ergeben sich Kriterien für das Hören von Geräuschen, etwa die Orientierung im Raum, sodann Unterscheidung, Vergleich und Vorstellung von Zahl und Dauer der Geräusche. Das Beispiel für die psychotechnische Programmierung lieferte Francis Ford Coppolas Film *The Conversation* (1974), worin der ›Weg des Abhörspezialisten‹ in einen pathologischen Akt mündet. Die als Psychotechnik beschriebene Verschränkung unterschiedlicher Wissensgebiete bringt die stabil geglaubte Differenz zwischen Information und Rauschen zum Kollaps. Die kulturelle Programmierung erläutert Schlüter am Bespiel von Dubravka Ugresics Essays »Alle Fremden piepsen«, wodurch das »chauvinistische Ohr« als ein diskriminierendes Organ hervortritt. Ein abschließendes Kapitel zum ›Weg des Avatars‹ durch seine virtuelle Umgebung‹ am Beispiel des Computerspiels *Doom 3* untersucht die wichtigsten Faktoren digitaler Programmierung und stellt sowohl die lautlichen Effekte (Layertechnik, Grundrauschen, *sound emitter*, Radius, sound-Pfad, Reflexion, Simulation, Okklusion) als auch die Produktion eines *listener object* vor.

DANK

Das Projekt wurde durch die Finanzierung der VolkswagenStiftung und der Dr. German Schweiger-Stiftung ermöglicht. Ihnen und Innokentij Kreknin, der die Publikation der Beiträge betreut hat, sowie allen Autorinnen und Autoren gilt unser großer Dank.

BIBLIOGRAPHIE

Andrada, Damián Vicente: Cacerolas Y Plumas. La primera protesta contra los Kirchner y el posicionamiento político de los medios, Saarbrücken 2012.
Attali, Jacques: The Political Economy of Music, Minneapolis 1985.
Augoyard, Jean-François und Henry Torgue (Hg.): Sonic Experience. A Guide to Everday Sounds, Montreal u.a. 2005.
Azar, Betty S.: Understanding and Using English Grammar, White Plains/NY 1999.
Bailey, Peter: Breaking the Sound Barrier, in: Mark M. Smith (Hg.): Hearing History: A Reader, Athens und London 2004, S. 23-35.
Battista, Kathy: E.A.T. – The Spirit of Collaboration, in: Sabine Breitwieser (Hg.): E.A.T. – Experiments in Art and Technology. Ausstellungskatalog Museum der Moderne Salzburg, Köln 2015, S. 28-37 (dt. S. 17-26).
Bijsterveld, Karin: Mechanical Sound. Technology, Culture, and Public Problems of Noise in the Twentieth Century, Cambridge/MS 2008.
Bijsterveld, Karin and Trevor Pinch (Hg.): The Oxford Handbook of Sound Studies, Oxford und New York 2012.
Bijsterveld, Karin und Fefje Cleophas: Selling Sound: Testing, Designing, and Marketing Sound in the European Car Industry, in: Karin Bijsterveld und Trevor Pinch (Hg.): The Oxford Handbook of Sound Studies, Oxford und New York 2012, S. 102-124.

Bijsterveld, Karin, Eefje Cleophas, Stefan Krebs und Gijs Mom: Sound and Safe: A History of Listening Behind the Wheel, Oxford 2013.
Bosmann Julie: Painting With Sound, in: The New York Times Magazine, 15.1.12, http://www.nytimes.com/interactive/2012/01/15/magazine/painting-with-sound.html?ref=magazine&_r=0 (30.9.16).
Bull, Michael und Les Back (Hg.): The Auditory Culture Reader, Oxford und New York 2004.
Bull, Michael: Sound Moves. iPod Culture and Urban Experience, Abingdon und New York 2007.
Cage, John: The Future of Music: Credo (1937), in: Ders.: Silence: Lectures and Writings by John Cage, Middletown/CT 1961, S. 3-6.
Cage, John: Experimental Music: Doctrine (1955), in: Ders.: Silence: Lectures and Writings by John Cage, Middletown/CT 1961, S. 13-15.
Cage, John: Composition as Process (1958), in: Ders.: Silence: Lectures and Writings by John Cage, Middletown/CT 1961, S. 18-56.
Connor, Steven: Dumbstruck. A Cultural History of Ventriloquism, Oxford 2000.
Daiber, Jürgen: Franz Kafka und der Lärm. Klanglandschaften der frühen Moderne, Paderborn 2015.
Dolar, Mladen: A Voice and Nothing More, Boston/MS und London 2006.
Erlmann, Veit: Reason and Resonance: A History of Modern Aurality, Boston 2014.
Ernst, Wolf-Dieter und Arno Mungen (Hg.): Sound und Performance. Positionen – Methoden – Analysen, Würzburg 2015.
Ernst, Wolfgang: Im Medium erklingt die Zeit. Technologische Tempor(e)alitäten und das Sonische als ihre privilegierte Erkenntnisform, Berlin 2014.
Felderer, Brigitte (Hg.): Phonorama. Eine Kulturgeschichte der Stimme als Medium, Berlin 2004.
Geisel, Sieglinde: Nur im Weltall ist es wirklich still. Vom Lärm und der Sehnsucht nach Stille, Berlin 2010.
Gess, Nicola, Florian Schreiner und Manuela K. Schulz (Hg.): Hörstürze: Akustik und Gewalt im 20. Jahrhundert, Würzburg 2005.
Goodman, Steve: Sonic Warfare. Sound, Affect, and the Ecology of Fear, Cambridge/MS 2010.
Grimshaw, Marc und Tom Garner: Sonic Virtuality. Sound as Emergent Perception, Oxford und New York 2015.
Grüny, Christian: Von der Sprache des Gefühls zum Mittel der Qual. Musik als Folterinstrument, in: Musik und Ästhetik 57 (2011), S. 68-83.
Heinz, Solveig M.: Urban Opera. Navigating Modernity through the Oeuvre of Strauss und Hofmannsthal, University of Michigan (Diss.) 2013, https://deepblue.lib.umich.edu/handle/2027.42/102451 (30.9.16).

Helmholtz, Hermann: Die Lehre von den Tonempfindungen als physiologische Grundlage für die Theorie der Musik, Braunschweig 1863, http://echo.mpiwg-berlin.mpg.de/MPIWG:FEMV3VNX (30.9.16).

Hendy, David: Noise. A Human History of Sound and Listening, London 2013.

Herrmann, Britta (Hg.): Dichtung für die Ohren. Literatur als tonale Kunst der Moderne, Berlin 2015.

Hongler, Camille, Christoph Haffter und Silvan Moosmüller (Hg.): Geräusch – das Andere der Musik. Untersuchungen an den Grenzen des Musikalischen, Bielefeld 2012.

Jenny, Hans: Kymatik. Wellenphänomene und Schwingungen, Aarau 2009 (Neuausgabe der beiden Teilbände, Basel 1967 und 1972).

Kahn, Douglas: Noise Water Meat. A History of Voice, Sound, and Aurality in the Arts, Boston 1999.

Keizer, Garret: The Unwanted Sound of Everything We Want. A Book About Noise, New York 2010.

Kittler, Friedrich, Thomas Macho und Sigrid Weigel (Hg.): Zwischen Rauschen und Offenbarung. Zur Kultur- und Mediengeschichte der Stimme, München 2002.

Kolesch, Doris und Sybille Krämer (Hg.): Stimme. Annäherung an ein Phänomen, Frankfurt/M. 2006.

Kümmel, Albert und Erhard Schüttpelz: Medientheorie der Störung / Störungstheorie der Medien. Eine Fibel, in: Dies. (Hg.): Signale der Störung, München 2003, S. 9-13.

Kursell, Julia: Epistemologie des Hörens. Helmholtz' physiologische Grundlegung der Musiktheorie, München 2016 (angekündigt).

LaBelle, Brandon: Acoustic Territories. Sound Culture and Everyday Life, New York 2010.

Meyer, Petra Maria (Hg.): ə'ku:stik tə:n, München 2008.

Mieszkowski, Sylvia: Resonant Alterities: Sound, Desire and Anxiety in Non-Realist Fiction, Bielefeld 2014.

Nancy, Jean-Luc: Listening, New York 2007.

Nieberle, Sigrid: FrauenMusikLiteratur. Deutschsprachige Schriftstellerinnen im 19. Jahrhundert, 2., verb. Aufl. Herbolzheim 2002.

Noppeney, Gerda: Erkenntnisfortschritt und fehlende Umsetzung. Zum Konservatismus in der Politik. Zehn Jahre ärztliches Engagement in der Fluglärmproblematik, in: Friedrich Thießen (Hg.): Die Grenzen der Demokratie. Die gesellschaftliche Auseinandersetzung bei Großprojekten, Wiesbaden 2012, S. 149-159.

O'Callaghan, Casey: Sounds. A Philosophical Theory, Oxford und New York 2007.

Papenburg, Jens Gerrit und Holger Schulze (Hg.): Sound as Popular Culture. A Research Companion, Boston/MS 2016.

Pieslak, John: Sound Targets. American Soldiers and Musik in the Iraq War, Bloomington 2009.
Ross, Alex: The Rest is Noise, New York 2007.
Schlüter, Sabine: Musikwissenschaft als Sound Studies. Fachhistorische Perspektiven und wissenschaftstheoretische Implikationen, in: Axel Volmar und Jens Schröter (Hg.): Auditive Medienkulturen. Techniken des Hörens und Praktiken der Klanggestaltung, Bielefeld 2013, S. 207-225.
Schoon, Andi und Axel Volmar (Hg.): Das geschulte Ohr. Eine Kulturgeschichte der Sonifikation, Bielefeld 2012.
Schulze, Holger (Hg.): Sound Studies: Traditionen – Methoden – Desiderate. Eine Einführung, Bielefeld 2008.
Schwartz, Hillel: On Noise, in: Mark M. Smith (Hg.): Hearing History: A Reader, Athens und London 2004, S. 51-53.
Smith, Bruce R.: The Acoustic World of Early Modern England. Attending to the O-Factor, Chicago und London 1999.
Smith, Mark M.: (Hg.): Hearing History: A Reader, Athens und London 2004.
Smith, Mark M.: Listening to Nineteenth-Century America, Chapel Hill/NC 2001.
Spehr, Georg (Hg.): Funktionale Klänge. Hörbare Daten, klingende Geräte und gestaltete Hörerfahrungen, Bielefeld 2009.
Sterne, Jonathan: The Audible Past. Cultural Origins of Sound Reproduction, Durham/NC 2003.
Sterne, Johnathan (Hg.): The Sound Studies Reader, Abingdon und New York 2012.
Thompson, Emily Ann: The Soundscape of Modernity. Architectural Acoustics and the Culture of Listening in America, 1900–1933, Cambridge/MS und London 2002.
Umweltbundesamt (Hg.): Auswahlbibliographie Lärmschutz, Dessau 2016, http://www.umweltbundesamt.de/publikationen/auswahlbibliografie-laermschutz-0 (30.9.16).
Voegelin, Salomé: Listening to Noise and Silence: Towards A Philosophy of Sound Art, New York und London 2010.
Weheliye, Alexander G.: Phonographies. Grooves in Sonic Afro-Modernity, Durham/NC und London 2005.

II Epistem und Geräusch

Das Rauschen bei Foucault

Marion Schmaus

Grenzphänomene der Akustik: Geräusche, Lärm, ein »Rauschen«, »Murmeln« oder das »Schweigen« spielen in Michel Foucaults Texten vielfach eine Rolle. Sie werden allerdings metaphorisch gebraucht und kennzeichnen strategische Allianzen, durch die er sein Modell der Diskursanalyse mit anderen zeitgenössischen Theorien kontextualisiert. Dem Rauschen bei Foucault nachzugehen, verspricht daher zweierlei: einerseits einen genaueren Blick auf sein Theoriemodell und dessen sprachanalytische und medientheoretische Implikationen, andererseits einen Beitrag zur kulturgeschichtlichen Erfassung des Lärms bzw. Rauschens, da es gerade das Verdienst von Foucaults historischer Wissenschaft der Diskursanalyse sein könnte, den eher geschichtsvergessenen Modellen der Informations- und Kommunikationstheorie, der Nachrichtentechnik sowie der Linguistik ein historisches Gedächtnis einzuschreiben. Ich werde im Folgenden den Blick ausführlicher auf zwei kürzere, auch unbekanntere Texte Foucaults richten: auf seinen Vortrag »Botschaft oder Rauschen?« aus dem Jahr 1966 und auf seinen Hölderlin-Essay aus dem Jahr 1962, in denen er dem Rauschen besondere Aufmerksamkeit widmet und Begrifflichkeiten verwandter Theorieansätze erprobt. Es sind dies zum einen nachrichtentechnische und linguistische Kommunikationsmodelle, zum anderen die psychoanalytische Sprachphilosophie.

I. Botschaft oder Rauschen?

Einleitend beziehe ich mich auf jenen Text Foucaults, in dem das Rauschen am prominentesten ins Feld geführt wird. Es handelt sich um den mit »Message ou bruit?«, also »Botschaft oder Rauschen?«, überschriebenen Vortrag, den Foucault 1966 bei einem »Kolloquium über das Wesen des medizinischen Denkens« vor Ärzten gehalten hat. Er unternimmt hier eine Reformulierung des medizinischen Krankheitsbegriffs aus linguistischer und nachrichtentechnischer Perspektive. Wenn es abschließend heißt, eine »Theorie der medizinischen Praxis« solle auf »Grundlage von Begriffen neu durchdacht werden«, die aus »der Sprachanalyse und der Datenverarbeitung stammen«,[1] so beschreibt Foucault die Allianz aus Linguistik und Informationstheorie, die sich in den 1950er und 1960er Jahren vollzog und für die die Namen Claude Shannon und Roman Jakobson stehen. Beide entwerfen in gegenseitiger Wahrnehmung kompatible Kommunikationsmodelle, die dem Rauschen eine besondere Stellung einräumen.

Vor dem Hintergrund der Datenübertragung durch Medien wie Telegraf und Telefon entwickelt Shannon 1948 einen für die Computer- und Medientheorie, ja für das digitale Zeitalter insgesamt richtungsweisenden Ansatz in seinem Beitrag »A Mathematical Theory of Communication«. Es ist ein Ansatz, der sich im Hinblick auf pragmatische Anwendungen, d.h. technologische Neuerungen, dem ›Kampf gegen den Lärm‹, »combating noise«,[2] verschrieben hat. Die kriegerische Metaphorik ist hier eher metonymisch zu nehmen, denn es besteht ein Zusammenhang zwischen der Entwicklung dieser mit Codierung / Decodierung befassten Sender-Empfänger-Modelle und der Kriegstechnologie des Zweiten Weltkriegs. Shannon war, ebenso wie Norbert Wiener, der Begründer der Kybernetik, dem er in seinem Beitrag besondere Reverenz erweist, während des Zweiten Weltkriegs in der amerikanischen Rüstungsforschung tätig.[3]

Als eine Zwischenbemerkung sei hier eingefügt, dass diese Verbindung von Rauschen, *noise*, Lärm und Krieg auch für Foucaults Denken prägend ist. Denn es handelt sich um einen agonalen Theorieansatz. Nicht umsonst streicht Foucault in Vorlesungen der 1970er Jahre das erkenntnisfördernde »Licht des Krieges« heraus: »Wer hat im Lärm und im Wirrwarr des Krieges, wer hat im Schlamm der Schlachten das Erkenntnisprinzip der Ordnung, des Staates und seiner Institutionen gesucht?«[4] Auf eine etymologische Verbindung von Lärm und Krieg im Hinblick auf das deutsche Wort hatte bereits das Grimmsche Wörterbuch verwiesen. Der »Lärm« habe sich aus dem »romanische[n] schlachtruf, ital. all arme, [...] franz. al arme (zu den waffen)« entwickelt, der »lautete zu ende des 15. jahrh. im munde burgundischer Franzosen al erme«.[5]

Doch zurück zu Shannons ›combating noise‹ und seinem Kommunikationsmodell, das dem Rauschen eine nicht zu umgehende, konstitutive Funktion zuweist. Es wird von der Unvermeidbarkeit des Rauschens gesprochen

---

1 | Foucault: Botschaft oder Rauschen, S. 722.
2 | Shannon: A Mathematical Theory of Communication, S. 407.
3 | Ebd., S. 652, und Markowsky: Claude Shannon; Sterne: MP3. The Meaning of a Format, S. 76f.
4 | Foucault: Vom Licht des Krieges zur Geburt der Geschichte, S. 7.
5 | Deutsches Wörterbuch, Bd. 12, Sp. 202.

und die Störung zum Bestandteil normaler Kommunikation gemacht. Kanal und Rauschen sowie Botschaft und Rauschen treten üblicherweise – es gibt Ausnahmen bei Shannon – gemeinsam auf. »Since, ordinarily, channels have a certain amount of noise [...], exact transmission is impossible.«[6] Und es heißt weiterhin: »If the channel is noisy it is not in general possible to reconstruct the original message or the transmitted.«[7] Diese Äußerungen scheinen Bernhard Siegerts Auffassung in »Die Geburt der Literatur aus dem Rauschen der Kanäle« zu rechtfertigen, Shannon habe »der Störung (dem Rauschen) eine eigenständige und gegenüber den anderen Instanzen gleichberechtigte Rolle zugewiesen«.[8] Er führt unter anderem Shannons Graphik des Kommunikationsmodells als Argument an. Die Kastengröße der Störquelle darin gilt ihm als Zeichen der Gleichberechtigung von Rauschen und Botschaft bzw. Sender und Empfänger:

Abbildung 1: Shannons Kommunikationsmodell

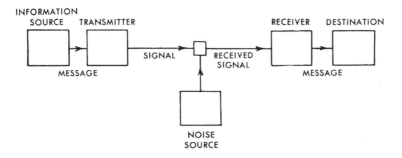

Quelle: Shannon: A Mathematical Theory of Communication, S. 381.

Diese Informationstheorie hat Einfluss auf linguistische Kommunikationsmodelle gehabt, wie Roman Jakobson in dem 1960 gehaltenen Vortrag »Linguistics and Communication Theory« bestätigt.[9] Das Begriffspaar *langue-parole* wird durch *code* und *message* abgelöst. Von den sechs Funktionen des Sprachzeichens, die Jakobsons Kommunikationsmodell in »Linguistik und Poetik« (1960) festhält (als da wären: emotive, poetische, konative,

---

6 | Shannon: A Mathematical Theory of Communicationy, S. 646.
7 | Ebd., S. 407.
8 | Siegert: Die Geburt der Literatur aus dem Rauschen der Kanäle, S. 12.
9 | »Today, with respect to the treatment of coding problems in communication theory, the Saussurian dichotomy langue-parole can be restated much more precisely and acquires a new operational value«, Jacobson: Linguistics and Communication Theory, S. 247.

referentielle, metalinguale und phatische), lassen sich im Besonderen die beiden letzten als Reaktionen auf die Informationstheorie verstehen.[10]

Was die Linguistik und auch Foucault an einem informationstheoretischen Kommunikationsmodell interessieren konnte, war die Einführung von Statistik und Stochastik sowie die Ausklammerung von Semantik und Hermeneutik. Es geht bei der Datenübertragung nicht um den Transport von Bedeutungen und es geht nicht um ein Verstehen der Nachricht. Es dürfte dem Posthumanismus des Foucault der 1960er Jahre sehr zupass gekommen sein, dass das mathematische Kommunikationsmodell nicht von einem sich ausdrückenden und einem rezipierenden Individuum ausgeht, sondern der Kryptologie und Nachrichtentechnik gemäß die sendende Instanz aufspaltet in Nachrichtenquelle und Sender und die empfangende Instanz in Empfänger und Nachrichtenziel.

Dieser Posthumanismus zeigt sich in »Botschaft oder Rauschen?« u.a. in der Wendung, dem Arzt begegneten in seiner Praxis keine Patienten, schon gar keine »menschlichen Wesen«, sondern nur ein Rauschen. Und er zeigt sich auch in seiner kritischen Abgrenzung von Michael Balint. Dieser Psychoanalytiker ungarisch-jüdischer Herkunft lehrte in den 1920er Jahren am Berliner Institut für Psychoanalyse, musste in den 1930er Jahren nach England emigrieren und trug dort entscheidend zu einer ganzheitlichen, psychosomatisch ausgerichteten Weiterbildung der Allgemeinmediziner bei, u.a. durch seinen 1957 veröffentlichten Klassiker *The Doctor, His Patient and the Illness*. Balints Anliegen zielt auf eine Optimierung des Arzt-Patienten-Gesprächs durch Wahrnehmung der Prozesse von Übertragung und Gegenübertragung in der Therapie. Der psychoanalytischen Hermeneutik zufolge gilt es, die Krankheit zum Sprechen zu bringen, unter der Oberfläche des manifesten Sinns der Symptome den unbewussten, latenten Sinn zu dekodieren. Einem solchen, auf Sender und Empfänger sowie Sinn zentrierten, psychoanalytischen Kommunikationsmodell begegnet Foucault in »Botschaft oder Rauschen?« mit einer knappen Polemik:

---

10 | Vgl. hierzu Siegert: Die Geburt der Literatur aus dem Rauschen der Kanäle, S. 15: »Wie aus einem 1987 im Magazin *Omni* veröffentlichten Interview mit Shannon hervorgeht, war Shannon offenbar bekannt, daß der zentrale Bezug seiner ›information theory‹ auf den Kanal als ›phatische Funktion‹ Eingang in die Linguistik gefunden hatte. ›A similar thing happens in the social system where we have lots of aids to communication. If you're talking to me I might say ›what?‹ which is a feedback system to overcome some of the noise, and to get correct transmission.‹«

Seit Balint heißt es immer wieder, der Kranke sende eine ›Botschaft‹ oder ›Botschaften‹ aus, die der Arzt höre und interpretiere. Daraus lassen sich allerlei segensreiche Humanismen zum fragwürdigen Thema des Arzt-Patienten-Verhältnisses ableiten.[11]

Dem psychoanalytischen Kommunikationsmodell hält Foucault ein nachrichtentechnisches bzw. linguistisches entgegen, das andere Referenzgrößen ins Spiel bringt: nicht Patient und Arzt, noch Sender und Empfänger, noch Sinn der Botschaft sind hier entscheidend, sondern Kanal bzw. Rauschen, die systemische Betrachtung von Rauschen und Botschaft sowie der Code als Bezugsgröße für eine Botschaft. Die Spiegelstriche im nachfolgenden Zitat schreiten diese drei Aspekte nacheinander ab:

Wenn es eine ›Botschaft‹ geben soll, müssen mehrere Bedingungen erfüllt sein:
- Zunächst einmal muss es ein Rauschen geben (im Fall der Medizin ist dieses Grundrauschen das ›Nichtschweigen der Organe‹);
- dieses Rauschen muss aus verschiedenen diskontinuierlichen, das heißt nach sicheren Kriterien gegeneinander abgrenzbaren Elementen ›bestehen‹ oder zumindest deren ›Träger‹ sein;
- diese Elemente müssen in eindeutiger Weise mit anderen Elementen verknüpft sein, die deren Bedeutung darstellen (in der Medizin können diese Elemente die ›Krankheit‹, die ›Prognose‹ oder die ›therapeutische Indikation‹ sein);
- und schließlich müssen diese Elemente nach bestimmten Regelmäßigkeiten miteinander verknüpft sein. Nun sendet aber die Krankheit keine ›Botschaft‹ aus, denn Botschaften basieren auf einem ›Code‹, der nach den oben beschriebenen Regeln geschaffen ist. In der Natur gibt es keine Codes, so denaturiert sie auch sein mag. Die Krankheit erzeugt allenfalls ein Rauschen, und das ist bereits viel. Alles Übrige tut die Medizin hinzu, und sie tut in Wirklichkeit sehr viel mehr, als sie selbst glaubt.[12]

Insofern Foucault den Kanal hier mit dem Rauschen gleichsetzt, distanziert er sich allerdings auch deutlich von dem nachrichtentechnischen Kommunikationsmodell Shannons, das auf eine technische Minimierung des Rauschens angelegt ist, diesem also keinen Eigenwert zubilligt. Foucault hingegen geht es darum, das Rauschen jenseits der durch Botschaft und Code in der Medizin legitimierten Elemente hörbar zu machen. Wissenschaftskritisch und in historischer Perspektive gilt es, die »klinische Erfahrung« »seit anderthalb Jahrhunderten«,[13] also seit dem Epistemewechsel zur Moderne um 1800, als Technik der Ausblendung von »diversen Formen von

---

11 | Foucault: Botschaft oder Rauschen?, S. 719.
12 | Ebd.
13 | Ebd.

Rauschen«[14] wahrzunehmen. Als Akteure des vermeintlichen »Siegs über das Rauschen« werden im Folgenden die medizinischen Codes ausgemacht, die das Rauschen in Krankheitsbotschaften überführen, die Ärzte, die »das Rauschen ausblenden und sich die Ohren für alles verstopfen, was nicht Element der Botschaft ist«[15] und schließlich medizinische Modelle, die eine Zuordnung der Elemente von Botschaften zu Signalgruppen erlauben.

II. Diskurs und Gegendiskurs oder vom Pathos des Rauschens

Das Vokabular der Informations- oder Kommunikationstheorie von Botschaft, Rauschen und Code findet sich bei Foucault nicht allzu oft. Es stellt aber, wie in »Botschaft oder Rauschen?« ersichtlich, eine Profilierungs- und Übersetzungsmöglichkeit für seinen eigenen, in ständiger Überarbeitung begriffenen Theorieansatz dar. Für Rauschen bzw. Kanal, Code und Botschaft verwendet Foucault überwiegend eine alternative Begrifflichkeit, nämlich Diskurs, Gegendiskurs, Dispositive, Wissens- und Machtkomplexe. ›Diskurs‹ und ›Dispositiv‹ sind, wie Walter Seitter unterstrichen hat,[16] Foucaults terminologische Beiträge zur Medientheorie, und sie zeichnen sich durch eine bis in die 1980er Jahre stetig weitergeführte Verbindung von Kommunikations- und Handlungstheorie aus.

Wenn in anderen Texten Foucaults noch vom Rauschen die Rede ist, dann ist die Diktion eine gänzlich andere, keine nachrichtentechnisch-nüchterne, sondern eine rhetorisch-emphatische, die an das Ethos, die Utopie und das politische Engagement von Foucaults Diskursanalyse rührt. Die akustische Metaphorik transportiert eine Gleichzeitigkeit zwischen Sender und Empfänger als Hörgemeinschaft und dem, was die Diskursanalyse zum Sprechen bringt: Wahnsinnige, Ausgegrenzte, Delinquenten oder infame Menschen – allesamt unterdrückte Wissensarten.[17] Ihre in Schrift archivierten Aussagen werden metaphorisch als Affektausdruck, als ›Schrei‹ qualifiziert. In besonderen Textformen, an den Rändern seiner großen Studien, in Vorwort, Essay und Interview erlaubt sich Foucault solche strategisch-rhetorischen

---

14 | Ebd.
15 | Ebd., S. 721.
16 | Siehe Seitter: Wahrheit, Macht, Medien.
17 | Hier schließt der Beitrag an Brandon LaBelle und ›noise as production of the social‹ an. Michel Serres war Foucaults zeitweiliger Kollege an den Universitäten Clermont-Ferrand und Vincennes und wohl auch sein Gesprächspartner in Bezug auf die Informationstheorie; vgl. Eribon: S. 129, 137f.

Operationen, die kenntlich machen, dass die Geschichte ein uns alle angehender Kampfschauplatz ist. Im Fall Foucault vollzieht sich ein Kampf für das Rauschen. Mit Jakobson gesprochen dominieren in dieser Emphase für das Rauschen die phatische, emotive und konative Funktion.

Das erste Vorwort von *Wahnsinn und Gesellschaft* von 1961 kennt eine solche Emphase des Rauschens:

Die Fülle der Geschichte ist allein möglich in dem zugleich leeren und bevölkerten Raum all jener sprachlosen Worte, die dem, der ihnen ein Ohr leiht, einen dumpfen Lärm von unterhalb der Geschichte vernehmbar machen, das hartnäckige Gemurmel einer Sprache, die *ganz allein* sprechen würde – ohne sprechendes Subjekt und ohne einen Mitsprechenden, über sich selbst gebeugt, mit zugeschnürter Kehle, zusammenbrechend, bevor sie überhaupt zu einer Formulierung gelangt ist, und glanzlos ins Schweigen zurückkehrend, von dem sie sich niemals befreit hat.[18]

In *Wahnsinn und Gesellschaft* unternimmt Foucault den Versuch, die Geschichte des Anderen der Vernunft zu erzählen, um den »Punkt Null«[19] zu markieren, an dem die Vernunft die Herrschaft über den Wahnsinn übernommen hat und diesen zum Schweigen verurteilt. Während in Mittelalter und Renaissance noch ein »dramatisches Gespräch«[20] zwischen Vernunft und Unvernunft stattgefunden hat, wird in der Aufklärung, in einer Allianz von epistemologischem Ausschluss des Wahnsinns als Denkunmöglichkeit und politischer Ausgrenzung, der Wahnsinn zum Schweigen gebracht. Am Ende des 18. Jahrhunderts entsteht dann, im Zuge einer vermeintlichen »Humanisierung«, die wissenschaftlich-moderne Form der Objektivierung des Wahnsinns als Geisteskrankheit, und damit gekoppelt findet die Einschließung der Kranken in Asyle statt. In »ein und derselben Bewegung« etablieren sich in der Moderne zwei Diskurse, die beide, so Foucault, die »geheimen Wahrheiten des Menschen« im Wahnsinn suchen, der jetzt die »Kraft eines Spiegels«[21] angenommen hat: der humanwissenschaftlich-psychiatrische Monolog der Vernunft über den Wahnsinn und das lyrische Selbstgespräch des Wahnsinns.

Seit dem Ende des achtzehnten Jahrhunderts manifestiert sich das Leben der Unvernunft nur noch im Aufblitzen von Werken wie Hölderlins, Nervals, Nietzsches oder Artauds, die unendlich irreduzibel auf jene Alienationen sind, die heilen, weil sie durch ihre eigene Kraft jenem gigantischsten moralischen Gefangenendasein widerstehen,

---

18 | Foucault: Vorwort, S. 228f.
19 | Foucault: Wahnsinn und Gesellschaft, S. 7.
20 | Ebd., S. 14.
21 | Ebd., S. 545.

das man gewöhnlich, wahrscheinlich in einer Antiphrase, die Befreiung der Irren durch Pinel und Tuke nennt.[22]

Diese beiden Diskurse kommunizieren jedoch nicht miteinander, denn die wissenschaftliche »Reflexion«[23] weigert sich, in dem zum Ding objektivierten Irren ihr Spiegelbild wiederzuerkennen, während sich die lyrische Erfahrung gleichsam zu einem freiwilligen Wahnsinn bekennt. Damit etabliert Foucault das Modell von Diskurs und Gegendiskurs, das für sein Denken der sechziger Jahre kennzeichnend wird, wobei einer der Diskurse, der wissenschaftliche, sich auf die Festschreibung von Grenzen – zwischen Psychiater und Irren, Arzt und Patient – spezialisiert, während der andere in konstanter Grenzüberschreitung die Antinomien, und vornehmlich die zwischen Subjektivität und Objektivität, miteinander versöhnt.[24] Das Ungleichgewicht dieser beiden Diskurse wird jedoch sogleich vermerkt: Der lyrischen Erfahrung des Wahnsinns ist nur ein »kurze[s] Glück«[25] vergönnt. An der Bruchstelle zwischen Klassik und Moderne scheint für einen Moment die »Möglichkeit einer Poesie der Welt«, einer »Poesie des Herzens«[26] auf, deren Weiterleben dann nur noch »ein Blitz, ein Schrei«[27] in den Werken Nervals, Nietzsches, Roussels oder Artauds ist. Emphase lässt diese Wortwahl zwar erkennen, aber auch eine Machtlosigkeit gegenüber dem Diskurs der »Reflexion«, der das antinomische Denken in der Form verfestigt, dass die Gegensätze immer weiter auseinandergetrieben und festgeschrieben werden.

Das Rauschen wandert also in den Gegendiskurs moderner Literatur ab, die trotz ihrer hochkomplexen ästhetischen Textur als Affektausdruck, als ›Schrei‹ wahrgenommen wird. Dieses Rauschen der Literatur analysiert Foucault am ausführlichsten in seinem Hölderlin-Essay »Das ›Nein‹ des Vaters« aus dem Jahr 1962. Es handelt sich um eine zum Essay erweiterte Rezension von Jean Laplanches Studie *Hölderlin et la question du père* aus dem Jahr 1961. Dieser Hölderlin-Artikel gehört zu Foucaults frühesten Schriften zur Literatur, in der er dem Zusammenhang von Wahnsinn, Werk und Sprache nachgeht und damit das in *Wahnsinn und Gesellschaft* skizzierte Verhältnis von Sagbarkeit und Schweigen weiter differenziert. Hier entwickelt er in Auseinandersetzung mit Hölderlin und Lacan eine Sprachauffassung, die

---

22 | Ebd., S. 536.
23 | Ebd., S. 545.
24 | »In der unmittelbaren Totalität der poetischen Erfahrung und in der lyrischen Anerkennung des Wahnsinns waren sie bereits in der ungeteilten Form einer mit sich selbst versöhnten Dualität vorhanden«. Ebd., S. 547.
25 | Ebd.
26 | Ebd., S. 544.
27 | Foucault: Psychologie und Geisteskrankheit, S. 132.

für seinen Umgang mit moderner Literatur in den sechziger Jahren kennzeichnend bleiben wird. Die Erwähnung Hölderlins in den weiteren Texten zur Literatur verweist auf dessen bedeutende Rolle für Foucaults Denken:

Könnte man vielleicht, ohne zu weit zu gehen, sagen, daß [...] Hölderlin durch die Entdeckung, daß die Götter sich abwenden und durch die Spalte einer sich verlierenden Sprache entschwinden, [...] für das kommende Jahrhundert, allerdings in gewisser Weise chiffriert, in unser Denken die Erfahrung des Draußen gelegt ha[t]?[28]

Hölderlins Leben ebenso wie der Zusammenhang zwischen seinem Leben und Werk wird auf den Spuren von Laplanche im Modus von Spiegelszenarien, Prä- und Postfiguration, Antizipation und Wiederholung gelesen. Gegenüber einer klinischen Psychologie, die in einem einfachen Kurzschluss Leben und Text zusammenführt, und daher den Wahnsinn nur im Kollaps des Werks verorten kann, wird Laplanches »psycho-biographie«[29] hoch angerechnet, dass sie die Frage auf das Problem der gemeinsamen Sprache von Wahnsinn und Poesie lenkt. Diesem geht Foucault nach, indem er mit Laplanche die Stationen Hölderlins, Jena, Frankfurt und Homburg, nachzeichnet und dabei zugleich den Weg Lacans vom ›Spiegelstadium‹ zum ›Gesetz des Vaters‹ folgt. Foucault lehnt sich hier stark an die Terminologie von Laplanche / Lacan an, jedoch mit einer interessanten Auslassung: Die imaginären Spiegelverhältnisse werden nicht als narzisstische gefasst. Kennzeichen von Lacans Spiegelstadium ist, dass das Ich *(moi)* in der spiegelbildlichen Identifikation mit dem anderen sein »wahres« Ich *(je)* gerade verkennt, sich selbst als einheitliches gespiegelt findet und aus diesem Kreis narzisstischer Selbstdarstellung erst durch Einführung eines Dritten, des großen Anderen entlassen wird. Im ›Namen-des-Vaters‹ wird die duale Mutter-Kind-Beziehung des Spiegelstadiums aufgebrochen und der Eintritt in die symbolische Ordnung der Sprache und der Geschlechterdifferenz ermöglicht.[30] Lacan hat Freuds Ödipus-Komplex konsequent auf die Ebene der Sprache verschoben, sodass bei der ödipalen Anerkennung des ›Gesetzes des Vaters‹ das Augenmerk auf der symbolischen Vaterfunktion, nicht auf der realen liegt. Durch die kindliche Identifikation mit dem Vater wird der Phallus als fundamentaler

---

28 | Foucault: Schriften zur Literatur, S. 134. »Das ist der Augenblick (oder er steht bevor), als Hölderlin sich bis zum Geblendetsein gewahr wurde, er könne nur noch in einem Raum sprechen, von dem sich die Götter abgewandt hatten, und daß es das Sprechen nur noch sich selbst verdanke, wenn es den Tod umginge. Damals tat sich am Fuße des Himmels eine Öffnung auf, auf die sich unser Sprechen immer mehr zubewegt.« Ebd., S. 95.
29 | Ebd., S. 267.
30 | Vgl. Lacan: Das Spiegelstadium als Bildner der Ichfunktion.

Signifikant der symbolischen Ordnung eingesetzt, der fortan als Wunsch der Mutter (Phallus zu sein) und als das, was Vater und Kind nicht haben, das unbewusste Begehren strukturiert. Bei der Psychose nun werden das väterliche Gesetz und der phallische Signifikant nicht urverdrängt, sondern ursprünglich verworfen. Das bedeutet, wie Foucault in Anschluss an Lacan formuliert, »dass der Vater niemals Zugang zur Benennung erlangt hat und dass dieser Platz des Signifikanten, durch den der Vater sich benennt und durch den er dem Gesetz gemäß benennt, leer geblieben ist.«[31] Das psychotische ›Nein-des-Vaters‹ als Fehlen des transzendentalen Signifikanten (Phallus) reißt ein wirkliches »Loch«[32] in die Signifikantenkette der symbolischen Ordnung, aus dem das Imaginäre ausfließt und das im psychotischen Prozess auf dem Wege einer Sprachverdoppelung zu schließen versucht wird.

Was uns Foucault mit Hölderlin in »Das ›Nein‹ des Vaters« vorführt, ist die historische Etablierung zweier Diskurse: Der eine ein »therapeutisch-wissenschaftlicher« Diskurs, der seine Positivität dem Gesetz oder dem Phallus verdankt.[33] Der andere ein »psychotisch-schizoider« Diskurs, der das Gesetz des Vaters verworfen hat und in Richtung auf diese Abwesenheit als einem wirklichen Loch in der Signifikantenkette spricht. Hier eröffnet sich der Sprachraum moderner Literatur, in der der Wahnsinn – im Inneren der Sprache als Abwesenheit des Herrensignifikanten situiert – den Prozess der Signifikation zum Scheitern bringt.

Doch zugleich eröffnet sich der Bereich einer an ihren äußersten Begrenzungen verlorenen Sprache, dort, wo sie sich selbst am fremdesten ist, der Bereich der Zeichen, die auf nichts hinzeigen, und eine Ausdauer, die nicht leidet: »*Ein Zeichen sind wir, deutungslos ...*«. Die Eröffnung der letzten Lyrik ist selbst die Eröffnung des Wahnsinns.[34]

Mit Laplanche / Lacan erkennt Foucault die Psychoanalyse als legitimen Zeugen der psychotischen Sprache Hölderlins an, da es ihr gelungen ist, den Wahnsinn als Sprachproblem zu sehen. Die Psychoanalyse grenzt an die moderne Literatur, da sie den Wahnsinn zum Sprechen gebracht hat.[35] An ihm, und mit ihm an der modernen Literatur, findet sie aber auch ihre Grenze: Die Psychose ist dasjenige, an dem sich die Psychoanalyse als »unmächtig« erweist, in ihr als dem Nicht-Therapierbaren findet sie ihre

---

31 | Foucault: Das ›Nein‹ des Vaters, S. 277.
32 | Lacan: Über eine Frage, S. 91.
33 | »Denn der Phallus ist ein Signifikant, [...] der bestimmt ist, die Signifikatswirkungen in ihrer Gesamtheit zu bezeichnen, soweit der Signifikant diese konditioniert durch seine Gegenwart als Signifikant«. Ebd., S. 126.
34 | Foucault: Das ›Nein‹ des Vaters, S. 278f.
35 | Vgl. Foucault: Psychologie und Geisteskrankheit, S. 106.

»unüberwindlichste Qual«.³⁶ In gleicher Weise entzieht sich auch die moderne Literatur ihren Entschlüsselungstechniken, denn als eine »Theorie der Bedeutung«,³⁷ oder wie es auch heißt als »Theologie der Bedeutungen«,³⁸ bleibt sie einem binären, klassischen Zeichensystem verhaftet, das die Absage moderner Literatur an das Paradigma der Repräsentation nicht nachvollziehen kann.

Foucaults Originalität gegenüber Laplanche / Lacan besteht darin, dass er den ›Fall Hölderlin‹ zum Epochenphänomen der abendländischen Kultur erklärt, zur Geburtsstunde moderner Literatur, die fortan den Tod Gottes im Innern ihrer Sprache als Abwesenheit eines Herrensignifikanten, als Schweigen verzeichnet: »[I]n unserer Sprache [hat] der Tod Gottes durch das Schweigen, das er an ihren Anfang gesetzt hat [...] eine tiefe Wirkung gezeitigt«.³⁹ Damit wird Literatur zu einer Sprachform, die sich über dem strukturellen Defekt der symbolischen Ordnung, über der Verlustzone von Bedeutungen als Zweitsprache etabliert. Begriffe wie nicht-diskursive Sprache, nicht-dialektische Grenzsprache, zirkelhafte Sprache, Rückwendung der Sprache zu sich selbst, Selbstinfragestellung der Sprache, unendliches Sprechen, doppeltes Sprechen, Selbst-Implikation, Selbst-Überlagerung werden in der Folge in den »Schriften zur Literatur« diesem Sachverhalt Rechnung tragen, dass Sprache auf nichts anderes als auf sich selbst verweist. Das ist Sprache in ihrem »rohen Sein« jenseits ihrer »repräsentativen oder bedeutenden Funktion«,⁴⁰ das Murmeln und Raunen, das Foucaults Texte fortan durchzieht und das den Ort der Sprache als ein »Draußen« der Kultur und des Diskurses ausweist. Die moderne Literatur wird im Denken Foucaults zu einer Form von Selbstverhältnis, das »vorlebt«, worauf Foucaults späte Technologien des Selbst zielen: Anders-Denken, Selbsttransformation.

Der in »Das ›Nein‹ des Vaters« praktizierte kritisch-archäologische Blick auf die Psychoanalyse tritt in den Texten der sechziger Jahre zugunsten einer strategischen Allianz zwischen moderner Literatur und Psychoanalyse zurück, die sich beide in ihrer Überschreitung des humanwissenschaftlichen Bildes des Menschen als Gegendiskurs qualifizieren. Mit Beginn der siebziger Jahre rückt Foucault von der archäologischen Kritik der Humanwissenschaften ab, die sich der Darstellung von Brüchen und Erfahrungsstrukturen der Wissenschaftsgeschichte verschrieben hatte, und wendet sich der Verschränkung von sozialer Praxis und Wissensstrukturen, den sogenannten Macht-/Wissens-Komplexen zu. Mit Foucaults genealogischer Wende,

---

36 | Foucault: Die Ordnung der Dinge, S. 449.
37 | Ebd., S. 77.
38 | Foucault: Einleitung, S. 15.
39 | Foucault: Das ›Nein‹ des Vaters, S. 280.
40 | Foucault: Die Ordnung der Dinge, S. 76.

die das duale Denken nach dem Schema Diskurs und Gegendiskurs verabschiedet, fallen sowohl Literatur als auch Psychoanalyse unter das Verdikt der Machtanalysen. Das ehemalige »Draußen« des Diskurses wird nun im Innern der Macht-/Wissens-Komplexe verortet; Rauschen und Diskurs erscheinen als deckungsgleich.

Es herrscht zweifellos in unserer Gesellschaft [...] eine tiefe Logophobie, eine stumme Angst vor jenen Ereignissen, vor jener Masse von gesagten Dingen, vor dem Auftauchen all jener Aussagen, vor allem, was es da Gewalttätiges, Plötzliches, Kämpferisches, Ordnungsloses und Gefährliches gibt, vor jenem großen unaufhörlichen und ordnungslosen Rauschen des Diskurses.[41]

Das ehemals der Literatur zugebilligte subversive Potential wandert für Foucault hingegen in solche Texte ab, die die Schwelle zur Literatur nicht erreichen. An den autobiographischen Aufzeichnungen des Elternmörders Paul Rivière, den »Lettres de cachet« und den Memoiren des Hermaphroditen Herculine Barbin lässt sich beobachten, dass sich Foucaults Interesse auf diese Form nicht-literarischer »Gebrauchstexte« verlagert. Diese zeugen von »der seltsamen Intensität und einer Art Schönheit«,[42] die das Sprechen im Angesicht der Macht erlangt. Als »Novellen« bzw. »befremdende Gedichte« bezeichnet Foucault diese Texte, deren »Intensität« darin besteht, dass diese »Diskurse [...] wirklich Leben gekreuzt [haben]; diese Leben sind tatsächlich riskiert und verloren worden in diesen Wörtern.«[43] Es ist nun dieser ›kleine Lärm‹ der infamen Menschen,[44] der ihn interessiert und der als Schlachtruf konnotiert ist: »Sich zur Sprache bringen, um nicht zur Sprache zu kommen: Subjekt bleiben, ohne irgend jemandem, nicht einmal dem König, die Möglichkeit zu geben, einen zum Objekt zu machen.«[45]

In diesem erweiterten Diskursverständnis, das Aussageweisen, Technik, Institution, soziale Praxis, Codes und Medien, Regeln der Sagbarkeit und Unsagbarkeit sowie SprecherInnenpositionen umfasst, liegt Foucaults Beitrag für eine kulturwissenschaftliche Wahrnehmung von *noise/bruit*. Diese Begrifflichkeit bezeichnet eher ein Zuviel als ein Zuwenig an Strukturierung, Ordnung, Reglementierung, das Sprach- und Handlungsmöglichkeiten eröffnet. So wird das Produktive und Formative von Rauschen und Diskurs herausgestellt, denn der »Diskurs [...] ist auch nicht bloß das, was die Kämpfe oder die Systeme der Beherrschung in Sprache übersetzt: er ist dasjenige,

---

41 | Foucault: Die Ordnung des Diskurses, S. 35.
42 | Foucault: Das Leben der infamen Menschen, S. 50.
43 | Ebd., S. 44.
44 | Foucault: Familiäre Konflikte, S. 45.
45 | Ebd., S. 283.

worum und womit man kämpft; er ist die Macht, deren man sich zu bemächtigen sucht.«[46] Und diese Macht ist »produktiv; und sie produziert Wirkliches. Sie produziert Gegenstandsbereiche und Wahrheitsrituale: das Individuum und seine Erkenntnis sind Ergebnisse dieser Produktion.«[47]

BIBLIOGRAPHIE

Deutsches Wörterbuch von Jacob Grimm und Wilhelm Grimm, Leipzig 1885.
Eribon, Didier: Michel Foucault, Cambridge/MS 1991.
Foucault, Michel: Botschaft oder Rauschen, in: Ders.: Botschaften der Macht. Reader Diskurs und Medien, hg. v. Jan Engelmann, Stuttgart 1999, S. 140-144.
Foucault, Michel: Das ›Nein‹ des Vaters, in: Ders.: Schriften in vier Bänden, Bd. 1: 1954-1969, Frankfurt/M. 2001, S. 263-281.
Foucault, Michel: Das Leben der infamen Menschen, in: Tumult 4 (1982), S. 41-57.
Foucault, Michel: Die Ordnung der Dinge. Eine Archäologie der Humanwissenschaften, Frankfurt/M. 1974.
Foucault, Michel: Einleitung, in: Ders. und Ludwig Binswanger: Traum und Existenz, Bern, Berlin 1992, S. 5-93.
Foucault, Michel: Familiäre Konflikte. Die ›Lettres de cachet‹. Aus den Archiven der Bastille im 18. Jahrhundert, Frankfurt/M. 1989.
Foucault, Michel: Psychologie und Geisteskrankheit, Frankfurt/M. 1968.
Foucault, Michel: Schriften in vier Bänden, Bd. 1: 1954-1969, Frankfurt/M. 2001.
Foucault, Michel: Schriften zur Literatur, Frankfurt/M. 1988.
Foucault, Michel: Überwachen und Strafen. Die Geburt des Gefängnisses, Frankfurt/M. 1994.
Foucault, Michel: Vom Licht des Krieges zur Geburt der Geschichte, Berlin 1986.
Foucault, Michel: Vorwort, in: Ders.: Schriften in vier Bänden, Bd. 1: 1954-1969, Frankfurt/M. 2001, S. 223-234.
Foucault, Michel: Wahnsinn und Gesellschaft. Eine Geschichte des Wahns im Zeitalter der Vernunft, Frankfurt/M. 1973.
Jacobson, Robert: Linguistics and Communication Theory, in: Structure of language and its mathematical aspects. Proceedings of the Twelfth Symposium in Applied Mathematics, Providence/RI 1961, S. 245-252.

---

46 | Foucault: Die Ordnung des Diskurses, S. 8.
47 | Foucault: Überwachen und Strafen, S. 250.

Lacan, Jacques: Das Spiegelstadium als Bildner der Ichfunktion, in: Ders.: Schriften I, Olten u.a. 1973, S. 61-70.

Lacan, Jacques: Über eine Frage, die jeder möglichen Behandlung der Psychose vorausgeht, in: Ders.: Schriften II, Olten u.a. 1975, S. 61–117.

Markowsky, George: Claude Shannon, in: Encyclopaedia Britannica, http://www.britannica.com/EBchecked/topic/538577/Claude-Shannon (14.12.16).

Seitter, Walter: Wahrheit, Macht, Medien. Zum Wirkenkönnen nach Michel Foucault, http://www.walterseitter.at/nova/nachfoucault.htm (16.12.16).

Shannon, Claude E.: A Mathematical Theory of Communication, in: The Bell System Technical Journal 27.3/4 (1948), S. 379-423, 623-656.

Siegert, Bernhard: Die Geburt der Literatur aus dem Rauschen der Kanäle. Zur Poetik der phatischen Funktion, in: Michael Franz u.a. (Hg.): Electric Laokoon. Zeichen und Medien, von der Lochkarte zur Grammatologie, Berlin 2007, S. 5-41.

Sterne, Jonathan: MP3. The Meaning of a Format, Durham u.a. 2012.

Multiplicities: Sound, Noise and Silence

Ben Byrne

Sound is commonly treated as a *thing*. As such, it is opposed with silence and contrasted with noise. This article sets out to argue that this approach is problematic, as a sound – rather than being simply a thing – is a multiplicity. Although this is hard to conceive, it is easy to demonstrate. The sound of a piano is a good example. Often people talk of the sound of a particular piano, whether it is heard being played live or recorded, and such an approach presents that sound as a thing, a discrete sound, a sound with particularity, which represents the piano. However, what is being heard is fingers on keys, feet on pedals and hammers on strings, resonating from the body of the instrument and resounding around a room. In other words: what is heard is many sounds, a multiplicity of sound. Sound, as demonstrated with the example of a piano, is never simple, discrete and particular, although it may be heard as such. Instead, it is always multiple.

Interestingly, John Cage is most famous for his work *4'33"* in which – at least in the canonized version – a performer at a piano is instructed to sit silently at the instrument, interacting with it only to open and close the lid several times. In this work, the sound of the piano is silenced in favour of the noise of the performance environment, heard by an audience as music. Here, along with the sound of the piano – which, if not heard, is perhaps imagined or implied as a possibility – silence and noise are not absolutes but multiplicities.

In this article, I will show how the work of Cage, along with that of Fluxus artist Yasunao Tone and the Wandelweiser group of composers, all of whom are influenced by Cage's work, calls into question the relationships between sound, noise and silence. With reference to the writing of Henri Bergson, Gilles Deleuze and Michel Serres, I will describe noise, sound and silence as mutually constitutive multiplicities, demonstrating my points with examples of the artists' work. There is evidence that the writing of these three theorists has influenced the work of the artists mentioned. This not only supports my argument but also is interesting in that it shows how experimental music and sonic art exists in dialogue with the work of other disciplines. Demonstrating how these practices assist in the theorization of sound, I will offer an account of the relationship between noise, sound and silence that avoids absolutes in favour of addressing each as interdependent, contingent on and coexistent with the others, avoiding hierarchical valorisations to, instead, emphasize the dynamic character of each. Along with Cage's *4'33"*, premiered in 1952, I will address in particular Yasunao Tone's performance at the UTS Music.Sound. Design Symposium in 2008, and the Wandelweiser box set *Wandelweiser und so weiter*, released in 2012.

In his book *Silence* (1973), Cage notes that many composers object to the use of the term »experimental music« to define their work, arguing that, while they may experiment when *making* their work, the *result* is very much determined. While Cage accepts their reasons, he points out that when attention is on the »observation and audition« of multiple things at the same time, »the word ›experimental‹ is apt, providing it is understood not as descriptive of an act to be later judged in terms of success and failure, but simply as of an act the outcome of which is unknown«.[1] I shall approach the work of Cage, Tone and Wandelweiser as experimental in just such a way, particularly as heard by audiences. All are significant for how they explore noise, sound and silence, as well as for the relationships they share. However, as I will explain, I find that *4'33"* is particularly significant as a demonstration of the existence of sound as a multiplicity while Tone's performance is interesting as a presentation of noise as a multiplicity and *Wandelweiser und so weiter*, in turn, is notable for its emphasis on silence as a multiplicity.

It is the work of Michel Serres that has led me to approach sound as a multiplicity, particularly his book *Genesis* (2009), in which he offers an account of the multiple based on a metaphysics of noise. He writes, in the book's introduction, »I hear sound and I lose it, I have only fragmentary information on this multiplicity«,[2] succinctly summing up the quandary of my interest in sound. He explains of the multiple:

Locally, it is not individuated; globally, it is not summed up. So it's neither a flock, nor a school, nor a heap, nor a swarm, nor a herd, nor a pack. It is not an aggregate; it is not discrete. It's a bit viscous perhaps. A lake under the mist, the sea, a white plain, background noise, the murmur of a crowd, time.[3]

---

1 | Cage: Silence, p. 13.
2 | Serres: Genesis, p. 5.
3 | Ibid., pp. 4-5.

The multiple, he argues, »is not an epistemological monster, but on the contrary the ordinary lot of situations«.[4] This is also the case with sound, noise and silence. As Frances Dyson writes in her book *Sounding New Media: Immersion and Embodiment in the Arts and Culture*, »›Sound‹ – the term itself – is already abstracted: there is sound, inasmuch as there is atmosphere; like a dense fog, it disappears when approached, falling beyond discourse as it settles within the skin«.[5] Many of those that have turned their attention to sound have attempted to clear the fog so that they may see but I wish instead to listen through it.

Sound, as I will show, is a multiplicity with physical, perceptual and conceptual dimensions comprised of many events, experiences and ideas, which can be considered distinct but are nonetheless intimately entangled with each other. The same holds true for both noise and silence. To discuss any of these as merely phenomenal is to ignore important dimensions of their existence. As I have shown above, with the example of the piano, sound is always multiple when produced and heard. There is never simply a sound. Instead, there are many sounds that may be heard as, that is identified as or resolved into being, one particular sound. In addition, sound exists conceptually as a multiplicity. Sound is conceived in many ways, by different subjects and with a variety of characteristics, but is irreducible to any of these. Principally, as a *thing*, sound is conceived and so it is a cultural artefact, but one that involves physical and perceptual dimensions, even if only implied or imagined. As I will explain, perception of sound as a phenomenon, involving necessarily physicality, is only possible with a conception of sound. That is, it is necessary to conceive sound in order to perceive it. It is only possible to hear sound if you know it in some way. A conception of sound can even be used to *hear* sound without ears (for instance by feeling low frequency vibrations or by synesthetic experience), to remember or imagine it (as may happen with a melody, drawing out sound's associative and mnemonic qualities) and, perhaps most powerfully of all, to consider it as a resource that can be recorded, stored and traded. Still, however, a conception of sound depends on involvement with the perceptual and physical, on sound as *heard* in some way. To demonstrate the multiplicity of sound, noise and silence it is necessary to offer a more thorough grounding in the concept of multiplicity. While it is the work of Serres that I have found particularly influential, his work is to a large extent based on that of Deleuze and Bergson.

---

4 | Ibid., p. 5.
5 | Dyson: Sounding New Media, p. 4.

Multiplicities

Henri Bergson has been central to developing philosophies of multiplicity. Outlining his theory of duration, he explains multiplicity in his book *Time and Free Will: An Essay on the Immediate Data of Consciousness*.[6] He argues that number is a collection of units and as such »the synthesis of the one and the many«.[7] Therefore, he finds, every number is one, a unity, but »covers a multiplicity of parts which can be considered separately«.[8] He sees it as necessary, however, to distinguish between two kinds of multiplicity – quantitative multiplicities and qualitative multiplicities. Quantitative multiplicities involve number in a way that can be expressed or measured, such as a flock of sheep comprised of a number of sheep that, considered to be identical and mapped in space, can be counted.[9] Qualitative multiplicities, meanwhile, are heterogeneous and contain number only potentially such that »consciousness, then, makes a qualitative discrimination without any further thought of counting the qualities or even of distinguishing them as *several*«.[10]

In *The Creative Mind* (1992) Bergson elucidates his concept of duration as »what we have always called *time*« but »time perceived as indivisible«.[11] It is, for him, an example of qualitative multiplicity with particular significance. He explains the concept using the example of a melody, »when we listen to a melody we have the purest impression of succession we could possibly have [...] yet it is the very continuity of the melody and the impossibility of breaking it up which make that impression upon us«.[12] A melody, as heard, relies on time as duration, rather than time as linear and divisible and such a conception of time is a qualitative multiplicity. Subsequently, Gilles Deleuze and Felix Guattari explain in their book *A Thousand Plateaus: Capitalism and Schizophrenia* (1987) that the creation of multiplicity as a substantive marks »a very important moment« because it allows escape from »the abstract opposition between the multiple and the one«, and thus dialectics, such that it is possible »to succeed in conceiving the multiple in the pure state«.[13] Keeping all of this in mind, I base my own work on the openness of Michel Serres's

---

6 | Bergson: Time and Free Will. Originally published in 1889 as *Essai sur les données immédiates de la conscience*, first English translation in 1910.

7 | Ibid., p. 75.

8 | Ibid., pp. 75-76.

9 | Ibid., pp. 76-77, 121.

10 | Ibid., pp. 76-77, 121.

11 | Bergson: The Creative Mind, p. 149. Originally published in 1934 as *La pensée it le mouvant*, first English translation in 1946.

12 | Ibid., p. 149.

13 | Deleuze and Guattari: A Thousand Plateaus, p. 32.

account of multiplicity, approaching sound, accordingly, as a multiplicity that is known predominantly qualitatively but that is still both temporal and spatial. Sound, as such a multiplicity, is conceived including a seemingly ever expanding number of elements, such as infrasound, ultrasound, non-sound, recorded sound and digital sound, heard by a variety of different organs, individuals and machines.

Instead of considering sound ontologically as people consider *things*, it is necessary to theorize its existence in a way that accounts for its multiplicity. This is possible using Deleuze's concept of *difference*. In *Difference and Repetition*, Deleuze argues that »difference must become the element, the ultimate unity; it must therefore refer to other differences which never identify it but rather differentiate it. Each term of a series, being already a difference, must be put into a variable relation with other terms, thereby constituting other series devoid of center and convergence«.[14] Differentiating and defining sound in this way, it cannot be considered as merely phenomenal. Nor can it be considered as simply perceptual or conceptual and thought to exist in sites such as the ear or *high-fidelity* recording. Instead, sound, in the way Deleuze outlines, »must be shown *differing*«.[15] Sound, as I will show, has been differentiated in complex ways from silence and noise.

Deleuze believes empiricism becomes transcendental when the being of what is experienced is approached as based in difference, positioning »difference, potential difference and difference in intensity as the reason behind qualitative diversity«.[16] He explains, drawing on Bergson's work, »this empiricism teaches us a strange ›reason‹, that of the multiple, chaos and difference (nomadic distributions, crowded anarchies)«.[17] Therefore, what Deleuze's theory of difference offers this study is a concept to underpin a new approach to sound, an approach based on differentiation rather than essentialism. Using this approach it is possible to avoid seeking sound's essence or attempting to define it.

Deleuze further claims that »identity, produced by difference, is determined as ›repetition‹«.[18] For him, repetition »consists in conceiving the same on the basis of the different«.[19] Moreover, he argues »individuation is mobile, strangely supple, fortuitous and endowed with fringes and margins [...] the individual is far from indivisible, never ceasing to divide and change its

---

14 | Deleuze: Difference and Repetition, p. 56. Originally published in 1968 as *Différence et Répétition*, first English translation in 1994.
15 | Ibid., p. 56.
16 | Ibid., pp. 56-57.
17 | Ibid., p. 57.
18 | Ibid., p. 41.
19 | Ibid.

nature«.[20] Employing Deleuze's concept, sound as a multiplicity based in difference can be and is individuated; but only as part of a process of differentiation that is itself unstable. Sound is still multiple when individuated, comprised of yet more *individual* sounds. Although sound is generally contrasted with silence, conceived as a multiplicity, it is differentiated from noise.

In *Genesis*, Michel Serres proposes a metaphysics of noise that emphasizes the multiple and encompasses all examples of noise. He argues that »noise cannot be a phenomenon; every phenomenon is separated from it, a silhouette on a backdrop, like a beacon against the fog«.[21] He claims that »what are called phenomena alone are known and knowable« and this can, as I will show, be effectively applied to sound and its relationship to noise.[22] Sound is typically defined as meaningful and, therefore, knowable, differentiated from noise of many kinds. However, whenever sound is defined, it is surrounded by and drenched in noise. Building on Serres's theory, Frances Dyson comments: while »the meaning that a signal might convey results from its serialization and periodicity«, »what in fact defines the signal [...] is an aesthetic, technological and metaphysical process that both filters and is constituted by noise«.[23] However, she finds that the »ceaseless movement« of noise »between signal, music, rumour, and language unhinges any dialectic with which it is engaged, or to which it is applied«.[24] Noise, approached in this way, is always multiple and as such cannot easily be grasped. *Noise*, meanwhile, is, for Serres, chaos, the undifferentiated. He uses the archaic French word *noise* rather than the more commonly used *bruit* to differentiate his conception of *noise* from everyday examples of noise.[25] *Noise* generally denotes »ado, strife, contention«[26] and, thus, is related to but distinct from other definitions of noise, including auditory noise and information noise, both of which are usually referred to as *bruit* in French. In Serres's conception, *noise* precedes and underlies not only all sound but everything. Explaining his concept further, Serres argues that »the *noise* is incapable of differentiation, everything in it is indistinguishable«.[27] His point is that if *noise* is what lies outside meaning, then it is necessarily, in any kind of pure form, indecipherable.

---

20 | Ibid., p. 257.
21 | Serres: Genesis, p. 13. Originally published in 1982 as *Genèse*.
22 | Ibid., p. 18.
23 | Dyson: Sounding New Media, p. 188.
24 | Ibid.
25 | Here and throughout this article *noise* – in italics – refers to Serres's conception and noise – without italics – to other, more common, conceptions of noise.
26 | Serres: Genesis, p. 141.
27 | Ibid., p. 118.

Consequently, the noises people hear, themselves multiple in the same way as sound, are at most only ever a momentary suggestion of an all encompassing *noise* that exists as an inaccessible multiplicity. Serres argues that »noises that come and go are contingent on an observer, they hinge on a listening post, on a channel, on an aperture, open or closed, door or window.«[28] These noises, in that moment in which they pierce right through me when I hear them, can give an inkling of the multiplicity of *noise* but never constitute it themselves – when I hear something I regard as a noise, I render it meaningful just in perceiving it, even if only in the subtlest way, diffusing and discarding it. These noises are thus examples of noise that, for Serres, »is a turbulence, it is order and disorder at the same time, order revolving on itself through repetition and redundancy, disorder through chance occurrences«.[29] Despite his use of the word, Serres finds disorder to be a negative term and so prefers *noise*.[30] Bergson's take on disorder illuminates this point. He argues, in support of Serre's approach, that »one cannot suppress one arrangement without another arrangement taking its place, or take away matter without some other matter taking its place« and so »disorder« refers only to »the presence of a thing or an order which does not interest us, which blunts our effort or our attention; it is our disappointment being expressed when we call this presence absence«.[31] *Noise*, then, as thought by Serres, is only an unruly swirl of order (meaning that we are interested in) and disorder (meaning that is not of interest), which is thought to interfere with the meaningful. Bergson goes on to argue that »when the philosopher speaks of chaos and nothingness, he is only carrying over into the order of speculation – raised to the absolute and consequently emptied of all meaning, of all effective content – two ideas made for practical use«.[32] Clearly, this could be positioned in opposition to Serres's theory of *noise*, but I do not think this to be the case. Instead, I read these theories as compatible, for when Serres writes of *noise* as chaos, he does not mean »nothingness« but a kind of universal totality from which everything known is differentiated.

Turbulence can be found in many places, in the tumultuous roar of the ocean, the play of the wind in the trees, the hum of the city and even in the brain. It is particularly important for Serres because »the turbulent state mixes or associates the one and the multiple, systematic gathering together and distribution«.[33] He writes, »turbulence is widespread everywhere, almost

---

28 | Ibid., pp. 62-63.
29 | Ibid., p. 59.
30 | Ibid., p. 20.
31 | Bergson: The Creative Mind, p. 64.
32 | Ibid.
33 | Serres: Genesis, p. 109.

everywhere, yet it is not universal«.[34] Instead, he finds, it is »diversal,« – »a mix of foreseeable regions and chaotic regions, a mix of concepts in the classical, unitary sense of the term, and of pure multiplicity«.[35] He continues: »turbulence is an intermittence of void and plenitude, of lawful determinism and underdeterminism«.[36] *Noise,* meanwhile, is for Serres »a saturation of differences« such that »no signal will pass through the innumerable plurality«.[37] He claims that »no difference or complete difference both produce the undifferentiated. The sense of hearing is lost in silence and also in pure noise«.[38] Applying Serres theory, sounds that are heard are always turbulent, containing and surrounded by noise but differentiated from *noise.*

Sound as meaningful, drawing on Serres work, exists within a swell of noise with the »mere appearance«[39] of silence. Nonetheless, if sound and noise are to be approached as multiple, then the same must be done with silence. It is easy to argue that silence does not exist, but such an approach does not account for the specific and multiple silences in the world. After all, silence is something that Cage did use in his work; it may not have been *absolute* silence but that does not make it insignificant, since it constituted the prescribed absence of *intentional* sound. Silence and noise, then, both imply an absence of sound, at least, in any specific instance, of a particular sound. However, each can coexist with the other *and* with sound, which – it follows – has no clear horizon. Instead, all three need to be thought of as multiple and coexistent. In the following, I shall demonstrate this, drawing on the work of Cage, Tone and Wandelweiser.

Sound

John Cage's influence on the study of sound is profound and, as I have argued and will show in greater detail now, his work is helpful in developing an understanding of the multiplicity of sound. *4'33"* is particularly significant in this respect, but to explain its importance, I must start with the story of its development. As has been recited many times, during a visit to an anechoic chamber Cage discovered that what he thought was silence was in fact a whole world of new sounds just beyond the reach of the human ear. He declared:

---

34 | Ibid., p. 110.
35 | Ibid., pp. 110-111.
36 | Ibid., p. 109.
37 | Ibid., p. 118.
38 | Ibid., p. 119.
39 | Ibid., p. 13.

There is always something to see, something to hear. In fact, try as we may to make silence, we cannot. For certain engineering purposes, it is desirable to have as silent a situation as possible. Such a room is called an anechoic chamber, its six walls made of special material, a room without echoes. I entered one at Harvard University several years ago and heard two sounds, one high and one low. When I described them to the engineer in charge, he informed me that the high one was my nervous system in operation, the low one my blood in circulation. Until I die there will be sounds. And they will continue following my death.[40]

There is debate about the science of Cage's claim – Peter Gena, for one, argues that humans cannot in fact hear the operation of their nervous system nor indeed, normally, their blood in circulation, and suggests that Cage may simply have suffered from tinnitus – but as Kyle Gann notes: »medical fact leaves Cage's basic point unscathed: our bodies do produce sounds of their own, and in the vast continuum of human experience true silence is virtually unknown«.[41] Inspired by the possibilities around him, Cage employed amplification, microphones and loudspeakers to render audible previously unheard sounds, from his »own vital signs to the (musical) vibrational resonances of all matter«.[42] Indeed, Cage's interest in, to use his own words, »the physicality of sound and activity of listening«,[43] can be described as phenomenological. However, it turns out that Cage had a broader interest in philosophy.

In his essay »Chance, Indeterminacy, Multiplicity«, Brandon W. Joseph examines Bergson's influence on Cage's work.[44] As Joseph recounts, Cage, in his essay »Where are we going? What are we doing?« included in *Silence*, claims: »I believe, of course, that what we're doing is exploring a field, that the field is limitless and without qualitative differentiation but with multiplicity of differences«.[45] The influence of Bergson here is clear. Furthermore, Joseph points out that »Cage's use of the term ›multiplicity‹ in describing the heterogeneous and unlimited space of all sound«[46] was not occasional but had come up in his correspondence with Pierre Boulez about his work *Music of Changes*. Moreover, Joseph claims that Cage had most likely discovered Bergson's work on multiplicity in 1951, before the premiere of *4'33"*.[47] More supportably,

---

40 | Cage: Silence, p. 8.
41 | Gann: No Such Thing as Silence, p. 164.
42 | Kahn: Noise Water Meat, p. 192.
43 | Gann: No Such Thing as Silence, p. 88.
44 | Joseph: Chance, Indeterminacy, Multiplicity, p. 213.
45 | Cage: Silence, pp. 204-205; Joseph: Chance, Indeterminacy, Multiplicity, pp. 219-220.
46 | Joseph: Chance, Indeterminacy, Multiplicity, p. 220.
47 | Ibid.

as Joseph writes, »Cage's mature understanding of silence as formulated in that year can be related to (if it did not, in fact, derive from) Bergson's critique of non-being as expressed in *Creative Evolution*«.[48] Bergson's argument is that »judgments that posit the non-existence of a thing [...] formulate a contrast between the possible and the actual (that is between two kinds of *existence*, one thought and the other found)«.[49] This relates back to Bergson's account of disorder, discussed above. Joseph further finds that Cage »mobilized the idea of multiplicity (as a complex interaction that was in line with the actual, ontological existence of sound) against an idea of relationships as generally understood by the human mind« to conceive existence, like sound, as a multiplicity that is not cognizable as a totality but from which the actual is differentiated.[50] This echoes Bergson's conception of multiplicity and uncannily suggests both Deleuze's concept of difference and Serres's metaphysics of noise. Having decided that absolute silence does not exist, Cage regarded silence as the absence of intention, most often articulated with the example of music, which is why silence, for him, is a chance to hear life. Silence, approached in this way, rather than being understood as the opposite of sound (which is omnipresent for Cage), replaces noise as the label for everything that is not *intended* sound. Apart from setting into motion sound's rise in contemporary arts and the acceptance of all sound (otherwise frequently considered noise) into the contemporary musical palette, Cage's music and ideas, particularly as expressed with *4'33"*, have left those that follow to deal with the implications of a world where there is always a multiplicity of sound.

Noise

While Cage's music explores sound as multiplicity, Yasunao Tone's work demonstrates the multiplicity of noise. I organized for Tone to attend the UTS Music.Sound.Design Symposium in 2008, and it is the performance he gave as part of that event I will discuss in this essay. Tone is well known for his live performances using prepared CDs, but has also produced a significant body of work based on the use of a WACOM tablet to transcribe Chinese characters into noise. His performance at UTS forms part of the latter. The performance, based on one he gave for Lovebytes 2007 in Sheffield, England titled *495,63*, involved the artist transcribing a series of Chinese characters in Japanese calligraphic style. The characters were both projected on a screen in front of the audience and fed into a Max/MSP based system which, in turn,

---

48 | Ibid.
49 | Bergson: Creative Evolution, p. 186.
50 | Joseph: Chance, Indeterminacy, Multiplicity, pp. 222-224.

produced a complex flood of noise, using an eight channel surround audio system. The technical details of the influence of Tone's transcriptions on the resulting sound were not revealed to the audience or myself and were, to my ears, incomprehensible. The performance continued for almost an hour and by the end most of the audience had left. It was in witnessing the performance that I began to consider Tone's work in new ways.

Due to the sound he achieves with what he calls his *wounded CDs*, prepared with scotch tape, Tone's sonic output has commonly been described as *glitch* – referring to the so called *post-digital* style of electronic music that developed in the 1990s and proliferated early this century. But this label represents at best a limited understanding of Tone's work. Considering Tone's practice in detail, I have found he is focused on dealing with what is outside meaning – that is, *noise*. Demonstrating my point, his release *Musica Iconologos* (1993), and in particular his explanation of it, is of interest here. He explains how he produced the release in his article »John Cage and Recording«.[51] He scanned images and had a computer store the resulting data as sound files (deliberately forcing the computer to *misread* the data, decoding it as if it represented sound, when, in fact, it represented the scanned image), which, in turn, were encoded to the individual CDs when they were manufactured. Moreover, he claims:

Now, when playing the CD, what is received are not images as message, but sound that is simply an excess. According to information theory the resultant sound is nothing other than noise. As the French word for (static) noise, *parasite*, indicates, noise is parasitic on its host, that is, the message. But in this case there is no host, only a parasite on the CD. Therefore, this CD is pure noise. Technically speaking, the sound of the CD is digital noise.[52]

---

51 | Tone: John Cage and Recording, p. 12. Interestingly, Cage attended the premiere of Tone's *Music for 2 CD Players* in 1986, for which Tone employed his CD preparation technique. Tone recounts that, as soon he had finished the performance, Cage rushed up to him and shook his hand (Tone: John Cage and Recording). Tone explains the importance of Cage to his work in his article »John Cage and Recording«. Specifically, he details the complexity of Cage's approach to recording and its relationship to his own (ibid.), pointing out that although Cage had told him he did not like records, he was clearly happy to have his own music recorded for preservation (ibid.). Indeed, Tone adds, Cage perhaps encouraged the publishing of multiple recordings of his pieces to avoid any one recording becoming canonical (ibid.). Moreover, Tone notes that Cage used recordings in his own music and so seemingly did not mind their creative use, he just »hated repeating the known« (ibid.). It this impulse, above all, that Tone shares with Cage, as his work with CDs shows.

52 | Ibid.

I disagree with Tone's claim that the CD is pure noise. Even if the content of the CD is noise when produced, the fact that it can then be listened to as music means that meaning can be ascribed to it. This noise cannot be pure, as both noise and music are polysemic. Nonetheless, the above quotation articulates very clearly Tone's approach. As Federico Marulanda notes, »Tone's playback technique is not an instrument for effacing the boundary between the musical and non-musical«.[53] Writing about one of Tone's releases,[54] Marulanda convincingly argues that Tone's »sonic transliteration [...] represents a deliberate effort to recuperate, and then dissipate, specific bits of information, leaving as a trace only noise«.[55] Primarily, as is indicated in his quote above, Tone seems to be interested in the dissolution of meaning that occurs in any act of transcription, foregrounding the noise that exists in all communication. Therefore, as with these earlier examples, it is possible to approach *495,63* and Tone's performance at UTS as works concerned primarily with the production and dissolution of meaning, producing and emphasizing the presence of noise.

For his performance in Sydney, Tone dedicated his attention to fastidiously copying Chinese characters from a book he picked up in nearby Chinatown earlier the same day, choosing them from pages at random, but attempting to transcribe them, using a WACOM tablet projected onto a screen before the audience, as accurately, beautifully and meaningfully as possible. Having offered some, seemingly indeterminate, input to the spatialization of noise around the room, each transcribed character was – once completed – wiped from the projection before the audience's eyes. The spatialization, meanwhile, was carried out by the Max / MSP system, which drew on sound files stored on the computer's hard drive along with a live audio stream coming from a radio to produce a clamorous noise. Demonstrating its indefinite qualities, the piece Tone performed in Sydney was not even titled because the name of its predecessor – *495,63* – refers to the call number of the library book Tone chose to transcribe for the earlier Sheffield performance. In Sydney, he did not find a suitable book in the university library and so decided, instead, to make the most of the proximity of the venue to Chinatown, choosing one from a local bookshop.

It is an interest in the transcription of meaning, as demonstrated by the performance at UTS and a number of Tone's other works, which I believe is most central to this artist's practice. Perhaps unsurprisingly then, he has been profoundly influenced by the theory of Serres, who is himself

---

53 | Marulanda: From Logogram to Noise, p. 89.
54 | *Wounded Man'yo 2/2000*, for which he used the ancient *Man'yoshu* poems and employed a technique similar to the one he used for *Musica Iconologos*.
55 | Marulanda: From Logogram to Noise, p. 90.

particularly interested in messages. Tone has used Serres's theory of the parasite as a basis for his own concept – *paramedia* – which he has, in turn, used to explain why much of his work, using a variety of techniques, explores the presence and role of noise in media. Despite the many references to paramedia and their basis in Serres's theory of the parasite by Tone and others, the concept has to date not been expanded on by theorists at any length. Serres's theory suggests that parasitic noise exists with, and indeed *in*, every signal. It forms part of all meaning in the world: »mistakes, wavy lines, confusion, obscurity are part of knowledge; noise is part of communication«.[56] This regard for the *unmeaningful* is central to Tone's practice. As Serres points out, »parasite« in French means noise – specifically static or interference – along with »to eat next to«.[57] It is the significance of these multiple meanings that Serres explores in his theory of the parasite. He claims: »what passes might be a message but parasites (static) prevent it from being heard, and sometimes, from being sent«.[58] The parasite is also a place of difference. However, it is one that already exists with a signal. It cannot exist alone. As Serres writes: »the difference is part of the thing itself, and perhaps it even produces the thing«.[59] He is referring here to Deleuze's theory of difference, articulated as a kind of differential; not focusing on the difference between *things* but stressing abstract difference as an underlying principle.

Turbulence of the kind Serres theorizes is what Tone produces in drawing out *noise* in his paramedia explorations. He produces a cacophony in which meanings surface only to disappear once more, not a singular, determined, meaning but a range of possible meanings. Listening to and watching, witnessing, Tone's performance in Sydney, I found myself confronted with a disjuncture between his *work*, which I could see, and the excess it created, which I could only hear – the characters he drew as signal, and noise as parasite. Bits of discernable radio transmissions, granulation and static bobbed to the surface only to disappear again, denied even a discrete source as they were strewn around the room using the multi-channel setup. I was challenged to, if possible, chart my own passage through the signals and noise that comprised the work, comprehending the *noise* along the way. Tone's work is, therefore, notable for the way in which it continually contrives situations in which the artist himself, as much as audiences, is confronted with *noise*. That is, the *noise* his work produces is as much *noise* for the artist as it is for audiences. Tone's work shifts constantly between order and chaos, a multiplicity of meanings and *noise*, challenging listeners to open themselves to that

---

56 | Serres: The Parasite, p. 12.
57 | Ibid., p. 7.
58 | Ibid., p. 11.
59 | Ibid., p. 13.

which is other to them – offering an opportunity to comprehend, if only for a moment, *noise* as it spills turbulently into the meaningful, known, world. He achieves this by avoiding codifying works with his own meanings. Instead, he evacuates meaning in favour of the parasite within it and the noise around it, urging listeners to find their own path and dare to stray from it. *Noise*, as theorized by Serres and exemplified in Tone's work, is a fertile and nourishing outside that overflows any and all boundaries, productively challenging the confines of meaning, identity and individuality, a multiplicity full of potential that is, nonetheless, inaccessible.

SILENCE

Despite the emancipatory rhetoric Cage employed, as Douglas Kahn notes, »silencing would, in fact, run concurrently with his progressive opening up to all sound, and at the most fundamental level, it would entail a silencing of the social and ecological within an ever expanding domain of music«.[60] For instance, the bars of silence in *4'33"* that allow everyday sounds to be considered music, in doing so can be considered to strip these everyday sounds of all other meaning and significance. Although, contrarily, as Dyson explores, »part of the brilliance of *4'33"* is the way it reveals the presence of meaning and culture in the reception of sound«.[61] Kahn, too, notes how performances of the piece were, in fact, dependent on silencing such that »it can also be understood that he extended the decorum of silencing by extending the silence imposed on the audience to the performer«.[62] Along with sound and noise as multiplicities, silence as a multiplicity clearly plays a vital role in Cage's work. However, as Kahn points out,

> *4'33"*, by tacitly instructing the performer to remain quiet in *all* respects […] disrupted the unspoken audience code to remain unspoken, transposed the performance onto the audience members both in their utterances and in the acts of shifting perception toward other sounds, and legitimated bad behavior.[63]

Paradoxically, the silencing employed by Cage in *4'33"* in being ignored by audiences frees them from existing social expectations of silence. In hindsight, this is relatively easily explained, as Gann notes: »*4'33"* cannot be bracketed as a purely sonic phenomenon […] the pianist's refusal to play calls a

---

60 | Kahn: Noise Water Meat, pp. 159-160.
61 | Dyson: The Ear That Would Hear Sounds in Themselves, p. 391.
62 | Gann: No Such Thing as Silence, p. 19.
63 | Kahn: Noise Water Meat, p. 166.

whole network of social connections into question and is likely to be reflected in equally unconventional responses on the part of the audience«.[64] This demonstrates Dyson's point, that *4'33"* »reveals the presence of meaning and culture in the reception of sound«,[65] showing the significance of the multiplicity of silences that permeate the work.

Gann details the story of *4'33"* in his book *No Such Thing as Silence: John Cage's 4'33"*. The piece was premiered at the Maverick Concert Hall in Woodstock, New York on August 29, 1952.[66] It was written using an indeterminate process involving the ancient Chinese text the *I-Ching* that Cage had developed and employed for determining the pitches, dynamics and durations in his previous work *Music of Changes*. However, as he had already decided that the piece would be silent, indeterminate procedures were used only to define the duration of the piece.[67] Interestingly, Cage claims to have used the process to build up each movement from shorter silences until he arrived at *4'33"* for the entire piece.[68] Also, it suggests that perhaps he had already planned the piece to be approximately that length, which seems likely given its parallels with his earlier, proposed but unrealized, work *Silent Prayer*.[69] Moreover, it demonstrated his theory that »there can be no right making of music that does not structure itself from the very roots of sound and silence – lengths of time«.[70] Cage's process indicates that ultimately, for him, the piece is based on non-intentionality and its fundamental characteristic is duration. According to the premiere's program, on the night the durations of the individual movements were 30", 2'23" and 1'40". But Cage's performance direction states the lengths of the three movements at the premiere were 33", 2'40" and 1'20".[71] All in all, Cage published three different scores of *4'33"*, culminating in the version published by C.F. Peters in 1961 that replaces all musical notation with the use of the term *tacet* – which means »be silent« – and states that »the work may be performed by any instrumentalist or combination of instrumentalists and last any length of time«.[72] This demonstrates clearly that Cage's thinking about the piece changed over the years and, in fact, he eventually made comments which indicated that he considered the piece, as Gann

---

64 | Gann: No Such Thing as Silence, p. 19.
65 | Dyson: The Ear That Would Hear Sounds in Themselves, p. 391.
66 | Gann: No Such Thing as Silence, p. 2.
67 | Ibid., p. 174.
68 | Ibid., pp. 174-175.
69 | Ibid., p. 128, 177.
70 | Cage: Defense of Satie, pp. 81-82.
71 | Gann: No Such Thing as Silence, p. 186.
72 | Ibid., pp. 176-187.

writes, »simply an act of listening«.[73] As such it did not even need a performer. This shows the complexity, multiplicity, of silence as employed in Cage's work. Moreover, the role silence plays in Cage's work has served as inspiration for the Wandelweiser group of composers. As I will show, their work explores the role of silence in music and, as a result, its relationship with sound and noise.

Michael Pisaro, one of the more prominent composers involved in the group, explains: »*Wandelweiser* is a word for a particular group of people who have been committed, over the long term, to sharing their work and working together«.[74] Telling the story of his own encounter with the group, before becoming a member, he explains that he met the composer Kunshu Shim, who is no longer a part of the collective but still »crucial to the aesthetic development of the group«,[75] when he was in Chicago in the autumn of 1992. Cage had visited Northwestern University, where Pisaro was teaching, in the spring of 1992 and then died that August so »his name was still very much in the air«,[76] and Pisaro was struck by Shim's thoughts on Cage. While in Pisaro's experience most musicians had seemed more interested in Cage's ideas than his music, he found Shim to be focused on the music, considering it »more radical and more useful than the writing: because it had so many loose ends and live wires still to be explored«.[77] Pisaro explains that he later discovered other Wandelweiser composers shared the same approach to Cage's work, thus hearing *4'33"* as music and considering it unfinished work that created new possibilities for combining sound and silence. He writes, »put simply, silence was a material and a disturbance of material at the same time«.[78] Interest in silence, as recounted and demonstrated by Pisaro, is pivotal to the group. The collective started in 1992 but has only gradually gained prominence, most of all with the release of the *Wandelweiser und so weiter* compilation on the Another Timbre label in 2012.[79] Writing a review of *Wandelweiser und so weiter* for *Dusted*, Bill Meyer notes of the compilation:

Its name translates as ›Wandelweiser and so on‹ [...] which not only foregrounds its self-conscious refusal to be comprehensive, but also the implicit hope that it will set the listener on a path of discovery, as well as the fact that Wandelweiser is not a fixed entity but a moving target. This box doesn't document the end of something,

---

73 | Ibid., p. 186.
74 | Pisaro: Wandelweiser.
75 | Ibid.
76 | Ibid.
77 | Ibid.
78 | Ibid.
79 | Wandelweiser: Wandelweiser und so weiter.

like so many nostalgia-based boxes do; it opens a window onto a living music [...]. It affords you the chance to hear the same piece done by different musicians, and to hear different approaches by the same composer. You could spend months simply digesting its contents.[80]

The compilation draws together a considerable sample of the collective's work but in a way that presents that work as on-going, even in the act of listening, and so reflects ideas explored in the group's music.

Listening to the compilation, Wandelweiser's preoccupation with silence is clear but, crucially, it is not silence as *absolute* or silence as a *concept*, but silence that is *heard*. Specifically, multiple silences and their relationship to the sound and noise around them. The inclusion of Cage's *Prelude for meditation* is instructive. Written for prepared piano and including only four tones, the piece, in only 1 minute 14 seconds, provides a model – if indeed one can be said to exist – for a Wandelweiser piece. The tones and the melody created seem to somehow draw the listener into the silence around them. Pisaro explains the group's interest in Cage, referencing Antoine Beuger's essay »Grundsätzliche Entscheidungen« which he describes as »important«:

What seemed to be at stake here was not only the status of silence, but of the relationship between silence and noise (›the noise of the world‹), and the function of tone within that continuum.[81]

In the essay, published in 1997, Beuger details his thoughts at the time on the relationship between silence and noise.[82] Echoing Cage, he suggests that the matter of music is the noise of the world, and music *cuts* sounds from its timeless variety. Clearly following Cage, Beuger's thoughts juxtapose the work of Serres, Bergson and Deleuze, suggesting an approach to sound, noise and silence as multiplicities. Pisaro himself explicitly mentions Deleuze, in particular his suggestion that philosophy creates *concepts* while science creates *functions* and art *percepts*. He explains that »each of us, without being anything like a professional philosopher (we're more like non-professional philosophy readers), has drawn inspiration from philosophical work«.[83] He offers no detail and instead writes: »this is very hard to talk about in depth without sounding pretentious, so I'm not going to. However, not mentioning it also seemed wrong – it's an important part of the Wandelweiser atmosphere«.[84]

---

80 | Ibid.
81 | Pisaro: Wandelweiser.
82 | Beuger: Grundsätzliche Entscheidungen.
83 | Pisaro: Wandelweiser.
84 | Ibid.

Of the pieces by Wandelweiser composers on the compilation, Manfred Werder's *2 ausführende seiten 357-360* is particularly clear in its reliance on many silences. The recording is part of the *performer series*, which includes nine scores, each consisting of 160'000 units of time on 4000 pages (533 hours 20 minutes) to be performed, in sections, in succession.[85] The actualization of the series is recorded online along with a note written by Werder, detailing that »one question constitutes *ein(e) ausführende(r)*: action or silence«.[86] The score involves the use of two signs – ».« and »1« – to represent silence and action respectively. Each represents time units of 12 seconds, and Werder dictates that »one action consists of six seconds of sound, followed by six seconds of silence«[87] but leaves the rest up to the performer. Jürg Frey's *Time Intent Memory*, meanwhile, is particularly striking for the way it employs noise alongside tone and silence. As the compilation's liner notes explain, it is a »composition without a fixed architecture, though pitches are all written out« with »an extra part for a musician with non-pitched instruments, who adds backgrounds and shadows«.[88] Lastly, the inclusion of three separate realizations of Sam Sfirri's *Little By Little* is notable, demonstrating a refusal to canonize one particular take of the piece, supporting Meyer's claim that »Wandelweiser is not a fixed entity but a moving target«.[89] Each is very different from the others, such that it is not clear what exactly constitutes the score. Just as Meyer details:

One consists of fuzzy electronic textures; another, draws of a violin bow contrast with stark single notes passed from one instrument to the next; and in the third, variously sourced low pitches loom in and out of the silences that are each performance's common denominator.[90]

Wandelweiser und so weiter demonstrates the way in which music produced by the group delicately counterbalances a multiplicity of seemingly divergent elements – composition with improvisation, silence with noise (mediated by tone) and notation with music as living.

Wandelweiser's music, moreover, reflects the interests and activities of the group more broadly. Despite clear aesthetic and conceptual commonalities in a great deal of the work produced by the group, there is, at the same time, heterodoxy to their approach. Pisaro describes how Wandelweiser events have

---

85 | Werder: performer series.
86 | Ibid.
87 | Ibid.
88 | Wandelweiser: Wandelweiser und so weiter.
89 | Meyer: Wandelweiser und so weiter.
90 | Ibid.

taken place in various locations around the world, organized by a variety of people and often with little or no money. Also, he mentions that for him, as I find myself, a recording involves sound stored for »use« and so is, in some way, »open«.[91] He describes a recording as an »instrument« which produces »a limited set of sounds that can nonetheless have a variable relationship in the environment in which they are played«.[92] He find this »plays a role«[93] in how he listens to Wandelweiser recordings. Perhaps most importantly, he focuses on the importance to the group of playing one another's work, describing it as »the most important conversation«,[94] and while critique does occur, mutual support and dialogue are considered more valuable. He mentions the influence and involvement of artists, other musicians, composers (particularly improvisers) and what he calls »The Tokyo Connection«[95] along with various philosophers[96] and their work. Still it is clear that the sharing of music among members of the group is particularly central to its practice.[97] A focus on experimentation, discourse and collaboration is characteristic of Wandelweiser. The organization and operation of the group, then, reflects the existence of sound, noise and silence, as multiplicities – emphasizing contact, mutuality and contingency, and embracing a plurality of perspectives. Simon Reynell, the producer of *Wandelweiser und so weiter*, articulates this well, comparing the group and its work with a sound, that is »a narrow passage of water between the mainland and an island, or between two larger bodies of water« – »something without precisely defined boundaries that takes from and gives back to the expanses around in an ongoing process of exchange«.[98] Along with providing an analogy for Wandelweiser, this is an affective figuration of sound as multiplicity, articulating its most challenging and exciting feature – the ambiguity of its existence.

Conclusion

Addressed as mutually constitutive multiplicities, sound, noise and silence coexist in complex ways, and their relationships cannot be reduced to simple

---

91 | Pisaro: Wandelweiser.
92 | Ibid.
93 | Ibid.
94 | Ibid.
95 | Pisaro refers to musicians such as Taku Sugimoto, Toshiya Tsunoda and Taku Unami.
96 | For example, Pisaro mentions Deleuze immediately before making this point.
97 | Pisaro: Wandelweiser.
98 | Reynell: Wandelweiser sound.

hierarchies. Instead, their physical, perceptual and conceptual dimensions are intermingled, each intimately entangled with the others. This is demonstrated in the work of Cage, Tone and Wandelweiser, showing the important role of the experimental arts in sound studies. Influenced variously by Bergson, Deleuze and Serres, the work of these artists exemplifies how the work of philosophers can be used to approach sound, noise and silence as multiplicities. Cage's work, clearly related to that of Bergson, demonstrates sound as multiple, constant beyond the experience of an individual. Despite his complicated and problematic approach and relationship to silence, his denial of the existence of absolute silence has formed a basis for accounts of silence as multiple, allowing noise to be heard in new ways. In turn, Tone, influenced by both Cage and Serres, demonstrates in his work the differentiation of the meaningful, such as sound, from *noise,* and the importance of turbulence, the multiplicity of noises that are heard. Most recently, Wandelweiser in their music explore silence as multiple, enmeshed with both noise and sound in the form of tone, taking Cage's music as inspiration along with a variety of philosophy and art. All these artists demonstrate particular concern for the multiplicity of sound, noise and silence heard by audiences, their work exemplifying the complex relationships that exist between each. Also, the artists all produce work that involves the transduction of sound in some way – be it with a score, a performed transcription and / or through recordings. However, they do so in such a way that the transduction does not serve to prescribe, place or reproduce sound, but rather to multiply its existence and function. Consequently, the approaches of each problematize the position of the author, placing emphasis, instead, on listening and sounding, association, exchange and mutuality. They do so without replacing the one with the many, foregrounding instead a multiplicity of relationships. Approaching sound, noise and silence as multiplicities allows, as I have shown, complex readings of works such as *4'33"*, Tone's performance at the UTS Music.Sound.Design Symposium and *Wandelweiser und so weiter.* These readings, which are not otherwise possible, demonstrate how such an approach, in which sound as a multiplicity is differentiated from *noise* and may be silenced in many ways, assists in addressing the complexity of many sonic interactions.

Bibliography

Bergson, Henri: The Creative Mind, New York 1992.
Bergson, Henri: Time and Free Will: An Essay on the Immediate Data of Consciousness, New York 2001.
Bergson, Henri: Creative Evolution, New York 2007.
Beuger, Antoine: Grundsätzliche Entscheidungen (1997), from http://www.timescraper.de/_antoine-beuger/texts.html (7.3.16).
Cage, John: Defense of Satie, in: Richard Kostelanetz (ed.): John Cage, New York, Washington/DC 1970, pp. 81-82.
Cage, John: Silence, London 1973.
Deleuze, Gilles: Difference and Repetition, New York 1994.
Deleuze, Gilles and Guattari, Félix: A Thousand Plateaus: Capitalism and Schizophrenia, Minneapolis 1987.
Dyson, Francis: The Ear That Would Hear Sounds in Themselves: John Cage 1935-1965, in: Douglas Kahn and Gregory Whitehead (eds): Wireless Imagination: Sound, Radio and the Avant-Garde, Massachusetts 1994, pp. 373-407.
Dyson, Francis: Sounding New Media: Immersion and Embodiment in the Arts and Culture, Los Angeles 2009.
Gann, Kyle: No Such Thing as Silence: John Cage's 4'33", New Haven 2010.
Joseph, Branden W.: Chance, Indeterminacy, Multiplicity, in: Ana Jiménez Jorquera (ed.): The Anarchy of Silence: John Cage and Experimental Art, Barcelona 2009, pp. 210-238.
Kahn, Douglas: Noise Water Meat: A History of Sound in the Arts, Cambridge/MS 2001.
Marulanda, Federico: From Logogram to Noise, in: Yasunao Tone: Noise Media Language, Copenhagen 2007, pp. 79-92.
Meyer, Bill: Wandelweiser und so weiter, in: Dusted, 7.1.13, http://www.dustedmagazine.com/reviews/7511 (7.3.16)
Pisaro, Michael: Wandelweiser, in: erstwords, 23.9.12, http://erstwords.blogspot.com.au/2009/09/wandelweiser.html (7.3.16).
Reynell, Simon: Wandelweiser sound, in: Wandelweiser und so weiter (CD), Sheffield 2012.
Serres, Michel: The Parasite, Baltimore 2007.
Serres, Michel: Genesis, Ann Arbor 2009.
Tone, Yasunao: John Cage and Recording, in: Leonardo Music Journal 13 (2003), pp. 11-15.
Wandelweiser: Composer Information: Time Intent Memory, in: Wandelweiser und so weiter (CD), Sheffield 2012.

Wandelweiser: Wandelweiser und so weiter (CD). Sheffield 2012.

Werder, Manfred: performer series (1999-), http://www.performerseries.blogspot.com.au/ (7.3.16).

Wie kommen Geräusche in die Sprache?
Wort und Geräusch aus linguistischer Perspektive

Christine Ganslmayer

1. Einleitung

»Geräusche« sind akustisch wahrnehmbare Ereignisse und als solche kommunikationsrelevante Faktoren der menschlichen Erfahrungswelt. Sprachtheoretisch betrachtet sind sie referier- und prädizierbare Bestandteile der außersprachlichen Wirklichkeit: Sprecher können mittels der Sprache auf Geräusche verweisen und über sie Aussagen tätigen.

Der vorliegende Beitrag widmet sich aus sprachwissenschaftlicher Perspektive der Relation zwischen Geräuschen als außersprachlicher Kategorie und ihren Bezeichnungen mittels Wörtern als lexikalischen Einheiten des Sprachsystems. Von Interesse ist dabei nicht nur, wie »Geräusche« sprachlich kodiert werden, sondern auch inwieweit der Sprachgebrauch Rückschlüsse auf die Relevanz der Geräuschkategorie für die menschliche Wahrnehmung zulässt.

2. Sprachgebrauchsanalyse »Geräusch«

Folgt man Wittgenstein, so konstituiert sich Wortbedeutung im Gebrauch.[1] Anhand einer pragmatisch fundierten Wortgebrauchsanalyse lässt sich nicht nur kontextbezogen die Bedeutung eines Lexems fassen, sondern zugleich auch die Einstellung der Sprecher zu dem jeweiligen außersprachlichen »Objekt«. Daher bietet sich dieses Analyseverfahren für eine erste Annäherung an den Gegenstand an: Was verrät der aktuelle Sprachgebrauch über die Einstellung der Sprecher zur außersprachlichen Kategorie »Geräusch«?

---

1 | »Die Bedeutung eines Wortes ist sein Gebrauch in der Sprache.« Wittgenstein: Philosophische Untersuchungen, § 43.

Mit dem DWDS-Wortprofil[2] steht hierfür ein nützliches Instrumentarium zur Verfügung. Die korpusbasierte, automatisierte Analyse der syntaktischen Relationen des Lexems »Geräusch« vermag Aufschluss über dessen statistisch signifikante Wortbeziehungen und im Kontext stark assoziierte Wörter zu bieten. Da die Wortumgebung zudem syntaktisch differenziert wird, können relativ spezifische Angaben zum Wortgebrauch entnommen werden. Zusätzlich wird ermöglicht, das Abfragewort mit einem Vergleichswort – bei der folgenden Analyse »Klang« – zu kontrastieren, wodurch das Wortprofil noch klarer hervortritt.

Abbildung 1: Wortwolke 1 – »Geräusch« bzw. »Klang« als Aktivsubjekt

Geräusch: ablenken anschwellen aufschrecken dämpfen erschrecken ersterben herrühren irritieren nerven stören verebben

Geräusch und Klang: dringen dröhnen durchdringen erklingen ertönen erzeugen hallen klingen mischen nachhallen schallen tönen umgeben verschmelzen verstummen wecken widerhallen übertönen

Klang: aufblühen daherkommen durchströmen entfalten erschallen faszinieren inspirieren locken mitschwingen scheppern schweben schwingen strömen untermalen verhallen verklingen verwischen verzaubern wabern wandern wehen

DWDS: Wortprofil 3.0: *Geräusch*. (21.4.14)

---

2 | Das DWDS-Wortprofil (aktuelle Version 2014: 3.0) basiert auf der Analyse sehr großer Korpora mit über 4.000.000 Einzeldokumenten (ca. 115.000.000 Sätze und 1.800.000.000 Tokens) unterschiedlicher Textsorten (vorwiegend Zeitungstexte). In der sog. Wolkenansicht ist durch die Schriftgröße die Stärke der jeweiligen statistischen Assoziation angedeutet, vgl. https://www.dwds.de/d/ressources#wortprofil.

Abbildung 2: Wortwolke 2 – Attribute zu »Geräusch« bzw. »Klang«

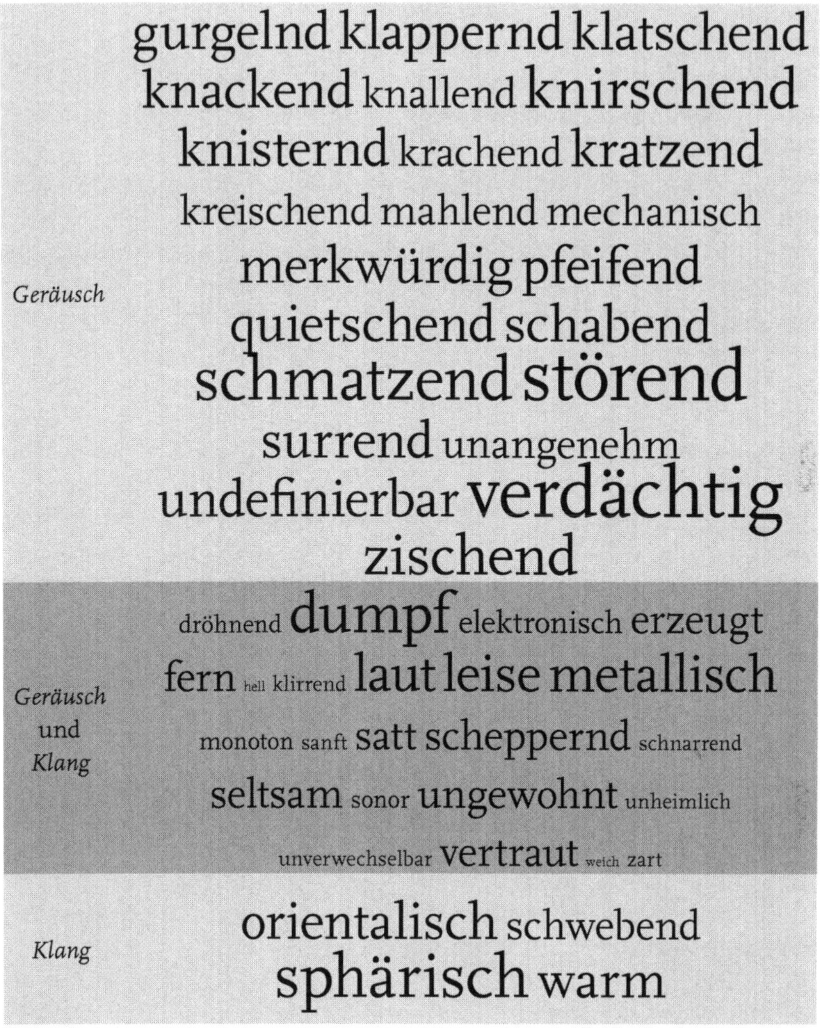

Geräusch

gurgelnd klappernd klatschend
knackend knallend knirschend
knisternd krachend kratzend
kreischend mahlend mechanisch
merkwürdig pfeifend
quietschend schabend
schmatzend störend
surrend unangenehm
undefinierbar verdächtig
zischend

Geräusch und Klang

dröhnend dumpf elektronisch erzeugt
fern hell klirrend laut leise metallisch
monoton sanft satt scheppernd schnarrend
seltsam sonor ungewohnt unheimlich
unverwechselbar vertraut weich zart

Klang

orientalisch schwebend
sphärisch warm

DWDS: Wortprofil 3.0: *Geräusch* (21.4.14)

Die Sprechereinstellung tritt vor allem anhand zweier unterschiedlicher Kontexte hervor: zum einen in Sätzen, in denen das Lexem als Subjekt der Verbalhandlung fungiert und prädiziert wird (vgl. Abb. 1), zum anderen anhand der Attribute, mittels derer dem Lexem Eigenschaften zugeschrieben werden (vgl. Abb. 2).

Die Analyse zeigt, dass in Verbindung mit beiden Lexemen als Subjekt fast ausschließlich Verben belegt sind, die das Schallereignis als solches bzw. seine Intensität etc. bezeichnen (vgl. Abb. 1). Entsprechende Verben begegnen auch bei »Geräusch« bzw. »Klang« separat. Auffällig ist jedoch, dass mit »Klang« häufig Verben assoziiert sind, die eine positive Wirkung ausdrücken (z.B. »faszinieren«, »verzaubern«; lediglich »scheppern« ist negativ konnotiert). Dagegen finden sich im Zusammenhang mit »Geräusch« vorwiegend Verben, die eine negative Auswirkung auf den Hörer beschreiben (z.B. »aufschrecken«, »stören«). Das Verb »herrühren« belegt, dass im Sprachgebrauch außerdem die Geräuschquelle hohe kommunikative Relevanz hat.

Auch die Analyse der Adjektivattribute zu beiden Lexemen ist aufschlussreich und vermag die Beobachtungen der bisherigen Analyse zu ergänzen (vgl. Abb. 2). Bereits auf den ersten Blick fällt auf, dass mit »Geräusch« verhältnismäßig viele Adjektive stark assoziiert sind. Betrachtet man die Struktur dieser Adjektive, so handelt es sich ausschließlich um sekundäre, durch Wortbildungsprozesse entstandene Lexeme: Zu 80% liegen Konversionen aus einem Partizip I vor (z.B. »knackend«). Entsprechend sind ursprünglich verbale Konzepte in der Wortart »Adjektiv« zur Verfügung gestellt; die Bedeutung dieser Adjektive ist daher dynamisch geprägt. Mit »störend« und »verdächtig« sind zwar am stärksten zwei Adjektive assoziiert, die eine negative Wirkung auf den Hörer bezeichnen, jedoch bezeichnen die meisten Attribute zu »Geräusch« eine spezifische, auditiv wahrnehmbare Qualität (z.B. »gurgelnd«, »zischend«). Hervorzuheben ist, dass wiederum die meisten dieser Adjektive (15 von 19) onomatopoetischen Charakter aufweisen. Ausschließlich mit »Klang« sind dagegen relativ wenige und ausnahmslos solche Adjektive assoziiert, die eine angenehme Qualität benennen. Diejenigen Attribute, die bei beiden Lexemen statistisch signifikant belegt sind, spezifizieren einerseits die Quantität des akustischen Ereignisses (»laut«, »leise«) – eine Kategorie, die erwartungsgemäß für beide Konzepte relevant ist; andererseits bezeichnen sie wiederum eine (eher negativ konnotierte) Wirkung auf den Hörer (»ungewohnt«, »seltsam«, »unheimlich«) und besonders häufig die Qualität, worunter nun auch deutlich positiv konnotierte Adjektive belegt sind (z.B. »sonor«, »zart«), die freilich vergleichsweise stärker mit »Klang« als mit »Geräusch« assoziiert werden. Denn insgesamt ist das akustische Ereignis »Klang« deutlich positiver konnotiert als »Geräusch«.

Es lässt sich also festhalten, dass bei der Spezifizierung der beiden akustischen Ereignisse im Sprachgebrauch deren eher negative bzw. befremdliche Wirkung auf den Hörer thematisiert wird, außerdem die akustische Qualität und weitere Eigenschaften. Gerade letztere verweisen nun häufig indirekt auf die Schallquelle. So beinhalten abgesehen von den Lautstärkebezeichnungen auch die beiden, ebenfalls in der Schnittmenge belegten Adjektive »erzeugt« und »fern« Informationen, durch die der Hörer das akustische Ereignis situativ verorten kann: Hinter dem akustischen Ereignis steht etwas oder jemand, der dieses erzeugt (Schallquelle); relevant für den Hörer ist zudem die Entfernung von der Schallquelle, die sich dimensional bzw. indirekt über die Lautstärke erschließen lässt. Anscheinend ist bei der näheren Beschreibung eines Höreindrucks demnach nicht nur das akustische Ereignis als solches relevant, sondern darüber hinaus auch das Wesen der jeweiligen Schallquelle. Dies scheint bei »Geräusch« noch ausgeprägter der Fall zu sein als bei »Klang«. Denn über ihre deverbale Semantik verweisen die zugehörigen Adjektivattribute direkt auf Eigenheiten der Schallquelle: Ein »knackendes Geräusch« ist kausallogisch mit etwas oder jemandem verbunden, das oder der knackt. Zugleich kann lautlich mittels der sprachlichen Imitation des Geräuschs eine unmittelbare Verbindung zur Schallquelle hergestellt sein, indem als geräuschspezifizierende Attribute häufig solche Adjektive gewählt sind, die onomatopoetischen Charakter zeigen.

Diese Wortgebrauchsanalye wird durch philosophische und wahrnehmungspsychologische Beobachtungen gestützt, die davon ausgehen, dass bei der menschlichen auditiven Wahrnehmung neben dem Schallereignis und seiner lautlichen Qualität vor allem die Schallquelle relevant ist:

We commonly listen to their sources, not to the sounds themselves. We seldom pay attention to the sensory qualities of sounds, but we focus instead on what is producing them. We mostly perceive sounds in terms of the objects that produced them. We hear the sound *of* a violin, the sound *of* a dog barking [...] We hear and are interested in these distal sources of the sounds, and we hear them because the experience of a sound represents its source and the properties of its source.[3]

Aus der bisherigen Sprachgebrauchsanalyse wurde ersichtlich, dass Äußerungen über akustisch wahrnehmbare Phänomene vor allem dann üblich sind, wenn das akustische Ereignis für das wahrnehmende Subjekt in der augenblicklichen Situation in irgendeiner Weise auffällig ist, d.h., dass der Hörer das Schallereignis direkt auf seine individuelle Situation bezieht. Entsprechende Kontexte erlauben Rückschlüsse auf seine Einstellung zum Geräusch als Schallereignis. Diese Einschätzung wird von situationsspezifischen Faktoren wie Bekanntheit/Vertrautheit, mögliches Gefährdungspotenzial, Störungsgrad etc. beeinflusst; ein Schallphänomen wird also eher ignoriert (und nicht versprachlicht), wenn es dem Hörer bekannt ist und ihn in seiner momentanen Situation nicht stört. Die Kategorisierung des Schallereignisses bezieht Qualität und Quantität ein und basiert somit wiederum auf situationsbedingten Informationen. Indirekt lassen sich mögliche Reaktionen des Hörers ableiten, die in der Regel eine ungestörte Fortsetzung seiner augenblicklichen Handlung bzw. den Erhalt seiner persönlichen Unversehrtheit intendieren: Der Hörer wird umso unmittelbarer von einem

---

3 | Smith: Speech Sounds and the Direct Meeting of Minds, S. 203.

akustischen Phänomen beeinflusst, je intensiver (im positiven bzw. negativen Sinn) dieses ist bzw. wenn es für ihn unbekannt ist und er Schallquelle und damit Schallverursacher nicht einordnen kann.

3. ONOMATOPOETIKA – BESONDERE LEXEME FÜR DEN ZUGRIFF AUF DIE AUSSERSPRACHLICHE WIRKLICHKEIT

Wie die Wortgebrauchsanalyse unter anderem zeigen konnte, ist bei den geräuschbezeichnenden Lexemen im Deutschen ein bestimmter Wortschatzausschnitt besonders stark beteiligt, nämlich derjenige der sogenannten Onomatopoetika.

Der besondere Zeichencharakter der »lautmalenden« Wörter wurde bereits in der antiken Philosophie thematisiert und in der modernen Sprachwissenschaft von Ferdinand de Saussure aufgegriffen. Infolge ihrer natürlichen Motiviertheit beschreibt de Saussure die Onomatopoetika als (seltene) Ausnahme von der grundlegend geltenden Arbitrarität des sprachlichen Zeichens:

> Man könnte unter Berufung auf die Onomatopoetika sagen, daß die Wahl der Bezeichnung nicht immer beliebig ist. Aber diese sind niemals organische Elemente eines sprachlichen Systems. Außerdem ist ihre Anzahl viel geringer als man glaubt.[4]

Onomatopoetika sind phonetisch motivierte sprachliche Zeichen, die auf einer auditiv wahrnehmbaren Ähnlichkeitsbeziehung zwischen bezeichnender Lautkette und bezeichnetem außersprachlichen Objekt basieren (vgl. Abb. 3). Ausgehend von den Zeichenklassen nach Charles Sanders Peirce werden Onomatopoetika daher den ikonischen Zeichen zugeordnet, und zwar genauer den sogenannten bildikonischen Zeichen (»images«), die den höchsten Ähnlichkeitsgrad mit dem repräsentierten Objekt aufweisen und mit diesem sog. einfache Qualitäten (z. B. Farbe, Form oder sonstige Merkmale) teilen.[5] Im Falle der lautnachahmenden Wörter handelt es sich um gemeinsame akustische Eigenschaften mit dem bezeichneten Objekt.

---

4 | de Saussure: Grundfragen der allgemeinen Sprachwissenschaft, S. 81.

5 | Auf der Basis des unterschiedlichen Similaritätsgrades des Zeichens zum bezeichneten Objekt differenzierte Peirce mit Ikon, Index und Symbol drei grundlegende Zeichenklassen. Unter einem Ikon verstand er ein Zeichen, »which represents its object mainly by its similarity«, Peirce: Collected Papers, Bd. 2, Elements of Logic, S. 157, § 2.276. Die Ikone unterteilte er nach abnehmendem Ikonizitätsgrad: »Those which partake of simple qualities [...] are *images*; those which represent the relations, mainly

Abbildung 3: Phonetische Motivation bei Onomatopoetika

Signifikant (Bezeichnendes) ↕ Signifikat (Bezeichnetes)	Ticktack ['tık'tak] ↕ ›Uhr‹	lautliche Ähnlichkeit: von einer mechanischen Uhr ausgehendes Geräusch

Es wäre jedoch verfehlt, den Onomatopoetika infolge ihrer Nicht-Arbitrarität den abstrakten Zeichencharakter gänzlich abzusprechen. Denn bereits de Saussure erkannte, dass die lautnachahmenden Wörter das außersprachliche akustische Ereignis nicht unmittelbar abbilden, sondern mittels der sprachlich gegebenen Einheiten vielmehr imitieren.[6] Peirce spricht den Onomatopoetika entsprechend eine »eingebildete Ähnlichkeit mit Lauten« zu, »die mit ihren Objekten verbunden sind«.[7]

Abbildung 4: Phonetische Motivation als übereinzelsprachliches Phänomen[8]

Sprachfamilie / Sprachzweig	Sprache	›Ruf des Hahns‹
Indoeuropäisch / Westgermanisch	Deutsch	kikeriki
	Englisch	cock-a-doodle-doo
Indoeuropäisch / Nordgermanisch	Isländisch	gaggala gó
	Schwedisch	kukkeliku
Indoeuropäisch / Ostromanisch	Italienisch	chicchirichì

---

dyadic, [...] of the parts of one thing by analogous relations in their own parts, are *diagrams;* those which represent [...] by representing a parallelism in something else, are *metaphors«* (ebd., § 2.277). Vgl. zusammenfassend Nöth: Handbuch der Semiotik, S. 59-67, 193-198, sowie Pusch: Ikonizität, S. 371-373.

6 | »Was die eigentlichen Onomatopoetika betrifft [...], so sind diese nicht nur gering an Zahl, sondern es ist auch bei ihnen die Prägung schon in einem gewissen Grad beliebig, da sie nur die annähernde und bereits halb konventionelle Nachahmung gewisser Laute sind [...].« de Saussure: Grundfragen der allgemeinen Sprachwissenschaft, S. 81.

7 | Peirce: Collected Papers, Bd. 2, Elements of Logic, S. 350.

8 | Die Zusammenstellung in Abb. 4 basiert auf dem freien Online-Wörterbuch »Wiktionary« sowie einer internationalen Sammlung des Hahnenschreis von Alain J. Schneider, der darüber hinaus viele weitere Beispiele bietet. Die Angaben zu Sprachfamilien und -zweigen orientieren sich an Glück: Metzler Lexikon Sprache.

Indoeuropäisch/Westromanisch	Französisch	cocorico
	Spanisch	quiquiriquí
Indoeuropäisch/Slavisch	Polnisch	kukuryku
	Russisch	кукареку (koukariékou)
	Weißrussisch	кукарэку (koukareku)
Indoeuropäisch/Indoarisch	Hindi	kukru:ku
Uralisch (Finnisch-Ugrisch)	Finnisch	kukko kiekuu
	Ungarisch	kukurikú
Semitisch/Kanaanäisch	Hebräisch	ליפורבפ הצפ (kukuriku)
Sino-Tibetisch/Ostasiatisch	Chinesisch	喔喔 (wōwō)
Altaisch/Turksprache	Türkisch	kuk-kurri-kuuu
Altaisch bzw. Austroasiatisch (?)	Japanisch	コケコッコー (kokekokkō)

Auch Onomatopoetika können also konventionalisierte Einheiten des Lexikons einer Sprache sein. Dies ist auch ein Grund dafür, dass sie sich in verschiedenen Einzelsprachen unterscheiden (vgl. Abb. 4), wenngleich die ikonisch basierte Benennungsstrategie als solche übereinzelsprachlich nachweisbar ist. Daraus wiederum lässt sich die Hypothese ableiten, dass dieser Typus des sprachlichen Zeichens kommunikative Vorteile aufweisen muss, die vermutlich in der einfachen und raschen Perzipierbarkeit zu suchen sind: Die Ähnlichkeitsbeziehung zwischen Zeichen und bezeichnetem Konzept erleichtert den kognitiven Verstehensprozess und beschleunigt realiter das Reaktionsvermögen. Anhand von Reaktionszeitexperimenten konnte erwiesen werden, dass die Bedeutungsbeurteilung bei ikonisch motivierten Sprachzeichen schneller erfolgt als bei arbiträren.[9]

Einen weiteren wichtigen Aspekt erwähnt Nöth in seinem grundlegenden Beitrag zur sprachlichen Ikonizität:[10] Da die Onomatopoetika mit dem außersprachlichen Ereignis über den identischen (auditiven) Wahrnehmungskanal verbunden sind, liegt ein Fall von »intramedial iconicity« vor. Ausgehend von der Typologie des »sound symbolism«[11] handelt es sich im

---

9 | Vgl. Hinton, Nichols und Ohala: Introduction, S. 11.
10 | Vgl. Nöth: The Semiotic Potential for Iconicity, S. 193f.
11 | Hinton, Nichols und Ohala: Introduction, S. 3.

engeren Sinn also um »imitative sound symbolism«, bei dem die Lautkette eines Wortes einen Klang wiedergibt, den es zugleich bedeutet.[12]

Demzufolge werden mit den lautimitierenden Onomatopoetika in erster Linie akustische Ereignisse benannt, so dass aus dem primären Wortschatz der deutschen Standardsprache vor allem geräuschbezeichnende Verben zuzuordnen sind.[13] Diese benennen – systematisiert nach Art der Schallquelle – entweder Geräusche, die von Objekten ausgehen bzw. durch menschliche und tierische Aktivität verursacht sind (z.B. *knattern, ballern, summen*), Geräusche, die bei physikalischen bzw. chemischen Prozessen entstehen (z.B. *blubbern*), oder Lautäußerungen von Menschen bzw. Tieren (z.B. *wispern, zwitschern*).[14] Auch viele Lexeme, die im weitesten Sinn als Interjektionen klassifiziert sind, sind dem onomatopoetischen Wortschatz der deutschen Standardsprache zugehörig. Hier reicht das Spektrum von geräusch- bzw. klangimitierenden Einheiten (z.B. *peng, bim, klingelingeling*) bis hin zu Elementen, die tierische und menschliche Lautäußerungen nachahmen (z.B. *kikeriki, miau, bla bla bla*). Weiterhin können durch konzeptionelle metonymische Verschiebung auch die »Verursacher« der Geräusche oder Laute mittels Onomatopoetika bezeichnet sein. Neben Tier-, vor allem Vogelbezeichnungen (z.B. *Kuh, Kuckuck, Uhu*) sind häufiger Musikinstrumente (z.B. *Glocke, Trommel*) schallikonisch benannt.

---

12 | »[O]nomatopoeic words and phrases representing environmental sounds«, Hinton, Nichols und Ohala: Introduction, S. 3. Ullmann: Semantics, S. 84, spricht von »primary onomatopoeia« und »imitation of sound by sound«, Lyons: Semantics, Bd. 1, S. 103, von »primary iconicity«, Seebold: Etymologie, S. 35, von »Lautnachahmungen«. Davon abzugrenzen ist »corporeal sound symbolism«, Hinton, Nichols und Ohala: Introduction, S. 2, bei dem Laute einen emotionalen oder physischen Zustand des Sprechers ausdrücken wie z.B. *hick* ›Schluckauf‹, sowie »*Lautgebärden*, bei denen die Sprechwerkzeuge eine Bewegung des Gemeinten nachahmen«, Seebold: Etymologie, S. 35, wie z.B. *bibbern*.

13 | Eine Durchsicht des Großen Duden in zehn Bänden hat ergeben, dass von den insgesamt über 200.000 Lemmata lediglich 546 als »(ursprünglich) (vermutlich/wohl/wahrscheinlich) lautmalend« ausgezeichnet sind, darunter 262 Verben (= 48%), 169 Substantive (= 31%) und 101 Interjektionen (= 18%). Zu diesen Angaben ist dringend zu beachten, dass die ohnehin äußerst sparsam eingesetzte Auszeichnung »lautm.« in diesem Wörterbuch häufig vage bleibt, mitunter zeitlich entfernt auf der Wortetymologie basiert (vgl. z.B. *Knochen*: »mhd. *knoche* [...] zu einem urspr. lautm. Verb, das mit *knacken* verwandt ist«) und oftmals auf die Herkunftsangaben von Lehn- bzw. Fremdwörtern bezogen ist, ohne dass der lautmalende Charakter in der Zielsprache Deutsch eindeutig erhalten sein muss (vgl. z.B. *Klischee*: »frz. *cliché* = Abklatsch [...] von: *clicher* = abklatschen, urspr. wohl lautm.«). Dies zeigt, wie problematisch die Einschätzung eines Lexems als lautimitierend sein kann.

14 | Vgl. Nöth: The Semiotic Potential for Iconicity, S. 193f.

Der Anteil der Onomatopoetika am deutschen Wortschatz steigt an, wenn man über die Standardsprache hinaus auch sprachliche Subsysteme und Domänen des Sprachgebrauchs einbezieht. So sind in den Mundarten – in Abhängigkeit zum jeweiligen Lautstand – weitere lautimitierende Lexeme belegt, wie z.B. süddeutsch-fränkisch *pumpern* ['bʊmbɐn] ›heftig klopfen‹, *quenksen* ['gwɛŋsn] ›ein hohes, fast quietschendes Geräusch erzeugen‹, *Ziebelein* [dsi:balɑ] ›Hühnerküken‹.[15] Im Rahmen des Erstspracherwerbs gebrauchen ein- und zweijährige Kinder okkasionell lautmalende Einheiten (z.B. *boing, brr, bum, wauwau*).[16] Die kreative Verwendung lautimitierender Elemente ist in der Comicsprache belegt, die wiederum auf andere Bereiche zurückwirkt (z.B. Sprache der Werbung, Chat-Sprache). Havlik differenziert hier zwischen »eigentliche[n] und umschreibende[n] Onomatopöien«:[17] Während erstere Geräusche bzw. Laute möglichst getreu imitieren und stärker erlebnisgebunden sind, sind letztere sprachnäher und greifen Wortstämme von geräuschbezeichnenden Verben auf (sog. Inflektive). Beide Typen werden anhand bedeutungsgleicher Wortpaare verdeutlicht, wie z.B. *BUAAA – HEUL, BZZ – SUMM, DRR – RASSEL*.

Durch wortbildende Verfahren können im Deutschen ganze Wortfamilien phonetisch motiviert sein (vgl. Abb. 5).[18] Ausgangspunkt im gewählten Beispiel sind die in ablautendem Verhältnis stehenden lautmalenden Interjektionen *puff* und *paff*, die dumpfe, knallartige Geräusche bzw. das Entweichen von Luft bezeichnen können.[19] Durch die Wortbildungsverfahren (vgl. →) Konversion, Derivation und Komposition sind diese in unterschiedlichsten Lexemen motivierende Bestandteile; durch bedeutungsbildende

---

15 | Vgl. Handwörterbuch von Bayerisch-Franken, S. 136, 404, 552f.
16 | Vgl. Szagun: Sprachentwicklung beim Kind, S. 115.
17 | Havlik: Lexikon der Onomatopöien, S. 38.
18 | Viele indigene Substantive, die der Bezeichnung akustischer Ereignisse dienen, sind Wortbildungen zu lautmalenden Verben: *Krach* (ahd. *krah, krac*, mhd. *krach*, belegt seit dem 9. Jh.) ist eine Konversion zu den Verben ahd. *krahhen, krachhōn*, mhd. *krachen*, die wiederum auf eine schallnachahmende Interjektion *Krack, Krach* zurückzuführen sind, vgl. Kluge: Etymologisches Wörterbuch der deutschen Sprache, S. 535. Die Ablautbildung *Klang* (ahd. *chlanch*, mhd. *klanc*, belegt seit dem 11. Jh.) gehört zu vermutlich lautmalendem *klingen* (vgl. ebd., S. 495); bei *Geräusch* (mhd. *geriusche*, belegt seit dem 13. Jh.) handelt es sich um eine Derivation vom lautmalenden Verb mhd. *rûschen* (nhd. *rauschen*) (vgl. ebd., S. 350).
19 | Die Wortfamilie wurde mittels Duden-Universalwörterbuch, Kluge: Etymologisches Wörterbuch der deutschen Sprache und DWDS zusammengestellt. Die Abhängigkeitsverhältnisse sind etymologisch nicht vollständig geklärt. Vgl. außerdem kindersprachlich *piff paff*.

Verfahren (vgl. ↓) bezeichnen diese Lexeme nicht nur akustische Ereignisse der außersprachlichen Wirklichkeit (vgl. Abschnitt 5).

Abbildung 5: Phonetisch motivierte Wortfamilie

puff → *der ¹Puff* ›Stoß, Knall‹
  → *¹puffen* ›stoßen, knallen‹
    → *Puffer* → *Kartoffelpuffer*
    puffern → *Pufferbatterie, -speicher, -staat, -zone*
    auspuffen → *Auspuff* → *Auspuffanlage, -gas, -rohr, -topf*
    verpuffen → *Verpuffung*
  ↓
  das ⁴Puff ›Brettspiel‹ (nach d. Geräusch beim Aufschlag d. Würfel)
  ↓
  das ²Puff ›Bordell‹ → *Puffmutter*
→ *der ³Puff* ›Behälter für Schmutzwäsche‹ (eigentl. ›Aufgeblasenes‹)
  → *³puffen* ›bauschen‹ → *Puffärmel, -bohne, -mais, -otter, -reis*
    → *Puffe* ›Bausch‹, *Püffchen*

paff → *baff/paff sein* ›überrascht, sprachlos sein‹
  der Paff ›Knall, Zug aus der Tabakspfeife‹
    → *paffen* ›rauchen‹

Auch aus etymologischer Perspektive gilt als gesichert, dass Onomatopoetika als Bezeichnungsverfahren in verschiedenen Sprachen parallel genutzt werden. Der sprachübergreifende Charakter zeigt sich in »Elementarparallelen«,[20] so dass ähnliche Lautformen in nichtverwandten Sprachen begegnen können (vgl. auch Abb. 4). Bei Schallwörtern sind die etymologischen Beziehungen insgesamt aber oft nur schwer eruierbar, da sie »Urschöpfungen«[21] darstellen können, die nicht mit vorhandenen Wortwurzeln in Verbindung stehen. Unklar ist, wie groß der ursprüngliche Anteil derartiger »Urschöpfungen« am Wortschatz ist. Infolge ihres originären Charakters wurden die lautnachahmenden Wörter spätestens seit Herder in engen Zusammenhang mit der Frage nach dem generellen Sprachursprung gerückt.[22] Dies gilt jedoch als spekulativ. Auch die Lautnachahmungen sind erwiesenermaßen konventionalisierter Bestandteil des Lexikons einer Sprache und müssen von

---

20 | Seebold: Etymologie, S. 29.
21 | Ebd., S. 35-39.
22 | Aus dieser Perspektive wurde entsprechend die Ähnlichkeit der lautnachahmenden Wörter in verschiedenen Sprachen betont.

den Sprechern gelernt werden (vgl. oben). Die diachrone Entwicklung der Onomatopoetika zeigt zudem, dass diese durch Laut- und Bedeutungswandel den lautmalenden Charakter einerseits verlieren können, dass aber andererseits Lautgruppen auch neu bildikonisch funktionalisiert werden können.[23]

Unbestritten ist, dass im Wortschatz übereinzelsprachlich bildikonische Bezeichnungsverfahren genutzt werden. Während im Deutschen und in den indoeuropäischen Sprachen der Gesamtbestand lautmalender Wörter als eher gering zu veranschlagen ist, gilt dies für andere Sprachen nicht in gleichem Maße.[24] Beispielsweise ist das Japanische – angeblich die Sprache mit den meisten Onomatopoetika nach dem Koreanischen – sehr reich an bildikonischen Lexemen. Die primär lautmalenden Wörter wie *gasha-gasha* ›scheppernd, klappernd, klirrend, rasselnd‹ oder *gāgā* ›quakend, schnatternd; krächzend; gackernd; lärmend‹ werden in »Giongo« (von unbelebten Objekten ausgehende Geräusche) bzw. »Giseigo« (von Lebewesen produzierte Laute) differenziert.[25]

Infolge der Konventionalisierung muss der onomatopoetische Charakter im Bewusstsein der Sprecher nicht zwingend präsent sein, kann aber durch

---

23 | Beispielsweise zeigt Angelika Lutz, dass bestimmte germ. konsonantische Anlautgruppen durch Anlautschwund bzw. -stärkung regelmäßig zugunsten einer Optimierung des Silbenonsets abgebaut wurden. Bei onomatopoetisch funktionalisierten Lautverbindungen ist häufiger mit Anlautstärkung zu rechnen, wodurch der lautimitierende Charakter erhalten bleibt. Dies wird anhand der Entwicklung von germ. /fn-/ (bei Lexemen des Bedeutungsbereichs ›schwer atmen‹) nachvollziehbar, vgl. z.B. me. *fneesen* → spätme. *sneeze*; ahd. *fnehan* → mhd. *phnehen* → süddt. *pfnechen* ›schnauben, keuchen‹, vgl. Lutz: Lautwandel bei Wörtern mit imitatorischem oder lautsymbolischem Charakter, S. 218f. Auch Nöth: The Semiotic Potential for Iconicity, S. 207, bietet einige Beispiele für Ausnahmen von regulärem Lautwandel bei engl. Onomatopoetika. Vgl. außerdem Wescott: Linguistic Iconism, S. 426f., der beide Aspekte – Verlust von Ikonizität durch Sprachwandel sowie Entstehung neuer Ikone – erwähnt.

24 | Derzeit untersucht Mark Dingemanse vom Max-Planck-Institut für Psycholinguistik (Nijmegen) in einem Langzeit-Forschungsprojekt an über zwanzig Standorten lautmalende Wörter in verschiedenen Sprachen. Es bestätigt sich bereits, dass in den europäischen Sprachen verhältnismäßig wenige Onomatopoetika belegt sind, die zudem vorwiegend auf den geräuschimitierenden Bereich beschränkt bleiben. Dagegen »gibt es viele andere Sprachen auf der Welt, die über Hunderte oder gar Tausende solcher Ideophone verfügen, die ein weit größeres Spektrum an sinnlichen Bedeutungen abdecken«, Dingemanse: Wie wir mit Sprache malen, S. 3. Als Beispiele werden Koreanisch, Semai (Malaysia) und Siwu (Ghana) angeführt. Vgl. auch Abschnitt 5.

25 | Ivanova: Sound-symbolic approach to Japanese mimetic words, S. 103f., und Großes Japanisch-Deutsches Wörterbuch, Bd. 1, S. 1373f., 1306. Für einschlägige Hinweise zum Japanischen danke ich Dr. Günter Vogel, Nürnberg.

Remotivation wieder aktualisiert werden, so dass die lautmalenden Wörter ein bildikonisches Potenzial in sich tragen, das je nach Kontext aktivierbar ist. Dies kann beispielsweise durch eine Häufung onomatopoetischer Lexeme erreicht werden, wie folgendes Zitat aus einer Konzertkritik der »Nürnberger Nachrichten« zu demonstrieren vermag:

Es knarzt und zwitschert, pfopfert und strömt. So vielstimmig klingt, was aus Ray Andersons Trichter in der Nürnberger Tafelhalle beim Auftritt in der Reihe »The Art of Jazz Nr. 116« an kunstvoll verbeulten Tönen stürzt.[26]

Im Sprachgebrauch sind Onomatopoetika diastratisch bzw. diaphasisch markiert, d.h. sie werden von Sprechern / Schreibern in Abhängigkeit von sozialen Faktoren bzw. situationsbedingt als ausdrucksstärker vorgezogen oder aber bewusst vermieden. Onomatopoetika zeigen durch »involvement«, durch ihr expressives und affektives Potenzial sowie die enge Situationsverschränkung, Eigenschaften, durch die sie mehr oder weniger ausgeprägt dem nähesprachlichen Bereich zugeordnet werden können;[27] auch ist der Anteil an nicht-lexikalisierten Einheiten innerhalb des onomatopoetischen Wortschatzes vermutlich hoch. Dementsprechend ist das Vorkommen der lautmalenden Wörter in bestimmten Kommunikationsbereichen höher (Alltags- und Umgangssprache, Kindersprache und kindgerichtete Sprache; medial schriftliche, aber konzeptionell mündliche Sprache wie Comic, Chat, SMS u.a., vgl. oben). Durch diese skizzierten Merkmale weisen Onomatopoetika ein hohes stilistisches Potenzial auf und können in Texten Stileffekte erzeugen.[28]

4. Geräuschimitation mittels sprachlicher Strukturen

Eine Gemeinsamkeit zwischen außersprachlichen akustischen Ereignissen und menschlicher Sprache besteht darin, dass beide über den auditiven Kanal wahrnehmbar sind. Physikalisch betrachtet handelt es sich jeweils um Schallwellen, die sich jedoch in ihrem Schwingungsverlauf messbar unterscheiden. Zwischen lautnachahmendem Onomatopoetikon und dem entsprechenden Umgebungsgeräusch lässt sich die beschriebene Ähnlichkeitsbeziehung

---

26 | Nürnberger Nachrichten: Vielstimmig und Schrill, Herv. C. G.
27 | Koch und Oesterreicher: Sprache der Nähe – Sprache der Distanz, S. 23.
28 | Erinnert sei hier auch an literarische Texte, in denen Autoren das synästhetische Potenzial der Onomatopoetika nutzen und sogar neue kreieren, wie z.B. Harsdörffer und Klaj (1644) im »Pegnesischen Schäfergedicht in den Berinorgischen Gefilden« oder Goethe (1802) in »Hochzeitslied«.

(vgl. Abschnitt 3) zwar auch anhand von Messungen nachweisen; d.h., dass Schallwort und Umgebungsgeräusch in einem Sonagramm, das die akustische Struktur des Schalls abbildet, charakteristische Eigenschaften teilen.[29]

Dennoch kann mittels menschlicher Sprache ein Umgebungsgeräusch allenfalls annähernd wiedergegeben werden. Dies hat biologische, sprachstrukturelle und kognitive Ursachen: Zunächst ist die Beschaffenheit des menschlichen Sprechapparats anzuführen. Entscheidend ist hier vor allem der Bau des Kehlkopfs, der an der Phonation maßgeblich beteiligt und für die Wiedergabe bestimmter akustischer Eindrücke ungeeignet ist. Darüber hinaus ist die menschliche Sprache ein strukturiertes System, das aus konkreten, unterscheidbaren, wiederkehrenden Einheiten (Sprachlaute, Phoneme) besteht, dabei aber eine sog. doppelte Gliederung aufweist, welche die Basis für unbegrenzte Ausdrucksmöglichkeiten darstellt, indem ein begrenztes Inventar von Lauten (Phoneme) immer wieder neu zu sinntragenden sprachlichen Bausteinen (Morpheme) kombiniert werden kann.[30] Die Einzelsprachen unterscheiden sich dabei durch unterschiedliche Konventionen und Regeln. Weiterhin ist bekannt, dass die menschliche Wahrnehmung auf Umgebungsreizen basiert, die kognitiv verarbeitet werden. Auch diese Prozesse laufen nach bestimmten wahrnehmungspsychologischen Prinzipien ab. Dazu kommt, dass der menschliche auditive Sinn relativ begrenzt ist und akustische Ereignisse rasch verklingen, weshalb für die Analyse eines Umgebungsschalls (zumindest bei Nicht-Repetition) nur begrenzte Zeit zur Verfügung steht.

Von Interesse ist daher nun im Folgenden, wie wahrgenommene außersprachliche akustische Ereignisse im Rahmen ihrer Bezeichnung mittels Onomatopoetika sprachlich umgesetzt und somit »umstrukturiert« werden. Prinzipiell ist bei diesem Vorgang mit einem gewissen Umsetzungsspielraum zu rechnen, da außersprachliche Geräusche nicht in regelmäßige Segmente gegliedert sein müssen. Insgesamt kann die Wiedergabe von Geräuschen oder Lauten mittels menschlicher Sprache als Annäherungsprozess beschrieben werden, in dessen Verlauf Merkmale des Umgebungsschalls

---

29 | Ähnlichkeiten in der akustischen Struktur von Geräusch und Schallwort hinsichtlich Frequenz, Periodizität und Formantenstruktur werden in kontrastiven Sonagrammen erkennbar, in denen eine Geräuschstruktur (z.B. Türklingel, Uhr, Reißverschluss) abgebildet ist sowie die akustische Struktur der entsprechenden Schallwörter *dingdong, tictac, zip*, vgl. Pharies: Charles S. Peirce and the Linguistic Sign, S. 57, 62f.

30 | Die grundlegenden Eigenschaften menschlicher Sprache »semanticity«, »arbitrariness«, »discreteness«, »productivity« und »duality of patterning« sind Teil der bekannten, von Charles F. Hockett (1916-2000) beschriebenen Wesensmerkmale (»design-features«) menschlicher Kommunikation, vgl. Hockett: The Origin of Speech, S. 91 u. passim.

selektiert[31] und sprachlich imitiert werden. Dafür ist in jedem einzelsprachlichen System zunächst ein jeweils spezifisches Repertoire an Phonemen vorhanden, das in Kombination mit ebenfalls spezifischen Regeln der Phonotaktik (Lautkombination) und Prosodie (Intonation, Betonung) quasi die lautlichen Bausteine zur Verfügung stellt, mittels derer Geräusche einzelsprachlich gebunden nachgeahmt werden können:

> Nur einige relevante Merkmale werden entsprechend dem Phonemsystem der Sprache zur Bildung des Formativs gewählt. [...] Merkmale des Geräuschs werden durch Phoneme des Formativs abgebildet, aber die Auswahl der Merkmale und die Zuordnung zum Phonemsystem sind sprachliche Verallgemeinerungen. [...] Dennoch fällt die Klangähnlichkeit onomatopoetischer Wörter verschiedener Sprachen auf. Sie ist ohne Zweifel durch die ähnliche Sinneswahrnehmung und Ähnlichkeiten im Phonembestand bedingt.[32]

Im Rahmen sprachpsychologischer Experimente zur Neubenennung von Geräuschen in deutscher Sprache gelang es Heinz Wissemann, systematische Querbeziehungen zwischen verschiedenen sprachlichen Einheiten und Geräuscheigenschaften zu ermitteln, von denen einige im Folgenden angeführt werden:[33]

---

31 | Eco: Einführung in die Semiotik, S. 209, betont, dass ikonische Zeichen von »einer vorhergehenden Codifizierung von Wahrnehmungserfahrung« abhängen: »Die ikonischen Zeichen geben einige Bedingungen der Wahrnehmung des Gegenstandes wieder, aber erst nachdem diese auf Grund von Erkennungscodes selektiert und auf Grund von [...] Konventionen erläutert worden sind.« (ebd., S. 205).
32 | Schippan: Lexikologie der deutschen Gegenwartssprache, S. 99f.
33 | Heinz Wissemann führte 1950 insgesamt 14 Versuche durch, in deren Rahmen unterschiedliche Geräusche erzeugt wurden, z.B. durch Hammerschläge gegen ein eisernes Gewicht, durch Schütteln einer Bierflasche, durch Zerbrechen eines Holzstabs, durch Fallenlassen eines dünnwandigen Glasgefäßes aus der Höhe von 150 cm auf den Fußboden, so dass es zerbrach etc., vgl. Wissemann: Untersuchungen zur Onomatopoiie, S. 12-15. Für eine neue sprachliche Bezeichnung der gehörten Geräusche mussten Probanden entweder aus gegebenen Listen mit sinnlosen Wörtern auswählen (Welches gegebene Kunstwort benennt das Geräusch am besten?) und Fragen nach dem Grad der Eignung, nach Benennungsalternativen, nach bestimmenden Faktoren u.a. beantworten (Hauptversuche A) oder wurden gebeten, selbst eine Neubenennung zu kreieren (Erfinde ein Wort für das Geräusch!) (Hauptversuche B) (vgl. ebd., S. 15-20). Obwohl die Probanden aufgefordert waren, die Neubenennungen unabhängig von »sprachüblichen« Lexemen zu schaffen, wurden diese häufig durch Variation vorhandener Lexeme gebildet (ebd., S. 63-71), und zwar meist als erlebnisnahe Interjektionen auf der Basis vorhandener onomatopoetischer Verben (ebd., S. 72, 75, 83).

- Die Silbe fungiert als Ausdrucksmittel für Geräuschteile, indem die Silbenzahl der Zahl der Geräuschteile entspricht. Für den Ausdruck der Geräuschdauer ist die Silbenzahl dagegen weniger relevant; hier wurden z.B. offene Endsilben für unbegrenzte Geräuschdauer gewählt. Bei unklar segmentierten Geräuschen drückt die Silbenzahl den Intensitätsgrad der Gegliedertheit des Geräuschs aus.[34]
- Die Neubenennungen beinhalten häufig Laute und Lautverbindungen, die für die phonische Struktur des Deutschen untypisch sind, z.B. retroflexe Laute, Frikative als Silbenträger, Langkonsonanten in ungewöhnlicher Stellung, ungewöhnliche konsonantische Anlautgruppen etc.[35]
- Die Vokalqualität drückt Klangfarbe und Tonhöhe des Geräuschs aus, und zwar bei einsilbigen Wörtern bezogen auf das Geräusch als Gesamtheit, bei mehrsilbigen auf den entsprechenden Geräuschteil.[36] Dabei entsprechen die Vokale *i, ü, ö, e, a* einem hohen und hellen Geräusch(teil), *e, ə, a* einem mittelhohen und farblosen sowie *a, u, o* einem tiefen und dunklen.[37]
- Der Ausdrucksgehalt der Konsonanten ist insgesamt vielfältiger als derjenige der Vokale, da die Konsonanten nicht nur eine Eigenschaft des Geräuschganzen bzw. von Geräuschteilen ausdrücken können, sondern zusätzlich auch eine bestimmte Stelle (Anfang, Ende) des Geräuschs sowie eine Pause.[38] Er ist von der Stellung in der Silbe abhängig, z.B. drücken im Auslaut Nasale ein Klingen aus, stimmlose Plosive den plötzlichen Abbruch eines Geräusch(teil)s und Frikative ein allmähliches Beenden; im Anlaut signalisieren Nasale einen weichen, allmählichen Geräuscheinsatz oder die Weichheit des Gesamtgeräuschs und umgekehrt stimmlose Plosive einen harten Einsatz bzw. Härte des Gesamtgeräuschs sowie Frikative einen allmählichen Geräuschbeginn. Der absolute Anlaut ist insgesamt die ausdrucksstärkste Stellung.[39]
- Reduplikation wird eingesetzt, um die Gleichheit von Teilgeräuschen auszudrücken.[40]
- Der Akzent wird funktionalisiert, um Geräuschteile zu zentrieren; Geräuschschwerpunkte liegen auf der Akzentsilbe.[41]

---

34 | Wissemann: Untersuchungen zur Onomatopoiie, S. 97, 110-113.
35 | Ebd., S. 122-127.
36 | Ebd., S. 144.
37 | Ebd., S. 148.
38 | Ebd., S. 148f.
39 | Ebd., S. 152-165, 173.
40 | Ebd., S. 193.
41 | Ebd., S. 194.

Lexikalisierten Schallwörtern geht eine Kategorisierung des außersprachlichen Schallphänomens voraus. Christian Lehmann stellt fest, dass das Wortfeld der deutschen Schallverben noch nicht adäquat erschlossen ist und die Parameter für die Kategorisierung von Schällen durch sprachliche Ausdrücke aus lexikalisch-semantischer Perspektive noch nicht einheitlich ermittelt sind.[42] Die Kategorisierung akustischer und visueller Phänomene scheint sich jedenfalls zu unterscheiden. Denn visuelle Eindrücke werden um ihrer selbst willen kategorisiert, während die Schallkategorien im Sprachbewusstsein größtenteils unbewusst sind und akustische Eindrücke funktional interpretiert werden. Daher charakterisieren Versuchspersonen einen Schallbegriff niemals anhand auditiver Merkmale, sondern bieten situativ bedingte Umschreibungen:[43]

> Wir haben hier mit einem wichtigen Unterschied zwischen visueller und auditiver Wahrnehmung zu tun: *Visuelle Wahrnehmung* als solche ist gegenüber der Dynamizität der wahrgenommenen Situation indifferent; [...] Visuelle Wahrnehmung hat wesentliche Funktionen in räumlicher und sozialer Orientierung. *Auditive Wahrnehmung* ist auf dynamische Situationen beschränkt. Sie hat wichtige Funktionen in der Anpassung des Verhaltens des Wahrnehmenden an den Stimulus.
>
> Hieraus ergibt sich die folgende Hypothese: menschliche auditive Wahrnehmung ist darauf ausgerichtet, Schälle funktional zu interpretieren. Die Leitfrage bei der Kategorisierung eines auditiven Perzeptes ist: Was bedeutet dieser Schall für mich?[44]

Lehmann beschreibt insgesamt drei relevante Parameter für die Kategorisierung von Schällen, die von der Situation des Schallereignisses ausgehen, und überprüft sekundär deren sprachliche Umsetzung anhand einer

---

42 | Lehmann: Zur sprachlichen Kategorisierung von Schällen, S. 1-3.
43 | Ebd., S. 2, 13. »Wenn Versuchspersonen einen Schallbegriff charakterisieren sollen, rekurrieren sie lieber auf die Selektionsrestriktionen und die den Schall hervorbringende Bewegung / Manipulation, anstatt eine rein auditive Charakterisierung zu geben. Sie charakterisieren also *peng* als »das Geräusch, das typischerweise durch einen Schuß entsteht« und nicht als »ein lautes, momentanes, aperiodisches, ausklingendes Geräusch«. Daraus kann man schließen, dass Menschen Schälle nicht wie visuelle Perzepte kategorisieren, nämlich um ihrer selbst willen. Statt dessen dient auditive Kategorisierung typischerweise dazu herauszubekommen, von welcher Relevanz der Schall für den Rezipienten ist.« (ebd., S. 2). Diese Bemerkungen ausgehend von der lexikalisch-semantischen Ebene entsprechen den Ergebnissen der in Abschnitt 1 geleisteten Wortgebrauchsanalyse.
44 | Ebd., S. 13.

systematischen strukturellen und semantischen Analyse von 192 deutschen Schallverben:[45]
- auditive Merkmale der bezeichneten Situation,[46] d.h. aus akustisch-phonetischer Perspektive ist die vertikale Struktur des Schalls (Intensität, Klangfarbe, Qualität) relevant. Sprachlich wird im Deutschen niedrige Intensität durch das Wortbildungssuffix -el- kodiert (vgl. z.B. *zischen* – *zisch<u>el</u>n*), die Qualität wird durch Lautwahl bezeichnet: »Wörter, die Töne bezeichnen, enthalten mehr Sonoranten; Wörter, die Schälle bezeichnen, enthalten mehr Obstruenten«.[47] Unklar ist, inwieweit die Klangfarbe des Geräuschs sprachlich umgesetzt wird.
  Zum anderen weist Schall eine horizontale Struktur auf (Impulsrate, Homogenität, Ausklang). Sprachlich wird die als Kontinuum beschreibbare Impulsrate relativ genau ausgedrückt (z.B. iterative Schallverben durch -er-, vgl. *klappen* vs. *klappern*; in semelfaktiven Schallverben ist durch -s- ein Einzelimpuls bezeichnet, vgl. z.B. *knacken* vs. *knack<u>s</u>en*; vibrative Schallverben enthalten typischerweise den Laut /r/, z.B. *kna<u>rr</u>en*). Die Homogenität des Schalls wird sprachlich morphologisch und phonologisch umgesetzt: »Wörter, die heterogene Schälle bezeichnen, haben auch eine komplexe Silbenstruktur«.[48] Der Ausklang des Schalls wird häufig durch die Lautwahl ausgedrückt, vgl. z.B. ausklingender Schall durch Wurzeln auf Sonorant oder Frikativ (*kli<u>rr</u>en*, *kra<u>ch</u>en*).
- Bewertung der Situation, d.h. die positive bzw. negative Einschätzung des Schalls. Die Wortanzahl für negativ bewertete Schälle überwiegt deutlich (z.B. *kreischen*): »Diese Tatsache ist die Basis für eine ganze Subdisziplin der Psychoakustik, nämlich die Lärmforschung«.[49]
- Eigenschaften der Schallquelle. Für die Kategorisierung der Schall- und Energiequelle ist die Belebtheits- oder Empathiehierarchie entscheidend.[50] Diese zeigt sich im Sprachgebrauch in »Selektionsrestriktionen von Schallverben« (z.B. *husten* → menschlich, *zirpen* → niederes Tier, *klicken* → technisches Objekt, *rascheln* → loses Material).[51]

Prinzipiell erfolgt die sprachliche Kodierung des Schalleindrucks niemals eindeutig im physikalischen Sinn, sondern ist von Oppositionsbildung im

---

45 | Ebd., S. 4-12. Um den »onomatopoetische[n] Zirkel« bei der Analyse zu durchbrechen, fordert er eine getrennte Beschreibung von Bedeutungs- und Ausdrucksseite der Schallwörter (vgl. ebd., S. 4).
46 | Ebd., S. 5-10.
47 | Ebd., S. 5f.
48 | Ebd., S. 9.
49 | Ebd., S. 10.
50 | Ebd., S. 10f.
51 | Ebd., S. 11.

Sprachsystem abhängig.[52] Daher wird das bildikonische Potenzial in Schallverben oftmals erst im Kontrast zu einem lautverwandten Lexem deutlich, vgl. z.B. *klicken – klacken*.[53]

Sowohl Wissemann als auch Lehmann zeigen, dass bestimmte Schalleigenschaften durch bestimmte sprachliche Strategien umgesetzt werden. Die menschlichen Sprachlaute lassen sich in Konsonanten (Geräuschlaute mit aperiodischer Schwingung) und Vokale (Klanglaute mit periodischer Schwingung) differenzieren, die systematisch bei der Imitation des akustischen Schalleindrucks funktionalisiert werden. Phonotaktische, prosodische und morphologische Strategien ergänzen diese phonologische Basis. Infolge der Imitation des Umgebungsschalls können die Onomatopoetika im Vergleich zu den arbiträren Lexemen der deutschen Sprache als »markierte«, d.h. auffällige, Wortschatzeinheiten gelten. Diese Markiertheit kann mehr oder weniger stark ausgeprägt sein und wird auf allen Ebenen des Sprachsystems erkennbar:

- phonologisch/silbenstrukturell: In Onomatopoetika lässt sich eine Konzentration bestimmter Laute/Lautverbindungen (bes. Konsonanten) an bestimmten Positionen beobachten (z.B. anlautend *kn-* in *knacken, knallen, knarren, knarzen, knattern, knistern, knittern, knurren* etc.).[54] Durch minimale phonologische Varianten kann die paradigmatische Opposition reduziert sein (vgl. *klicken – klacken, sirren – surren, piff – paff*). In weniger sprachnahen Onomatopoetika werden bei der Silbenfüllung extreme Oppositionen bei der Konsonanten- und Vokalverteilung ausgenutzt (z.B. KVKVKVKV in *ki-ke-ri-ki*). Statt prototypischer Stammsilbenbetonung (trochäisches Wortbetonungsmuster) kann der Wortakzent verlagert sein (z.B. *kikeri'ki*); häufig beinhalten die Lexeme außerdem Nebenakzente, verfügen über eine ungewöhnlich hohe Silbenzahl und weisen eine auffällige Rhythmisierung auf (z.B. *klingelingeling, holterdipolter*). Phonotak-

---

52 | »Nirgends ist ein absoluter physikalischer Wert relevant; stets bekommt ein Merkmal seine Identität durch seine paradigmatischen Oppositionen und seine syntagmatischen Kontraste [...].« Ebd., S. 12.

53 | Im Sprachgebrauch sind lautverwandte lexikalisierte Schallverben in bestimmten Kontexten oft nicht vollständig differenziert, wie anhand einer kontrastiven Analyse der Umgebungen von *klicken* und *klacken* deutlich wird: Beide Lexeme bezeichnen lt. DWDS helle, kurze Geräusche. Während *klicken* eindeutiger mit Bezug auf (elektronische) Geräte (bes. im Computerkontext) gebraucht wird, hat *klacken* insgesamt ein weiteres Kollokationsspektrum, wird zugleich aber auch in identischen Kontexten wie *klicken* und mit diesem (scheinbar) austauschbar gebraucht.

54 | Die Mehrzahl der im Duden-Universalwörterbuch, S. 1006-1013, mit *kn-* anlautenden Lexeme ist lautmalend oder steht mit einem Onomatopoetikon in direktem Zusammenhang.

tisch sind besondere Lautstellungen bzw. -verbindungen möglich (z.B. d*oi*ng, b*rr* mit Vibrant als Silbenträger); in unbetonten Nebensilben können statt des üblichen Reduktionsvokals volle Vokale erscheinen (z.B. *blabla*). Häufig begegnet Reduplikation, oft in Verbindung mit Ablaut (z.B. *bumbum, bimbam*).

- graphisch: Bei der Verschriftung von Onomatopoetika in der Comicsprache werden häufig zusätzlich parasprachliche Merkmale mit abgebildet, wie z.b. Affektheit und Lautstärke durch Majuskelgebrauch, Abbildung der Wortlänge durch Graphemvervielfältigung im Auslaut.
- morphologisch: Onomatopoetika entziehen sich mitunter der herkömmlichen Wortartenklassifikation, vgl. z.b. *kikeriki* als Interjektion(?) oder Inflektive wie *knarz*. Bei lexikalisierten Onomatopoetika scheinen gelegentlich Restriktionen hinsichtlich der Auslastung des Flexionsparadigmas vorzuliegen, vgl. z.B. *der Kikeriki – die Kikerikis*(?). Durch besondere Wortbildungsmorpheme sind Schallverben morphologisch markiert, auch wenn sie häufig auf keine Motivationsbasis beziehbar sind, wie z.B. durch *-(e)l-* (z.B. *babbeln, bimmeln, quasseln*), *-(e)r-* (z.B. *gluckern, knistern, schmettern*).[55]
- syntaktisch: Manche Onomatopoetika sind im Satz nur eingeschränkt kombinierfähig und in feste Konstruktionsmuster eingebunden (häufig in Verbindung mit »machen«, vgl. *Das macht bumbum*).[56]

Auch wenn zwischen unterschiedlichen Sprachen deutliche Abweichungen im onomatopoetischen Wortschatz bestehen (vgl. auch Abb. 4),[57] sind viele der beschriebenen sprachlichen Strategien zur bildikonischen Umsetzung der Schallphänomene übereinzelsprachlich nachweisbar.[58] Dies gilt für die Reduplikation (z.B. engl. *ding-dong*, jap. *jiri-jiri* ›Läuten einer elektrischen Klingel‹) ebenso wie für ungewöhnliche Lautverbindungen, die von Lautwandel unberührt bleiben, bis hin zur Assoziation bestimmter Phonemklassen mit bestimmten semantischen Feldern (vgl. Abschnitt 5).

---

55 | Vgl. Fleischer und Barz: Wortbildung der deutschen Gegenwartssprache, S. 430f.

56 | Vgl. auch Pesot: Ikonismus in der Phonologie, S. 8.

57 | Wie unterschiedlich und den lautlichen und prosodischen Konventionen ihrer Muttersprache gemäß Kinder verschiedener Herkunft im Alter von zwei bis sieben Jahren die Laute von Tieren und Objekten nachahmen, stellt eindrucksvoll die mit mehreren Medienpreisen ausgezeichnete internationale Sammlung kindsprachlicher Onomatopoesien von Agathe Jacquillat und Tomi Vollauschek unter Beweis.

58 | Vgl. Hinton, Nichols und Ohala: Introduction, S. 8-10.

5. Ausblick: Phoneme und geräuschbezeichnende Lexeme im kognitiven Prozess

Durch kognitive Prozesse wie Analogie (Regelübertragung bzw. -erweiterung) und Reanalyse (Umdeutungen) kann das sprachliche Wissen der Sprachbenutzer stetig verändert und erweitert werden; d.h., dass sprachliche Elemente im Sprachgebrauch neue Bedeutungen entwickeln können. In unserem Zusammenhang ist hier abschließend auf Phänomene der sog. sekundären phonetischen Motivation hinzuweisen sowie auf Aspekte des Bedeutungswandels bei geräuschbezeichnenden Lexemen.

Bei sekundärer phonetischer Motivation[59] bezeichnet eine Lautkette ein nichtakustisches Ereignis der außersprachlichen Wirklichkeit, wobei die beteiligten Laute physische oder psychische Eigenschaften des Referenten wie Größe, Farbe, Bewegungen, emotionale Zustände u.a. imitieren. Es handelt sich also um Fälle der »intermedial iconicity«, die im Gegensatz zur »intramedial iconicity« (vgl. Abschnitt 3) davon gekennzeichnet ist, dass ein ikonisches Sprachzeichen und das bezeichnete außersprachliche Objekt über einen unterschiedlichen Wahrnehmungskanal verbunden sind.[60] Seebold spricht von »*Lautbilder[n]*, die einen Sinneseindruck, an dem nicht notwendigerweise ein Laut beteiligt ist, durch lautliche Mittel wiederzugeben suchen«.[61] Da Empfindungen mittels verschiedener Sinnesorgane miteinander verbunden sind, können derartige Ausprägungen der sekundären Ikonizität dem Bereich der Synästhesie zugeordnet werden.[62]

Unter den einschlägigen deutschen Beispielen begegnen nicht nur solche, bei denen visuell wahrgenommene Ereignisse lautlich umgesetzt

---

59 | Ullmann: Semantics, S. 84, nennt das Phänomen »secondary onomatopoeia« (»sounds evoke, not an acoustic experience, but a movement [...] or some physical or moral quality, usually unfavourable«); Lyons: Semantics, Bd. 1, S. 104, verwendet die Termini »secondary iconicity« und »sound symbolism (or phonaesthesia)« als Spezialfall der »secondary onomatopoeia«.
60 | Nöth: The Semiotic Potential for Iconicity, S. 193.
61 | Seebold: Etymologie, S. 35.
62 | Karl Bühler differenziert zwischen »*erscheinungstreuer* Wiedergabe« (bei »Geräuschnamen«) und »*relationstreue[n]* Wiedergaben«; bei letzteren wird nicht »Akustisches auf Akustischem abgebildet, sondern Nicht-akustisches auf Akustisches. [...] Es sind Bewegungsarten und dynamische Gestalten, die hier wiedergegeben werden. Sie gehören nicht zu den spezifischen Sinnesqualitäten, sondern zu den überspezifischen, d.h. mehreren Sinnesorganen zugleich verdankten Daten«, Bühler: Sprachtheorie, S. 208. Zur »Synästhesie« vgl. Jakobson und Waugh: Die Lautgestalt der Sprache, S. 206-214; Posner und Schmauks: Einführung. Synästhesie; Volke: Lautsymbolik und Synästhesie.

werden, wie z.B. *glitzern*, *glimmen* oder *flimmern*, sondern darüber hinaus auch Lexeme wie *tätscheln*, *bummeln* oder *zappeln*, mit denen taktile Eindrücke oder Bewegungsabläufe bezeichnet werden. Entscheidend ist jedenfalls, dass keine akustischen Ereignisse repräsentiert werden, obwohl die Lexeme eine auditiv ähnlich auffällige Lautstruktur aufweisen wie die Onomatopoetika. Daher stellt – aus Perspektive des Themas »Wort und Geräusch« – das sprachliche Ereignis als solches das relevante akustische Ereignis dar.

Diesem Typus der sekundären Ikonizität gehen analogische und assoziative Prozesse voraus, bei denen Laute bzw. Lautkombinationen »Lautbedeutsamkeit«[63] entwickelt haben und mit anderen, nichtauditiven Qualitäten assoziiert werden. Entsprechend differenzieren Hinton, Nichols und Ohala zwischen »synesthetic sound symbolism« (»acoustic symbolization of non-acoustic phenomena«) und »conventional sound symbolism« (»analogical association of certain phonemes and clusters with certain meanings«).[64]

Der Bereich der Lautbedeutsamkeit[65] ist häufig dem Vorwurf der Spekulation ausgesetzt. Denn oft scheint es, als würde den Lauten bzw. Lautverbindungen erst aus Kenntnis des außersprachlichen Phänomens sekundär Bedeutung zugesprochen.[66] Jedoch gibt es für Lautbedeutsamkeit verschiedene Evidenzen: In verschiedenen sprachpsychologischen Experimenten[67] wurde erwiesen, dass zwischen Sprachlauten und Sinneseindrücken gewisse Ähnlichkeitsbeziehungen bestehen, die zumindest als überindividuell, eventuell sogar als universell gelten können; Sprachbenutzer können mit Einzellauten bzw. Lautkombinationen bestimmte Eigenschaften assoziieren. Systematische Lautoppositionen und Bedeutungsrelationen zwischen Lauten bzw. Lautverbindungen und bestimmten semantischen Bereichen wurden

---

63 | Seebold: Etymologie, S. 36.
64 | Hinton, Nichols und Ohala: Introduction, S. 4f.
65 | Vgl. zur Lautsymbolik grundlegend Jakobson und Waugh: Die Lautgestalt der Sprache, S. 195-206.
66 | So kann ein Laut bzw. eine Lautverbindung letztlich immer dann expressives Potenzial entfalten, wenn der Laut zur Bedeutung passt. In literarischer Sprache wird dieses Assoziationspotenzial bewusst genutzt, wie z.B. Ernst Jandls »Schtzngrmm« (1957) eindrucksvoll zeigt, in dem über die Konsonanten mittels auditiver Assoziationen nicht nur ein Kriegsereignis als solches, sondern sogar dessen Abläufe dargestellt werden.
67 | Vgl. zusammenfassend Ertel: Psychophonetik.

und werden aktuell für verschiedene Einzelsprachen ermittelt.[68] Auch kindsprachliche Wortkonstruktionen zeigen ähnliche Korrelationen.[69]

Als relevante kognitive Prozesse, die auf lexikalischer Ebene Bedeutungsbildungen durch Um- oder Neudeutungen bewirken können, gelten Metonymien und Metaphern. Diese können in vielfältiger Weise auch im Zusammenhang mit geräuschbezeichnenden Lexemen beobachtet werden.

Die in Abschnitt 4 herausgestellte Vagheit bei der Kategorisierung und sprachlichen Bezeichnung akustischer Phänomene zeigt sich im Sprachgebrauch nicht zuletzt darin, dass Klangeindrücke vorwiegend metaphorisch bezeichnet werden, indem Wahrnehmungsadjektive, die primär der Prädizierung von Wahrnehmungen mittels anderer Sinne dienen, für die Bezeichnung von Klangqualitäten herangezogen werden. Beispielsweise werden Klänge vorwiegend mit Adjektiven beschrieben, die primär visuelle oder taktile Wahrnehmungen bezeichnen, wie z. B. *hell – dunkel* (Klang<u>farbe</u>), *weich – rauh – hart*.[70]

Bei Perzeptionsadjektiven lässt sich insgesamt beobachten, dass diese »häufig auf unterschiedliche Sinnesbereiche angewendet werden«.[71] Im

---

68 | Bekanntheit hat besonders die bereits von Otto Jespersen 1933 beschriebene Laut-Inhalt-Korrelation zwischen vorderen/hellen vs. hinteren/dunklen Vokalen erlangt, wobei /i/ »Kleinheit« ausdrückt, dagegen /a/ (oder /o/) »Größe«, wie z. B. in engl. *little, teeny, bit, slim* vs. *large, vast, grand;* dt. *winzig* vs. *groß;* frz. *petit* vs. *grand;* griech. *mikrós* vs. *makrós* u. a. Für derartige Korrelationen macht John Ohala anthropologisch-biologische Gründe geltend: »High resonances are typical of short vocal tracts which, in turn, are indicative of a small vocalizer; and conversely, low resonances of a larger vocalizer«, Ohala: The frequency code underlies the sound-symbolic use of voice pitch, S. 333. Vgl. auch Wescott: Linguistic Iconism, S. 420-422, und Etzel: Untersuchungen zur Lautsymbolik, S. 29-31, mit weiteren Beispielen für Lautsymbolismus aus verschiedenen Sprachen sowie Nöth: The Semiotic Potential for Iconicity, S. 197-199, und Hinton, Nichols und Ohala: Introduction, S. 10 u. passim. Für das Englische hat Marchand: The categories and types of present-day English word-formation, S. 313-343, auf der Basis von Wort(bildungs)analysen positionsdifferenziert Lauten bzw. Lautgruppen bestimmte Bedeutungen zugeordnet. Zum Lautsymbolismus im Japanischen vgl. Ivanova: Sound-symbolic approach to Japanese mimetic words.

69 | Vgl. Jakobson und Waugh: Die Lautgestalt der Sprache, S. 202f.

70 | »Humans simply do not trust their ears to make fine acoustic distinctions, even when there is ample opportunity to repeat the sound under study. The poverty of human audition is reflected in the terminology employed in describing sounds, which is composed primarily of adjectives metaphorically extended to sound from other sensory modes, as ›soft‹, ›rough‹, ›bright‹, ›clear‹, ›dark‹, etc. (›loud‹ being a conspicuous exception).« Pharies: Charles S. Peirce and the Linguistic Sign, S. 54.

71 | Fritz: Historische Semantik, S. 138.

diachronen Verlauf zeigt sich, dass einige der Wahrnehmungsadjektive, die primär auditive Eindrücke bezeichneten, heute generell oder zusätzlich in anderen Bezeichnungsbereichen verwendet werden. Dies gilt für *grell*, das zunächst ausschließlich im auditiven Bereich spezialisiert war und erst ab dem 16. Jh. auf visuelle Eindrücke ausgedehnt wurde,[72] ebenso für *hell*, das erst ab dem Mhd. visuelle Wahrnehmungen bezeichnet.[73] Auch *schrill* ist zunächst ausschließlich auf auditive Eindrücke festgelegt.[74] Ein weiteres interessantes Beispiel für Bedeutungsentwicklung ausgehend vom auditiven Quellbereich bietet *toll*, das ursprünglich im Sinne von ›lärmend‹ gebraucht wurde (vgl. *herumtollen*) und eine stufenweise Bedeutungsveränderung erfuhr, indem ein lärmendes Verhalten als Anzeichen für Wahnsinn interpretiert wurde (metonymischer Schluss), so dass das Adjektiv die Bedeutung ›verrückt‹ entwickeln konnte.[75]

Auch ursprünglich geräuschbezeichnende Verben können durch Metaphorisierung ihr Bedeutungsspektrum erweitern, wie z.B. eine korpusbasierte Auswertung[76] der Kontexte von *klacken* und *klicken* zeigt: Während *klacken* nur als Geräuschbezeichnung belegt ist, begegnet *klicken* inzwischen vorwiegend als Handlungsbezeichnung im Bereich der Computerverwendung (›auf etwas klicken‹), die immer weniger von dem typischen Geräusch begleitet sein muss. Weiterhin sind Belege mit Metaphorisierung in den geistigen Bereich (›bei jemandem hat es geklickt‹) vorhanden.

Insgesamt kann die Relevanz des auditiven Bereichs im Rahmen kognitiver, bedeutungsbildender Prozesse letztlich noch nicht genau eingeschätzt werden, da umfassende diachrone und synchrone Wortschatzstudien fehlen. Während solche Beispiele im Deutschen eher selten sind, begegnet derartige Bedeutungsbildung durch systematische konzeptionelle Metonymik und Metaphorik ausgehend vom akustischen Quellbereich in anderen Sprachen wesentlich häufiger, und zwar nicht nur in lexikalisierter Form, sondern auch okkasionell.[77] Beispielsweise können im Japanischen lautimitieren-

---

72 | Pfeifer: Etymologisches Wörterbuch des Deutschen, S. 474.

73 | Ebd., S. 529.

74 | Ebd., S. 1244.

75 | Vgl. Keller und Kirschbaum: Bedeutungswandel, S. 53-55. Der Bereich der Wahrnehmung wird mit dieser Bedeutung sowie der aktuell präferierten (›sehr gut‹) verlassen.

76 | Diese Ergebnisse basieren auf Recherchen im Zeit-Korpus (1957 bis 2011) und Kernkorpus des DWDS.

77 | Bekannt ist folgende von Diedrich Westermann, einem Begründer der Afrikanistik, geschilderte Beobachtung über die Neuprägung von Lautbildern durch westafrikanische Sprecher: »Auf Reisen mit Eingeborenen kann man erleben, wie diese etwa für eine in weiter Ferne sichtbare, aber noch unhörbare Bewegung, einen plötzlich aufstoßenden

de Onomatopoetika (vgl. Abschnitt 3: »Giongo«, »Giseigo«) auch »mimetisch« zur Bezeichnung physischer Zustände und Handlungen (»Gitaigo«) sowie psychischer Zustände (»Gijōgo«) gebraucht werden,[78] die visuell, taktil oder in anderer Form nicht-auditiv wahrgenommen werden können, wie abschließend die folgenden Beispiele demonstrieren sollen:

jap. pō? ›Ton einer Dampfpfeife u.ä.‹ (Giongo) → ›Zustand des Errötetseins‹ (Gitaigo) → ›Zustand des Abgelenktseins durch Beschäftigung mit Anderem‹ (Gijōgo).[79]

jap. *gara-gara* ›verschiedene reibende Geräusche beim Zusammenstoßen oder Einstürzen von Gegenständen; auch: ›Baby-Rassel‹ (Giongo) → ›heiserer Laut der Stimme‹ (Giseigo) → ›Zustand der trockenen, entzündeten Kehle; Zustand des abgemagerten Körpers; Zustand, dass Gräser vertrocknet sind und zu Staub zerfallen‹ (Gitaigo) → ›Zustand, sich nicht zurückzuhalten und mit lauter Stimme zu sagen, was man denkt; auch: Unhöflichkeit, Grobheit‹ (Gitaigo / Gijōgo) → ›Zustand, dass etwas nicht da und freier Raum vorhanden ist‹ (Gitaigo).[80]

6. Fazit: Geräusche und Sprache

Der vorliegende Beitrag hat einen weiten Bogen gespannt und Geräusche als Schallereignisse in mehrfache Beziehung zur menschlichen Sprache gesetzt: Im Rahmen einer kontrastiven Sprachgebrauchsanalyse der Lexeme »Klang« und »Geräusch« (Abschnitt 2) wurde erwiesen, dass Geräusche vom Hörer bevorzugt in Bezug auf seine augenblickliche Situation interpretiert werden und tendenziell negativ konnotiert sind. Bei der Bezeichnung und näheren Charakterisierung von Geräuschen mittels sprachlicher Lexeme ist mit den sogenannten Onomatopoetika – einem übereinzelsprachlichen Phänomen – auch im Deutschen ein besonderer Wortschatzausschnitt funktionalisiert, da phonetische Motivation im Bereich des Lexikons eher die Ausnahme als die Regel darstellt (Abschnitt 3). Da auch die menschliche Sprache über den auditiven Kanal wahrnehmbar ist und somit selbst ein Schallereignis darstellt, war in Abschnitt 4 von Interesse, wie bei Onomatopoetika die bezeichneten Geräusche und andere Schallereignisse sprachlich imitiert werden; der Umsetzung von Geräuschen mittels sprachlicher Strukturen geht die

---

eindringlichen Geruch, sogleich einen Ausdruck bereit haben, der von den Anwesenden durch Wiederholung oder durch ein Schmunzeln als zutreffend quittiert wird.«, Westermann: Laut, Ton und Sinn in westafrikanischen Sudansprachen, S. 319.

78 | Vgl. Ivanova: Sound-symbolic approach to Japanese mimetic words, S. 103.
79 | Vgl. Ono: A Practical Guide to Japanese-English Onomatopoeia & Mimesis, S. 341.
80 | Vgl. Großes Japanisch-Deutsches Wörterbuch, Bd. 1, S. 1365.

Kategorisierung des außersprachlichen Schallphänomens voraus; die sprachliche Nachahmung der Geräusche kann infolge dieser Kategorisierung und durch die Gesetzmäßigkeiten einzelsprachlicher Strukturen allenfalls eine Annäherung an das Geräuschereignis darstellen. Welche Mechanismen und Regularitäten hier im Einzelnen wirken, ist gesamthaft noch nicht hinreichend erforscht. Die kognitive Linguistik widmet sich typischen Prozessen, durch die sprachliches Wissen mittels Übertragungen und Umdeutungen erweitert werden kann. Entsprechend bieten Sprachlaute ihrerseits ein Deutungspotenzial, das es erlaubt, sie zur Charakterisierung von Phänomenen heranzuziehen, die mittels anderer Sinneskanäle wahrgenommen werden (sog. sekundäre phonetische Motivation). In ähnlicher Weise sind im Wortschatz Wahrnehmungsadjektive und geräuschbezeichnende Verben nicht nur als eigentliche Bezeichnungen im auditiven Bereich funktionalisiert, sondern auch im übertragenen Sinn, so dass der auditive Bereich den Ausgangspunkt für Bedeutungsbildung durch konzeptionelle Metonymik und Metaphorik darstellen kann. Einen Ausblick auf derartige kognitive Prozesse, die in anderen Sprachen in vermutlich noch größerem Ausmaß als im Deutschen beobachtet werden können, bot abschließend der fünfte und letzte Abschnitt.

Bibliographie

Bühler, Karl: Sprachtheorie. Die Darstellungsfunktion der Sprache. Mit einem Geleitwort von Friedrich Kainz, 3. Aufl., Stuttgart 1999, Neudruck der 1. Aufl., Jena 1934.
Dingemanse, Mark: Wie wir mit Sprache malen. How to paint with language. Forschungsbericht 2013. Max-Planck-Institut für Psycholinguistik, http://www.mpg.de/6683977/Psycholinguistik_JB_2013 (25.4.14).
Duden. Das große Wörterbuch der deutschen Sprache, 10 Bde., hg. v. Wissenschaftl. Rat der Duden-Redaktion. 3., völlig neu bearb. und erw. Aufl., Mannheim u.a. 1999, CD-ROM 2000.
Duden. Deutsches Universalwörterbuch. Hg. v. der Dudenredaktion. 7., überarb. und erw. Aufl. Mannheim, Zürich 2011.
DWDS = Digitales Wörterbuch der deutschen Sprache des 20. Jahrhunderts. Projekt der Berlin-Brandenburgischen Akademie der Wissenschaften, http://www.dwds.de/ (25.4.14).
Eco, Umberto: Einführung in die Semiotik, München 1972.
Ertel, Suibert: Psychophonetik. Untersuchungen über Lautsymbolik und Motivation, Göttingen 1969.
Etzel, Stefan: Untersuchungen zur Lautsymbolik. Diss., Frankfurt/M. 1983.

Fleischer, Wolfgang und Irmhild Barz: Wortbildung der deutschen Gegenwartssprache, 4., völlig neu bearb. Aufl., Berlin, Boston 2012.

Fritz, Gerd: Historische Semantik, Stuttgart, Weimar 1998.

Glück, Helmut (Hg.): Metzler Lexikon Sprache. 2., überarb. und erw. Aufl., Stuttgart, Weimar 2000.

Großes Japanisch-Deutsches Wörterbuch, Bd. 1 (A-I), hg. v. Jürgen Stalph u.a., München 2009.

Handwörterbuch von Bayerisch-Franken, hg. v. der Kommission für Mundartforschung der Bayerischen Akademie der Wissenschaften, bearb. v. Eberhard Wagner und Alfred Klepsch, 3. Aufl., Bamberg 2008.

Havlik, Ernst J.: Lexikon der Onomatopöien. Die lautimitierenden Wörter im Comic, Frankfurt/M. 1981.

Hinton, Leanne, Johanna Nichols und John J. Ohala: Introduction, in: Dies. (Hg.): Sound symbolism, Cambridge 1994, S. 1-12.

Hockett, Charles F.: The Origin of Speech, in: Scientific American 203.3 (1960), S. 89-96.

Ivanova, Gergana: Sound-symbolic approach to Japanese mimetic words, in: Toronto Working Papers in Linguistics 26 (2006), S. 103-114.

Jacquillat, Agathe und Vollauschek, Tomi: http://www.bzzzpeek.com/index.html (25.4.14).

Jakobson, Roman und Linda R. Waugh: Die Lautgestalt der Sprache, Berlin, New York 1986.

Keller, Rudi und Ilja Kirschbaum: Bedeutungswandel. Eine Einführung, Berlin, New York 2003.

Kluge, Friedrich: Etymologisches Wörterbuch der deutschen Sprache. Bearb. v. Elmar Seebold, 25., durchges. und erw. Aufl., Berlin, Boston 2011.

Koch, Peter und Oesterreicher, Wulf: Sprache der Nähe – Sprache der Distanz. Mündlichkeit und Schriftlichkeit im Spannungsfeld von Sprachtheorie und Sprachgeschichte, in: Romanistisches Jahrbuch 36 (1985), S. 15-43.

Lehmann, Christian: Zur sprachlichen Kategorisierung von Schällen. Vortrag bei der Jahrestagung der Koreanischen Gesellschaft für Deutsche Sprachwissenschaft, Pusan (Korea), 23.6.04 (Manuskriptüberarbeitung 3.7.04), http://www.christianlehmann.eu/publ/Spr_Kat_Schall.pdf (25.4.14).

Lutz, Angelika: Lautwandel bei Wörtern mit imitatorischem oder lautsymbolischem Charakter in den germanischen Sprachen, in: Kurt Gustav Goblirsch, Martha Berryman Mayou und Marvin Taylor (Hg.): Germanic Studies in Honour of Anatoly Liberman, Odense 1997, S. 213-228.

Lyons, John: Semantics, Bd. 1, Cambridge 1977.

Marchand, Hans: The categories and types of present-day English word-formation. A synchronic-diachronic approach, Wiesbaden 1960.

Nöth, Winfried: The Semiotic Potential for Iconicity in Spoken and Written Language, in: Kodikas / Code 13.3-4 (1990), S. 191-209.

Nöth, Winfried: Handbuch der Semiotik. 2., vollständig neu bearb. und erw. Aufl., Stuttgart, Weimar 2000.

Nürnberger Nachrichten: Vielstimmig und schrill – Verlässlicher Dauerläufer: »Bassdrumbone« in der Tafelhalle Nürnberg, 3.12.2003.

Ohala, John J.: The frequency code underlies the sound-symbolic use of voice pitch, in: Leanne Hinton, Johanna Nichols und Ders. (Hg.): Sound symbolism, Cambridge 1994, S. 325-347.

Ono, Hideichi: A Practical Guide to Japanese-English Onomatopoeia & Mimesis, Tokyo 1984.

Peirce, Charles Sanders: Collected Papers, Bd. 2, Elements of Logic, hg. v. Charles Hartshorne und Paul Weiss, Cambridge/MS 1932/1960.

Peirce, Charles Sanders: Naturordnung und Zeichenprozeß. Schriften über Semiotik und Naturphilosophie, hg. u. eingeleitet v. Helmut Pape, Frankfurt/M. 1991.

Pesot, Jürgen: Ikonismus in der Phonologie, in: Semiotik 2 (1980), S. 7-18.

Pfeifer, Wolfgang: Etymologisches Wörterbuch des Deutschen, 6. Aufl., München 2003.

Pharies, David A.: Charles S. Peirce and the Linguistic Sign, Amsterdam, Philadelphia 1985.

Posner, Roland und Dagmar Schmauks: Einführung. Synästhesie: Physiologischer Befund, Praxis der Wahrnehmung, künstlerisches Programm, in: Semiotik 24.1 (2002), S. 3-14.

Pusch, Claus D.: Ikonizität, in: Language Typology and Language Universals. Sprachtypologie und sprachliche Universalien. La typologie des langues et les universaux linguistiques. An international Handbook. Ein internationales Handbuch. Manuel international, hg. v. Martin Haspelmath, Ekkehard König, Wulf Oesterreicher und Wolfgang Raible, 1. Halbbd., Berlin, New York 2001, S. 369-384.

de Saussure, Ferdinand: Grundfragen der allgemeinen Sprachwissenschaft, hg. v. Charles Bally und Albert Sechehaye unter Mitwirkung v. Albert Riedlinger, 3. Aufl., Berlin, New York 2001.

Schippan, Thea: Lexikologie der deutschen Gegenwartssprache, 2., unveränd. Aufl., Tübingen 2002.

Schneider, Alain J.: http://alain.j.schneider.free.fr/cocorico1.htm (25.4.14).

Seebold, Elmar: Etymologie. Eine Einführung am Beispiel der deutschen Sprache, München 1981.

Smith, Barry C.: Speech Sounds and the Direct Meeting of Minds, in: Matthew Nudds und Casey O'Callaghan (Hg.): Sounds and Perception. New Philosophical Essays, Oxford 2009, S. 183-210.

Szagun, Gisela: Sprachentwicklung beim Kind. Ein Lehrbuch., 4. Aufl., Weinheim, Basel 2011.

Ullmann, Stephen: Semantics. An introduction to the science of meaning, Oxford 1964, Neudruck der 1. Aufl. von 1962.

Volke, Stefan: Lautsymbolik und Synästhesie – Beiträge zu einer leiborientierten Phonosemantik, in: Anna Blume (Hg.): Zur Phänomenologie der ästhetischen Erfahrung, Freiburg i. Br., München 2005, S. 92-120.

Wescott, Roger W.: Linguistic Iconism, in: Language 47.2 (1971), S. 416-428.

Westermann, Diedrich: Laut, Ton und Sinn in westafrikanischen Sudansprachen, in: Franz Boas u.a. (Hg.): Sprachwissenschaftliche und andere Studien. Festschrift Karl Meinhof, Hamburg 1927, S. 315-328.

Wictionary. Das freie Wörterbuch, http://de.wiktionary.org/wiki/kikeriki (25.4.14).

Wissemann, Heinz: Untersuchungen zur Onomatopoiie, 1. Teil. Die sprachpsychologischen Versuche, Heidelberg 1954.

Wittgenstein, Ludwig: Philosophische Untersuchungen. Spätfassung 1953. Kritisch-genetische Edition, hg. v. Joachim Schulte in Zusammenarbeit mit Heikki Nyman, Eike von Savigny u. Georg Henrik von Wright, Frankfurt/M. 2001.

Der Dreck in der Stimme – eine Spurensuche

Uta von Kameke-Frischling

Wann immer Musikinstrumente oder Stimmlippen in Schwingung versetzt werden, entstehen periodische Schwingungen, die wir als Klang hören, und unregelmäßige Schwingungen, die den Geräuschanteil bilden. Es gibt also in *allen* Stimmen einen Geräuschanteil, bei Tom Waits oder Janis Joplin ebenso wie bei Maria Callas oder Placido Domingo. Wie kommt es, dass das gleiche Ausgangsmaterial, die Vibration der Stimmlippen, so verschiedene ›Endprodukte‹ liefert? Oder anders gefragt: Wie schafft es die klassische Gesangspädagogik, Stimmen so auszubilden, dass deren Geräuschanteile so wenig zu *hören* sind?

Klassische Sänger und Sängerinnen[1] werden wie Hochleistungs-Athleten ausgebildet. In den allermeisten Fällen muss sich ihre Stimme über ein Orchester hinweg behaupten können; nur in Ausnahmen (z. B. in Open-Air-Aufführungen) wird ihnen ein Mikrofon zur Verfügung gestellt. Dass sich die Stimme als mühelos und tragfähig erweist, ist Voraussetzung dafür, dass Sänger und Sängerinnen ihren Beruf lange ausüben können. Im Hinblick auf den Geräuschanteil jeder menschlichen Stimme stellen sich hierzu folgende Fragen: Ist Tragfähigkeit an Geräuscharmut gekoppelt? Was hat der Geräuschanteil mit dem Timbre und der Authentizität der Stimme zu tun? Was sagt der Umgang mit dem Geräuschanteil aus über unsere klassische Musikkultur? Über unser Verhältnis zum eigenen Körper? Und wie wirkt sich das Unterrichts-Setting auf den Umgang mit dem Geräuschanteil aus?

Bei einer Stichprobe im Bestand der Berliner Zentral und Landesbibliothek (Standort Amerika-Gedenkbibliothek) im März 2016 finden sich nur in 11 von 57 Lehrwerken zur Stimmbildung etwaige Hinweise auf die Begriffe ›Geräuschanteil‹ bzw. ›Nebengeräusche‹. Höhere Trefferquoten erzielen hingegen die Stichworte ›Heiserkeit‹ oder ›Stimmfehler‹. Sofern es überhaupt Erwähnung findet, wird das Geräusch im Stimmklang bereits mit diesen Bezeichnungen abgewertet. Wie kommt es zu dieser Haltung? Hat diese

---

1 | Im weiteren Text verwende ich das generische Maskulinum, sofern keine geschlechtsneutralen Begriffe vorhanden sind.

Abwertung mit dem unterschwelligen Kompetenz-Streit zwischen theoretischem Musikwissen und praxisnaher Ausübung zu tun? Gerade unter Sängern galt es lange als überflüssig, sich Gedanken darum zu machen, wie sie singen, solange es gut funktionierte. Richtige Intuition sollte nicht von allzu viel abstraktem Wissen überlagert werden.[2] Von Enrico Caruso ist die Anekdote überliefert, dass er sich, nachdem er einem Gesangsprofessor zugehört hatte, der die Caruso-Methode beschrieb, lakonisch äußerte: »Er weiß mehr als ich.«[3]

Ein weiterer wichtiger Faktor für die Abwertung unstrukturierter Laute, die sich in den Gesangsklang mischen, könnte die Abscheu vor unserem Verdauungstrakt sein. In den meisten Gesangslehrbüchern finden wir nur anatomische Darstellungen von sauber durchlüfteten Atemräumen. Dabei ist unser Atemtrakt eine Spezialisierung des Verdauungsrohrs, das uns von Mundlippen bis Anus durchzieht. Im Embryo knospen sich von diesem Einheitsrohr, ab etwa der vierten Schwangerschaftswoche, die verschiedenen anderen Räume ab bzw. stülpen sich ein (Mittelohr, Nasenraum, Kehlkopf, Lungen).[4] Diese Doppelnutzung von Verdauungs- und Atemräumen hat noch weitgehend unterschätzte Auswirkungen auf das Verhalten des Kehlkopfs beim Singen. Die Muskelgruppe, die hauptsächlich für die Spannung der Stimmlippen und damit die Tonhöhen-Einstellung zuständig ist, ist gleichzeitig in die Schluck-Peristaltik eingebunden, was häufig zu Fehlspannungen in diesem Bereich führt.[5] Obwohl es selbstverständlich ist, dass die Mundhöhle und der Rachen zum Verdauungstrakt gehören (und in Anatomiebüchern dort zugehörig beschrieben werden), finden wir in den meisten Gesangslehrbüchern darüber nichts. Ist die Vorstellung davon, dass wir mit ausdifferenzierten Teilen des Verdauungstrakts singen, mit einem Tabu belegt? Es stellt sich die Frage, ob dieses Tabu sich in gleichem Maße auf alle Lautäußerungen, die nicht ›klar und rein‹ sind, erstreckt. Mit zunehmender Liberalisierung der Reinlichkeitserziehung im Laufe des 20. Jahrhunderts konnte sich dieses Tabu nur allmählich lockern.

Neben Gesangstechnik und anatomischen Modellierungen spielen auch akustische Aspekte eine wichtige Rolle für die Abwertung des Geräuschanteils im Gesang. Wie kommt es, dass in unserer Musiktradition die Periodizität der Schwingungen so wichtig ist? Die periodischen Schwingungen

---

2 | Dazu ausführlich: Hammar: Gesang lehren und lernen im Spannungsfeld zwischen Instinkt und Wissenschaft.

3 | Zitiert nach: Fischer: Die Stimme des Sängers, S. 267.

4 | Vgl. dazu Shubin: Der Fisch in uns, S. 108-116, sowie Nawka und Wirth: Stimmstörungen, S. 27f.

5 | Reid: Das Erbe des Belcanto; sowie: Rohmert und Landzettel: Lichtenberger Dokumentationen.

bilden unser Bezugssystem und, als Tonhöhen geordnet, unsere Tonarten. Das Geräusch war auch in der Musiktheorie über viele Jahrhunderte hinweg kein Thema.[6] (Der Vergleich mit außereuropäischer Musik zeigt, dass diese Festlegung auf die Tonhöhe keinesfalls zwingend sein muss.)[7]

In einem aktuellen Lehrbuch der Phoniatrie lautet die Definition von Schall: »Er entsteht immer dann, wenn die Gleichverteilung der Dichte (oder des Druckes) eines Gases, einer Flüssigkeit oder eines festen Körpers gestört wird.«[8] Auch bei dem Physiker Ernst Terhardt, der sich an der TU München vorwiegend mit akustischer Kommunikation beschäftigt hat, finden wir eine ähnliche Vorstellung. Er bezieht sich dabei auf Helmholtz und sein Konzept von Konsonanz als »gradueller Abwesenheit von *Störungen des Zusammenklanges* (Helmholtz). In dieser Definition des Begriffes Sonanz steckt die Auffassung, daß jeder hörbare Schall grundsätzlich eine Art Störung darstellt [...].«[9]

Schall wird in diesen beiden Zitaten, unabhängig von der Einteilung in Klang oder Geräusch, als Störung einer gegebenen Ordnung verstanden. Die stabile Ordnung ist der eigentliche Zustand, den die Bewegung des Schalls durcheinanderbringt. Und wenn eine solche Störung nicht zu vermeiden ist, dann sollte sie zumindest regelmäßig sein. Die Periodizität und damit die Tonhöhe galten sowohl in der Theorie als auch in der Ausübung von Musik als zentrale Toneigenschaft. Es herrschte ein *Periodizitätsdogma*, das sehr lange Zeit nicht hinterfragt wurde. Diese Denkweise erinnert an das *Stabilitätsdogma*, das die Physik bis in die 1960er Jahre dominierte. Seit der griechischen Antike wurde die Natur als stabile Ordnung konstituiert und ausschließlich als stabil wahrgenommen. Phänomene, die mit Instabilität zu tun haben, wurden ignoriert oder auf menschliches Versagen (›Messfehler‹) zurückgeführt.[10] In solchen stabilen, geordneten Welten findet man für jedes Problem eine konvergente Lösung.

Ebenfalls seit der griechischen Antike kennen wir zwei Sagen über den Ursprung der Musik. Die eine steht im Zusammenhang mit Dionysos, einem Sohn des Zeus und Gott des Weines, des Tanzes und der Sinnenfreuden. Auf Dionysos-Festen erklingt die Aulos, eine Doppeloboe, deren Klang der menschlichen Stimme sehr nahekommt. Der Sage nach wurde sie von Athene

---

6 | Vgl. Borsche: Geräusch, Musik, Wissenschaft. Eine Bestandsaufnahme, S. 33-46. Zwar gibt es Klangfarbenmelodie, Vierteltonmusik, graphische Notation, Geräuschmusik etc., aber das, was in den Musik- und Musikhochschulen erarbeitet wird, orientiert sich größtenteils immer noch am tonalen System.
7 | Dazu z. B. Graf: Zur Verwendung von Geräuschen in der außereuropäischen Musik.
8 | Nawka und Wirth: Stimmstörungen, S. 49.
9 | Terhardt: Akustische Kommunikation, S. 400.
10 | Schmidt: Instabilität in Natur und Wissenschaft, S. 88.

nach der Enthauptung der Medusa für die Totenklage erfunden.[11] Das dionysische Element der Musik hat demnach mit berauschenden Urkräften, körperlicher Bewegung, Kontrollverlust und dramatischen Begebenheiten zu tun.[12] Dem steht das apollinische Element entgegen: Apollon, ebenfalls ein Sohn des Zeus, spielt auf der Lyra, einem Saiteninstrument. Diese Musik steht für Heiterkeit, Exaktheit, die Mathematik und die Harmonie der Sphären.[13]

Diese gegensätzlichen Elemente stehen in einer dialektischen Spannung zueinander, was bedeutet, dass sie jeweils zwei extreme Daseinsformen repräsentieren, die Teile *eines* Ganzen sind. Im Mythos versöhnen sich Apollon und Dionysos jedoch nicht, sondern treten gegeneinander an: Bei einem Wettstreit zwischen Apollon und Marsyas, einem Aulosbläser aus dem Gefolge von Dionysos, gewinnt Apollon mit seiner Lyra.[14]

Vor der Analyse, wie Gesangslehren mit dem Geräuschanteil umgehen, gilt es, kurz in einigen Linien zu skizzieren, welche Entwicklung die westliche Kultur in ihrem Empfinden für Klang und Geräusch genommen hat und wie sich die Mechanisierung auf die Musikdidaktik auswirkte.

DAS STREBEN NACH REINEM KLANG

Seit der Antike zieht sich die Vorstellung, dass die mathematisch erfassbaren, rationalen Elemente der Musik über die sogenannten irrationalen zu stellen seien, wie ein roter Faden durch die abendländische Musikgeschichte. Die quantifizierbaren Klangeigenschaften – insbesondere die Tonhöhe – wurden zur Grundlage für die Musiktheorie, die bis ins Mittalalter hinein als mathematische Wissenschaft betrieben wurde. Die ganzzahligen Proportionen bildeten die Ordnung des Universums ab; Musik definierte sich über Ordnungsbeziehungen, wonach Irreguläres abgewertet wurde. Die »Mathesis« hatte über die »Emotion« gesiegt.[15] Es verwundert daher nicht, dass der turbulente Geräuschanteil aus der Wahrnehmung verdrängt wurde. Musik sollte rein, klar und hell sein.

Der verdrängte Geräuschanteil kann in Analogie zu einem Phänomen aus der Tiefenpsychologie C. G. Jungs gesehen werden: der Verdrängung des

---

11 | Schafer: Klang und Krach, S. 11.
12 | Zum Thema Opferkult als Ursprung der Musik vgl. Türcke: Zurück zum Geräusch. Die sakrale Hypothek der Musik, S. 509-519.
13 | Schafer: Klang und Krach, S. 11.
14 | Die Trennung der Musik in geräuschhafte Tanzmusik und klangvolle ›klassische Musik‹ ist nach wie vor in unserem Denken und Bewerten präsent, wie man an der im Rundfunk und Streaming-Diensten üblichen Einteilung in U- und E-Musik erkennen kann.
15 | Vgl. Eggebrecht: Musikbegriff und europäische Tradition, S. 41.

Schattens. Danach trägt jeder Mensch in sich positive und negative Aspekte, wobei oft dem eigenen Ich gegenüber so getan wird, als existierten diese negativen Anteile nicht. Sie werden ins Unbewusste verdrängt und bilden dort einen »immer gegenwärtigen und potentiell zerstörerischen ›Schatten‹ unseres Bewusstseins.«[16] Laut Jung geht es bei der »Selbstwerdung« des einzelnen Menschen, der »Individuation«, darum, das Bewusste und das Unbewusste zu integrieren. Dabei muss auch der Schatten realisiert werden, d.h. die dunklen Aspekte der Persönlichkeit werden als vorhanden anerkannt, damit sie als kreative Ressource genutzt werden können.[17] Diese dunklen Aspekte sind »nicht einfach die Umkehrung des bewussten Ego. Ebenso wie das Ich unvorteilhafte und zerstörerische Einstellungen enthält, hat auch der Schatten gute Eigenschaften – normale Instinkte und schöpferische Impulse. Ich und Schatten sind in Wirklichkeit, obgleich getrennt, unentwirrbar miteinander verbunden, in ganz ähnlicher Weise wie Denken und Fühlen aufeinander bezogen sind.«[18]

Bei dem oben beschriebenen Wettstreit zwischen Marsyas und Apoll kommt ein weiterer interessanter Aspekt ins Spiel: die *Sichtbarkeit* der Vorgänge. Die Schwingungen der Saiten folgen nicht nur mathematisch berechenbaren Regeln, sondern sind auch für das Auge klar zu erkennen, während das Geschehen in der Aulos (oder auch in der Stimme) wie in einer *black box* verborgen bleibt. Seit Heraklit wird unser Begriff von ›wissenschaftlicher Objektivität‹ maßgeblich durch Sichtbarkeit geprägt; die Augen sind nach seiner Vorstellung im Vergleich zu den Ohren »die besseren Zeugen.«[19] Die Wahrnehmung über das Ohr verbindet uns mit der Materialität dessen, was da gerade zum Klingen gebracht wird.[20] Das Auge hingegen rückt die Welt als ein Gegenüber von uns ab.[21] Das Subjekt kann sich so von dem zu erforschenden Objekt distanzieren. Vorgänge sichtbar zu machen, ist eine Voraussetzung dafür, sie wissenschaftlich darzustellen. Zählen, ordnen, messen, kartographieren – all das sind Strategien, das Irreguläre (zumindest visuell) zu bezähmen; die Welt wird vertraut und beherrschbar, sie wird zu unserer »Wohnstube«.[22] Nach der Ansicht Christina von Brauns droht sich unsere Identität als West-Europäer in der unstrukturierten Komplexität des Fremden zu verlieren, was latente Todesängste heraufbeschwört. Indem wir in das

---

16 | Jung: Zugang zum Unbewussten, S. 93.
17 | Jung: Welt der Psyche, S. 71.
18 | Henderson: Der moderne Mensch und seine Mythen, S. 120.
19 | Kolesch und Krämer: Stimmen im Konzept der Disziplinen, S. 7f.
20 | Sowodniok: Stimmklang und Freiheit, S. 62. Vgl. auch: Nancy: A l'écoute, S. 10, sowie Barthes: Die Rauheit der Stimme, S. 269.
21 | Sowodniok: Stimmklang und Freiheit, S. 64.
22 | Vgl. von Braun: Der Einbruch der Wohnstube in die Fremde, S. 8f. und S. 23f.

Unbekannte wiedererkennbare Strukturen hineinprojizieren, machen wir es verfügbar. Dies gilt für fremde Länder ebenso wie für das eigene Unbewusste. Die Natur liefert dieser Weltanschauung zufolge z.B. Laute als rohes Material, das der Mensch dann ordnet und veredelt, sodass Musik daraus entsteht. Im folgenden Zitat aus einem Musik-Nachschlagewerk der 1970er Jahre zum Begriff »Geräuschmusik« wird deutlich, wie sehr sich die westeuropäische Musiktheorie von der natürlichen Lautsphäre abgrenzt:

> Geräuschmusik ist die erste Musik der Primitiven. Das Geräusch des abfliegenden Pfeils, der Ton des angeschlagenen Holzstammes oder der Metallscheibe werden als magische Zeichen gehört. Im Augenblick, da aus den Geräuschen Töne und Klänge entwickelt werden, beginnt die Musikgeschichte. Es ist ein Zeichen ihrer Ermüdung, wenn sie zu Geräuschen zurückkehrt.[23]

Hier wird die Tatsache ignoriert, dass Geräusch und Klang nicht klar zu trennen sind, sondern ein Kontinuum bilden. Auch kommt die Furcht vor der subversiven Kraft des so sorgsam abgespaltenen dionysischen Anteils zum Vorschein, die sich in der Abgrenzung gegenüber anderen, sogenannten »primitiven« Kulturen äußert.[24] Vor allem aber fragt man sich: Was hat die Musikgeschichte »ermüdet«?

TECHNISIERUNG DER MUSIK

Die Trennung der Musik in mathematisch streng erfassbare und emotional bewegende Anteile hatte ganz praktische Auswirkungen: Die Musik ließ sich in einen geistigen (Komposition) und in einen körperlichen Vorgang (Ausübung) aufspalten. In den instrumental- und vokalpädagogischen Schriften, die seit dem 17. Jahrhundert überliefert sind, dominiert die auf René Descartes basierende Denkweise:

> Der Körper enthält nichts, was dem Geist zugeordnet werden könnte, und der Geist beinhaltet nichts, was zum Körper gehörig wäre [...]. Ich sehe keinerlei Unterschied zwischen Maschinen, die von Handwerkern hergestellt wurden, und den Körpern, die allein die Natur zusammengesetzt hat.[25]

---

23 | Herzfeld: Ullstein-Lexikon der Musik, S. 191.
24 | Das Dionysische war latent immer in der Tanzmusik präsent und brach sich schließlich Bahn in Luigi Russolos Manifest »Die Geräuschkunst« am 11. März 1913.
25 | Zitiert nach: Biesenbender: Von der unerträglichen Leichtigkeit des Instrumentalspiels, S. 18.

Akzeptiert man diese Mechanisierung des Körpers, »verwandelt sich der Prozess lebendigen Musizierens [...] in einen Kanon komplexer Bedienungsregeln.«[26] Musizieren-Können wird zu einer Frage der Technik, und erst wenn man diese Technik »beherrscht«, kommt man in die Nähe des geistigen Konstrukts »Musik«. Denn so gut man auch singt oder spielt, stets ist »Musik besser als ihre best-mögliche Aufführung.«[27] Die Lehrperson kann so ihre Machtposition gegenüber den Lernenden behaupten (»›Meister-Schüler‹-Prinzip«)[28] und in ihrer Rolle des »Besser-Wissers« bleiben.[29]

Lernende werden in dieser »Erzeugungsdidaktik«[30] als »triviale Maschinen«[31] betrachtet, von denen erwartet wird, dass sie bei gleichem *input* auch den gleichen, vorhersehbaren *output* bringen. Sie sind »defizitäre Wesen«, die sich in ihrer Lernentwicklung an einer von außen festgelegten Norm orientieren müssen. Normabweichungen, also Fehler und Irrtümer, werden negativ bewertet.[32] Die Unterrichtsstunde gleicht einer Prüfungssituation, in der sich die Lernenden möglichst perfekt präsentieren wollen, ja, sie übernehmen sogar selbst das defizitäre Denken der Lehrperson.[33] In einer solchen Lernumgebung ist kein Raum gegeben, mit unkonventionellen Klangfarben zu experimentieren oder gar den Geräuschanteil zu explorieren.

Vergleichbar mit Naturwissenschaftlern und Ingenieuren, die Instabilitäten als Störungen wahrnehmen, die sie zu eliminieren trachten,[34] sollen Instrumental- und Gesangslehrpersonen nur den Klang zu akzeptieren, der frei von »ineffizienten Betriebsgeräuschen« ist.[35] Dabei sind es gerade

---

26 | Ebd., S. 19.
27 | Kingsbury: Music, Talent and Performance, S. 107.
28 | Winkler: Pädagogik ›Als-Ob‹, S. 106. Kingsbury weist darauf hin, dass sich klassische Musiker darüber definieren, bei wem (welchem Meister) sie studiert haben. Jazz-Musiker hingegen berufen sich darauf, mit wem sie zusammen auf der Bühne musizierten. Kingsbury: Music, Talent and Performance, S. 167f.
29 | Winkler: Pädagogik ›Als-Ob‹, S. 106. Vgl. auch dazu Reich: Systemisch-konstruktivistische Pädagogik, S. 260.
30 | Vgl. Winkler: Pädagogik ›Als-Ob‹, S. 103.
31 | von Foerster: Das Gleichnis vom blinden Fleck, S. 23f.
32 | Winkler: Pädagogik ›Als-Ob‹, S. 106f.
33 | Kruse-Weber et al.: Umgang mit Fehlern: Konstruktivistische Einstellungen und Strategien für Musiker/innen und Instrumentallehrkräfte, S. 109.
34 | Schmidt: Instabilität in Natur und Wissenschaft, S. 88.
35 | Jukic: The Sound of Obsolence, S. 158f. Ein Vergleich mit dem klassischen Ballett bietet sich an: Dabei wurden ebenfalls Schritt- und Körpergeräusche vermieden, da sie den Tanz, der überirdisch und schwebend wirken sollte, hörbar mit der Schwerkraft in Verbindung brachten. Vgl. dazu: Arend: Steppen, Schleifen, Schlagen. Eine tanzwissenschaftliche Sicht auf das Geräusch, S. 139f.

diese Nebengeräusche, die oft als »trübe« oder »dreckig« abgewertet werden, die uns Auskunft darüber geben, welches *Material* da schwingt. Schon Carl Stumpf konnte Ende des 19. Jahrhunderts in mehreren Versuchen nachweisen, dass Instrumentalklänge bis zu einem gewissen Grade nicht mehr identifizierbar sind, wenn man die Einschwinggeräusche unhörbar macht.[36] Als Rauschuntergrund (oder Nebengeräusch) halten sich Spuren der Einschwinggeräusche auch im quasi-stationären Teil der Klänge und sorgen so dafür, dass diese für unser Ohr weiterhin *belebt* wirken.[37] Der Geräuschanteil bringt uns mit der Materialität der Klangerzeuger in Kontakt. Dieser Kontakt wird in der Gesang- und Instrumentalpädagogik kaum (und wenn, dann nicht explizit) gefördert.

Interessant ist auch, dass seit dem Mittelalter bei unseren klassischen Instrumenten der Klanganteil immer weiter optimiert wurde – auf Kosten des Geräuschanteils. Gewünscht waren mehr Klangfülle und damit mehr dynamische Möglichkeiten sowie ein größerer Tonumfang. Auch eine höhere Präzision beim Treffen der Töne wurde angestrebt und machte so den Weg frei für virtuose solistische Einsätze. Die bessere Tonansprache machte die perfekte Beherrschung des Instruments möglich. Sie war jedoch mit dem Verlust des lebendigeren ›Innenlebens‹ des Klangs erkauft, da die Ein- und Ausschwingvorgänge eingeebnet wurden.[38] Der Klang entledigt sich seiner materiellen Grundlagen, der sogenannten ›Schlacken‹, verliert dadurch aber auch an Flexibilität und Expressivität.

DIE VEREDELUNG DER ›SCHLACKEN‹

Wie gehen Gesangslehrpersonen nun konkret in der Unterrichtssituation mit dem Geräuschanteil in der Stimme um? In Gesangslehrbüchern kann man dazu folgende Anweisungen lesen:

> Ein Ton kann Nebengeräusche mit sich führen, die so stark wirken, dass seine regelmäßige Form fast verloren geht und er kaum noch zu erkennen ist. [...] Das den Ton begleitende Geräusch führt in die Wissenschaften der Resonanzverhältnisse und zur

---

36 | Stumpf: Tonpsychologie, S. 516ff.

37 | Winckel: Phänomene musikalischen Hörens, S. 27, 35.

38 | Am Beispiel der Rohrblattinstrumente lässt sich diese Entwicklung gut nachvollziehen: Die schnarrenden Windkapselinstrumente (Nachfahren der Aulos) wurden von den Vorläufern der Oboen (Schalmeien und Pommern) verdrängt, die präziser ansprachen und damit kontrollierbarer waren. Vgl. dazu Krüger: Die Entwicklung der Konstruktionsprinzipien von Holz- und Metallblasinstrumenten seit 1700, S. 49.

Technik des Tones. Die Geräuscherscheinungen in Resonanz [...] umwandeln, also dem Gesangston das Geräusch zu nehmen, ist Aufgabe des Tonbildners. [1905][39]

Mit den drei Hauptforderungen der Gesangskunst kristallisieren sich die Bemühungen der alten Meister heraus,
- aus den eigentlich uninteressanten krächzenden, knarrenden Geräuschen, die unsere Stimmbänder als Primärtöne herausgeben
- durch richtige Atembenutzung
- Vollausnutzung der Resonanzräume

einen edel klingenden, herrlichen Gesangston zu erreichen. [2005][40]

Die beiden Beschreibungen liegen ein Jahrhundert auseinander, aber an der Kernaussage hat sich nicht viel geändert: Aus dem vorliegenden stimmlichen ›Material‹ soll durch Veränderung der Resonanzverhältnisse der Klang optimiert werden. Anfang des 20. Jahrhunderts ist klar, wer da »umwandelt«: der »Tonbildner«, also die Lehrperson. Sie ist eindeutig die treibende Kraft in der Entwicklung der Stimme und entscheidet darüber, welche Technik angewandt wird. Sie ist also nicht nur ein »Mehr-Wisser«, sondern auch ein »Besser-Wisser«[41] par excellence; der Lernende hat nach dem Modell »triviale Maschine« zu funktionieren. Szemzö-Goese äußert sich unbestimmter, wenn sie den »edel klingenden, herrlichen Gesangston« als Stimmideal definiert und sich damit auf die »alten Meister«, also Lehrer des Belcanto, beruft. Wer oder was dieses Stimmideal aber umsetzt, bleibt diffus.

Gerade von der traditionellen italienischen Gesangslehre setzt sich Boruttau 1941 deutlich ab, wenn er schreibt: »Die deutsche Stimmbildung soll vom schlackigen Rohklang über den gereinigten Klang zum Edelklang geleiten.«[42] Sieht man einmal von der völkischen, ideologisch begründeten Wortwahl ab, findet sich hier erneut die Vorstellung, dass das Materielle der Stimme unbedingt der Läuterung durch den Geist des Stimmbildners bedarf. Noch deutlicher bringt es der französische Phoniater Husson auf den Punkt: »Mit seinem Kehlkopf macht der Mensch Geräusch, er spricht und singt mit seinem Gehirn.«[43] Auch im sogenannten Werbeck-Singen, das im Zusammenhang mit der Anthroposophie Rudolf Steiners entstand, wird der immaterielle Ton angestrebt: »Ohne die Erkenntnis, daß Sprache und Ton geistigen Ursprungs sind, ist jeder Kampf gegen Schmutz und Schund im Singen aussichtslos. [...] Der Ton muß genauso klar bleiben wie im ng, keine

---

39 | Böhme-Köhler: Lautbildung beim Singen und Sprechen, S. 6.
40 | Szemzö-Goese: Singen als akustisches Erlebnis, S. 10.
41 | Reich: Systemisch-konstruktivistische Pädagogik, S. 260.
42 | Boruttau: Grundlagen, Ausbau und Grenzen der Stimmkunst, S. 133.
43 | Husson: La voix chanté; zitiert in: Baum: Abriss der Stimmphysiologie, S. 64.

Trübung darf hörbar werden.«[44] Auffallend ist in diesen Zitaten, wie stark das Geräuschhafte und damit das Materielle, aus dem der Stimmklang entsteht, abgewertet wird.

Geräusch als Indikator für Ineffizienz

Fast alle Stimmbildner sind sich darüber einig, dass eine Stimme »frei von Nebengeräuschen« sein sollte.[45] »Das ›Singen auf dem Atem‹ ist [...] der Ausdruck für das Gehörserlebnis des von Nebengeräuschen freien und damit von der Materie unabhängigen ausgeschälten Gesangstones.«[46] Auch in dieser kanonischen Darstellung von Martienßen dominiert die Sehnsucht nach einem Klang, der von der Materie unabhängig ist, und dies soll sich in Geräuschlosigkeit manifestieren. Martienßen spezifiziert an anderer Stelle weiter, was sie mit den »Nebengeräuschen« meint: »Jeder Ton, der sich vermischt mit Reibungsgeräuschen ausströmender sogenannter wilder Luft, ist eben nicht auf dem Atem gesungen, sondern steckt im Atem darin [...].«[47] Das Reibungsgeräusch war spätestens seit der Industrialisierung zu einem Indikator für ineffiziente Abläufe geworden.[48] So werden über den Geräuschanteil der hörenden Lehrperson Vorgänge aus dem Inneren des Körpers angezeigt. Im Lauf des 20. Jahrhunderts findet allmählich eine Umwertung statt: Anstatt den Geräuschanteil nur negativ zu beurteilen und ihn letztlich zu eliminieren, gibt das Geräusch nun, sofern man sich ihm zuwendet, Auskunft über die Art der Klangerzeugung. Mit anderen Worten: Das Geräusch generiert Wissen.

Cornelius L. Reid, der in der Tradition der Belcanto-Lehrer[49] steht, schreibt dazu: »Wenn ein Mechanismus – so auch der Stimmmechanismus – leistungsfähig arbeitet, sind Reibung und Widerstand minimal.«[50] Reids Zugang zum Geräusch in der Singstimme bleibt ambivalent: Sein Stimmkonzept ist zwar einerseits mechanistisch, und ein erhöhter Geräuschanteil gilt als Stimmfehler. Andererseits aber sollte die Klangvorstellung

---

44 | Hensel: Die geistigen Grundlagen des Gesanges, S. 44.
45 | Welches sind die *Haupt*geräusche?, könnte man zunächst einmal fragen.
46 | Martienßen: Das bewußte Singen, S. 118.
47 | Ebd.
48 | Vgl. Keizer: The unwanted Sound of Everything we want, S. 265.
49 | Mit Geburt der Oper, also vom Beginn des 17. Jahrhunderts an, bis in die Mitte des 19. Jahrhunderts hatte die italienische Gesangstechnik des Belcanto ihre Blütezeit. Als die Orchester immer größer wurden, veränderten sich die Anforderungen an die Sänger und dementsprechend auch die Gesangstechniken.
50 | Reid: Erbe des Belcanto, S. 90.

von Lernenden und Lehrperson nicht zu rigide vordefiniert sein, da ja beide noch nicht wissen können, in welche Richtung sich der Stimmklang entwickeln wird.[51] Sein didaktischer Ansatz beruht vor allem darauf, die beiden Haupt-Stimmregister (Brust- und Falsettregister) erst einmal einzeln in ihrer Qualität wahrzunehmen und herstellen zu lernen, damit sie sich danach umso besser koordinieren können. Auf dem Weg dorthin schreckt er auch vor geräuschhaften Klangfarben nicht zurück: »Um die grobe und rauhe Qualität des reinen Brustregisters hören zu können, benutze man den Vokal ›a‹.«[52]

In der Belcanto-Tradition, aus der nur wenige konkrete Anweisungen für den Gesangsunterricht überliefert wurden, steht auch Giovanni Battista Lamperti, dessen Schüler William Earl Brown die Gesangsstunden, die er von 1891 bis 1893 in Dresden erhielt, protokollierte. Lamperti selbst verhält sich gegenüber dem Thema Nebengeräusch eher pragmatisch. Für ihn sind klassisch ausgebildete, tragfähige Stimmen und ihr Geräuschanteil also kein Gegensatz:

Oft sind Nebengeräusche in der Stimme unvermeidbar. [...] Diejenigen, die durch Phlegma, Emphase, emotionale Effekte, deklamatorische Ausrufe, hauchige Lautäußerungen oder übertriebene Aussprache etc. entstehen, sollten die Vibration und Resonanz der Stimme nicht daran hindern, Kopf, Mund und, bei tiefen Tönen, die Brust zu füllen. [...] Nebengeräusche ›tragen‹ nicht und werden von den Zuhörern nicht bemerkt, wenn die anschließende Resonanz reich und die nachfolgende Vibration brillant genug sind. [...] Vibration und Resonanz können eine Menge Geräusche überdecken.[53]

Derart tolerant mag man in der Phoniatrie den Geräuschanteil der Stimme, dessen Existenz unbestritten ist, nicht betrachten. In einer phoniatrischen Anamnese finden viele verschiedene Untersuchungen statt: Zunächst wird der Stimmklang analytisch gehört, um sich »ein Bild [sic] über die technische Beherrschbarkeit der Stimme, die Atem- und Stimmökonomie, den Grad der stimmlichen Anstrengung und Belastbarkeit sowie möglicher unerwünschter Geräuschanteile zu verschaffen.«[54] Liegt bei einer Stimme das Symptom »Heiserkeit« vor, wird diese nach dem *RBH-Index (Rauigkeit/Behauchtheit/*

---

51 | Reid: Voice: Psyche and Soma, S. 18 (Übers. U.v.K.-F.).
52 | Reid: Funktionale Stimmentwicklung, S. 16. Im vorliegendem Beitrag bleibt die Behandlung der Konsonanten (stimmhaften und stimmlosen) in der Gesangspädagogik außen vor. Überwiegend orientiert man sich in der Belcanto-Tradition an Übungen auf reinen Vokalen, /a/ für das Brust- und /u/ für das Kopfregister.
53 | Lamperti und Brown: Vocal Wisdom, S. 40 (Übers. U.v.K.-F.).
54 | Richter: Die Stimme, S. 67.

Heiserkeit) auf einer Skala von 0 bis 3 beschrieben.[55] Ergänzend dazu gibt es den Tastbefund und die Selbsteinschätzung der Untersuchten *(VHI – Voice Handicap Index).* Ferner werden eine Menge apparategestützter Verfahren durchgeführt, die stimmliche Aktivitäten sichtbar machen, messen und darstellen.[56] Es geht der Phoniatrie darum, die Stimme wieder funktionstüchtig zu machen und dafür den Geräuschanteil zu eliminieren, weil man davon ausgeht, dass er die stimmliche »Durchschlagskraft« vermindert.[57] Deswegen wird der Geräuschanteil von dieser Disziplin, bei aller Zuwendung, letztlich doch nur als Symptom einer Störung bewertet.

DAS GERÄUSCH IN JAZZ- UND POPGESANG

Eine Ausnahme bildet, aus phoniatrischer Sicht, die »artifizielle Heiserkeit«, bei der eine störungsfrei funktionierende Stimme »Heiserkeit bewusst als künstlerisches Ausdrucksmittel« einsetzt, »wie dies beim Popgesang häufig geschieht.«[58] Sofern die Künstler wieder zu einer »dichten und klaren Stimmgebung«[59] zurückkehren können, sei gegen den bewussten Einsatz des Geräuschs von phoniatrischer Seite her nichts einzuwenden.[60] Geradezu hymnisch idealisiert Emmi Sittner den Jazzgesang als Ausdrucksmöglichkeit,

> vor allem aber das ›Dirty Play‹, eine Art [...] des Singens, welche die vielen als Untugenden verpönten Praktiken (unreine Intonation, denaturierte Tongebung, Schmieren, [...] Glottisschläge, Falsettieren, heiseren Sprechgesang, Hochziehen der Bruststimme u. a. m.) kultiviert, in der Absicht, [...] die Persönlichkeit des Sängers [...] mit all ihren Schlacken und Lichtern ins Treffen zu führen. Also der höchste Subjektivismus im Gesang, der überhaupt denkbar ist.[61]

---

55 | Dazu: Nawka und Wirth: Stimmstörungen, S. 157f. Ein Wert von 0 repräsentiert die ungestörte Stimmfunktion, bei der schwerstmöglichen Störung wählt man die Zahl 3.
56 | Z.B. Stroboskopie, Hochgeschwindigkeitsglottografie, Stimmfeldmessung, *Harmonic to Noise Ratio (HNR), Relative Average Perturbation (RAP), Normalized Noise Energy (NNE)* und kombinierte Verfahren wie das »Göttinger Heiserkeitsdiagramm«.
57 | Nawka und Wirth: Stimmstörungen, S. 111.
58 | Seidner: Dysodie, S. 172f.
59 | Ebd., S. 175.
60 | In Pop-Lehrbüchern pflegt man einen eher pragmatischen Umgang mit dem Geräusch: Vor zu viel Rauheit wird gewarnt, aber der Geräuschanteil gehört dort ganz selbstverständlich zum Stimmklang mit dazu. Vgl: Baxter: The rock-and-roll singer's survival manual, S. 40.
61 | Sittner: Wege zum Kunstgesang, S. 65.

Sittner zeigt sich hier, trotz ihrer klassischen Ausbildung, beeindruckt von der Authentizität, die dem Jazzgesang eigen ist, und die ohne das Geräuschhafte nicht möglich wäre.

Husler und Rodd-Marling, ebenfalls Vertreter der klassischen Gesangsausbildung, bewerten diese Art von Gesang hingegen völlig anders. In dem Kapitel »Schönheit der Stimme« ihres Buches *Singen* aus dem Jahr 1965, einem Standardwerk unter den gesangspädagogischen Lehrbüchern, diskutieren sie zunächst die verschiedenen Stimmideale »exotischer Völker«,[62] und kommen dann zu dem Schluss, dass »Schönheit kein einheitlich-gültiges Kriterium für eine rationell-physiologische Stimmforschung liefern kann.«[63] Ihr Kriterium ist die »Güte, d.h. die physiologische Intaktheit«,[64] die sie z.B. bei Jazzsängern auf gar keinen Fall gewährleistet sehen, da sie ihre Stimmen zu »gesangsfremden Zwecken« gebrauchen; dieser Gebrauch stellt aus der Perspektive von Husler/Rodd-Marling eine »Denaturierung« dar.[65]

Wer erfahren hat, mit welchem Bedacht und Aufwand diese ›Sänger‹ alle natürliche Klangschönheit aus ihren Stimmen auszumerzen trachten, um sie mit wüsten, hektisch hervorgebrachten geräusch-durchsetzten Lauten beim Hörer einzig und allein orgiastische Zustände aus seinen kreatürlichen Tiefen heraufzubeschwören, wer das erfahren hat, der wird einsehen, daß ein solches Ideal und ähnliche solche ›gesanglichen‹ Strebungen mit singen nicht mehr zu vergleichen sind.[66]

Dieses Urteil über den Jazzgesang ist zwar vernichtend, aber aus Sicht von Husler/Rodd-Marling ist es nicht ausgeschlossen, selbst Jazz-Sänger für das westliche Stimmideal zu gewinnen, nämlich durch das Hören von abendländisch ausgebildeten Sängern.

Und übrigens sind jene exotischen Völker mit den verkünstelten Stimmen ausnahmslos unseres ›Geschmackes‹, sobald sie sich einmal für wirkliches Singen zu interessieren beginnen. Eine Erfahrungstatsache. Es ist das nicht weiter verwunderlich, sie finden eben nur zur Natur ihres Gehöres zurück, die ihnen verfremdet war.[67]

Hier wird das in unserem Kulturkreis tradierte Stimmideal (»wirkliches Singen«) nicht nur eindeutig über die »wüsten geräusch-durchsetzten Laute« gesetzt, sondern es wird der fremde Gesangsstil zugleich auch als »denaturiert«

---

62 | Husler und Rodd-Marling: Singen, S. 123.
63 | Ebd.
64 | Ebd.
65 | Ebd., S. 128.
66 | Ebd.
67 | Ebd.

und »verfremdet« bezeichnet. Dies lässt vermuten, dass die Begegnung zwischen »exotischen« Sängern und westlichen Gesangspädagogen nicht auf Augenhöhe stattfand. Wie wir sehen werden, ist dies nicht nur ein Problem zwischen Vertretern verschiedener Kulturkreise oder Kontinente.

DIE HIERARCHIE ZWISCHEN LEHRENDEN UND LERNENDEN

In Franziska Martienßens kanonischem Lehrbuch wird das wichtige Verhältnis zwischen Lehrenden und Lernenden als zuweilen notwendige, einseitige Überlistung charakterisiert:

> Viele Fehler und Schwächen, namentlich bei verbildeten Stimmen, können nur durch ein feines Überlisten von Seiten des Lehrers bezwungen werden. Die technischen Studien müssen jedem Schüler zunächst wie auf den Leib geschnitten sein, so daß er möglichst keine Hemmungen vor sich sieht und spielend lernt, wie ein Kind. Erst wenn eine gewisse Urteilsfähigkeit da ist, treten dann von selbst die großen Aufgaben ins Bewusstsein.[68]

Von ihrer höheren Warte aus sucht die Lehrperson demzufolge individuell passende Gesangsübungen aus, die den Lernenden direktiv instruieren, bis er (in den Augen der Lehrperson) selbst so weit ist, sich ein Urteil zu bilden. Die Didaktik ist die eines »›Meister-Schüler‹-Prinzips, bei dem die Schüler das Produkt eines bestimmten Plans darstellen, das umso besser ist, je näher es an die Vorstellungen des Meisters herankommt.«[69] Die Machtposition der Lehrperson bleibt so immer gewährleistet.

Bei Reid klingt dieser Vorgang partnerschaftlicher. Lernende und Lehrperson nehmen die neu auftauchenden Klangqualitäten in einem gemeinsamen Lernprozess wahr.[70] Die Lehrperson bringt die stimmliche Entwicklung in Gang, indem sie reflektorisch ablaufende Vorgänge stimuliert. Reid wendet sich in vielen seiner Schriften klar gegen die »Mach-es-so«-Instruktionen, die so tun, als gäbe es konvergente Lösungen für sämtliche Stimmprobleme. Dennoch ist an vielen Stellen seiner Bücher von »Beherrschung« und »Kontrolle der Stimmfunktion« die Rede, da für ihn die Koordination der Vorgänge beim Singen anders nicht möglich erscheint.

Einen Ausweg aus dem Dilemma, in dem Reid steckt, sucht die Gesangspädagogik mit Hilfe von Körpertechniken. In der Feldenkrais-Arbeit,

---

68 | Martienßen: Das bewußte Singen, S. 137f.
69 | Winkler: Pädagogik ›Als-Ob‹, S. 106. Ein anschauliches Beispiel für einen typisch direktiven Unterricht findet man z.B. in der Darstellung bei Morsbach: Opernroman, S. 250f.
70 | Reid: Funktionale Stimmentwicklung, S. 72f.

Alexandertechnik, Eutonie oder auch der Dispokinesis (um nur einige zu nennen) findet man einen alternativen Ansatz, der die Gesangsdidaktik in einen ganz neuen Kontext stellt. Anstatt den Körper zu beherrschen, lässt man sich von seinem impliziten Wissen leiten; anstatt die Klangproduktion zu kontrollieren, exploriert man die Laute unvoreingenommen; anstatt konvergente Lösungen für Stimmprobleme anzustreben, bietet man individuelle, divergente Möglichkeiten an. Das Lernziel – die getreue Widergabe eines Notentextes – tritt für die Lernphase der Stimmbildung in den Hintergrund. Im prozessorientierten Lernen können sich den Lernenden neue Bewegungsabläufe von selbst erschließen.[71] In der Stimmbildung haben wir es zu gleichen Anteilen zum einen mit der Entwicklung von kognitiven Fähigkeiten und Konzepten und zum anderen mit der Ausübung bzw. Verfeinerung von körperlichen Bewegungsmustern zu tun. Die Körpertechniken bieten sich als gute Möglichkeit an, Gewohnheiten durch Fragen (Fragepädagogik) zu durchbrechen, mentale Konzepte zu dekonstruieren[72] und Bewegungen zu destabilisieren, um mehr Entscheidungsfreiheit zu erhalten: Denn »(w)er keine Wahl hat, dem wird Anstrengung zur Gewohnheit.«[73] Die Lehrperson wird damit zum Katalysator für die Selbstorganisation der Bewegungsabläufe, der Lernende zum Experten seiner Wahrnehmung. In der Physik erscheinen Instabilitäten nicht mehr nur als Problem, sondern implizieren mittlerweile Strukturneubildung und Wachstum.[74] Ebenso wendet sich nun auch die Gesangspädagogik dem vollständigen Klang inklusive seines Geräuschanteils zu und nutzt ihn als Ressource.

DAS GERÄUSCH ALS KREATIVER FUNDUS

In der angewandten Stimmphysiologie des Lichtenberger Instituts ist die Wahrnehmung des Stimmklangs mit all seinen Anteilen, ob nun periodisch oder irregulär, zentral für die Weiterentwicklung der Stimme.[75] Genauso

---

71 | Dazu ausführlicher v. Kameke-Frischling: Prozessorientiertes Lernen als *missing link* zwischen Körpertechnik und Gesang, S. 23-29.
72 | Reich: Systemisch-konstruktivistische Pädagogik, S. XI.
73 | Feldenkrais: Bewusstheit durch Bewegung, S. 120.
74 | Schmidt: Instabilität in Natur und Wissenschaft, S. 15.
75 | Das Lichtenberger Institut für angewandte Stimmphysiologie wurde 1982 von der Sängerin Gisela Rohmert und ihrem Mann, dem Arbeitswissenschaftler Prof. Walter Rohmert, in dem Dorf Lichtenberg im Odenwald gegründet. Ausgangspunkt war ein Forschungsprojekt am Institut für Arbeitswissenschaften der TU Darmstadt. Mittels umfangreicher Messmethoden wurden Physiologie und Akustik des Stimmklangs und des Instrumentalspiels erfasst, untersucht und interpretiert. Das Ziel des Instituts ist es,

achtsam, wie in den Körpertechniken mit der Bewegungswahrnehmung umgegangen wird, explorieren Lehrperson und Lernende hier gemeinsam den Klang. Dieser stellt in der Arbeit nach Lichtenberger nicht das Endprodukt einer raffinierten Tätigkeit (Singen) dar, sondern wirkt als Teil des komplexen Systems Mensch direkt wieder auf den Körper zurück, in dem er entsteht. Dies geschieht vor allem über das Vibrato und die hochfrequenten, energiereichen Anteile im Klang, z.B. den Sängerformanten bei 3 kHz (Brillanz).[76] Hören und Singen stehen in einem unmittelbaren Zusammenhang, denn »die Stimme enthält als Obertöne nur die Frequenzen, die das Ohr hört.«[77] Besonders empfindlich (d.h. dämpfungsarm) ist unser Ohr für hochfrequente Klänge, die in den Bereichen um 3 kHz, 5 kHz oder 8 kHz liegen.[78] Entscheidend ist also, wie wir unsere Ohren beim Singen nutzen: Sie können entweder wie Filter fungieren, dann hören wir kultiviert-selektiv und wertend, wie es natürlicherweise geschieht, wenn wir z.B. Lärm ausblenden wollen bzw. wenn wir zielgerichtet üben; oder aber wir stellen die Ohren ein wie beim Lauschen, und so werden sie zu »Pforten, durch die große Informationsmengen Einlass finden.«[79] Dieses sogenannte *responsive* Hören[80] kann Tonus-Einstellung und Bewegungseffizienz in direkter Weise verbessern. Das Lauschen auf unterschiedliche Klang- und Geräuschqualitäten führt Lehrperson und Lernende in neues, unbekanntes Terrain. Wenn sich alte Fehlspannungen auflösen, kann das umliegende Gewebe meist besser in den Schwingungsprozess mit einbezogen werden. Es absorbiert dann nicht den Klang, sondern wird von Vibration durchdrungen und kann so mit seiner eigenen Materialität zur Klangmischung mit beitragen.[81] Wie hört sich das an?

Alle Gewebe haben ihre eigenen Klangcharaktere. Feinporiger Knochen klingt anders als Schleimhaut – etwa im Verhältnis von feinkörnig summend zu etwas schlierig. Schleimhaut kann viele Qualitäten in sich haben – und verwandelt sich sehr schnell in der Schwingung von rau zu glatt, von feucht zu trocken etc. [...] Wenn die klanglichen Oberflächen dieser inneren Membranen zunächst unzugänglich und fest erscheinen – so zeigen sie eine erste Veränderung, indem sie eine Brüchigkeit und Rauigkeit bis hin zu einer Rissigkeit anklingen lassen.[82]

---

neueste Erkenntnisse aus der Gesangs- und Instrumentalforschung in die pädagogische Praxis zu transferieren.

76 | Rohmert: Der Sänger auf dem Weg zum Klang.
77 | Tomatis: Der Klang des Lebens, S. 11.
78 | Rohmert und Landzettel: Lichtenberger Dokumentationen, S. 60f.
79 | Krause: Das große Orchester der Natur, S. 23f.
80 | Vgl. dazu Sowodniok: Stimmklang und Freiheit, S. 63.
81 | Rohmert und Landzettel: Lichtenberger Dokumentationen, S. 46.
82 | Sowodniok: Stimmklang und Freiheit, S. 158.

Je wahrnehmungsfähiger und unbefangener wir für diese nie gehörten Qualitäten sind, umso leichter fällt es, diese anzuerkennen und zu integrieren. Damit einher geht oft auch ein psychischer Prozess, in dem sich unbewusste, unbeabsichtigte Anteile der Persönlichkeit (›Schatten‹) als Material in Stimme und Musik entfalten dürfen.[83] Verändert sich das Schwingungsverhalten der Stimmlippen, erhöht sich häufig der Geräuschanteil. Dieses Phänomen kann man als *Transit-Geräusch* bezeichnen, weil es

1. ein *Durchgangsstadium* in der Stimmbildung darstellt,
2. mit Perturbationen und Fluktuationen zu tun hat, also den unsteten Anteilen der Schwingungen, die in der Akustik, als *Transienten* bezeichnet[84] werden und
3. hierbei die Bewegungen der bindegewebigen Anteile der Stimmlippen *(Transition)* eine große Rolle spielen.[85]

Aus systemischer Sicht ist leicht zu verstehen, was in einem solchen Fall passiert: Eine Anregung (eine Frage oder Übung), die das bestehende Schwingungsmuster destabilisiert, bringt die Schleimschicht sowie die Schleimhaut dazu, sich anders als sonst und vorerst unregelmäßiger zu bewegen. Turbulenzen werden hörbar (in der konstruktivistischen Pädagogik spricht man ebenfalls von »Perturbation«[86]) und fordern damit Lehrperson und Lernende heraus. Die plötzlich auftretenden, irritierenden Geräuschemissionen sind oft besser zu ertragen, sobald man sich klar macht, was dort zwischen Luftschwingung, Schleimschicht, Bindegewebe und Muskel physiologisch geschieht:

Wichtig ist hierbei, dass die physiologische Bewegung im Kehlkopf an der Schleimhautummantelung der Stimmlippen ansetzt. Nach der sog. ›Body-Cover-Theorie‹ mit den Funktionseinheiten ›*Cover-Transition-Body*‹ dominiert die Oberflächenschwingung das darunter liegende Gewebe, d.h. die Flatterbewegungen von Schleim und Schleimhaut an der Oberfläche – *Cover* – informieren und gestalten das Schwingungsverhalten des darunter liegenden Muskels – *Body*. Das Bindegewebe – *Transition* – der umkleidenden Membran des Stimmbandmuskels ist auf diesem in hohem Maße frei verschieblich. [...] Allein angesprochen wirkt sie [= die bindegewebige *Lamina profundis;* U.v.K.-F.] klanglich rauer und matter als die äußeren Schichten.[87]

---

83 | Siehe dazu auch: Arye: Unbeabsichtigte Musik.
84 | Pilaj: Singen lernen mit dem Computer, S. 61.
85 | Eine wissenschaftliche Untersuchung der *Transit-Geräusche* im Unterrichtsfeld steht noch aus.
86 | Krause: Perturbation als musikpädagogischer Schlüsselbegriff?!, S. 46f.
87 | Sowoniok: Stimmklang und Freiheit, S. 129f.

Der Geräuschanteil wird auf diese Weise zum Indikator für Veränderung und damit zu einer wichtigen Informationsquelle, die verloren ginge, wenn das Geräusch als ›Fehler‹ bewertet oder ganz vermieden würde. Es ist dann wichtig, dass die Lehrperson das Vertrauen der Lernenden in den begonnenen Prozess fördert. Die Stimmtherapeutin Uta Feuerstein schreibt dazu:

> Eine schwierige Aufgabe ist es auch, die Schülerin davon zu überzeugen, dass gewisse geräuschhafte Anteile im Stimmklang die in der Entstehung begriffene Brillanz darstellen und zu verhindern, dass der Geräuschanteil sofort wieder durch erhöhte Muskelkompensation retuschiert wird.[88]

Vor allem bei Menschen, die ihre Stimme professionell nutzen, herrscht große Angst vor der Berührung mit dem Geräuschanteil, da dieser meist mit Stimmstörungen gleichgesetzt und so pathologisiert wird. Dabei können Geräusche in der Stimme sogar als *Stimuli* die Entwicklung der Stimme befördern, wenn entsprechend achtsam damit umgegangen wird. Zum Beispiel können im Falle einer Erkältung die verschleimten Luftwege zum Ort der Erkundung gemacht werden: Wenn Schleim-Geräusche hörbar werden, entsteht dadurch die Möglichkeit, differenziert unsere Wahrnehmung für die Vorgänge an der Glottis, in der Luftröhre, im Nasenraum u.a. zu schulen und darüber besser in Kontakt zu treten mit Abläufen, die ganz ohne Störung glatt und unbewusst geblieben wären. Wie lassen sich die Schleim-Geräusche beschreiben? Knisternd? Blubbernd? Knatternd? Reibend? Wenn es Schleifpapier wäre, welche Körnung hätte es? Kommt das Geräusch eher von links oder von rechts? etc.[89] Das Eintauchen in diesen Kosmos der Laut-Phänomene kann manchmal für Lehrende und Lernende so faszinierend sein, dass darüber die Arbeit an Arie oder Lied ganz in den Hintergrund tritt. Kritisch könnte man daher einwenden, dass es oft schwierig ist, dieses Explorieren in eine Hochschulausbildung zu integrieren, wenn diese in erster Linie effizient sein soll.

Im responsiven Hören nehmen unsere Ohren nicht nur äußere Schallereignisse wahr, sondern auch Laute, die aus dem Inneren des Körpers dringen. Besonders interessant sind die feinen Sinneshärchen (Zilien) im Innenohr, die ihre eigene Erregung hören können[90] und die *formatio reticularis*,

---

88 | Feuerstein: Stimmig sein. Die Selbstregulation in Gesang und Stimmtherapie, S. 77.
89 | Siehe v. Kameke-Frischling: Schleim als Chance.
90 | Die Eigenschwingungen der Zilien (sogenannte Oto-akustische Emissionen OAE) werden mittlerweile beim Neugeborenen-Hör-Screening genutzt. Die dabei verwendeten Sende-Frequenzen liegen zwischen 2 und 4 kHz. Quelle: MAICO ERO SCAN OAE-Screener Datenblatt von 2008.

eine Struktur im Hirnstamm, von der Ähnliches berichtet wird.[91] Diese Areale generieren feine, sirrende Klänge, die zumeist unterhalb der Wahrnehmungsschwelle bleiben und an das Schwirren von Insekten erinnern. Gelingt es, diese zirpenden Grillen-ähnlichen Geräusche zuerst im Wechsel und dann zusammen mit dem eigenen Stimmklang zu erleben, kann diese Erfahrung für die »Klangerzeugung – Stimme und Instrument – [...] strukturbildend werden.« Der Klang reichert sich an, und die hochfrequente, geräuschhafte »Grillenessenz« lässt »Klangliches und Körperliches verschmelzen.«[92] Die unstrukturierten, irregulären Schallerscheinungen, die üblicherweise Geräusche heißen, werden nun nicht mehr abgewertet und hinausgefegt, sondern können durchaus Positives zur Stimmbildung beitragen. Voraussetzung dafür ist, dass im Unterricht achtsam und respektvoll mit den Lernenden (und deren Geräuschanteilen im Stimmklang) umgegangen wird. Dann steht das Entwicklungspotenzial und nicht das Entwicklungsdefizit im Vordergrund, und beide, Lernende wie Lehrende können sich vertrauensvoll und staunend der Selbstorganisation der Stimme überlassen.

Von Rumi, dem großen persischen Mystiker, ist der Satz überliefert: »Die Musik ist das Knarren der Pforten des Paradieses.« Als ein vorlauter Zuhörer ihm ins Wort fiel und sagte: »Mir gefällt das Knarren von Pforten nicht«, antwortete ihm Rumi: »Ich höre die Pforte, die sich auftut, du aber die Pforte, die sich schließt.«[93]

Bibliographie

Arend, Anja K.: Steppen, Schleifen, Schlagen. Eine tanzwissenschaftliche Sicht auf das Geräusch, in: Camille Hongler, Christoph Haffter und Silvan Moosmüller (Hg.): Geräusch. Das Andere der Musik, Bielefeld 2015, S. 139-149.
Arye, Lane: Unbeabsichtigte Musik, Petersberg 2004.
Barthes, Roland: Die Rauheit der Stimme, in: Ders.: Der entgegenkommende und der stumpfe Sinn, Frankfurt/M. 1982, S. 269-278.
Baxter, Mark: The rock-and-roll singer's survival manual, Milwaukee 1990.
Biesenbender, Volker: Von der unerträglichen Leichtigkeit des Instrumentalspiels, Aarau 1992.
Borsche, Dahlia: Geräusch, Musik, Wissenschaft. Eine Bestandsaufnahme, in: Camille Hongler, Christoph Haffter und Silvan Moosmüller (Hg.): Geräusch. Das Andere der Musik, Bielefeld 2015, S. 33-46.

---

91 | Rohmert und Landzettel: Lichtenberger Dokumentationen, S. 83-87.
92 | Ebd., S. 86.
93 | Zitiert nach: Cramer: Das Buch von der Stimme, S. 255.

Boruttau, Alfred Julius: Grundlagen, Ausbau und Grenzen der Stimmkunst, München und Berlin 1941.
Böhme-Köhler, August: Lautbildung beim Singen und Sprechen, Leipzig 1905.
Braun, Christina von: Der Einbruch der Wohnstube in die Fremde, Bern 1987.
Cramer, Annette: Das Buch von der Stimme, Zürich und Düsseldorf 1998.
Eggebrecht, Hans-Heinz: Musikbegriff und europäische Tradition, in: Hans-Heinz Eggebrecht und Carl Dahlhaus (Hg.): Was ist Musik?, Wilhelmshaven 1985, S. 43-54.
Feldenkrais, Moshe: Bewusstheit durch Bewegung, Berlin 1989.
Feuerstein, Uta: Stimmig sein. Die Selbstregulation in Gesang und Stimmtherapie, Paderborn 2000.
Fischer, Peter-Michael: Die Stimme des Sängers, Stuttgart 1993.
Foerster, Heinz von: Das Gleichnis vom blinden Fleck, in: Gerhard Johann Lischka (Hg.): Der entfesselte Blick, Bern 1993, S. 14-47.
Graf, Walter: Zur Verwendung von Geräuschen in der außereuropäischen Musik, in: Jahrbuch für musikalische Volks- und Völkerkunde, Bd. 2, Berlin 1966, S. 59-90.
Hammar, Jan: Gesang lehren und lernen im Spannungsfeld zwischen Instinkt und Wissenschaft, Augsburg 2012.
Henderson, Joseph L.: Der moderne Mensch und seine Mythen, in: Carl Gustav Jung: Der Mensch und seine Symbole, Freiburg i. Br. 1988, S. 106-157.
Hensel, Olga: Die geistigen Grundlagen des Gesanges, Kassel 1952.
Herzfeld, Friedrich: Ullstein-Lexikon der Musik, Frankfurt/M. 1957.
Husler, Frederick und Yvonne Rodd-Marling: Singen, Mainz 1965.
Husson, Raoul: La voix chanté, Paris 1960. Abdruck in: Günther Baum: Abriss der Stimmphysiologie, Mainz 1972.
Jukic, Nina: The Sound of Obsolence, in: Camille Hongler, Christoph Haffter und Silvan Moosmüller (Hg.): Geräusch. Das Andere der Musik, Bielefeld 2015, S. 151-162.
Jung, Carl Gustav: Zugang zum Unbewussten, in: Ders.: Der Mensch und seine Symbole, Freiburg i. Br. 1988, S. 20-103.
Jung, Carl Gustav: Welt der Psyche, München 1962.
Keizer, Garret: The unwanted Sound of Everything we want. A Book about Noise, New York 2010.
Kameke-Frischling, Uta von: Schleim als Chance [unveröffentlichter Vortrag], Symposium der Deutschen Gesellschaft für Musikphysiologie und Musikermedizin, Hannover 2015.
Kameke-Frischling, Uta von: Prozessorientiertes Lernen als *missing link* zwischen Körpertechnik und Gesang, in: Zeitschrift der Deutschen Gesellschaft für Musikphysiologie und Musikmedizin 21.1 (2014), S. 23-29.
Kingsbury, Henry: Music, Talent and Performance, Philadelphia 1988.

Kolesch, Doris und Sybille Krämer: Stimmen im Konzept der Disziplinen, in: Dies. (Hg): Stimme, Frankfurt/M. 2006, S. 7-15.

Krause, Bernie: Das große Orchester der Natur, München 2013.

Krause, Martina: Perturbation als musikpädagogischer Schlüsselbegriff?!, in: Christoph Richter (Hg.): Konstruktivismus in der Musikpädagogik und im Musikunterricht? Diskussion Musikpädagogik 40.4 (2008), S. 46-51.

Kruse-Weber, Silke, Barbara Borovnjak und Cristina Marín: Umgang mit Fehlern: Konstruktivistische Einstellungen und Strategien für Musiker/innen und Instrumentallehrkräfte, in: Zeitschrift der Deutschen Gesellschaft für Musikphysiologie und Musikmedizin 22.3 (2015), S. 106-117.

Krüger, Walther: Die Entwicklung der Konstruktionsprinzipien von Holz- und Metallblasinstrumenten seit 1700, in: Jürgen Meyer (Hg.): Qualitätsaspekte bei Musikinstrumenten, Celle 1988, S. 35-50.

Lamperti, Giovanni Battista und William Earl Brown: Vocal Wisdom, Boston 1957.

Martienßen, Franziska: Das bewußte Singen, Frankfurt/M. 1923/1951/1989.

Morsbach, Petra: Opernroman, München 1998.

Nancy, Jean Luc: A l'écoute, Berlin 2010.

Nawka, Tadeus und Günter Wirth: Stimmstörungen, Köln 2007.

Pilaj, Josef: Singen lernen mit dem Computer, Augsburg 2011.

Reich, Kersten: Systemisch-konstruktivistische Pädagogik, Neuwied u.a. 1996.

Reid, Cornelius Lawrence: Voice: Psyche and Soma, New York 1975.

Reid, Cornelius Lawrence: Funktionale Stimmentwicklung, Mainz 1984.

Reid, Cornelius Lawrence: Erbe des Belcanto, Mainz 2009.

Richter, Bernhard: Die Stimme, Leipzig 2013.

Rohmert, Gisela: Der Sänger auf dem Weg zum Klang, Köln 1991.

Rohmert, Gisela und Martin Landzettel: Lichtenberger Dokumentationen, Lichtenberg/Odw. 2015.

Schafer, Robert Murray: Klang und Krach. Eine Kulturgeschichte des Hörens, Frankfurt/M. 1988.

Schmidt, Jan Cornelius: Instabilität in Natur und Wissenschaft, Berlin 2008.

Seidner, Wolfram: Dysodie, in: Bernhard Richter: Die Stimme. Grundlagen. Künstlerische Praxis. Gesunderhaltung, Leipzig 2013, S. 172-180.

Shubin, Neil: Der Fisch in uns, Frankfurt/M. 2009.

Sittner, Emmi: Wege zum Kunstgesang, Wien 1968.

Sowodniok, Ulrike: Stimmklang und Freiheit, Bielefeld 2013.

Stumpf, Carl: Tonpsychologie, Bd. 2, Leipzig 1883.

Szemző-Goese, Elisabeth: Singen als akustisches Erlebnis, Norderstedt 2005.

Terhardt, Ernst: Akustische Kommunikation, Heidelberg 1998.

Tomatis, Alfred A.: Der Klang des Lebens. Vorgeburtliche Kommunikation – Die Anfänge der seelischen Entwicklung, Reinbek b. Hamburg 1990.

Türcke, Christoph: Zurück zum Geräusch. Die sakrale Hypothek der Musik, in: Merkur 55.6 (2001), S. 509-519.

Winckel, Fritz: Phänomene musikalischen Hörens, Berlin 1960.

Winkler, Christian: Pädagogik ›Als-Ob‹, in: Peter Röbke und Natalia Ardila-Mantila (Hg.): Vom wilden Lernen, Mainz 2009, S. 99-116.

III Technologien und Bedeutsamkeit von Geräuschen

»Automobile gehen über mich hin.«
Urbane Dispositive akustischer Innervation um 1900[1]

Daniel Morat

> Daß ich es nicht lassen kann, bei offenem Fenster zu schlafen. Elektrische Bahnen rasen läutend durch meine Stube. Automobile gehen über mich hin. Eine Tür fällt zu. Irgendwo klirrt eine Scheibe herunter, ich höre ihre großen Scherben lachen, die kleinen Splitter kichern. Dann plötzlich dumpfer, eingeschlossener Lärm von der anderen Seite, innen im Hause. Jemand steigt die Treppe. Kommt, kommt unaufhörlich. Ist da, ist lange da, geht vorbei. Und wieder die Straße. Ein Mädchen kreischt: Ah tais-toi, je ne veux plus. Die Elektrische rennt ganz erregt heran, darüber fort, fort über alles. Jemand ruft. Leute laufen, überholen sich. Ein Hund bellt.
>
> *Rainer Maria Rilke: Die Aufzeichnungen des Malte Laurids Brigge*[2]

Der Protagonist und Ich-Erzähler aus Rainer Maria Rilkes 1910 veröffentlichtem Roman *Die Aufzeichnungen des Malte Laurids Brigge* erlebt die (nächtliche) Stadt als Aufeinanderfolge akustischer Reize, die körperlich erfahren werden und in den Wahnsinn treiben können.[3] Rilkes Roman erinnert mit dieser Passage an eine häufig vernachlässigte Wahrnehmungsdimension der urbanen Moderne. Denn Großstädte waren und sind nicht nur verdichtete Bildräume, wie in der kulturhistorischen Forschung zur Stadt immer wieder

---
1 | Eine kürzere Fassung dieses Textes ist auf Englisch erschienen, vgl. Morat: Urban Soundscapes and Acoustic Innervation around 1900.
2 | Rilke: Die Aufzeichnungen des Malte Raurids Brigge, S. 455f.
3 | Vgl. dazu auch Cowan: Imagining Modernity Through the Ear.

betont wird, sondern auch dynamisierte Hör- und Klangräume. Besonders in der Phase der Hochurbanisierung seit dem letzten Drittel des 19. Jahrhunderts veränderte sich mit den rapide wachsenden Großstädten auch deren Klanggestalt, zum einen durch die Verdichtung, Elektrifizierung und Motorisierung des Verkehrs und zum anderen durch das schiere Anwachsen der Wohnbevölkerung und deren Zusammendrängung in eng gestaffelten Mietskasernen. Beide Dimensionen sind in der Rilke-Passage mit dem Verkehrslärm von der Straße und dem Lärm der Nachbarn im gleichen Haus angesprochen.

Dass die durch das schnelle Städtewachstum um 1900 entstandenen urbanen Lebensverhältnisse unmittelbare Auswirkungen auf den Wahrnehmungs- und Nervenapparat der Stadtbewohner haben konnten, wurde ebenfalls schon zeitgenössisch festgestellt und diskutiert. Das wahrscheinlich berühmteste Zeugnis dieser Reflexion auf die kognitiven Effekte des Großstadtlebens ist wohl der Text über »Die Großstädte und das Geistesleben« von Georg Simmel aus dem Jahr 1903. In diesem Text spricht Simmel von der »Steigerung des Nervenlebens« in der Großstadt, die er zunächst allgemein auf den »raschen und ununterbrochenen Wechsel äußerer und innerer Eindrücke« zurückführte.[4] Bei diesen »eng zusammengedrängten Nervenreizen« schien Simmel allerdings in erster Linie an die optischen Eindrücke, an die »rasche Zusammendrängung wechselnder Bilder« gedacht zu haben.[5] In einem anderen Text spricht Simmel vom »Übergewicht des Sehens über das Hören Andrer«[6] im Großstadtverkehr.

In der Nachfolge Simmels haben sich die Kulturgeschichtsschreibung und die Soziologie der Stadt in vielfältiger Weise mit der visuellen Kultur der Großstädte befasst und etwa den Flaneur als primär visuell orientierten Großstadtkonsumenten und -beobachter analysiert.[7] Neben Simmel sind die anderen beiden Säulenheiligen dieser Art der historischen Rekonstruktion urbaner Erfahrung, Siegfried Kracauer und Walter Benjamin, zu nennen.[8] Tatsächlich lassen sich auch bei Benjamin viele Argumente für die These einer primär visuell geprägten Großstadtkultur finden, vom Flaneur aus dem *Passagen-Werk* bis zu den Anmerkungen zum Kino im Kunstwerk-Aufsatz,

---

4 | Simmel: Die Großstädte und das Geistesleben, S. 116.

5 | Ebd., S. 121 u. 117.

6 | Simmel: Soziologie, S. 727.

7 | Vgl. etwa Neumeyer: Der Flaneur; Ward: Weimar Surfaces. Sabina Becker spricht in ihrer Untersuchung zur literarischen Großstadtwahrnehmung im frühen 20. Jahrhundert allgemein von einer »Visualisierung und Optisierung des großstädtischen Lebens«, Becker: Urbanität und Moderne, S. 47.

8 | Vgl. zu dieser intellektuellen Trias Frisby: Fragmente der Moderne; zu Simmel als Ahnherr der Großstadtreflexion Müller: Die Großstadt als Ort der Moderne.

nach denen der Schockcharakter der bewegten Bilder dem Apperzeptionstraining für das Überleben in der Großstadt dienen könne. Der von Benjamin in diesem Kontext verwendete Begriff der »Innervation« lässt sich jedoch vom Visuellen auch auf das Akustische übertragen.

Der Mensch, so Benjamin im Kunstwerk-Aufsatz, dem die entwickelte Technik als eine »zweite Natur« gegenüberstehe, die er »zwar erfand aber schon längst nicht mehr meistert«, sei auf einen »Lehrgang« angewiesen, um die »neue[n] Aufgaben der Apperzeption« in der technischen Welt bewältigen zu können.[9] Für Benjamin war das Kino der Ort, an dem das Auge diese notwendig gewordene Anpassung einüben könne:

Der Film dient, den Menschen in denjenigen neuen Apperzeptionen und Reaktionen zu üben, die der Umgang mit einer Apparatur bedingt, deren Rolle in seinem Leben fast täglich zunimmt. Die ungeheure technische Apparatur unserer Zeit zum Gegenstand der menschlichen Innervation zu machen – das ist die geschichtliche Aufgabe, in deren Dienst der Film seinen wahren Sinn hat.[10]

Benjamin ging dabei von einer weitgehenden Analogie zwischen Film und modernem Großstadtleben aus:

Der Film ist die der gesteigerten Lebensgefahr, der die Heutigen ins Auge zu sehen haben, entsprechende Kunstform. Das Bedürfnis, sich Chockwirkungen auszusetzen, ist eine Anpassung der Menschen an die sie bedrohenden Gefahren. Der Film entspricht tiefgreifenden Veränderungen des Apperzeptionsapparates – Veränderungen, wie sie im Maßstab der Privatexistenz jeder Passant im Großstadtverkehr, wie sie im geschichtlichen Maßstab jeder heutige Staatsbürger erlebt.[11]

In seinen Überlegungen »Über einige Motive bei Baudelaire« schrieb Benjamin in ähnlicher Weise, dass durch den »Verkehr in der großen Stadt« sich zu bewegen »für den einzelnen eine Folge von Chocks und von Kollisionen« zur Folge habe, wodurch »das menschliche Sensorium einem Training komplexer Art« unterworfen werde.[12] Diese Wahrnehmungsanalyse muss jedoch nicht auf das Sehen reduziert werden. So hat etwa Peter Bailey vorgeschlagen, Benjamins Analyse der visuellen Wahrnehmungscodierung in der

---

9 | Benjamin: Das Kunstwerk im Zeitalter seiner technischen Reproduzierbarkeit (Erste Fassung), S. 444 u. 466.
10 | Ebd., S. 444f.
11 | Benjamin: Das Kunstwerk im Zeitalter seiner technischen Reproduzierbarkeit (Dritte Fassung), S. 503.
12 | Benjamin: Über einige Motive bei Baudelaire, S. 630.

Moderne und besonders in der modernen Großstadt auch auf die Codierung des Hörens zu übertragen:

> It may be instructive [...] to extend to hearing Benjamin's proposition that distraction has superseded contemplation as the habitual state of modern visual reception. Thus we may understand modern street noise as a montage of sounds with shocklike juxtapositions of dissimilars and constant dissolves met and mastered by a newly developed sonic subconscious.[13]

Im Folgenden soll diese Anregung aufgegriffen werden, um mithilfe von Benjamins Begriff der Innervation über den Zusammenhang von akustischer Reizstruktur und »gesteigertem Nervenleben« (Simmel) in der Großstadt um 1900 nachzudenken. Dazu ist zunächst eine kurze Charakterisierung der akustischen Veränderungen in der Großstadt um 1900 notwendig. Im längsten Abschnitt wird es dann um das Verhältnis von Nervositäts- und Lärmdiskurs gehen. Abschließend kann dann nur noch mit einigen wenigen Bemerkungen darauf hingewiesen werden, dass sich die Frage nach den urbanen Dispositiven akustischer Innervation nicht auf die Frage nach der neuropathogenen Qualität des Großstadtlärms reduzieren lässt.

Lärm und Lärmbekämpfung in der Grossstadt um 1900

Dass Städte laut sind, ist ein Gemeinplatz, der nicht nur auf moderne Großstädte zutrifft. Als Zentren von Handwerk, Handel und Verkehr waren Städte auch schon in der Vormoderne Orte der vielfältigen akustischen Kommunikation und Emission, die man sich nicht als leise vorzustellen hat.[14] Im Zuge der Hochurbanisierung und der Metropolenbildung um 1900 veränderte sich aber durch Städtewachstum und Verkehrsverdichtung sowie durch Elektrifizierung und Motorisierung auch die Klanglandschaft der Großstadt in den entscheidenden Parametern.[15] Während etwa der Straßenlärm in New York kurz vor der Jahrhundertwende, so eine zeitgenössische Beobachtung, in erster Linie durch Pferdewagen, Händler, Straßenmusiker, Klingeln und Tiere hervorgerufen worden und damit weitgehend organischen Ursprungs gewesen sei, katalogisierte das New Yorker Gesundheitsamt 1930 in einer Bestandsaufnahme des »City Noise« hauptsächlich technische Geräuschquellen wie

---

13 | Bailey: Popular Culture and Performance in the Victorian City, S. 206.
14 | Vgl. etwa Garrioch: Sounds of the City; Smith: Tuning into London c. 1600; Wright: Speaking and Listening in Early Modern London.
15 | Vgl. zum Begriff der »Klanglandschaft« als Übersetzung des englischen »Soundscape« Schafer: The Soundscape.

Autos, Züge und Straßenbahnen, Bauarbeiten, Lautsprecher und Radios.[16] Wie aus dieser Aufzählung hervorgeht, kann man für die Zeit um 1900 von einer doppelten »Technisierung des Auditiven«[17] sprechen: einer primären durch Maschinenlärm und Großstadtverkehr und einer sekundären durch die neuen akustischen Aufzeichnungs-, Speicherungs- und Übertragungsmedien. Denn seit dem Ende des 19. Jahrhunderts entwickelten sich mit der Erfindung des Phonographen, des Telefons und schließlich des Radios auch die akustischen Medien auf einer qualitativ neuen Stufe. Sie fanden ihre Verbreitung und Anwendung zunächst vor allem in den großen Städten.

Allerdings führte nicht allein die doppelte Technisierung des Auditiven zu einer neuartigen großstädtischen Klanglandschaft, sondern auch die oben schon angesprochene Verdichtung der Lebens- und Wohnverhältnisse. Der Sozialhistoriker Klaus Saul katalogisiert folgende Faktoren, die um 1900 zu einem gesteigerten Lärmbewusstsein geführt haben:

Mit der rapiden Großstadtentwicklung und der Entstehung industrieller Ballungsräume, der Gemengelage von Wohnhäusern, Fabriken und Handwerksbetrieben in zahlreichen Stadtvierteln und der Motorisierung auch des Kleinbetriebs, der Intensivierung des innerstädtischen Verkehrs, der Verwendung neuer, den Schall vorzüglich leitender Baumaterialien, der Verbreitung des Massenmiethauses von den Mietskasernen der Arbeiter bis zu den großbürgerlichen Etagenwohnungen, der beginnenden Technisierung des bürgerlichen Haushaltes, der Ausdehnung des großstädtischen Vergnügungsbetriebes gewann der Lärm in der Zeit des Kaiserreichs eine neue Qualität.[18]

Eine Folge dieser Entwicklung war, dass seit dem Ende des 19. Jahrhunderts der Lärm zunehmend als großstädtisches Problem thematisiert wurde und sich bürgerliche Initiativen zu seiner Bekämpfung formierten. Eine Vorreiterin dieser Antilärmbewegungen war die New Yorker Verlegergattin und Philanthropin Julia Barnett Rice, die 1906 die *Society for the Suppression of Unnecessary Noise* in New York gründete und mit dieser Vereinigung relativ erfolgreich Lobbyarbeit für Antilärmverordnungen und Ruhezonen besonders um Krankenhäuser und Schulen herum betrieb.[19] Rice wurde mit ihrer

---

16 | Vgl. Thompson: The Soundscape of Modernity, S. 117f., sowie den Bericht des New York Department of Health: Brown u. a. (Hg.): City Noise.

17 | Knoch: Die Aura des Empfangs, S. 133.

18 | Saul: »Kein Zeitalter seit Erschaffung der Welt hat so viel und so ungeheuerlichen Lärm gemacht …«, S. 189; vgl. für das Beispiel Wiens auch Payer: »Großstadtwirbel«; Payer: Der Klang von Wien.

19 | Vgl. zu Rice und ihrem Verein neben Thompson: Soundscape, S. 120-130, die frühen Arbeiten von Smilor: Cacophony at Thirty-fourth and Sixth; Smilor: Personal Boundaries in the Urban Enviroment; Smilor: Toward an Enviromental Perspective.

Vereinigung zum Vorbild ähnlicher Gründungen in anderen Ländern und Großstädten. So berief sich auch der Philosoph und Kulturkritiker Theodor Lessing auf das New Yorker Vorbild, als er 1908 den Deutschen Lärmschutzverband ins Leben rief, der auch als Antilärmverein bekannt wurde.[20] Der Vereinsgründung unmittelbar vorausgegangen war die Publikation von Lessings Kampfschrift *Der Lärm*, in der er, wie es im Untertitel heißt, »gegen die Geräusche unseres Lebens« zu Felde zieht.[21] Lessing klagt darin vor allen Dingen von der Warte des »Geistesarbeiters« aus, dessen Konzentration und Produktivität durch das »Übermass von Geräusch im gegenwärtigen Leben« empfindlich gestört werde.[22] Für Lessing war der Lärm Ausdruck der weit verbreiteten Unkultur der Menschen und damit nicht spezifisch großstädtisch. In den Großstädten nahm er durch die dortige Verdichtung der Wohn- und Lebensverhältnisse jedoch besonders quälende Formen an, die die geistige Sammlung verunmöglichten:

Die Hämmer dröhnen, die Maschinen rasseln. Fleischerwägen und Bäckerkarren rollen früh vor Tag am Hause vorüber. Unaufhörlich läuten zahllose Glocken. Tausend Türen schlagen auf und zu. Tausend hungrige Menschen, rücksichtslos gierig nach Macht, Erfolg, Befriedigung ihrer Eitelkeit oder roher Instinkte, feilschen und schreien, schreien und streiten vor unsern Ohren und erfüllen alle Gassen der Städte mit den Interessen ihrer Händel und ihres Erwerbs. Nun läutet das Telephon. Nun kündet die Huppe ein Automobil. Nun rasselt ein elektrischer Wagen vorüber. Ein Bahnzug fährt über die eiserne Brücke. Quer über unser schmerzendes Haupt, quer durch unsere besten Gedanken. [...] Alle Augenblicke ein neues unangenehmes Geräusch! Auf dem Balkon des Hinterhauses werden Teppiche und Betten geklopft. Ein Stockwerk höher rammeln Handwerker. Im Treppenflure schlägt irgend jemand Nägel in eine offenbar mit Eisen beschlagene Kiste. Im Nebenhaus prügeln sich Kinder.[23]

Diese Litanei macht deutlich, dass der quälende Lärm für Lessing vor allen Dingen zwei Ursachen hatte: die Geschäfte und Geschäftigkeiten der Mitmenschen, der Nachbarn und Händler, sowie den großstädtischen Verkehr. Mit seinen Publikationen und Aktionen zog Lessings Antilärmverein daher auch gegen beides zu Felde. Allerdings überwog eindeutig die Stoßrichtung gegen den Lärm der Mitmenschen. Forderungen nach technischen Verbesserungen etwa der Straßenpflasterung oder der Schalldämmung von Gebäuden und Verkehrsmitteln wurden ebenfalls erhoben, standen aber eher im

---

20 | Vgl. dazu neben Saul: Zeitalter; auch Baron: Noise and Degeneration; Lentz: »Ruhe ist die erste Bürgerpflicht«; zum Kontext Bijsterveld: Mechanical Sound, S. 91-104.
21 | Lessing: Der Lärm.
22 | Ebd., S. 2.
23 | Ebd., S. 14f.

Hintergrund. In erster Linie stellte sich das Lärmproblem für Lessing und seine Mitstreiter als Problem der Rüpelhaftigkeit des Großteils der Mitmenschen dar. Dementsprechend hieß auch die im Herbst 1908 erstmals veröffentlichte Vereinszeitschrift *Der Anti-Rüpel* (auch *Antirowdy; Das Recht auf Stille*). *Monatsblätter zum Kampf gegen Lärm, Roheit und Unkultur im deutschen Wirtschafts-, Handels- und Verkehrsleben*.[24] Schon in der zweiten Ausgabe wurde *Das Recht auf Stille* zum Obertitel gemacht und der *Antirüpel* wurde in den Untertitel verschoben, da die Bezeichnung Kritik hervorgerufen hatte. Das Problem des Elitismus und des kulturellen Dünkels gegenüber der »Unkultur« der Bevölkerungsmehrheit blieb aber bestehen.

Dieser Elitismus war es wohl auch, der den Erfolg und die Reichweite des Vereins, etwa im Vergleich zu seinem New Yorker Vorbild, letztlich beschränkte. Nach ersten Erfolgen stagnierte die Mitgliederzahl ab 1910 bei wenig mehr als 1000. Fast ein Viertel davon kam aus Berlin, der Rest aus weiteren Großstädten wie (in der Reihenfolge der Mitgliederstärke) Hannover (wo Lessing die Geschäftsstelle des Vereins betrieb), München, Frankfurt am Main, Hamburg, Wien, Bremen, Düsseldorf, Dresden, Leipzig, Breslau, Königsberg und Köln.[25] Trotz der (bildungs-)bürgerlichen Herkunft der Mitglieder war deren Zahlungs- und Spendenbereitschaft gering, so dass Lessing die Vereinsaktivitäten und -publikationen, die er ohnehin weitgehend im Alleingang bestritt, zum Teil privat finanzieren musste. Im Juni 1911 gab Lessing seine Bemühungen daher einigermaßen desillusioniert auf. Die Geschäftsstelle des Antilärmvereins wurde nach Berlin verlegt, wo der Verein noch bis 1914 am Leben gehalten wurde, allerdings ohne ein eigenes Publikationsorgan wie den *Antirüpel*, dessen Erscheinen mit dem Ausscheiden Lessings eingestellt wurde.

DIE STADT, DER LÄRM UND DIE NERVEN

Zum Problem für den Antilärmverein wurde nicht nur sein bildungsbürgerlicher Elitismus, sondern auch die Art und Weise, in der dieser Elitismus und die Lärmproblematik mit dem zeitgenössischen Nervositätsdiskurs verbunden waren. Schon in der ersten Nummer des *Anti-Rüpel* vom November 1908 musste sich Theodor Lessing unter der Überschrift »Kultur und Nerven« mit

---

24 | In ganz ähnlicher Weise forderte der Wiener Volkskundler Michael Haberlandt schon 1900 die »Entpöbelung unserer Cultur«, denn die »entsetzliche, nie endende Kakophonie des Großstadtlärms« war auch für ihn in erster Linie auf die »Barbarei« seiner Mitmenschen zurückzuführen, die er folgerichtig als »elendes Lärmgesindel« bezeichnete; vgl. Haberlandt: Cultur im Alltag, S. 177-183.
25 | Vgl. Lentz: »Ruhe ist die erste Bürgerpflicht«, S. 90.

der Behauptung auseinandersetzen, bei den Antilärmaktivisten handele es sich lediglich um eine schmale Schicht nervöser Gelehrter, deren Anliegen man nicht ernst nehmen müsse:

> Als der ›Antilärmverein‹ ins Leben gerufen wurde, da brachte eine Berliner Wochenschrift einen Artikel, in dem es hieß: »Man kann sich denken, wie solch ein deutscher ›Lärmprofessor‹ aussieht; zunächst ist er natürlich ›nervös‹; sodann wohnt er sicher in einer Großstadt und drittens wird er nicht Geld genug haben, um sich eine Villa mieten zu können!« Dies wurde gesagt, um unser Vorhaben lächerlich zu machen. Aber man könnte diese drei Voraussetzungen: Nervosität, Großstadt, Armut, getrost auch in gutem Ernste als die wichtigsten Hebel der ›Antilärmbewegung‹ gelten lassen. Auch von vielen anderen Seiten wurde der Kampf gegen den Lärm als ein Auswuchs ›moderner Nervosität‹ oder als ›Produkt der Großstadt‹ hingestellt. [...] Nun wollen wir ruhig annehmen, die ›Antilärmbewegung‹ wäre eine Folgeerscheinung der städtischen Neurasthenie, der Reizbarkeit und zunehmenden nervösen Verletzlichkeit des heutigen Menschen. Was wäre damit gegen sie gesagt?[26]

Nicht viel nach Ansicht Lessings. Denn eine »Auslese der Lärmstumpfesten«[27] könne kaum im Sinne der Kulturentwicklung liegen. Diese beruhe vielmehr auf der Verfeinerung der Nerven. Es gäbe »keinerlei Geistesleben, das nicht ein feines und kompliziertes Leben der Sinne voraussetzt!«:

> Ein waches, scharfes, immer reges Bewußtsein kann nicht inmitten des Lärms von Dampfbahnen ruhig schlafen. Wer für die Reize des heutigen Lebens, für heutige Künste *Sinne* hat, der kann unmöglich Nerven haben, wie der Metallarbeiter, der sein Leben in einem Eisenwalzwerk verbringt![28]

Man könne sagen, so Lessing weiter, die »Kulturstufe eines jeden Menschen ermesse sich an der Feinheit seines Gehirn- und Nervenapparates«, die »wachsende Nervosität« sei »der Kaufpreis, um den wir *Kulturmenschen* sind«. Deshalb müssten die »Bedingungen des Verkehrs, des Handels, der Städteordnung mit der Verfeinerung des Leibes und der Seele Schritt halten«.[29]

---

26 | L[Lessing]: »Kultur und Nerven«, S. 2.
27 | Ebd.
28 | Ebd., S. 3.
29 | Ebd., S. 3. Es ist nicht ohne bittere Ironie, dass der 1933 im tschechischen Exil von nationalsozialistischen Attentätern ermordete Lessing in diesem Zusammenhang mit der Eugenik argumentierte, die als »soziale Hygiene« zur »menschliche[n] Aufzucht« beitragen solle. Die unter dem Lärm Leidenden erschienen Lessing im Sinne dieses eugenischen Gedankens als die kulturell Höherentwickelten, die zur Zeit jedoch noch

Mit dieser Argumentation verwahrte Lessing sich nicht einfach gegen die Bezeichnung als nervös, sondern eignete sie sich an und deutete sie im Sinne einer Höherentwicklung der Kultur positiv um. Die Frage, ob Lärmempfindlichkeit Zeichen einer pathologischen Veranlagung oder vielmehr Ausdruck einer Kultiviertheit der Sinne sei, und die damit zusammenhängende Frage, ob Lärm nervös machte oder ob nur der Nervöse unter dem Lärm litt, war damit jedoch noch nicht beantwortet. Beide sich überkreuzende Fragen begleiteten die Diskussion um das Lärmproblem kontinuierlich. 1910 kam der *Antirüpel* mit einem Beitrag von Rudolf Christ-Brenner erneut darauf zurück:

> Das ›unter dem Lärm leiden‹ ist – darüber muß sich der Kritische klar sein – ein ›Vorrecht‹ nervös veranlagter Menschen. Allerdings hat dieser ›nervöse‹ Teil der Menschheit heute eine derart starke Ausdehnung erfahren, daß man schlechthin diese allgemeine Sensibilität, Ueberempfindlichkeit, Widerstandsunfähigkeit des modernen Gehirns als typisch für eine Riesenzahl der Kultivierten von heute ansehen muß und nicht mehr von einer Teilerscheinung, von Ueberempfindlichkeit einzelner Nervenschwacher reden kann.[30]

Woher stammten diese Stichworte der Nervosität und Nervenschwäche? Wieso konnte Rudolf Christ-Brenner im *Antirüpel* behaupten, die nervöse Überempfindlichkeit des Gehirns sei eine typische Erscheinung der Zeit? 1910 war diese Behauptung tatsächlich Ausdruck einer weit verbreiteten Überzeugung. Schon in den letzten beiden Jahrzehnten des 19. Jahrhunderts hatte sich ein breiter Diskurs über das Problem der modernen Nervosität bzw. Neurasthenie entfaltet, der um 1900 seinen Höhepunkt erreichte und bis zum Beginn des Ersten Weltkriegs fortgeführt wurde. Es handelte sich dabei zunächst um einen medizinisch-wissenschaftlichen Diskurs, der aber bald allgemein zeitdiagnostische Qualität annahm und Nervosität nicht allein als Krankheit, sondern als modernen Kulturzustand behandelte.[31] Das Problem des Lärms und der akustischen Reizüberflutung spielte in diesem Diskurs nur eine Nebenrolle. Die moderne Nervosität galt vielmehr allgemein als »Folge unserer gesamten industriell-individualistischen Kultur«,[32] wie Willy Hellpach schrieb, wobei mit individualistisch auch kapitalistisch gemeint

---

»eine ›leidende Minorität‹ inmitten schreiender, feilschender, roh sich überlärmender Millionen« bildeten (ebd., S. 4).

30 | Christ-Brenner: »Das ›Leiden unter dem Lärm‹«.

31 | Vgl. dazu Radkau: Das Zeitalter der Nervosität; Eckart: Nervös in den Untergang; zum Zusammenhang von Großstadt und Nervosität vgl. besonders Killen: Berlin Electropolis.

32 | Hellpach: Soziale Ursachen und Wirkungen der Nervosität, S. 46.

war.³³ Richard von Krafft-Ebing nannte in diesem Sinn die allgemeine »Jagd nach Gelderwerb und Sinnengenuss«³⁴ als Hauptursache der Nervosität.

Da sich diese Jagd vor allen Dingen in den urbanen Zentren des Kaiserreichs abspielte, wurde im Rahmen dieses Diskurses auch immer wieder über die Frage nach dem Zusammenhang von Großstadt und Nervosität diskutiert. Um das »Dasein des modernen Culturmenschen in seinen Geist und Körper schädigenden Bedingungen zu erkennen«, so Krafft-Ebing, genüge es, »einen Tag das Leben und Treiben der Leute in einem Centrum der Cultur, in einer Grossstadt zu betrachten«.³⁵ Krafft-Ebing kommt dabei zwar nicht gesondert auf den Großstadtlärm zu sprechen.³⁶ Von anderen wird er in diesem Kontext jedoch immer wieder thematisiert. So ist sich etwa auch Wilhelm Erb sicher, dass das »rapide Anwachsen der Grosstädte« für die »Nervosität unserer Zeit«³⁷ mitverantwortlich sei, denn »das Leben in den grossen Städten ist immer raffinierter und unruhiger geworden«.³⁸ Zu den »Schädlichkeiten des Alltagslebens« zählt Erb dabei »den Lärm, die Hast und Unruhe, die mechanischen Erschütterungen in unserem heutigen Leben und Verkehr«.³⁹ Der Lärm erscheint hier als eine unter vielen Schädlichkeiten, auf die Erb jedoch mehrfach zu sprechen kommt: »Und wie entsetzlich, ohrenbetäubend und hirnerregend ist der Lärm in vielen Strassen und Städten, wie erschwerend wirkt er auf die Kopfarbeit!«⁴⁰ August Cramer unterscheidet endogene und exogene Ursachen der Nervosität und zählt zu den exogenen auch die »Schall- und Lichtreize, wie sie das Großstadtleben mit sich bringt«:⁴¹

> Bei weitem die wichtigere Rolle spielen die akustischen Reize. Wenn ich auch auf Grund umfangreicher forensischer Erfahrung auf diesem Gebiete sagen muß, daß es meist mehr oder weniger disponierte Menschen sind, welche unter bestimmten Geräuschen, welche namentlich von industriellen Unternehmungen ausgehen, schwer leiden, so muß

---

33 | Vgl. Hellpach: Soziale Ursachen und Wirkungen der Nervosität, S. 52.
34 | Krafft-Ebing: Über gesunde und kranke Nerven, S. 11.
35 | Ebd., S. 8f.
36 | Er sprach stattdessen nur von »nervenerschütternder und aufregender Musik« (ebd., S. 10). Auch in seiner späteren Aufzählung der möglichen Ursachen von Nervosität nannte Krafft-Ebing zwar die »Ueberanstrengung der Gehörnerven«, (ebd., S. 70), dachte dabei aber wiederum in erster Linie an die »grelle[...] und geräuschvolle[...] Musik« (ebd., S. 71) seiner Zeit.
37 | Erb: Über die wachsende Nervosität unserer Zeit, S. 7.
38 | Ebd., S. 23.
39 | Ebd., S. 31.
40 | Ebd., S. 37.
41 | Cramer: Die Ursachen der Nervosität und ihre Bekämpfung, S. 71.

ich doch andererseits auch hervorheben, daß namentlich im großstädtischen Leben eine Menge von akustischen Reizen produziert werden, die vermeidbar sind. Der Höllenlärm, der heute in den belebten Straßen der Großstädte vorhanden und für empfindliche Individuen sicher schädlich ist, läßt sich bei gutem Willen wohl verringern.[42]

Auch Willy Hellpach vertrat die Meinung, das moderne Großstadtleben wirke sich negativ auf die Nerven aus. Die meisten Leute täuschen sich, so Hellpach 1902 in seiner Abhandlung über *Nervosität und Kultur,* »wenn sie meinen, sie seien an den Lärm, das grelle Licht, das Drängen und Stossen des modernen Strassenbildes gewöhnt«. In Wahrheit brächte »ein längerer Gang durch die Grossstadt auch dem völlig Eingelebten eine ganze Kette kleiner und kleinster Ärgernisse und Unzuträglichkeiten«.[43] Allerdings führt Hellpach das nicht primär auf die Technisierung der Großstädte zurück. Im Gegenteil, er ist der Meinung, »dass das Gesamtbild unserer technischen Arbeit die Tendenz zeigt, unsere Sinne zu schonen, nicht aber, sie zu schädigen«.[44] An anderer Stelle wiederholt er, »dass die technische Signatur unserer Zeit, weit entfernt davon, die Nerven zu schädigen, uns gerade von früheren Einflüssen ungünstiger Art mehr und mehr befreit«.[45] Als Beispiele führt er »elektrisches Licht« und »geräuschloses Pflaster« an, zwei »Wahrzeichen der modernen Stadt«, die zur »Schonung der Sinne« beitrügen:

Oder ist das Pferdegetrappel auf Asphalt und Holzpflaster nicht beinahe ästhetisch schön gegenüber dem Lärm, mit dem auch das eleganteste Gefährt über die granitenen Katzenköpfe einer alten Stadt rasselte? [...] Ist der Griff zum Wandkontakt beim Eintritt ins Zimmer nicht etwas unvergleichlich Ruhigeres gegenüber dem Herumtappen nach Streichhölzern, dem Träufeln der Stearinkerze, dem Anschirren der Lampen?[46]

Selbst der Maschinenlärm der Fabriken sei, auch wenn er die ihm unmittelbar ausgesetzten Arbeiter durchaus schädigen könne, für die Gesamtheit der Stadtbevölkerung weniger störend als der Handwerkslärm:

---

42 | Ebd., S. 79. In seiner Studie *Die Nervosität, ihre Ursachen, Erscheinungen und Behandlungen* von 1906 kamen die akustischen Reize als pathogene Momente der Nervosität nicht gesondert vor. Umgekehrt zählte Cramer hier die »Ueberempfindlichkeit für nicht vermeidbare Geräusche« aber zu den Symptomen der Nervosität, vgl. Cramer: Die Nervosität, ihre Ursachen, Erscheinungen und Behandlungen, S. 142.
43 | Hellpach: Nervosität und Kultur, S. 28.
44 | Ebd., S. 31.
45 | Ebd., S. 35.
46 | Ebd., S. 31.

Was von der [Fabrik] nach aussen dringt, ist meist ein gedämpftes Rauschen, das einen ursprünglich gesunden Menschen sowenig stört, wie das Rauschen eines nahen Stromwehres. Was aber ein Schlosser, ein Feilenhauer, ein Tischler, ein Stellenmacher, ein Schuster im Hause oder Nebenhause für die Anwohner bedeuten, das bedarf wohl keiner Schilderung.[47]

Für die Nachbarn sei das »Verschwinden des selbständigen Handwerkes« daher kein Verlust.[48] Was die modernen Großstädte für Hellpach 1902 zu Quellen der Nervenreize und Nervenleiden machte, waren daher lediglich ihr ungeordnetes Wachstum und die vielen »Überreste des Alten«,[49] die in ihnen noch erhalten seien. Die »konsequente Trennung der Wohnstätte vom Arbeitsschauplatz«[50] werde aber, verbunden mit der allgemeinen »Tendenz des technischen Fortschritts zur Ruhe und Lautlosigkeit«,[51] in Zukunft zu ruhigen und nervenschonenden urbanen Lebensverhältnissen führen, so die fortschrittsoptimistische Prognose von Hellpach.[52]

Auch in seinem zeitgleich publizierten Aufsatz über die sozialen Ursachen und Wirkungen der Nervosität thematisierte Hellpach die »Großstadtnervosität«, die für ihn die Folge einer »passiven Überreizung« durch den »unaufhörliche[n] Wechsel von übermäßig starken Sinneseindrücken verschiedener Modalität« war: »das ›Laute‹ und das ›Grelle‹ unseres modernen Lebens«.[53] Die Großstadtnervosität, die besonders in den betriebsamen Geschäfts- und Vergnügungsvierteln gedeihe und mit der oben genannten kapitalistischen

---

47 | Ebd., S. 34.
48 | Ebd.
49 | Ebd., S. 36.
50 | Ebd., S. 34.
51 | Ebd., S. 32.
52 | Hellpach beendete diesen Abschnitt mit der in die Technik vertrauenden Aussage: »Des Nervenarztes bester Helfer ist heute – der Ingenieur.« (ebd., S. 38). Auch in dem zuvor zitierten Aufsatz glaubte Hellpach an einen möglichen »Sieg über die Nervosität«, Hellpach: Soziale Ursachen und Wirkungen der Nervosität, S. 134. Im Hinblick auf die Großstadtnervosität sei dieser vor allen Dingen durch eine Eindämmung der »Sinnesüberreizung« (ebd., S. 132) zu erlangen, wobei Hellpach seine Hoffnungen auch hier auf den sozialen und technischen Fortschritt setzte, der dazu beitragen werde, »das großstädtische Straßenleben ruhiger, behaglicher, weniger lärmend und vor allem auch gefahrloser zu machen« (ebd., S. 133).
53 | Hellpach: Soziale Ursachen und Wirkungen der Nervosität, S. 126. Interessanterweise thematisiert Hellpach die Großstadtnervosität im Zusammenhang mit »kindlicher Nervosität«. Diese sei »Großstadtnervosität in ihrer reinsten Ausprägung«, da Kinder noch nicht am kapitalistischen und am Kulturleben teilnähmen und man also an ihnen die Folgen der »passiven Überreizung« am klarsten erkennen könne (ebd.).

Hatz einhergehe, ist für Hellpach vor allen Dingen eine »Krankheit der besitzenden, der unternehmenden Klassen«.[54] Daneben kennt Hellpach allerdings auch die »Nervosität im Arbeiterstande«, die jedoch nicht dieselben Ursachen habe wie die bürgerliche Nervosität. Die Arbeiternervosität sei zumeist Folge einer »Unfallneurose« und damit den »psychopathogenen Wirkungen« der Maschinenarbeit zuzuschreiben. In diesem Kontext nennt Hellpach an erster Stelle die »Fabrik mit ihrem Lärm«: »Einmal ist die Maschine laut; die Sinneseindrücke, die sie vermittelt, sind betäubend, unlustvoll.«[55] Allerdings handele es sich im Unterschied zum »unaufhörliche[n] Wechsel der Sinneseindrücke verschiedener Modalität« in den Konsum- und Vergnügungsvierteln der Großstadt beim Maschinenlärm um eine »rumorende Monotonie«, bei der sich Hellpach unschlüssig ist, ob sie im selben Maße krankmachend sei wie der »kaleidoskopische Wechsel bunter Eindrücke«. Hellpach müsse »offen bekennen, daß wir über die nervöse Wirkung monotonen Lärms noch nichts Sicheres wissen«.[56] In jedem Fall sei »die echte Nervosität innerhalb der industriellen Arbeiterschaft noch etwas Selteneres [...] im Vergleich zu ihrer Verbreitung in den besitzenden Ständen«.[57] Mit dieser Thematisierung der Arbeiter-Nervosität und des Fabriklärms unterscheidet sich Hellpach vom Gros der Diskursteilnehmer, die Nervosität in erster Linie als bürgerliche Krankheit und Lärm als ein Problem der »Geistesarbeiter« ansahen.[58]

In einem Aufsatz über »Nervenhygiene in der Großstadt« hält es Otto Dornblüth zwar grundsätzlich für einen »Irrtum, daß die Großstadt die Nervosität besonders begünstige.«[59] In seinen weiteren Ausführungen räumt er aber doch ein, dass »der Großstadtverkehr durch die beständigen Reizungen der Augen und der Ohren«[60] schädlich für die Nerven sei, und beschäftigt sich des Längeren mit geeigneten Maßnahmen zur Reduzierung des Straßenlärms. Ähnlich wie Willy Hellpach glaubt er, dass der technische und hygienische Fortschritt bald zur Beseitigung der meisten schädlichen Geräusche aus der Stadt führen werde.

Waren die bisher Zitierten mehrheitlich medizinische und wissenschaftliche Experten, so zeichnete sich der Nervendiskurs gerade dadurch aus, dass er sich nicht auf diese Diskursteilnehmer beschränkte. Vielmehr verbreitete

---

54 | Ebd., S. 127.
55 | Ebd., S. 128f.
56 | Ebd., S. 130.
57 | Ebd., S. 130.
58 | Vgl. zum hier ausgeklammerten Problem des Arbeitslärms im Kontext der Nervositätsdebatte auch Lentz: »Ruhe ist die erste Bürgerpflicht«, S. 96-99.
59 | Dornblüth: Nervenhygiene in der Großstadt, S. 353.
60 | Ebd., S. 354.

sich die Rede von der Nervosität der Zeit auch in nicht-wissenschaftlichen und nicht-medizinischen Zusammenhängen. In Bezug auf das Problem des Großstadtlärms zeigt sich das etwa beim Berliner Stadtbauinspektor Georg Pinkenburg, der in einem kurzen Beitrag zum *Lärm in den Städten* ebenfalls auf die genannten Topoi des Nervositätsdiskurses zurückgriff. So geht er grundsätzlich davon aus, »daß der Straßenlärm von schädigendem Einfluß auf das Nervensystem« sei:

Kurzum, der Straßenlärm ist eine höchst lästige Zugabe des Straßenverkehrs, der unsere Nerven ungünstig beeinflußt, zumal sie durch das sonstige Großstadtgetriebe, durch die ewige Hetze, in der wir uns befinden und durch das angestrengte Arbeiten, zu dem wir gezwungen sind, bereits ohnehin stark gereizt und erregt werden.[61]

An anderer Stelle führt er aus:

Ganz besonders qualvoll wird der Straßenlärm aber dann für uns, wenn auch unsere Nachtruhe durch vorüberfahrende Straßenbahnen, Droschen [sic], Hochbahnzüge u.s.w. beeinträchtigt wird. Diese Störungen dürften für unsere Nerven ganz besonders schädlich sein, da sie den uns so unentbehrlichen Schlaf verkürzen.[62]

Der Rekurs auf die nervenaufreibende Qualität des Großstadtlärms konnte sogar als Verteidigungsstrategie vor Gericht eingesetzt werden. So berichtet der *Antirüpel* von einem geständigen Falschmünzer, der laut eigener Aussage nur straffällig geworden war, um im Gefängnis dem Straßenlärm zu entkommen:

›Herr Gerichtsdirektor,‹ erwiderte der Angeklagte, ›ich wohne im Herzen Berlins in einer Nebenstraße, welche, weil sich ausnahmsweise keine Kirche in ihr befindet, auch nicht mit Asphalt gepflastert ist. Das Lärmen der Kinder, das Rattern der Automobile, das Geknalle der Brau- und anderer Wagen, das Gefauche der Elektrischen, das Getingel der Grammophone und all die sonstigen Faktoren des jetzt in Berlin so beliebten Straßenlärms, sie bringen mich bei den papierdünnen Wänden meiner Wohnung dem Wahnsinn nahe. Ausziehen kann ich nicht, weil mich ein langjähriger Mietskontrakt bindet und meine, wenn auch nicht geringen, doch auch nicht übermäßigen Mittel mir den Wegzug nicht gestatten. Meine juristischen Beiräte, die ich befragte, zuckten mitleidig die Achseln. Da ging ich neulich zufällig bei der Strafanstalt in Tegel vorbei und ich sah darin die glücklichen Leute, deren Nerven verschont bleiben von dem disharmonischen Getobe des Straßenlärms und denen die Ruhe durch dicke Mauern vollkommen verbürgt ist.

---

61 | Pinkenburg: Der Lärm in den Städten und seine Verhinderung, S. 6.
62 | Ebd., S. 7.

Da beschloß ich, meine Gesundheit, und sei es auch auf Kosten meiner Ehre, mit aller Macht zu sichern, und deshalb, nur deshalb verübte ich die Tat.‹⁶³

Selbst wenn es sich hierbei nur um eine kuriose Ausrede gehandelt haben mag, so belegt die Tatsache, dass der Angeklagte gerade auf *diese* Ausrede verfallen konnte, doch einen gewissen Bekanntheits- und Verbreitungsgrad der in ihr zum Einsatz gebrachten Lärm- und Nerventopoi.

Bisher sind nur Quellen aus dem deutschen Kontext zitiert worden, und tatsächlich kann die Nervositätsdebatte in vielem als ein typisch deutsches Phänomen gelten. Der medizinische Begriff der Neurasthenie, der zusammen mit dem der Nervosität als Leitbegriff der Debatte diente, stammte jedoch aus den USA, und zwar von dem Mediziner Georg M. Beard. Dessen Buch *American Nervousness. It's Causes and Consequences* von 1881 wurde noch im selben Jahr ins Deutsche übersetzt und fand hier eine breite Aufnahme.⁶⁴ In diesem Buch spielte der Lärm unter den Ursachen der Neurasthenie zwar keine herausgehobene Rolle. An anderer Stelle lassen sich jedoch auch im amerikanischen Kontext Belege für die diskursive Verknüpfung von Nerven, Großstadt und Lärm finden. So spricht etwa Hollis Godfrey in seiner Abhandlung *The Health of the City* von 1910 allgemein von der »nerveexhaustion which is drawing so heavily on the forces of the city« und nennt »the noise of the city« einen zentralen Faktor dieser Nervenerschöpfung.⁶⁵ Godfrey zitiert den Mediziner Richard Olding (nicht George M.) Beard mit der Aussage »Noise is fast becoming a neurotic habit with the American people«, um dann fortzufahren:

Noise, acting upon the nervous system of the nervously worn city-dweller, produces so real and constant an irritation that quiet becomes an abnormal state, to which exhausted nerves find great difficulty in responding.⁶⁶ [...]
 Officers of hospitals for the insane consider the increasing noise of the city a potent factor in the recent increase of insanity [...]. Dr. Hyslop of London says, in his monograph on ›Noise in its Sanitary Aspect‹: ›There is in city life no factor more apt to produce brain unrest, and its sequel of neurotism, than the incessant stimualtion of the brain through the auditory organs.‹⁶⁷

---

63 | Zitiert in: Recht auf Stille 1.4 (1909), S. 70. Dass die dicken Mauern der Strafanstalt Tegel vor der Reizüberflutung der Großstadt schützen, ist später auch Thema in Döblins *Berlin, Alexanderplatz*.
64 | Zu Beard und seiner Rezeption in Deutschland vgl. Radkau: Das Zeitalter der Nervosität, S. 49-57.
65 | Godfrey: The Health of the City, S. 232.
66 | Ebd., S. 233f.
67 | Ebd., S. 236.

Im Unterschied zur deutschen Antilärmbewegung spielte das Thema der Nervosität in den um die Kampagnen von Julia Barnett Rice geführten Debatten jedoch keine herausgehobene Rolle, weder bei den Befürwortern noch bei den Gegnern. Vielleicht hat das ihren Erfolg begünstigt. Denn im deutschen Fall war die Verbindung von Nervositäts- und Lärmdiskurs für Lessing und seinen Verein letztlich eher nachteilig. Lessings Versuch, sich affirmativ zur Nervosität und Geräuschempfindlichkeit zu bekennen und die »Kulturstufe eines jeden Menschen« an der »Feinheit seines Gehirn- und Nervenapparates« ermessen zu wollen,[68] verfing offenbar nicht in einem Diskurskontext, in dem Nervosität mehrheitlich als Zeichen von »Degeneration«[69] angesehen wurde.

DIE SYMPHONIE DER GROSSSTADT

Trotz dieses Misserfolgs verweist Lessings Argumentationsstrategie jedoch auf eine grundlegende Ambivalenz im Nervositätsdiskurs. Denn Nervosität konnte auch in anderen Diskussionskontexten nicht nur als Zeichen von Krankheit und Degeneration verstanden werden, sondern ebenso als Zeichen von Kultiviertheit und moderner Zivilisation. Diese Ambivalenz ist auch dem Benjaminschen Begriff der Innervation und Georg Simmels Formulierung von der »Steigerung des Nervenlebens« in der Großstadt eigen. Denn das Nervenleben konnte sowohl in Richtung der krankhaften Nervosität als auch in Richtung einer erhöhten Aufmerksamkeit und Feinsinnigkeit gesteigert werden. In diesem Sinn musste auch der Straßenlärm nicht zwangsläufig als Beeinträchtigung des Geisteslebens wahrgenommen werden. Im Gegenteil, manche konnten ihn geradezu als dessen Stimulans betrachten. So postulierte etwa Edmund Wengraf in Reaktion auf Lessing Forderung nach einem »Recht auf Stille« sein »Recht auf Lärm« und schrieb dazu: »Gestehen wir's doch offen: wir Großstadtmenschen […] können tatsächlich ohne diesen Straßenlärm nicht leben. Er ist die geistige Anregung unserer Tage und die einwiegende Musik unserer Nächte.«[70]

In ähnlicher Weise beschreibt auch August Endell, Jugendstil-Architekt und Herausgeber der Kunstzeitschrift *Pan*, die Geräusche der Großstadt in seiner Eloge auf *Die Schönheit der großen Stadt* von 1908 als Quelle des ästhetischen Vergnügens:

---

68 | L[Lessing]: »Kultur und Nerven«, S. 3.
69 | Krafft-Ebing: Über gesunde und kranke Nerven, S. 12.
70 | Zit. nach Payer: »Großstadtwirbel«, S. 95.

Man muss nur einmal hinhören und den Stimmen der Stadt lauschen. Das helle Rollen der Droschken, das schwere Poltern der Postwagen, das Klacken der Hufe auf dem Asphalt, das rasche scharfe Stakkato des Trabers, die ziehenden Tritte des Droschkengauls, jedes hat seinen eigentümlichen Charakter, feiner abgestuft als wir es mit Worten wiederzugeben vermögen. [...] Wie vielfältig sind die Stimmen der Automobile, ihr Sausen beim Herannahen, der Schrei der Huppen, und dann, allmählich hörbar werdend, der Rhythmus der Zylinderschläge, bald rauschend, bald grob stoßend, bald fein in klarem Takte, metallisch klingend. Und schließlich ganz in der Nähe die Sirenentöne der Räder, deren Speichen die Luft schlagen, und das leise rutschende Knirschen der Gummireifen. [...] Wie wundervoll braust der satte, dunkle Ton einer Trambahn in voller Fahrt, rhythmisch gegliedert durch das schwere Stampfen des Wagens, dann allmählich hineinklingend das harte Schlagen auf den Schienen, das Klirren des Räderwerks, das Schlirren der Rolle und das lang nachzitternde Zischen des Zuführungsdrahtes. Stundenlang kann man durch die Stadt wandern und ihren leisen und lauten Stimmen zuhören, in der Stille einsamer Gegenden und dem Tosen geschäftiger Straßen ein viel verschlungenes seltsames Leben spüren. Es fehlen die Worte, den Reiz all dieser Dinge zu sagen.[71]

Tatsächlich wurden die Geräusche der Großstadt um 1900 nicht nur in Worten wie diesen besungen, sondern auch zum Gegenstand und zur Inspiration der zeitgenössischen Musik gemacht, von Charles Ives' *Central Park in the Dark* über Edgard Varèses *Amériques* bis hin zu George Antheils Maschinenmusik und Luigi Russolos *Kunst der Geräusche*.[72] Schließlich ist auch die vielfältig aufblühende Musik- und Vergnügungskultur der Metropolen in der Jahrhundertwende als Faktor der großstädtischen akustischen Innervation zu verstehen, der zur kulturellen Steigerung des Nervenlebens beitrug.[73] In diesem Sinn sollte Benjamins Begriff der Innervation (der als medizinischer Begriff ja die Versorgung von Gewebe mit Nervenzellen meint) hier in seinem Doppelcharakter verstanden werden, der sowohl die krankmachende wie die Kreativität stimulierende Dimension der großstädtischen Klanglandschaft aufzuschließen in der Lage ist. Das akustisch innervierte Metropolensubjekt ist nicht nur als nervös, sondern auch als auditiv agil und aufmerksam zu denken.

Wie die eingangs zitierten Passagen deutlich machen, bezog Benjamin den Begriff der Innervation allerdings nicht unmittelbar auf die »Chockwirkungen« des Großstadtverkehrs selbst, sondern auf den Film, der als

---

71 | Endell: Die Schönheit der großen Stadt, S. 31ff.
72 | Vgl. dazu Thompson: The Soundscape of Modernity, S. 130-144; Bijsterveld: Mechanical Sound, S. 137-158.
73 | Vgl. neben Bailey: Popular Culture and Performance in the Victorian City; stellvertretend für eine breite Literatur Scott: Sounds of the Metropolis.

Medium die »ungeheure technische Apparatur unserer Zeit zum Gegenstand der menschlichen Innervation«[74] machen und damit dem Apperzeptionstraining dienen solle. Es stellt sich daher abschließend die Frage, welche Rolle den akustischen Medien in Bezug auf die akustische Innervation in der Großstadt zukam und ob man hier in ähnlicher Weise von einem auditiven Apperzeptionstraining sprechen kann. Eine der Montagetechnik des Films – auf die Benjamin in seiner Argumentation besonders abhob – vergleichbare Möglichkeit der Toncollage gab es erst seit Anfang der 1930er Jahre. Das berühmteste Beispiel einer solchen Toncollage ist Walter Ruttmanns *Weekend* von 1930, das allerdings noch viele Jahre lang keine wirklichen Nachahmer fand.[75] Das Radio, in dem Ruttmanns Hörstück ausgestrahlt wurde, verbreitete sich seit den 1920er Jahren und wurde erst nach dem Zweiten Weltkrieg im eigentlichen Sinn zum Massenmedium.[76] Das Grammophon war dagegen schon um 1900 weit verbreitet und trug mit der erstmaligen Möglichkeit der Tonaufzeichnung und -wiedergabe nicht unwesentlich zur Veränderung der Hörgewohnheiten bei.[77] Das Apperzeptionstraining bestand hierbei aber weniger in der Gewöhnung an schockförmige Wahrnehmungsreize und mehr darin, den Umgang mit körperlosen Stimmen und Geräuschen zu erlernen.[78] Größere Nähe zum Phänomen der Innervation bestand beim in den 1880er Jahren eingeführten Telefon, besonders bei den Telefonistinnen – den sprichwörtlichen »Fräuleins vom Amt« –, die an den Schaltbrettern tatsächlich für die ›Nervenverbindungen‹ zwischen den Gesprächsteilnehmern sorgen mussten und die dabei nicht selten selbst dem Nervenzusammenbruch nahe gebracht wurden.[79] Allerdings konnte das Telefon auch die Ruhe des bürgerlichen Haushalts empfindlich stören und zur häuslichen Gereiztheit beitragen, wie sich Benjamin in seiner *Berliner Kindheit um neunzehnhundert* erinnert:

> Nicht viele, die den Apparat benutzen, wissen, welche Verheerungen einst sein Erscheinen in den Familien verursacht hat. Der Laut, mit dem er zwischen zwei und vier, wenn wieder ein Schulfreund mich zu sprechen wünschte, anschlug, war ein Alarmsignal, das

---

74 | Benjamin: Das Kunstwerk im Zeitalter seiner technischen Reproduzierbarkeit (Erste Fassung), S. 445.

75 | Vgl. dazu Goergen: Walter Ruttmanns Tonmontagen als Ars Acustica; Hagen: Walter Ruttmanns Großstadt-Weeked.

76 | Vgl. dazu Hagen: Das Radio; Lenk: Die Erscheinung des Rundfunks.

77 | Vgl. Gauß: Nadel, Rille, Trichter. Siehe auch den Beitrag von George Brock-Nannestad im vorliegenden Sammelband.

78 | Vgl. Hörisch: Der Sinn und die Sinne, S. 250-283; Kittler: Grammophon, Film, Typewriter, S. 37-173.

79 | Vgl. Killen: Die Telefonzentrale; Siegert: Das Amt des Gehorchens.

nicht allein die Mittagsruhe meiner Eltern sondern das Zeitalter, in dessen Herzen sie sich ihr ergaben, gefährdete. Meinungsverschiedenheiten mit den Ämtern waren die Regel, zu schweigen von den Drohungen und Donnerwettern, die mein Vater gegen die Beschwerdestelle ausstieß. Doch seine eigentlichen Orgien galten der Kurbel, der er sich minutenlang und bis zur Selbstvergessenheit verschrieb. Seine Hand war dabei ein Derwisch, den der Taumel überwältigt. Mir schlug das Herz, ich war gewiß, in solchen Fällen drohe der Beamtin als Strafe ihrer Säumigkeit ein Schlag.[80]

Im Telefon waren die akustische und die elektrische Innervation unmittelbar miteinander verschaltet. In den oben skizzierten Debatten um Großstadt, Lärm und Nervosität spielte es jedoch keine besondere Rolle. Die urbane akustische Innervation war um 1900 tatsächlich noch nicht im gleichen Maße mediatisiert wie später nach dem Ersten Weltkrieg. Vielleicht trug das Fehlen geeigneter medialer Trainingsmethoden für das Ohr im Sinne Benjamins gerade zur Virulenz der Verbindung von Lärm und Nerven bei. Für den nächtlich wach liegenden Malte Laurids Brigge stellten die durch seine Stube rasenden elektrischen Bahnen und die über ihn hingehenden Automobile jedenfalls eine Nerventortur dar, an die er sich offenbar noch nicht gewöhnt hatte und vor der ihn kein mediales Apperzeptionstraining bewahrte.

BIBLIOGRAPHIE

Bailey, Peter: Popular Culture and Performance in the Victorian City, Cambridge u.a. 1998.
Baron, Lawrence: Noise and Degeneration. Theodor Lessing's Crusade for Quiet, in: Journal of Contemporary History 1 (1982), S. 165-178.
Becker, Sabina: Urbanität und Moderne. Studien zur Großstadtwahrnehmung in der deutschen Literatur 1900-1930, St. Ingbert 1993.
Benjamin, Walter: Berliner Kindheit um neunzehnhundert. Fassung letzter Hand, Frankfurt/M. 1987.
Benjamin, Walter: Das Kunstwerk im Zeitalter seiner technischen Reproduzierbarkeit (Erste Fassung), in: Ders.: Gesammelte Schriften I.2, hg. v. R. Tiedemann und H. Schweppenhäuser, Frankfurt/M. 1991, S. 431-469.
Benjamin, Walter: Das Kunstwerk im Zeitalter seiner technischen Reproduzierbarkeit (Dritte Fassung), in: Ders.: Gesammelte Schriften I.2, hg. v. R. Tiedemann und H. Schweppenhäuser, Frankfurt/M. 1991, S. 471-508.
Benjamin, Walter: Über einige Motive bei Baudelaire, in: Ders.: Gesammelte Schriften I.2, hg. v. R. Tiedmann und H. Schweppenhäuser, Frankfurt/M. 1991, S. 605-653.

---

80 | Benjamin: Berliner Kindheit um neunzehnhundert, S. 18f.

Bijsterveld, Karin: Mechanical Sound. Technology, Culture, and Public Problems of Noise in the Twentieth Century, Cambridge/MS 2008.

Brown, Edward u. a. (Hg.): City Noise, New York 1930.

Christ-Brenner, Rudolf: Das ›Leiden unter dem Lärm‹, in: Der Antirüpel (Recht auf Stille). Monatsblätter zum Kampf gegen Lärm, Roheit und Unkultur im deutschen Wirtschafts-, Handels- und Verkehrsleben 2.1 (1910), S. 4.

Cowan, Michael: Imagining Modernity Through the Ear. Rilke's »Die Aufzeichnungen des Malte Laurids Brigge« and the Noise of Modern Life, in: arcadia 41.1 (2006), S. 124-146.

Cramer, August: Die Nervosität, ihre Ursachen, Erscheinungen und Behandlungen, Jena 1906.

Cramer, August: Die Ursachen der Nervosität und ihre Bekämpfung, in: Deutsche Vierteljahrsschrift für öffentliche Gesundheitspflege 41 (1909), S. 66-82.

Dornblüth, Otto: Nervenhygiene in der Großstadt, in: Blätter für Volksgesundheitspflege 23.2 (1908), S. 353-356.

Eckart, Wolfgang U.: Nervös in den Untergang. Zu einem medizinisch-kulturellen Diskurs um 1900, in: Zeitschrift für Ideengeschichte 3.1 (2009), S. 64-79.

Endell, August: Die Schönheit der großen Stadt, Stuttgart 1908.

Erb, Wilhelm: Über die wachsende Nervosität unserer Zeit. Akademische Rede zum Geburtstagsfeste des höchstseligen Grossherzogs Karl Friedrich am 22. November 1893, Heidelberg 1893.

Frisby, David: Fragmente der Moderne. Georg Simmel – Siegfried Kracauer – Walter Benjamin, Rheda-Wiedenbrück 1989.

Garrioch, David: Sounds of the City. The Soundscape of Early Modern European Towns, in: Urban History 20.1 (2003), S. 5-25.

Gauß, Stefan: Nadel, Rille, Trichter. Kulturgeschichte des Phonographen und des Grammophons in Deutschland (1900-1940), Köln u. a. 2009.

Godfrey, Hollis: The Health of the City, Boston, New York 1910.

Goergen, Jeanpaul: Walter Ruttmanns Tonmontagen als Ars Acustica, Siegen 1994.

Haberlandt, Michael: Cultur im Alltag. Gesammelte Aufsätze, Wien 1900.

Hagen, Wolfgang: Das Radio. Zur Geschichte und Theorie des Hörfunks. Deutschland/USA, München 2005.

Hagen, Wolfgang: Walter Ruttmanns Großstadt-Weeked. Zur Herkunft der Hörcollage aus der ungegenständlichen Malerei, in: Nicola Gess, Florian Schreiner und Manuela Schulz (Hg.): Hörstürze. Akustik und Gewalt im 20. Jahrhundert, Würzburg 2005, S. 183-200.

Hellpach, Willy: Nervosität und Kultur, Berlin 1902.

Hellpach, Willy: Soziale Ursachen und Wirkungen der Nervosität, in: Politisch-Anthropologische Revue. Monatsschrift für das soziale und geistige Leben der Völker 1 (1902 / 03), S. 43-53 und S. 126-134.

Hörisch, Jochen: Der Sinn und die Sinne. Eine Geschichte der Medien, Frankfurt/M. 2001.

Killen, Andreas: Berlin Electropolis. Shock, Nerves and German Modernity, Berkeley 2006.

Killen, Andreas: Die Telefonzentrale, in: Alexa Geisthövel und Habbo Knoch (Hg.): Orte der Moderne. Erfahrungswelten des 19. und 20. Jahrhunderts, Frankfurt/M., New York 2005, S. 81-90.

Kittler, Friedrich: Grammophon, Film, Typewriter, Berlin 1986.

Knoch, Habbo: Die Aura des Empfangs. Modernität und Medialität im Rundfunkdiskurs der Weimarer Republik, in: Ders. und Daniel Morat (Hg.): Kommunikation als Beobachtung. Medienwandel und Gesellschaftsbilder 1880-1960, München 2003, S. 133-158.

Krafft-Ebing, Richard von: Über gesunde und kranke Nerven, Tübingen 1909.

Lenk, Carsten: Die Erscheinung des Rundfunks. Einführung und Nutzung eines neuen Mediums 1923-1932, Opladen 1997.

Lentz, Matthias: »Ruhe ist die erste Bürgerpflicht«. Lärm, Großstadt und Nervosität im Spiegel von Theodor Lessings ›Antilärmverein‹, in: Medizin, Gesellschaft und Geschichte 13 (1994), S. 81-105.

Lessing, Theodor: Der Lärm. Eine Kampfschrift gegen die Geräusche unseres Lebens, Wiesbaden 1908.

L[Lessing, Theodor]: Kultur und Nerven, in: Der Anti-Rüpel (= Antirowdy; Das Recht auf Stille). Monatsblätter zum Kampf gegen Lärm, Roheit und Unkultur im deutschen Wirtschafts-, Handels- und Verkehrsleben 1.1 (1908), S. 2-4.

Morat, Daniel: Urban Soundscapes and Acoustic Innervation around 1900, in: Robert Beck, Ulrike Krampl und Emmanuelle Retaillaud-Bajac (Hg.): Les cinq sens de la ville. Du Moyen Age à nos jours, Tours 2013, S. 71-83.

Müller, Lothar: Die Großstadt als Ort der Moderne. Über Georg Simmel, in: Klaus R. Scherpe (Hg.): Die Unwirklichkeit der Städte. Großstadtdarstellungen zwischen Moderne und Postmoderne, Reinbek 1988, S. 14-36.

Neumeyer, Harald: Der Flaneur. Konzeptionen der Moderne, Würzburg 1999.

Payer, Peter: Der Klang von Wien. Zur akutischen Neuordnung des öffentlichen Raumes, in: Österreichische Zeitschrift für Geschichtswissenschaften 4 (2004), S. 105-131.

Payer, Peter: »Großstadtwirbel«. Über den Beginn des Lärmzeitalters, Wien 1850-1914, in: Informationen zur modernen Stadtgeschichte 2 (2004), S. 85-103.

Pinkenburg, Georg: Der Lärm in den Städten und seine Verhinderung, Jena 1903.

Radkau, Joachim: Das Zeitalter der Nervosität. Deutschland zwischen Bismarck und Hitler, München, Wien 1998.

Recht auf Stille. Der Antirüpel. Antirowdy. Monatsblätter zum Kampf gegen Lärm, Roheit und Unkultur im deutschen Wirtschafts-, Handels- und Verkehrsleben, 1.4 (1909).

Rilke, Rainer Maria: Die Aufzeichnungen des Malte Laurids Brigge. In: Ders.: Werke. Kommentierte Ausgabe in vier Bänden, Bd. 3, Frankfurt/M. 1996, S. 453-635.

Saul, Klaus: »Kein Zeitalter seit Erschaffung der Welt hat so viel und so ungeheuerlichen Lärm gemacht ...«. Lärmquellen, Lärmbekämpfung und Antilärmbewegung im Deutschen Kaiserreich, in: Günter Bayerl, Norman Fuchsloch und Torsten Meyer (Hg.): Umweltgeschichte. Methoden, Themen, Potentiale, Münster u. a. 1996, S. 187-217.

Schafer, R. Murray: The Soundscape. Our Sonic Environment and the Tuning of the World, Rochster/VT 1994.

Scott, Derek B.: Sounds of the Metropolis. The 19th-Century Popular Music Revolution in London, New York, Paris, and Vienna, Oxford u. a. 2008.

Siegert, Bernhard: Das Amt des Gehorchens. Hysterie der Telephonistinnen oder Wiederkehr des Ohres 1874-1913, in: Jochen Hörisch und Michael Wetzel (Hg.): Armaturen der Sinne. Literarische und technische Medien 1870 bis 1920, München 1990, S. 83-106.

Simmel, Georg: Die Großstädte und das Geistesleben, in: Ders.: Aufsätze und Abhandlungen 1901-1908, Bd. 1, Frankfurt/M. 1995, S. 116-131.

Simmel, Georg: Soziologie. Untersuchungen über die Formen der Vergesellschaftung, Gesamtausgabe Bd. 11, Frankfurt/M. 1992.

Smilor, Raymond W.: Cacophony at Thirty-fourth and Sixth. The Noise Problem in America, 1900-1930, in: American Studies 18 (1977), S. 23-38.

Smilor, Raymond W.: Personal Boundaries in the Urban Enviroment. The Legal Attack on Noise 1865-1930, in: Enviromental Review 3.3 (1979), S. 24-36.

Smilor, Raymond W.: Toward an Enviromental Perspective. The Anti-Noise Campaign 1893-1932, in: Martin V. Melosi (Hg.): Pollution and Reform in American Cities 1870-1930, Austin, London 1980, S. 135-151.

Smith, Bruce R.: Tuning into London c. 1600, in: Michael Bull und Les Back (Hg.): The Auditory Culture Reader, Oxford, New York 2003, S. 127-135.

Thompson, Emily: The Soundscape of Modernity. Architectural Acoustics and the Culture of Listening in America 1900-1933, Cambridge/MS, London 2004.

Ward, Janet: Weimar Surfaces. Urban Visual Culture in 1920s Germany, Berkeley 2001.

Wright, Laura: Speaking and Listening in Early Modern London, in: Alexander Cowan und Jill Steward (Hg.): The City and the Senses. Urban Culture Since 1500, Aldershot 2007, S. 60-73.

Fragrant Steam

Anthony Moore

Foreword

This essay falls somewhere between a talk and an article. It is derived from a reading given at the workshop *Noise – Geräusch – Bruit*. There was a decision to perform the text as an exploration of noise in speech. Thus phonosemantic prose as a kind of *poésie sonore* was intended to unfold content by its very form; speaking out loud is noise too. Whilst not wishing to conceal wishy-washiness by the artful use of art, this dramatic sounding out, being its own argument, resulted in an apparent absence of argument in the text. »It's all bluster«, you might say. »Well yes, precisely – that's noise.«

What may serve well for a participatory reading out loud as *akousmata*, might not function with the same efficacy as a contribution towards a collection of scientific texts to be made into a book. Hence this foreword, whose purpose is to plea for a kind of inner listening, to discern through the din of malfunctioning ears and brain (in my case), the humming, rumbling, zinging of tinnitus, intermingled with all that, the unarticulated fricatives of the ever-present, interior locutor. In other words, I am calling upon the inner voice in each reader of this text to stand in for the absent voice of its author.

Before submitting to this persistent and sometimes unwanted speaker in the mind, it may be wise to reflect upon some aspects of its nature, for it is this per-son[1] who should now replace the real thing in the absence of a medium and any pressure waves between us. It, too, will be considered to arise from the realm of noise or unstructured sound. At the outset, then, an introduction to the inner voice – variously known as the subvocaliser, the tacit dictator, your nebulousness, the soundless one, the interior locutor and so on. The conceit is that the unsounding voice be granted autonomy, wilful and replete with both fear and desire. What it wishes most is to hear itself. It

---

1 | See http://www2.khm.de/news/per_SON2002/index.html (19.3.14).

realises that for such a thing to occur, it would need to emerge and become a sounding voice. By encountering the cold of the outer air, it hopes to gain an understanding of the actual physical nature of the sonosphere. As yet soundless, the inner locutor expresses itself in the silent act of writing. This is more a sign of trepidation than any suggestion of precocious, literary talent on the part of the unborn non-entity. A further sign of its timidity is displayed by a predilection for dwelling on one particular topic of the acoustic, namely its necessarily ethereal and silent history. It is as if the subvocaliser is already preparing a safe haven, a further soundless realm to scuttle back to, should the outer air prove too inhospitable.

...

So this is a written recording of a voice, mouthing, whispering sometimes, but usually confined to the silent realm of the skull (in fact, it is far from silent in there, full as it is with the roar of blood and the hissing, whistling drone of dubious machinery; more noise then). To what extent writing informs the inpourings of this interior locutor remains a moot, if mute, point to which a return is planned. Feverish with intention, the tacit dictator wishes to accost the physical nature of sound and its perception in air, matter and liquid, its speed, its duration and directionality; in other words, precisely all those very attributes the inner voice itself, as if in a vacuum, peculiarly lacks.

Paradoxically however, and perhaps reluctant to forgo the silent realm to which it is accustomed, it turns to the essentially soundless past as a subject for consideration – sound's history. Once disclosed, sound must fade, just as the present slips into the past: the history of sound can only be done silently. Even Edison will bring us no more than the sound of sound in the present. So no returning then, even if played back on original devices, for our ears have aged inexorably, they are contemporary ears and the past must come to them in the here and now. The inner voice writes in silence as a means of expression and, to linger in soundlessness, invites mute history as its subject, the silent past as potential present whose fate is to become the soundless future.

Like that very first howl for air which cocoons the newborn in an expanding, spherical wave of sound, inside which the infant and all its proceeding sounds are re-enwombed (whilst hearing may be pre-natal, projecting your voice into your own outer ear requires the medium of air), so the inner voice desires to give birth to itself. The homunculus wants to break out of the hermetic vacuum of the alembic but in the moment of so doing, with its first, resounding yell, surrounds itself once more with a skin. This time however, it is not sealed but porous, a permeable and expanding shell of sound. Through this wavefront, this penetrable membrane, emergent sentience struggles to make traces, scribbles, writings and recordings to delay, with reflections, the inevitable, entropic dispersal back into silence.

Right now, however, that inner voice is called upon to help with the sounding of the first of two parts of reading out loud.

READING OUT LOUD I

HCN, Here Comes Noise; noise in Joyce has been done to some extent in, amongst other works, Cage's Roaratorio,[2] so instead of Finnegan's HCE (Here Comes Everybody),[3] I offer HCN. And here, indeed, comes noise arising perhaps from the amplification connected to Jimi Hendrix's guitar...

These half-silvered valves glowing in the back of the amplifier are like time-holders, brief moments of memory gathered in the ionised dust and giving off a scent of hot metal. The tentative fingers that move inside the back of the machine are belonging and feelable (like do-it-yourself surgery on your own brain). A couple of RCA ET USA 6V6 GTAs, and a big, fat motherfucker Colomor 5U4G, they have spent plenty of time being extremely loud and smoking the glass black, a cloud of free electrons driven crazy with current. And the sound that came screaming through the vacuum was sheer, unmediated information setting all a-bristle the hair cells of the inner ear and the skin's surface alike...

and wireless, funk...?

At lighting-up time the street lamps in the village of the soul gradually begin to glow like the valves in the back of a radio, warming up until the first voices break through the circuitry: dust, God of Ears, heterodyning Theremin The Unhearable, eating out, heterodining out on Bordeaux, systole diastole, loudspeakers as microphones, voices emerging from the ear, The Invisibles; broadcasters tracing their own history back to the groundwave radio freaks at the end of the 1800s with telluric tellings across impossible gaps, telegraphing through the earth itself. So who actually needs pre-laid connections?

At which point the sound of the voice is overwhelmed by noise and re-emerges as music, a song...

Hot repetition of signals chime,
Feeble reception, couldn't get the meantime.
Blood-flecked voices, distortion and gain,
Static interference, shortwave rain,

---

2 | Cage: Roaratorio.
3 | See Joyce: Finnegans Wake, p. 32.

Waiting for the monsoon,
No lighting in the ballroom.[4]

The signal collapses in waves of phase-cancelled interference. Then spoken words float back up onto the surface of the noise like a flotilla of submersibles breaking through the skin of the ocean, to form some kind of meaning, a set of instructions, a manual on time storage: quicksilver, quartz crystal, a tank, some cable... »You simply need to collect the elements and assemble them accordingly.« A mercury acoustic delay line in order to attach a tail on the moving point of now, a trace of past so that the radar trackers can better anticipate the future. Turing was happy to hook up this liquid metal RAM from the old war machine, from the years of no lighting-up time, bombs and black-outs. Time storage, a recent history of recorded time with memory devices – from the discovery of electricity and its practical applications to the memory of genes and the genes of memory – the precursors of RAM and the history of memory! The radio drew a picture...[5]

SOME REFLECTIONS

The hypothesis of both the contribution to the original workshop and this essay is to suggest that in noise we begin, that noise is the start of everything. The mapping of the background radiation of the cosmos reveals traces of the big bang, which can hardly have been silent as it devoured the unbeing of non-spacetime.

It is as if matter was formed from the density and random amplitudes of noise itself. And as time, too, comes into existence, there can be no better measure of it than noise. Silence is untime, motionless. Whereas movement, friction, heat, entropy are dynamic systems all; and, in one way or another, noisy, on the move and alive. This applies to acoustic and atomic behaviour alike. At the mortal scale, ears develop extremely early in the human embryo, otic placodes, thickenings of the rhombencephalon. But only when we emerge do we hear ourselves for the first time, summoning self-consciousness via the bi-directional feedback loop of spontaneous output and active perception.

The Howl for Air (or the art of slapping newborns): speaking of a tradition perhaps more liberally applied before the middle of the 20th century, of delivering a sharp smack to kick-start breathing and life. This howl for air, the expanding sphere, the first feedback loop, the yell to the ears, this first sound

---

4 | From the song »World Service« on the L.P. of the same name recorded by the author originally in 1979 and released on Do It Records 1981.

5 | Moore: Electricity that shines into the light, p. 194.

both made and heard re-enwombs the infant and becomes an expanding bubble inside which all other proceeding sounds, heard or made, continue to be contained. To paraphrase Charles Babbage writing in *The Ninth Bridgewater Treatise:* the air becomes one vast library on whose pages are forever written all that commons and sages alike have ever uttered.[6]

The permeable and elastic membrane that surrounds the expanding, spherical after-life of a sound is pervious to carrier waves of information flowing in. These waves are themselves other sounds moving out from their sources and passing through; and all is recorded by us, notwithstanding that our most significant memories are those we have forgotten, all this noise becomes filtered by the existential encounters that time's passing ceaselessly throws at us.

Additive synthesis is, after Fourier and electronic music, the superimposition of individual sine waves stacked up one by one in harmonic or inharmonic layers, to model the timbre of natural sounds such as the voice. This recalls the additive method of modelling with clay. Alternatively, there is reductive synthesis. Here, one commences with the simultaneous, chaotic totality of all possible frequencies, which is then passed successively through filters to remove unwanted, interstitial waves. This, in turn, recalls the reductive method of carving away at, or sculpting in, stone. Another term for the original, raw ›mass‹ of primal sound might be – noise.

Noise, then, as a beginning carrying within it two fundamental attributes; the first one being simultaneity, for noise simply cannot be made up of a single event, it is by nature multitudinous and the coherence, the linearity of non-displacing waves allows them to co-exist in what is, for the ear, the same place at the same time; and the second one being duration. The resulting cacophony can only emerge in a continuum. Noise gives rise to space and time and – as individuals, societies and cultures within it – we function as active filters to form our shifting identities out of it.

One can hardly speak of primal sound without recalling the Ur-Geräusch of Rainer Maria Rilke:

Zur Zeit, als ich die Schule besuchte, mochte der Phonograph erst kürzlich erfunden worden sein. Er stand jedenfalls im Mittelpunkte des öffentlichen Erstaunens, und so mag es sich erklären, daß unser Physiklehrer, ein zu allerhand emsigen Basteleien geneigter Mann, uns anleitete, einen derartigen Apparat aus dem handgreiflichsten Zubehöre geschickt zusammenzustellen. Dazu war nicht mehr nötig, als was ich im Folgenden

---

6 | Babbage: The Ninth Bridgewater Treatise, p. 112: »The air itself is one vast library, on whose pages are for ever written all that man has ever said or woman whispered. [...] [T]he air we breathe is the never-failing historian of the sentiments we have uttered, earth, air, and ocean, are the eternal witnesses of the acts we have done.«

aufzähle. Ein Stück biegsamerer Pappe, zu einem Trichter zusammengebogen, dessen engere runde Öffnung man sofort mit einem Stück undurchlässigen Papiers, von jener Art, wie man es zum Verschlusse der Gläser eingekochten Obstes zu verwenden pflegt, verklebte, auf diese Weise eine schwingende Membran improvisierend, in deren Mitte, mit dem nächsten Griff, eine Borste aus einer stärkeren Kleiderbürste, senkrecht abstehend, eingesteckt wurde. Mit diesem Wenigen war die eine Seite der geheimnisvollen Maschine hergestellt, Annehmer und Weitergeber standen in voller Bereitschaft, und es handelte sich nun nur noch um die Verfertigung einer aufnehmenden Walze, die, mittels einer kleinen Kurbel drehbar, dicht an den einzeichnenden Stift herangeschoben werden konnte. Ich erinnere nicht, woraus wir sie herstellten; es fand sich eben irgendein Cylinder, den wir, so gut und so schlecht uns das gelingen mochte, mit einer dünnen Schicht Kerzenwachs überzogen, welches kaum verkaltet und erstarrt war, als wir schon, mit der Ungeduld, die über dem dringenden Geklebe und Gemache in uns zugenommen hatte, einer den andern fortdrängend, die Probe auf unsere Unternehmung anstellten.[7]

He goes on to describe the effect on the schoolchildren of hearing a playback of their own recorded voices which, needless to say, stunned them into silence. At first Rilke believes it will be those very sounds that remain unforgettable, but more than 20 years later he realises it is not the sound so much as the image of marks traced by the bristle stylus. Whilst casually observing a skull he has purchased during life-drawing classes in the École de Beaux Arts in Paris, his gaze falls upon the coronal suture, that fine zigzagging line where the two halves of the growing skull-bone have joined together. This jagged line, he claims, brings to his mind the markings of the bristle in the wax cylinder and the idea comes to him to speculate what sound might emerge if he were to place the stylus of a phonograph into it.

Yet, there is a problem here. The impressions of the clothes brush bristle would either not have caused any sound to emerge at all or, if sounding, would then not have caused marks recalling the appearance of the coronal suture. Using the homemade device described, the action needed to produce the sound of a recorded voice would have been a vertical, ›hill & dale‹ movement resulting in variations in the depth of the etching, and not lateral movements at all. This is a technical detail, but it is thinkable that Rilke was compounding two different memories, recalling, in fact, the many illustrations of other lateral ›sound-to-writing‹ machines such as the inscriptions produced by Édouard-Léon Scott de Martinville 20 years earlier than Edison.

However, there is no doubt that the invention of sound recording, the imprinting of the pressure waves of a voice, is in itself somehow miraculous. That the simple ›hill & dale‹ action, the vertical modulation known as *Tiefenschrift* (as opposed to *Seitenschrift*) can encode such *klangfarbige*, timbral

---

7 | Rilke: Ur-Geräusch, pp. 1085-1086.

complexity, all the noise of hissing fricatives and sharp plosives, is counterintuitive. Furthermore, it leads to startling and previously unthinkable notions, such as the idea of a sound emerging backwards, the playing of a recording in reverse. It is no surprise, then, that time-travelling in literature appears increasingly often,[8] what with time's arrow so challenged here.

Reversibility can also be seen in the mechanics of the recording device itself. Initially, the sound-collecting horn, the equivalent of today's microphone, an ear, is also used as the loudspeaker. So now we have a transmitting ear! The active sensing of noise in the human organ involves the output of signals. These are known as oto-acoustic emissions. Their presence, as an emerging stream of sound produced by the ear, helps physicians determine the hearing abilities, or lack of them, in very young children.

Are we limited to only listening outwards for noise? Might we consider tinnitus as the object of inward listening? Well, the difficulty here is that we should first have to locate that singularity known as the ›sweet spot‹ (the ideal listening position) and ask whether it resides at the centre or the periphery, which might be thought of as the brain or the ear. What's more, due to the action of oto-acoustic emissions, it might even be argued that hearing actually takes place just outside the body, beyond the entrance to the ear. In whichever case, the humming, throbbing, zinging, whistling, hissing noises of tinnitus certainly qualify as noise in whatever world – unbeknownst to physicians – they exist.

Concerning direction and flow, Empedocles in his Theory of Pores[9] formulated an idea of perception that was located between two alternative hypotheses of the day. In the case of vision, simply put, one hypothesis stated that objects emanated light which shone into the eye. The second posited the reverse, that the eye functioned like a projector, illuminating the object. The thinking of Empedocles, however, embraced both these notions with the proposition that the eye did indeed engage the object by casting its gaze upon it. But at the same time the object shone back toward the viewer. This means that perception of the object is located more or less in between the seer and the seen.

---

8 | See Booker and Thomas: The Science Fiction Handbook, pp. 15-17. They mention Edward Page Mitchell's »The Clock that Went Backwards« (1881), Edward Bellamy's *Looking Backward* (1888), Mark Twain's *A Connecticut Yankee in King Arthur's Court* (1889) and H. G. Wells's »The Chronic Argonauts« (1888), *The Time Machine* (1895) and *When the Sleeper Wakes* (1899).

9 | I owe these reflections on Empedocles to conversations with Siegfried Zielinski. He explores these thoughts far more profoundly in: Deep Time of the Media - Toward an Archaeology of Hearing and Seeing by Technical Means. For further reading see Diels: Die Fragmente der Vorsokratiker, pp. 347-353.

Empedocles principally describes the sense of hearing much as he does the other senses within his Theory of Pores. In particular he remarks that auditive perception comes from inner noises, when the inner air produces a sound by being moved through resonance. For Empedocles, the system of the ear, which he calls a fleshy twig or branch, is some kind of a bell or ground of resonance that produces sounds to match those in the outer world. By being moved, the inner air is beating against the bell-like, solid parts and thus produces sound.[10]

So once again, perception of the object is located in between the hearer and the heard, the seer and the seen, at an interface, an ethereal skin of interference outside the body caused by the two streams of information colliding. We are at the centre and the periphery simultaneously because feedback or memory reflects inwards, off the inner skin of that first, primal noise, and the inside is as voluminous as the knowable universe.

As the inner voice expresses an abiding fascination with what it calls ›a necessarily silent history of sound and noise‹, it is worth reflecting on what historiographical potentialities it has in mind. The inner voice sometimes speaks of four paths, rivers or areas. I have even seen it written thus.

> The intention [...] is to present a continuous record of fragments in the hope of identifying a topology of unforetold correspondences across a landscape ›eroded‹ by the action of sound. Despite repeated and extensive inundations it does seem possible to define four, near-distinct tributaries that flow across this geography, even if they do burst their banks again and again.[11]

So we can safely assume there are four regions, each over-lapping and ill-defined, in this approach to the archaeology of noise. (i) Its perception or, how we hear. (ii) The more recent history of recording and technical devices, drawing parallels with the development of computing machines and memory storage. This flows into (iii) a deeper time of sound and inscription by considering the well-known orality/literacy shift, from the ancient sonosphere to the invention of alphabets and writing. And lastly (iv) the relationship of sound to number; attempting to rethink the long-standing bond between acoustics and mathematics.

It is the uncertain notion of time, flowing beneath all four, that causes the over-lappings and correspondences mentioned above. However, time and arithmetic can be strange bedfellows. A not inconsiderable aim of mathematics is to arrive at formulae, which, once conceived, do away with the need to work things through; in a sense, discarding the process. It seems the very

---

10 | See Kirk et al.: Die vorsokratischen Philosophen, pp. 340-343.
11 | Moore: Transactional Fluctuations 2, p. 300.

idea of a mathematical formula is to purge time. Beneath the surface, nevertheless, are the gears, the turning wheels, found inside any timepiece. This suggests that a different connection between acoustics and mathematics and its unfolding over time might be discovered, not through pictorial geometry, but rather within the more abstract realm of numbers; in particular those numbers and ratios which result in non-halting, irrational, divergent, convergent, limit processes and remainders; and thus are based not so much on the visual symmetry and patterns of a Bach score, but rather on the dynamics of time and processuality. Furthermore, mathematical theories of tuning offer up a rich plethora of irrational functions from the attempt to divide the octave into twelve equal steps to the Pythagorean comma.

The doing of history itself is, at least partly, to confront the diabolical task of unravelling the nature of time. To occupy the site of someone else's listening is, of course, impossible. To then seek to do this over a time span of say three millennia, creates yet greater challenges! What holds true for sound also applies to time; they both depend on disappearing as they come into existence. It turns out that to think about listening in the past is to probe the nature of history itself. Evidently, this task is furthered by the archaeological exploration of music instruments, technical devices and the history, not just of tuning theory, but of systems of measurement from all branches of science, from medicine to mathematics, from celestial motion to the casting in bronze of – amongst other artefacts – bells.

From the limited perspective of European history, it is thinkable that the orality/literacy shift, positioned some 2,800 years ago in the ancient Mediterranean, was preceded by an earlier transitions: the shift from the acoustic into number and then from number to geometry. These, again, are moves from ear to eye, particularly given that the rendering of irrational number in geometrical form imposes a means of expression, which seems profoundly inimical to the nature of what it seeks to describe. 2,000 years will pass before the Calculus appears in the West. With its unfreezing action this time machine opens a way back past the visual to the abstractly numerical and ultimately, to two voices, where a child and adult singing an octave apart would, on sounding that interval, be doing the equivalent of a multiplication by two in an arithmetic without signs. Let us turn from its musings, back to the voicing of our tacit dictator.

READING OUT LOUD II – OTHERS' POETIC DESCRIPTIONS

Here follow two quotations. It seems there should be some comment in addition, but in fact we are required to do no more than listen to ourselves, reading them out loud.

Fourier succeeded in proving a theorem concerning sine waves which astonished his, at first, incredulous contemporaries. He showed that any variation of a quantity with time can be accurately represented as the sum of a number of sinusoidal variations of different amplitudes, phases, and frequencies. The quantity concerned might be the displacement of a vibrating string, the height of the surface of a rough ocean, the temperature of an electric iron, or the current or voltage in a telephone or telegraph wire. All are amenable to Fourier's analysis.[12]

And now Hermann Helmholtz, from a lecture given in Bonn in 1857:

Endlich möchte ich nun Ihre Aufmerksamkeit noch einem lehrreichen Schauspiel zulenken, was ich nie ohne ein gewisses physikalisches Vergnügen gesehen habe, weil es dem körperlichen Auge auf der Wasserfläche anschaulich macht, was sonst nur das geistige Auge des mathematischen Denkers in der von Schallwellen durchkreuzten Luft erkennen kann. Ich meine das Uebereinanderliegen von vielen verschiedenen Wellensystemen, deren jedes einzelne seinen Weg ungestört fortsetzt. Wir können es von jeder Brücke aus auf der Oberfläche unserer Flüsse sehen, am erhabensten und reichsten aber, wenn wir auf einem hohen Punkte am Meeresufer stehen.

Oft habe ich an den steilen, waldreichen Küsten des Samlandes, wo uns Bewohnern Ostpreussens das Meer die Stelle der Alpen vertrat, Stunden mit seiner Betrachtung verbracht.

Selten fehlt es dort an verschieden langen, in verschiedener Richtung sich fortpflanzenden Wellensystemen in unabsehbarer Zahl. Die längsten pflegen vom hohen Meer gegen das Ufer zu laufen, kürzere entstehen, wo die grösseren brandend zerschellen, und laufen wieder hinaus in das Meer. Vielleicht stösst noch ein Raubvogel nach einem Fische, und erregt ein System von Kreiswellen, die, über die anderen hin auf der wogenden Fläche schaukelnd, sich so regelmässig erweitern, wie auf dem stillen Spiegel eines Landsees. So entfaltet sich vor dem Beschauer von dem fernen Horizonte her, wo zuerst aus der stahlblauen Fläche weisse Schaumlinien auftauchend die herankommenden Wellenzüge verrathen, bis zu dem Strande unter seinen Füssen, wo sie ihre Bogen auf den Sand zeichnen, ein erhabenes Bild unermesslicher Kraft und immer wechselnder Mannigfaltigkeit, die nicht verwirrt, sondern den Geist fesselt und erhebt, da das Auge leicht Ordnung und Gesetz darin erkennt.[13]

---

12 | Pierce: Symbols, Signals and Noise, pp. 31-32.
13 | Helmholtz: Über die physiologischen Ursachen der musikalischen Harmonie, pp. 70-71.

From whence came the Title

The whole subject [acoustics; A. M.] is one of particular interest from the point of view of the history of science because it was one of the earliest fields, both in East and West, where quantitative measurement was applied to natural phenomena.[14]

Needham goes on to say:

Sound was regarded as but one form of an activity of which flavour and colour were others. The background for Chinese acoustic thinking was largely determined by a concept which stemmed from the vapours of the cooking pot, with its fragrant steam [...].[15]

I suggest, if the Chinese were cooking the acoustic soup with its aromatic vapours, then perhaps we could say that Pythagoras was chopping up the carrots for it. As we begin to sprout limbs and prostheses with which to hold pens and measure distances, to record impressions, facts and numbers, so we become separated from ourselves in a uniquely visual way. The possibility for the simultaneous co-existence of differences, in fact noise itself, begins to be a matter of survival. The notion of an immersive »either and both« (a three-part voicing of the one, the other and the both), becomes thinkable through music, sound and noise, and the coherence of waves whose physical properties, analysed by Fourier, form the basis for much of our contemporary communication channels.[16] Long live noise!

Bibliography and Discography

Babbage, Charles: The Ninth Bridgewater Treatise – A Fragment, 2nd ed., London 1838.
Booker, M. Keith and Anne-Marie Thomas: The Science Fiction Handbook, Chichester et al., 2009.
Cage, John: Roaratorio: An Irish Circus on Finnegans Wake, 1976/79.
Diels, Hermann: Die Fragmente der Vorsokratiker, ed. by Walther Kranz, 17th ed., Vol. 1, Hildesheim 1974.
Helmholtz, Hermann von: Über die physiologischen Ursachen der musikalischen Harmonie, in: Populäre wissenschaftliche Vorträge, Braunschweig 1865, pp. 55-91.
Joyce, James: Finnegans Wake, London 1975.

---

14 | Needham: Science and Civilisation in China, p. 126.
15 | Ibid., p. 132.
16 | See Moore: ›Aromatic Vapours‹.

Kirk, Geoffrey S., John E. Raven and Malcom Schofield: Die vorsokratischen Philosophen, transl. by Kalheinz Hülser, Stuttgart, Weimar 1994.

Moore, Anthony: ›Aromatic Vapours‹. Tuning and Measurement in Greek and Chinese Antiquity, in: Friedrich Kittler and Ana Ofak (eds): Medien vor den Medien, Paderborn 2007, pp. 161-168.

Moore, Anthony: Electricity that shines into the light, in: Peter Berz, Annette Bitsch and Bernhard Sieeert (eds): FAKtisch. Festschrift für Friedrich Kittler zum 60. Geburtstag, München 2003, pp. 193-199.

Moore, Anthony: Transactional Fluctuations 2. »Reflections on sound«, in: Siegfried Zielinski and Eckhard Fürlus (eds): Variantology 4. On Deep Time Relations of Arts, Sciences and Technologies in the Arabic–Islamic World and Beyond, Köln 2010, pp. 289-304.

Needham, Joseph: Science and Civilisation in China, Vol. 4.1., Cambridge 2004.

Pierce, John R.: Symbols, Signals and Noise, New York 1961.

Rilke, Rainer Maria: Ur-Geräusch, in: Sämtliche Werke, Vol. 6, Frankfurt/M. 1966, pp. 1085-1093.

Zielinski, Siegfried: Deep Time of the Media – Toward an Archaeology of Hearing and Seeing by Technical Means, Cambridge, London 2006.

Audio Technology and Extraneous Noises – All Past and No Present?

George Brock-Nannestad

Introduction

Modern access to sound is even easier than turning a tap, because a tap sits in the wall. Access to sound, however, is wireless, digital and its selection and playing occurs after pressing your finger silently on an imaginary button on an interactive screen. Traditionally, sound reproduction has always been associated with effort, and extraneous noises that had to be left out of consideration or disregarded when submitting to the illusion of hearing a performance. The long association with these noises, even though there has been a constant development to reduce them, has given certain forms of sound reproduction an iconic status. Now, all the noises that used to be associated with playing recordings have gone. If we want to put ourselves in the places of listeners of times past, however, we have to know about and understand the operations that had to be performed in order to hear something reproduced. Some of these operations were associated with particular noises that were partly used as feedback in the performance of the operations, and were contributors to a ritual[1] of reproduction. Others permeated the reproduction and had to be considered as unavoidable.

One may consider that the modern lack of effort to obtain a replay entails a lack of ritual and this causes a lack of respect for the recorded sounds. They are taken for granted. This is also reflected in present-day lack of respect for the intellectual property rights associated with recordings, although they are as much the result of composing and performing as other musical activities. It is the author's thesis that knowledge about replay access in earlier times may enlighten a discussion on the meaning of recordings in present

---

1 | The word ›ritual‹ is here used with its colloquial connotations and without its association to religious beliefs and/or rites.

everyday life. This article aims at putting the noises associated with traditional reproduction into a context that will stand as a conscious contrast to modern reproduction.

In the following, we shall consider instants of audio reproduction as they would have appeared from the beginnings about 1900 to just before our days, while focussing on the noises and extraneous sounds associated with them. Although these decades cover a time of fierce development of technical detail, it is worth considering that, in the pre-digital world, only minimal adjustments were necessary in order to be able to use equipment from a later period to reproduce recordings from an early one. The present is not a history of technical development as such, but a discussion of operations and sounds typical of particular years that have been chosen because they represent a period of relative »stability« of technology, a pause in the technical progress that we, retrospectively, may observe. Leaving out technological history completely would create a narrative without anchors in reality. If much of this article's argument might have appeared pedestrian to readers fifty years ago, it is because the noises discussed here were sounds encountered daily, although their almost subliminal nature may have meant they were registered mostly on a pre-conscious level. The fact that these sounds have disappeared and are, thus, largely forgotten today, qualifies them for historical re-evaluation.

1900 CYLINDER OR DISC

Around the turn from the 19th to the 20th century, those who could afford luxury goods, or liked to experiment, could acquire sound recording and reproducing equipment. The machine invented by Edison and Bell & Tainter used a wax cylinder as its medium; and if a cylinder was still empty, the user could record on it for later replay. If a recording had lost its interest, it could be »shaved« by means of a sharp tool that was pressed against the cylinder's surface while it rotated. This created a weak whistling-type of noise, depending on the hardness of the wax. A similar noise is known from a mechanical workshop where a lathe is used to turn a workpiece into a perfect cylinder. Indeed, one could argue that a mechanical sound recorder is merely a lathe used for a special purpose. The same type of noise was emitted when the phonograph was used to record, and to the performers' displeasure, the very horn or funnel that collected the sound of the performance would project this noise right into their faces. Moreover, the noise was recorded along with the performance and could, thus, be heard when the cylinder was played. With the various distortions inherent in the system it was a wonder that the idea of the phonograph-recording caught on.²

Just about the same time a democratisation of access occurred in that the expensive and finely constructed phonographs from Edison, Columbia, and Pathé met with competition from cheap and primitive German constructions. These, however, could not record, only reproduce, had to be wound like clocks, and could only play one cylinder on one winding. As far as this limitation is concerned they were reminiscent of music boxes, which also had to be wound. While the more expensive machines were in fact silent during winding, the cheaper constructions made a characteristic ›click-click‹³ noise, which was integrated into music and given iconic status by the performance of Olympia's Aria »Les Oiseaux dans la charmille« in Jacques Offenbach's *The Tales of Hoffmann* in 1881.

If home recording was not a function essential to the owner of a sound-reproducing apparatus, buying the much more practical flat gramophone discs, made in a material that was much more durable than wax, was an alternative. The first gramophones had been hand-operated; you had to turn the handle at a precise and regular speed. The inevitable imprecision and lack of stability caused the distortion that we later came to know as ›wow and flutter‹. This was improved by Eldridge R. Johnson, who invented the archetypical gramophone motor with a large and strong helical spring that could last several records before rewinding – at least in the expensive gramophone models. This now permitted winding to take place by means of a crank instead of a key. The motor was not noiseless, but it was enclosed in a heavy wooden cabinet, which silenced it considerably. If it was well lubricated, the only noise came from the centrifugal governor, a fast-revolving system of rotating weights, supported on springs, which pulled a brake disk harder if the speed was increased. Thereby, equilibrium at the intended speed established itself. If the gramophone motor and spring were less well lubricated, one would hear internal clonking noises, both during winding and the playing of a record. A hardened lubricant would make windings adhere to each other, and the clonking noise would be produced by the sudden release of one winding in the spring from the next. If the adhering and release happened frequently, the spring would eventually break with a resounding ›clong‹.

---

2 | See Brock-Nannestad: What Are the Sources of the Noises We Remove.

3 | In the present text, noise phenomena associated with audio technology are in several places described by onomatopoetics. It is worth noting that the same period, which saw the technical development of audio technologies, also saw the introduction of such onomatopoetics for sounds, not specifically related to audio technology – from Filippo Tommaso Marinetti: »Zang Tumb Tumb« (1914) to Kurt Schwitters: »Ursonate« (1932).

Playing a cylinder or a disc meant taking it out of its container, placing it carefully on the apparatus, guided by the sound it made against the mechanical parts of the apparatus. A soft clonking noise during this operation meant that everything was going well. The brake would be released, the motor would produce a soft whirring that was only audible if you sat in attention, waiting for it as a signal. The needle of the soundbox would engage the groove, and a more or less soft hissing noise would become audible as the introduction to the music. This noise really consisted of two sounds, which emanated from two locations: one directly from the soundbox and the other through the horn. Theodor Adorno (Wiesengrund at the time) commented on this noise, in his aphoristic musings on ›Nadelkurven‹, that it was »[…] das Recht des Interpreten zu jener Freiheit, die die Maschine mit andächtigem Rauschen begleitet«.[4] What better way to express a sense of ritual!

This noise was caused by the medium's material. Although the discs were called »shellac records«, this compound only accounted for about 20 % of their content. The rest was mainly fine stone dust. While it created a strong material that could resist the huge pressure from the tip of the reproducing needle, the dust grains could be heard in chorus when the record was played.[5]

Cylinder reproducers, in other words phonographs, had a virtually everlasting permanent stylus that was made to fit the groove perfectly. Disc gramophones, by contrast, used a single-use needle that had to grind itself into a properly fitting shape during the first revolutions of the record. Before playing, an unused and suitable needle had to be fitted to the soundbox by means of a minute thumbscrew provided for this purpose. This type of interaction with the most sensitive part of the gramophone was clearly audible as clonking noises emanating from the horn. Those who had a feel for it would sneak the needle into its hole and turn the screw carefully, thereby reducing the noises. Wearing into shape meant that during the first 10-15 revolutions the groove was worn more, while grinding the needle to fit, and on a frequently played record one would, over time, be able to hear the music emerging out of the noise like one might see Venus rising from the frothy ocean.

Dropping a record made of shellac-based material on a hard surface meant that it shattered, if it was larger than the standard for the time, 7 inches (17.5 cm) in diameter. Not a very pleasant sound, and unfortunately a noise with finality. Over the years, the cracking of records for example when someone sat on a pile of them left carelessly in a chair, became well known to most record owners. Records were expensive and the loss was felt. Very rarely the records could be glued together successfully, but two or more clicks per revolution were the unavoidable accompaniment when the record was played in the future.

---

4 | Wiesengrund-Adorno: Nadelkurven, p. 48.
5 | See Bryson: The Gramophone Record, pp. 150-186.

More frequent and less damaging was the accidental brushing or bumping against the soundbox while playing a record. This caused the needle to be pushed out of the groove, which resulted in breaking the wall between neighbouring grooves;[6] a movement that continued as long as the brush's or bump's momentum lasted. The sound created and transmitted with great volume from the horn was one of tearing, while the physical result created was a crossing groove of damage that looked like a steep spiral and gave one click per revolution of the record when it was subsequently played.

It was also not unknown that the soundbox would slip from one's hand when poised to place the needle in the groove. The sharp needle in the heavy soundbox would fall down and gouge a crater in the record surface, and this would create great problems for subsequent playings. The result was a distinct risk of repeating the reproduction, of »sticking in the groove« and a heavy clicking once per revolution until this place had been passed, and this only if the crater or »needle dig« was not too deep.

1920 RECORD ALBUMS AND SETS

Already before 1910 a few complete operas had been recorded on a series of consecutive records, but they were very expensive, not the least because the records were usually single-sided. Single-sided records were the norm because aligning both sides to the centre hole was too difficult in the beginning. It did not become feasible to record other long works like symphonies, until it became standard practice to press also classical recordings on both sides of a record. Such recordings would typically come in albums of 6-8 records, and they were heavy. As it was impossible to fit a whole movement of a symphony or a piano sonata onto one record side, the musical piece had to be interrupted at suitable places, so the switch to the other side or the next record could be made.

The playing of a symphony or any other long work thus entailed an almost ritual ›ballet‹ on the part of the gramophone operator – mostly the proud owner. Getting the first record ready on the turntable, winding and waiting for people to sit down was easy, but 4½ minutes after starting the gramophone, the operator had to get up, lift the soundbox out of the way, stop the motor, remove the record, turn it over, change the needle and – perhaps – re-wind the gramophone, if this had not already been done during the playing of the record – with the risk of rattling the gramophone. Many gramophones were fitted with an automatic brake that went into action when the

---

6 | In reality, there is only one groove from beginning to end, but on the record surface it looks as if there were a series of grooves.

needle was close to the label, which saved at least one of the operations. While some brakes were silent, others made a shrieking noise. Then the next side was played, and after another 4 ½ minutes the ›ballet‹ needed to be repeated. After 12-16 sides had been played, the symphony – accompanied by the final sliding noises of replacing the records in their album sleeves – was over. What had been the purpose of this ballet? To create an illusion of a concert performance.

From ca. 1910 onwards, a trend started to move away from an open horn and towards a gramophone as a piece of furniture enclosing the horn. This permitted a closing of the lid on a playing record. As a result, the high-frequency noise that mostly came directly from the soundbox's diaphragm could be eliminated, and the hiss emanated only through the horn opening in the cabinet. Two decades into the 20th century, there was a distinct awareness of the record's noise among the users of classical music recordings, as evidenced in the correspondence columns and some reviews in early issues of the journal *The Gramophone*, first published in 1923. Certain chamber music records from the National Gramophonic Society were blamed for being recorded at too low a volume, which made the background noise much more conspicuous.[7]

For the piano repertoire there was an expensive solution to the problem of long musical pieces: the roll for the reproducing piano.[8] This was a wide strip of paper, which contained music encoded as instructions to the player piano, and moved from a storage roll onto an uptake roll. There were two fundamentally different kinds of piano roll. One type was slavishly copied in perforation from printed music. The other type was called »Künstlerrolle« or »Artist's Roll«, because the perforations were based on a particular performance by a famous soloist, which had been recorded by means of a recording piano, an apparatus of considerable complexity.

The whole piano keyboard was represented across the width of the strip (about 25 cm), and a perforation represented a position, i.e. a particular key to be struck. Several perforations could be made in a row, establishing a long slit, which meant that the struck key was held down until the slit ended. Accordingly, the simultaneous presence of a number of perforations or slits provided a chord. The operation of the decoder for the perforations was ingenious: the whole width of the strip was transported past a carrier for the ends of hollow tubes, each once again representing one key. Air was continuously sucked through the tubes, but as long as there was unbroken paper strip covering the ends of the tubes, no air could enter. When a hole gave access to air, it passed into one of the actuators. Since there was one actuator per key, a

---

7 | Nicholas T. Morgan, personal communication May 2013.
8 | See Permut: Reproducing Piano.

combination of holes placed in a representation corresponding to the written music would make the piano play that music.

This reproduction of piano music was not without its own internal sound, however. Some versions used treadle bellows, like a harmonium, to pump air, others used electric motors driving a pump. The air passing through the perforations and tubes gave out a faint hissing noise, which was usually dampened by means of a glass window in the upright piano. The treadle bellows would make the usual pumping noises, while the motor would produce a hum. Two types of reproducing piano were generally available: the built-in mechanism that acted directly on the hammers, and the so-called *vorsetzer*. The latter had the complete roll reading mechanism in a piece of furniture with an overhang that just came above the keyboard of an ordinary piano when the *vorsetzer* was pushed in place. Inside the overhang were as many leather-covered actuators as there were keys, and each actuator would hit a key to play a tone. If you were close to the *vorsetzer*, you would notice a slight but constant clicking noise when the leather hit the keys.

The reproducing piano was a luxury instrument, and it was perfected before World War I ended. It offered the only really satisfactory reproduction of piano sound, because the apparatus that produced it was, in fact, a piano. Its popularity disappeared in the same period as the cylinder for phonographs, towards 1930. By then, electrical recording had improved the sound of piano recordings, and the radio was broadcasting live recitals.

The advent of commercial electrical recording in 1925, although it was a huge development, did not influence record users very much. All the motions for obtaining the sound still had to be gone through. As the quality of acoustic reproduction improved vastly, due to better understanding of the scientific principles behind recording and reproduction, acoustic reproduction, paradoxically, was better and less distorted than the new and contemporary electrical reproduction.

1935 THE RECORD CHANGER

By the mid 1930s, electrical reproduction was quite widespread, and the sound in most cases came out of a radio loudspeaker. One simply switched the radio from receiving broadcasts to reproducing records.

The availability of longer works on the market finally made the constant changing of record sides intolerable, and the time was ripe for the record changer. This was a mechanical construction which demanded that one would first have to take all the records out of their covers and put them in a stack, the first side lowermost, facing upwards. Sets of records for use on the record changer were made differently from ordinary, sequential sets (sides

1+2, sides 3+4, sides 5+6),⁹ as they were ›auto-coupled‹ (sides 1+6, sides 2+5, sides 3+4). This meant that you could have consecutive sides in the stack, facing upwards, and when the last side of the stack (halfway through the set) had been played, you simply turned the whole stack over to continue. Accordingly, one manual change would be enough to cover all 6 sides, instead of five individual changes.

The records were stacked on a long centre pin – »the broken thumb«[10] – at a level above the turntable. They were, thus, prevented from reaching the turntable until the mechanism released them one by one. Everything was automatic: the music was interrupted, the pickup arm lifted, swivelled out of the way, and the pickup was momentarily switched off. By the time the record changer had been invented, needles were of a semi-permanent type, which meant there was no need for manual intervention. Then the mechanism released a record so it fell on top of the one below on the stacking pin, then the pickup arm swivelled to the beginning of the rotating record now on top and the pickup, switched on again, was lowered with the needle in the run-in groove. This changing of the record made a clonking noise that was usually dampened by closing the lid. However, the illusion of a continuous, live performance was not perfect – the changing still took up to 10 seconds, and the music was still interrupted in ›unmusical‹ places. For this reason at least a couple of companies – RCA Victor and HMV – introduced fade-ins/fade-outs to open/end each side. This created a different illusion of a produced performance that was actually similar to many scene changes in movie productions.

The record changer, furthermore, became a useful addition to partying. The host would have a record changer and the guests would bring records to provide music for dancing. With a possibility of stacking 10 records, one would have a reasonable »set«,[11] and a savvy host would mix the dance records accordingly. The less fortunate, who had to make do completely without a gramophone, tuned in to the special weekly dance night programs on the radio.

With the increasing proliferation of electrical reproduction, home recording came back, this time for discs. Strong gramophone turntables could also form the basis for recording, and the recording head was very similar in construction to a pickup of the time. Various kinds of blank records were developed, and when they had been recorded, they could be instantly reproduced. However, one had to use special, »leant-back« needles because the

---

9 | For simplification only a small set of three records is described here.
10 | A professional nickname for the stacking pin of record changers (Otto Ring, personal communication September 1973).
11 | A term taken from dance establishments.

record material was not as hard as commercial records. As these home recordings produced more noise than commercial records, home recording was never considered a commercial threat to professional record distribution.[12] The noise came from the cutting process, which took place in a hard and reasonably durable blank record, in contrast to the soft wax used commercially.

The broadcasting houses also utilised instantaneous records for delaying transmission or for storing programs for later use. They had high quality equipment and recording blanks of a higher quality. But even on the wavebands then in use, *long wave* and *medium wave*, it was possible to hear the increased background noise when these recordings were played. Even the magnetic recording media of the time had a discernible background noise. It was, hence, a major achievement when Walter Weber, who worked at the German broadcasting authority in 1942, discovered how to apply an inaudible high frequency signal to magnetic recording. The so-called »bias« reduced the background noise dramatically. It formed the basis for all professional analogue tape recording to this day, and was incorporated when private tape recording took off in the early 1950s. Although tape brought its own extraneous noises and disturbances with it, such as ›wow and flutter‹, it was still considered a vast improvement in sound recording and reproduction.

1950 BIRTH OF THE 45

When CBS Columbia introduced the long-playing record in 1948, they, in fact, provided everybody with the possibility of obtaining long playing time without the need for a special apparatus – like the record changer for dance music – or the double turntable in classical music for seamless transfer from one record to the next.

RCA Victor did not tread in Columbia's footsteps, but used a different approach when they introduced the vinyl »45« in 1949.[13] This was a small record of 17.5 cm diameter, which rotated at 45 rpm and contained the same amount of sound as a 25 cm record had contained at 78 rpm. At the same time, RCA Victor introduced a record changer that would perform the change in about one second, that is, within one revolution of the record. For this changer a large centre hole in the record was required. This robust record completely took over the jukebox industry, which had been developed based on shellac records. Now, a compact and efficient jukebox mechanism could provide entertainment in public places without any background noise from the record.

---

12 | See Brock-Nannestad: The Lacquer Disc for Immediate Playback.
13 | See Magoun: The Origins of the 45-RPM Record.

All the noise that remained was the clonking of coins, while one obtained the heavy bass, so characteristic of jukeboxes.

The 45 »singles« became the medium for distributing popular music in the 1950s. They did get just as worn, and their sound distorted with heavy use as most popular record players were unkind on the records. Nevertheless, the »singles« were considered a vast improvement on the old shellac records they replaced.

1955 LP – NO ACTION FOR 15 MINUTES

When Columbia initiated the era of the Long Playing record, they also introduced to the commercial market a record material that had the lowest inherent noise ever: the vinyl compound. This was the absolute prerequisite for obtaining the low noise from a slowly rotating record at $33\frac{1}{3}$ rpm instead of at 78 rpm. However, in the beginning it was not simple. A story is told of the introduction of this new format to dealers during the summer of 1948 in Atlantic City. The windows were kept open – for the heat, it was purported; but in reality Columbia needed the swell of the Atlantic to drown the noise from the first vinyl pressings.[14]

The sounds associated with the LP were different from those that listeners had grown used to with the old shellac records. A good wide-range High Fidelity (HiFi) installation would bring the whole audible range of sound to you, including the bass. This frequently created a problem, because the turntable's vibrations and unevenness in the record's surface were reproduced as »rumble«. The actions of dancers on the floor would also create »rumble«. Good quality records and a high-end turntable reduced this very much. Many HiFi owners took to mounting the turntable on a concrete wall. Modern users of records took just as much care over them as their predecessors, and modern records had the distinct advantage that dropping them did not do any damage.

Before playing, the record had to be brushed to remove dust, and this was tricky, because dry brushing charged the insulating record surface electrostatically. When the record was subsequently played, there was a distinct risk of small local discharges that sounded like clicks, only sharper than the clicks that came from specks of dust in the groove. The stylus, too, was prone to getting dirty and had to be brushed before playing. For this reason, when playing a record you would hear the swishy noise of a brush moving against the stylus, very reminiscent of someone testing a microphone by blowing,

---

14 | Personal communication from Barney Pisha (equipment reviewer at the journal Audio), April 1986.

followed by a slight thump when the stylus was lowered onto the record surface and the stylus found the run-in groove. After this, the record would play with only the little clicks to break the relative silence that this new technology meant, until you reached the run-out groove. The quality of the run-out groove was different, and you heard a different background noise. This noise repeated itself every 1.8 seconds. Who has not tried to fall asleep during an LP and woken up to the repeating sound of the stylus starting yet another round of run-out groove? Some turntables had an automatic switching-off mechanism, and then this would never happen.

When the pickup was accidentally pushed across the record (and it required very little force), it still gave a tearing noise from the loudspeaker, but the damage to the record was minimal, since the pickup's weight was so slight that the stylus tip did not break any walls. It merely slid across the surface, the tip moving violently up and down every time it fell into the groove.

The LP was originally the medium for the wealthier, who invested in a Hi-Fi system, whereas the less wealthy used the »single«. Usually, when a pop »group« had made a number of singles, a compilation was made available as an »album« on an LP. The mix for each track on the LP was slightly different from the single version, and the reason was the expected quality of replay equipment. Also, an LP frequently had stereo sound (starting in 1957), while singles were mostly recorded with mono sound. In the popular and dance music market from the mid 1960s, there was a move away from the single and towards the LP, and two distinct developments occurred in the 1970s that were related to the dance establishments called Discotheques.

One of these developments related to the way that disc jockeys or DJs used records when creating dance music programs. They would have access to several turntables and the facility to cross-fade the sound from them, to use the combination to get the sound for the amplifiers and loudspeakers. At one stage it was discovered that flicking an LP back and forth with the stylus engaging a part of the groove with a relevant piece of music would create a rhythmic breathing noise that could be mixed into the dance music. This was the development of »scratching« or »turntablism« as it became known.[15] The LP is the only record that lends itself to this kind of action, because it has a suitable recorded speed which, treated to the flicking back-and-forth of »scratching«, will produce the desired high-pitched sound.

The other development was technical in nature and had to do directly with the »rumble« mentioned above. An efficient Discotheque had to supply a very heavy bass sound, which was able to physically shake the dancers' inner organs. Unfortunately, the same strong vibrations also enhanced the

---

15 | See Hansen: The Basics of Scratching; Hansen: The acoustics and performance of DJ scratching.

»rumble« by vibrating the turntables on which the pickups played. This, in turn, created feedback that limited the intensity of the bass deemed feasible, as simply turning up the volume created a howling distortion. For this reason the »Disco Singles« were developed; 30 cm diameter 45 rpm records with coarse grooves that would take a very strongly recorded bass and needed less amplification, so the rumble was less prominent. Greater satisfaction all around!

1970 Compact Cassette

The Compact Cassette was developed in 1962 by Philips and became the most successful small-format sound carrier with the widest distribution of all time. Industrial standardisation, that relied on freely available patents from Philips, the developer, on the condition that equipment and cassettes were completely interchangeable between manufacturers. The cassette started out as a mono medium, but stereo cassettes quickly became available. Originally they were intended for dictation, but as early as 1965 they were used for music distribution. While the tapes' speed was very low, the recorded time was high – 30 or 45 minutes per side – and the tapes' hiss was noticeable. This was improved considerably by a consumer version of noise reduction systems developed for movies by Dolby Laboratories. The Dolby-B® noise reduction became the new standard, and even HiFi-listeners who preferred classical music accepted the »MusiCassette« as a sound carrier. The cassette was the most democratic medium imaginable – it was recordable, it could be carried in a pocket, and it worked most times because of a simple basic mechanism. Many local recording productions came out on cassette only, because it did not make sense, economically, to invest in the complete processing chain for obtaining a pressed record, if you only expected a low volume distribution. The iconic sound of a cassette about to be played was the insertion of the cassette, the closing of the lid and the reassuring, springy »click« of the play button, just before the music started.

In the wake of the cassette's introduction, two basic methods for providing portable sound were developed: the heavy battery-driven cassette player with built-in stereo loudspeakers known as a »boombox« or »ghetto-blaster« from 1976;[16] and from 1979 the small cassette player with earbuds: the Walkman® by SONY.[17] The latter came to embody the essence of the personal stereo, which at the same time provides entertainment and exclusion of extraneous noises. It also marked the start of the hearing loss epidemic in young

---

16 | See Benson: Boombox.
17 | See Benson: Walkman®.

people, because the sound pressure from earbuds frequently exceeds industrial noise protection standards.[18]

1985 NOISES GONE!

Historically, the record industry earned part of its money by giving access to back catalogues and, ideally, by providing reissues to a new format because the production was much cheaper than new recordings. While the LP had also brought compilations of earlier recordings, the cassette led to material from the LP repertoire being reissued. Technical developments in information technology enabled a new format, the Compact Disc or CD. This was introduced in 1983 and offered noise-less recording as well as easy navigation between tracks. In the beginning it was a luxury item, but as electronics in the players became more integrated and plastics replaced glass in the optics, it became an overwhelming success as a medium for reproduction. The CD permitted a dynamic range that was higher than any previous recording system, and the background noise was gone. During the first years the recording engineers did not fully understand the medium, and the lack of noise became a problem: previously a sound dying out would gradually disappear into the noise – sometimes called ambience – but with the early CDs the gradual disappearance ended audibly and very abruptly to total silence. It was perceived as frightening and some listeners felt cheated out of an experience: that of a sound trailing off into a soft background noise. Later, the engineers invented methods to inject a digital noise called ›dither‹, which succeeded in suiting the medium to consumer taste.

At the same time, digital audio workstations took over record production, and complex computer programmes were written for editing and modifying sound, including the removal of background noise. When early records were broadcast directly from the originals, excuses were inevitably made for the age-related noise. It became fashionable to remove background noise from earlier recordings, in particular recordings taken from the period of shellac records. This noiselessness, however, was perceived (especially by old-timers)

---

18 | The technical issue here is that the pop (hard rock and even tougher genres) distributed via radio and as files on the internet can be demonstrated to have very limited dynamic range: > 95 % of the time the volume is maximum. This makes the sound stand out more in competition with traditional, more dynamic sound. Maximum volume is 1000 times (60 decibels more than) the noise in ordinary listening environments. But you virtually never get below the maximum volume – another reason for the hearing damage. Compared to this, occasional exposure to rock concerts is generally much less damaging.

to kill the atmosphere, while it also distorted voices beyond recognition. Recognition requires a reference, and this is what the new audience / customers did not have to start with. For them the noiseless CDs became the new point of reference.

The sound of the CD player is inaudible, unless one rested one's ear against the cabinet. In this case, one would hear the faint sound of the motor for the reproducing optics, finding the right track, and the whirr of the CD accelerating to its working speed, which is between 500 and 200 rpm, all controlled automatically by the equipment and the signals from the CD. The only real problem occurs if a CD is scratched on the label side, which is the more fragile, since virtually no protection is provided for the recorded signal. In case of such a scratch, the CD player will try to repair the signal or reject the track as unplayable. Ultimately, a rejection is to the listener's benefit, since if the player continued to produce what the optical head sees, this would result in sounds similar to thunderbolts and noises sharp enough to destroy both loudspeakers and ears.

The most recent development of access via computer files has been no different from the use of a CD-player as concerns the noise or lack of it – but in the most modern times the buttons are virtual buttons on a screen. After the user has decided which track to play, the music – robbed of its last ›click‹ – begins smoothly and noiselessly.

Today: small revival of some noises

If we miss the noises, it is because they provided identity! It is not just a question of getting acoustic confirmation of an action – we were used to a ›click‹ as feedback, and it is now replaced by the well-known little ›beep‹ that accompanies pressing a key on a virtual keyboard. If this were merely a replacement, a camera, too, could provide feedback by a small and subdued ›beep‹. Instead, we hear the synthesised sound of a shutter, or even the click of the mirror as it occurred in a pre-digital SLR camera when we pressed the button. And for years now, the palette of modern mobile phone ring tones has included the sound of a 1940s telephone. All is not forgotten!

What about Public Address?

Modern public sonic events are inevitably linked to the use of what, in the old days, used to be called Public Address and PA-systems. This is a completely different environment from the private use of sound reproduction systems but, nonetheless, the associated noises share roots with those with which we are by now familiar. Almost all singers and speakers in a live performance now use a microphone, and an adjustable amplifier sends the amplified signal to one or more loudspeakers in the venue. Numerous extraneous noises are still associated with the use of PA.

The earliest PA was the use of speech trumpets, for instance out-of-doors and in rowdy theatres. This was followed by experiments to use electricity, for instance the friction amplifier.[19] These constructions had the disadvantage of producing a constant background hiss that was audible through the loudhailer. On the other hand, this background noise heralded the fact that a message would be given. Modern microphone users, who address crowds, frequently blow on the microphone in order to check the system and create attention at the same time.

The same happens during train station announcements – an often incomprehensible message is always heralded by the noise of hum and crackling from the switch on the microphone. The microphone technique of many such announcers is terrible and almost invariably there is no wind noise limiter, which adds a spitting noise to the message.

Since the presentation of the first fully electromagnetic PA systems during the Pacific Panama Exhibition in San Francisco 1915,[20] it has been known that too much amplification results in an acoustic feedback loop that makes the system overload and howl. Even before these noises begin, it is very noticeable that the system is about to oscillate, because certain tones remain ›hanging‹ after an utterance has stopped.

The worst and most frequent noise in PA is the hum, which is mostly produced by a defective design or a broken wire in a shielded cable.[21] In recent times the hum has been joined by the sound of a mobile phone sending out its call of identification. A mobile phone has such a strong transmitter that the very spiky digital signal penetrates the shielding of the wires, which carry the minute signals of a modern microphone. A more irritating buzzing sound comes from the injection of noise signals produced by fluorescent

---

19 | According to Frederik Johnsen and Knud Rahbek, US Patent 1,533,757 (1919-25) a handle turned a cylinder made in a semi-conducting material, and applying a voltage from a microphone to a metal strip in contact with the rotating cylinder would change the friction in accordance with the sound. The strip pulled on a large diaphragm, and the sound was amplified.

20 | The Magnavox Company by Edward Pridham and Peter L. Jensen, US Patents 1,329,928 (1916-20) and 1,448,279 (1920-23).

21 | To prevent injection of noise signals in an audio circuit, the wires carrying the signal are surrounded by a mesh of wire, a shield that is usually connected to the chassis of the amplifiers and the casing of the microphone. If that connection is broken, hum ensues.

lighting and electronic dimmers. All systematic sounds related to mains frequency can today be removed by computer-based methods,[22] which are, indeed, used on modern film sets, as digital filtering »on the fly« is faster and cheaper than having to create the perfect sonic environment for shooting.

Conclusion

It is strange that in a world which has become increasingly noisier for everybody, the noises associated with the transmission of the sounds themselves have been reduced almost to the absurd. At the same time the way that music is now distributed has developed into the consistent use of maximum volume. The dynamic range of modern pop music is frighteningly small,[23] and if logic had a role to play, the question of background noise would never come up in such an environment. There isn't a moment of silence! However, to the degree that we use noises related to our daily activities to orient ourselves in life, we need them, and there is no doubt that relevant noises will come back and support the little rituals that we engage in. And who knows, perhaps a future *app* will automatically attach little LP noises to frame a music selection when nostalgia becomes once more the new style.

Bibliography

Benson, Carl: Boombox, in: Frank Hoffman (ed.): Encyclopedia of Recorded Sound, 2nd ed., Vol. 2., New York 2005, p. 120.
Benson, Carl: Walkman®, in: Frank Hoffman (ed.): Encyclopedia of Recorded Sound, 2nd ed., Vol. 2., New York 2005, p. 1170.
Brock-Nannestad, George: What Are the Sources of the Noises We Remove, in: Zoltán Vajda and Heinrich Pichler (eds): Proceedings of AES 20th Int. Conf. ›Archiving, Restoration, and New Methods of Recording‹, Budapest 5–7 October 2001, New York 2001, pp. 175-182.
Brock-Nannestad, George: The Lacquer Disc for Immediate Playback: Professional Recording and Home Recording from the 1920s to the 1950s, in: Simon Frith and Simon Zagorski-Thomas (eds): The Art of Record Production. An Introductory Reader for a New Academic Field, Farnham 2012, pp. 13-28.
Bryson, H. Courtney: The Gramophone Record, London 1935.

---

22 | For instance the stand-alone equipment ›BRX +‹ debuzzer pioneered by CEDAR®.
23 | See Milner: Perfecting Sound Forever, p. 237.

CEDAR Audio Ltd: BRX+ debuzzer, AZX+ azimuth corrector, Owners' Manual Version 1.00, February 1999, pp. 20-24.

Hansen, Kjetil Falkenberg: The Basics of Scratching, in: Journal of New Music Research 31.4 (2002), pp. 357-365.

Hansen, Kjetil Falkenberg: The acoustics and performance of DJ scratching, Doctoral Thesis, KTH School of Computer Science and Communication, Stockholm 2010.

Magoun, Alexander B.: The Origins of the 45-RPM Record at RCA Victor, 1939-48, in: Hans-Joachim Braun (ed.): ›I sing the body electric‹ – Music and Technology in the 20th Century. Hofheim 2000, pp. 160-169.

Milner, Greg: Perfecting Sound Forever. The Story of Recorded Music, London 2010.

Permut, Steven: Reproducing Piano, in: Frank Hoffman (ed.): Encyclopedia of Recorded Sound. 2nd Ed., Vol. 2, New York 2005, pp. 918-919.

Wiesengrund-Adorno, Theodor: Nadelkurven, in: Musikblätter des Anbruch (1928), pp. 47-50.

On the overheard

Brandon LaBelle

Studies in sound continue to emerge as a dynamic field spanning multiple disciplines, from sociology to literature, technology to aesthetics, and crossing over between theory and practice, academic scholarship and artistic projects. The intensity of such a range of subjects and work gives compelling suggestion for understanding sound as more than an object of study, and it is this *more than* which rests at the center of this article. Rather than being a mere object, it is my argument that sound is an event that acts to connect or hinge together a disparate range of things and bodies; and in doing so it spirits a rather forceful sense for what it means to be a body amongst others. Such primary qualities also extend beyond the purely physical. The continual fluctuations of sound lead us toward a type of poetical engagement – I would say sound is fundamentally poetic, in that it starts from a concrete thing or body, while immediately leading away, into a certain ethereal space. The ephemeral nature of any sound speaks toward the imagination; I might even argue, it requires it. Sound is thus a dynamic link between our concrete realities and metaphysical imagination. To my ear, these qualities of sound – an event which says: something is happening! – may be appreciated as lending to a type of public expression: the formulation of a radical animation. Might sound be embraced as a vehicle, a sort of mobilization, for creating types of inhabitation that hinge together private and public life?

My interest is to think through sound, then, as such a space, from which we might learn more fully of each other; a type of experiential platform from which different interactions may materialize and be imagined. As part of this larger project I am keen to also write as a listening subject, as a body caught within the dynamics of acoustic space, that tries to write its way through, or deeper in; in other words, to take seriously what happens if we place sound at the center of our critical and creative thinking, not to mention as a means for relating to a crowd. I would stress this relational aspect as being inherent to auditory experience: by forcing into contact a range of disparate events, as well as conditioning the spaces shared amongst people with a certain unpredictability, sound fosters what I refer to as ›radical empathy‹. In this regard, I have come to recognize how sound is deeply connected to experiences of not only intimate sharing, social bonding and reassurance, but also of disruption, interruption and threat. The fact that these acoustic territories overlap so easily, or brush against each other so frequently suggests, to my listening at least, that sound is precisely an opportunity for vulnerability: of the body and the senses, as well as of our knowledge-boundaries.

I am interested to extend such thinking, and such vulnerability – which Christof Migone refers to as *the porous body* shaped by sound[1] – by focusing on noise *and* the other: noise as the production of the social, that is, as a generative experience by which we may come to share space. Noise, in this regard, need not be thought of in terms of volume, nor as having any particular sonic quality. Rather, I emphasize noise as the beginning of confrontation and negotiation; noise, as Michel Serres suggests, as the »rending« of any system or order that fundamentally promotes new social and bodily configurations.[2]

I want to locate noise, then, as the initiation of a new sociality constituted by bodies meeting on the threshold of possible community. Although I write ›community‹, I am still searching for another word, and this very text must be understood as a search for this other, as yet unnamed, type of collectivity. In this regard, noise may be heard or defined as a sound which *over-steps* particular limits, that which is *out of place,* and forms the basis for an art of listening. Such a perspective finds resonance with Luigi Russolo's original »art of noises«, in which he calls for a broader appreciation for those surges of urban sound; that is, for an ear for the »continuous, very strange and marvelous hubbub of the crowd.«[3]

To develop this thinking, I want to bring into the spotlight a particular memory of attending a concert in Los Angeles in 1998 – an event that, while arising out of an extremely personal situation, has come to suggest a greater and more general set of ideas. I would like to dwell on this concert so as to situate noise as a form of ›interruption‹, linked to a place as well as collective experience, that is, connected to those always already beside me, whose presence conditions, interferes with and shapes my own. What I may call: You, They or Them, and which may become Us, though never fully, which is precisely one of the forms of the *more than,* which can never be captured completely, to which this article is devoted.

To map this further I'll draw upon what I may call ›three coordinates‹ of listening to noise:

---

1 | See Migone: Sonic Somatic.
2 | Serres: Genesis; see also LaBelle: Acoustic Territories, pp. 61-62.
3 | See Russolo: Art of Noises, p. 45.

1. Acoustics multiplied
2. The Supplement
3. Difference-making

I imagine these as coordinates within the field of sound by which to open a view onto noise, and by which to explore the particular forms and spatial vocabularies, which noise may be heard to produce. Some of the key questions which arise here are: If noise can be thought of as the production of the social, of an acoustic space, what forms of inhabitation does it make possible? Is interference the beginning of a new public? A stage for a certain proliferation of what is suddenly proximate, or all too near?

Concert

Los Angeles, 1998: I'm at a club with a group of friends. We've gone out to see a band, and the place is packed. I'm standing a bit to the back, drink in hand, sandwiched between friends and strangers, and the band in front, not too far, but not exactly close: it's a small club, and everyone is listening, focused, interested. All, except a few: to my right, about 6 or 7 meters away, a few guys are standing, drinking beers and talking, laughing, having a good time and rather oblivious to the situation. The consequence is that they are breaking the mood, disrupting the scene, and causing a ruckus.

Suddenly, I am caught between two perspectives, two performances, and two forms of listening: in front of me, the band, the object of attention, the thing I am here to witness, and to the right, a group of talkers, conversing somewhere between quiet and loud, but still, loud enough to unsettle my main focus, my main perspective onto the band.

The situation continues for some time; other people start to yell at the group, who keep talking; then, the group starts to yell back, and even the band begins to get annoyed. In this moment though, something changes for myself: I begin to notice that what is happening is extremely provocative, and extremely suggestive, and in this moment, I begin to realize what it means to listen: that sound, of course, is never an isolated event; that there are always sounds to the side of another sound, which we constantly over-hear; and that listening is a process of confronting the expressive movements occurring around us, which act to broaden our attention – sometimes even by force.

This experience of disruption was neither necessarily new to me, nor did it stand out within the patterns of rock club behavior. Still, at this instant, it brought forward a sudden recognition. I became aware that my own annoyance was actually an opportunity, that if listening is to deepen one's experience of the world, then noise provides a dynamic instantiation of such depth, an active education of sound's particular knowledge structure. A chance of knowing, and of being known; not as composition, but as association. In this sense, over-hearing points the way for a consideration of not so much what is in front, but rather next to; that is, a sensitivity for the crowd.

It is my interest to embrace this moment of disturbance, this noise, this *over-here*, and understand it as a special kind of acoustic, and something to add to how we perceive and understand sounds around us. I would venture to say that the ›over-here‹, this group of guys over here, is the horizon of every sound. It is the promise that every sound makes: to say – ›here, I am over here‹.

I contend that this notion of ›over-hearing‹, of sounds that appear *over-here*, and produce this moment of interruption, is worth exploring as a fundamental theory of the sound arts, but also a central theme within the field of the auditory, which merits an appreciation for noise as a productive and generative (social) event. Over-hearing should be understood as an expanded listening, which complements what is in front by what is beyond. In other words: over-hearing, as I will suggest, is a form of listening to *more than*.

To unfold these thoughts, I will begin by drawing out my three coordinates of listening, which are, at the same time, three forms of spatial thinking, of *over-stepping, over-hearing*, and *eaves-dropping*.

1. Acoustics Multiplied

Following such experience as that at the LA concert, I would suggest that sounds can be understood to multiply perspectives. In other words, there is always a sound outside the frame of a particular listening, which often interferes or occurs to the side, yet immediately becomes part of the experience. To put it differently: sound promises the outside, as well as the making of a second space within. As an event, sound links together seemingly incongruous or even dichotomous elements, creating spaces that easily connect inside and outside. For example, the talking occurring during the concert, the thing that is to the side of the band, creates a second acoustical space, there in the room. *To the side*, then, is actually *inside*; it is *within* the parameters of the expected event, while also being *outside*, appearing as interruption.

The complexity of this situation is suggestive for understanding sound's particular relationship to spatiality. As Barry Truax proposes: »the sound wave arriving at the ear is the analogue of the current state of the physical environment, because as the wave travels, it is changed by each interaction with the environment.«[4] Subsequently, space can be understood according to

---

4 | Truax: Acoustic Communication, p. 15.

a temporal element, an explicit time-based flux toward which our attention is continually drawn, fixed and then unfixed, made and then unmade. Sound *conditions* space as a fluctuating event, during which each interaction with the environment must be heard to bring into relief, at each moment, the materiality around us.

Yet, such inherent dynamics of sound also open out onto experiences of noise, which might be said to inflect this acoustics with degrees of agitation. While sound may multiply perspectives, in a fundamental acoustic operation, noise, and its instant of interference, conditions such perspectives with a confrontation with what is *out of place*. While invading one's personal space, or unsettling any particular quietude, noise grants potential to each instant of rupture. That is, it leads us to hear what is *out of reach*.

Noise, in this regard, is pluralistic: it registers and highlights our spatial surroundings by explicitly connecting us to often difficult, complex or intense events. To follow this sound wave as it is charged by each interaction with what is surrounding, is certainly to arrive at what might be called »pure intensity«, which must simultaneously be emphasized as impure. Acoustic space, in other words, is a primary animation that might envelope me in a supportive embrace, but might also overwhelm, threaten and unsettle me. It might return me to lost voices, in a sudden moment of rememberance, *and* it may surround me in absolute banality. In other words, acoustic space is a multiplication that shifts between reassuring enfoldment and its agitating disruption.

This operation can also be found at work in numerous sound art projects, in which sound is used not only as material, but as an extension of a given architectural space, in order to bring up the volume on our locational perspective. Joel Sanders's *Mix House* project from 2006, for example, depicts a domestic architecture fitted or bursting with audio-visual extensions. Installing multiple cameras and microphones to the exterior of a house, the work functions to bring the outside *into* the home. These exterior perspectives are amplified through windows that act as screens, as well as through a speaker system wired throughout the house, which can be controlled in the kitchen area, from a sort of DJ platform integrated into the counter. Various controls are added, which allow active surveying of the exterior, such as cameras that can scan the landscape outside, or microphones that can zoom in on particular events. The *Mix House* in this way literally extends the single home, creating links to a broader environment. What I appreciate about Sanders's speculative vision is how it images a space in dialogue with a greater environmental surrounding. Its implication is that an ›audio-visual‹ perspective is precisely one that unsettles the stable borders between interior and exterior, by amplifying their meeting point as an architecture of intensity, a tension that subsequently explodes its geometry.

Mix House finds a certain material realization in a work by the artist Mark Bain. Titled *Bug*, this work is a permanent installation in a building in Berlin. Bain's interest in or obsession with vibration as a phenomenon found within buildings has led the artist to produce works that often aim to capture the embedded resonance of architectural structures. With *Bug* this takes shape through the insertion of transducers directly into the concrete foundations of a building. The transducers essentially amplify existing vibrations, which pass through the foundations to an earphone plug, which is permanently fitted to the building's façade. Passersby are invited to tap into the building and listen to the noises therein. Bain's work leads us to recognize buildings less in terms of visual boundaries and more as manifestations of vibrational connectivity. Rooms no longer end at their visual thresholds, but extend deeper in, through and down, or up and above, where vibrations link and ultimately redraw perspectival space.

I take these two projects, then, as echoes of Truax's environmental listening, whereby a sound wave not only brings forward but actually multiplies our understanding of the current state of a place. The acoustics of an environment is precisely a territorial layer that often brings into contact things and bodies, events and voices, and from which alliances and resonances, as well as ruptures and agitations, are experienced and produced. Such productions radically shift attention from sightlines to a deeper, vital materiality.

2. The Supplement

Having dealt with multiplied acoustics, the second coordinate of listening I would like to map is that noise *challenges my sense of what I am listening for*. In other words, what I am expecting, what I am waiting for, is constantly supplemented by something else – by that sound there, and then, another there.

Returning again to the club in Los Angeles, it is clear that my own expectations, that is, what I had been waiting for, were supplemented by the laughter and the chattering occuring to the side: what I over-heard did not necessarily block out the presence of the band, the experience of the music, rather, it appeared *alongside*, as a contributing element. Such an instant of expanded listening, of multiplied perspectives, highlights, I would like to suggest, sound's ability to always demand more, that is, to support the production of an *encounter*. Noise, then, might be understood as the acoustical multiplication that forces negotiation as a by-product of such an encounter.

We can understand the supplement, following Jacques Derrida's account in *Of Grammatology*, as something that *adds* onto something else;[5] rather

---

5 | Derrida: Of Grammatology, pp. 141-164.

than appearing as a substitute for something of an ›original nature‹, the supplement introduces a critical addition. A sort of appendix that, in adding onto an ›original‹ object or action or phenomenon, enacts a type of rupture; the supplement empties out the seemingly stable presence of what we imagine as being complete, whole, or immutable. In this regard, the supplementing force of noise brings into question the stability of an event, such as the band, or the expectation of fulfilled listening, by introducing a *more than* onto the scene. Yet in doing so it also *opens up* the original to undo the appearance of a stable meaningful reference. The supplement, in other words, makes the ›original‹ available for sampling, for appropriation, and for comment. It unsettles and dislocates the fixity of any form, allowing for unexpected entry.

To return once more to the club in LA; the talking happening over-here interfered with what I had been expecting, with what I had been waiting for – that is, the band. Yet in doing so it also started to supplement the band, by creating an appendix to my listening; and, in that moment, the full presence of the band, as the point of my attention, was undone. To take another example: listening in the mode of the over-here is like being in a cinema during an intensely serious moment in a film, and suddenly someone in the audience starts laughing – this laughter, this noise, completely disrupts the scene, but it also begins something else. It delivers the understanding that every expectation, every *hoping for*, is also prone to surprise. This I take as an extremely vital element of sound and listening: that the process of supplementing – *of that sound over there, and then there* – creates the possibility for another narrative, an opening precisely for what we did not expect, yet might further imagine. This might also be thought of as an echo to what Paul Carter calls »the erotic ambiguity of sound.«[6] For Carter, this ambiguity is importantly the exceeding of representation – a positive, productive ambiguity found within sound that generates what we might think of as ›extra-expressivities‹: something that slips through, or overflows from an instant of representation: a *more than*.

To explore this idea further, I would like to refer to two works I produced in the last few years – *The Sonic Body* (2009-11) and *Lecture on Nothing* (2011) –, which I imagine as expressions of supplementing. Starting with John Cage's »Lecture on Nothing«, originally presented in 1950 and later published in *Silence* (1961), I proceeded to record a deaf man reading the text. Through this gesture I was interested to explore and complicate the ways in which silence is often understood, namely as forming the basis for a dedicated listening. For Cage, silence operates as a frame within which non-intentional sounds appear, as well as a subsequent opening up of our auditory sense, our auditory behavior, to a greater social situation. Following Cage's important

---

6 | Carter: Ambiguous Traces, Mishearing, and Auditory Space, p. 61.

example, silence continues to inform the sound arts in various ways, often functioning as a positive, nurturing platform for our listening. In recording a deaf individual reading the original text, silence, from my perspective, may also appear in another way: rather than understand it as the pre-condition for sound, or as an optimistic, democratic frame for *all sounds*, my work poses silence as a particular force, one that carries its own ideological contour, and ultimately performs to exclude or territorialize.[7] Supplementing the Cage lecture the deaf man is reading out, his voice gives us a silence to listen to, that is, a deafness found in the voice, but one that may reposition Cage's silence, to make audible an additional referent. I take this work, then, just like acts of supplementing in general, as a possible footnote to Cage's lecture; a footnote, that, as Derrida suggests pulls against the original.

A second work in line with this approach is *The Sonic Body*. It is based on making audio recordings of different individuals, as well as selected groups, while they are dancing to music heard through headphones. I was interested to capture the movements of people dancing, and to hear these movements as a detailed translation of the music heard only by them. The subsequent recordings start to give another version of the particular song. For example, the sounds of a body moving to Joy Division's *Transmission*, I would propose, *are* the song. They are the song, and they are something *more*. They are the song ingested by a body and forced back out in various pivots and breaks, gyrations and hops. This combination of sounds is a song *and* a body, together, as an assembly: a sonic body. In paying attention to this sonic body, the work gives us a supplementing elaboration of music to suggest, or possibly to lay bare, the ways in which listening moves us (and makes us move). These supplementing additions and stagings initiate a form of over-hearing, that is, a form of listening that hears *past* or *through* the original referent – whether this be Cage's lecture or a musical track – to arrive somewhere *alongside*. It is my view that noise explicitly introduces this potential, this operation, into the sonic imagination to suggest a method for narrative and creativity, and for countering the encounter.

---

7 | Questions on the ideological tensions of silence were first developed in my work in LaBelle: Acoustic Territories: Sound Culture and Everyday Life. It has been my aim to query in what way silence performs to reduce and limit forms of social participation, and how it appears within disciplinary practices (for example, within prisons). Silence and silencing are examined to ultimately challenge some of the overarching assumptions pervasive within the sound arts and related sound culture discussions that cast silence as a positive, ›pure‹ horizon for deep listening and social improvement (e.g. the quiet home initiative in the UK). For more see LaBelle: Acoustic Territories, particularly chapter 2.

3. Difference-making

After having discussed multiple acoustics and the supplement, my last coordinate to explore is that of difference-making, since noise *introduces the other onto the scene*. In other words, noise brings the one that is over there to here, in front of me. This elaborates both the idea of the supplement and that of the multiplying of acoustic perspective, to suggest that noise, as *the over-here of the here*, delivers a confrontation with the unexpected. And if we have to give a name to this unexpected, to the supplement, I would propose we call it the ›stranger‹. The ›stranger‹, in a sense, gives a body to the over-here, a shape to the supplement that also suggests a social situation, a fuller negotiation.

I would propose that if noise multiplies perspectives, as a spatial acoustic, and supplements what I am expecting, enabling or forcing other narratives, it does so by explicitly introducing something, or someone, I do not yet know. It is to bring to my attention something I was not waiting for – in other words, it is to introduce a difference. As Aden Evens proposes: »sound is fundamentally a difference of difference« – that is, a continual introduction of something which was not there before.[8]

The operations of this *difference-making* can also be found at play in various artistic works. For instance, Richard Serra's video *Boomerang* from 1974 can be appreciated as a piece of difference-making, in this case one instigated by a voice and its echo. For the work, the artist places a microphone in front of a woman. The woman wears headphones and can hear her speaking voice, yet only delayed, as it comes back to her slightly behind her own speaking. The woman then speaks, talks about the experience she is having at this very moment, she refers to the situation, and tries to describe what she is hearing, how this echoing disrupts her speech, her conscious thought. Something is always coming back to interrupt her speech. Here is a transcription of what she says:

Yes, I can hear my echo and the words are coming back on top of me
Uh, the words are spilling out of my head
and then returning into my ear
It puts a distance between the words and their apprehension, or their comprehension
The words coming back seem slow, they don't seem to have the same forcefulness as when I speak them
I think it's also slowing me down
I think that it makes my thinking slower
I have a double-take on myself
I am once removed from myself

---

8 | See Evens: Sound Ideas.

I am thinking and hearing and filling up a vocal void
I find that I have trouble making connections between thoughts
I think that the words forming in my mind are somewhat detached from my normal thinking process
I have a feeling that I am not where I am
I feel that this place is removed from reality [...][9]

Serra's *Boomerang* stages the evocative dynamics of echoing sound. As the woman states, it's as if she leaves her own body, to become a stranger to herself, with her voice coming back to her as though from another reality. Everything seems to stagger within the multiplying movements of the echo; the interfering echo introduces a *difference* into her speech. Such ruptures instantiate the sonorous dynamics I am aiming for here – over-hearing herself, the performer perfectly describes a state of *listening subjectivity* that, I maintain, is intrinsic to experiences of noise. The differentiating production announced in her speech acts as a metaphor for what I'm defining as noise's potent exacerbation of an existing situation.

I understand the notion of difference-making as something that necessarily broadens my horizon: the multiplying of perspectives, the supplementing of representation, forces me to meet the one that is separate from me, but it does so by collapsing distance: this difference that is over-here, forces its way inside, that is, inside myself. It comes directly into me. As Steven Connor eloquently reminds us: »The self defined in terms of hearing rather than sight is a self imaged not as a point, but as a membrane; not as a picture, but as a channel through which voices, noises, and musics travel.«[10] In this regard, the worldly intensities of sound *others my horizon*, it *others my body*, as a differentiating production: as the noise found in relating to a ›stranger‹, even the ›stranger‹ of oneself. The self defined in terms of hearing, then, might be a self always already extra, an extra to itself, and always already involved in more.

Emergent Public

The acoustic space that I am mapping here is one defined by what I would like to refer to as *radical sharing*: a generative and messy space brought into play by the disjointedness of interference, where community may appear more as a crowd, and where the private body is interrupted by those around it. If we

---

9 | A sample of Serra's video can be found on *YouTube:* https://www.youtube.com/watch?v=8z32JTnRrHc (10.6.14).
10 | Connor: Sound and Self, p. 57.

map this spatially, we start to have an acoustic picture that, as I would suggest, reconfigures conventional understandings of what is inside, and what is outside; and especially, and importantly, what is mine and what is yours and what is the others. Accordingly, I am keen to emphasize sound as a property of relationships – a linkage, a hinge; an economy of the in-between that generates and supports a dynamics of inclusion, even if we do not want it to do this.

To conclude, I would like to elaborate this thought by drawing on the work of cultural and urban historian Richard Sennett, in particular on *The Uses of Disorder* from 1970, in which he makes an interesting claim for »disorder« as a productive tool for nurturing social life. As he states:

> What is needed is to create cities where people are forced to confront each other so as to reconstitute public power [...]. The city must then be conceived as a social order of parts without a coherent, controllable whole form. [...] Rather, the creation of city spaces should be for varied, changeable use.[11]

What I take from Sennett is an extremely provocative inversion: Urban planners and social organizers may draw upon concepts of harmony, of togetherness, of cohesion or concensus, as means for establishing community, as in the legacy of suburban development in the United States. Sennett, in contrast, sees disorder, difference, and discord as productive for spaces of sharing, that is, for a spatial form composed by and nurturing multiplicity. Place-making, in other words, can be enriched precisely through experiences of displacement.

I take all this as the very condition of listening in general. Might we appreciate the irksome interventions of noise as a discordant opportunity? One that might give way to new social encounters? Following Sennett, is not the irritating force of noise at times delivering explicitly what we might not understand?

I would suggest that to listen is to always already over-hear: it is to live within multiple perspectives, to experience noise, and to deal with strangers (and *strangeness*) whose voice may suddenly surprise us. In this sense, I would propose that sound, as an event and also as a certain perspective of thought, recovers a view of the private and the public, not as distinct or separate, but rather as integrated and interwoven. It fully supports a model of spatial relations shaped equally by contamination and interruption, as well as association and unexpected solidarity.

---

11 | Sennett: The Uses of Disorder, p. 141.

Bibliography

Carter, Paul: Ambiguous Traces, Mishearing, and Auditory Space, in: Veit Erlmann (ed.): Hearing Cultures: Essays on Sound, Listening and Modernity, Oxford 2004, pp. 43-63.
Connor, Steven: Sound and Self, in: Mark M. Smith (ed.): Hearing History: A Reader, Athens 2004, pp. 54-66.
Derrida, Jacques: Of Grammatology, Baltimore 1997.
Evens, Aden: Sound Ideas: Music, Machines, and Experience, Minneapolis 2005.
LaBelle, Brandon: Acoustic Territories: Sound Culture and Everyday Life, New York 2010.
Migone, Christof: Sonic Somatic: Performances of the Unsound Body, Berlin 2012.
Russolo, Luigi: Art of Noises, New York 1986.
Sennett, Richard: The Uses of Disorder: Personal Identity and City Life, New York 1970.
Serres, Michel: Genesis, Ann Arbor 1997.
Truax, Barry: Acoustic Communication, Norwood 1994.

Artworks

Bain, Mark: *Bug* (2009).
Serra, Richard: *Boomerang* (1974).
LaBelle, Brandon: *The Sonic Body* (2009-2011).
LaBelle, Brandon: *Lecture on Nothing* (2011).
Sanders, Joel: *Mix House* (2006).

IV Noise of the Art: Geräusch und literarischer Text

Noise, Whirling Sounds and Narrative Dizziness in M. P. Shiel's *The House of Sounds*

Sylvia Mieszkowski

Noisy Beginnings

Famous for the »frenetic vigour«[1] of his flamboyant prose style, Matthew Phipps Shiel was a late Victorian author of gothic fiction, »existential horror«[2] and apocalyptic ›future history‹ Sci Fi, who attained cult status after his death. Born in 1865 in the West Indies and of mixed-race extraction,[3] Shiel was educated as a gentleman at Harrison College, Barbados, and migrated to London in 1885 to make a living as a writer. In 1901 he published an autobiographical sketch titled *About Me*. Setting the scene on Montserrat, Shiel's native Caribbean island, it fantasises the author's origin as a promisingly noisy affair:

> I was born at the moment of an earthquake and a storm, or, rather, these were born at the moment of me. Nature sneezed at my coming. The sheet-lightning, like a sheeted ghost, came peering into the chamber, winking a million to the second. And, with lullaby rough enough, this mixture of Heaven and Earth and Hell which I call ›I‹, and sometimes ›We‹, came out, and began to cry.[4]

---

1 | Morse: Works of M. P. Shiel, p. 480, quoted in Vogeler's article on Shiel in the *Oxford Dictionary of National Biography*.
2 | Mullen: M. P. Shiel's *The Purple Cloud*.
3 | Matthew Dowdy Shiell [sic], the writer's father, had Irish ancestors. Vogeler: Shiel, Matthew Phipps, p. 1. Records seem to indicate that Shiel's mother might have been either a freed slave herself or born to freed slaves. Svitavsky: From Decadence to Racial Antagonism, p. 4, quoting Morse: Works of M. P. Shiel, p. 457.
4 | Squires: Some Closing Thoughts.

Playing with the cliché of the author-subject's birth as an act of creation by cosmos unbound, this passage flirts with concepts like Edmund Burke's definition of the sublime,[5] John Keats's »negative capability«[6] and Rimbaud's »je est un autre«:[7] it showcases a narrative I, which sees itself as a hybrid (of »Heaven and Earth and Hell«); who lacks a stable sense of individual identity as the »I« sometimes dissolves into a »We«, only to re-cohere at other times; and it retrospectively installs an identity from which the future writer's career – whose imagination will give life to many characters – is foreshadowed. At the same time, the passage's bathetic metaphor pokes fun at the author-subject's sense of self-importance. After all, by depicting the sublime trembling of sky and earth and, presumably, the accompanying rain as nature's sneezing spasm, an involuntary, uncontrollable and, above all, noisy impulse is held responsible for pushing the narrated I into being. If the total absence of the maternal body in this nativity scene is conspicuous, it is hardly surprising. Given the cultural *topos* which, from around 1900, feminises nature while naturalising women, it is obvious why all mention of maternal materiality is superfluous: If nature ›herself‹ is there to sneeze the hero-artist into existence, the story does not need a human female presence to provide him with an origin or genealogy. Incidentally, Shiel's narration thus stages a scenario that draws on Edward Young's concept of the »*Original* author that is born of himself, is his own progenitor«,[8] while adding to it a noisy note.

More importantly for an exploration of noise, the writer's beginning of existence is imagined here as a predominantly sonic event. In a gesture of self-fashioning that exemplifies the »grandiloquence«,[9] which has been found

---

5 | In section fourteen of his *Philosophical Enquiry* (1756) Burke maintains that light can only »make a strong impression on the mind« and thus become »a cause of producing the sublime«, if it is »attended with some circumstances«. Lightning, one of the circumstances listed, is described as »certainly productive of grandeur«, yet it owes its sublime effect »chiefly to the extreme velocity of its motion«. Burke: A Philosophical Enquiry, p. 73. In Shiel's scene, where sheet-lightning personified is »winking a million to the second«, the hyperbole seems to be a tongue-in-cheek reference to Burke's condition for lightning to turn into a source of the sublime.
6 | According to Keats it is an asset for a poet to be »capable of being in uncertainties«. John Keats: Letter to George and Tom Keats. 21, 27 (?) [sic] December 1817, in: Keats: The Complete Poems, p. 539.
7 | Arthur Rimbaud used this phrase »[For] I is someone else« twice, in the two so-called »letters of the visionary« he wrote from Charleville on May 13 and 15 1871 to Georges Izambard Charles Demeney. Rimbaud Complete: Vol. I, Poetry and Prose, pp. 365, 366.
8 | Young: Conjectures on Original Composition, p. 68, italics in the original.
9 | Bulfin: Review of: Harold Billings. M. P. Shiel: The First Biography, p. 389.

typical for Shiel's writing in general, the autodiegetic narrator confidently puts himself at the centre of a meteorological as well as seismic occurrence. As the tiny human and the massive storm come into being simultaneously, these events are hierarchised. Far from being presented as beyond human control, the forces of nature are made to appear as incidents which literally ›accompany‹ the future author's birth, providing it with a soundtrack that uses the natural spectacle to mark the birth as a more momentous occasion. Instead of being deemed disturbing, thunderstorm and earthquake are presented as having the soothing effect of a »lullaby« on this special child.

While this autobiographical fragment *About Me* is a good introduction to Shiel's stylistic idiosyncrasy, it also provides evidence that he, as a writer, pays attention to the sound *of* the text, as it describes the sounds *in* the text; in other words, Shiel attributes importance to the feature which Garrett Stewart has theorised as the »phonotext«.[10] Another sounding of the same quotation provides evidence: the italicised words and syllables highlight the phonemic rather than the semantic level, by marking the overlapping or interlinking sound fields created by the vowels in ›born – storm – born‹, by ›these – me – sneezed – sheet – sheet – peering‹, by ›rough enough‹ and by ›I – lullaby – I – I – cry‹:

> *I* was *born* at the moment of an earthquake and a *storm*, or, rather, *these* were *born* at the moment of me. Nature *sneezed* at my coming. The *sheet*-lightning, like a *sheeted* ghost, came *peering* into the chamber, winking a million to the second. And, with lulla*by rough enough,* this mixture of Heaven and Earth and Hell which *I* call ›*I*‹, and sometimes ›We‹, came out, and began to *cry*. (italics added)

As this article is going to argue, in the *The House of Sounds* the same principle of »phonemic«[11] manipulation is at work in a more consistent fashion and charged with performative purpose. In contrast with the fragmentary *About Me*, which stages an elemental blessing of its hero by the noises of nature, the re-written short story *The House of Sounds* foregrounds how natural noises bring about the mental as well as physical destruction of the protagonists.

Described by one of his anthologists, as the »Grand Viscount of the Grotesque«[12] and, in his obituary, as »an Irish Dumas *père*«, who cultivated

---

10 | According to Stewart the »phonotext« is »a materialized part of the phenotext, accessible only in phonemic reading« or »endophony«, a »silent sounding of a text«, which takes account of the »slippery interdependence of phonemes and graphemes«. Stewart: Reading Voices, p. 28.
11 | Ibid.
12 | August Derleth as quoted by Gullette: M. P. Shiel (1865-1947). The Lord of Language.

»an original if bizarre prose style«,[13] the prolific Shiel not only experimented with a number of genres such as poetry, romance, fantasy, detective fiction, tales of adventure, mystery and horror,[14] but was also seen as a source of inspiration by some of his colleagues. Sam Moskowitz hails him as »a writer's writer«, and underscores particularly that »[h]is mad literary rhythms, seemingly improvised, like a jazz artist's at a jam session, were a bubbling fountain at which new techniques of phrasing could be drunk«.[15] A controversial figure already at his time, Shiel as a person – due to his racist attitudes, his antisemitism and sexual preference for underage girls[16] – is even more problematic today. In his professional life he nourished a sustained interest in topics that caused collective anxiety. The *Oxford Dictionary of National Biography* lists »imperialism, the yellow peril, spiritualism, scientism and evolution«[17] as amongst his favourite subjects. To this one could add the theory of degeneration, yet another system of belief to which a number of late Victorian semi-scientific discourses and individual writers contributed. As William Svitavsky has demonstrated, Shiel's depiction of »racial denigration shades into dread of evolutionary superior rivals«. While his »visions of progress [...] are shaped by fears of decline«, his »disturbing views regarding race«, too, are »crystallized out of Decadent ideologies of social decay and degeneration«.[18] As Shiel picked up subjects that worried many of his contemporaries, he was and is credited to have done so with a »grandiose sweep of imagination«, in prose characterised by »vigour and inventiveness«, and with a pronounced penchant for »surreal images of obsession, hysteria and horror«.[19]

The House of Sounds is typical both of Shiel's extravagant style and his interest in tales of decline and extinction. An early version, titled *Vaila*, characterised by Roger Luckhurst as »a genuinely unhinged tale«,[20] had already come out in 1896, as one of the »five Poesque stories«[21] collected in *Shapes of Fire*. For the purpose of this article I shall concentrate on the text's

---

13 | John Gawsworth in Shiel's obituary in *The Times* on 20th Feb 1947, Gawsworth: Obituary M. P. Shiel.
14 | Vogeler: Shiel, Matthew Phipps, p. 2.
15 | Sam Moskowitz quoted by Gullette: M. P. Shiel (1865-1947). The Lord of Language.
16 | Shiel was actually convicted under the infamous *Lambouchère Amendment Act*, see MacLeod: M. P. Shiel and the Love of Pubescent Girls, p. 355.
17 | Vogeler: Shiel, Matthew Phipps, p. 2.
18 | Svitavsky: From Decadence to Racial Antagonism, p. 1. John D. Squires mentions Shiel's connection with the English Decadent movement through John Lane, who published Shiel's *Shapes of Fire* in 1896. Squires: Rediscovering M. P. Shiel.
19 | Vogeler: Shiel, Matthew Phipps, p. 1.
20 | Luckhurst: Introduction, p. xxx.
21 | Gullette: An Annotated Bibliography of M. P. Shiel.

final version, which was published in 1911 as *The House of Sounds*.[22] Some of Shiel's contemporaries viewed *The Purple Cloud* as his outstanding literary contribution,[23] a text which has been continuously in print since its publication in 1901. H. P. Lovecraft, however, Shiel's American fellow author of supernatural literature,[24] considered *The House of Sounds* his colleague's »undoubted masterpiece«.[25] Vaguely reminiscent of Edgar Allan Poe's *The Fall of the House of Usher* (1839), it presents an unnamed autodiegetic narrator, who tells the story of how he witnessed the extinction of his friend's ancient family, and the seemingly time-programmed self-destruction of their ancestral seat after half a millennium. While *The House of Sounds* shares with *The Fall of the House of Usher* its atmosphere of decay, its tale of destruction and its queer subtext,[26] it differs from Poe's story by the degree to which it is pervaded by noise.

Lovecraft, having made his way through Shiel's short story, described his reading experience in a letter. Mentioning the story's »hideous, insistent, brain-petrifying, Pan-accursed cosmic SOUND«,[27] he put his finger on the very feature which qualifies *The House of Sound* for an investigation that turns an inquisitive ear. »[C]osmic« suggests that, for Lovecraft, Shiel's story successfully performed on a larger scale what *About me* had done in a nutshell, namely creating a sound effect of overwhelming, and therefore sublime, volume. Perhaps Lovecraft spells »SOUND« in capital letters, although Shiel's story never uses this visual technique to suggest amplified sound, because it achieves in a sentence what the story builds up over twenty-one pages: ›silent‹ letters creating the impression of ›noise‹. In any case, the aesthetic judgment »hideous« seems to be linked with the moral one of »Pan-accursed«, both not uncommon in connection of what, in effect, is pandemonium. I would like to use the »insistent« quality of the sound, which Lovecraft mentions, as well

---

22 | All quotations refer to: Shiel: The House of Sound.
23 | H. G. Wells, for example, thought *The Purple Cloud* was »brilliant«, and the critic Andrew Block listed it as Shiel's »key book«. Wells: The discovery of the future, p. 55. Block: Key Books of British Authors, p. 300.
24 | Squires points out that Lovecraft is not the only American writer who thought highly of *The House of Sounds*, naming August Derleth and Clark Ashton Smith as two other admirers. Squires: Rediscovering M. P. Shiel.
25 | Lovecraft: Supernatural Horror in Literature, section ix: »The Weird Tradition in the British Isles« (n. p.).
26 | For a queer reading of *The Fall of the House of Usher* see Kraß: Aschertorte. Queerer Witz bei Streeruwitz. An interpretation that focuses on the queer aspects of *The House of Sounds* remains to be undertaken.
27 | H. P. Lovecraft, letter to Frank Belknap Long, 7th Oct 1923, quoted by Joshi in: Introduction, p. 9.

as his suggestion that it produces a psychosomatic effect, as stepping-stones for my own argument. While agreeing that the relentless persistence of noise in/of the story does something to the reader's as well as to the protagonist's mental faculties, I shall be arguing for the opposite *effect*. Rather than acting as »brain-petrifying«, producing a lack of motion where there should be some, the soundscape *in* and the sounds *of* Shiel's text produce a mental impression of too much, even uncontrollable, movement where there should be none: of vertigo.

In the description of his reading experience of *The House of Sounds* Lovecraft could have been referring primarily to the dominant role sound plays in the story's plot; after all a castle made of brass sinks into the sea during a terrible storm. On the other hand, he may have had the sound of the story's *narration* in mind as well. If he had thought of that, he would have been in good company: that of the American science fiction author E. F. Bleiler, who hailed Shiel's writing as »a welter of stylistic sound effects«;[28] and that of Shiel-editor S.T. Joshi, who proclaims the author to have »cultivated a mannered, almost *recherché* style to create a kind of incantatory effect upon the reader«.[29] As the *OED's* entry for »incantation« records, the Latin verb ›incantare‹, literally ›to sing into‹, implies »[t]he use of a formula of words spoken or chanted to produce a magical effect; the utterance of a spell or charm; more widely, the use of magical ceremonies or arts; magic, sorcery, enchantment«.[30] Joshi's description of Shiel's style as »incantatory« is neither tailored to a particular text, nor is it backed up by any analysis. Building on his general insight, however, this article will now turn its attention on *The House of Sounds* to pursue a »phonemic«[31] reading. Focusing on the role of noise, it will trace how Shiel's tale re-creates the sensation of uncontrollable motion, which is described by the narrator-auscultator-protagonist, for the reader; thereby installing narratively induced dizziness as part of *The House of Sound's* aesthetics.

Synopsis

The House of Sounds is divided into two segments of unequal length, connected, as far as narrative logic is concerned, by a story-within-the-story. This intradiegetic narration is told in part one and seems to find its fulfilment at the end of part two. Set in 1877, the shorter first section introduces the nameless

---

28 | E. F. Bleiler quoted by Gullette: M. P. Shiel (1865-1947). The Lord of Language.
29 | Joshi: Introduction, p. 12.
30 | Entry for »incantation« in: Oxford English Dictionary Online (21.10.16).
31 | Stewart: Reading Voices, p. 28.

narrator-protagonist, who is the text's main focaliser-auscultator.[32] Having come to Paris to study medicine, he runs into his boyhood friend Haco Harfager, and the two unattached young men decide to share a house. While relating a few case studies of mental illness linked to noise, the protagonist refers several times to »the great Carot« (53). Whether or not this is a thinly veiled allusion to ›the great Charcot‹,[33] he presents himself as a keen student of neurology. Meanwhile, his friend – unmarried, childless and living with a man – is last youngest member of an ancient family and an amateur historian, who spends his time »rapt back into the past« (54).

One evening, Haco drags an old chronicle off the shelf, which tells a tale of original violence from the late 14th century, committed by Sweyn Harfager against his brother Harold on the family's native island in the Shetlands. This is the story-within-the-story that connects the two parts of *The House of Sounds*. Coveting Harold's wife, Sweyn cuts off his brother's ears, stabs him, throws him into the sea, weds his widow, and commissions a house to be built during the couple's prolonged absence. Without the new master's knowledge, the architect and his crew are drowned during their journey to the Shetlands. When the couple returns from their journey, they find the old castle destroyed and a new house, made entirely of brass, built on the island of Rayba. Despite the suspicion that Harold or his ghost might have constructed the uncanny mansion with malicious intent by, the newlyweds move in and their heirs have lived there ever since. The chronicle ends by quoting the curse which has been put on the »House« of Harfager in both senses of the word ›house‹: »upon all who dwell there falleth a wicked madness and a lecherous anguish; and that by way of the ears do they drinck the cup of the furie of the earless Harold, till the time of the House be ended«. (56-57) Haco confesses to his friend that the ancestral seat, even from a great distance, emits a siren's song, a call to return, which he finds increasingly hard to resist. When the narrator-protagonist has to leave Paris for a while, Haco, seemingly mortally afraid, begs him to stay to prevent the house's uncanny power

---

32 | The term ›auscultator‹, developed as an equivalent to the well established ›focaliser‹, has been coined by Melba Cuddy-Keane, who first used it in her article on »Virginia Woolf, Sound Technologies and the New Aurality« and expanded it in »Modernist Soundscapes and the Intelligent Ear«.

33 | The neurologist Jean-Martin Charcot was made professor at the University of Paris in 1872. From 1879 onwards, he gave public lectures and had been teaching at the Salpêtrière, as the first chair of »maladies du système nerveux«, for four years by the time *Vaila*, the first version of *The House of Sounds*, was written in 1886. His Tuesday-lectures had been available to the reading public for over twenty years when Shiel finished *The House of Sounds*. Micale: The Salpetrière in the Age of Charcot, p. 709.

from forcing him to return to Rayba. Despite this plea, the narrator leaves and, upon his return, finds Haco gone.

Part two of *The House of Sounds*, set twelve years later, commences with a letter. On the occasion of his mother's death Haco invites his friend for a visit to Rayba. Honouring it, the protagonist travels to the Shetlands. During the few days of his sojourn in the brazen mansion he is tortured by incessant pandemonium. When a gigantic storm hits the island, he discovers that the house is not actually fixed to the rock but sits loosely on a central column. Driven by the force of the gale, it snaps the chains that kept it in place for five hundred years and begins to rotate around its brazen axis. While the noises created by the tempest, the ocean, the waterfall nearby, the rain and, the turning house itself build up in a huge crescendo, the narrator-protagonist witnesses the extinction of the last members of the Harfager family. As the house sinks into the North Sea, dragging the insane Haco and the corpses of his mother and aunt down with it, the protagonist manages a narrow escape.

RAYBA: ISLAND OF NOISES

In *The Tempest*, Shakespeare's Caliban tells the shipwrecked newcomers to Sycorax's island: »Be not afeard«, assuring them that they will encounter »[s]ounds and sweet airs, that give delight and hurt not«. In contrast to Caliban, who claims to happily behold »twangling instruments«, which »hum around mine ears«,[34] the protagonist of *The House of Sounds* finds himself fiercely attacked by the tumultuous noises which surround and inhabit Rayba.

Particularly the passages that describe the narrator-auscultator's approach to the island are a good example of the »poetic function«[35] of literary language, described by Roman Jakobson in a classic piece of criticism. More recently, Philip Nel has referred to »choosing particular words because of their sound and look« as producing »language as sculpture«,[36] the aim of which is to »create visual and aural connection«, so the words »look [...] balanced on the page and sound [...] harmonious to the ear«.[37] Shiel's narrator, too, chooses his words with great care, based on how they look and sound. Nel's metaphor however, suggests solidity and stability, explicitly stressing its »balanced« and »harmonious« effects. By contrast in *The House of Sounds* the look and sound of words is carefully selected and set at odds with each

---

34 | All quotations from Shakespeare: The Tempest, III.2, 138-141. For an analysis of noise in *The Tempest*, see Ina Schabert's article in this volume.
35 | Jakobson: Linguistics and Poetics, p. 27.
36 | Nel: Don DeLillo's Return to Form, pp. 738, 739 and 749.
37 | Ibid., p. 749.

other with the effect of creating a *dis*harmonious noise and a *loss* of balance. Discussing the aesthetics of fin de siècle literature of horror, a period and genre of which Shiel's work forms part, Suzanne Navarette has coined the term »lacquered language«.³⁸ Without a doubt the kind of aesthetic perfection achieved by superior craftsmanship foregrounded by her metaphor can be detected in Shiel's writing. Its connotation of layers of inflexible, mirroring smoothness, however, fails to capture the chaotic, dynamic vortex the sounds in this short story produce, and the effect of vertigo they achieve.

To understand how the sound *of* Shiel's short story is manipulated to reproduce for the reader the effect the sound *in* the text has on the narrator-protagonist, attention needs to be paid to phonemic details. As demonstrated above, the early fragment *About Me* already plays with vowel sounds to form assonances and alliterations. In order to achieve what I – instead of using Nel's »language as sculpture« or Navarette's »lacquered language« – would like to call the ›whirling language‹ of *The House of Sounds*, one vowel starts shifting into another, and then into another, while consonants are pressed into service as well:

*Ray*ba [...] was the centre of quite a ne*st* of those *rösts* (eddies) and cross-curren*ts* which the tidal wave *hurls* with complicated *swirl*ings among all the islands: but at *Ray*-ba they *ran* with more than usual *angr*iness [...]. We came sufficiently close to see the mane of foam which *rai*led *round* the coast-wall. Its *shock*, according to the captain, had often more than all the efficiency of artillery, tossing tons of *rock* to heights of six hundred feet upon the island. (58; italics added)

While the ›s‹ in ›nest‹ connects to the ›sts‹ in ›*rösts*‹ and the ›ts‹ in ›currents‹, the ›r‹ in ›*rösts*‹ echoes back as well as foreshadows the ›R‹ in ›Rayba‹. At the same time, the vowel sound of ›Ray‹ in the twice-mentioned ›Rayba‹ is phonemically shifted into ›ran‹, repeated in ›angriness‹, and then shifted back and picked up again by the ›rai‹ in ›railed‹. This results in a gliding motion of sound bent into a turn (/reɪ/, /reɪ/, /ran/, /æŋgrɪnɪs/, /reɪ/). That this gliding vowel sound does *not* lead back to the point of its origin (›Ray‹), and thus does *not* form a perfect circle, but instead – like in a whirl – leads around to a point at a slight distance from this origin (›rai‹), cannot be detected by the ears, but only by the eyes. This phenomenon, which linguists call a ›homophone‹ (one word-sound that can be spelled in different ways), and which is the basis of every pun, is known to music theorists as an ›enharmonic equivalent‹³⁹ (one note that can be ›spelled‹ in different ways). Each written version of a homophone produces a different meaning, but the alternative

---

38 | Navarette: The Soul of the Plot, p. 104.
39 | Entry for »enharmonic« in Oxford Music Online (21.10.16).

meaning/s continue/s to echo in the word-sound, once the written version is pronounced. In *The House of Sounds*, the fact that readers' eyes have to disagree with their ears on the question whether ›rai‹ (/reɪ/) is identical to ›Ray‹ (/reɪ/), adds to the performative effect of instability that the text subsequently intensifies to narrative vertigo, once the protagonist has set foot on the island proper.

Several of the ›whirling words‹ in the passage quoted above are not only linked by their phonemes, in assonances and alliterations, but also connected on the level of meaning: ›rösts‹ and ›cross-currents‹, ›hurls‹ and ›swirling‹, ›railed round‹ and ›tossing‹ all belong to the semantic field of motion, which is further enhanced by force, and the anthropomorphising notion of rage. Together, motion, force and rage produce a ›shock‹ the impact of which echoes back phonemically and is underlined in its intensity by the very material which it ›shocks‹ – alongside the protagonist, first person narrator and auscultator – namely ›rocks‹.

Having landed on Rayba, the nameless hero starts searching for the Harfager mansion. The house turns out to be situated in a bay, in the middle of »an amphitheatre« of rock in »the form of a Norman door« (both 59), the circumference of which is a giant waterfall:

Fancy such a *door*, half a mile wide, flat on the *ground*, the *round*ed part farthest from the sea; and all *round* it let a wall of rock *tower* perpendicular *forty* yards: and *now down* this *rounded door*-shape, and over its whole extent, let a *roar*ing ocean roll its tonnage in *hoary fury*. (59; italics added)

Once again, phonemic connections created by alliteration and assonance abound. While ›fancy‹, ›forty‹, and ›fury‹ share initial and final phonemes, the first vowel sound of ›fan-cy‹ /æ/ is homophonic with the first vowel sound in ›flat‹. All the italicised words, however, share their tail-phoneme /i/ with ›hoary‹ which, in turn, is connected through its vowel sound /ɔː/ with ›roar‹, ›door‹ and the ›for‹ in ›forty‹. Introduced by the half-rhyme ›mile wide‹, the following combination of eye-rhyming consonance and alliteration in ›part farthest from‹, the dominant group of homophones in this quote, is formed by ›ground‹, ›rounded‹, ›round‹, ›tower‹, ›now‹, ›down‹ and, again, ›rounded‹, with elements of two properly rhyming combinations (›all‹, ›wall‹ and ›whole‹, ›roll‹) scattered amongst them.

Behind all this ›whirling‹ and grouping of sounds lies a contradiction. In the *histoire*, on the level of events happening in the story, the auscultator-protagonist perceives some unstructured, chaotic sounds produced by uncontrolled as well as uncontrollable forces. In fact, according to Hermann Helmholtz's study *On The Sensations of Tone*, first published in 1863, »the soughing, howling, and whistling of the wind, the splashing of water«⁴⁰ are some of the paradigmatic sounds defined as natural ›noises‹. Meanwhile on the level of *discours* the same character, in his capacity as the story's narrator, performs a meticulous grouping and calculated ›whirling‹ of sounds (manifest in rhymes, half-rhymes, eye-rhymes, alliterations and assonances), which can only be described as the result of vigorous control over the narration. With the help of this contradiction of incalculable chaos and rigorous control, indeed in its production of an *impression* of *chaos* through a *performance* of *control*, Shiel's short story provides an example how literature positions itself between these two poles, thereby also destabilising the dichotomy between ›meaningful‹ and ›meaningless‹ sounds that defines the acoustic field. It does so by deliberately employing a technique of structuring its phonotext in order to produce the very icon of unstructured sound. Meanwhile, these noise-producing phonemic and metric patterns of ›sound whirling‹ in *The House of Sounds* combine with and support the text's equally carefully constructed semantics of vertigo.

Vertigo

S.T. Joshi's general suggestion that Shiel's writing achieves a crossover from the level of the diegesis to that of text-reader communication is certainly true for *The House of Sounds*, and he is also correct in implying that this crossover's success has everything to do with sound. At the same time, as I argued above, it is hard to concur that the effect of Shiel's style is best described as »incantatory«. Instead, I want to suggest, the phonemic patterns in *The House of Sounds* seem to be aiming for a ›vertiginous‹ effect, a narrative dizziness that tries to transmit the protagonist's feeling of losing firm ground both – physically and psychologically – to the level of narration and, thus, to the reader. By creating relations between words, syllables and single phonemes, which form a concatenation of incomplete circles, or ›whirls‹, in which sounds slide and shift and bend and almost return, Shiel's textual techniques re-create the protagonist's loss of balance, a classically gothic sense of disorientation, for the reader. It is significant that while the characters in the fictional world are attacked through their very organ of balance – their inner ears – the texts reenacts this by appealing to the reader's ›inner‹ ear, i.e. the one that perceives the »phonotext«, even while reading silently, using what Stewart calls »endophony«.⁴¹

---

40 | Helmholtz: On the Sensations of Tone, p. 7.
41 | Stewart: Reading Voices, p. 28.

The House of Sounds, however, not only manipulates phonemic structure. Occasionally, it also messes with metre. There is one particularly beautiful example, not long after the protagonist has entered the brazen mansion for the first time and remarks: »Wáter, wáter wás the wórld – a níghtmare ón my bréast« (60, stresses added). As the accents indicate, these two short phrases are metrically stable: four feet of regular trochee are followed by a clear caesura and then by another four feet of regular iamb. Partly because of this and partly due to the reference to water, they echo one of the best-known stanzas of English Romantic poetry. All the stylistic means Shiel's line employs (number of feet, caesura, semantic field) evoke Samuel Taylor Coleridge's »The Rime of the Ancient Mariner« (1797/98) as an intertext.

> Water, water, every where,
> And all the boards did shrink;
> Water, water, every where,
> Nor any drop to drink.[42]

Helped along further by the fact that the iamb is the metre to which the English language lends itself most easily, Shiel's line creates reader expectation. In this case, the expectation that the metric pattern established at this moment is going to be repeated in the next phrase, and will, eventually, lead up to a rhyme, thus continuing to echo Coleridge's ballad. But at this very moment, Shiel's prose not only refuses rhyme and changes rhythm, but gives up metric structure altogether, segueing from poetry back into prose:

> Water, water was the world – a nightmare on my breast, a desire to gasp for breath, a tingling on my nerves, a sense of being infinitely drowned and buried in boundless deluges; [...] the feeling of giddiness, too, increased [...]. (60)

Of course it is possible to claim that Shiel's text is merely clumsy, here. Given the continued ›whirling of sounds‹,[43] which indicates how carefully his prose is constructed on the phonemic level however, this is not a terribly satisfying assumption. What seems more likely is that this moment of ›metric stumbling‹ is deliberate; purposefully planted as a kind of ›rhythmic noise‹. As such, the breach of metre does more than merely re-affirm that, despite all its techniques pinched from poetry, *The House of Sounds* is a piece of prose. By establishing a metric pattern and reader expectation, and then deliberately breaking through both, the text disrupts the reader's breathing patterns, ›trips her/him up‹, causes confusion. In other words, Shiel's short story uses

---

42 | Coleridge: The Rime of the Ancient Mariner, p. 242.
43 | ›breast‹ – ›breath‹, ›drowned‹ – ›boundless‹, ›feeling‹ – ›giddiness‹ – ›increased‹.

syntax to mess further with the reader's sense of orientation and control – which had already destabilised by ›sound whirling‹ –, moving his/her another step along towards sharing the protagonist's experience of ›giddiness‹. Both phonemic and metric techniques thus combine to support the story's narrative of dizziness. The semantic level is next.

Already at the first visual contact with Rayba, the protagonist has »the impression of some *spinning* motion of the island«, which he rationalises as »due probably to the swirling movement of the water« (58). After he has stepped ashore, though, the feeling of dizziness does not go away:

We affected [sic] a landing [...] I began to climb the island. [...] [D]uring the night in the boat, I had been aware of a booming in the ears for which even the roar of the sea around the coast seemed insufficient to account; and this now, as we went on, became immensely augmented – and with it, once more, that conviction with me of *spinning* motions. (58, italics in the original)

Instead of a regaining a sense of balance, the protagonist experiences increased disorientation as he makes his way across firm land. Attacked every now and then by »a singular sickness of giddiness« (59), he arrives at the Harfager mansion where he finds Haco haunted by even worse fits of dizziness:

He himself, indeed, confessed to me his own [...] proneness to paroxysms of *vertigo*. I was startled! For I had myself shortly previously been roused out of sleep by feelings of reeling and nausea; and an assurance that the room furiously flew round me. The impression passed away, and I attributed it, perhaps hastily, to some disturbance of the nerve-endings of »**the labyrinth**«, or inner ear. In Harfager, however, the conviction of whirling motions in the house, in the world, got to so horrible a degree of certainty, that its effects sometimes resembled those of lunacy or energumenal possession. Never, he said, was the sensation of giddiness altogether dead in him; seldom the sensation that he gazed with stretched-out arms over the brink of abysms which wooed his half-consenting foot. Once, as we walked, he was hurled as by unearthly powers to the ground, and there for an hour sprawled, bathed in sweat, with distraught bedazzlement and **amaze** in his stare, which watched the racing walls. (63, italics in the original, bold print added)

Although it no longer dominates, ›sound whirling‹ as a narrative technique that produces disorientation continues in this passage, to intensify the semantics of vertigo. The rather unusual noun »amaze«, which refers to »loss of one's wits, mental stupefication, craze«, »bewilderment, mental confusion«, »loss of presence of mind through terror, panic« or »extreme astonishment, wonder«,⁴⁴ is not only linked semantically to the (failing) organ of balance, it also harkens back to it phonemically. After all a »labyrinth«, otherwise known ›a maze‹, is not only a part of the inner ear responsible for the sense of balance, but also the paradigmatic space designed to make one lose one's bearings.

Moving on from rationalising his dizziness as caused by external factors, such as »the swirling movement of the water« (58), to attributing it to internal ones, the protagonist speaks of his own »paroxysms of *vertigo*« in terms of »feelings«, »assurance« and »impression«, attributing the information his body produces that »the floor furiously fl[ies] around« to a disorder in his labyrinth. For the much more seriously afflicted Haco, vertigo is not only a »sensation« but a »conviction« characterised by »certainty« that marks him as having crossed into »lunacy« and »possession«. His sense of »whirling motions« spreads far beyond the immediate surroundings, is attributed to »unearthly« forces and, as »wooed [...] half-consenting foot« suggests, invested with seductive power that tempts Haco to give in to the temptation of vertigo and letting himself fall.

Sigrid Nieberle, too, investigates such link between seduction and vertigo in *FrauenMusikLiteratur*, her study on nineteenth-century German women writers. One of its sub-chapters discusses the autobiographically inspired epistolary novel *Die Günderode* (1840), which celebrates Bettine von Arnim's homoerotically charged friendship with the poet Caroline von Günderode.⁴⁵ During the correspondence, the two principal characters' discourse takes on a seductive quality. As Nieberle shows, this is tied to vertigo by the reversal of an old *topos* of instruction. Usually, the metaphor for a (male-male) didactic relationship, ›gradus ad Parnassum‹,⁴⁶ invokes a path that leads uphill. Bettine and Caroline re-define it as a form of guidance on a »downward gradient«, as two women take turns in helping each other down the dizzying slope of understanding the relation between music and language.⁴⁷

Two points, here, are illuminating for a reading of *The House of Sounds*. First, that vertigo in the mid-19th century, as Nieberle shows, continues to be understood to be a heavily gendered condition, since women were thought to be, by nature, more prone to dizziness than men.⁴⁸ I would claim that this

---

44 | Entry for »amaze« in: Oxford English Dictionary Online (21.10.16).
45 | Nieberle: FrauenMusikLiteratur.
46 | More specifically, this is the title of a textbook on counterpoint published in 1725 by the composer and musical theoriest Johann Joseph Fux.
47 | My translation. Nieberle's original reads: »Der ›gradus ad Parnassum‹ führt in vorliegendem Fall nach unten und nicht nach oben [...]«. Nieberle: FrauenMusikLiteratur, p. 71.
48 | Nieberle offers proof for this by quoting Marcus Herz's *Versuch über den Schwindel*.

gendering is still active in the culture that forms the backdrop for Shiel's tale. It has the effect that the two male protagonists, one of whom threatens to ›lead‹ the other ever downwards, are characterised by their very vertigo as effeminate and – according to fin de siècle discourse that sees vertigo as a collective problem – thus as degenerates.[49] Max Nordau, one of the most influential proponents of degeneration as a cultural theory, even makes the connection between vertigo and a particular kind of literature:

> In English fiction ghost-stories have begun to occupy a large place [...] a society has been formed which has for its object the collecting of ghost-stories, and testing their authenticity; and even literary men of renown have been seized with the vertigo of the supernatural, and condescend to serve as vouchers for the most absurd aberrations.[50]

Although *The House of Sounds* is not a straightforward ghost-story, it is a literary example of »the vertigo of the supernatural« and there is no doubt that Shiel is one of the authors Nordau sees as pursuing a ›gradus ad Parnassum‹ that leads them ever *down*ward – meant, this time, as a judgment of morals as well as literary quality –, as they »condescend« to pen »absurd aberrations«.

The second point made by Nieberle that enriches an interpretation of vertigo in *The House of Sounds* goes back to Shiel's phonemic manipulations, that is, to the narrative technique to which I have referred above as ›sound whirling‹. In German the word for vertigo happens to be a special case of homophone, since ›Schwindel‹ is a homonym that also denotes ›fraud‹. In von Armin's novel, one of Caroline's letters puns on this double meaning. Commenting on enharmonic equivalents in music, she claims they produce disorientation in the listener through the kind of ›fraud‹ that allows a musician the shift from one musical key into another.[51] Exactly like Shiel's ›whirling‹ of sounds, this shift in musical key (or ›meaning‹) is immediately apparent to the eye – that is, in musical notation – while it remains undetectable by the ear until the following notes make it apparent.[52]

In the introductory chapter of her study on the cultural history of dizziness, *Versuch über den Schwindel*, Christina von Braun characterises the ›vertiginous subject‹ as symptomatic of the mid-19th century: »The term ›vertigo‹

---

49 | »All the symptoms enumerated are the consequences of states of fatigue and exhaustion, and these, again, are the effect of contemporary civilisation, of the vertigo and whirl of our frenzied life [...].« Nordau: Degeneration, p. 42.
50 | Ibid., p. 214.
51 | Nieberle: FrauenMusikLiteratur, p. 72.
52 | »Der ›enharmonische Schwindel‹, den Bettine betreibt, so formuliert Caroline in einem ihrer vernünftlerischen Briefe (BvA, S. 405), ist poetologisches Konzept in diesem Spiel um Musik, Sprache und Geschlecht [...].« Ibid., p. 71.

condenses hi/stories about the self's fragility, about a failing of the senses and a suffering from dizziness, only to arrive at an enjoyment of vertigo, which is a product of techniques of space as much as of techniques of simulation – the performed swindle.«[53] Florian Rötzer, on whom von Braun relies as a source on self-loss in late twentieth century emersion culture, clothes the cultural relish of vertigo in more psychoanalytic terms: »The trauma [of falling] turns into wish fulfilment, the very vertigo, which drags us into the deep, and which according to Kierkegaard can reveal freedom to us, can be experienced as pleasure.«[54] Shiel's story, I contend, needs to be read as positioned within a genealogy of literary texts that dedicate themselves to representing the suffering from dizziness as delightful.

In *The House of Sounds*, fragility, failing sensual perception, loss of orientation, which threatens to erase the subject, are all part of the characters' vertiginous experience on Rayba. The irony of Haco's unstable relationship with the boundaries of space – the ground to which he is repeatedly »hurled« by his vertigo, yet which he feels falling away from him unless he is »sprawled« against it; and the walls that seem to be »racing« (all 63) – lies in the foreshadowing. Once the storm breaks the chains, which attach the house to the bedrock, and once the agitated sea starts spinning the castle on its central axis, the walls *are*, of course, racing. And once the ancestral seat sinks into the North Sea, the ground *does* fall away from the last Harfager. Shiel's story thus externalises its hero's vertigo staging a gigantic maelstrom that drags him into the deep. Before the mansion goes down, however, the text also knits together intense pain and enjoyment in typically decadent fashion. Not only in the dizziness experienced by both main characters but in a second aural condition, which Haco presents during the last few days before the fall of the house of Harfager.

---

53 | My translation. Just like Caroline in *Die Günderode*, von Braun draws on the pun permitted by the homonymic German word for ›vertigo‹. The original reads: »Im Begriff des ›Schwindels‹ verdichtet sich eine Geschichte, die von der Fragilität des Selbst, vom Schwinden der Sinne und vom erlittenen Schwindel erzählt, um schließlich bei einer Lust am Schwindel anzukommen, die sich den Techniken der Eroberung des Raums wie denen der Simulation – des verübten Schwindels – verdankt.« von Braun: Versuch über den Schwindel, p. 33.

54 | My translation. The original reads: »Das Trauma wird zur Wunscherfüllung, der Schwindel, der uns in die Tiefe zieht und der uns nach Kierkegaard die Freiheit offenbart, kann als Lust erlebt werden.« Ibid., p. 32.

Oxyecoia: Decadence »By way of the ears«

Haco, despite being »somewhat deaf«, is characterised from the start as »liable to a thousand delights at certain sounds«. Some of the sources of these pleasures are conventional enough – like »the note of a bird« –, even if the degree of delight they cause seems unusual. Other sources of Haco's auditory pleasure, like »the whine of a door« (all 54), are less common. The very first sentence of *The House of Sounds* already forge an explicit connection between abnormal hearing and »mind-malady« (53), as the narrator shares three neurological case histories, reported by his teacher Carot, with his friend.

In the first case, a young girl apparently[55] diagnosed with hysteria reports she can hear »*the sound of the world*« as the earth turns around its own axis while circling the sun. »Within six months«, the narrator comments, »she was as mad as a March-hare« (53, italics in the original). The second case is that of a young man, who, after excessive reading of political pamphlets, goes insane because he cannot bear »the rushing shriek of being« (54) any longer. The third case is that of a man who claimed to be able to hear the chemical composition of two metal rods as they were struck against each other, and »[h]im also did the Harpies snatch aloft« (54). In all three medical tales madness is presented as the final outcome to which privileged, seemingly impossible, knowledge derived through superhuman hearing inevitably leads. Unsought information enters the three patients aurally, and is translated into knowledge at the cost of their mental equilibrium, the loss of which eventually destroys the hearers. These case stories open the frame that Haco's knowledge about the destruction of his ancient house – in the double sense of ›mansion‹ and ›genealogy‹ – closes. While he is still in Paris, he, too, gains knowledge through hearing that which he should not be able to hear. In this case it is his castle's hall-sized ›clock‹, a countdown built into the structure of the house that has been ›ticking away‹ for centuries hundreds of miles away, which ›calls him‹ back to Rayba. And Haco, too, eventually loses his mind, penetrated by the medieval curse, like the rest of his family, »by way of the ears«. (57) When it is fulfilled, the last three Harfagers share the fate of the three patients the narrator had introduced at the beginning of the tale as examples of pathological hyperaurality.

The term *oxyecoia*, first mentioned on the second page of *The House of Sounds* in connection with the reported medical cases, is derived from *oxys*, the Greek word for ›sharp‹ and *akoe*, meaning ›sensitivity‹. It is a medical condition defined as »abnormal acuteness of hearing«, »excessive sensitivity

---

55 | At least if »the Great Carot«, who treats her as one of the cases »of which he was such a master«, is indeed a reference to Jean-Martin Charcot.

to sounds«,[56] particularly of low frequency, or »acoustic hyperesthesia«.[57] The link Shiel's story makes to insanity is taken up again as the protagonist first sets foot in the brazen house. This time, he is not cast in the role of the observing medical student but as an afflicted party:

> I seemed to stand in the centre of some yelling planet, the row resembling the resounding of many thousand of cannon, punctuated by strange crashing and breaking uproar. And a madness descended on me; I was near to tears. (60)

The narrator-auscultator's impression upon having entered the eponymous 14th century Harfager mansion harkens back to medieval cosmology, seemingly indicating the degeneration of the Pythagorean harmony of the spheres.[58] Not only has the *musica universalis* been replaced here by anthropomorphised (»yelling«) noise, the listening subject's position, too, has changed dramatically. According to ancient geocentric cosmology, the earth was *surrounded* by the heavenly bodies, which produced a celestial form of acoustic order between them. In Shiel's own early fragment *About me*, the noisy forces of nature are *outside* the house and wink at the newly-born future author through the window. In *The House of Sounds*, by contrast, the hearing subject feels as if he were *inside* an astronomic body that is itself the source of noise. The scenario has changed from a background of distant harmony to friendly contact by potentially dangerous powers to terrifying entrapment without hope of escape. A second metaphor in the short passage above describes the noise inside the house through a hyperbolical reference to war, which in itself is a classic *topos* for historians and theoreticians of noise.[59] »[M]any thousand of cannon« is, on the one hand, an oddly archaic expression; on the other, the sound of canons is not only typical of the soundscape of warfare around the turn of the century, but actually reminiscent of fantasies formulated only a couple of years after the final version of *The House of Sounds* was published.

---

56 | Both Oxford English Dictionary Online (21.10.16).

57 | Reuter: Springer Medical Dictionary, p. 406.

58 | As a philosophical concept it was credited with epistemological reach since antiquity and referred to until well into the mid-19th century. The OED lists Dante Gabriel Rossetti's »On the Site of a Mulberry-Tree, planted by William Shakespeare, felled by Rev. F. Gastrell« (1853) as the most recent literary reference to the »music of the spheres«, entry for »sphere«, Oxford English Dictionary Online (21.10.16).

59 | For the intimate connection between noise and war see the work of Jacques Attali, Philip Schweighauser and Steve Goodman. The latter comments extensively on the »politics of frequency« and ensuing »production, transmission, and mutation of affective tonality«. Goodman: Sonic Warfare, p. xv.

When Luigi Russolo sketched his »Futurist Manifesto: The Art of Noises« in 1913, he made the argument that ›noise-sound‹ was supposed to extend the all too limited sonic repertoire of Western classical music. Not only was noise going to be accepted as the adequate form of modern artistic expression. It was, in future, to be considered as a source of aesthetic appreciation. This step into modernity[60] seems beyond the scope of Shiel's gothic tale. Yet the gothic tale does present a positive take on noise by characterising this painful path to »madness« and »tears« as pleasurable to Haco, as a mix of disturbance and delight Russolo might have appreciated. As the protagonist enters the mansion the short story stages a scenario in which the futurists might have revelled, since its noises are a choice selection from what Russolo was going to categorise as »6 *families of noises*«.[61]

Apart from the noises associated with a »yelling planet« and the mechanical explosion like a thousand cannons' »row«, what is perceived as sending the protagonist, like his friend, towards madness is the »strange crashing and breaking uproar«, which »punctuates« the general din. The house, after all, is made of brass and thus acts as a giant percussion instrument. To borrow Anthony Moore's term it is an »inharmonic metallophone«,[62] which intensifies the noises of the rain, the rising storm and the increasingly agitated sea. While the plot unleashes the amplified cacophony of the storm's natural noises, which the resonator-house turns into cultural ones, the intricate ›sound whirling‹ on the level of narration continues.[63] From this moment on, the diegetic noise never lets up again, but steadily increases in intensity throughout the story's last eleven pages.

Oxyecoia is referred to for the third time when the protagonist describes what is happening to his friend. Haco has been permanently exposed to the brazen mansion's sonic environment for the last twelve years, and displays

---

[60] | Russolo projects that contemporary and future humans take pleasure in noise, due to their ›modernly‹ educated ears: »Today, Noise is triumphant and reigns sovereign over the sensibility of men. [...] But our ear takes pleasure in it, since it is already educated to modern life, so prodigal in different Noises«. Russolo: The Art of Noises, pp. 10-11.

[61] | »1. Roars, Thunderings, Explosions, Hissing roars, Bangs, Booms; 2. Whistling, Hissing, Puffing; 3. Whispers, Murmurs, Mumbling, Muttering, Gurgling; 4. Screeching, Creaking, Rustling, Humming, Crackling, Rubbing; 5. Noises obtained by beating on metal, woods, skins, stones, pottery etc.; 6. Voices of animals and people, Shouts, Screams, Shrieks, Wails, Hoots, Howls, Death rattles, etc.«. Ibid., p. 13.

[62] | Moore made this point while discussing a presentation at the conference »noise - geräusch - bruit: Medien und Kultur unstrukturierter Laute«, held in 2012 at the Friedrich-Alexander-University of Erlangen-Nürnberg.

[63] | »[D]welling« - »yelling«; »row‹ - »resembling‹ - »resounding‹; »near to tears‹.

symptoms, which the narrator diagnoses as the result of a permanent ear inflammation or »a *tinnitus* infinitely sick« (63). Early on in the text it is suggested that Haco might already be mad in Paris and that his hearing of the castle clock's ticking is an auditory hallucination. Now the protagonist considers the »morbid state of his hearing« (63), a mechanical hearing problem, as the original cause and Haco's madness the effect of Rayba's incessant noise.

> When I passionately shouted that I could gather no fragment of sound from his moving mouth, he clapped both his palms to his ears [...]. Once more he clapped his palms to his ears; then wrote: »Do not shout: no whisper in any part of the building is inaudible to me«. (60-61)

The loudest of places, where culturally amplified natural noises drown out words spoken nearby for the less afflicted protagonist, is where not the slightest sound is lost to Haco; and not *despite* the high level of ambient noise but *because* of it. When Harfager indicates that his friend's shouting over the sound wall[64] causes him acute pain, this prompts the student of neurology to cite yet another medical precedent and diagnosis:

> I named the disease to him as the »Paracusis Wilisü« [sic]. When he frowned dissent, I, quite undeterred, proceeded to relate the case (that had occurred within my own experience) of a very deaf lady who could hear the drop of a pin in a railway*[65] train. (63)

Haco's »paradoxical deafness«[66] is mixed up in the text with symptoms of other medical conditions. That »blood frequently guttered from his ears« (69) seems to indicate ruptured eardrums caused by an abrupt penetration of the tympani by extreme pressure. Yet the emphasis of Shiel's story is not on physical trauma inflicted by sudden noise but on the slow psychological progression toward madness caused by a permanent level of noise maintained

---

64 | Schafer: The Tuning of the World, p. 96.

65 | The asterisk is part of the original text and leads to a footnote that reads: »Such cases are known to many medical men. The concussion of the deaf nerve is the cause of the acquired sensitiveness; nor is there any limit to that sensitiveness when the tumult is immensely augmented.« (63).

66 | »Paracusis Willisii«, a symptom of tinnitus, is named after the 17th century physician Thomas Willis and also known as »false paracusis« or »paradoxical deafness«. For a medical discussion see Sullivan and Hodges: Paracusis Willisii. It is defined as »the ability to hear sounds better in a noisy environment [...] because the patient is not able to hear the background noise but can hear the voices raised above it.« Carruth: Ear, Nose and Throat, p. 142, quoted in entry for »paracusis«, Oxford English Dictionary Online (21.10.16).

over years. Before his death Haco confesses that there is a dimension of intense enjoyment to his suffering:

»[T]o be in love with pain – to pine after aching – is not that a wicked madness?« [...] He then spoke of a prospect at the terror of which his whole soul trembled, yet which sometimes laughed in his heart in the form of a *hope*. It was the prospect of any considerable increase in the volume of sound about his ears. At *that*, he said, the brain must totter. On the night of my arrival the noise of my boots and, since then, my voice, occasionally raised, had produced acute pain in him. To such an ear, I understood him to say, the luxury of torture involved in a large sound-increase around was an allurement from which no human virtue could turn. (66)

Phrases like »to be in love with pain«, »pine after aching« and »luxury of torture« this passage marks *The House of Sounds* as part of the decadent literary tradition and its glamorous perversions. Immediately after its publication Joris Karl Huysman's *À Rebours* (1884) had been translated into English, published as both *Against Nature* and *Against the Grain*, and greeted by Arthur Symonds as the »beviary of decadence«.[67] Its protagonist, Count Floressas des Esseintes, cultivates a philosophy according to which art is superior to life, life imitates art, and art, in turn, simulates nature in a state of sickness, reaching back to Baudelaire's beauty of rotting corpses in *Les Fleurs du Mal* (1857). First and foremost, however, Algernon Swinburne's ecstatically masochistic lyrical I in »Dolores (Notre Dame des Septs Douleurs)«[68] springs to mind as a literary predecessor for Haco. By exposing the ear as an erotic organ susceptible to the decadent enjoyment of pain caused by the violent aural penetration through noise, Shiel's story adds a sonic turn to English decadence, which is absent from its intertexts. As a late addition to the genealogy of the aestheticist tradition, *The House of Sounds* provides the link between fin de siècle cult of the beautifully disgusting, the pleasurably painful and Russolo's pre-WW I fantasy of the role noises were going to play in modernity.

In Shiel's story the feverishly anticipated »sound-increase« is finally provided by the breaking rainstorm, which causes the waterfall that surrounds the mansion to swell. As the din without reaches its climax and »the greatly augmented baritone of the cataract« assumes »a fresh character – a shrillness – the whistle of rapture – a malice [...]« (70), it is joined by »a queer sound – a crash« (71) from within the house, as a demented servant seizes two brass shields and starts »dashing them viciously together« (71). It is this combination of the »roaring and screeching chaos around« caused by the »cry of the now redoubled cataract, mixed with the mass and majesty of the now

---

[67] | Cevasco: The Breviary of Decadence, p. ix.
[68] | Originally published in *Poems and Ballads* in 1866.

climactic tempest [that] took on too intentional a *shriek* to be longer tolerable to any reason« and the servant's »grisly cymbaling«, which brings Haco's »auditory fever« (all 71, italics in the original) to a crisis. Fittingly for a text obsessed with imagining degeneration as a hearing problem, the improvised »cymbals« are medieval shields, presumably bearing family crests. In any case, they harken back to the family curse that destroys the Harfagers »by way of the ears«. While the destabilising narrative technique of ›sound whirling‹ seems to be drowned out by the din of the text's plot-crescendo, it nevertheless continues to operate in the background. After all, these »cymbals« are ›symbols‹ of the House (mansion/family) that is now going down as Haco, whose aural apparatus is in a state of permanent inflammation, falls prey to the temptation of giving in to the delicious agony caused by the noise.

Conclusion

If M. P. Shiel's early fragment *About me* imagines a scene of origin as productively noisy, *The House of Sounds* conjures up his fantasy of eschatological destruction as pandemonium. As a late addition to English decadence, the short story presents degeneration as a problem of hypersensitive hearing. Imagining the pathologically afflicted ear as the privileged site at which noise, impossible knowledge and madness intersect it stages the masochistic enjoyment of painful pleasure and pleasurable pain as a result of violent aural penetration.

The House of Sounds makes an effort to characterise Haco and, to a lesser degree, his friend the narrator-protagonist as ›effeminate degenerates‹ by taking up notions that have been highlighted by scholarship on vertigo as a cultural concept from the mid-19th century onwards. Sigrid Nieberle has drawn attention to the gendering of vertigo and to its close connection with disorientation in music created by enharmonic equivalents as a kind of semiotic ›fraud‹. Christina von Braun has emphasised the link between vertigo as a source of pleasure and an indicator for a symptomatic fragility of the self the simulation of which becomes a pressing topic towards the end of the century. Florian Rötzer has stressed for late 20th century emersion culture that dizziness is the privileged signifier for trauma turned delight, as the experience of being dragged into the deep is deliberately sought out. Interlocking noise, vertigo and tinnitus, *The House of Sounds* activates all of these cultural *topoi*, which confirms the cultural space Shiel's story occupies by bringing the gothic narrative tradition right up to the brink of modernity.

In addition I hope to have shown that *The House of Sounds* performs a meticulous manipulation of its »phonotext«.[69] The impression of unstructured sound in the diegesis is the result of extremely controlled prose. Existing terminology, it was argued, fails to capture the vertiginous effect of Shiel's narrative technique: Philip Nel's notion of »language as sculpture«[70] was rejected for its connotations of stability and durability; Susanne Navarette's description of fin de siècle prose as »lacquered language«[71] for its shiny rigidity; and T. S. Joshi's take on Shiel's own prose as having an »incantatory effect upon the reader«[72] for its magical associations. Instead, this article proposed to think of *The House of Sounds* as characterised by its ›whirling‹ of sounds. Understood as a narrative technique, it operates through phonemes and rhythms: producing gliding (from sound to identical sound in a different word) and bending (from sound to a similar but not identical one in a different word); and disturbing expectations of rhythm that ›trip up‹ the reader's endophonic reader or disrupt rhythms of breathing. Understood as an effect, ›whirling sounds‹ are at the core of Shiel's narrative of dizziness, through which the characters' loss of balance and orientation are translated into the reader's experience of language-induced vertigo; a feeling of reeling that might dish out discomfort as well as delight.

BIBLIOGRAPHY

Attali, Jacques: Noise: The Political Economy of Music, Minneapolis 1985.
Bleiler, Everett Franklin: A Guide to Supernatural Fiction, Kent/OH 1983.
Bleiler, Everett Franklin: M. P. Shiel 1865–1947, in: Everett Franklin Bleiler (ed.): Science Fiction Writers, New York, 1982, pp. 31-37.
Block, Andrew: Key Books of British Authors, 1600–1922, London 1933.
Brandy, William T. and James M. Lynn: Audiologic Findings in Hyperacusic and Nonhyperacusic Subjects, in: American Journal of Audiology 4.1 (1995), pp. 46-51, DOI: 10.1044/1059-0889.0401.46.
Braun, Christina von: Versuch über den Schwindel: Religion, Schrift, Bild, Geschlecht, Zürich and München 2001.
Bulfin, Ailise: Review of: Harold Billings. M. P. Shiel: The First Biography: The Middle Years 1897–1923. Austin: Roger Beacham, 2010, in: English Literature in Transition 54.3 (2011), pp. 387-391.

---

69 | Stewart: Reading Voices, p. 28.
70 | Nel: Don DeLillo's Return to Form, p. 749.
71 | Navarette: The Soul of the Plot, p. 104.
72 | Joshi: Introduction, p. 12.

Burke, Edmund: A Philosophical Enquiry into the Origin of our Ideas of the Sublime and Beautiful, ed. by Adam Phillips, Oxford 1990.

Carruth, J. A. S.: Ear, Nose and Throat, Oxford 1986.

Cevasco, George A.: The Breviary of Decadence: J.-K. Huysman's *A Rebours* and English Literature, New York 2001.

Coleridge, Samuel Taylor: The Rime of the Ancient Mariner, in: Harold Bloom and Lionel Trilling (eds): Romantic Poetry and Prose (The Oxford Anthology of English Literature), New York et al. 1973, pp. 238-254.

Cuddy-Keane, Melba: Virginia Woolf, Sound Technologies and the New Aurality, in: Pamela L. Canghie (ed.): Virginia Woolf in the Age of Mechanical Reproduction, New York and London 2000, pp. 69-96.

Cuddy-Keane, Melba: Modernist Soundscapes and the Intelligent Ear: An Approach to Narrative Through Auditory Perception, in: James Phelon and Peter Rabinowitz (eds): A Companion to Narrative Theory, Oxford 2005, pp. 382-398.

Gawsworth, John: Obituary M. P. Shiel – Master of Fantasy, in: The Times, February 20th, 1947, http://www.alangullette.com/lit/shiel/essays/ShielObituaryTimes.htm (21.10.16).

Goodman, Steve: Sonic Warfare: Sound, Affect and the Ecology of Fear, Cambridge/MS 2010.

Gullette, Alan: An Annotated Bibliography of M. P. Shiel, http://www.alangullette.com/lit/shiel/mpsbiblio.htm (21.10.16).

Gulette, Alan: M. P. Shiel (1865–1947). The Lord of Language, http://www.alangullette.com/lit/shiel/ (21.11.16).

Helmholtz, Hermann: On the Sensations of Tone, New York 1954.

Herz, Marcus: Versuch über den Schwindel, Berlin, 1791, zweyte umgeänderte und vermehrte Auflage, https://books.google.ie/books?id=Moo_AAAAcAAJ (12.12.16).

Jakobson, Roman: Linguistics and Poetics, in: Roman Jakobson: Selected Writings Volume III: Poetry of Grammar and Grammar of Poetry, The Hague et al. 1981, pp. 18-51.

Joshi, Sunand Tryambak: Introduction, in: Matthew Phipps Shiel: The House of Sounds and others, ed. by S. T. Joshi, New York 2005, pp. 7-13.

Keats, John: The Complete Poems, ed. by John Barnard, London 1988.

Kraß, Andreas: Aschertorte. Queerer Witz bei Streeruwitz: *Partygirl* und *The Fall of the House of Usher*, in: Jörg Born et al. (eds): »Aber die Erinnerung davon«. Materialien zum Werk von Marlene Streeruwitz, Frankfurt/M. 2007, pp. 183-205.

Lovecraft, Howard Phillips: Supernatural Horror in Literature, http://www.hplovecraft.com/writings/texts/essays/shil.asp (21.10.16).

Luckhurst, Roger: Introduction, in: Roger Luckhurst (ed.): Late Victorian Gothic Tales, Oxford 2005, pp. ix–xxxi.

MacLeod, Kirsten: M. P. Shiel and the Love of Pubescent Girls: The Other »Love That Dare Not Speak Its Name«, in: English Literature in Transition, 1880–1920 51.4 (2008), pp. 355-380.
Micale, Mark S.: The Salpetrière in the Age of Charcot: An Institutional Perspective on Medical History in the Late Nineteenth Century, in: Journal of Contemporary History 20.4 (1985), pp. 703-731.
Morse, A. Reynolds: The Works of M. P. Shiel: A Study in Bibliography, Los Angeles 1948.
Moskowitz, Sam: M. P. Shiel, in: Sam Moskowitz (ed.): Explorers of the Infinite: Shapers of Science Fiction, Cleveland and New York 1963, pp. 142-156.
Mullen, Richard D.: M. P. Shiel's *The Purple Cloud*, in: Science Fiction Studies 13.4 (1977), http://www.depauw.edu/sfs/reviews_pages/r13.htm#shiel (21.10.16).
Navarette, Susan J.: The Soul of the Plot: The Aesthetics of Fin de Siècle Literature of Horror, in: George Edgar Slusser and Eric S. Rabkin (eds): Styles of Creation: Aesthetic Technique and the Creation of Fictional Worlds. Athens/GA 1992, pp. 88-113.
Nel, Philip: Don DeLillo's Return to Form: The Modernist Poetics of The Body Artist, in: Contemporary Literature 43.4 (2002), pp. 736-759.
Nieberle, Sigrid: FrauenMusikLiteratur. Deutschsprachige Schriftstellerinnen im 19. Jahrhundert, 2., verb. Aufl. Herbolzheim 2002.
Nordau, Max: Degeneration, Lincoln and London 1993 [1895].
Oxford English Dictionary, http://www.oed.com (21.10.16).
Reuter, Peter: Springer Großwörterbuch Medizin – Medical Dictionary: Deutsch-Englisch / English-German. Berlin and Heidelberg 2005.
Rimbaud, Arthur: Rimbaud Complete: Vol. I Poetry and Prose, transl. and ed. by Wyatt Mason, New York 2002.
Rushton, Julian: enharmonic, in: Oxford Music Online (21.10.16).
Russolo, Luigi: The Art of Noises: Futurist Manifesto, in: Christopher Cox and Daniel Werner (eds): Audio Culture: Readings in modern music, New York 2004, pp. 10-14.
Schafer, R. Murray: The Tuning of the World, New York 1977. Reprinted as: The Soundscape: Our Sonic Environment and the Tuning of the World, Rochester 1994.
Schweighauser, Philipp: The Noises of American Literature 1890–1985: Toward a History of a Literary Acoustics, Gainesville/TN. et al. 2006.
Shakespeare, William: The Tempest, in: William Shakespeare: The Complete Works, ed. by Stanley Wells et al., Oxford 1988, pp. 1167-1189.
Shiel, Matthew Phipps: The House of Sound, in: Matthew Phipps Shiel: The House of Sounds and others, ed. by Sunand Tryambak Joshi, New York 2005, pp. 53-73.

Squires, John D.: Rediscovering M. P. Shiel (1865–1947), http://www.alangul lette.com/lit/shiel/essays/RediscoveringMPShiel.htm (21.10.16). Originally published in: The New York Review of Science Fiction 153, 13.9 (2001), pp. 12-15.

Squires, John D.: Some Closing Thoughts on M. P. Shiel Or The Frustrations of a Putative Biographer, http://www.alangullette.com/lit/shiel/essays/SomeClosingThoughts.htm (21.10.16). Originally published as afterword in: M. P. Shiel and the Lovecraft Circle: A Collection of Primary Documents, Including Shiel's Letters to August Derleth, 1929–1946, Edited with Notes by John D. Squires, Kettering/OH 2001, pp. 103-111.

Stewart, Garrett: Reading Voices: Literature and the Phonotext, Berkeley et al. 1990.

Sullivan, Joseph A. and William E. Hodges: Paracusis Willisii, in: The Laryngoscope 62.7 (1952), pp. 678-703.

Svitavsky, William: From Decadence to Racial Antagonism: M. P. Shiel at the Turn of the Century, in: Science Fiction Studies 31.1 (2004), pp. 1-24.

Swinburne, Algernon: Dolores. Notre-Dame des Sept Douleurs, http://rpo.library.utoronto.ca/poems/dolores-notre-dame-des-sept-douleurs (21.10.16).

Vogeler, Albert R.: Shiel, Matthew Phipps (1865–1947), in: Oxford Dictionary of National Biography (21.10.16).

Wells, H. G.: The discovery of the future, New York 1913, http://archive.org/stream/discoveryoffuturo0welliala/discoveryoffuturo0welliala_djvu.txt. (21.11.16).

Young, Edward: Conjectures on original composition. In a letter to the author of Sir Charles Grandison. London, 1759, https://books.google.de/books?id=h1IJAAAAQAAJ (21.10.16).

»Ur-Geräusch«
Rilkes Betrachtungen eines Unmusikalischen

Thomas Martinec

Am 15. August 1919 entwirft Rilke in einem kleinen, zunächst titellosen Aufsatz ein Experiment, das er in einem Brief an Katharina Kippenberg als »skurril« bezeichnet.[1] Rilke schlägt vor, die Kranznaht des menschlichen Schädels, die er »Kronennaht« nennt, mit einer Phonographennadel abzutasten, um etwas zu erzeugen, das er gleichlautend als »Ton«, »Musik« und »Geräusch« bezeichnet.[2] Diesen Versuch, der darauf ausgerichtet ist, visuelle in auditive Informationen umzusetzen, macht Rilke dann zum Ausgangspunkt von Überlegungen zu einer Lyrik, die sich nicht auf einen sensitiven Bereich konzentriert, sondern sämtliche Sinne miteinander kombiniert, um so einen möglichst großen Seinsbereich zu erfassen.

Abgesehen davon, dass der von Rilke entworfene Versuch medienkritischen Klärungsbedarf zu erkennen gibt, fällt vor allem der unbekümmerte Brückenschlag zwischen »Geräusch« und »Musik« auf, mit dem Rilke, unausgesprochen freilich, die Helmholtzsche Unterscheidung zwischen »*Geräuschen* und *musikalischen Klängen*« entkräftet.[3] Was auf den ersten Blick wie eine terminologische Unschärfe oder auch Unaufmerksamkeit erscheinen mag, die mit Rilkes notorischer Unmusikalität zusammenhängen könnte, gibt bei genauerem Hinsehen eine Vorstellung zu erkennen, die nicht zuletzt an musikästhetischen Entwicklungen des frühen 20. Jahrhunderts teilhat. Rilkes Interesse an der Musik gilt in erster Linie einer lautlosen Kraft, die sich in ihr äußert, nicht aber der sinnlichen Äußerung selbst, also jenem Hörbaren, das man gemeinhin als Musik bezeichnet. Wie sich Rilke diese Kraft vorstellt und auf welche Quellen er dabei zurückgreift, wird im Einzelnen zu zeigen sein. Für die These des vorliegenden Beitrags ist zunächst

---

1 | Rilke an Kippenberg, 17.8.1919, in: Dies.: Briefwechsel, S. 369.
2 | Rilke: Ur-Geräusch, S. 702. Alle Seitenangaben im Fließtext beziehen sich auf diese Ausgabe.
3 | Helmholtz: Die Lehre von den Tonempfindungen, S. 13, Herv. i. Orig.

maßgeblich, dass Rilke einen gewissermaßen theoretischen Teil der Musik von deren sinnlich wahrnehmbarer Seite absetzt, um ihn (im Unterschied zu dieser sinnlichen Seite) für poetologische Vorstellungen fruchtbar zu machen. Die fehlende Unterscheidung zwischen Geräusch und Musik bzw., um es affirmativ zu formulieren, die Gleichschaltung von beiden ist insofern symptomatisch für diesen Zugriff, als die Fokussierung auf die übersinnliche Dimension der Musik mit der Überwindung traditioneller Grenzen auf der sinnlichen Seite einhergeht: Die Grenzen des Klangs werden gesprengt, indem die Musik für den Bereich der »*nicht periodische[n] Bewegungen*«[4] geöffnet wird; dasselbe gilt im übrigen für den Bereich der völligen Bewegungslosigkeit, also die Stille. Geräusch und Stille werden musikästhetisch legitimiert. Nur so kann sich jene lautlose Kraft, an der Rilke interessiert ist, uneingeschränkt entfalten, denn sie ist nicht länger an die Klanggrenzen einer traditionellen Musikästhetik gebunden.

Vor dem Hintergrund der hier skizzierten poetologischen Funktionalisierung eines um das Geräusch erweiterten Musikbegriffes, bei dessen Konstituierung Nietzsches *Geburt der Tragödie*, Fabre d'Olivets *La musique* und Busonis *Entwurf einer neuen Ästhetik der Tonkunst* Pate gestanden haben, gewinnt Rilkes sogenannte Unmusikalität einen ästhetischen Stellenwert. Das, was Rilke unter ›unmusikalisch‹ versteht, bezieht sich nämlich in erster Linie auf ein Unvermögen mit dem technischen, performativen Teil der traditionell tonalen Musik umzugehen. Man kann Noten lesen, eine Melodie erkennen, ein Musikinstrument spielen bzw. singen, oder man kann es nicht: Rilke konnte es nicht. Genau dieses Unvermögen aber bildet in Rilkes poetologischen Überlegungen die Grundlage für einen auffallend experimentierfreudigen Umgang mit Vorstellungen, die den performativ-sinnlichen Teil der Musik und damit zugleich die Grenzen konventioneller Musikpraxis hinter sich lassen. Auf diese Weise beinhaltet Rilkes Unmusikalität im herkömmlichen Sinne auch einen ästhetischen Impuls, denn ›unmusikalisch‹ bedeutet hier zugleich ›nicht vorbelastet‹ durch Traditionen, die es nun zu überwinden gilt – und hierzu gehört eben auch die traditionelle Unterscheidung zwischen »Geräusch« und »Musik«.

I. Das Kranznaht-Experiment. Eine medienkritische Analyse

Der Aufsatz »Ur-Geräusch« entstand am 15. August 1919 in Soglio und wurde im Oktober desselben Jahres im ersten Heft des ersten Jahrganges von *Das*

---

4 | Helmholtz: Die Lehre von den Tonempfindungen, S. 16, Herv. i. Orig. *»Die Empfindung eines Klanges wird durch schnelle periodische Bewegungen der tönenden Körper hervorgebracht, die eines Geräusches durch nicht periodische Bewegungen«*, S. 15f.

Inselschiff. Zweimonatsschrift für die Freunde des Insel-Verlages veröffentlicht.[5] Mit Blick auf das Verhältnis von Geräusch und Musik ist der erste der zwei Aufsatzteile maßgeblich, in dem der Verfasser über Medien, Geräusche und Musik nachdenkt. Rilke schildert zunächst ein Experiment, an dem er sich als Schüler im Physikunterricht beteiligte: Mit Hilfe eines selbst gebastelten Phonographen wurde die eigene Stimme zunächst aufgezeichnet und dann wiedergegeben. Im Anschluss an dieses Experiment sowie anatomische Studien in Paris (1902/03) entwirft Rilke ein Experiment, das auf dem ersten aufbaut: Er schlägt vor, die Kranznaht des Schädels mit dem Stift eines Phonographen abzutasten; als mögliches Ergebnis dieses Experiments stellt er eine »Ton-Folge« in Aussicht, die er als »Ur-Geräusch« bezeichnet.[6] Die zentrale Passage lautet:

Die Kronen-Naht des Schädels (was nun zunächst zu untersuchen wäre) hat – nehmen wirs an – eine gewisse Ähnlichkeit mit der dicht gewundenen Linie, die der Stift eines Phonographen in den empfangenden rotierenden Cylinder des Apparates eingräbt. Wie nun, wenn man diesen Stift täuschte und ihn, wo er zurückzuleiten hat, über eine Spur lenkte, die nicht aus der graphischen Übersetzung eines Tones stammte, sondern ein an sich und natürlich Bestehendes –, gut: sprechen wirs nur aus: eben (z.B.) die Kronen-Naht wäre –: Was würde geschehen? Ein Ton müßte entstehen, eine Ton-Folge, eine Musik ...

Gefühle –, welche? Ungläubigkeit, Scheu, Furcht, Ehrfurcht –: ja, welches nur von allen hier möglichen Gefühlen? verhindert mich, einen Namen vorzuschlagen für das Ur-Geräusch, welches da zur Welt kommen sollte ... (702)

Die Überwindung herkömmlicher Grenzen in der Betrachtung akustischer Phänomene zeigt sich bereits in Rilkes Ausführungen zur Entstehung jenes Geräusches, das ihm als Musik erscheint. Schon in seiner Darstellung des Schulexperiments mit dem selbst gebastelten Phonographen zeichnet sich diese Überwindung ab. Der Phonograph und das mit ihm verwandte Grammophon stellten zu Beginn des 20. Jahrhunderts vielbeachtete technische Medien dar, von denen eine große Faszination ausging. »Zur Zeit, als ich die Schule besuchte, mochte der Phonograph erst kürzlich erfunden worden sein. Er stand jedenfalls im Mittelpunkte des öffentlichen Erstaunens [...]« (609), erklärt Rilke zu Beginn seines Aufsatzes. 1877 hatte Thomas Alva Edison »[d]en ersten funktionierenden Apparat zur Speicherung und

---

5 | Vgl. Nalewski: Kommentar zu Rilke, Ur-Geräusch, S. 1042f.

6 | Der zweite, kürzere Teil des Aufsatzes befasst sich mit dem Verhältnis der einzelnen Sinne zueinander im Gedicht sowie dem der Sinne zu den übersinnlichen Bereichen des Lebens.

Reproduktion von Musik und Sprache« konstruiert.[7] Nachdem die Tonqualität des Geräts von Alexander Graham Bell, Chichester Bell und Charles Sumner Tainter durch den Einsatz einer Wachswalze erheblich verbessert worden war, konstruierte Edison den »Improved Phonograph« (1888), der über einen elektrischen Motor zum Antrieb der Walze verfügte und mit dem ihm auf der Weltausstellung 1889 in Paris der Durchbruch gelang.[8]

Die Neuartigkeit des Mediums, an dem Rilke seine poetologischen Überlegungen aufhängt, äußert sich nicht zuletzt darin, dass in dem »Ur-Geräusch«-Aufsatz die Aufzeichnungs- bzw. Abspieltechnik des Phonographen mit der des Grammophons durcheinander gebracht wird.[9] Ein technischer Vorzug des Grammophons, das 1887 von Emil(e) Berliner zum Patent angemeldet worden war, gegenüber dem Phonographen besteht darin, dass es dessen Tiefenschrift durch die Seitenschrift ersetzt, wodurch der Nadel die Berg- und Talfahrt erspart bleibt. Dies schont nicht nur die Nadel, sondern ermöglicht überdies die Verwendung von Platten, die im Vergleich zum Zylinder des Phonographen wesentlich handlicher und aufgrund der verwendeten Materialien Hartgummi sowie Schellack widerstandsfähiger sind; außerdem können Platten mechanisch vervielfältigt werden.[10] Rilke bezeichnet das selbst konstruierte Gerät, mit dem er im Physikunterricht experimentierte, zwar als »Phonographen«, der zudem über einen »Cylinder« verfügt, wenn er dann aber den Vergleich mit der gezackten Kranznaht anstellt, wird deutlich, dass er keineswegs an die geradlinige Tiefenschrift des Phonographen, sondern an die Seitenschrift des Grammophons denkt.

Sowohl der Phonograph als auch das Grammophon zogen viele Menschen zur Jahrhundertwende in ihren Bann, da sie eine völlig neuartige Möglichkeit im Umgang mit dem gesprochenen Wort boten:

---

7 | Hiebel: Die Medien, S. 138.

8 | Ebd.

9 | Hierauf hat Anthony Moore während der Tagung »noise – geräusch – bruit: Medien und Kultur unstrukturierter Laute« (Erlangen, 17. bis 19. September 2012) hingewiesen, wofür ihm an dieser Stelle ausdrücklich gedankt sei.

10 | Vgl. Hiebel: Die Medien, S. 141. Jenseits der technischen Unterschiede gab es auch Differenzen im Einsatz und der damit einhergehenden Vermarktung der beiden Gerätetypen. Während Edison nicht zuletzt wegen seiner »immer wieder zitierten Unmusikalität« (ebd., S. 138) die revolutionäre Möglichkeit betonte, die menschliche Stimme aufzeichnen und speichern zu können, und am Umbau des Phonographen zur Musikbox kein Interesse zeigte, war das Grammophon von vornherein darauf ausgelegt, als musikalisches Unterhaltungsmedium zu dienen. Das ästhetische Potential, das Phonograph und Grammophon mit Blick auf das *Zusammenwirken* (nicht die Konkurrenz) von Sprache und Musik mit sich brachten, untersucht Hiebler: Sprache und Musik im Kontext der Medienkulturgeschichte der literarischen Moderne, S. 46.

Mit Telefon und Radio war der Schall nicht mehr an seinen ursprünglichen Ort im Raum gebunden; mit dem Phonographen war er auch frei von seinem ursprünglichen Ort in der Zeit. Die Beseitigung dieser Beschränkungen hat dem modernen Menschen eine erregende neue Macht verliehen [...]. Wir haben den Laut von seinem Urheber abgespalten.[11]

An der hier skizzierten »Schizophonie«, jener »Spaltung eines Lautes in den ursprünglichen Laut und seine elektroakustische Übertragung oder Reproduktion« also,[12] war Rilke nicht zuletzt deshalb interessiert, weil er zu jenen Autoren der Jahrhundertwende zählte, die sowohl dem lauten Lesen als auch dem Vortrag des literarischen Textes durch dessen Autor, der Dichterlesung also, große Bedeutung beimaßen. Wenige Monate, nachdem er seinen »Ur-Geräusch«-Aufsatz verfasst hatte, unternahm Rilke eine Lesereise durch die Schweiz (27.10.-28.11.1919), in deren Rahmen er neben Gedichten aus der mittleren Schaffensphase auch diesen Aufsatz vorlas.

In der Technik des Phonographen entdeckte Rilke nun die Möglichkeit, den Vortrag des Dichters aufzuzeichnen und zu speichern, um ihn an anderer Stelle und zu einer anderen Zeit wiederzugeben – unabhängig vom Dichter und doch authentisch, da ursprünglich von ihm aufgenommen. Über die Vorzüge dieses Verfahrens lässt sich Rilke in einem Brief an Dieter Bassermann, den Herausgeber der *Schallkiste. Illustrierte Zeitschrift für Hausmusik*, ausführlich aus:

Ich stelle mir (nach einigem Widerstreben) einen Lesenden vor, der, mit einem Gedichtbuch in der Hand, mitlesend, eine Sprechmaschine abhört, um von der Existenz des betreffenden Gedichts besser unterrichtet zu sein [...]. Voraussetzung für eine solche Übung wäre allerdings, daß die Maschine das Tonbild der Versreihe durch den eigenen Mund des Dichters empfangen hätte und nicht etwa auf dem Umweg über den Schauspieler. [...] Aufbewahrt in den Platten, bestände dann, jeweils aufrufbar, das Gedicht in der vom Dichter gewollten Figur: ein beinah unvorstellbarer Wert![13]

---

11 | Schafer: Klang und Krach, S. 120 u. 122.
12 | Ebd., S. 121.
13 | Rilke an Bassermann, 19.4.1926, in: Briefe aus Muzot, S. 387. So sehr Rilke sich einerseits für die Speicherung des Dichtervortrags begeistern konnte, so groß war andererseits sein Unbehagen gegenüber den neuen technischen Möglichkeiten. Im unmittelbaren Anschluss an die eben zitierte Passage wendet er ein: »Aber freilich für unsereinen, dem bestimmte Offenbarungen aus ihrer unerhörten Einmaligkeit ihr Unbeschreiblichstes an Größe, Wehmut und Menschlichkeit zu gewinnen scheinen, wäre ein solches mechanisches Überleben der heimlichsten und reichsten Sprachgestalt fast unerträglich.«

Wenn Rilke in seinem Aufsatz den Moment schildert, in dem der selbst gebastelte Phonograph seinen medialen Zweck erfüllt, ist die Faszination an der neuartigen Möglichkeit, Stimme zu speichern und, losgelöst von einem sprechenden Körper, wiederzugeben, deutlich spürbar: »Man stand gewissermaßen einer neuen, noch unendlich zarten Stelle der Wirklichkeit gegenüber, aus der uns, Kinder, ein bei weitem Überlegenes doch unsäglich anfängerhaft und gleichsam Hülfe suchend ansprach« (700). Schon bald aber nimmt der Gedankengang eine überraschende Wendung. Die Aufmerksamkeit wird von dem wiedergegebenen Ton als dem eigentlichen Zweck des Experiments auf die Walze verlagert, die ja bloß als Speichermedium dient. Der Zweck und sein Mittel werden verkehrt: »Nicht er, nicht der Ton aus dem Trichter, überwog, wie sich zeigen sollte, in meiner Erinnerung, sondern jene der Walze eingeritzten Zeichen waren mir um vieles eigentümlicher geblieben« (700). Rilke schildert nun sein anatomisches Interesse, das ihn schließlich dazu führte, den menschlichen Schädel näher zu untersuchen. Von hier aus ergibt sich eine Verbindung zu dem eingangs geschilderten Schulexperiment:

> In dem oft so eigentümlich wachen und auffordernden Lichte der Kerze war mir soeben die Kronen-Naht ganz auffallend sichtbar geworden, und schon wußte ich auch, woran sie mich errinnerte: an eine jener unvergessenen Spuren, wie sie einmal durch die Spitze einer Borste in eine kleine Wachsrolle eingeritzt worden waren! (701)

Die hier wahrgenommene »Ähnlichkeit« führt Rilke dann zum Entwurf des Kranznaht-Experiments.

Vernachlässigt Rilke im Fall des Phonographen über seinem Interesse an dem aufzeichnenden Zylinder den wiedergegebenen Ton, so ignoriert er im Fall der Kranznaht über seinen Spekulationen zum entstehenden Ton die Tatsache, dass diesem kein ursprünglicher Ton zugrunde liegt, da er sich aus einer graphischen Figur ergibt, die *nicht* die analoge Übersetzung eines Tones darstellt, sondern anatomischen Ursprungs ist. »Eine Schrift ohne Schreiber also, die denn auch nichts anderes archiviert als das unmögliche Reale am Grund aller Medien: weißes Rauschen, Ur-Geräusch.«[14] So lautet die Lesart in Friedrich Kittlers viel zitierter Interpretation von Rilkes Experiment in den *Aufschreibesystemen 1800/1900*, die in *Grammophon, Film, Typewriter* bekräftigt wird: »Niemand vor Rilke hat je vorgeschlagen, eine Bahnung zu decodieren, die nichts und niemand encodierte.«[15] Auf diese Weise, so Kittler weiter, »feiert ein Schriftsteller das genaue Gegenteil seines eigenen

---

14 | Kittler: Aufschreibesysteme 1800/1900, S. 323.
15 | Kittler: Grammophon, Film, Typewriter, S. 71.

Mediums – weißes Rauschen, wie keine Schrift es speichern kann.«[16] Diese Kritik verfehlt allerdings den Kern von Rilkes Idee.[17] Vor dem Hintergrund des Schulversuchs mit dem selbst gebauten Phonographen erscheint das später vorgeschlagene Kranznaht-Experiment auf den ersten Blick ebenfalls als Versuch mit einem technischen Medium. Doch der Schein trügt: Nur in dem ersten Versuch geht es um die *Speicherung und Wiedergabe* eines ursprünglichen Tones; in dem zweiten aber geht es um die *Verwandlung* einer optischen Linie in Musik. In der oben zitierten Passage fragt Rilke ausdrücklich: »Wie nun, wenn man diesen Stift *täuschte* und ihn, wo er zurückzuleiten hat, über eine Spur lenkte, die *nicht* aus der graphischen Übersetzung eines Tones stammte, sondern ein *an sich und natürlich* Bestehendes [...] wäre [...].« Wenig später spricht er von dem »Ur-Geräusch, welches da *zur Welt kommen* sollte ...«, nicht also bereits existierte, um nun bloß wiedergegeben zu werden. Die Kontur, so Rilke weiter, soll »verwandelt« werden (alle Zitate 702; Herv. T. M.). »Ur« bedeutet hier also nicht ›alt‹ im Sinne von ›vormals‹, in ›Urzeiten‹ aufgezeichnet, sondern ›neu‹ im Sinne von ›ursprünglich‹, erstmals zu hören:

Das Abtasten der Kranznaht ist im strengen Sinne also keine Dekodierung. Vielmehr fasst Rilke diesen Vorgang als entwerfenden bzw. verwandelnden Akt, der gewissermaßen zwischen Entdeckung und Erfindung oszilliert. Das hierbei entstehende Geräusch wäre folglich neu, unerhört, aber nicht ursprünglich, weil es dieses Geräusch nie gegeben hat.[18]

Dasselbe Bewusstsein dafür, dass es sich bei dem Ur-Geräusch nicht um Wiedergabe, sondern um Verwandlung handelt, tritt zutage, wenn Rilke knapp sechs Jahre später, am 5. April 1926, in dem bereits angeführten Brief an Dieter Bassermann erklärt:

Da das Wesen des Grammophons im graphischen Niederschlag von Tönen seinen Ursprung hat, warum sollte es nicht gelingen, Linien und Zeichnungen elementarischer Herkunft, die in der Natur vorkommen, in Klangerscheinungen zu verwandeln? [...]

---

16 | Ebd., S. 72.
17 | Zur Kritik an Kittlers Rilke-Interpretation vgl. vor allem Pasewalck: »Die fünffingrige Hand«, S. 16f., Anm. 30. Dem »Ur-Geräusch«-Aufsatz wird in dieser Studie ein ganzes, zumal ergiebiges Kapitel gewidmet. Vgl. ferner Pasewalck: Die Maske der Musik. Weitere Interpretationen des »Ur-Geräusch«-Aufsatzes mit Blick auf Rilkes Poetologie findet man u.a. bei Fick: Sinnenwelt und Weltseele, S. 189f.; Steiner: Die Zeit der Schrift, S. 412 und Fabian Stoermer: »Dann wuchs der Weg zu den Augen zu [...]«, S. 165-168.
18 | Pasewalck: »Die fünffingrige Hand«, S. 12.

> [W]äre es nicht ein Unerhörtes [...], die zahllosen Namenszüge der Schöpfung, die im Skelett, im Gestein ..., an tausend Stellen dauern, in ihren merkwürdigen Abwandlungen und Wendungen, zu ... vertonen? Der Riß im Holz, der Gang eines Insekts: unser Auge ist geübt, sie zu verfolgen und festzustellen.[19]

Die »Linien und Zeichnungen« sind hier »elementarischer Herkunft« und werden also nicht als analoge Speicher von Informationen aufgefasst. Konsequenterweise sollen auch keine akustischen Informationen wiedergegeben werden, sondern die Linien sind »in Klangerscheinungen zu verwandeln« bzw. zu »vertonen«. Auch hier erscheint die Linie also als Ursprung, nicht als Medium, und der Klang ist Ergebnis einer Verwandlung bzw. einer Vertonung, nicht einer Rückübersetzung im Sinne der ›Wiedergabe‹. Gerade in dieser Verwandlung liegt die poetologische Funktion des Experiments, denn es geht Rilke im zweiten Teil seines Aufsatzes ja darum, die Grenzen zwischen den Sinnesorganen zu überwinden, um auf der Basis von sinnlich Gegebenem ein neuartiges Erleben der Wirklichkeit zu ermöglichen. Silke Pasewalck hat dies ausdrücklich hervorgehoben: »Die *Übersetzung* der Kranznaht als graphische Zeichenfolge in eine Tonfolge wird dort aufgefasst als entwerfender, schöpferischer Akt, insofern er eine unerhörte, noch nie wahrgenommene Schicht der Wirklichkeit wahrnehmbar macht.«[20]

II. GERÄUSCH UND MUSIK IN RILKES POETOLOGIE

Wieso aber erscheint das Ergebnis der Kranznaht-»Verwandlung« unterschiedslos als »Geräusch« und »Musik«? Gewiss, der Titel »Ur-Geräusch« stammt nicht von Rilke, der den Aufsatz »Experiment« nennen wollte,[21] sondern von Katharina Kippenberg, der Rilke seine Arbeit zwei Tage nach Fertigstellung zusandte. Rilke verwendet diesen Ausdruck dann in dem Aufsatz allerdings in unmittelbarer Nachbarschaft zur Musik. Hier noch einmal die entscheidende Passage: »Ein Ton müßte entstehen, eine Ton-Folge, eine Musik ... / [...] welches nur von allen hier möglichen Gefühlen? verhindert mich, einen Namen vorzuschlagen für das Ur-Geräusch, welches da zur Welt kommen sollte ...«. Ferner verwendet Rilke mit »Musik« einen *ästhetischen* Terminus, um über das Ergebnis eines *physikalischen* Experiments zu spekulieren. Ausgangspunkt des Aufsatzes ist immerhin ein Experiment, das im Physikunterricht durchgeführt wurde und an das sich Rilke im Rahmen seiner anatomischen Studien, also wiederum in einem naturwissenschaftlichen

---

19 | Rilke an Bassermann, 5.4.1926, in: Briefe aus Muzot, S. 384.
20 | Pasewalck: »Die fünffingrige Hand«, S. 25, Herv. i. Orig.
21 | Vgl. Rilke an Bassermann, 5.4.1926, in: Briefe aus Muzot, S. 384.

Kontext, erinnert, bevor er sein Kranznaht-Experiment vorschlägt, das er von einem »Experimentator und Laboranten« durchgeführt wissen möchte.[22] Die *ästhetische* Benennung eines *wissenschaftlich-experimentell* generierten Geräuschs scheint für Rilke also kein Problem darzustellen.

Die fehlende Differenzierung zwischen Geräusch und Musik ist auch noch in anderer Hinsicht auffallend. In der Schilderung des Phonographen-Experiments im Physikunterricht hebt Rilke die schlechte Tonqualität der Wiedergabe ausdrücklich hervor: Der Klang »zitterte, schwankte aus der papierenen Tüte [...], unsicher zwar, unbeschreiblich leise und zaghaft und stellenweise versagend, auf uns zurück« (699). Auch wenn Rilke hier keine Kritik äußert oder sich gar über die schlechte Tonqualität beschwert, so zeigt diese Passage doch deutlich, dass ihm der qualitative Unterschied zwischen menschlicher Stimme im Original und deren Wiedergabe durch den Phonographen durchaus bewusst ist, denn im Grunde schildert er hier Verzerrungen und Nebengeräusche. In der Tat war die Tonqualität des Phonographen und auch des Grammophons noch so schlecht, dass Störgeräusche den natürlichen Klang des Aufgezeichneten beeinträchtigten. Dies war für jedermann hörbar – auch für Rilke. Als Beleg mag z.B. Hugo von Hofmannsthals berühmte Aufnahme von »Manche freilich ...« gelten, die am 22. April 1907 im Rahmen des seit 1901 existierenden Wiener Phonogrammarchivs gemacht wurde. Noch knapp zehn Jahre, nachdem Rilke über das Ur-Geräusch nachgedacht hatte, beschwerte sich Hesses Steppenwolf (1927) über die miserable Tonqualität eines Grammophons:

> In der Tat spuckte, zu meinem unbeschreiblichen Erstaunen und Entsetzen, der teuflische Blechtrichter nun alsbald jene Mischung von Bronchialschleim und zerkautem Gummi aus, welchen die Besitzer von Grammophonen und Abonnenten des Radios übereingekommen sind, Musik zu nennen – und hinter dem trüben Geschleime und Gekrächze war wahrhaftig, wie hinter dicker Schmutzkruste, ein altes köstliches Bild, die edle Struktur dieser göttlichen Musik zu erkennen, der königliche Aufbau, der kühle weite Atem, der satte breite Streicherklang.[23]

Während Hesse zwischen der aufgezeichneten Musik und der medialen »Schmutzkruste« unterscheidet, identifiziert Rilke das erwartete »Geräusch« ohne technischen Abzug von Verzerrung und Nebengeräuschen mit Musik. Der »Unterschied zwischen *Geräuschen* und *musikalischen Klängen*«, den Helmholtz als »Hauptunterschied verschiedenen Schalls, den unser Ohr auffindet« bestimmte,[24] spielt für Rilke also keine Rolle.

---

22 | Rilke an Kippenberg, 17.8.1919, in: Dies.: Briefwechsel, S. 369.
23 | Hesse: Der Steppenwolf, S. 198.
24 | Helmholtz: Die Lehre von den Tonempfindungen, S. 13, Herv. i. Orig.

Hier zeigt sich erneut, dass Kittlers medienkritischer Ansatz bei Rilke ins Leere läuft. Kittler führt Rudolph Lothars 1924 in Leipzig veröffentlichte Schrift *Die Sprechmaschine. Ein technisch-aesthetischer Versuch* an, in der der Sprechmaschine »eine besondere Stellung in der Ästhetik und in der Musik« attestiert wird, da sie »eine doppelte Illusionsfähigkeit« fordere: »Einerseits verlangt sie, daß wir alles Maschinelle überhören und übersehen. Jede Platte arbeitet, wie wir wissen, mit Nebengeräuschen. Die Nebengeräusche dürfen wir als Genießer nicht hören.«[25] Die zweite Illusionsfähigkeit, die dem Zuhörer abverlangt wird, bestehe darin,

> daß wir den Tönen, die aus ihr quellen, einen Körper geben. Wir spielen zum Beispiel eine Opernarie mit einem berühmten Sänger. Dabei sehen wir die Bühne, auf der er steht, sehen den Sänger im Kostüm der Rolle. Die Platte wird um so stärker wirken, je inniger sie mit Erinnerungen verbunden ist.

Aus diesen beiden Illusionsfähigkeiten leitet Lothar dann den »Kernpunkt der phonographischen Ästhetik« ab: »Nur dem musikalischen Menschen kann die Sprechmaschine künstlerischen Genuß gewähren, denn nur der Musiker hat die zu jedem Kunstgenuß erforderliche Kraft der Illusion.«

Kittler weist zwar zu Recht darauf hin, dass Rilkes Kranznaht-Experiment beide von Lothar aufgestellten Illusionsforderungen unterläuft, denn:

> Beim Abspielen jener Nahtstelle am Schädel sind Geräusche alles, was entsteht. Und beim Abhören von Zeichen, die nicht aus der graphischen Übersetzung eines Tones stammen, sondern anatomische Zufallslinien sind, braucht kein Körper optisch hinzuphantasiert zu werden.[26]

Wenn er in diesem Zusammenhang jedoch konstatiert, »[w]omöglich war Rilke kein musikalischer Mensch [...],«[27] dann bringt er hier einen Musikalitätsbegriff zur Anwendung, mit dem Rilkes Nachdenken über Geräusche nicht beizukommen ist. Rilkes Musikalität lässt sich nämlich nicht auf jenen performativen Bereich des Musikalischen einschränken, der im Sinne von Helmholtz durch die klare Struktur vom unstrukturierten Geräusch abzugrenzen und dabei zugleich mit dem Körper des vortragenden Musikers zu verbinden ist. Da Rilke mit Blick auf sein Kranznaht-Experiment gar nicht an strukturierte Töne denkt, können Nebengeräusche weder stören noch sich im Sinne Kittlers verselbständigen; und auch die Unmöglichkeit, das

---

25 | Alle Zitate dieses Absatzes nach Kittler: Grammophon, Film, Typewriter, S. 73f.
26 | Ebd., S. 73.
27 | Ebd.

entstehende Geräusch mit einem Körper in Verbindung zu bringen, zeigt in Rilkes musikalischer Vorstellungswelt keine Relevanz.

Wieso aber fasst Rilke ein Geräusch so ohne weiteres als Musik auf? Diese Frage zieht eine weitere nach sich: Wieso glaubt der für seine Skepsis gegenüber der Musik so berühmte Rilke überhaupt, in einem als Musik aufgefassten Ur-Geräusch irgendeine sinnvolle Basis für das Gedicht zu finden? In einem Brief an Lou Andreas-Salomé, in dem Rilke 1903 den für seine mittlere Werkphase so wichtigen Einfluss Rodins reflektiert, führt er die Musik noch als Antipode einer sinnvollen Ästhetik an. Rodins Kunst erscheint dabei als

das Gegentheil von Musik, als welche die scheinbaren Wirklichkeiten der täglichen Welt verwandelt und noch weiter entwirklicht zu leichten, gleitenden Scheinen. Weshalb denn auch dieser Gegensatz der Kunst, dieses Nicht-ver-dichten, diese Versuchung zum Ausfließen, so viel Freunde und Hörer und Hörige hat, so viel Unfreie und an Genuß Gebundene, nicht aus sich selbst heraus Gesteigerte und von außen her Entzückte [...].[28]

Zehn Jahre später beschreibt Rilke (erneut gegenüber Lou Andreas-Salomé) seine »Krise der Wahrnehmung«[29] als ein schutzloses Sich-Öffnen für die Welt, das den Betrachter überfordert. Auch in diesem Zusammenhang erscheint das Geräusch in erster Linie als störend:

Ich bin auch so heillos nach außen gekehrt, darum auch zerstreut von allem, nicht ablehnend, meine Sinne gehn, ohne mich zu fragen, zu allem Störenden über, ist da ein Geräusch, so geb ich mich auf und *bin* dieses Geräusch, und da alles einmal auf Reiz Eingestellte, auch gereizt sein will, so will ich im Grund gestört sein und *bins* ohne Ende.[30]

Genau aus diesem Dilemma, »heillos nach außen gekehrt« zu sein, führt Rilke ein Musikbegriff, der von einer stummen Rückseite der Musik ausgeht. Ein solcher Begriff versetzt die Musik nicht nur in die Lage, durch die Abkehr vom sinnlichen Eindruck »das durchaus lebensordnende Element« erfahrbar zu machen,[31] sondern er führt auch auf der sinnlichen Vorderseite der Musik zu jener Entgrenzung, die eine Unterscheidung zwischen Musik und Geräusch hinfällig macht.

---

28 | Rilke an Andreas-Salomé, 8.8.1903, in: Dies.: Briefwechsel, S. 94.
29 | Wermke: Landschaft als ästhetische Konstruktion zur Überwindung der gedeuteten Welt, S. 281.
30 | Rike an Andreas-Salomé, 26.6.1914, in: Dies.: Briefwechsel, S. 337, Herv. i. Orig.
31 | Rilke an von Thurn und Taxis, 17.11.1912, in: Dies.: Briefwechsel, Bd. 1, S. 235.

III. »JENSEITS DER PFORTE ERTÖNT MUSIK. KEINE TONKUNST.« (BUSONI) – ENTGRENZUNG DES HÖRBAREN IN DER MUSIKÄSTHETIK

Die Unterscheidung zwischen einer hörbaren Vorder- und einer stummen Rückseite der Musik ist charakteristisch für Rilkes Musikauffassung insgesamt und damit zugleich ausschlaggebend dafür, dass das Problem der Überwältigung durch sinnliche Eindrücke nur durch die Musik, genauer: durch deren unsinnliche Rückseite, zu lösen ist.[32] Bereits 1900 notiert Rilke in seinen Marginalien zu Nietzsches *Die Geburt der Tragödie*:

> Es ist zu auffallend, daß man für »Musik« in allen erwähnten Wirkungen immer jenes Andere setzen kann, das *nicht* Musik *ist*, sondern, welches nur durch Musik am reinsten ausgedrückt wird. [...] Und sollte mit Musik nicht überhaupt jene erste dunkle *Ursache der Musik* gemeint sein und somit die Ursache aller Kunst? Freie bewegte Kraft, Überfluß Gottes? Auch Malerei und Bildhauerei hat nur den Sinn, jene »Musik« zu interpretieren, an Bildern zu verbrauchen. Und dann wäre etwa die Musik schon der Verrat jener Rhythmen, die *erste* Form sie *anzuwenden*, noch nicht an den Dingen der Welt, sondern an den Gefühlen, an uns.[33]

Hier zeigt sich sehr deutlich, dass Rilke unter »Musik« zweierlei versteht: Zum einen das musikalische Kunstwerk, das gemeinsam mit dem Gedicht, der Plastik und dem Drama auf einer Art ästhetischer Stufenleiter angeordnet wird, und zum anderen eine Kraft, die diese Leiter hält und die Anordnung der Künste auf ihr bewirkt. Im Grunde unterscheidet Rilke also zwischen dem Musikalischen und der Musik als performativer Fassung des Musikalischen. Diesem Umstand entspricht auch die von Pasewalck hervorgehobene Tatsache, dass später Maltes Huldigung an Beethovens Musik nicht von einem »akustischen Eindruck«, sondern von einem »plastischen Gegenstand«, Beethovens Totenmaske nämlich, ausgeht.[34] Ebenso wie diese Maske stumm ist, erscheint die Musik, der hier gehuldigt wird, in erster Linie als Kunst eines Tauben:

> Das Antlitz dessen, dem ein Gott das Gehör verschlossen hat, damit es keine Klänge gäbe, außer seinen. Damit er nicht beirrt würde durch das Trübe und Hinfällige der Geräusche. Er, in dem ihre Klarheit und Dauer war; damit nur die tonlosen Sinne ihm Welt

---

32 | Pasewalck: Die Maske der Musik, S. 211, attestiert Rilke ein Verständnis von Musik, »das diese nun nicht auf die Klangkunst beschränkt«. Neuerdings grundlegend zu Rilkes Verhältnis zur Musik: Egel: »Musik ist Schöpfung«.
33 | Rilke: Marginalien zu Friedrich Nietzsche, S. 171, Herv. i. Orig.
34 | Pasewalck: Die Maske der Musik, S. 216.

eintrügen, lautlos, eine gespannte, wartende Welt, unfertig, vor der Erschaffung des Klanges.[35]

1912 findet Rilke seine Auffassung von den zwei Seiten der Musik durch die Lektüre von Antoine Fabre d'Olivets *La musique* (Paris 1828) bestätigt.[36]

Denn die Musik ist nicht, wie man sich das heute vorstellt, reduziert auf die Kunst, Töne zu kombinieren oder die Begabung, sie für das Gehör auf die angenehmste Weise zu reproduzieren: dies ist nur ihre zweckmäßige, praktische Seite, die vorübergehende Erscheinungen hervorbringt [...].[37]

Mit Blick auf die alten Hochkulturen betont Fabre d'Olivet den Zusammenhang von Musik und Mathematik (»Le nombre est donc le principe de la musique«)[38] und bezieht sich dabei auf die pythagoreische Vorstellung, dass die Musik die Ordnung der Zahlen widerspiegele:

Betrachtet man die Musik auf ihre theoretische Seite hin, so ist sie nach der Definition der Antike das Bewusstsein von der Ordnung aller Dinge und die Wissenschaft von den harmonischen Verhältnissen, die das Universum bestimmen; die Musik beruht auf unveränderlichen Regeln und Gesetzen, auf die kein Einfluß genommen werden kann.[39]

Die kulturelle Aufnahme dieses Zusammenhangs belegt Fabre d'Olivet z. B. an einem »Rohr, das den hoang-tchong erzeugt [und] in China stets als Grundlage für sämtliche Maße diente [...].«[40]
In einem Brief an Marie von Thurn und Taxis skizziert Rilke diejenigen Ideen d'Olivets, die seinen eigenen Vorstellungen von Musik entsprechen:

---

35 | Rilke: Die Aufzeichnungen des Malte Laurids Brigge, S. 508. Rilkes Interesse an der unhörbaren Seite der Musik wird auch hervorgehoben von Allemann: Zeit und Figur beim späten Rilke, S. 164f.
36 | Fabre d'Olivet: La musique expliquée comme science et comme art et considérée (zit. n. Pasewalck: Maske der Musik, S. 212, Anm. 16). Die Bedeutung Fabre d'Olivets für Rilke wurde erstmals gesehen von Herbert Deinert, vergl. Deinert: Rilke und die Musik, vor allem S. 70-76. Mit Blick auf Fabre d'Olivets Bedeutung für Rilkes späte Gedichte vgl. Eckel: Musik, Architektur, Tanz, S. 248-255; ferner Pasewalck: Die Maske der Musik, S. 212-215; neuerdings auch Egel: »Musik ist Schöpfung«, S. 121-127.
37 | Fabre d'Olivets Buch liegt nicht in deutscher Übersetzung vor. In meiner Skizze seiner Schrift verwende ich die Übersetzung einiger Passagen, die Pasewalck: Die Maske der Musik, anbietet; hier S. 213, Anm. 17.
38 | Fabre d'Olivet, zit. n. Pasewalck: Die Maske der Musik, S. 213.
39 | Fabre d'Olivet, übers. v. u. zit. n. Pasewalck: Die Maske der Musik, S. 214, Anm. 24.
40 | Fabre d'Olivet, übers. v. u. zit. n. Pasewalck: Die Maske der Musik, S. 213, Anm. 20.

> Was er von der Musik sagt, ihrer Rolle bei den alten Völkern, mag auch im Recht sein, – daß das Stumme in der Musik, wie soll ich sagen, ihre mathematische Rückseite, das durchaus lebensordnende Element z.b. noch im chinesischen Reiche war, wo der für das ganze Kaiserthum angenommene Grundton (dem *Fa* [i.e. romanische Bezeichnung für den Ton F; T. M.] entsprechend) die Großheit eines obersten Gesetzes hatte, sosehr, daß das Rohr, das diesen Ton erzeugte, als Maaßeinheit [sic], seine Fassungsmenge als Raumeinheit u.s.w. ausgegeben wurde und von Herrschaft zu Herrschaft in Geltung blieb. Musik war jedenfalls in allen alten Reichen etwas namenlos Verantwortliches und sehr Konservatives; hier ist die Stelle, wo manches zu erfahren wäre, was mit meinem Gefühl, Musik gegenüber, zu thun hat, ich meine, diesem äußerst unberechtigten rudimentären Gefühl eine Art nachträglichen Stammbaums lieferte: daß diese wahrhaftige, ja diese einzige Verführung, die die Musik ist, (nichts ver-führt doch sonst im Grunde) nur so erlaubt sein darf, daß sie zur Gesetzmäßigkeit verführe, *zum Gesetz selbst*. [...] Darum besticht es mich so, Fabre d'Olivet zu glauben, daß nicht allein das *Hörbare* in der Musik entscheidend sei, denn es kann etwas angenehm zu hören sein, ohne daß es *wahr* sei; mir, dem es überaus wichtig ist, daß in allen Künsten nicht der Anschein entscheidet, ihr »Wirken« (nicht das sogenannte »Schöne«,) sondern die tiefste innerste Ursache, das vergrabene Sein, das diesen Anschein, der durchaus nicht gleich als Schönheit muß einsehbar werden, hervorruft [...].[41]

Die Sinnlichkeit der Musik, der Rilke mit so großer Skepsis gegenüberstand, wird hier in den Status eines Mittels zum Zweck überführt. So wird aus der Not eine Tugend: Sinnlichkeit verführt zum Gesetz, das Hörbare wird abgewertet, insofern es nicht mehr an sich als sinnlicher Eindruck interessiert, sondern als »Anschein«, der durch die »tiefste innerste Ursache, das vergrabene Sein« hervorgebracht wird.[42] Durch die Verbindung der Musik über die Mathematik mit einer kosmischen Ordnung, die sich in ihr äußert, entwickelt Rilke einen Zugang zur Musik, der deren verstörende Wirkung auf ihn entkräftet. An die Stelle eines sinnlichen, emphatischen, tonkünstlerischen, performativen, ja rauschhaften Verhältnisses zur Musik tritt ein Interesse an der Natur, deren Gesetze sich in der Musik äußern: »Aufgefaßt wird die Musikerfahrung nun nicht als Kunsterlebnis, sondern wie die Konfrontation mit einem natur- und gesetzhaften Element [...].«[43] Die Trennung des Wahren

---

41 | Rilke an von Thurn und Taxis, 17.11.1912, in: Dies.: Briefwechsel, Bd. 1, S. 235f.

42 | »Akustisch gesprochen ist diese Rückseite die absolute Stille, die hinter dem ›Klangmaterial‹ wohnt und mitten durch das musikalische Kunstwerk hindurchgreift« Allemann: Zeit und Figur beim späten Rilke, S. 164.

43 | Pasewalck: Die Maske der Musik, S. 214; Eckel: Musik, Architektur, Tanz, S. 249, hebt die poetologische Konsequenz dieser Musikauffassung hervor: »Rilke entwickelt in der Beschäftigung mit der Musik die Konzeption seines späten nicht mehr mimetisch, sondern figural bestimmten Gedichts, das auf die Krise des Dinggedichtansatzes

von dem Schönen in der Musik bringt im Umkehrschluss eine Vorstellung mit sich, die für das »Ur-Geräusch« relevant ist: Nicht alles, was unschön klingt, ist deshalb auch unbedeutend. Rilke gibt diese Vorstellung in dem Brief an Marie von Thurn und Taxis selbst zu erkennen, wenn er denjenigen »Anschein«, der durch die »tiefste innerste Ursache, das vergrabene Sein« hervorgerufen wird, attribuiert mit dem Hinweis: »Anschein, der durchaus nicht gleich als Schönheit muß einsehbar werden [...].«[44] In diesem Sinne kann auch das Geräusch als Musik gelten.

Mit der hier skizzierten Vorstellung bewegt sich Rilke in auffallender Nähe zur Ferruccio Busonis *Entwurf zu einer neuen Ästhetik der Tonkunst* (1907), deren zweite Auflage Leipzig 1916, ihm gewidmet ist mit den Worten: »Dem Musiker in Worten / Rainer Maria Rilke / verehrungsvoll und freundschaftlich dargeboten.«[45] Auch Busoni, den Rilke durch dessen Schülerin Magda von Hattingberg 1914 kennenlernte, unterscheidet zwischen einer hörbaren und einer stillen Seite der Musik: »[...] das musikalische Kunstwerk steht, vor seinem Ertönen und nachdem es vorübergeklungen, ganz und unversehrt da.«[46] Vor dem Hintergrund dieser Vorstellung ist es ausgerechnet die Pause, die »in unserer heutigen Tonkunst ihrem Urwesen am nächsten rückt«, denn: »Die spannende Stille zwischen zwei Sätzen, in dieser Umgebung selbst Musik, lässt weiter ahnen, als der bestimmtere, aber deshalb weniger dehnbare Laut vermag.«[47] Insbesondere Busonis Auffassung von Musikalität legitimiert Rilkes eigene Distanz zur Musik gewissermaßen ästhetisch. Nachdem Busoni den musikalischen Menschen bestimmt hat als jemanden, »der dadurch Sinn für Musik bekundet, daß er das Technische dieser Kunst wohl unterscheidet und empfindet«,[48] fährt er fort: »[I]n Deutschland macht man eine Ehrensache daraus, ›musikalisch‹ zu sein, das heißt, nicht nur Liebe zur Musik zu empfinden, sondern hauptsächlich sie in ihren technischen Ausdrucksmitteln zu verstehen und deren Gesetze einzuhalten.« Genau hierin aber findet Busoni – ebenso wie Rilke – keine wahre Musikalität, sondern vielmehr deren Störung:

Tausend Hände halten das schwebende Kind und bewachen wohlmeinend seine Schritte, daß es nicht auffliege und so vor einem ernstlichen Fall bewahrt bleibe. Aber es ist

---

antworten soll. Es ist die Konzeption eines Gedichts, das nicht einfach auf ›Bilder‹ der Dinge zielt, seien diese statisch oder bewegt, sondern diese Dinge in musikalischen Ordnungen oder Bewegungen, in ›Figuren‹, aufheben will.«
44 | Rilke an von Thurn und Taxis, 17.11.1912, in: Dies.: Briefwechsel, Bd. 1, S. 235f.
45 | Busoni: Entwurf einer neuen Ästhetik der Tonkunst.
46 | Ebd., S. 30.
47 | Ebd., S. 46.
48 | Ebd., S. 32.

noch so jung und ist ewig; die Zeit seiner Freiheit wird kommen. Wenn es aufhören wird, »musikalisch« zu sein.[49]

Die Kritik an der Fixierung auf die technisch-performative Seite der Musik setzt sich fort in der Kritik an den Musikinstrumenten. Damit wird eine weitere Komponente der traditionellen Auffassung von Musikalität zum Hindernis der Musik erklärt. Busoni behauptet, »daß die Entfaltung der Tonkunst an unseren Musikinstrumenten scheitert«,[50] denn: »Die Instrumente sind an ihren Umfang, ihre Klangart und ihre Ausführungsmöglichkeiten festgekettet, und ihre hundert Ketten müssen den Schaffenwollenden mitfesseln.«[51] Das Fazit dieser Kritik für eine neue Ästhetik liegt auf der Hand: Es ist die Überwindung sämtlicher durch »Erschöpftheit« charakterisierten Elemente der Musik hin »zum abstrakten Klange, zur hindernislosen Technik, zur tonlichen Unabgegrenztheit [!]. Dahin müssen alle Bemühungen zielen, daß ein neuer Anfang jungfräulich erstehe.« Erst durch die Überwindung traditioneller Fesseln sei es dem Künstler möglich, »den inneren Klang zu erlauschen und zur weiteren Stufe zu gelangen, diesen auch den Menschen mitzuteilen.«[52]

Auch jene Unterscheidung von hörbarer Musik und deren mathematischer Rückseite, in der sich die Harmonie des Universums zu erkennen gibt, kann man bei Busoni finden: »Jenseits der Pforte ertönt Musik. Keine Tonkunst.«[53] Aber im Unterschied zu Rilke, dem Dichter, den diese Idee fasziniert, ohne dass er sich weiter mit der hörbaren Seite auseinandersetzt, kritisiert Busoni, der Musiker, die traditionellen Formen dieser Seite als bloß rudimentären Abklatsch einer universellen Ordnung: »›Zeichen‹ sind es auch, und nichts anderes, was wir heute unser ›Tonsystem‹ nennen. Ein ingeniöser Behelf, etwas von jener ewigen Harmonie festzuhalten; eine kümmerliche Taschenausgabe jenes enzyklopädischen Werkes; künstliches Licht anstatt Sonne.«[54] Nachdem sowohl die Unterteilung in Halbtonschritte als auch die Unterscheidung verschiedener Dur- und Molltonarten als künstlicher Notbehelf, ein »Fall von Zurückgebliebenheit« ausgewiesen wurden,[55] bekräftigt Busoni den fragmentarischen, keineswegs zwangsläufig sich aus der Natur ergebenden Charakter des abendländischen Tonsystems, indem er erklärt, »unser ganzes Ton-, Tonart- und Tonartensystem ist in seiner

---

49 | Ebd., S. 34.
50 | Ebd., S. 43.
51 | Ebd., S. 44.
52 | Ebd., S. 45.
53 | Ebd., S. 61.
54 | Ebd., S. 46.
55 | Ebd., S. 52.

Gesamtheit selbst nur der Teil eines Bruchteils eines zerlegten Strahls jener Sonne ›Musik‹ am Himmel der ›ewigen Harmonie‹.«[56] Dieser Kritik hält Busoni dann emphatisch sein ästhetisches Programm entgegen:

> Nehmen wir es uns doch vor, die Musik ihrem Urwesen zurückzuführen; befreien wir sie von architektonischen, akustischen und ästhetischen Dogmen; lassen wir sie reine Erfindung und Empfindung sein, in Harmonien, in Formen und Klangfarben [...]; lassen wir sie der Linie des Regenbogens folgen und mit den Wolken um die Wette Sonnenstrahlen brechen; sie sei nichts anderes als die Natur in der menschlichen Seele abgespiegelt und von ihr wieder zurückgestrahlt; ist sie doch tönende Luft und über die Luft hinausreichend; im Menschen selbst ebenso universell und vollständig wie im Weltenraum; denn sie kann sich zusammenballen und auseinanderfließen, ohne an Intensität nachzulassen.[57]

Ebenso wie Rilke unterscheidet Busoni zwischen akustisch wahrnehmbarer Tonkunst und einer »ewigen Harmonie« hinter aller Musik. Bei Rilke heißt die Dichotomie »Musik« vs. »Gesetz«, bei Busoni »Tonkunst« vs. »Musik«. Außerdem sieht auch Busoni das Verhältnis beider Seiten zueinander äußerst kritisch, wobei er mit Blick auf die Tonkunst radikaler argumentiert als Rilke; immerhin gibt aber auch Rilke zu bedenken, dass nicht alles, was schön klinge, deshalb auch wahr sei. Schließlich ist auch festzuhalten, dass Busoni durch die Verabschiedung der tonalen Tradition die Musik für jene Geräusche öffnet, in denen Rilke einen musikalischen Ausdruck des Universums findet.

So deutlich sich hier Parallelen zu Rilkes musikästhetischen Überlegungen abzeichnen, so wichtig ist allerdings auch der zentrale Unterschied zwischen dem Komponisten und dem Dichter. Als Musikästhetiker und praktizierender Musiker setzt sich Busoni mit den Grenzen der Tonkunst auseinander, um die Mittel einer neuen Musik zu entwickeln. Bemühungen dieser Art wird man bei Rilke, der sich in diesem Punkt als unmusikalisch im herkömmlichen Sinne erweist, vergeblich suchen. Am 4. Februar 1914 schreibt er an die Pianistin Magda von Hattingberg: »Wirklich, ich behalte keine Melodie, ja ein Lied, das mir nahe ging, das ich dreißigmal hörte, ich erkenn es wohl wieder, aber ich wüsste auch nicht den mindesten Ton daraus anzusagen, das ist wohl die dichteste Unfähigkeit selber.«[58] Im Unterschied zu Nietzsche, der sich in der *Geburt der Tragödie* u.a. mit dem Musikdrama Richard Wagners befasst, zu Fabre d'Olivet, der die kosmische Ordnung hinter exakt bestimmten Tönen erklärt, und zu Busoni, der musikalische

---

56 | Ebd., S. 51.
57 | Ebd., S. 58.
58 | Rilke an von Hattingberg, 4.2.1914, in: Dies.: Briefwechsel, S. 34f.

Grenzen sprengt, um eine neue Tonkunst zu ermöglichen, nähert sich Rilke der Rückseite der Musik *nicht* über deren Vorderseite.[59] Gerade hierdurch aber gelingt ihm, dem Unmusikalischen, jene Öffnung des traditionellen Musikbegriffs hin zum Geräuschhaften, die auch die zeitgenössische Avantgarde vollzieht. Die Fremdartigkeit des Hörbaren im Nachdenken über Musik bietet Rilke dabei die spekulative Freiheit, mit seinen poetologischen Vorstellungen an einer progressiven Musikästhetik anzuknüpfen.

BIBLIOGRAPHIE

Allemann, Beda: Zeit und Figur beim späten Rilke. Ein Beitrag zur Poetik des modernen Gedichts, Pfullingen 1961.

Busoni, Ferruccio: Entwurf einer neuen Ästhetik der Tonkunst. Zweite, erweiterte Ausgabe. Leipzig: Insel 1916. Mit Anmerkungen von Arnold Schönberg und einem Nachwort von H. H. Stuckenschmidt, Frankfurt/M. 1974.

Deinert, Herbert: Rilke und die Musik, Dissertation Yale 1959, Yale 1973, http://courses.cit.cornell.edu/hd11/Rilke-und-die-Musik.pdf (8.3.16).

Eckel, Winfried: Musik, Architektur, Tanz. Zur Konzeption nicht-mimetischer Kunst bei Rilke und Valéry, in: Manfred Engel und Dieter Lamping (Hg.): Rilke und die Weltliteratur, Düsseldorf 1999, S. 236-259.

Egel, Antonia: »Musik ist Schöpfung«. Rilkes musikalische Poetik, Würzburg 2014.

Eidt, Jacob-Ivan: Rilke und die Musik(er). Überlegungen zu Rilkes Musikverständnis im Kontext seiner Zeit, in: Andrea Hübener und August Stahl (Hg.): Rilkes Welt. Festschrift für August Stahl zum 75. Geburtstag, Frankfurt/M. 2009, S. 127-134.

Fabre d'Olivet, Antoine: La musique expliquée comme science et comme art et considérée dans ses rapports analogiques avec les mystères religieux, la mythologie ancienne et l'histoire de la terre, Paris 1828.

Fick, Monika: Sinnenwelt und Weltseele. Der psychophysische Monismus in der Literatur der Jahrhundertwende, Tübingen 1993.

Helmholtz, Hermann von: Die Lehre von den Tonempfindungen. Als physiologische Grundlage für die Theorie der Musik, 6. Ausgabe, Braunschweig 1913, Nachdruck Hildesheim u.a., 2. Auflage 1983.

Hesse, Hermann: Der Steppenwolf, in: Ders.: Sämtliche Werke, hg. v. Volker Michels, Bd. 4: Die Romane, Frankfurt/M. 2001. S. 5-203.

Hiebel, Hans H.: Die Medien. Logik – Leistung – Geschichte, München 1998.

---

59 | Zu Rilkes distanziertem Verhältnis zur Vorderseite der Musik vgl. Schoolfield: Rilke and Music; Eidt: Rilke und die Musik(er).

Hiebler, Heinz: Sprache und Musik im Kontext der Medienkulturgeschichte der literarischen Moderne, in: Joachim Grage (Hg.): Literatur und Musik in der klassischen Moderne. Mediale Konzeptionen und intermediale Poetologien, Würzburg 2006, S. 33-59.

Kittler, Friedrich A.: Aufschreibesysteme 1800 / 1900, München 1987.

Kittler, Friedrich A.: Grammophon, Film, Typewriter, Berlin 1986.

Nalewski, Horst: Kommentar zu Rilke, Ur-Geräusch, in: Rainer Maria Rilke Werke. Kommentierte Ausgabe in vier Bänden, hg. v. Manfred Engel u.a., Frankfurt/M., Leipzig 1996, Bd. 4: Schriften, hg. v. Horst Nalewski, S. 1042-1044.

Pasewalck, Silke: »Die fünffingrige Hand«. Die Bedeutung der sinnlichen Wahrnehmung beim späten Rilke, Berlin u.a. 2002.

Pasewalck, Silke: Die Maske der Musik. Zu Rilkes Musikauffassung im Übergang zum Spätwerk, in: Hans Richard Brittnacher, Stephan Porombka und Fabian Störmer (Hg.): Poetik der Krise. Rilkes Rettung der Dinge in den »Weltinnenraum«, Würzburg 2000, S. 210-229.

Rilke, Rainer Maria u.a.: Briefe aus Muzot 1921 bis 1926, hg. v. Ruth Sieber-Rilke und Carl Sieber, Leipzig 1936.

Rilke, Rainer Maria und Katharina Kippenberg: Briefwechsel, hg. v. Bettina von Bomhard, Wiesbaden 1954.

Rilke, Rainer Maria und Lou Andreas-Salomé: Briefwechsel, hg. v. Ernst Pfeiffer, Frankfurt/M. 1975.

Rilke, Rainer Maria und Magda von Hattingberg: Briefwechsel mit Magda von Hattingberg »Benvenuta«, hg. v. Ingeborg Schnack und Renate Scharffenberg, Frankfurt/M. 2000.

Rilke, Rainer Maria und Marie von Thurn und Taxis: Briefwechsel, hg. v. Ernst Zinn, Zürich 1951.

Rilke, Rainer Maria: Marginalien zu Friedrich Nietzsche / Die Geburt der Tragödie, in: Ders.: Werke. Kommentierte Ausgabe in vier Bänden, hg. v. Manfred Engel u.a., Frankfurt/M., Leipzig 1996, Bd. 4: Schriften, hg. v. Horst Nalewski, S. 161-172.

Rilke, Rainer Maria: Ur-Geräusch, in: Ders.: Werke. Kommentierte Ausgabe in vier Bänden, hg. v. Manfred Engel u.a., Frankfurt/M., Leipzig 1996. Bd. 4: Schriften, hg. v. Horst Nalewski, S. 699-704.

Schafer, Murray R.: Klang und Krach. Eine Kulturgeschichte des Hörens, Frankfurt/M. 1988.

Schoolfield, George C.: Rilke and Music. A Negative View, in: James M. MacGlathery (Hg.): Music and German Literature. Their Relationship since the Middle Ages, Columbia 1992, S. 269-291.

Steiner, Uwe C.: Die Zeit der Schrift. Die Krise der Schrift und die Vergänglichkeit der Gleichnisse bei Hofmannsthal und Rilke, München 1996.

Stoermer, Fabian: »Dann wuchs der Weg zu den Augen zu [...].« Rilkes Poetik des Erblindens, in: Hans Richard Brittnacher, Stephan Porombka und Fabian Störmer (Hg.): Poetik der Krise. Rilkes Rettung der Dinge in den »Weltinnenraum«, Würzburg 2000, S. 155-177.

Wermke, Jutta: Landschaft als ästhetische Konstruktion zur Überwindung der gedeuteten Welt. Ein Interpretationsansatz für Rainer Maria Rilke, in: Jahrbuch des Freien Deutschen Hochstifts (1990), S. 252-307.

Noise and Voice
Female Performers in George Meredith, George Eliot and Isak Dinesen

Barbara Straumann

FEMALE PERFORMERS

As readers of nineteenth and early-twentieth-century narrative fiction, we encounter a striking abundance of female performer figures that vocally articulate themselves in public, especially actresses and singers but also political speakers and religious preachers.[1] But how are we to read this literary preoccupation with the female voice performing in public? What is the cultural fascination that nourishes these texts? Given their overriding interest in performers who either have or attain star status, the cultural phenomenon of these texts may be seen in relation to the rise of modern stardom in the nineteenth century. After all, early in the century, following the disappearance of the castrati, the female soprano was established as a central voice on the operatic stage alongside the male tenor voice, which meant that female singers gained unprecedented cultural prominence.

Yet the cultural development of stardom alone does not fully account for literature's remarkable concern with female performer figures in the theatrical, political and religious cultural domains. Paradoxically, the production of these texts with their interest in the public female voice coincides with the period in which women in bourgeois culture are largely relegated and restricted to the private sphere. Interestingly enough, however, this is also the moment

---

[1] | Examples include the genius improviser Corinne in Germaine de Staël's *Corinne, ou l'Italie* (1807), the feminist speakers Zenobia in Nathaniel Hawthorne's *The Blithedale Romance* (1852) and Verena Tarrant in Henry James's *The Bostonians* (1886), the preacher Dinah Morris in George Eliot's *Adam Bede* (1859), the singers in George Du Maurier's *Trilby* (1895) and Willa Cather's *The Song of the Lark* (1915) among many others.

in which the so-called woman's question emerges as one of the key sociopolitical concerns and in which the first organized women's movement comes to revolve around tropes such as ›finding a voice‹, ›getting a voice‹ and ›raising one's voice‹. In fact, what these literary texts foreground through their female performer figures are questions concerning the voice women have – or do not have – in the public sphere. What does it mean to speak and/or sing in public? What is the difference between having a voice and having a voice of one's own? Who can speak and/or sing with a voice of her own? And who is actually heard? Can the performer speak for herself? Or is her voice absorbed by other voices?

This essay explores the ways in which narrative fiction imagines and constructs the public female voice during the period of first-wave feminism and thus on the threshold of modernity. Focusing on texts by three writers that centrally deal with the voice of a fictional singer – George Meredith's *Sandra Belloni* (1864), which was originally entitled *Emilia in England*, and its sequel *Vittoria* (1867), George Eliot's *Daniel Deronda* (1876) and Isak Dinesen's »The Dreamers« (1934) – I discuss the specific ways in which these examples, written at different cultural moments, treat the female voice as part of their textual aesthetics. As we shall see, the distinct modes in which they deal with the female voice performing in public becomes particularly palpable in the ways in which they link their singers to various effects of noise. While all the fictional singers discussed in this essay have a voice, it is only those whose voices are associated with effects of noise that have a voice of their own.

Attending a concert or an opera performance we usually expect to listen to voices that sing with seeming ease, technical accuracy and great beauty, even while we also wish them to simultaneously explore the very limits of the human voice. The elaborate training that this vocal mastery requires often forms an important element in fictional treatments and (auto)biographical accounts of singers alike.[2] Even while the individual singer has to subject herself to scripted roles and scores, the development of an accomplished singing voice is often seen as synonymous with the gain of a subject position; the concrete voice thus translates into the attainment of a ›voice‹ in a figurative sense.[3] However, just as important as the controlled harmonious voice

---

2 | See for example Renée Fleming's autobiography *The Inner Voice: The Making of a Singer* (2007) and the personal accounts of famous singers collected by Rieger and Steegmann (eds): Göttliche Stimmen.

3 | See for example Fleming: The Inner Voice, p. 118: »An interpretation exists because of what we find between the notes, and it is the only way for us, other than by timbre, to make ourselves distinctive. A brilliant execution of any phrase is only the beginning. Can something fresh be said with it? Can something personal be expressed? We dream that one day our talent, intelligence, and inspiration can take us from being a singer to the exalted station of artist«.

in these narratives are their noisy disturbances. In the area of singing, noise becomes audible as a disturbing factor when voices are as yet untrained, or when professional voices start to fall out of tune and into disharmony, which more often than not signals the end of a career.[4]

In narrative fiction, there are numerous female performers who lose their professional voices. In Eliot's *Daniel Deronda*, for instance, the former star singer Alcharisi recounts how she decided to leave the stage when she began to sing out of tune. The interference of noise in her singing brings her artistic career to an abrupt end. Together with her singing voice, she also loses the figurative ›voice‹ she had gained by transforming herself into a consummate artist against the patriarchal will of her father – a loss that is all the more painful since she regains her singing voice once it is too late to resume her career. However, noise is not just significant from a thematic standpoint, nor does it only articulate itself as a disturbance of the singer's voice and her singing alone. Quite on the contrary, effects of noise can also be produced by a particular textual aesthetics, for example if a performer's voice, its position and the values for which it stands do not harmonize but, instead, jar with other voices that make up the text's vocal soundscape. While the implied author Meredith allegorizes his Victorian singer as a voice of harmony, Eliot and Dinesen both closely relate their singers' voices to textual effects of noise. Eliot's text highlights the dissonance of Alcharisi's self-absorbed voice, who goes as far as abandoning her child in order to pursue her career and realize her full potential as an artist. Dinesen, on the other hand, allows us to hear the voice of her singer through the strange noise effect evoked by her modernist poetics.

THE VOICE AND NOISE OF NARRATIVE FICTION

A number of critics have written about the relationship between voice and noise, about the concrete sonic intrusions, as well as the figurative disturbances of the voice. Roland Barthes, for example, talks about the »grain of the voice«, a bodily component that resonates in certain voices and that addresses us as desiring subjects with an inescapable urgency.[5] Tracing the powerful hold opera has on its fans, Michel Poizat discusses instances of the pure ›cry‹

---

4 | Again see Fleming: The Inner Voice, p. 214, who articulates her anxiety in the following way: »I also worry about injury in a demanding role. It's amazing how even now I'll sing a phrase slightly wrong and think, *That's it! It's over. My voice is ruined.* That may sound neurotic, but it's certainly possible: you never know exactly when you are going to oversing and shut down your vocal cords for good«.
5 | Barthes: The Grain of the Voice.

in opera history – moments when the singer's voice screams, shouts, shrieks, moans, wails or whimpers – which suspend verbal articulation and, in so doing, potentially trigger an extreme form of ecstasy in the listener.[6] Voices do not only (and not always) transport meaning, but they also harbor a disturbing surplus. The philosopher Mladen Dolar is also concerned with a dimension of voice which exceeds verbal language and, therefore, suggests that the voice forms a surplus or excess.[7] Challenging Jacques Derrida's discussion of voice as the privileged trope of transparent meaning and self-presence, he points out that there is a vocal dimension which moves us beyond symbolic and imaginary codes and which disrupts, rather than supports, meaning and self-presence.[8]

But how can we conceptualize voice and noise for a discussion of literary texts? None of the critics mentioned above speak about voice and noise as literary phenomena, which is hardly surprising given that their voice theories are not conceived as text theories. Does it actually make sense to talk about sound in narrative fiction? In contrast to other literary genres such as performed drama and poetry, there are obviously no concrete sounds in novels that can actually be heard. Voice and noise are, in other words, alien to the type of literary language under discussion. Nevertheless, novels can be seen to evoke textually what escapes them medially. But how exactly do narrative prose texts produce voice and noise as aesthetic special effects? Similar to concrete voices, which are shot through with various colors, affects, moods and intonations, textual voices also mark a surplus, namely in the form of a multi-layered complexity they introduce into a text.

According to Mikhail Bakhtin, the novel constitutes the multi-voiced genre *par excellence*.[9] In his discussion, the novel occupies a special status as a literary form and an aesthetic medium, which juxtaposes different textual ›voices‹ and hence confronts different social accents, positions and perspectives with each other. His concept of heteroglossia foregrounds the clash and

---

6 | Early on in his discussion Poizat describes his interest in »the thrill or shiver that courses through the body in those supreme moments of musical ecstasy« in the following way: »Tears ... shivers ... Tears of joy? Is that what they are? These moments are not exactly moments of jubilation, or are so only very rarely; rather they are moments of physical thrill, of stupefaction, as the listener seems on the verge of disappearing, of losing himself, of dissolving in this voice, just as the singer on the stage seems on the verge of disappearing as a human subject to become sheer voice, sheer vocal object, all for the gratification of the fan«. Poizat: The Angel's Cry, pp. 3-4.
7 | See for instance Dolar: A Voice and Nothing More, pp. 20, 35.
8 | Dolar: A Voice and Nothing More, pp. 38, 52; Derrida: Of Grammatology, p. 20.
9 | See for example Bakhtin: Discourse in the Novel, p. 261: »The novel as a whole is a phenomenon multiform in style and variform in speech and voice.«

collision between antagonistic voices and social positions.[10] Using Bakhtin as my theoretical reference point, I want to suggest that it is in and through heteroglossia that narrative fiction creates ›noise‹ in a metaphorical sense. In other words, the conflict between the different characters' voices, the voice of the narrator and the position of the implied author produces what I want to call a noise effect. Narrative texts create 'noise' in the way in which they juxtapose different voices and, in so doing, point to the conflict between the different positions and values they stand in for. Bakhtin's theory of the novel provides a useful framework because it allows us to go beyond a purely thematic representation of noise. Rather than stopping at noise as a narrative theme, it invites us to consider noise as the effect of a particular textual aesthetics.

Moreover, we can speak of the effects of voice and noise in narrative fiction in analogy to what Shoshana Felman calls a »reading effect«.[11] As Felman points out, the effect of a text lies not simply in its thematic aspects but also in the ways in which it speaks to its readers.[12] In other words, a text's effect resides in our relation to it as well as in the impact it has on us. As readers and critics, we not only interpret but also actively reproduce the text.[13] Given that any sound in narrative fiction is entirely spectral and acousmatic, voices and noises have to be evoked by the reader in the solitary act of reading. This is why Felman's notion of a reading effect lends itself so well to a discussion of textual voice and noise effects: In narrative fiction, noise and voice are always effects of reading. Moreover, the literary effects of voice and noise as I define them also allow us to bring into play the tone, ›voice‹ or ›noise‹ of a text as we pay attention to, and indeed foreground, the dialogue and/or dissonance between the various voices in and of a text.

My close readings of the texts by Meredith, Eliot and Dinesen illustrate what we gain by focusing on voice and what noise effects this allows us to hear. There are various levels of voice that we can isolate in these texts: 1) voice

---

10 | »The novel can be defined as a diversity of social speech types (sometimes even diversity of languages) and a diversity of individual voices, artistically organized. [...] The novel orchestrates all its themes, the totality of the world of objects and ideas depicted and expressed in it, by means of the social diversity of speech types [raznorečie] and by the differing individual voices that flourish under such conditions. Authorial speech, the speech of narrators, inserted genres, the speech of characters are merely those fundamental compositional unities with whose help heteroglossia [raznorečie] can enter the novel; each of them permits a multiplicity of social voices [...] this is the basic distinguishing feature of the stylistics of the novel«. Bakhtin: Discourse in the Novel, pp. 262-263.
11 | Felman: Writing and Madness, pp. 15-22.
12 | Ibid., p. 18.
13 | Ibid., p. 21.

as a narrative theme, 2) voice as a trope of self-expression, 3) the voices (of the characters and the narrator) in the text, and 4) the tone or ›voice‹ of the text. Since Meredith, Eliot and Dinesen each trace the story of a singer, it comes as no surprise that the most obvious dimensions in their texts are voice as a narrative theme and the ways in which the concrete voices of these performers are used to develop narratives about the figurative ›voice‹ they have as women who realize their potential as artists, who appear in the public sphere and make themselves heard. Equally important, however, is the way in which these aspects feed into an aesthetic of noise. A number of questions are relevant here. How is the performer's voice evaluated and judged by other characters and the narrator? Is the relationship between the singer and these other voices one of concord or discord? And what is ultimately the tone or ›voice‹ of the overall text that emerges as a result of the way in which the implied author orchestrates and responds to all these voices?

THE ALLEGORICAL VOICE OF HARMONY

Meredith's *Sandra Belloni* (1864) and *Vittoria* (1867) revolve around the voice of a singer, who is called Emilia in the first novel and Vittoria in the second. The first novel opens with a description of the heroine's voice and characterizes its sound as being »so wonderfully sweet and richly toned«.[14] This emphasis on Emilia's voice at the very beginning of the text is no accident; the singer's beautiful voice forms the very center and pivot of the narrative. Meredith's female *Bildungsroman*, which is set in England, traces the personal and artistic development of the half-Italian singer and, in so doing, uses her voice as a narrative trope of self-discovery. Emilia, having been introduced as a natural talent at the beginning of the novel, temporarily loses her voice, because of her lovesickness, before she realizes that she is meant to be an artist and decides to train as a professional singer in Italy at the end of the novel. By the time the second novel *Vittoria* (1867) begins, she has already completed her musical training and makes her operatic debut in Milan. Her performance is a great success, but her career never actually takes off, because of the turmoil of the 1848 uprisings against the Austrian occupation in the context of the Italian Risorgimento. In both novels, the voice of Meredith's singer is characterized by its cohesive effect: Her singing brings her listeners together as an audience and even transforms them into social communities. On the one hand, this unification testifies to the immense power of the singer's voice, while on the other, it undermines the voice she has as an individual.

---

14 | Meredith: Sandra Belloni, p. 1.

The unifying force of Emilia's singing voice is evident from the very start. Early on in *Sandra Belloni,* Meredith describes the noisy concert of an English lower-class musical club. Emilia, who has witnessed the disharmonious performance of the lower-class musicians, promises to sing for the club members in the evening. When she does, they listen to her Italian song with its foreign words and strange style with attention, but their applause lacks enthusiasm. As soon as Emilia starts to sing a British song, however, her audience is enraptured.

No sooner had Emilia struck a prelude of the well-known air, than the interior of the booth was transfigured; legs began to move, elbows jerked upwards, fingers fillipped: the whole body of them were ready to duck and bow, dance and do her bidding: she had fairly caught their hearts. For, besides the pleasure they had in their own familiar tune, it was wonderful to them that Emilia should know what they knew. This was the marvel, this the inspiration. [...] the women and the men were alive, half-dancing, half-chorussing: here a baby was tossed, and there an old fellow's elbow worked mutely, expressive of the rollicking gaiety within him: the whole length of the booth was in a pleasing simmer, ready to overboil with shouts humane and cheerful, while Emilia pitched her note and led; archly, and *quite one with them all* [...].[15]

Taking great pleasure in Emilia's performance, the listeners are overcome by an impulse to dance and move along with her singing, and they also join in her song. This underlines the harmonizing effect of Emilia's voice. It is thanks to her singing that the lower-class musicians are all of a sudden capable of producing harmonious music instead of the noise generated earlier. When Emilia first hears their disharmonious music-making, her face is »screwed up at the nerve-searching discord«.[16] »*Can't* they be stopped«, she asks, »clenching her little hands«.[17] Given their initial noise, the harmonious sound, which they produce under Emilia's guidance, is all the more remarkable. But this is not the only effect she has on them. The singer also inspires her listeners with a sense of unity as her voice merges with their voices; as emphasized in the passage quoted above, she is »quite one with them all«. The harmony called forth by her voice is sustained until her song is drowned by the noisy arrival of a competing musical club.

Noise in Meredith is figured as disharmony. And as suggested by this episode, Meredith's singer has the power to supersede noise and create temporary harmony. Moreover, by leading and fusing with the voices of her listeners who join her in singing, her voice creates an acoustic community that is held

---

15 | Ibid., pp. 78-79, emphasis added.
16 | Ibid., p. 54.
17 | Ibid., p. 57.

together by her performance of a familiar song. This cohesion produced by her voice is even more prominent in the sequel entitled *Vittoria*. By the beginning of the second novel, Meredith's singer, now called Vittoria, is about to make her debut at the opera in Milan. Significantly enough, she makes her first stage appearance in a fictional opera, which revolves around a political allegory alluding to the Italian Risorgimento, the political movement working towards a unified Italian nation state in the mid-nineteenth century. Vittoria's part is Young Italy, that is, an allegorical personification of the future nation state. But this is not the only political role Vittoria plays on stage. At the end of her operatic performance, she goes on to sing an additional aria which repeats the line »Italia, Italia shall be free!«[18] as its refrain. The aria, which is not included in the libretto submitted to and passed by the Austrian censorship, serves as the call-to-arms for the real off-stage revolutionary fight for Italy's liberation.

Importantly enough, the allegorical mode of the fictional opera also extends to the novel itself. In turning his heroine into the allegorical voice of Italy, Meredith closely intertwines two allegorical layers, namely the struggle for feminine self-expression, on the one hand and the fight for national self-determination on the other. Vittoria's striving for personal freedom and artistic independence – that is, her attempt to gain a voice of her own – feeds into the narrative about the Risorgimento and vice versa. It is as an allegorical figure that she has a prominent public voice, even as a woman artist. Or put differently, Meredith's singer gains a political voice in public because she lends her voice to the national cause. The political movement, on the other hand, finds expression through the figure of the triumphant singer.

Before the opera performance, the revolutionaries quarrel about their strategy. As soon as they are at the opera, however, they are brought together by Vittoria's voice. In fact, even before she makes her first appearance on stage, the various members of the audience are united by their shared expectation as they are all »waiting for the voice of the new primadonna«.[19] As the text emphasizes, after the opera's second act, »she had won the public voice«.[20] The audience accepts and applauds her as the new star. At the same time, their collective enthusiasm for her voice unites them and anticipates the social community that she attempts to sing into existence. In fact, the singer represents her audience by giving voice to their patriotic sentiments and, in her allegorical role as Young Italy, proleptically embodies the nation that is still to be founded.

The unifying effect of Vittoria's voice is, however, at its most powerful when she sings the explicitly political aria mentioned before. After the actual

---

18 | Meredith: Vittoria, p. 253.
19 | Ibid., p. 221.
20 | Ibid., p. 230.

opera performance, the audience shouts her name: »The whole house had risen insurgent with cries of ›Vittoria‹«.²¹ It is at this moment that the singer's change of name becomes plausible. After all ›Vittoria‹ means ›victory‹, and by shouting her name, the Italian audience calls for a revolutionary triumph over their Austrian oppressors. Moreover, ›Vittoria‹ also alludes to Vittorio Emanuele, the future king of Italy. Historically, the Italian unification movement used the name of Giuseppe Verdi, the composer and passionate supporter of the unification movement, as its acronym V.E.R.D.I., referring to ›Vittorio Emanuele, Re d'Italia‹. Fusing opera and politics in an analogous way, the audience in the novel makes a political statement in their acclamation of the new *prima donna*.²² The listeners call her name united in one voice, but again it is the performer's voice that evokes the national community still to be created as she is singing the aria about Italy and its liberation. Although the Austrian authorities want to lower the curtain, Vittoria defends the floor. »She was seen, and she sang, and the whole house listened«.²³ While she sings her aria, all the Italian listeners rise and murmur its refrain, which calls for a free Italy, as if it were a national anthem. And even the Austrian members of the audience are fascinated by her voice despite the political project, which it represents.

As in the scene in which she sings for the lower-class musical club in *Sandra Belloni*, the voice of Meredith's singer has the power not only to hold the attention of her listeners but also to bring them together and turn them into an inspired, even enthusiastic community. The temporary social cohesion created by her aria is reminiscent of what Benedict Anderson writes about the significant role that songs and especially national anthems play in the formation of imagined communities. As Anderson argues, »there is in this singing an experience of simultaneity«.²⁴ Although we may not know the people with whom we are singing together, the fact that we sing the same song(s) allows us to experience a sense of what Anderson calls »unisonance« and »unisonality«.²⁵

In the case of Meredith's performer, the temporary unisonance, first among the lower-class musical club and then in the opera house, is produced by the performer's singing pieces with which her audiences identify. In other words, it is the performer's voice that focuses the attention of all the individual listeners and binds them together, as she herself turns into a collective

---

21 | Ibid., p. 253.
22 | Also see Phyllis Weliver's analysis of Meredith's novels in her broader discussion of music and national unity, Weliver: The Musical Crowd in English Fiction.
23 | Meredith: Vittoria, p. 253.
24 | Anderson: Imagined Communities, p. 145.
25 | Ibid.

voice, giving expression to a joint political project. The unifying effect of Vittoria's voice – or its unisonality – is also underscored after the conclusion of her aria, when her listeners again shout her name and, in so doing, merge in a single monotonous sound: »Vittoria's name was being shouted with that angry, sea-like, horrid monotony of iteration which is more suggestive of menacing impatience and the positive will of the people, than varied, sharp, imperative calls«.[26]

Prior to her performance, several revolutionaries are skeptical of Vittoria's prominent political role, but the text as a whole has great sympathy for its performing heroine. Given the novel's allegorical mode, one can go as far as to argue that it uses the Italian Risorgimento, its fight for national independence and freedom, as a trope for feminine self-expression and vice versa. In fact, both the implied author and the text position her as a proto-feminist voice by foregrounding her central political role. At the same time, however, Vittoria's public voice is clearly dependent on a national project. She only has a public voice because she sings for the patriotic cause, because she lends her voice to a collective movement. She does make herself heard in public – but she can do so only as the allegorical voice of Italy. Rather than singing and speaking for herself and her own interests, she serves the fight for national independence and unification. Ultimately, this means that as a collective voice, she is subsumed under the imagined community that she has helped inspire in and through her song.[27] On the one hand, the implied author and the text greatly valorize the performer's political voice. On the other hand, the allegorical mode of the text means that in the end, the voice she has as an individual comes to be curtailed by the larger national project. The contradiction between the celebration of her voice and its eventual silence is not thematized by the text itself, but as readers we notice its loss as we carefully ›listen‹ to the text and its various voices.

---

26 | Meredith: Vittoria, p. 256.
27 | For a general discussion of the tendency in the Western cultural tradition to represent nations and other abstract concepts by virtue of female allegories see Warner: Monuments and Maidens. In her study of »the allegory of the female form«, Warner focuses on visual examples and does not consider the allegorical role female voices can play. However, note that etymologically derived from the Greek *allos* (another, different) and *agoreuein* (speak), allegory literally means ›speaking about something else‹, which is precisely what the text has Vittoria do when she lends her voice to Italy rather than singing with a voice of her own. As mentioned above, the fight for national independence and feminine self-expression seem to stand in for each other. By providing its singer with an important political role, the text also seems to give her a powerful public voice. Yet in the end the singer appears to be reduced to her function as the allegorical voice of Italy instead of being given the opportunity of articulating a position and a voice of her own.

The absorption of Vittoria's voice into the larger national community becomes particularly obvious at the very end. The novel closes with a short epilogue, which describes the national unification of Italy under »an Emperor and a King«[28] several years later. At the proclamation, »a peal of voices« is heard, rendering »thanks to heaven for liberty«.[29] It is on this occasion that Vittoria is said to raise her voice one last time: »And then once more, and but for once«, the text closes, »her voice was heard in Milan«.[30] Given the elliptical character of this last sentence, we do not learn whether her voice is heard as part of the collective concert of voices greeting liberty and possibly acclaiming the new king, Vittorio Emmanuele, or whether she goes on to sing a final aria at the close of the text. Nor do we know whether the singer will ever perform again in other places, or whether her public voice disappears for good. The epilogue can be seen to offer a parallel scene to Vittoria's debut. Indeed the national community that is anticipated in the earlier scene of her operatic performance has been founded by the time the final scene takes place. However, while it is Vittoria who inspires her audience at the opera with a (temporary) sense if unity in and through her song, it is the figure of Vittorio Emmanuele, the king, who unifies Italy in the end. The public voice of the performer, on the other hand, can no longer be heard in the political entity, which she has helped to found.

All of this means that Meredith's performer can have a powerful public voice only as long as she lends it to the political movement and sings *for* as well as instead *of* a larger national community. Her voice inspires both musical and social harmony. But once the social cohesion for which she has been singing has been established, she is no longer heard as a professional singer. The overall tone or ›voice‹ of Meredith's novels is remarkably attuned to the public voice of its heroine and supports her striving for individual independence as an artist as well as her political fight for collective independence: Their narrative not only traces her individual development as a singer, but it also exalts her by turning her into the leading voice of a political movement and an entire national community in an almost megalomaniac fashion. At the same time, however, her individual voice is undermined by her role in the political cause. *Vittoria* draws a great deal of its narrative driving force from the allegorical interplay between the political struggle for national independence, on the one hand, and the singer's individual striving for personal and artistic independence, on the other. In the end, however, the singer is reduced to her allegorical function. This suggests that in keeping with Victorian gender

---

28 | Meredith: Vittoria, p. 629.
29 | Ibid.
30 | Ibid.

ideology, Meredith's singer can have a public voice only because she sings for a larger entity and, in so doing, effaces herself.

THE ›NOISE‹ OF RADICAL DIFFERENCE

In what follows I want to use Meredith's Victorian novels as a foil for my discussion of the female singer's voice in the texts by Eliot and Dinesen. How is Meredith's emphasis on harmony refigured by these more modern examples and their pronounced aesthetics of noise? While *Vittoria* culminates in the silencing of the singer's individual voice, Eliot's novel *Daniel Deronda* (1876) presents us with a performer's voice that stands for radical individualism. Indeed, in stark contrast to Meredith's allegorical treatment of the public female voice, Eliot's singer Alcharisi sings and speaks for herself alone. It is her self-interested voice that triggers a complex noise effect, which is at the very center of the novel's aesthetics. As we have seen, Meredith's novels repeatedly describe actual sounds, both the disharmonious music of the lower-class musicians and the harmonious song of their performer, in order to comment on the state of social communities. By contrast, Eliot's novel refers us to a metaphorical ›noise‹ effect, which is produced by the unresolvable tension between the modern subjectivity of the performer, on the one hand, and the traditionalist values of the other characters and the text as a whole, on the other.

Alcharisi appears in two chapters towards the end of the novel in which she tells the story of her life to her adult son, the novel's eponymous protagonist. Although she only makes two appearances on the occasion of the two meetings to which she has summoned him, she is crucial, as a character, for the noise effect produced by the dissonant clash between the position of her voice and all the other voices of the novel. In contrast to Meredith's Vittoria, who functions as the voice of a national movement, Alcharisi is not associated with any community. Quite on the contrary, in her account she underlines that she rejected the patriarchal tradition represented by her Jewish father, and used her exceptional voice in order to fundamentally remake, and fashion herself as a brilliant artist, against his will. Having been forced into marriage by her father, she even gave up her son, thus violating traditional nineteenth-century norms of femininity, in order to pursue her stellar career as »the greatest lyrical actress of Europe«.[31] »I wanted to live out the life that was in me, and not to be hampered with other lives« (688), she explains to the son she abandoned as a small child in order to lead a life of freedom and independence. The voice of Eliot's singer, thus, stands both for her artistic achievement and her creation of herself as an independent individual.

---

31 | Eliot: Daniel Deronda, p. 703. All page numbers in the text refer to this edition.

Crucial for the noise effect of Eliot's novel is not just Alcharisi's radical individualism but also the fact that she tells her life story in her own words. This is all the more remarkable given that her individualistic position is fundamentally opposed to the traditionalist values embraced both by her son and the text as a whole. Indeed, what characterizes Alcharisi's story more than anything else is her insistence on her radical self-creation. Regarding all bonds and ties as a form of bondage and enslavement, she says about her family: »I was born among them against my will. I banished them as soon as I could« (723). Driven by her desire for an unfettered existence, she severed all family ties and fashioned herself as a completely free-floating figure, a cosmopolitan artist who kept transforming herself through her operatic roles. »I was living a myriad lives in one« (689), she remarks early on in her first meeting with her son. Refusing to pattern herself on the domestic ideal of the Jewish wife and mother, which her father had wanted to impose on her, she followed her ambition for a far more worldly existence: »I cared for the wide world, and all that I could represent in it« (693).

Unlike Meredith's novels, *Daniel Deronda* does not suggest a positive valorization of the public feminine voice. Instead, the novel passes severe moral judgment on Alcharisi's self-centeredness, and quite literally destroys her. By the time she appears in the text, her career is long past. According to her own narrative, she left the stage when she realized that she began to sing out of tune. When she later recovered her voice, she bitterly regretted having given up her career as a celebrated star performer. As if her premature exit from the stage were not enough, the former singer also finds herself on the verge of death, suffering from a fatal disease. That is the reason why she feels compelled to explain herself to her son. The loss of her singing voice, her fatal illness as well as her sense that the paternal law is catching up with her, can all be read as a symbolic punishment of the female performer who insists on her individual voice.

In the novel, Alcharisi's wish for freedom and independence is juxtaposed with all those values of connectedness and rootedness she rejects, and which are embodied by her father and, even more, by her son. In fact, what characterizes Daniel Deronda is his family romance. Because he has never known his origin, he has been fantasizing about it for much of his life. What is more, after finding out from Alcharisi that he is Jewish, he comes to devote himself to the founding of a Jewish homeland. This means that in contrast to Meredith's novel, where Vittoria sings for Italy, the foundation of the community in Eliot's narrative is attributed to the male non-performer's political voice rather than the female performer's artistic voice. By juxtaposing the radical independence and self-realization of the singer with the cultural affiliation and tradition embraced by her son, Eliot's text emphasizes the dissonance between their different values.[32] While Deronda embraces the family background from which his mother cut him off and commits himself to the altruistic cause of his Zionist project, Alcharisi always remains interested in herself. Instead of lending her voice to others, she insists on her individual desire and personal ambition.

It is precisely for this that Daniel Deronda as well as the narrator and the implied author criticize and even demonize her and the fact that, in her singing, she refuses to represents anyone but herself. What renders her a problematic character within the novel's moral imagination, is her ambitious self-assertion; that is, the very characteristic that allowed her to become a great artist in the first place. Although the two chapters in which Eliot's star performer makes her appearance occupy only a small fraction of a very long text, they are pivotal because they crystallize the novel's ideological tension. In fact, it is here that I would like to locate the noise effect of this text: in the dissonance that is produced by incompatible positions and values. In contrast to Meredith's singer, who is eventually subsumed under the political community she has helped to inspire through her song, Alcharisi can neither be absorbed by a larger entity nor by the text itself. Instead, her voice persists as a dissonant element.

In the text this dissonance is further underlined by the fact that the two meetings of Alcharisi and her son are characterized by real difference. In his fantasy, Deronda has often imagined what his unknown mother might be like and has »often pictured her face in his imagination as one which had a likeness to his own« (687). But when he is confronted with the radically different voice and subjectivity of the actual person, he cannot read her. Rather than the loving mother he has been expecting and longing for, he finds a remote and harsh figure. According to the text's description, »her eyes were piercing and her face so mobile that the next moment she might look a different person« (687). She examines her son but stays unexaminable herself as the expression of her face keeps changing, and thus remains true to her identity as an arch-performer. From the beginning, Alcharisi seems to her son »as if she were not quite a human mother, but a Melusina, who had ties with some world which is independent of ours« (687-688). When he offers her his affection, she neither refuses nor reciprocates the gesture, telling him: »I reject nothing, but I have nothing to give« (697). What she definitely rejects, however, is being identified with the role of »a human mother« because as she points out later: »I am not a loving woman« (730).

Alcharisi ends their second encounter by telling Deronda that they will never meet again. But although she literally has the last word, the text and

---

32 | Also see Rachel Brownstein on the significant role played by »separateness and connectedness« in *Daniel Deronda*, Brownstein: Tragic Muse, p. 245.

the implied author are aligned with Deronda's perspective rather than hers. This is underscored by the fact that the scene of their second meeting closes with the text focalizing his affective response to their final separation. In fact, Deronda emerges as the central focalizer and we, as readers, are encouraged to join the narrator and implied author in adopting his perspective. Moreover, the values privileged and, eventually, shown to be viable by the plot are not feminine independence and self-articulation but the reinstallation of the patriarchal family tradition and its consolidation of a Jewish homeland. This, too, underlines the attunement of the overall text with Deronda's moral outlook.

Yet the rejection of Alcharisi and her self-absorbed voice by the novel is not as straightforward as it may seem. Although her position is repudiated by the implied author, narrator, and protagonist alike, her voice is granted significant space in the text. Rather than having the narrator tell the reader about the exchange between the singer and her son, Eliot adopts a quasi-dramatic mode; she presents the confrontation of the two character voices with each other in direct speech, thus staging a dialogue with relatively few comments from the narrator. Because Alcharisi is the principal speaker, the former singer dominates the two chapters with her life story, which she tells in her own words. Indeed, she has far more vocal presence than either Deronda or the narrator.

The narrative mode chosen by Eliot means that although Alcharisi has lost her voice as a star singer, she makes herself heard and produces a significant amount of noise with the voice she has in the text. The strong presence of her speaking voice points to a tension, a contradiction and thus to the limitation of the traditional value system that underpins *Daniel Deronda*, the last novel Eliot completed. Alcharisi's voice plays a decisive role in this late Victorian text and can be called ›modern‹ in so far as it disrupts the idea of a homogeneous set of values, signaling that it is no longer viable to uphold a single moral code. Indeed, her vocal presence in the text underscores that there are several stories, positions and perspectives, even if not all of them meet with the implied author's approval.

The noise effect of *Daniel Deronda* is further reinforced by the conflictedness of the overall text and its implied author Eliot. Still holding onto Victorian values, Eliot has to reject Alcharisi's self-absorbed ambition. She can imagine Alcharisi's position, but it is not a position she can envisage adopting for herself as a female writer. However, by creating the self-determined voice of her singer character, her novel does anticipate a modern feminine subjectivity. Alcharisi stands for a modern model of the female self-fashioning artist, which became more readily available later and was turned into an art practice by avant-garde women artists in the twentieth century.

What renders *Daniel Deronda* so complex in both its moral imagination and poetics, is the fact that the implied author Eliot acknowledges and recognizes Alcharisi in her radical difference, even though her voice is not the one she prefers. The former star singer violates the norms privileged by the text and is yet given space to show that she is justified from her own point of view. »Every woman«, she observes, »is supposed to have the same set of motives, or else be a monster. I am not a monster, but I have not felt exactly what other women feel – or say they feel, for fear of being thought unlike others« (691). Alcharisi is aware that her deviation from the traditional feminine gender norms makes her seem monstrous in the eyes of others, but she insists on her position and argues that this does not make her a monster.

Eliot's performer can be seen to stand for what Stanley Cavell would call a radical separateness,[33] because she emphasizes that she has a desire and a fantasy space of her own. In the text, this comes to be reflected by the fact that she has a voice in her own history, both because she has shaped her life as a self-fashioning performer and because she tells her story in her own voice. After her interviews with her son, Alcharisi disappears from the text, but her voice and the antagonism to which it points cannot be written out of the text. Instead, the text keeps reverberating with the unmistakable noise of her voice, which is radically different from and out of harmony with all the other textual voices. Eliot's novel punishes her singer because she has a voice of her own, yet despite this punishment her voice retains great resonance, precisely because of its noise effect. Her self-centeredness is dissonant with the moral norms and values of all the other textual voices and the values they represent. But it is precisely because of her dissonant voice that she becomes audible in the text and can be heard to speak for herself.

THE POETICS OF A STRANGE SOUND

Isak Dinesen's story »The Dreamers« from her first collection *Seven Gothic Tales* (1934) revolves around the self-fashioning of the modern female artist that is anticipated in *Daniel Deronda*. Pellegrina Leoni, the singer in Dinesen's text, resembles Alcharisi. Another arch-performer, she continually transforms herself both on and off stage. However, while Alcharisi's self-creation stands for a radical difference that cannot be fully integrated into the social system and value code upheld by Eliot's text, Pellegrina's protean voice, and the strange noise in which it culminates, directly reflect Dinesen's poetics.

---

33 | See Cavell: Contesting Tears, and Cavell: Cities of Words.

But how does Pellegrina fashion herself?[34] As pointed out by her impresario, the old Jew Marcus Cocoza, the singer is characterized by two great passions, namely her boundless love for her audience and her uncompromising commitment to her star persona. It is in a dialogic exchange with her rapt audience that the protagonist constitutes herself as a performer: She sings for the audience, which, in turn, confirms her in her role as a universally adored public voice. At the same time, Pellegrina sacrifices herself in order to transform into a great star soprano, who is worshipped both by herself and her audience as an object of quasi-religious devotion.

On the one hand, the voice of Dinesen's singer is multiple because she performs various operatic roles. Pellegrina will weep and die the numerous deaths demanded by the operatic scripts only to constantly resurrect herself on stage. On the other hand, her voice becomes monologic because she privileges one single persona. As mentioned by Marcus, the singer wishes to be able to perform several roles within the same opera: »she needs must have all the parts for Pellegrina«.[35] But her aim is not a protean performance of multiple roles. Rather than actually transforming herself into the various operatic characters she enacts, she claims all parts so as to subsume them under her one superlative role, »the great soprano Pellegrina Leoni«.[36]

One night during a performance at the opera house in Milan, a fire breaks out and a falling beam hits the singer. She narrowly escapes death but, as a result of the shock, loses her singing voice. With this near-fatal accident, Dinesen's tale can be seen to rewrite the type of nineteenth-century narrative, also developed by Meredith and Eliot, in which the performer loses her professional public voice. Seemingly in this tradition, »The Dreamers« reverberates with a tragic sense of loss. Like Vittoria and Alcharisi, Pellegrina leaves the stage, never to be heard again. However, by using what would be a classic ending in a nineteenth-century text as her point of departure, Dinesen revises the narrative argument. In fact, the accident can be seen to point to a deadlock in Pellegrina's static star persona. Investing everything in one single role, the incident suggests, is fatal.

Dinesen's protagonist loses her professional voice and her social role as a singer but, in compensation, she gains a different kind of ›voice‹. After the star soprano has been buried at a fake funeral, she explains to her former impresario: »There are many that I can be. [...] I will not be one person again, Marcus, I will be always many persons from now. Never again will I have my

---

34 | For a more detailed discussion of the singer and the effects of voice in Dinesen's tale see Straumann: The Effects of Voice in Isak Dinesen's ›The Dreamers‹.
35 | Dinesen: The Dreamers, p. 402.
36 | Ibid.

heart and my whole life bound up with one woman, to suffer so much«.[37] What Pellegrina opts for is a protean performance of the self, which harks back to Alcharisi and her practice of »living a myriad lives in one« (689). Yet while Alcharisi's multiple lives as an artist were aided by her stage performances, Pellegrina does not need the theatre. Having realized the lethal effects of a single self-construction, Dinesen's singer fragments her former persona into a plethora of masks and masquerades. Following her wish, never again to be caught up in a single role, Pellegrina turns into a traveller and adopts a new mask for each lover she encounters on her journey. To the Englishman Lincoln Forsner in Rome, she presents herself as the courtesan Olalla; to Friedrich Hohenemser in Lucerne as the milliner and revolutionary Madame Lola: and to Baron Guildenstern in Saumur as the saint Rosalba.

The actual theatre may have burnt down, but for Pellegrina, the wanderer, all the world becomes a stage. In fact, her extremely mobile and boundless self-performances seem to literalize the ambition articulated by Eliot's cosmopolitan artist Alcharisi when she says: »I cared for the wide world, and all that I could represent in it« (693). At the same time, the protean self-dramatizations on which Pellegrina embarks, after the symbolic burial of her singer persona, follow a typically modern trajectory. By transposing her theatrical scenarios into everyday life, she recreates herself as her own work of art. Although (or rather because) Pellegrina has lost her singing voice, she has gained a ›voice‹ of her own in articulating her self, and this time her performances are indeed multiple. Whenever she starts to feel tied down to a particular role, Marcus helps her disappear and adopt a new mask. Her self-performance is sustained by a continual reinvention and renewal. Or put differently, her self-performance is one of fleeting evanescence, of ceaseless disappearance and re-emergence.

Pellegrina serves as a character that reflects Dinesen's poetics. She refers us to a voice, which disappears and resounds as pure text. Her voice can no longer be attached to an individual person but, instead, dissolves into writing. At the same time, it is important to note that her voice is refracted and mediated by the narration of other characters voices. Her stellar career, the loss of her voice and her adoption of multiple roles are the chronological events we can reconstruct once we reach the end of »The Dreamers«. The text's actual structure, however, consists of several narratives that frame Pellegrina, who is almost the only character that does not tell a story: The diegetic narrative of the authorial narrator frames a intra-diegetic narrative, namely the story that Lincoln Forsner tells to the famous but weary storyteller Mira Jama. According to Lincoln, he was searching for the prostitute Olalla, who had made

---

37 | Ibid., pp. 417-418.

him a dreamer, when he met his two friends, Hohenemser and Guildenstern, who, in turn, told him their stories about Madame Lola and Rosalba.

This complex narrative structure refers us to the tension between the various voices in the text or, as Bakhtin would say, its heteroglossia.[38] »The Dreamers« enacts a heightened form of heteroglossia, in which the tension is not just between the various character-narrators, namely Lincoln, Hohenemser and Guildenstern, all of whom derive a narcissistic sense of identity from their love object. The fiercest conflict can be observed between their narrative desire and Pellegrina's protean performances. While Pellegrina keeps reinventing herself, so as to avoid being read and appropriated by another voice, each of the three men seeks to reduce her to the particular role, which she plays in his story, thus turning her into an allegory of his desire.

This conflict comes to a climax on a stormy winter night. The three men have just finished telling each other their stories about Olalla, Madame Lola and Rosalba in a hotel in the Swiss Alps when, all of a sudden, they catch sight of a veiled woman. They all believe to recognize their respective object of desire and chase the woman as she is running towards a mountain pass. When Lincoln finally catches up with her, he asks her who she is. His question will eventually turn out to be fatal. Pellegrina, who literally seeks to escape any one defining role or mask, throws herself into an abyss and disappears from sight so as to flee from this scene, in which Lincoln tries to pin her down to one identity.

But what is the ›voice‹ *of* Dinesen's text? By asking this question, I am not suggesting that the various textual voices are unified by a single voice. Rather, the question is one of tone, namely the tone that emerges as a result of the way in which the implied author orchestrates the various voices in the text. The narrative mode of »The Dreamers« appears as ›feminine‹, or even feminist, in the way in which it shows, and actually performs, the violence implicit in the narrative framing of the male figures. Significantly, it is only as the woman lies dying that Marcus reveals the great soprano's name and story. In a deft gesture, Dinesen has his belated commentary on the stable persona of the singer coincide with the woman's actual death. Or put differently, the text implies that death is brought about by a narrative desire that seeks to reduce her to a single role.

Yet the feminine mode of Dinesen's text goes further than that; shortly before Pellegrina's death, as her dying body is surrounded by her former

---

38 | According to Bakhtin, prose »often deliberately intensifies difference between [ideological languages], gives them embodied representation and dialogically opposes them to one another in unresolvable dialogues«. Bakhtin: Discourse in the Novel, p. 291.

impresario and three former lovers, her narrative containment is disrupted by a strange voice effect.

> Her whole body vibrated under her passion like the strings of an instrument.
> ›Oh,‹ she cried, ›look, look here! It is Pellegrina Leoni – it is she, it is she herself again – she is back. Pellegrina, the greatest singer, poor Pellegrina, she is on the stage again. To the honour of God, as before. Oh, she is here, it is she – Pellegrina, Pellegrina herself!‹
> It was unbelievable that, half dead as she was, she could house this storm of woe and triumph. It was, of course, her swan song. [...]
> The old Jew was in a terrible state of pain and strain. [...]
> Of a sudden he took up his little walking stick and struck three short notes on the side of the stretcher.
> ›Donna Leoni,‹ he cried in a clear voice. ›*En scène pour le deux* [sic].‹
> Like a soldier to the call, or a war horse to the blast of the trumpet, she collected herself at his words. Within the next minute she became quiet in a gallant and deadly calm. She gave him a glance from her enormous dark eyes. In one mighty movement, like that of a bellow rising and sinking, she lifted the middle of her body. A strange sound, like the distant roar of a great animal, came from her breast. Slowly the flames in her face sank, and an ashen grey covered it instead. Her body fell back, stretched itself out and lay quite still, and she was dead.[39]

Initially, Pellegrina's famous singer persona seems to be reconstituted by the cue given by her impresario. She slips into her former symbolic role, ready to resume her part at precisely the point at which she was interrupted by the near-fatal accident. The accumulation of the words »she«, »herself«, »Pellegrina Leoni« in her speech suggests unreserved identification with the role of the singer. However, ironically, the singer Leoni, a character to whom she refers in the third person, is just as much a mask as all of her other roles. Rather than coming back on stage, she has actually never left the theatrical boards. And, indeed, while the other character voices seek to unmask her, this last performance shows not just the fatality but also the impossibility of their attempt to lay bare her identity.

What is even more disruptive, however, is the culmination of Pellegrina's swan song in a monstrous utterance towards the end of the passage – »a strange sound, like the distant roar of a great animal«. Even though a written text cannot move beyond verbal language, the passage aesthetically evokes the effect of a voice beyond meaning by comparing her utterance to a non-human noise. The sheer sound of her non-verbal emission subverts not just the narrative desire of the three men. It also undercuts all symbolic and imaginary

---

39 | Dinesen: The Dreamers, pp. 426-427.

codes and, hence, all social roles. The sublime song Pellegrina used to produce as a singer allowed her and her audience to mirror themselves in each other. The animal-like noise that serves as her swan song accentuates the very opposite: a voice of radical alterity. It is here that we can invoke Mladen Dolar's notion of voice as a surplus or excess. The passage marks a moment where the voice refers to a radical subjectivity beyond cultural interpellation, thus allowing a part of the subject that is utterly intimate to be heard.

The strange noise in Dinesen's text can be read as a critique of the way in which the female character is reified. When Hannah Arendt reviewed a biography of Isak Dinesen, who was a consummate self-performer in her own right, she noted that for Dinesen, »the chief trap in one's life is one's identity«.[40] By creating her protean performer, Dinesen refigures earlier, more traditional performer narratives. Like them her tale also provides an implicit commentary on the so-called woman's question, which was first formulated in the nineteenth century, and at the same time, criticizes the way in which the individual female voice is elided, as the performer comes to be fetishized and allegorized as is for example the case in Meredith's *Vittoria*. »The Dreamers« is not just the very first text Dinesen wrote as she refashioned herself as a literary storyteller, but it also forms a quasi-manifesto of her poetics.[41] The text demonstrates, and indeed performs, a radical dispersal of a self-identical role into a multiplicity of masquerades. It is because Pellegrina abandons her monolithic star persona that she can articulate herself through her myriad of masks.

Yet even more important for Dinesen's poetics is the effect of the noise Pellegrina produces on her deathbed. The strange sound that she utters as her final one undercuts her social role as a star singer together with the narrative desire of her former lovers. At the same time, the noise of her radical utterance, which we are left to imagine for ourselves, also shows how literary texts invite us as readers to fill them with our critical tone, namely by listening to the various voices of a text and tracing both their consonance and dissonance. The voice as an aesthetic category in the sense of Bakhtin's heteroglossia[42] is closely connected to a political dimension. Or put differently, both voice and noise are reading effects in Felman's sense because they involve us as readers and refer us to an ethical dimension of literature. It is by discerning the different voices and their noise effects that we lend our ears to the moral imagination of literature. Pellegrina may die and fall silent. But it is clearly her voice that is ultimately granted the greatest resonance by Dinesen's poetics of noise.

---

40 | Arendt: Foreword, p. viii.
41 | On Dinesen's self-fashioning see Thurman: Isak Dinesen: The Life of a Storyteller; Straumann: The Effects of Voice in Isak Dinesen's ›The Dreamers‹.
42 | Bakhtin: Discourse in the Novel, p. 263.

Bibliography

Anderson, Benedict: Imagined Communities: Reflections the Origin and Spread of Nationalism, London, New York 1991.

Arendt, Hannah: Foreword: Isak Dinesen, 1885-1962, in: Isak Dinesen: Daguerreotypes and Other Essays, Chicago 1984, pp. vii-xxv.

Bakhtin, Mikhail: Discourse in the Novel, in: Mikhail Bakhtin: The Dialogic Imagination: Four Essays, Austin 1981, pp. 259-422.

Barthes, Roland: The Grain of the Voice, in: Roland Barthes: Image – Music – Text, London 1977, pp. 179-89.

Brownstein, Rachel M.: Tragic Muse: Rachel of the Comédie-Française, Durham, London 1995.

Cavell, Stanley: Contesting Tears: The Hollywood Melodrama of the Unknown Woman, Chicago and London 1996.

Cavell, Stanley: Cities of Words: Pedagogical Letters on a Register of the Moral Life, Cambridge/MS 2004.

Derrida, Jacques: Of Grammatology, Baltimore 1997.

Dinesen, Isak: The Dreamers, in: Isak Dinesen: Seven Gothic Tales, London 1969, pp. 327-430.

Dolar, Mladen: A Voice and Nothing More, Cambridge/MS and London 2006.

Eliot, George: Daniel Deronda, London 1986.

Felman, Shoshana: Writing and Madness – From ›Henry James: Madness and the Risks of Practice (Turning the Screw of Interpretation)‹, in: Emily Sun, Eyal Peretz and Ulrich Baer (eds): The Claims of Literature: A Shoshana Felman Reader, New York 2007, pp. 15-50.

Fleming, Renée: The Inner Voice: The Making of a Singer, London 2005.

Meredith, George: Sandra Belloni (Originally *Emilia in England*, 1864), London 1910.

Meredith, George: Vittoria, London 1914.

Poizat, Michel: The Angel's Cry: Beyond the Pleasure Principle in Opera, Ithaca and London 1992.

Rieger, Eva and Steegmann, Monica (eds): Göttliche Stimmen: Lebensberichte berühmter Sängerinnen. Von Elisabeth Mara bis Maria Callas. Frankfurt/M. and Leipzig 2002.

Straumann, Barbara: The Effects of Voice in Isak Dinesen's ›The Dreamers‹, in: Variations 17 (2009), pp. 157-69.

Thurman, Judith: Isak Dinesen: The Life of a Storyteller, New York 1982.

Warner, Marina: Monuments and Maidens: The Allegory of the Female Form, London 1987.

Weliver, Phyllis: The Musical Crowd in English Fiction, 1840-1910: Class, Culture and Nation, Houndmills/Basingstoke 2006.

Viel Lärm um *Noise*
Die Aktualität von Shakespeares Caliban

Ina Schabert

»Be not afeard. The isle is full of noises« – diese schlichte Aussage, die Shakespeare dem Caliban im Drama *The Tempest* in den Mund legt, ist in den letzten Jahren erstaunlich populär geworden. Inzwischen hat sie vermutlich Hamlets »To be or not to be« den Rang abgelaufen. Dies dürfte einem Lebensgefühl unserer Zeit entsprechen. Einer trennscharfen Alternative wird offene Pluralität vorgezogen. Statt introvertiertem Grübeln ist extrovertierte Aufmerksamkeit gefragt. Mehr als mit einem Helden, der sich in philosophischen Grundsatzüberlegungen der Frage nach dem Jenseits zuwendet, identifiziert man sich jetzt, so will es scheinen, mit einem Nicht-Helden, der mit den Sinnen, vor allem mit seinem Gehör, das immanente Mysterium seines Lebensraums erspürt.

Caliban ist ein Grenzwesen, angesiedelt zwischen Mensch und Tier, Opfer und Rebell, Naturwesen und Teufel. Er steht jenseits unserer Kultur und stellt deren Setzungen und Grenzziehungen infrage. Der intellektuell nicht kontrollierbare, semantisch fluide Raum der Klänge ist kennzeichnend für ihn: er hört, erinnert, erträumt und imaginiert verschiedenartige Geräusche. In den Versen, in denen die vielzitierte Zeile erscheint, verbleiben diese in einem Schwebezustand zwischen Wachen und Traum:

Cal. Be not afeard. The isle is full of *noises*,
    Sounds, and *sweet airs*, that give delight, and hurt not.
    Sometimes a thousand *twangling* instruments
    Will *hum* about mine ears; and sometimes *voices*
    That if I then had waked after long sleep,
    Will make me sleep again; and then in dreaming
    The clouds methought would open and show riches
    Ready to drop upon me, that when I waked
    I cried to dream again. (3.2.130-138, Herv. I.S.)

Gern wird diese Passage als selbständige Texteinheit behandelt, als abgerundetes Ganzes, gleichsam wie ein kleines Gedicht. Sie ist ein Glanzstück für Rezitationen von Schauspielern. Joseph Fiennes (der Hauptdarsteller von *Shakespeare in Love*) stellt sich mit ihr in seinem Album *When Love Speaks* und im Internet vor.[1] Geoffrey Rush, der den Sprachtherapeuten Lionel Logue in *The King's Speech* spielt, deklamiert sie im Film als Unterhaltung für seine Kinder. Fiennes spricht sie als geheimnisvolles Raunen, beruhigend und mit einschläferndem Effekt, im Sinne des im Text angesprochenen Traummotivs. Rush hingegen realisiert sie mit lebhaften Gesten und Worten als groteskes Kindertheater.

DIE POLYSEMIE DER *NOISES*

Derart losgelöst vom ursprünglichen dramatischen Kontext entfalten sich die Ausdeutungen von Calibans Rede in verschiedenste Richtungen. Das gilt schon für den banalen Textsinn. Die erwähnten Geräusche können als Gegenüberstellung von unterschiedlichen oder als Zusammenstellung von ähnlichen akustischen Effekten verstanden werden. Denn die Syntax klärt nicht, ob die *noises* als ›wohllautende Klänge‹ zu verstehen sind und die *sounds and sweet airs* als ›Töne und süße Weisen‹ diese Bedeutung weiterführen, oder ob ein Kontrast zwischen letzteren als schönen Klängen und den *noises* im Sinne von ›störendem Lärm‹ gemeint ist. Die nachfolgend genannten *thousand twangling instruments* und ihr Geräusch des *humming* können im Sinne von Instrumentalmusikeffekten als Spezifizierung für die *sounds* und die sodann erwähnten *voices* im Sinne von Gesangsstimmen als Erläuterung zu den *sweet airs* aufgefasst werden. Doch das Geräusch des *twangling* (ein Shakespearescher Neologismus abgeleitet von *twang*, ›klingen, näseln, schwirren, scharf klingen, zupfen‹) benennt auch mechanisch produzierten, nicht unbedingt angenehmen Lärm, und das *humming* muss nicht menschlich erzeugte Melodie sein, sondern kann wiederum mechanischem Lärm oder auch dem von Bienen oder anderen Kleintieren erzeugten Gesumme gelten. Die Unklarheit ist typisch für diesen Wortbereich: Begriffe, die Geräusche benennen, sind oft mehrdeutig; in unserer vom Intellekt kontrollierten Sprache sind Gehörsempfindungen und das dafür verfügbare Vokabular nicht optimal aufeinander abgestimmt – hier nimmt man es nicht so genau. So lassen sich in diesem Fall die Verse als eine Aussage sowohl über Störgeräusche als auch

---

[1] | Höre http://www.youtube.com/watch?v=tbjLqvUTuHo (29.7.13).

musikalischen Wohlklang oder auch über eine vom Kontrast zwischen beiden bestimmte Klangkulisse verstehen.²

In Wort- und Ton-Interpretationen zeigt das Zitat eine vitale, in seinen Bedeutungen ständig changierende Präsenz. Odilon Redon hat ihm sogar ein in mehreren Varianten überliefertes Gemälde mit dem Titel *Le sommeil de Caliban* (1895-1900) gewidmet. Die Klänge breiten sich hier in blumenartigen Farbeffekten aus. Auch im Internet findet man eine synästhetische Betrachtung der Zeilen als »colourful text«.³ Die Skala der akustischen Ausdeutungen reicht bis in klangliche Extreme – fast bis zum reinen Lärm. So zu hören im Theaterstück *Sturmspiel: Nach Motiven aus Shakespeares Sturm* von Gerald Thomas, das 1990 am Münchener Cuvilliés-Theater uraufgeführt wurde. Sturmgetöse, Donner und der Krach von Tiefffliegern, kombiniert mit lautem Getrommel bestimmen hier das Soundscape der Insel. Prospero muss sich die Ohren zuhalten.⁴ In anderen Rezeptionszeugnissen wird hingegen von Calibans Traumsituation (obgleich auf sie nur im Irrealis angespielt wird) darauf geschlossen, dass es sich um unhörbare Töne handelt, um Laute, die nur im Kopf des Protagonisten existieren. Gert Jonke, der in seinem literarischen Werk diesen Tönen im Kopf nachspürt, deutet das, was Caliban wahrnimmt, so im Roman *Der ferne Klang* (1979).

Im Sinne einer äußeren Klangkulisse stellt man sich die von Caliban evozierten *noises* gern als Geräusche der Natur vor, als das Rauschen von Wind und Wasser, wie es auf einer Insel im Meer ständig vernehmbar ist. Dieses Soundscape hat etwas Faszinierendes, Geheimnisvolles an sich, auch wenn man nicht so weit gehen muss wie der Komponist R. Murray Schafer, der aus ihm eine Erinnerung an den mythischen Ursprung des Kosmos und an die pränatale Existenz des Menschen heraushört. Als akustische Illustration der Passage ist ein solches Meeresrauschen, zum Teil durchsetzt von metallischen Klängen (die möglicherweise dem *twangling* entsprechen sollen), mehrfach elektronisch simuliert worden.⁵ Alternativ hat man die *noises* aber auch verstanden als die vielen feinen Geräusche, die durch Pflanzen

---

2 | Ein Vergleich von neun Übersetzungen von *The Tempest* 3.2.133-136 ins Deutsche, von Schlegel/Tieck bis Frank Günther, bestätigt die Polysemantik. Die *noises* werden als ›Klang‹ oder ›Klänge‹, als ›Stimmen‹, ›Geräusche‹, ›Lärm‹ oder ›Getöse‹ wiedergegeben, die *sweet airs* als ›süße‹ oder ›anmutige‹ ›Weisen‹, ›Melodien‹ oder ›Lieder‹; die *twangling instruments* sind ›helle‹, ›schwirrende‹, ›schwirre‹ oder ›klimpernde‹ ›Instrumente‹, und *to hum* wird als ›summen‹, ›sumseln‹, ›surren‹, ›klimpern‹, ›umklingeln‹, ›schwirren‹ oder als ›leichtes Murmeln‹ verstanden.
3 | Siehe http://Suite101.com/article/be-not-afeard/the-isle-is-full-of-noises-a411294 (25.7.13).
4 | Hörprobe unter http://geraldthomas.net/PP-Sturmspiel.html (25.7.13).
5 | Höre z.B. https://soundslikenoise.org/2011/08/01/caliban-253/ (25.7.13).

und Kleintiere in einem Feuchtgebiet entstehen, bevorzugt im Ökosystem der mittelamerikanischen Golfküste, der vermutlichen Heimat von Caliban, wenn man in ihm einen aus Afrika nach Mittelamerika gebrachten Sklaven sieht.[6] Der Kochbuchautor Robin Ellis wiederum findet sich durch die morgendlichen Tiergeräusche in seiner eigenen, ländlichen Umgebung an Calibans *noises* erinnert.[7] Mit solchen Interpretationen wird der neu entdeckte ökologische Shakespeare (›Green Shakespeare‹) assoziiert.

Zahlreich sind die Ausdeutungen der Zeilen durch Vertonungen. Unvermeidlich werden hier die *noises*, die Caliban meint, zu kunstvoll gestalteten Klängen veredelt. Zwischen 1871 und 1992 entstanden mindestens sechs Liedfassungen, jeweils für Gesang (Sopran oder/und Bariton, hohe oder mittlere Stimme) und Klavier oder Instrumentalensemble oder für einen a capella-Chor. Die Singstimme benennt die Klänge, gemeinsam mit den Instrumenten führt sie sie zugleich vor.[8] Der Textstelle wird regelmäßig auch eine prominente Position in Vertonungen zum gesamten Drama eingeräumt. Eine *Tempest Fantasy* von Paul Moravec (2002/03) setzt in Teil 4, der mit dem Zitat »Sweet Airs« überschrieben ist, mit Calibans Rede ein. Die Oper *The Tempest* von Lee Hoiby (Uraufführung 1996) bringt im 2. Akt Calibans Arie »Be not afeard« als Glanzstück des Werks. Eine Komposition des norwegischen Komponisten Daniel Bjarnason mit dem Titel *The Isle Is Full of Noises* (Uraufführung 2012) übersetzt die *noises* in einen vibrierenden großen Septakkord, kombiniert mit Glissandi, die vermutlich das *twangling* hörbar machen sollen, und mit Summtönen für das *humming*. Das Blechbläser-Quintett *Be Not Afraid: The Isle is Full of Noises* (1999) von Samuel Adler interpretiert die Inselgeräusche entsprechend der Instrumentenwahl als machtvolle Musik. Im Sommer 2011 gab es in der Wilton's Music Hall in London das Puppenspiel *The Isle is Full of Noises*, mit Musik von Nick McCarthy von der schottischen Rockband Franz Ferdinand. In den Nummern der deutschen Metalcore Band Caliban haben die *noises* einen besonders harten metallischen Sound.

---

6 | Z.B. Boelhower: Owning the Weather.

7 | http://www.robin-ellis.net/tag/caliban (25.7.13).

8 | Brian Dennis (1941-) »Be not afeard: the isle is full of noises« (1982), medium voice and piano; Joseph Francis Duggan (1817-1900) »Be not afear'd« (1871), high or medium voice and piano; Marjorie Merryman, no title (1978), soprano, clarinet, percussion and violoncello (from *Ariel*, No. 1); Arne Nordheim (1931-), »Be not afeard« (1977), soprano, baritone, celesta, harp, piano, and tape; Kaija Saariaho (1952-), »Caliban's Dream« (1992), bass-baritone, clarinet, harp, guitar, mandolin and contrabass (from *The Tempest Songbook*, No. 2); Tim Souster, »Voices« (1964), chorus a capella. Aufnahmen z.B. mit dem Tenor Gerald Seminatore (www.youtube.com/watch?v=TbdolBnjsxg, 24.9.13) und mit dem Tenor Oliver Mercer (www.youtube.com/watch?v=ceXEZWciUiQ, 24.9.13).

All diese Klänge wurden übertönt durch die Schläge der überdimensionalen, siebenundzwanzig Tonnen schweren Glocke, die am 20. Juli 2012 die Olympischen Spiele in England eingeläutet hat. In eingegossenen Lettern ist ihre Botschaft zu lesen, und diese lautet: »Be not afeard, the isle of full of noises«. Unter eben diesem Motto stand auch das Festspiel des Eröffnungsabends, das der Filmregisseur Danny Boyle arrangierte. Die vorgeführte Festspiellandschaft war Monate zuvor als ländliche Idylle mit gespielten Landbewohnern und echten Tieren angekündigt worden. Dies ließ eine von Glockenschlägen, Tierlauten und Volkslied bestimmte Klangkulisse erwarten und damit eine konservativ-selbstzufriedene Deutung der Insel, die von solchen Klängen erfüllt ist.

DAS PROTESTPOTENZIAL DER *NOISES*

Die südafrikanische Zeitung *Daily Maverick* konterte daraufhin mit einem ganz anderen Tonbild der Britischen Inseln:

Thing is, the noises the isle is full of are not »the sounds and sweet airs that give delight and hurt not,« they are the noises of bank balances dropping to the floor, of stores slamming forever shut, of landlords banging on the door. And the »thousand twangling instruments« are the failed financial models that brought the kingdom to this point.[9]

Damit wird eine alternative Deutungstradition in Bezug auf die von Caliban angesprochenen *noises* weitergeführt. Denn auch ihre potenzielle Kakophonie kann aktualisiert und interpretiert werden. Schon Jahre zuvor hatte der irische Dichter Seamus Heaney im Gedicht »Sybil« (1972) jene *noises* mit den Worten der Sibylle zu einer negativen Zeitdiagnose für seine Heimat Nordirland umgedeutet. »My people think of money / And talk weather. Oil rigs lull their future ... / Our island is full of comfortless noises«, sagt hier die Seherin.[10] Und die polnisch-jüdische Dichterin Rajzel Zychlinski beschwört 1993 in einem jiddischen Gedicht, dessen Titel »der indzl iz ful mit gerojschn« von Caliban übernommen ist, akustische Effekte von Gewalt, von erinnerter Gewalt in den Konzentrationslagern und erlebter Gewalt an ihrem späteren Exilort, der Insel von Manhattan:

Die Insel ist voll mit Geräuschen.
Klänge der Mondscheinsonate?
Herabgefallene, verloschene Sterne?

---

9 | Bloom: Danny Boyle's Olympic Vision.
10 | Heaney: New Selected Poems, Triptych II.

Nein!
Es ist das Weinen von Kindern, ...
Entführt,
verschleppt von ihren Heimen, [...]
Schüsse
Auf Straßen,
in Subways [...]
Die Insel ist voll mit Geräuschen.[11]

Die tatsächliche Eröffnungsshow der Olympischen Spiele brachte ziemlich unerwartet eine ähnliche Wende. Nach dem idyllischen Auftakt folgte zur allgemeinen Überraschung und zur Bestürzung der konservativen Regierung eine – von tausend Trommlern eingeleitete – anders geartete Sequenz von Bildern und Klängen, die ein England mit Industrieller Revolution, Krieg, sozialen Problemen und Reformen, Immigration, Skurrilitäten und viel Pop-Musik vorführte. Die *noises,* von denen die Britischen Inseln erfüllt sind, wurden damit ausgedeutet als kulturelle Stimmenvielfalt, in der die Missklänge nicht fehlen. Calibans Rede wurde vom Starschauspieler Kenneth Branagh gesprochen. Er trat auf als der Ingenieur Brunel, der in England allgemein als Pionier im Eisenbahn- und Schiffsbauwesen des 19. Jahrhunderts bekannt ist; aus seinem Mund ist der Verweis auf die *noises* der Insel nur für Technik-Fans wirklich beruhigend. Boyle selbst beschwichtigt: In einer vielzitierten Aussage möchte er die in der Show vorgeführte Pluralität von Klängen und Bildern in einem moralisch-konstruktiven Sinn verstanden wissen als Ausdruck von »the rich heritage, diversity, energy, inventiveness, wit and creativity that defines what is the British Isles«.[12]

Die *noises* im historischen Rückblick

Die neue Aufmerksamkeit für Calibans »The isle is full of noises«-Rede hat auch die Shakespeare-Forschung auf den Plan gerufen. Zuvor wurde bestenfalls eine Parallele zwischen dem von Caliban evozierten Soundscape und ähnlichen Klangangaben in elisabethanischen Berichten von exotischen Ländern wahrgenommen. Üblich war der Verweis auf das allerdings etwas später entstandene Reisebuch *Purchas His Pilgrimes* (1625). Hier ist vom Klang von Flöten und Zymbeln (»Phifes and the noise and sound of Cimbals«) die Rede, die auf einer entlegenen Insel jenseits des afrikanischen Kontinents

---

11 | In: Naje Lider, Tel Aviv 1993; deutsche Übersetzung in Tippelskirch: Rajzel Zychlinski, S. 272.
12 | Kelso: London 2012.

zu hören waren.[13] Wenn man die akustischen Informationen im Text nicht allzu genau nimmt, kann man annehmen, dass Calibans Klangerlebnis ähnlicher Art war. Eine neuere Arbeit von Christy Anderson stellt nun einen ganz anders gearteten Zusammenhang her. Im Kontext einer Geschichte der Gartenkunst wird hier die Klangwelt der Insel in *The Tempest* erklärt als Komposition aus kunstvoll simulierten Naturgeräuschen. Mittels einer hochentwickelten Hydraulik plätscherten in Renaissancegärten Fontänen, ertönten Wasserorgeln, Automaten bewegten sich und gaben ebenfalls Laute von sich. Zumal ein solcher Klanggarten zur Entstehungszeit von Shakespeares Drama gerade vom Ingenieur Salomon de Caus für Anna von Dänemark, die Gemahlin von James I., angelegt wurde, lässt sich vermuten, dass Prospero mit seinen magischen Kräften Calibans vormals wilde Insel in ähnlicher Art gestaltet hat. Die von Caliban evozierten *noises* werden damit in einer Kulturgeschichte der Geräuschproduktion verortet. Peter Greenaways *Tempest*-Film *Prospero's Books* (1991) kommt dieser Ausdeutung der Geräusche im Drama bereits zuvor.

THE TEMPEST ALS HÖRSTÜCK

Aber was hört Caliban auf der Insel ›wirklich‹? Welche Geräusche gibt es in Shakespeares Bühnenwelt? Diese naheliegende Frage wurde lange nicht energisch genug gestellt. Erst in jüngster Zeit setzte die systematische Erschließung der Dramen als Hör-Stücke ein. Mit dem ›geistigen Ohr‹ wurde daraufhin wahrgenommen, dass das in *The Tempest* vorgegebene Soundscape ungewöhnlich reich ausdifferenziert ist. Der Wortsinn wird kontinuierlich durch die Modulation von Sprech- und Singstimmen, durch Musik und Bühnengeräusche mitbestimmt, sodass selbst einem Zuschauer, der den Text nicht versteht, eine komplexe akustische Botschaft vermittelt wird, wenn er zu hören weiß.

Die Besonderheit mag mit der Entstehungssituation zu tun haben. Normalerweise bespielte Shakespeares Truppe das öffentliche Freilichttheater ›The Globe‹. Hier war mit einem relativ hohen äußeren Lärmpegel zu rechnen. *The Tempest* (1610) ist das erste Stück, das er für das private Innenraumtheater ›Blackfriars‹ konzipierte. Theatergeräusche konnten hier eine andere, subtilere Wirkung als im Globe entfalten; das mag Shakespeare dazu angeregt haben, das Stück als eine sorgfältig aufeinander abgestimmte Partitur der Klänge zu konzipieren. Glücklicherweise hat er seine Spätwerke (zu denen *The Tempest* zählt) im Unterschied zu seiner früheren Gewohnheit mit

---

13 | Vgl. Kermodes Anmerkung zu *The Tempest* 3.2.133 im Arden Shakespeare, die weite Verbreitung fand.

genauen Regieanweisungen versehen, selbst was die Begleitgeräusche betrifft. Die Aufführung als Klangkomposition lässt sich deshalb ungewöhnlich genau rekonstruieren.

Die hauseigene Attraktion des Blackfriars-Theaters war ein *Broken Consort*, d. h. ein Ensemble von Instrumentalisten. Es spielte vor und während der Aufführungen; bereits etwa eine Stunde vor einer Vorstellung pflegte das Konzert zu beginnen. Shakespeares *Tempest* setzt sodann kontrastiv mit dem gänzlich unharmonischen Lärm des Sturms ein. »*A tempestuous noise of thunder and lightning heard*« lautet die erste Bühnenanweisung (1.1.1). Die Schiffsmannschaft verständigt sich mit Schreien, der Kapitän mit einer schrillen Pfeife; von unterhalb der Bühne, aus dem Schiffsrumpf, ertönt der angstvolle Ruf von Passagieren: »*a cry within*«. Die knappen Wortwechsel bestätigen das Brüllen, *roaring*, des Winds, das Angstgeheul, *howling*, der Passagiere, das laute Rufen, *bawling*, der Besatzung. Schließlich zerbirst das Schiff unter dem wirren Schreien der unten Eingeschlossenen: »*A confused noise within*« ist zu hören. Gedeutet wird der Lärm – ansatzweise – als Unbotmäßigkeit, als Aufsässigkeit. Das Tosen der Elemente kümmert sich nicht um den hohen Rang der Passagiere: »*What cares these roarers for the name of king?*« fragt ein Bootsmann; und einer der vornehmen Passagiere beschimpft ihn im Gegenzug als »*whoreson insolent noisemaker*«. Man kann mit Andrew Gurr die akustischen Signale und ihre Kommentierung als klares Shakespearesches Gegenstatement gegen die Vornehmheit des neuen Theaterraums und seines Stammpublikums verstehen: Jetzt – so die Botschaft – wird es hier volkstümlich und subversiv laut![14]

Im Nachfolgenden wechseln sehr ruhige und ausgesprochen geräuschreiche Szenen einander ab; Instrumentalmusik und Gesang alternieren mit bloßem Lärm, feine mit burlesken Liedern, dunkle Männer- mit hohen Knabenstimmen in den Dialogen.[15] Die Personen selbst zeigen sich sehr empfänglich für Klänge; in ihren Reden machen sie häufig auf akustische Effekte aufmerksam, auf vorgeführte oder auch erinnerte Geräusche. Auch die Bedeutung eines Geräusches oder Klanges kann von ihnen diskutiert werden, kennzeichnender Weise kommen sie dabei nicht zu schlüssigen Ergebnissen, denn Klänge lassen sich nicht vollständig und endgültig in Sinn überführen. Durchgängig zugegen bleibt der bedrohliche und destruktive Lärm, der den Beginn des Dramas kennzeichnete. Als Prospero den Schiffbrüchigen ein Bankett herbeizaubert, verschwindet dieses kurz darauf mit »*Thunder and lightning*« (3.3.53); als er die Hochzeit von Ferdinand und Miranda mit einem Maskenspiel feiern lässt, bricht dieses abrupt ab mit »*a strange,*

---

14 | Vgl. Gurr: *The Tempest's* Tempest at Blackfriars.

15 | Genaueres bei Smith: The Acoustic World of Early Modern England, und Neill: »Noises / Sounds, and sweet airs«.

hollow, and confused noise« (4.1.142). Stephano und Trinculo werden an ihrem Raub von Prosperos Kleidern durch Jagdlärm, bellende Hunde und bedrohliche Ausrufe gehindert und beginnen ihrerseits zu brüllen: »Hark, they roar!« (4.1.257) Gegen Ende berichtet der Bootsmann, die Schiffsmannschaft sei für die Heimreise mit furchtbarem Krach aus ihrem magischen Schlaf geweckt worden:

> with strange and several noises
> Of roaring, shrieking, howling, jingling chains,
> And more diversity of sounds, all horrible. (5.1.235-237)

Während die Figuren innerhalb des Dramas solcherart *noises*, im Unterschied zu den Musik- und Liedeinlagen, als unerklärbare Störung erfahren, werden sie für die Zuschauer als Signale von Prosperos regelndem und rächendem Eingreifen durchschaubar. Un-sinnigen Lärm kann es in einem Kunstwerk letztlich ebenso wenig geben wie sinnlosen Text.

CALIBAN UND DIE *NOISES*

Caliban ist, neben Ariel, das einzige Wesen, das Prospero bei seiner Ankunft auf der Insel vorfand. Seinen Erziehungsversuchen gegenüber erweist er sich als unzugänglich; er ist für ihn »A devil, a born devil, on whose nature / Nurture can never stick«: an seiner Natur lässt sich keine Kultur festmachen (4.1.188-89). Die Sprache, die Prospero ihm beigebracht hat, nutzt er, nach eigener Aussage, um zu fluchen. Seine wohlklingenden und wirkmächtigen Verse über die Geräusche auf der Insel passen, isoliert betrachtet, überhaupt nicht zu solcher Fremd- und Selbstdeutung. Allerdings verfolgt Caliban mit der schönen Rede ein unschönes Ziel: Er hat mit seinen durch den Schiffbruch herbeigeführten Kumpanen Trinculo und Stefano einen Mordplan für Prospero ausgeheckt; daraufhin singt das Trio ein derbes Lied, und zwar völlig falsch: Böse Menschen kennen keine Lieder! Ariel stört den Mordplan und die Ausgelassenheit, indem er, unsichtbar, mit Trommel und Flöte die korrekte Melodie des Liedes erklingen lässt. Die anscheinend von niemandem gespielte Musik versetzt Calibans Kumpane in Angst. Es ist diese Situation, in der Caliban sie mit seiner Rede beruhigen und beim Mordplan halten will. Macht euch keine Sorgen, will er ihnen zu verstehen geben, auf dieser Insel tönt immer etwas; das bedeutet nichts.

Die Absicht der Rede ist also durchaus in Calibans Charakter eines »born devil«. Was im Dramengeschehen folgt, lässt die Rede noch negativer erscheinen. Schon die Sensibilität für Klänge als solche nahm in der Hierarchie der Werte, wie sie in der Renaissance galt, einen niederen Platz ein.

Sinneseindrücke rangierten unterhalb geistiger Einsichten; und in der Skala der Sinne wurde die akustische unter der optischen Wahrnehmung eingestuft, da das Hören nach damaliger Auffassung intensiver an die Materie gebunden ist und eine geringe geistige Distanz zum wahrgenommenen Objekt impliziert. Calibans Klanggefühl verweist auf seine Affinität zum niedersten der Elemente, zur dunklen, trägen Erdmaterie. Niedere Wesen wie Tiere oder Barbaren, so glaubte man, lassen sich mit Klängen anlocken und lenken: Die Mythen von Orpheus und Amphion galten als Beleg dafür. Menschen, die sich durch Klänge betören lassen, degenerieren, wie die Geschichte von Circe lehrt, zu groben Tieren. Solche entwürdigenden Bedeutungen werden aktiviert, wenn Ariel (in 4.1.171-184) mit Tiervergleichen berichtet, was nach Calibans Rede geschieht: Er schlägt seine Trommel, das Trio spitzt, unberittenen Jungpferden gleich, die Ohren; hebt die Augenlider und Nasen, da es Musik ›riecht‹ (der Hörsinn wird noch einmal, zum Geruchssinn, hinabgestuft); wie Kälber folgen die drei dem Laut der Trommel durch Dickicht und Dornen – bis sie in einer Jauchegrube nahe Prosperos Behausung einsacken. Anders als Ariels feine Lieder und anders als die von Prospero herbeigezauberte Musik des Maskenspiels wirken sich somit die für Caliban, Trinculo und Stefano inszenierten Trommelklänge keinesfalls als tröstend oder gar erhebend aus. Sie führen in Schmutz und Schande.

Postkoloniale Relektüren

Es ist ein lange wirksam gebliebener neuplatonischer Denkkontext, der das Hören als Wahrnehmung und damit zugleich den Bereich akustischer Effekte abwertet. Der Weg zur Erkenntnis führt in der westlichen Kultur traditionell weg von den materiellen Dingen, weg von den unteren Sinnen, und über das Schauen hinauf zum Reich des Geistes, der Ideen. Dem stellt sich in unserer Zeit ein konträres Postulat entgegen: *Bodies matter!* Das positive Interesse für Calibans Wahrnehmung der vielfältigen Inselgeräusche ist in einem gewandelten Werteverständnis begründet, in dem Körperlichkeit und sinnliche Erfahrung vorrangig sind. Die Umdeutung geschieht nicht nur, wenn (wie berichtet) die Zeilen aus dem Kontext herausgenommen werden. Sie vollzieht sich auch innerhalb einer gesamten Gegenlektüre des *Tempest*. Aus gesellschaftskritischer Sicht schon in der Romantik und in kolonialkritischer Absicht im postkolonialen Zeitalter werden Prosperos Kultur und seine Wertwelt als Instrument der Unterdrückung negativiert, während ein von ihm enteigneter, versklavter und sich auflehnender Caliban ins positive normative Zentrum des Dramas rückt. Er wird zum Repräsentanten erst einer klassenspezifischen und sodann einer ethnischen Gegenkultur, der die Zukunft gehört. Calibans akustische Sensibilität wird nun im Vergleich zu

Prosperos Bücherwissen als alternative, höherrangige Kompetenz gewertet; die Schönheit der Zeilen über »the isle is full of noises« gilt als Bestätigung dieser Aufwertung. Die Textpassage avanciert zu einer Schlüsselstelle für das neue *Tempest*-Verständnis.

Nach der antikolonialistischen Pionierstudie über Prospero und Caliban von Ottavo Mannoni (1950) und der ersten dramatischen Umdeutung *Une Tempête* von Aimé Césaire (1969) ist die Gegenlektüre allmählich Allgemeingut geworden. Vor allem wird sie gepflegt von karibischen anglophonen Autoren, die damit den ihnen zumeist aus dem Schulunterricht vertrauten kanonischen Shakespeare gegen den Strich bürsten und dabei in Caliban eine Spiegelfigur ihrer selbst finden. Caliban steht im Zentrum der Selbstdarstellung in Texten z. B. von George Lamming, Derek Walcott und Edward Kamau Brathwaite. Die Identifikation mit ihm über die »The isle is full of noises«-Rede wird dadurch erleichtert, dass sich die afro-karibische Kultur grundsätzlich Geräuschen gegenüber besonders aufgeschlossen zeigt.[16] Es ist, so Lamming, eine orale und aurale Kultur. Bevorzugtes Medium ist für Lamming der Hörfunk; vor allem in Form des BBC-Programms »Caribbean Voices« (1943–1958), das das karibische Selbstbewusstsein mitgeprägt hat. Die Zeilen, die von Calibans Empfindsamkeit für Klänge zeugen, werden immer wieder zum kreativen Kern für eigene Dramen, Erzählungen und Gedichte der karibischen Autoren. Brathwaite führt die alternative Kultur der Laute im Gedicht »Caliban« mit den für die afro-karibische Musik typischen abgehackten, scharf rhythmisierten, knappen, repetitiven Einheiten vor:

It was December second, nineteen fifty-six.
It was the first of August eighteen thirty-eight.
It was the twelfth October fourteen ninety-two.[17]
How many bangs and how many revolutions?
[...]
And
Ban
Ban
Cal-
iban
Like to play
Pan
At the Car-

---

16 | Vgl. Hart: Erosion, Noise and Hurricanes.
17 | 1956 kehrte Fidel Castro nach Cuba zurück, und begann den Kampf für die Revolution 1959. 1839 fand die Revolte auf dem Sklavenschiff Amistad statt. 1492 landete Columbus in Cuba.

nival;
pran-
cing up the lim-
bo silence
down
down
down [...].¹⁸

Der Text bezieht sich auf den während des karibischen Karnevals gepflegten *Limbo dance* zu den Klängen von *steel-band music*. Dieser Tanz findet unter einer Eisenstange statt und erinnert damit an das Sklavendasein. Caliban revoltiert, wie das Gedicht zeigt, in der Karibik in einem anderen Stil als bei Shakespeare. Kreolsprache klingt nicht wie Shakespearezeilen, sagt Brathwaite, der Hurrikan heult nicht wie Shakespeares Inselwind in Blankversen.¹⁹ In einem Spottlied von Shakespeares Caliban deutet sich jedoch schon die Rhythmik von Brathwaites Gedichts an: »'Ban, 'Ban, Cacaliban / Has a new master. – Get a new man!« (2.2.175-76)

Der Shakespearesche Gegensatz von Prosperos Buchkultur und Calibans auraler Vorzivilisiertheit wird in diesen Lektüren zu einem Kontrast von kolonialer Arroganz und sinnenfroher Gegenkultur ausgestaltet und damit auch völlig anders bewertet. Caliban avanciert zu einem Kronzeugen für die Zielsetzungen postkolonialer Literatur- und Kulturwissenschaft.²⁰ Die neue selbstbewusste Abgrenzung des Subalternen von der britischen Herrenkultur klingt mit an, wenn im Film *The King's Speech* der Sprachtherapeut Lionel Logue Calibans Rede rezitiert. Bei Shakespeare lehrte Prospero Caliban das Sprechen; im Film hingegen ist es der Spezialist aus Australien, dem es gelingt, den englischen König vom Stottern abzubringen.

Calibans *noises* als alternative Erkenntnisquelle

Kenneth Gross geht in seiner Untersuchung *Shakespeare's Noise* (2001) wiederum einen Schritt weiter in der subversiven Ausdeutung von Calibans Rede. Die *noises*, von denen sie handelt, seien, so befindet er, das Zeichen eines alternativen Hörens, das seinem Herrn völlig abgeht. Sie geben ihm

---

18 | Vgl. den gesprochenen Text: https://media.sas.upenn.edu/pennsound/authors/Brathwaite/5-1-04/Brathwaite-Kamau_Caliban_Segue_NY_5-1-04.mp3 (14.12.16).
19 | Brathwaite: History of the Voice, S. 365.
20 | Siehe dazu vor allem Vaughan und Vaughan: Shakespeare's Caliban, sowie Lie und D'haen (Hg.): Constellation Caliban.

Kunde von etwas, das jenseits aller Sprache, jenseits aller Kultur liegt.[21] Auch der postkoloniale Kulturwissenschaftler Abdennebi Ben Beya deutet die »the isle is full of noises«-Rede in diesem nicht primär politischen, antikolonialistischen, sondern in einem philosophisch-dekonstruktiven Sinn. »The ›textual empire‹ is shaken by the unknown: The island is full of noises«.[22] Im präverbalen Medium der von Caliban gehörten Klänge sei Nichtgewusstes verborgen und werde erahnbar. Michel Serres thematisierte diese transgressive Bedeutung des Hörens in einem Essay über »Bruits« bereits im Buch *Le parasite* (1980). Nach Serres öffnet der Gehörsinn einen Zugang zum primordialen Chaos jenseits jeder Kultur.[23]

Die Ahnung von solch fundamentaler Alterität, die sich gleichsam in unartikulierten, vorsprachlichen ›Lauten‹ äußert, wurde lange zuvor schon bei George Eliot in einer berühmt gewordenen Passage in *Middlemarch* zum Ausdruck gebracht. Hier ist von einem fatalen »Brüllen auf der anderen Seite des Schweigens« die Rede, gegen das wir uns mit geistiger Abgestumpftheit schützen und das paradoxerweise nur mit einem irreal feinen Gehör vernehmbar wäre:

it would be like hearing the grass grow and the squirrel's heart beat, and we should die of that roar which lies at the other side of silence. As it is, the quickest of us walk about well wadded with stupidity.[24]

Der eigenwillige schottische Dichter W. S. Graham befasst sich im Gedicht »The Beast in the Space« (1970) mit den Geräuschen auf der anderen Seite des Schweigens. Gleichsam wie ein großes Tier, so befindet er, lecken sie ihm seine gewohnten Bedeutungen weg. Seine Hoffnung ist es, mit Hilfe von Dichtung die alternative Botschaft hörbar zu machen:

If you think you hear somebody knocking
On the other side of the words, pay
No attention. It will be only
The great creature that thumps its tail
On silence on the other side.
If you do not even hear that
I'll give the beast a quick skelp
And through Art you'll hear it yelp.

---

21 | Gross: Shakespeare's Noise, S. 203.
22 | Zum Beispiel Ben Beya: Mimicry, Ambivalence, and Hybridity.
23 | Serres: Le parasite, S. 170.
24 | Eliot: Middlemarch, S. 226.

Das *yelp* (ein tierisches, schrilles Bellen) stößt Graham im eigenen Gedichtvortrag in lauter, grotesker Weise heraus, als akustische Entsprechung zur vorkulturellen sprachlichen Unartikuliertheit, in der sich alternatives Wissen verbirgt.[25]

Ein Roman des neuseeländischen Anthropologen Randolph Stow, *Visitants* (1979), der auf einer Insel in Papua-Neuguinea spielt, wählt Calibans Zeile »Be not afeard; the isle is full of noises« als sein Motto. Wiederum gelten in der Erzählung Geräusche als sinnliche Botschaft von etwas Übersinnlichem, als Kunde von geheimnisvoller Wahrheit, die unerklärt jenseits des Textes verbleibt. Weit intensiver nutzt ein späterer Roman, *Indigo* (1992) von Marina Warner, Calibans Soundscape als Bezugshorizont für eine alternative Sinnvermittlung. Warner, eine englische Autorin, deren Vorfahren als Kolonisatoren in die Karibik kamen und Jahrhunderte lang dort lebten, erzählt die Geschichte des fatalen Zusammentreffens der indigenen Bevölkerung einer karibischen Insel mit den englischen Eroberern um 1600 und die Geschichte ihrer Nachfahren in der Mitte des 20. Jahrhunderts; die Erzählebenen wechseln dabei in sinnträchtiger Verschachtelung miteinander ab. Auf beiden Ebenen beziehen sich eine Reihe von Figuren zurück auf Charaktere von Shakespeares *Tempest*, besonders prominent unter ihnen sind die Caliban-Figuren und die Figuren, die seine Mutter Sycorax repräsentieren – bei Shakespeare ist sie eine zu Dramenbeginn bereits verstorbene böse Hexe, hier hingegen eine weise Frau.

Detailliert zeichnet der Text das akustische Profil der ursprünglichen und der jetztzeitigen Insellandschaft auf. Durch das Ganze zieht sich leitmotivisch wiederum das Zitat »the isle is full of noises«, und diese Worte nehmen eine Bedeutung jenseits der Bedeutungen an. Sie verweisen auf Geräusche, die auf »der anderen Seite des Schweigens«, von Toten unter der Erde oder auf dem Meeresgrund, vernommen werden. Zugleich sind es Geräusche, mit denen die Verstorbenen, Opfer der brutalen Kolonialisierung wie auch der gewaltsamen Entkolonialisierung, sich über das Schweigen hinweg in den Lauten der Natur der Jetztzeit mitzuteilen versuchen. Vermittelt wird dies in einer lyrischen Sprache, die intensiv mit Klangeffekten arbeitet, mit suggestiven Rhythmen, mit Onomatopoesie, mit alliterativen Klangketten, volltönenden Vokalen und Diphthongen, Kontrasten von weicher und harter Konsonanz:

THE ISLE IS full of noises [...] and Sycorax is the source of many. Recent sound effects – the chattering of loose halyard against the masts of the fancy yachts riding at anchor in the bays, the gush and swoosh of water in the oyster pool at the luxury hotel – aren't of her making:

---

25 | »The Beast in the Space«, aus: *Malcolm Mooney's Land* (1970). Abdruck in Graham: Collected Poems. S. 147-148. Lesung durch den Autor: http://www2.warwick.ac.uk/fac/arts/english/writingprog/archive/writers/wsgraham/231079 (25.7.13).

Sycorax speaks in the noises that fall from the mouth of the wind. It's a way of holding on to what was once hers, to pour herself out through fissures of the rock, to exhale from the caked mud bed of the island's rivers in the dry season, and mutter in the leaves of the saman where they buried her. [...] When she sighs or clicks in the shaking of the palms and breathes out with the rip of the surf, you can hear her despair that her death will never come to an end.[26]

Erinnerungen, Gefühle und Vorahnungen kreuzen sich mit akustischen Wahrnehmungen; Hören, Empfinden und Denken werden auch für den Leser als Einheit erfahrbar.

In derartigen Texten beginnt sich in der europäischen Kultur des späten 20. Jahrhunderts eine der Frühen Neuzeit ganz fremde, neue geistige Hochschätzung von Geräuschen und Klängen anzudeuten. Wissen ist nicht mehr, wie die platonische Tradition es lehrt und wie es unsere Sprache mit vergeistigten optischen Metaphern suggeriert, an ›Einsicht‹, ›Durchschau‹ und ›Überblick‹ gebunden, sondern wird bewirkt durch eine besondere mentale Hörfähigkeit. Erkennen ist ein Lauschangriff auf das Unbekannte.

BIBLIOGRAPHIE

Anderson, Christy: Wild Waters: Hydraulics and the Forces of Nature, in: Peter Hulme und William H. Sherman (Hg.): ›The Tempest‹ and Its Travels, London 2000, S. 41-47.
Ben Beya, Abdennebi: Mimicry, Ambivalence, and Hybridity, https://scholarblogs.emory.edu/postcolonialstudies/2014/06/21/mimicry-ambivalence-and-hybridity/ (6.5.16).
Bloom, Kevin: Danny Boyle's Olympic Vision: The £ 27-million nervous breakdown, in: Daily Maverick, 16.4.2012.
Boelhower, William: Owning the Weather: Reading *The Tempest* after Hurricane Katrina, http://www.borrowers.uga.edu/782579/pdf (14.12.16).
Brathwaite, Edward Kamau: Caliban, https://media.sas.upenn.edu/pennsound/authors/Brathwaite/5-1-04/Brathwaite-Kamau_Caliban_Segue_NY_5-1-04.mp3 (14.12.16).
Brathwaite, Edward Kamau: History of the Voice, in: Roots: Essays in Carribean Literature, Ann Arbor 1993, S. 259-304.
Eliot, George: Middlemarch, hg. von W. J. Harvey, Harmondsworth 1965.
Graham, W. S.: Collected Poems, 1942-1977, London 1979.
Gross, Kenneth: Shakespeare's Noise, Chicago 2001.
Gurr, Andrew: *The Tempest's* Tempest at Blackfriars, in: Shakespeare Survey 41 (1989), S. 91-102.

---

26 | Warner: Indigo, S. 77-78.

Hart, David W.: Erosion, Noise and Hurricanes, in: Revista Mexicana del Caribe 6,xii (2001), S. 215-220.
Heaney, Seamus: New Selected Poems 1966-87, London 1990.
Kelso, Paul: London 2012: Shakespeare provides the inspiration for ›wondrous‹ Olympic Games opening ceremony, in: The Telegraph, 27.1.2012, http://www.telegraph.co.uk/sport/olympics/9045785/London-2012-Shakespeare-provides-the-inspiration-for-wondrous-Olympic-Games-opening-ceremony.html (14.12.16).
Kermode, Frank (Hg.): The Tempest: The Arden Shakespeare, London 1954.
Lie, Nadia und Theo D'haen (Hg.): Constellation Caliban: Figurations of a Character, Amsterdam 1997.
Neill, Michael: »Noises / Sounds, and sweet airs«: The Burden of Shakespeare's *Tempest*, in: Shakespeare Quarterly 59 (2008), S. 36-59.
Schafer, R. Murray: The Soundscape: Our Sonic Environment and the Tuning of the World, Rochester 1994.
Serres, Michel: Le parasite, Paris 1980.
Shakespeare, William: The Norton Shakespeare, hg. von Stephen Greenblatt et al., New York 1997.
Smith, Bruce R.: The Acoustic World of Early Modern England: Attending to the O-Factor, Chicago 1999.
Stow, Randolph: Visitants, London 1979.
Tippelskirch, Katharina von: »Also das Alphabet vergessen?«: Die jiddische Dichterin Rajzel Zychlinski, Marburg 2000.
Vaughan, Alden T. und Virginia Mason Vaughan: Shakespeare's Caliban: A Cultural History, Cambridge 1991.
Warner, Marina: Indigo, or, Mapping the Waters, London 1993.

Filmographie

Prospero's Books (1991), Regie: Peter Greenaway, UK, Farbe.
Shakespeare in Love (1998), Regie: John Madden, USA, Farbe.
The King's Speech (2010), Regie: Tom Hooper, UK, Farbe.

Diskographie

Adler, Samuel: Be Not Afraid: The Isle is Full of Noises (1999).
Bjarnason, Daniel: The Isle Is Full of Noises (UA 2012).
Hoiby, Lee: The Tempest (UA 1996).
Moravec, Paul: Tempest Fantasy (2002/3).
McCarthy, Nick: The Isle is Full of Noises (2011).

V Medieneinsatz: Geräusche in virtuellen Welten

Sounds and Vision
Geräusche in Jacques Tatis *Les vacances de Monsieur Hulot*
und David Lynchs *Eraserhead*

Kay Kirchmann

Erst seit wenigen Jahren beginnt auch die Medienwissenschaft sich systematisch mit den Figuren des Akustischen in medialen Artefakten auseinanderzusetzen, eine Verspätung, die vor allem auf die traditionelle Bildzentrierung der Disziplin zurückzuführen ist, wie Harro Segeberg anmerkt.[1] Angesichts dieser bisherigen Geringschätzung des Tons im Allgemeinen nimmt es nicht Wunder, dass auch das Geräusch im Besonderen wenig akademische Aufmerksamkeit auf sich gezogen hat. Dies gilt auch für den Teilbereich der Filmanalyse,[2] was dann doch insofern wieder verwunderlich ist, als die Filmgeschichte durchaus exponierte Beispiele für eine avancierte Handhabung des Geräusches als Tonquelle kennt. Das ist zunächst in der Phase unmittelbar nach Einführung des Tonfilms 1926 zu beobachten, die neben zahlreichen Experimenten mit der neuen Gestaltungsoption sogar eine (und bis dato zugleich letzte) programmatische Debatte um eine ästhetisch veritable Verwendung von Geräusch und Klang im Film hervorbrachte, auf die später noch einzugehen sein wird. Das Erbe dieser sogenannten Tonfilmdebatte und ihrer bekanntesten filmischen Beiträge wird dann unter dem Vorzeichen der Moderne von einzelnen Filmautoren wieder aufgegriffen und hinsichtlich der Abwendung von einem akustischen Repräsentationsparadigma sogar radikalisiert. Zwei dieser Regisseure – Jacques Tati

---

[1] | Vgl. Segeberg: Der *Sound* und die Medien.
[2] | Bedingt durch den starken Einfluss Pierre Schaeffers kam es aber wenigstens in Frankreich zu einer fruchtbaren Symbiose von Protagonisten der *musique concrète* und Filmanalytikern, wie dies vor allem in den wegweisenden Studien des Schaeffer-Schülers Michel Chion manifest wurde. Chion legte dann auch 1984 eine erste Systematik des Filmtons vor, die ihrerseits jedoch stark auf die Stimme als filmischem Ausdrucksträger fokussiert war: Chion: La voix au cinéma.

und David Lynch – und ihre diesbezüglich pointiertesten Filme stehen im Mittelpunkt der folgenden Erörterungen. Gezeigt werden soll dabei zum einen, dass die Nobilitierung des Geräusches in beiden Fällen Ausweis einer dezidiert *modernen* Filmästhetik ist, wobei Tati am Beginn, Lynch am Ende der filmischen Moderne steht. Gezeigt werden soll zum anderen, dass Tati gleichsam den Boden bereitete, auf dem Lynch dann das (den klassischen Film noch beherrschende) Junktim zwischen Bild und Tonquelle weiter aushöhlen konnte. Beide hier zu untersuchenden Filme haben, ungeachtet ihres historischen und generischen Binnenabstandes, gemein, dass gerade das Geräusch ihnen dazu dient, ein neues, enthierarchisiertes Verhältnis von Bild und Ton zu etablieren, welches das Visuelle *und* das Akustische als jeweils *autonome* Artikulationsformen des Filmischen begreift .

DIE (WIEDER-)ENTDECKUNG DES GERÄUSCHES IN JACQUES TATIS *LES VACANCES DE MONSIEUR HULOT*

Few films delight the ear more than Jacques Tati's *Les vacances de Monsieur Hulot*. From its 1953 release critics have remarked its sonic richness and the complex interaction between sounds and images, striving to put into words the film's unusual approach to the construction of the audio track.[3]

Mit derart emphatischen Zuschreibungen versucht der amerikanische Filmwissenschaftler Donald Kirihara den besonderen Stellenwert von Jacques Tatis zweitem Spielfilm für die Nachkriegsgeschichte des internationalen Films zu umreißen. Gedreht wurde *Les vacances de Monsieur Hulot* im kleinen Badeort Saint-Marc-sur-Mer bei Saint-Nazaire in der Bretagne, wo heute eine Hulot-Statue ebenso an den Film erinnert wie die Benennung des Strandes nach Tatis berühmter Figur. Ursprünglich auf Farbmaterial gedreht, schließlich aber doch in Schwarz-weiß veröffentlicht, erfuhr auch die Tonspur von *Les vacances de Monsieur Hulot* durch Tati eine für damalige Verhältnisse unüblich aufwändige Nachsynchronisation und -bearbeitung. Es wird zu zeigen sein, warum.

Der Plot des Films ist angesichts des technischen Aufwandes so dünn wie unerheblich. *Les vacances de Monsieur Hulot* besteht aus einer losen narrativen Koppelung vergleichsweise autonomer Segmente, die das gemächliche Strand- und Hotelleben in einem verschlafenen Badeort am Ende der Hauptsaison schildern: das tägliche Essen und das abendliche Kartenspiel im einzigen Hotel am Platze, kleinere sportliche Unternehmungen der

---

3 | Kirihara: Sounds in *Les Vacances de Monsieur Hulot*, S. 158.

Badegäste ... Die spärlichen sozialen Kontakte zwischen einzelnen Touristen, ja, selbst der annoncierte Saisonhöhepunkt, ein Maskenball, versickern nahezu unbemerkt in der gleichförmigen Spätsommerlethargie. In dieses somnambul vor sich hinbrütende Idyll bricht mit dem von Tati selbst gespielten (und in mehreren seiner späteren Filme reaktivierten) Monsieur Hulot ein tollpatschig-naiver Sonderling ein, der sich in jeder Hinsicht als *Ruhe*störer wider Willen erweist und eher geringe Begeisterung bei den meisten anderen Gästen auslöst. Denn mit Hulot dringen die Geräusche, vor allem jene seines von permanenten Fehlzündungen heimgesuchten vorsintflutlichen Autos, in den eher geräuscharmen Mikrokosmos ein, wie dies im *mise en abyme*-Verfahren, gleich bei Hulots Einzug in den Ferienort durchgespielt wird.[4] Letztlich kann aber auch Hulot die Homöostase des Ortes nicht wirklich destabilisieren. Ganz im Gegenteil integriert auch er sich gerne in die gezielte Ziellosigkeit des Urlaubstreibens; auch seinen Handlungen ist kein Kausalnexus, kein Telos eingeschrieben, außer dem, Zeit totzuschlagen, und die durch ihn ausgelösten Irritationen widerfahren ihm eher, als dass sie in ihm ein aktives Handlungssubjekt fänden.

Von der Handlung zum Seriellen: Die Krise des Aktions bildes im Film nach 1945

Wo aber das Band zwischen handlungsmächtigem Subjekt und Milieu sich lockert, da kommt es zu jener ›Krise des Aktionsbildes‹, die Gilles Deleuze in seiner zweibändigen Filmtheorie[5] als konstitutive Zäsur zwischen dem klassischen Film – dem *Bewegungs-Bild* – und dem modernen Film – dem *Zeit-Bild* – begreift und auf die 40er und frühen 50er Jahres des 20. Jahrhunderts datiert: »An die Stelle der Aktion oder der sensomotorischen Situation ist die Fahrt, das Herumstreifen und das ständige Hin und Her« getreten, die Bewegung im modernen Film »hat jede aktivistische oder affektive Struktur, die es vorher trug, die es anleitete und ihm [...] Richtungen gab, abgelegt«.[6] Aus der gerichteten Bewegung hin zu einem teleologisch aufgeladenen Ort ist ein Mäandern ohne jede Finalität geworden. Die Bewegungen der Figur und der Raum, den sie durchquert, treten auseinander, keine Handlung kann mehr dauerhaft auf ihren situativen Kontext ein- und rückwirken. Die *motorische Krise*, die der moderne Film nach 1945 ausstellt, ist also untrennbar verbunden mit der Etablierung neuer Figuren- und neuer Raumtypen

---

4 | *Les vacances de Monsieur Hulot* (1953), 00:03:12.
5 | Deleuze: Kino 1; Ders.: Kino 2.
6 | Deleuze: Kino 1, S. 278.

und sie führt im Gegenzug zur Aufwertung dessen, was Deleuze die »reine optische und akustische Situation« nennt: »Wir haben es nunmehr mit einem Kino des Sehenden und nicht mehr mit einem Kino der Aktion zu tun.«[7] Das Visuelle wie das Sonorische emanzipieren sich vom Primat der Handlungsketten und gewinnen einen Status der Autonomie, der sie zu reflexiven Parametern des Filmischen selbst werden lässt. Voraussetzung dafür ist jedoch das Aufbrechen des sensomotorischen Bandes (Wahrnehmung – Affekt[8] – Aktion), das dem klassischen Kino vor allem in Gestalt des sogenannten ›Aktionsbildes‹ seine Prägung gab, indem ein Handelnder eine vorgefundene Situation (S) durch sein Agieren (A) zu einer neuen Situation (S') transformierte, meist in der Form, dass eine gestörte Ordnung (z.B. eine von einer Verbrecherbande terrorisierte Stadt) durch die milieutransformierende Aktion wieder in die ursprüngliche Homöostase zurückverwandelt wurde. Wo die Homöostase aber vorgängig ist (wie in unserem Beispiel) oder sich als nicht rekonstituierbar erweist (wie in den von Deleuze paradigmatisch angeführten Filmen des italienischen Neorealismus), da wandeln sich die filmischen Ereignisketten zu Spiegelungen, Spiralen oder Serien und aus dem vormaligen Handlungsträger wird ein passiv ›Sehender‹ im angesprochenen Sinne.

Tatis Figuren, allen voran Monsieur Hulot, verkörpern geradezu idealtypisch jenen filmhistorischen Wandel, wie auch *Les vacances de Monsieur Hulot* schon in seiner eher seriell[9] als kausallogisch angelegten Erzählstruktur der Dramaturgie des klassischen Erzählkinos entsagt. So wie die Urlaubstage die Gestalt einer Serie relativ ereignisarmer und wiederholter Handlungsfragmente ohne wechselseitige Wirkungsfolgen annehmen, so sind auch die episodischen Narrateme des Films »zwanglos aneinandergereiht und [...] austauschbar wie die Glieder einer Kette«[10] und bleiben in sich geschlossene Einheiten, die allein durch rekurrierende Elemente zusammengehalten werden. Und dies sind vor allem Elemente des Raumes, des Geräusches und ihrer Interdependenz – so wie das Läuten der Hotelglocke eine dünne temporale wie spatiale Orientierungsfunktion im gleichförmigen Ereignisfluss des Urlaubslebens einnimmt.

Bevor ich auf die Funktion des Geräusches näher eingehe, sei angemerkt, dass dessen Aufwertung in *Les vacances de Monsieur Hulot* mit einer reziproken Entwertung der dominanten Tonsorte im klassischen Tonfilm, des Dialogs, einhergeht. *Les vacances de Monsieur Hulot* ist nicht nur ein extrem

---

7 | Deleuze: Kino 2, S. 13.
8 | Darunter versteht Deleuze ein Moment der abwägenden Reflexion des Wahrnehmungsreizes, bevor dieser in eine Handlung übersetzt wird.
9 | Vgl. Heller: Vom komischen Subjekt zur Konstruktion des Komischen, S. 216.
10 | Maddock: Die Filme von Jacques Tati, S. 63.

dialogarmer Film, sondern vor allem einer, der Sprache entweder bis zur Unverständlichkeit entstellt oder aber – weit häufiger noch – sie radikal als sinnentleert enttarnt. Einige der Figuren des Films bleiben vollständig oder nahezu stumm, wie auch Hulot selbst, dem sogar bei der Anmeldung im Hotel seine notorische Pfeife aus dem Munde genommen werden muss, damit er halbwegs verständlich seinen Namen herauspressen kann (vgl. Abb. 1).

Abbildung 1: Hulots Pfeife als Kommunikationshindernis und als Transformator der Sprache in Geräusche, Les Vacances de Monsieur Hulot *(1953), 00:10:57.*

Ansonsten wechseln die Gruppensituationen beliebig zwischen Schweigen und tosendem Geplapper. Die wenigen halbwegs verständlichen Dialogpassagen sind vollends asignifikant: *small talk*, Geschwätz, Floskeln, Leerformeln. Den einzigen zitierfähigen Satz legt Tati dann auch jenem jugendlichen Linksexistentialisten in den Mund, der sich direkt aus *Les Deux Magots* an den Strand verirrt zu haben scheint und die anderen Gäste mit seinen Rezitationen aus philosophischen Büchern nervt: »Der Kapitalismus redet zu viel und der Eklektizismus wird siegen« – nicht so bei Tati!

In dem Maße, wie der Dialog seine handlungstreibende und orientierende Funktion einbüßt, avanciert das Geräusch zur dominanten Tonsorte. Hierbei entwickelt Tati eine ganze Phalanx an ästhetischen Strategien, deren Gemeinsamkeit in der Substitution der Sprache durch Geräusche oder durch die technische Verzerrung des Gesprochenen liegt. Letzteres geschieht nun gerade in Kontexten, die eigentlich in hohem Maße auf Verständlichkeit angewiesen sind (wie in Abb. 2).

Abbildung 2: Die Lautsprecherdurchsage mobilisiert die Figuren, Les Vacances de Monsieur Hulot *(1953), 00:01:55.*

Die Eröffnungssequenz des Films[11] zeigt die ankommenden Besucherscharen auf den Bahnsteigen des kleinen Ferienortes, wo sie von einer metallisch scheppernden und gänzlich unverständlichen Lautsprecherdurchsage von einem Bahnsteig auf den anderen umdirigiert werden. An die Stelle gerichteter Handlungsimpulse tritt somit gleich zu Beginn des Filmes eine von Geräuschen initiierte, wellenartige Choreographie von Figuren und Objekten, eine Serie von non-linearen Handlungsfragmenten, die »zur Bildung und Auflösung von Gruppen, zum Zusammenschweißen und Trennen der Figuren in einer Art von modernem Ballett«[12] führt, wie Deleuze notiert.

DIE NOBILITIERUNG DES GERÄUSCHES IN DER TONFILMDEBATTE

Zugleich dürften es Sequenzen wie diese gewesen sein, die Tatis Film wie einen verspäteten Nachfahren der minimalisierten Zugeständnisse an den Tonfilm in den Filmen der frühen 30er Jahre erscheinen ließen. Schließlich erinnert die Anfangssequenz von *Les vacances de Monsieur Hulot* in ihrer Technisierung und Verzerrung von Sprache stark an den *opener* von Charlie Chaplins *City Lights* von 1932, in der Chaplin die sinnentleerten Politikerreden bei einer Denkmalenthüllung in vergleichbarer Weise verfremdete. Rufen wir zur besseren filmhistorischen Einordnung also noch einmal die sogenannte Tonfilmdebatte auf, in der die führenden Filmtheoretiker (wie etwa Rudolf Arnheim) sowie Filmpraktiker (René Clair, Sergei Eisenstein)

---

11 | *Les Vacances de Monsieur Hulot* (1953), 00:01:14.
12 | Deleuze: Kino 2, S. 93.

in Europa wie in Amerika, hier vor allem eben Chaplin, reserviert bis offen ablehnend auf die Einführung der *talkies* nach 1926 reagiert hatten. Gemeinsamer Tenor aller Proklamationen war die Befürchtung, die Einführung des Sprechfilms werde automatisch zu einer Verarmung der bis dato entwickelten Bildsprache führen, die ja mangels Sprache gezwungen war, narrative und rhetorische Sinnzusammenhänge durch visuelle Metaphern oder elaborierte Montagekonzepte zu ersetzen. Entsprechend warnte Chaplin 1929: »Die sogenannte Sprechfilmkunst will die unerhörte Schönheit des Schweigens zerstören. Und Schweigen ist das Wesen des Films.«[13] Und auch Eisenstein, Pudowkin und Alexandrow formulierten in ihrem berühmten »Manifest zum Tonfilm« von 1928:

> Eine falsche Auffassung von den Möglichkeiten innerhalb dieser neuen technischen Entdeckung könnte nicht nur die Entwicklung und Perfektionierung des Films als Kunst behindern, sondern sie droht auch alle seine gegenwärtigen formalen Leistungen zu zerstören. Gegenwärtig übt der mit visuellen Bildern arbeitende Film einen mächtigen emotionalen Effekt auf die Menschen aus und hat berechtigterweise eine der führenden Positionen unter den Künsten eingenommen. [...] Eine anfängliche Periode von Sensationen hält die Entwicklung einer neuen Kunstform nicht wirklich auf. Es ist in diesem Falle vielmehr die zweite Periode, die an die Stelle des naiven Gebrauchs der neuen technischen Möglichkeiten deren automatische Nutzbarmachung für *hochkultivierte Dramen* und andere fotografierte Bühnenaufführungen setzen wird. Den Ton in diesem Sinne zu verwenden, würde aber die Zerstörung der Montage-Kultur bedeuten, denn jegliche ÜBEREINSTIMMUNG zwischen dem Ton und einem visuellen Montage-Bestandteil schadet dem Montagestück [...]. NUR EINE KONTRAPUNKTISCHE VERWENDUNG des Tons in Beziehung zum visuellen Montage-Bestandteil wird neue Möglichkeiten der Montage-Entwicklung und Montage-Perfektion erlauben.[14]

Offensichtlich sind solche Befürchtungen, wenngleich sie durch die späteren Entwicklungen des Sprechfilms durchaus ihre retrospektive Berechtigung erhalten sollten, zum einen geleitet von der Sorge, der gerade mühsam errichtete Abstand zu den etablierten Künsten Theater und Literatur werde nunmehr wieder eingezogen. Zum anderen speisen sie sich aus der anhaltenden Wirkungsmacht der Sprachkritik des späten 19. Jahrhunderts, die ja noch den frühen Béla Balázs im stummen Film die Erlösung von der Allmacht der Sprache hatte erkennen lassen.[15] All dies erschien nunmehr hinfällig, und die Lösung konnte – da selbst die Avantgardisten am industriellen Siegeszug des Sprechfilms keine ernsthaften Zweifel hegten – nur in

---
13 | Chaplin: Was ich zum Sprechfilm zu sagen habe.
14 | Eisenstein, Pudowkin und Alexandrow: Manifest zum Tonfilm, S. 42f. Herv. i. Orig.
15 | Balázs: Der sichtbare Mensch oder die Kultur des Films.

einer dezidiert anti-naturalistischen Handhabung des Tons liegen, um die befürchtete Redundanz zwischen dem auditiven und dem visuellen Track zu umgehen. Und dies schien wiederum nahezu zwangsläufig den Verzicht auf das *gesprochene* Wort zu bedeuten, wie auch René Clair in seiner 1929 publizierten Stellungnahme betonte:

> Wir Stummfilmregisseure wollen uns der tönenden Invasion nicht länger verschließen. Machen wir gute Miene zum tönenden Spiel. Fassen wir den Stier bei den Hörnern. – Einen Ausweg sehe ich zum Beispiel im Tonfilm ohne Dialog. Vielleicht lässt sich durch ihn die Gefahr doch noch bannen. Man könnte sich doch vorstellen, dass die das Filmband begleitenden Geräusche und Klänge die Masse so unterhielten, dass sie auf den Dialog verzichtete.[16]

Neben Clairs eigenen Versuchen, diesem Programm in seiner Filmarbeit Rechnung zu tragen, war es bekanntlich vor allem Charlie Chaplin, der sich bis 1940, also bis zu *The Great Dictator*, weigerte, seine Trampfigur sprechen zu lassen und allein Geräusche oder Nonsens-Sprache (wie im Lied aus *Modern Times*, 1936) als neue Tonsorten in seinen Filmen zuließ. Allerdings greifen die in der Forschungsliteratur häufig gezogenen Vergleiche zwischen Chaplin und Tati zu kurz.[17] Die Ähnlichkeiten zwischen der Handhabung des Geräusches bei beiden Regisseuren sind nur vordergründig. Häufig verkannt wird, dass *Les vacances de Monsieur Hulot* eben *kein* »stummer Tonfilm«[18] ist, sondern dass ihn von der Ära der Tonfilmdebatte zuvorderst die Erfahrung der filmischen Moderne trennt. Entsprechend liegen Tatis Nobilitierung des Geräuschs bei gleichzeitiger Sprachskepsis völlig andere Motive zugrunde als noch bei Chaplin. Tatsächlich ist das Geräusch bei Tati eine »reine akustische Situation« im Sinne von Deleuze, und faktisch unterliegt der ganze Film bereits jener Enthierarchisierung der Ausdrucksebenen und -mittel, die Deleuze als konstitutiv für den Film nach 1945 erkannt hat. Während Chaplin bei aller Sprachskepsis sehr wohl noch dem Paradigma des linear-kausalen, aktionszentrierten Films verpflichtet bleibt, ist dies bei Tati eindeutig nicht mehr der Fall. Der Vergleich mit Chaplins Handhabung des Geräuschs läuft also schon insofern ins Leere, als bei Chaplin die Tonquelle stets identifizierbar ist: Sie ist im *on* und damit eindeutig Teil der diegetischen Welt.

---

16 | Clair: Drei Briefe aus London, S. 111.
17 | Vgl. Heller: Die Ferien des Monsieur Hulot, S. 206f.
18 | Haberer: Aspekte der Komik in den Filmen von Jacques Tati, S. 33.

Die Aufhebung der Klanghierarchien

Dass die Verwendung des Tons, zumal des Geräusches, bei Tati wesentlich vielfältiger und uneindeutiger ausfällt als in den angesprochenen Filmen der Post-Stummfilm-Ära, wird deutlich, vergegenwärtigt man sich noch einmal das Funktionsspektrum des Tons im klassischen narrativen Film:

- Orientierung im raumzeitlichen Geflecht der Handlung
- Orientierung in narrativen Strukturen
- Charakterisierung von Schauplätzen / Räumen und Zeit
- Charakterisierung der Relation von Figur und Umwelt
- Positionierung des Zuhörers im Raum
- Informationsvergabe v. a. durch Sprache und Dialog
- Kontinuitätsherstellung zwischen Einstellungen, Szenen[19]

Die naturalistische Mischung kontinuierlicher Klangquellen, wie sie vor allem für das Hollywood-Paradigma verpflichtend war und ist, also die hierarchische und an den Erfordernissen des *plot*-Nachvollzugs geeichte Abstufung zwischen laut und leise, vorne und hinten, Atmosphäre, Musik, Sprache und Geräusch wird bei Tati gezielt unterlaufen. Mal fehlt die Atmosphäre völlig, mal stehen Geräuschquellen überproportional im Vordergrund, mal stimmt das interne Lautstärkenverhältnis zwischen einzelnen Klangsorten nicht. Stattdessen arbeitet Tati mit einem wohlkalkulierten Ein- und Abblenden multipler Geräusche aus dem *on* wie dem *off*, aus dem intradiegetischen wie dem extradiegetischen Raum. Dies gilt sowohl für den einzigen Musiktrack des *score*, der immer wieder zwischen intra- und extradiegetischer Topik wechselt, als auch für das Radio in der Hotellobby, als auch ganz grundsätzlich für die Relationierung der Geräusche der Innen- und Außenwelt.

Dieses Prinzip dominiert bereits den Eintritt Hulots in die Hotellobby,[20] deren Geräuschkulisse – wider jede Wahrscheinlichkeit – trotz starkem Publikumsverkehr von den *off*-Geräuschen der spielenden Kinder am nahen Strand beherrscht wird. Als Hulot aber die Tür nach außen öffnet, dringt ein bis dahin nicht vernehmbarer starker Windzug mit entsprechender Klangstärke ins Innere, ohne dadurch jedoch die Kinderstimmen vollständig zu überdecken. Überproportional laut wiederum ist das Röhrenradio ausgesteuert, das einer der Hotelgäste nun anschaltet – jedoch auch nur solange, bis Hulot die Außentür wieder verschließt und dadurch die Windgeräusche aussperrt, nicht aber die Kinderstimmen, die nun wieder die Tonmischung dominieren, während das Radio nahezu verstummt. Die *Dynamik*

---

19 | Vgl. Flückiger: Narrative Funktionen des Filmsounddesigns.
20 | *Les Vacances de Monsieur Hulot* (1953), 00:09:46.

der Klangquellen unterliegt also einem kompositorischen, nicht einem repräsentationalen Prinzip, das sich an der Lautstärkenhierarchie einer vorfindlichen Realität orientieren würde. Dies gilt nicht minder für die natürlichen Umweltgeräusche bei den Außenaufnahmen. Auch hier werden »die Bezüge der Töne zueinander systematisch verzerrt«,[21] auch hier wechselt Tati beliebig die Optionen zur Akzentuierung einzelner Klänge und Geräusche (Stimmen, Wellenschlag, Wind, die Türen der Badehäuschen etc.), und enthierarchisiert somit das Ensemble der Töne zugunsten punktueller Betonung einer einzelnen Quelle.

So sehr Tati also den Konventionen eines naturalistischen Klangraums entgegenarbeitet, so sehr erteilt er aber auch einer *durchgängigen* Orchestrierung der Geräuschquellen eine Absage. Auch nach mehrmaligem Sehen und Hören ist kein durchgehaltenes Prinzip erkennbar, nach dem Dynamik, Auftauchen und Stellenwert einzelner Quellen in der auditiven Gesamtstruktur des Films organisiert wären. Offensichtlich kam es Tati vor allem darauf an, sowohl mit den *intradiegetisch* evozierten Klangerwartungen des Publikums zu spielen als auch mit den Erwartungen, die sich aus unserer *Alltagswahrnehmung* speisen. So unvorhersehbar die Eruptionen aus dem Motorraum aus Hulots Vehikel sind, so unvorhersehbar ist auch der Umgang mit den Geräuschen und ihren Quellen. Dies gilt auch und besonders für das berühmteste Geräusch des Films überhaupt, das sanfte Ploppen der Schwingtür im Hotelrestaurant, das sich eben keinesfalls immer dann einstellt, wenn die Tür aufgestoßen wird.[22]

Das anti-naturalistische Programm Tatis wird dabei auch auf die Frage der Klangtreue, der *fidelity*, ausgedehnt. So wie im Falle der Restauranttür das Zupfen einer Cello-Saite nachträglich auf die Tonspur gelegt wird und das reale Geräusch einer Schwingtür überschreibt, so werden auch die Geräusche eines Tennismatchs[23] zu einem merkwürdigen Hyperrealismus[24] überhöht. Tati transformiert das Geräusch des Aufschlages von Hulot zu einem harten, schussartigen Klang-Peak, auch dank der gezielten Ausblendung der Atmosphäre und der Reduktion aller anderen Geräuschquellen. Wenn es also offenbar unentwegt um die Aufhebung von Klanghierarchien geht, so ist das Geräusch natürlich besonders geeignet, ebendiese Konventionen zu unterlaufen. Die wesentlichen Orientierungsfunktionen des Tons im klassischen Film, nämlich die Verortung im raumzeitlichen Kosmos der Diegese, laufen ins Leere, sobald das Geräusch, wie bei Tati, eine Eigenständigkeit gewinnt, die sich jeglicher Hierarchisierung verweigert und die im

---

21 | Deleuze: Kino 2, S. 300.
22 | *Les Vacances de Monsieur Hulot* (1953), 00:13:05.
23 | Ebd., 00:47:19.
24 | Vgl. Chion: Jacques Tati: The Cow and the Moo.

Gegenzug »elementare Geräusche zu Personen werden«[25] lässt – der Tischtennisball, die Tür, der Tennisschläger, die Spielkarten, das Vogelzwitschern etc. avancieren zu den eigentlichen Handlungsträgern, emanzipieren sich von den Figuren und leiten nunmehr ihrerseits deren spärlichen Handlungsimpulse an.

Interessanterweise korrespondiert diese Egalität der Klänge mit jener der Räume. Strukturell gibt es in *Les vacances de Monsieur Hulot* keinen privilegierten Handlungsort, so wie überhaupt anzumerken ist, dass der Film mit sehr wenigen Schauplätzen auskommt, zwischen denen mehr oder weniger frei hin- und hergewechselt wird: der Strand, der Tennisplatz, das Hotel, die Pension von Martine, der heimlich von Hulot verehrten jungen Frau. Häufiger frequentierte Schauplätze, etwa die Hotellobby, erfüllen eher die Funktion einer Schnittmenge zwischen Parabeln, als dass sie zum wirklichen Handlungsmittelpunkt avancierten. So wie zwischen Innen und Außen – auch und gerade auf der Tonebene – fließende Übergänge herrschen, so fluten die Aktionen der Figuren ziellos zwischen den einzelnen räumlichen Fixpunkten hin und her. Auch hier dominiert das Prinzip der egalitären Serialität das der hierarchischen Kausalität oder Handlungsteleologie. Nur zwei Ausbrüche aus diesem eng abgesteckten Handlungsraum sind zu verzeichnen, die aber beide im Nichts versanden: eine angedeutete Verfolgungsjagd mit Hulots Auto, die bezeichnenderweise schon nach wenigen Metern auf dem Friedhof endet (einem wahren *dead end* also) und der große Ausflug der Hotelgäste (an dem Hulot nicht teilnehmen kann, weil er wieder einmal sein notorisch pannenanfälliges Gefährt reparieren muss), der uns in seiner potentiellen Öffnung eines Gegenraumes aber auch nicht genauer gezeigt wird.

Das formalsprachliche Äquivalent der egalitären Raumbezüge findet sich in Tatis Nutzung der Tiefenschärfe als Modus, die klassische Relationierung der Handlungsräume mittels der traditionellen analytischen Montage nun durch ein Prinzip der inneren Montage zu ersetzen. Die durch Tiefenschärfe hergestellte Gleichwertigkeit von Bildvorder-, -mittel- und -hintergrund, wie sie durch Orson Welles und William Wyler in den 1940er Jahren in den USA und durch die italienischen Neorealisten fast zeitgleich in Europa etabliert wurde, prägt die Bildkomposition von *Les vacances de Monsieur Hulot* mit der typischen Favorisierung diagonaler Achsen und aufsichtiger Perspektiven überdeutlich (vgl. Abb. 3).

Entsprechend dominieren Totalen und Halbtotalen, die fast 49 % der Einstellungsgrößen[26] ausmachen, sowie die lange Einstellung, die jenen frei wandernden Blick des Zuschauers vor dem tableauartigen Filmbild

---

25 | Deleuze: Kino 2, S. 300.
26 | Vgl. Heller: Die Ferien des Monsieur Hulot, S. 214f.

Abbildung 3: Diagonalen und Aufsicht als Konstituenten der Bildkomposition, Les Vacances de Monsieur Hulot *(1953), 00:08:17.*

ermöglichen, die André Bazin, wenige Jahre nach Tatis Film, ins Zentrum seiner Filmtheorie stellen sollte.[27] Auch diesbezüglich also verortet sich Tatis Filmsprache eindeutig in der filmischen Moderne, in der Abkehr vom Aktionsbild zugunsten einer neuen Gleichwertigkeit der filmischen Räume und der filmischen Bildebenen.

Das Prinzip der Dekonstruktion vorheriger Hierarchien im Register der filmischen Ausdrucksformen dehnt Tati an einer Stelle des Films sogar auf die Relationen von Ton- und Bildebene aus, indem er – erneut durch ein Geräusch (eine weitere Fehlzündung von Hulots Auto) – Ton und Bild zu einer Art *freeze frame* erstarren lässt.[28] So wie in der Apotheose des von Hulot vorzeitig und unfreiwillig entzündeten Feuerwerks die Figur ihre Ausweichbewegungen dem Jaulen und Pfeifen der Feuerwerkskörper unterwirft,[29] *so folgt auch hier das Bild dem Ton* und nicht länger umgekehrt. Das Auditive verkettet sich mit dem Visuellen zu einem Kreislauf, der sämtliche Handlungs- und Bildräume durchdringt, wie Deleuze anmerkt:

Der Kreislauf ist nicht nur Kreislauf der akustischen (einschließlich der musikalischen Elemente) in ihrem Verhältnis zum visuellen Bild, sondern er ist der Bezug des visuellen Bildes als solchen zum musikalischen Element *par excellence*, das überallhin gleitet ins ›On‹, ins ›Off‹, in Geräusche, Töne, Reden.[30]

---

27 | Vgl. Bazin: Die Entwicklung der kinematographischen Sprache.
28 | *Les Vacances de Monsieur Hulot* (1953), 00:46:53.
29 | Ebd., 01:16:10.
30 | Deleuze: Kino 2, S. 304.

JENSEITS DES REPRÄSENTATIONSPARADIGMAS: VON TATI ZU LYNCH

Tati greift in der Handhabung des Tons in Les vacances de Monsieur Hulot künstlerische Strategien aus den frühen Jahren des Tonfilms bei Clair und vor allem Chaplin zwar auf, überführt diese aber in ein dezidiert modernes Paradigma, indem von der Ebene der seriellen Erzählstruktur über die der egalitären Raumbezüge bis eben hin zur Aufwertung des Geräuschs gegenüber Sprache und Dialog jene von Deleuze beschworene Krise des Aktionsbildes sich in Gestalt einer unentwegten Umwertung vorgängiger Hierarchien auf allen filmischen Operationsebenen manifestiert. Was sich in all den hier dargestellten Funktionen des Geräuschs in Les vacances de Monsieur Hulot abzeichnet, kann nun in einem weiteren Abstraktionsschritt eben auch als Kritik am Repräsentationsparadigma gelesen werden, was wiederum durchaus konstitutiv für die filmische Moderne ist. Indem das Handlungsprimat nun durch eine reflexive Dimension abgelöst wird, entkoppeln sich Bild wie Ton von der Bewegung (der Handlung, der Figuren, des Diskurses) und verbinden sich auf einer Ebene jenseits der Repräsentation zu neuen Figuren, so dass »der Ton in ein außerordentlich schöpferisches Verhältnis zum Visuellen tritt, da beide nicht mehr in einfache sensomotorische Schemata integriert sind«.[31]

Tati bringt in seinem Film immer wieder Hinweise unter, die als Aussetzung des Indexikalischen auf der Bild- wie der Tonspur gelesen werden können. Interessanterweise ist es hier vor allem der visuelle Abdruck, der in seinem Repräsentationsanspruch ironisch in Frage gestellt wird, so in gleich zwei Szenen,[32] in denen Hulots heimlicher Gegner, der Oberkellner, vergeblich versucht, die Fußabdrücke in seinem Arbeitsbereich bis zu ihrem Verursacher, natürlich Hulot, zurückzuverfolgen (vgl. Abb. 4).

Spur und Repräsentiertes fallen auseinander, am deutlichsten in jener Sequenz,[33] in der Hulot die Füße gerade noch vor einem herannahenden Bus einzieht, der Abdruck (die Spur) der Reifen sich aber der Logik des Geschehens und des von uns Gesehenen scheinbar gleich wieder entzieht, indem die Suggestion entwickelt wird, der Reifenabdruck habe um Hulots Füße gleichsam einen Bogen gemacht. Gleiches gilt für den Spurcharakter der Klänge und Geräusche, die sich von ihren Quellen tendenziell abkoppeln, sich zu hyperrealistischen Sonozeichen im Sinne von Deleuze verdichten. Dadurch übersteigern sich die Klangqualitäten zu einer autonomen Dimension, die sich nicht länger als rein indexikalisch klassifizieren lässt.

---

31 | Ebd., S. 93.
32 | Les Vacances de Monsieur Hulot (1953), 00:37:55 und 01:09:25.
33 | Ebd., 01:11:20.

Abbildung 4: Das Brüchigwerden des Indexes, Les Vacances de Monsieur Hulot *(1953), 01:09:29.*

So notorisch wie Tati immer an den großen Komikern der Stummfilmära gemessen wurde, so unausweichlich erscheint bei David Lynch der Verweis auf den Einfluss des surrealistischen Films.[34] Doch auch hier gilt es der vorschnellen Konstatierung einer solchen Ahnenschaft mit Vorsicht zu begegnen, trennt doch auch Lynch die ›Krise des Aktionsbildes‹ von den Surrealisten der späten 1920er und 1930er Jahre. Auch Lynch durchbricht in seinen Filmen entsprechend das sensomotorische Band, wie Slavoj Žižek und Michel Chion beobachtet haben.[35] Und ebenso wie Tati operiert auch Lynch gegen das vorgängige Äquivalenzprinzip zwischen Ton und Bild:

> Jean-Luc Godard hat gesagt, der Ton leide unter der Tyrannei des Bildes; von Anfang an hat Lynch diese Tyrannei gebrochen, indem er den Ton als gleichberechtigte und nicht unbedingt gleichgestimmte Aussageform zum Bild verwendet hat.[36]

Bereits Lynchs erster Langfilm, *Eraserhead* von 1977, eine in jeder Hinsicht verstörende s/w-Fiktion über die Nachtmahren, Halluzinationen und sexuellen Phantasien eines unfreiwillig früh zum Vater eines missgebildeten, wurmähnlichen Frühchens avancierten jungen Mannes, war deutlich von der Durchbrechung der klassischen Handlungsketten geprägt. Wenn die Hauptfigur Henry von der Familie Marys, die er unwissentlich geschwängert

---

34 | Vgl. Lommel, Maurer Queipo und Roloff (Hg.): Surrealismus und Film.
35 | So verweist Slavoj Žižek in seinen Reflexionen über David Lynch auf Michel Chions Monographie über Lynch (*David Lynch*, Paris 1992) und den dort konstatierten »gap or discord between action and reaction that is always at work in Lynch's films«. Vgl. Žižek: The Lamella of David Lynch, S. 210.
36 | Seeßlen: David Lynch und seine Filme, S. 169.

hat, gezwungen wird, sie zu heiraten und das unerquickliche Baby mit zu versorgen, so verbleiben seine Reaktionen hierauf im Bereich purer Apathie. Auch später wird er keine Anstalten machen, den erotischen Avancen seiner Nachbarin in irgendeiner Art und Weise aktiv zu antworten. Generell bleibt jedes Handlungsmoment in dieser wahrhaft obskuren Kleinfamilie ohne unmittelbare, jedenfalls ohne kausallogische *response:* aus dem von Henry tranchierten Huhn quillt eine dunkle Substanz, woraufhin die Mutter einen spastischen Anfall erleidet; Henrys Versuch, die Hände der geheimnisvollen Frau hinter der Heizung zu ergreifen, werden durch einen grellen Lichtblitz hintertrieben; nachdem der von seiner Frau verlassene Henry schließlich das Baby tötet, löst sich der diegetische Raum in einem grellen Lichtraum auf etc. Der ganze Film ist überdies durchzogen von Träumen, Halluzinationen und phantastischen Sequenzen, deren ontischer Status mehr als einmal obskur bleibt. Immer wieder öffnet sich der enge Raum, in dem Henry mit dem Baby lebt, auf phantasmatische Interieurs, Bühnen und Figuren hin (Frau hinter der Heizung, Mann auf dem Planeten etc.).

Stärker noch als kraft solcher, tatsächlich surreal anmutender Handlungselemente erregte *Eraserhead* jedoch rasch internationale Aufmerksamkeit durch seinen ungewöhnlichen Soundtrack,[37] den Lynch und sein Toningenieur Alan Splet in zehnmonatiger Detailarbeit in einer zum Tonstudio umgebauten Garage produziert hatten.[38] Robert Fischer zählt in seiner Monographie die markantesten der generierten Geräusche und Klänge auf:

Das Wummern, Zischen und Heulen der Maschinen und Fabriken in Henrys Nachbarschaft, der Bullern der Heizkörper, das Summen des Tabernakels, in dem Henry den Wurm versteckt, den er eines Tages mit der Post erhält […], die Dampforgelmusik vom Plattenspieler in Henrys Zimmer, das Quietschen der saugenden Welpen an den Zitzen der Hündin in der Wohnung von Marys Eltern und vor allem natürlich das durch Mark und Bein gehende Quäken des Babys, das Mary und Henry nachts kein Auge schließen lässt […].[39]

Ersichtlich geht die Vielzahl der genutzten Klangsorten über Lynchs notorische Vorliebe für Elektrizität und industrielle Maschinen, die auch in vielen seiner anderen Filme überpräsent ist, weit hinaus. Keinen seiner späteren Filme hat Lynch *derart* stark vom Geräusch dominieren lassen wie seinen ersten, über den Frances Morgan kurz und bündig feststellt: »David Lynch's

---

37 | So urteilt Frances Morgan: »Its noisescape is still its most memorable element.« Morgan: Darkness Audible, S. 190.
38 | Vgl. Fischer: David Lynch, S. 60.
39 | Fischer: David Lynch, S. 60.

very first feature was a noise film.«[40] Tatsächlich ist das Geräusch *die* Kategorie, die in *Eraserhead* das Schisma zwischen Organischem (Geburt, Säugen, Wimmern, Tod) und Mechanischem transzendiert. Während die Maschinengeräusche von einer Wärme und Pulsation gekennzeichnet sind, die traditionell eher mit dem Organischen assoziiert werden, klingen die tierischen und menschlichen Laute merkwürdig artifiziell. Und es ist der *industrial noise*, der immer wieder die Songs und im engeren Sinne ›musikalischen‹ Elemente des *score* vorbereitet, rahmt und sich harmonisch mit ihnen verbindet:

Yet David Lynch, while creating iconic, successful films, with particularly influential musical soundtracks, is one director who has often approached noise in this more abstract way, using noise both on its own and interwoven with, or augmenting, more ›traditional‹ music to create atmospheres of disquiet and liminality.[41]

Während die Songs jedoch grundsätzlich Teil der intradiegetischen Welt und, als ausgewiesene *stage performances,* immer schon im *on* sind, fällt die Lokalisierung der Geräusche deutlich schwerer. Zwar suggerieren Lynchs Kamerafahrten auf die potentiellen Klangquellen (Heizung, Tabernakel, Baby) zu (und durch sie hindurch) eine traditionell anmutende Fokussierung der Geräuscherkunft, doch führen sie faktisch nur in einen weiteren phantasmatischen (Binnen-)Raum, in dem neue obskure Geräusche emanieren. Die qua Kameraoperation permeabel gemachte Dingwelt erschließt sich nicht in einer abschließbaren Bewegung, und kein letzter Ort rundet die Geräuscherkundung ab – so wie auch die Kamerafahrten durch die Grasoberfläche und in das abgeschnittene Ohr (!) in *Blue Velvet* (1986) letztlich nur eine *rite de passage* in neue Räume, Klang- und Bildwelten darstellen. Ein letzter Grund, eine nicht weiter zerlegbare Einheit von Klangobjekt und Bildraum, ist bei Lynch nicht zu finden. Die Stimme der Frau hinter der Heizung klingt, als käme sie aus einem Radio; der Aufprall der herabfallenden Würmer auf dem Bühnenboden findet keine Entsprechung im Volumen der Objekte; Lautstärke und Tonqualität der Heizkörpergeräusche sind nicht kausal identifizierbar etc.: »Therein lies the fundamental feature of post-modern hyperrealism: the very over-proximity to reality brings about the loss of reality. Uncanny details stick out and perturb the pacifying effect of the overall picture.«[42] War es im klassischen Film noch geboten, das

---

40 | Morgan: Lynchian noise, S. 189.
41 | Ebd. Morgan weist diesbezüglich auch auf den Einfluss der *musique concrete* (Pierre Schaeffer, Pierre Henry) und auf John Cages Aufwertung aller Klänge zu Musik als Inspirationsquellen von Lynch hin.
42 | Žižek: The Lamella of David Lynch, S. 207.

Geräusch visuell zu analogisieren, um »*the thing that made the sound*«[43] zu zeigen, so radikalisiert Lynch die neben anderen von Tati vorbereitete Autonomie des Geräusches und seine Loslösung von einem Referenten in derartigen infiniten Reihungen von Klangräumen, die ihrerseits die neuen Bildräume erst eröffnen und motivieren.

WUCHERUNGEN DES KLANG-RAUMES

Treffen sich Ton und Bild auch nicht im Modus der Referentialität, so verbindet sie doch ein *tertium:* das *Monströse.*[44] Monströs verunstaltet sind in *Eraserhead* nicht nur das Baby, das blutende Hühnchen und die seltsamen Würmer und Organe, auf die Henry trifft, sondern auch die Frau hinter der Heizung (vgl. Abb. 5), Henrys Haarschopf, die Fabriken und Innenräume. Monströs sind sämtliche Beziehungen der Figuren untereinander, die Fantasien und Halluzinationen Henrys, die sich nur graduell von der intradiegetischen Welt erster Ordnung abheben. Monströs sind die Bildkreationen Lynchs, die einer permanenten *Wucherung* in immer neue Räume und Bildwelten zu unterliegen scheinen. Und monströs ist auch die Phalanx von Geräuschen, die sich durch all diese Entitäten und Lokalitäten hindurch zu fräsen scheint, Räume öffnet, aufsprengt und durchquert, ontische Differenzen schleift und zum eigentlichen Motor der Bildgenese avanciert.

Abbildung 5: Figurationen des Monströsen, Eraserhead *(1977), 00:58:33.*

---

43 | Morgan: Lynchian noise, S. 189.
44 | Vgl. Geisenhanslüke und Hein (Hg.): Monströse Ordnungen.

Eraserhead ist beherrscht von visuellen, figurativen, narrativen und eben auch akustischen *Wucherungen*, die auf eine Ursprungdynamik verweisen, die in gewisser Weise außerhalb des diegetischen Horizonts liegen. Slavoj Žižek hat hierzu in seiner Lektüre der Filme David Lynchs einen interessanten Vorschlag unterbreitet:

> This noise is difficult to locate in reality. In order to determine its status, one is tempted to evoke contemporary cosmology which speaks of noises at the borders of the universe; these noises are not simply internal to the universe – they are remainders or last echoes of the Big Bang that created the universe itself. The ontological status of this noise is more interesting than it may appear, since it subverts the fundamental notion of the ›open‹, infinite universe that defines the space of Newtonian physics. That is to say, the modern notion of the ›open‹ universe is based on the hypothesis that every positive entity (noise, matter) occupies some (empty) space; it hinges on the difference between space as void and positive entities which occupy it, ›fill it out.‹ Space is here phenomenologically conceived as something that exists prior to the entities which ›fill it out.‹ [...] The primordial noise, the last remainder of the Big Bang, is on the contrary constitutive of space itself: it is not a noise ›in‹ space, but a noise that keeps space open as such.[45]

In einem filmischen Kontext, der so stark um Fragen der Hervorbringung und Geburt kreist, scheint diese Lesart durchaus ins Zentrum zu führen. Es sind die der Raumentstehung *vorgelagerten* Geräusche, die sich als infinite Wucherung ihren Weg durch alle Entitäten im Kosmos von *Eraserhead* bahnen, deren Physis deformieren und dadurch ihrerseits Neues generieren. Die Prinzipien von Kausalität und Repräsentation werden dadurch in einer finalen Volte in ihr Gegenteil verkehrt: Nicht länger gilt unser Interesse der Quelle des Geräusches, sondern dem, was das Geräusch als Quelle erst hervorbringt: den monströsen Wucherungen des Bildraumes.

Lynchs Inklination zum ›Zeit-Bild‹ im Sinne von Deleuze gewinnt dieser Konstellation indes auch immer medienreflexive Potentiale ab, wie gleichsam retrospektiv noch einmal einem seiner späteren Filme entnommen werden kann. Im Nachtclub in *Mulholland Drive* (2001), der auf den sprechenden Namen »Club Silencio« hört, liefert ein dämonisch ausgeleuchteter Conférencier dem Publikum eine geradezu brechtianische Lektion in Sachen Illusionismus. Immer wieder betont er, begleitet von Musikfetzen hinter dem Bühnenvorhang, dass es auf dieser Bühne keine Band, kein Orchester gebe, vielmehr käme alles vom Band (vgl. Abb. 6). Seine Ausführungen werden dadurch bestätigt, dass die hiernach auftretenden Musiker allesamt mit Playback agieren, was sich jedoch erst zeigt, wenn sie zusammenbrechen oder

---

45 | Žižek: The Lamella of David Lynch, S. 207f.

von der Bühne gebracht werden. Die vorherige Aufklärung verhindert jedoch nicht, dass die beiden weiblichen Hauptfiguren des Filmes im Zuschauerraum des Clubs angesichts einer sentimentalen Gesangseinlage auf der Bühne Tränen der Rührung vergießen. Der Zwang zum Illusionismus scheint stärker zu sein, denn es wird weiter ›romantisch geglotzt‹. Interessant hieran ist jedoch der Umstand, dass der Bühnenraum des Nachtclubs zwar dem Dispositiv eines Logentheaters entspricht (merkwürdig genug für einen Nachtclub), die Zuschauerreihen jedoch in der klassischen Kinobestuhlung angeordnet sind. Lynch scheint hier also weniger über die Wirkung der szenischen als über die der *filmischen* Illusion zu reden: »This is all a tape recording!«

Abbildung 6: »No hay banda!« Die mediale Ermöglichungsbedingung des Geräusches, Mulholland Drive *(2001), 01:42.22.*

Žižeks kosmologische Deutung des ›primordial noise‹ bei Lynch trifft sich indessen mit der hier vorgeschlagenen medienreflexiven Erweiterung im Moment der Transzendentalkategorie, also der Ermöglichungsbedingung. Das Geräusch, das in beiden Fällen den Raum offen hält (und insofern erst ermöglicht), ist entsprechend der Entstehung isolierbarer und identifizierbarer Entitäten vorgelagert. Der ›Big Bang‹ des Filmgeräusches wäre insofern als das *Rauschen der Aufzeichnungsapparatur* zu verstehen, und der imaginäre Bühnenraum in *Mulholland Drive* dient mithin lediglich als deren erste spatiale Manifestation in einem fiktionalen *locus*. Von hier aus dehnt sich das Geräusch des Films aus, quer durch alle Räume, quer durch *on* und *off*, in immer neuen Wucherungen und Wellen. Eine filmhistorisch frühe Welle schwappte an den Strand von Saint-Marc-sur-Mer, eine spätere flutete den »Club Silencio«.

Bibliographie

Balázs, Béla: Der sichtbare Mensch oder die Kultur des Films [1924], Frankfurt/M. 2004.
Bazin, André: Die Entwicklung der kinematographischen Sprache, in: Ders.: Was ist Kino? Bausteine zur Theorie des Films, Köln 1975, S. 28-44.
Chaplin, Charlie: Was ich zum Sprechfilm zu sagen habe, in: Mein Film 175 (1929), S. 5.
Chion, Michel: La voix au cinéma, Paris 1984.
Chion, Michel: David Lynch, Paris 1992.
Chion, Michel: Jacques Tati: The Cow and the Moo, in: Ders.: Film, a Sound Art, New York 2009, S. 189-198.
Clair, René: Drei Briefe aus London, in: Ders.: Kino. Vom Stummfilm zum Tonfilm. Kritische Notizen zur Entwicklungsgeschichte des Films 1920-1950, Zürich 1995, S. 111-123.
Deleuze, Gilles: Kino 1: Das Bewegungs-Bild, Frankfurt/M. 1989.
Deleuze, Gilles: Kino 2: Das Zeit-Bild, Frankfurt/M. 1991.
Eisenstein, Sergej M., Wsewelod I. Pudowkin und Grigorij W. Alexandrow: Manifest zum Tonfilm [1928], in: Franz-Josef Albersmaier (Hg.): Texte zur Theorie des Films, Stuttgart 1979, S. 42-45.
Fischer, Robert: David Lynch. Die dunkle Seite der Seele, München 1997.
Flückiger, Barbara: Narrative Funktionen des Filmsounddesigns: Orientierung, Setting, Szenographie, in: Harro Segeberg und Frank Schätzlein (Hg.): Sound. Zur Technologie und Ästhetik des Akustischen in den Medien, Marburg 2005, S. 140-156.
Geisenhanslüke, Achim und Georg Hein (Hg.): Monströse Ordnungen. Zur Typologie und Ästhetik des Anormalen, Bielefeld 2009.
Haberer, Peter: Aspekte der Komik in den Filmen von Jacques Tati, Alsfeld 1996.
Heller, Heinz-B.: Vom komischen Subjekt zur Konstruktion des Komischen: Die Ferien des Monsieur Hulot, in: Fischer Filmgeschichte, hg. von Werner Faulstich und Helmut Korte, Bd. 3: Auf der Suche nach Werten 1945-1960, Frankfurt/M. 1990, S. 206-221.
Kirihara, Donald: Sounds in *Les Vacances de Monsieur Hulot*, in: Peter Lehmann (Hg.): Close Viewings. An Anthology of New Film Criticism, Tallahassee 1990, S. 158-170.
Lommel, Michael, Isabel Maurer Queipo und Volker Roloff (Hg.): Surrealismus und Film. Von Fellini bis Lynch, Bielefeld 2008.
Maddock, Brent: Die Filme von Jacques Tati, München 1993.
Morgan, Frances: Darkness Audible. Sub-Bass, tape decay and Lynchian noise, in: Virginie Sélavy (Hg.): The End: An Electric Sheep Anthology, London 2010, S. 186-202.

Seeßlen, Georg: David Lynch und seine Filme, Marburg 1997.
Segeberg, Harro: Der Sound und die Medien. Oder: Warum sich die Medienwissenschaft für den Ton interessieren sollte, in: Ders. und Frank Schätzlein (Hg.): Sound. Zur Technologie und Ästhetik des Akustischen in den Medien, Marburg 2005, S. 9-23.
Žižek, Slavoj: The Lamella of David Lynch, in: Richard Feldstein, Bruce Fink und Maire Jaanus (Hg.): Reading Seminar IX. Lacan's Four Fundamental Concepts of Psychoanalysis, Albany 1995, S. 205-220.

FILMOGRAPHIE

Eraserhead (1977), Regie: David Lynch, USA, s/w.
Les vacances de Monsieur Hulot (1953), Regie: Jacques Tati, FR, s/w.
Mulholland Drive (2001), Regie: David Lynch, USA/FR, Farbe.

Rauschen im Fernsehen
Kommunikation mit Astronauten

Sven Grampp

»GROUND CONTROL TO MAJOR TOM«

Fünf Tage vor dem Start der Apollo-11-Mission, die die ersten Menschen auf den Mond bringen wird, veröffentlicht David Bowie, inspiriert durch Stanley Kubricks Film *2001: A Space Odyssey*, der wiederum einige Monate davor in die Kinos kam, die Single *Space Oddity*. Die *Space Odyssee* wird hier also zu einer *Oddity*, einer Merkwürdigkeit. Das Lied kreist um den Funkverkehr zwischen der Bodenstation, *ground control*, und dem Astronauten Major Tom, der gerade ins All fliegt.[1] Während des Fluges ergeben sich erhebliche Kommunikationsstörungen, bis schließlich der Funkkontakt gänzlich abbricht. Gegen Ende des Liedes funkt die Bodenstation vergeblich:

Ground control to Major Tom, your circuit's dead, there's something wrong.
Can you hear me, Major Tom?
Can you hear me, Major Tom?
Can you hear me, Major Tom?
Can you ...[2]

Damit ist recht präzise das Problem bezeichnet, dem ich im Folgenden näher nachgehen möchte, nämlich der Schwierigkeit bei der Kommunikation zwischen Erde und Weltraum. Solch eine Kommunikation setzt eine vergleichsweise komplizierte technologische Medienapparatur voraus. Schallwellen, die man im Weltraum ohnehin nicht hören könnte,[3] müssen in

---

1 | Vgl. dazu auch Geppert: European Astrofuturism, S. 6ff.
2 | Bowie: *Space Oddity*.
3 | Ein Umstand, mit dem z.B. der Science Fiction Horror Film *Alien* (1979) Werbung macht. Im Trailer und auf Kinoplakaten ist zu lesen: »In space no one can hear you scream.«

elektromagnetische Wellen umgewandelt, Tausende von Kilometer übertragen und wieder decodiert werden. Kommunikation ist in einem solchen Zusammenhang extrem störanfällig und voller Rauschen, was sie aber zumindest für den Kontext dieses Bandes besonders interessant machen dürfte, handelt es sich doch bei diesen Kommunikationsschwierigkeiten um *Noise*, präziser: um Interferenzen, die, wie es im Klappentext vorliegender Publikation heißt, »un-intendierte, un-sinnige, un-erwünschte Laute« verursachen.

Jedoch möchte ich mich nicht direkt mit den technischen Problemen dieser Kommunikation beschäftigen, sondern vielmehr ihrer Verarbeitung in der Fernsehberichterstattung über Weltraummissionen nachgehen. Denn dort werden die Störungen, so möchte ich zeigen, nicht einfach nur als Problem verhandelt, sondern ästhetisch und narrativ produktiv gemacht. Wie facettenreich die televisuellen Verarbeitungen der Kommunikationsprobleme zwischen Bodenstation und Astronauten sind und wie sie zur Demonstration der kommunikativen Kompetenz des Fernsehens funktionalisiert werden, das möchte ich an einigen Beispielen der Live-Berichterstattungen über Weltraummissionen untersuchen. Speziell an der Fernsehberichterstattung über die wohl bekanntesten bemannten Mond-Missionen, nämlich Apollo 11 und Apollo 13, lässt sich das Problem festmachen.

Den Analysen zur Berichterstattung über die Missionen vorgeschaltet wird ein medientheoretischer Exkurs. Der Sinn dieses Exkurses besteht erstens darin zu zeigen, warum und in welcher Weise der medientheoretische Diskurs sich seit jeher äußerst interessiert zeigt an Störungen. Geht es doch dabei immer auch um das spezifische Selbstverständnis und Erkenntnisinteresse kulturwissenschaftlicher Medialitätsforschung.[4] Zweitens lassen sich einige der dort recht abstrakt formulierten Annahmen im Fortgang dieses Beitrags sehr konkret an der televisuellen Berichterstattung über Weltraummissionen veranschaulichen und somit ›erden‹. Drittens sind umgekehrt, vom Blickwinkel medienwissenschaftlicher Störungstheorien aus betrachtet, die produktiven Aspekte televisueller Störungsverarbeitung im Fernsehen besonders gut zu erklären.

STÖRUNG IN DER MEDIENTHEORIE

Von Störungen verspricht man sich in der Medientheorie allerhand. Sie werden dort – in einer typisch dekonstruktivistischen Geste – nicht etwa als

---

[4] | Siehe zur Bezeichnung kulturwissenschaftliche Medialitätsforschung (vor allem in Differenzsetzung zur kommunikationswissenschaftlichen Medienforschung) die Einschätzungen und Empfehlungen des Wissenschaftsrates: Empfehlungen zur Weiterentwicklung der Kommunikations- und Medienwissenschaften in Deutschland.

defizitär verstanden, sondern als Mittel zur Erkenntnis gewendet, ja regelrecht gefeiert.[5] *Noise* ist in der Medientheorie nahezu immer eine gute Sache.

Um es etwas genauer und kleinteiliger zu fassen: Der Ausgangspunkt medientheoretischer Beschäftigungen mit Störung beinhaltet zumeist eine Referenz auf das mathematische Kommunikationsmodell von Claude E. Shannon, das dieser im Kontext seiner Anstellung bei dem Telefon- und Telefunkproduzenten Bell Lab entwickelt hat (vgl Abb. 1).[6]

Das Modell besagt in aller Kürze formuliert: Die Nachrichtenquelle *(information source)* wählt aus einem Repertoire von Elementen (z.B. Buchstaben) eine Nachricht *(message)*, die durch einen Transmitter zum Signal umgewandelt und über einen Kanal zu einem Empfänger übertragen wird, wo das Signal wiederum in eine Nachricht rückübersetzt wird. Dieses vergleichsweise einfache (und für seine Einfachheit zu Recht kritisierte)[7] Kommunikationsmodell beinhaltet mindestens zwei Aspekte, die es für die Medientheorie interessant macht. Da gibt es erstens eine eigens im Modell ausgewiesene Störungsquelle *(noise source)*. Störung wird somit *per se* als gewichtiger Faktor eines jeglichen Kommunikationsprozesses verstanden. Zweitens wird hier mit einem sehr spezifischen Informationsbegriff operiert: Der Informationsgehalt eines Signals ist umgekehrt proportional zu seiner Auftrittswahrscheinlichkeit. Einfacher formuliert: Je unerwarteter bzw. unerwartbarer ein Signal, desto informativer ist es. Das hat unter anderem eine zunächst vielleicht kontraintuitive Konsequenz: Je größer die Störung, desto höher der Informationswert.

---

5 | Siehe dazu z.B. Kümmel/Schüttpelz: Medientheorien der Störung, S. 9: »Er [der Sammelband] zielt auf eine Analyse von Störungsphänomenen, die diese nicht vornehmlich als destruktiv in Hinsicht auf bestimmte Ordnungen, sondern als konstitutiv für die Entstehung neuer Ordnung ansieht.« Siehe auch: Kümmel: Mathematische Kommunikationstheorie, S. 236, wo es zum Schluss heißt: »So endet der Aufsatz mit einer kleinen Hymne an das Rauschen [...].«
6 | Siehe dazu ausführlicher: Kümmel: Mathematische Kommunikationstheorie, S. 207ff.
7 | Siehe nur ein Beispiel unter vielen: Schmidt/Zurstiege: Orientierung Kommunikationswissenschaft, S. 63f. Die Autoren machen deutlich, dass bei diesem Kommunikationsmodell einzig die Frage nach technischer Informationsübermittlung gestellt wird, semantische Kommunikation, mithin menschliche Bedeutungszuweisungen innerhalb des Kommunikationsprozesses spielen hingegen keine Rolle und können mit diesem Modell nicht angemessen beschrieben werden. Dass aber eben auch technische Probleme wichtig für die menschliche Kommunikation, mithin für Bedeutungszuweisungen werden können, ist hingegen von dieser Art Kritik nicht tangiert. Eine Ehrenrettung des Kommunikationsmodells Shannons zur Beschreibung semantisch basierter Kommunikation unternimmt Baecker: Kommunikation, S. 65f.

Abbildung 1: Shannons Kommunikationsmodell

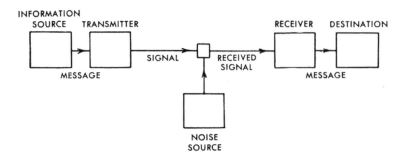

Quelle: Shannon: A Mathematical Theory of Communication, S. 381.

Obwohl das Modell die formale Struktur jedweder Informationsübermittlung beschreiben soll, stammen die Beispiele und Metaphern von Shannon sehr häufig aus dem akustischen Bereich. Bereits die Wahl für die Störungsbezeichnung als *Noise* macht das deutlich (möglich wären ja genauso *annoyance* oder *disruption*). Darüber hinaus stammen auch im Vorwort, das Warren Weaver für Shannons detaillierte Abhandlung über dieses mathematische Kommunikationsmodell 1949 verfasst hat, die Beispiele meist aus dem akustischen Bereich.[8] So schreibt Weaver:

> Im Fall der Telefonie ist der Kanal ein Draht, das Signal ein sich ändernder elektrischer Strom in diesem Draht; der Sender ist die Anlage (Telefonapparat usw.), der den Schalldruck der Stimme in einen sich ändernden elektrischen Strom übersetzt. [...] In der Funktechnik ist der Kanal einfach der Raum [...], und das Signal ist die elektromagnetische Welle, die übertragen wird. [...] Während des Übertragungsprozesses werden leider meistens dem Signal bestimmte Dinge hinzugefügt, die von der Nachrichtenquelle nicht beabsichtigt waren. Diese unerwünschten Zusätze können Tonverzerrungen sein [...] oder atmosphärische Störungen (in der Funktechnik) [...]. Alle diese Veränderungen im übertragenen Signal werden *Störungen* genannt.[9]

---

8 | Vgl. Weaver: Ein aktueller Beitrag zur mathematischen Theorie der Kommunikation. In den Kulturwissenschaften wird, jenseits der ›Kittler-Schule‹, ohnehin nahezu ausschließlich dieses Vorwort zitiert, wenn es um das mathematische Kommunikationsmodell geht. Das mag u. a. daran liegen, dass es im Gegensatz zu Shannons Abhandlung ohne mathematische Zeichensprache auskommt, dafür aber sehr viele anschauliche Beispiele anführt.

9 | Ebd., S. 198.

Bei Weaver heißt es noch deutlich: ›leider‹. Störung ist hier also etwas, das es am besten zu vermeiden gilt.[10] Den kanadischen Philologen Marschall McLuhan interessierte an dem Kommunikationsmodell von Shannon und Weaver hingegen vor allem die Störung – und zwar aus einem ganz bestimmten Grund und in einem ganz bestimmten Sinn. McLuhan versteht nämlich den technischen Übertragungskanal nicht als neutrales oder limitierendes Mittel, das von außen gestört werden kann. Vielmehr wird die Störung zu einem Merkmal des medialen Übertragungskanals selbst. In einem Brief aus dem Jahr 1976 heißt es dazu pointiert: »What they [Shannon und Weaver] call ›Noise‹ I call the medium, all the side effects, all the unintended patterns and changes.«[11] Was McLuhan also interessiert, ist nicht das Signal, das vom Sender zum Empfänger geht, sondern was dazwischen geschieht, was jenseits der Kommunikationsabsicht des Senders und der Dekodierung durch den Empfänger liegt, sie aber gleichwohl beeinflusst. Das Medium ist demgemäß nicht einfach ein Kanal, sondern als Milieu eine die gesamte Kommunikation beeinflussende, präformierende Größe. Mit *noise* ist hier also die Medialität des Mediums gemeint. Nach dieser Medialität will McLuhan fahnden. Damit ist auch der Grund genannt, warum McLuhan mit einigem Recht als Stammesvater aller *Medien*wissenschaft gilt.[12]

Legionen von Medienwissenschaftlern sind McLuhan nicht nur in seinem Interesse an der Medialität des Mediums gefolgt,[13] sondern ebenso in der Kopplung von Medium und *noise* oder doch zumindest in einer bestimmten Implikation dieser Verbindung. Zwar werden meist nicht, wie in der zitierten Briefstelle, Medium und *noise* synonym gesetzt. Jedoch wird *noise* zur *Erkenntnis stiftenden* Kraft stilisiert: Zuallererst oder zumindest insbesondere in der Störung zeigt sich die Medialität des Mediums – so lautet ein maßgebliches Axiom vieler medientheoretischer Verlautbarungen.[14]

---

10 | Wenn man sich den Kontext, dem die Forschung entstammt, klar macht – Shannon und Weaver sind in der Zeit der Veröffentlichung beim Telefon- und Telefunkproduzenten Bell Lab angestellt – dürfte das Interesse an der *Vermeidung* von Störung bei der Kommunikation nicht allzu verwunderlich sein.
11 | Marshall McLuhan: »Brief an Jerry Angel (1976)«, zitiert nach: Patterson: History and Communications, S. 100.
12 | Vgl. dazu ausführlicher Grampp: Marshall McLuhan, v. a. S. 11ff. und S. 190ff.
13 | Vgl. ebd., v. a. S. 11ff. und S. 190ff.
14 | Nur zwei Beispiele aus jüngerer Zeit sollen für eine große Anzahl solcher Projekte genannt sein. Zum einen ist Dieter Merschs Projekt einer negativen Medientheorie zu nennen: »Die Medialität des Mediums gegen den Strich bürsten und ihre Unkenntlichkeit selbst kenntlich zu machen: darin erfüllen sich jene Bewegungen der Verschiebung und Verwirrung [...], woran zugleich eine ›negative Medientheorie‹ ihr unverwechselbares Profil findet.«, Mersch: Medientheorien zur Einführung, S. 228. Zwei Seiten zuvor

Neben dieser medienreflexiven Wendung der Störung gibt es noch einen weiteren Strang in der medientheoretischen Diskussion. In diesem Fall findet sich der Ausgangspunkt in der Kybernetik. Dort wird die Frage nach der Störung funktional umformuliert. Gregory Bateson schreibt 1967 in *Kybernetische Erklärung* in diesem Sinne: »Alles, was nicht Information, nicht Redundanz, nicht Form und nicht Einschränkung ist – ist Rauschen, die einzige mögliche Quelle *neuer* Muster.«[15] Störung ist aus dieser Perspektive nicht nur nicht etwas, das es zu vermeiden gilt, weil es die Kommunikation verzerrt; es ist ebenso wenig nur Ausgangspunkt des Nachdenkens über die materiellen Aspekte medialer Kommunikation. Vielmehr ist es das entscheidende, ja notwendige Mittel zur Innovation: Ohne Störung nichts Neues in der Welt oder doch zumindest keine neuen Formen der Verarbeitung von Informationen. Störung steigert, streng nach Shannons Informationsbegriff, Komplexität.[16]

Vor allem durch Michel Serres findet das Nachdenken über die Störung unter diesen kybernetischen Vorzeichen Anschluss an medientheoretische Debatten. In seinem breit rezipierten Buch *Der Parasit* formuliert Serres, ebenfalls unverkennbar vorrangig der Metaphorik des Akustischen verpflichtet: »Der Lärm unterdrückt das System zeitweilig, er läßt es auf unbestimmte Weise oszillieren. [...] Theorem: Der Lärm bringt ein neues System hervor, eine Ordnung höherer Komplexität, als die einfache Kette sie hat.«[17]

---

heißt es: »Ihre Basis sind negative Praktiken wie Eingriffe, *Störungen*, Hindernisse, konträre Konfigurationen.« (Herv. S. G.). Etwas weniger poetisch, aber ganz in diesem Sinn formuliert der in der Medienwissenschaft der letzten Jahre stark rezipierte (Technik-) Soziologe Bruno Latour: »Nehmen wir [...] an, der Projektor hat plötzlich eine Panne. Erst die Krise macht uns die Existenz des Geräts wieder bewußt. [...] Eben war der Projektor noch kaum mit einer eigenen Existenz begabt, und nun hat sogar jedes seiner Teile ein Eigenleben [...].«, Latour: Die Hoffnung der Pandora, S. 223. In der Störung des Geräts liegt also Erkenntniswert, der uns das ›Eigenleben‹, mithin die Medialität des medientechnischen Apparats erkennen lässt. Bereits bei McLuhan ist diese Sicht der (Störungs-)Dinge zu finden, vor allem in den Passagen, in denen er über die Störung von Medien durch andere Medien nachdenkt – siehe: McLuhan: Understanding Media, v. a. das Kapitel »Hybrid Energy: Les Liaisons Dangereuses«, S. 71ff.

15 | Bateson: Kybernetische Erklärung, S. 529.

16 | Eine andere Frage ist freilich, wie groß die Komplexität sein darf, um tatsächlich als Innovationspotenzial attraktiv zu sein. Absolutes, sogenanntes weißes Rauschen hat zwar unendliche Information und ist unendlich komplex, führt aber so eben auch ins Indifferente. Alle Möglichkeiten zu haben, beinhaltet zwar logischerweise auch immer die Möglichkeit für Neues, ist aber nicht unbedingt ein Motivator neue Wege zu gehen. Vgl. dazu auch Luhmann: Die Realität der Massenmedien, S. 37f.

17 | Serres: Der Parasit, S. 29.

Um das an einem einfachen Beispiel zu verdeutlichen, das Serres selbst immer wieder aufgreift: Freunde sitzen zusammen in der Küche; plötzlich klingelt laut das Telefon. Das Telefon kann als Störung der Gespräche in der Küche gefasst werden. Vielleicht versteht man dadurch nicht mehr jedes Wort der Gesprächsteilnehmer oder die Anwesenden spekulieren darüber, wer da anrufen könnte (etwa der nicht eingeladene Freund, der nun einen Kontrollanruf macht oder das Krankenhaus, das einen der Anwesenden wegen eines Notfalls anruft etc.). Im ersten wie auch im zweiten Fall wird die Komplexität des Kommunikationssystems gesteigert. Wird, wie im ersten Fall, nicht mehr jedes Wort verstanden, müssen die einzelnen Teilnehmer darüber spekulieren oder nachfragen, was nun genau gesagt wurde. Die Leerstellen innerhalb der Kommunikation nehmen zu, also auch – streng nach Shannon und Weaver – der Informationsgehalt. Im zweiten Fall wird die Irritation des Klingelns zum Anlass genommen, über denjenigen zu spekulieren, der möglicherweise anruft. Das Kommunikationssystem wird so durch Irritation dynamisch. Man macht sich nun zusätzlich auch über anderes als zuvor Gedanken. Mit anderen Worten: Komplexität wird gesteigert.

Das Ganze ließe sich freilich noch medientechnischer wenden: Gesetzt den Fall, der Telefonhörer liegt nicht richtig auf dem Apparat, dann erfolgt nach einiger Zeit ein Signal im hohen Frequenzbereich, sodass alle Gespräche vor Ort massiv gestört werden.[18] Man wendet sich dem Hörer zu, erkennt, dass er nicht aufgelegt war, obwohl er doch eigentlich aufgelegt sein sollte. Denn andernfalls kann man nicht angerufen werden bzw. man besetzt unnötig eine Leitung. Genau diese mediale Eigenschaften (Telefonhörer muss aufgelegt sein, sonst kann man nicht angerufen werden bzw. es gibt eine begrenze Anzahl telefonischer Kommunikationskanäle) werden in dieser Störung reflexiv. Mit anderen Worten: Die Kommunikation wurde durch den Telefonlärm in komplexere Sphären gelenkt. Auch hier gilt im Sinne Serres', wie bereits bei Bateson: *noise* ist kreativ, verantwortlich für Neues, für Komplexitätszuwachs, für Dynamik.

Jedoch soll noch auf einen anderen Aspekt aufmerksam gemacht werden, der sich ebenfalls in Serres' *Der Parasit* findet. Nämlich die Idee, dass jede Störung *relativ* ist. Je nach Beobachter und System kann etwas entweder als Störung oder aber als Information verstanden werden.

---

18 | Wir befinden uns mit diesem Beispiel weder in Deutschland noch sonst wo auf dem europäischen Festland. Denn dort wird solch ein sogenannter *Receiver Off-Hook Tone* aufgrund möglicher Gefährdung des menschlichen Gehörs nicht (mehr) verwendet, anders als etwa in Asien und Amerika. Für ein Beispiel solch eines Tones siehe (und vor allem höre): »Receiver Off-Hook Tone«, http://www.youtube.com/watch?v=K0_YErq1M-M (27.7.13).

> Auf dem Fest gehen die Worte hin und her. An der Zimmertür ertönt ein Geräusch: das Telefon klingelt. Die Kommunikation unterbricht die Konversation, dieses Geräusch unterbricht jene Botschaften. Sobald ich das Gespräch mit dem neuen Gesprächspartner aufnehme, setzt die Unterhaltung an der Festtafel wieder ein, sie wird zum Lärm, zum Rauschen, für das neue Wir. Das System schaukelt. Nähere ich mich wieder der Tafel, so wird der Lärm nach und nach wieder zur Konversation. Im System tauschen Rauschen und Nachrichten ihre Rollen je nach der Stellung des Beobachters und nach den Handlungen des Akteurs, aber sie verwandeln sich auch ineinander ganz in Abhängigkeit von der Zeit und vom System. Sie machen Ordnung und Unordnung.[19]

Hier kommt es also darauf an, was ich als Kommunikationssystem verstehe. Im einen Fall ist das Telefon eine Störung für die Kommunikation; im anderen Fall ist das Telefonsignal Ausgangspunkt für eine andere Kommunikation, nämlich mit dem Anrufer. Wenn ich am Telefongespräch teilnehme, wird die sich miteinander unterhaltende Gruppe in der Küche zur Störung für die Telefonierenden. Je nach Beobachterperspektive wird etwas zur Störung oder eben nicht. Einmal ist die Küchenkommunikation die Störung, einmal das Telefongespräch. Störungen sind also strikt *beobachterrelativ*.[20]

Damit kommt auch die wichtige Differenz zwischen Materialität und Semantik in den Blick. Zwar kann eine Apparatur kaputt gehen oder deren Funktionsweise massive Einschränkungen erfahren, Kommunikation somit technisch gestört werden. Ob das aber tatsächlich als Störung, als problematische Störung oder als produktives Element von Anschlusskommunikation verstanden wird, entscheidet sich erst im jeweiligen Kontext und ist eine Leistung des Beobachters. Solch ein Beobachter kann beispielsweise das Fernsehen sein, das technische Kommunikationsprobleme zwischen Astronauten und der Bodenstation beobachtet und technische Störungen in bestimmter Weise semantisiert, wie im nächsten Abschnitt ausführlicher erläutert werden wird.

Alle bisher angeführten Aspekte der Störung sind in wünschenswerter Klarheit ausbuchstabiert und verdichtet in einer kurzen Passage eines

---

19 | Serres, Der Parasit, S. 102f.
20 | Störungen lassen sich freilich auch danach unterscheiden, ob sie beabsichtigt sind oder nicht, etwa ob sie eine künstlerische Strategie oder einfach ein Unfall sind. Da im Folgenden primär die unbeabsichtigte Variante in Form technischer Funkprobleme eine Rolle spielt, wird der intentional hergestellten Störung keine größere Aufmerksamkeit geschenkt (mit einer Ausnahme, wie noch näher auszuführen sein wird, nämlich der televisuellen Herstellung von ›Hintergrundrauschen‹). Das unterscheidet den hier gewählten Zugriff maßgeblich von der Herangehensweise, die z.B. Mersch wählt. Ihm geht es bei den Störungen vorrangig um künstlerisch beabsichtigte Intervention; vgl. Mersch: Medientheorie, S. 226ff.

Romans von John Griesemer, der den englischen Originaltitel *Signal & Noise* trägt. Erzählt wird darin die Geschichte der Verlegung des ersten transatlantischen Telegrafenkabels. Die im Folgenden zitierte Passage ist zeitlich nach der ersten erfolgreichen Auslegung des maritimen Telegrafenkabels situiert, dem aber ein Misserfolg auf dem Fuß folgte: Das Kabel wurde wieder durchtrennt. In einem Tagebucheintrag heißt es dazu:

Ich bin bald ein halbes Jahr hier und bemanne das Telegraphenhaus. [...] Ich warte auf Signale. [...] Dieses Kabel endet an einer Bruchstelle auf dem Meeresgrund, 1250 Seemeilen entfernt von meinem Stuhl. [...] Durch dieses gebrochene Kabel werden Botschaften gesandt. Woher sie kommen, das weiß ich nicht. Sie sind Ausbrüche der Klarheit inmitten sonst nicht entzifferbaren Gestammels. [...] Der gesamte Ozean spricht durch das Kabel. Seine Stürme, seine Magnetfelder senden Botschaften. Bestimmten Mustern haben wir eine Bedeutung zugeordnet, aber wer wollte behaupten, dem übrigen Zucken des Lichtes lägen keine Muster zugrunde?[21]

Hier liegt augenscheinlich eine medientechnische Störung vor. Das Telegrafenkabel ist durchtrennt. Durch diese Störung wird eine ›Klarheit‹ erzeugt hinsichtlich der Funktionsweise des Telegrafenkabels: Botschaften werden in Form von Lichtimpulsen gesandt. Durch die Störung wird zudem die Komplexität gesteigert: Neue Muster werden erkannt (oder doch zumindest vermutet). Hieran wird denn auch die Relativität von Signal und *noise* offenbar. Für den Tagebuchschreiber wird ja gerade das bloße Rauschen, das vermeintlich Bedeutungslose bedeutungsvoll, Erkenntnis stiftend.

STÖRUNG IM FERNSEHEN

In Literatur bzw. Kunst wird also ebenfalls das ausbuchstabiert, was die Medientheoretiker seit einigen Jahrzenten betonen: Störung ist produktiv, relativ und Erkenntnis stiftend. Im Folgenden geht es mir weder um ambitionierte Reflexionen in der (Roman-)Kunst, noch um die Fortsetzung der erkenntnistheoretisch ausgerichteten Reflexionen der Medientheoretiker über *Signal & Noise*. Vielmehr möchte ich mich, gerüstet mit den angeführten medientheoretischen Überlegungen zur Störung, in die Niederungen gängiger massenmedialer Praxis begeben und zeigen, in welcher Weise das Fernsehen mit Störungen umgeht. Konzentrieren werde ich mich auf televisuelle Strategien und Darstellungen bemannter Raumfahrtmissionen. Meine These lautet: Das Fernsehen geht mit technischen Störungen in bestimmter Weise um. Einerseits sollen solche Störungen kompensiert bzw. schnellstmöglich

---

21 | Griesemer: Rausch, S. 51ff.

beseitigt werden; andererseits werden Störungen aber auch produktiv gewendet, sei es, dass eine Störung als dramaturgischer Effekt Verwendung findet oder dass sie medienreflexiv gewendet – im Sinne Serres' – zum Komplexitätsaufbau und zur Erzeugung von Anschlusskommunikation funktionalisiert wird.

Das Fernsehen hat schon immer eine Affinität zur Störung.[22] Unfälle, Terrorangriffe, Naturkatastrophen, Strom- oder Satellitenausfälle – das sind allesamt außergewöhnliche Ereignisse, die massive Beeinträchtigungen und Schwierigkeiten mit sich bringen mögen, aber eben doch eine hohe Chance haben, den Weg in die massenmediale Berichterstattung zu finden. Schließlich wird doch dort, zumindest wenn man den Ausführungen Niklas Luhmanns dazu folgen will, die Welt primär nach Besonderem, Neuem, Überraschendem, Unvorhergesehenem und Unwahrscheinlichem durchforstet, um darüber zu berichten.[23] Unwahrscheinliches hat, wie wir spätestens seit Shannon wissen, hohen Informationswert – und ist deshalb insbesondere für die Massenmedien attraktiv.[24]

---

22 | Vgl. dazu ausführlicher Kirchmann: Störung und ›Monitoring‹.

23 | Vgl. Luhmann: Realität der Massenmedien, insb. S. 36ff. Luhmann geht davon aus, dass das System Massenmedien primär mit der Unterscheidung Information/Nicht-Information operiert und dabei den ersten Begriff in dieser Dichotomie präferiert. Luhmanns Informationsbegriff ist im Übrigen der, den Shannon als mathematische Informationstheorie eingeführt hat, und den Luhmann in der Variante von Bateson übernimmt (vgl. ebd., S. 39f.). Eine wichtige Verschiebung findet dabei jedoch statt: Was jeweils als Ereignis mit hohem Informationswert eingestuft wird, ist bei Luhmann eine semantische Beobachtung- und Bedeutungszuweisung des Systems Massenmedien. Bei Shannon ist es ein rein medientechnisches formales Problem der Informationsübertragung.

24 | Vgl. ebd., S. 36ff. Mit Bezug auf das System Massenmedien macht Luhmann auf einen wichtigen Punkt aufmerksam: Die Dichte einer neuen Information hat Grenzen. So hat die Suche der Massenmedien nach neuen Informationen auch immer etwas mit Anschlussfähigkeit an bereits Bekanntes zu tun. Genauer noch: Anschlussfähigkeit wird durch bestimmte Schemata erzeugt, die vorselektieren, Neues auf bereits Bekanntes beziehen und damit Komplexität reduzieren. Neues ist, so gesehen, also nicht absolut neu. Weiterhin müssen die Massenmedien das Vermögen besitzen, Neues in Altes umwandeln zu können, damit überhaupt erst wieder Neues beobachtet werden kann. »Wollte man den Horizont dessen, was möglicherweise geschehen kann, ins gänzlich Unbestimmte ausfließen lassen, würden Informationen als arbiträr erscheinen und nicht als Überraschung. Man würde mit ihnen nichts anfangen können, weil sie nichts anbieten, was man lernen könnte, und weil sie nicht in Redundanzen umgeformt werden könnten, die einschränken, was weiter zu erwarten ist. Deshalb ist alle Information auf Kategorisierungen angewiesen, die Möglichkeitsräume abstecken, in denen der

Technische Übertragungsstörungen und Fehlfunktionen bei der Signalübermittlung haben in diesem Zusammenhang eine ambivalente Stellung. Einerseits gilt es, solche Störungen tunlichst zu vermeiden. Wenn die Liveschaltung in das Krisengebiet ausfällt, kann die Krise nicht direkt sichtbar gemacht werden. Wenn der Fernsehempfang eine Fehlfunktion hat, ist nichts zu sehen.[25] Anderseits haben technische Störungen immer auch (und sei es auch nur im Nachhinein) hohen Informationswert oder können zumindest produktiv gewendet werden.[26] Fällt ein Fernsehkanal vorübergehend aus, wird ganz sicher auf den anderen Fernsehkanälen ausgiebig darüber berichtet. Doch wenn regelmäßig das Bild ausfallen würde, würden wohl kaum noch Zuschauer einschalten. Störungen gilt es also einerseits zu vermeiden, zumindest die damit zusammenhängenden Probleme zu minimieren. Anderseits erzeugen Störungen hohe Aufmerksamkeit und Anschlusskommunikation.

Im Fall der televisuellen Beobachtung der Kommunikation und der Kommunikationsstörungen zwischen Astronauten und Bodenstation wird diese Ambivalenz in gewisser Weise auf Dauer gestellt und (zumindest teilweise) vorhersehbar. Denn die Probleme der Kommunikationsstörungen sind ein ständiger Begleiter der Missionen, für die im Laufe der televisuellen

---

Auswahlbereich für das, was als Kommunikation geschehen kann, vorstrukturiert ist.« (ebd., S. 37f.). Als Beispiel für solche Selektionsbereiche nennt Luhmann u. a. Politik, Kunst, aber auch eigens »*Unfälle* oder *Katastrophen*« (ebd., S. 38; Herv. S.G.). Noch pointierter und auf Kommunikationsphänomene generell ausgedehnt formuliert Dirk Baecker die Notwendigkeit von komplexitätsreduzierenden Schemata im Kontext der Diskussion von Shannons Kommunikationsmodell und Informationsbegriff: »Der Inhalt einer Nachricht ist eine Selektivität, die nur an der mitgelieferten *Redundanz* überhaupt kenntlich wird.« Baecker: Kommunikation, S. 66; Herv. S. G.

25 | Anders liegt freilich der Fall, wenn über externe technische Störungen berichtet wird, etwa der Austritt radioaktiver Strahlung aus einem Atommeiler. Hier wird ja nicht die Fernsehberichterstattung selbst beeinträchtigt. Das Funksignal ist nicht gestört. Im Fall der Kommunikationsstörungen zwischen den Astronauten und der Bodenstation liegt der Fall weniger deutlich. Zwar geht es hier einerseits auch um externe Störungen; das Fernsehsignal selbst ist nicht gestört; wir sehen die Experten im Studio, hören ihre Aussagen etc. Anderseits schlägt die Störung sofort auf die Berichterstattung durch; wenn nicht verstanden wird, was die Astronauten sagen, wenn man keinen Kontakt zum Schiff mehr vernimmt, wird die Störung zu einem Problem, das die Live-Berichterstattung direkt betrifft, das kompensiert werden muss oder doch zumindest kommunikativ Bearbeitung erfährt.

26 | Selbst wenn das Fernsehen selbst ausfällt, hat das, wie angeführt, für die Fernsehberichterstattung hohen Informationsgehalt. Vgl. dazu auch Kirchmann: Störung, S. 92ff.

Übertragungen unterschiedliche Problemlösungsstrategien entwickelt wurden. Dieser Zustand *permanenter* und gleichsam zumindest partiell vorhersehbarer, also *operationalisierbarer* Störung macht die televisuellen Übertragungen der Raumfahrtmissionen zu einem besonders interessanten Untersuchungsgegenstand, will man die unterschiedlichen Facetten des Umgangs mit Störungen im Fernsehen untersuchen.

FUNKVERKEHR MIT ASTRONAUTEN IM FERNSEHEN

Beim Funkverkehr zwischen Bodenstation und Astronauten entstehen notwendigerweise medientechnisch bedingte Unschärfen, also Rauschen. Um Töne aus dem All auf der Erde hörbar zu machen, benötigt man einen hohen medientechnischen Aufwand. Kommunikation im All mit Astronauten hat vergleichsweise komplizierte technologische Medienapparaturen zur Voraussetzung, die extrem störanfällig sind. Gerade diese Unschärfen und Lücken werden wiederum in der televisuellen Berichterstattung nicht nur als Problem behandelt, sondern ebenso produktiv gewendet. In welcher Form dies geschieht, soll nun an einigen Beispielen des Funkverkehrs zwischen Apollo 11 bzw. Apollo 13 und der Bodenstation verdeutlicht werden. Mindestens vier unterschiedliche Strategien, mit Störung umzugehen, lassen sich in der Berichterstattung des Fernsehens über diese Missionen ausfindig machen:

(1) Kompensation des Rauschens durch Filterung des Signals
(2) Rauschen durch Überlagerung von Signalen als Anlass zur Spekulation
(3) Herstellung von Hintergrundrauschen aus Signalen
(4) Inszenierung des Wartens auf ein Signal im Rauschen

Diese vier Strategien sollen im Folgenden nacheinander näher beleuchtet und vorgestellt werden.

Strategie 1: Kompensation des Rauschens durch Filterung des Signals

Beginnen wir mit dem Satz, der bis dato der berühmteste aller Raumfahrtprojekte ist und wohl auch eine der berühmtesten Äußerungen überhaupt, die jemals von einem Menschen formuliert wurde. Ich meine den Satz, den Neil Armstrong in der Nacht vom 20. auf den 21. Juli 1969 geäußert hat, als er im Begriff war, als erster Mensch den Mond zu betreten. Über eine halbe Milliarde Menschen sollen die Live-Berichterstattung dieser ersten bemannten Mondmission im Fernsehen verfolgt haben, während Armstrong den ebenso poetischen wie pathetischen Satz sprach: »That's one small step for [a] man, one giant leap for mankind.«[27] So deutlich dieser Satz heute den damaligen historischen Augenblick markiert, so undeutlich war er indes damals zu hören. In der Live-Berichterstattung etwa auf dem US-amerikanischen Sender CBS verursachte die Aussage deshalb einiges Kopfzerbrechen.[28]

Während die Zuschauer die ersten gespensterhaft wirkenden Schwarz-Weiß-Bilder live vom Mond sehen und die Umrisse Armstrongs zu erkennen sind, als er die Leiter des Mondmoduls nach unten klettert, verweist der Moderator der CBS auf den historischen Stellenwert des Ereignisses, dessen Zeugen die Zuschauer gerade werden. Dann spricht Armstrong seinen berühmten Satz. Man versteht den Anfang vergleichsweise gut, den zweiten Teil aber eher schlecht. Das medientechnisch bedingte Rauschen ist hoch. Der Moderator versucht zu rekonstruieren, was Armstrong gesagt hat: »›One small step for man‹ – but I didn't get the second phrase.« Daran anschließend wird im Studio darüber spekuliert, was Armstrong gesagt oder gemeint haben könnte. Hier ist das Rauschen im Fernsehen eindeutig als Problem, ja als Störung identifiziert. Man würde doch so gerne wissen, was Armstrong im Augenblick dieses historischen Meilensteins genau gesagt hat. Das Rauschen soll kompensiert werden, indem man es in Sinn und Bedeutung übersetzt oder doch zumindest übersetzen will.[29]

Noch deutlicher wird dieses televisuelle Streben nach bedeutungstragenden Signalen durch alles Rauschen hindurch in so gut wie allen Rückblicksendungen, die sich mit der ersten bemannten Mondlandung befassen. Dort ist das geschilderte Problem schlicht verschwunden: Die Störungen sind herausgefiltert. Das Rauschen und die damit zusammenhängende semantische Unsicherheit sind weitestgehend beseitigt; der Satz ist deutlich zu verstehen.[30]

Der Satz bietet aber nichtsdestotrotz bis heute Anlass zu Spekulationen. Damit wird zudem offensichtlich, wie die Störung in der massenmedialen Kommunikation nicht nur kompensiert bzw. ausgeschaltet werden soll, sondern dort zum Zwecke der Anschlusskommunikation produktiv gemacht

---

27 | Vgl. dazu ausführlicher Grinsted: Die Reise zum Mond, v.a. S. 125ff. Vgl. auch Allen: Live From the Moon, v.a. S. 141ff.

28 | »CBS News Coverage of Apollo 11 – Moon Walk 01«, http://www.youtube.com/watch?v=WQDjy2csPP0 (1.8.13). Zu den genauen Daten der CBS-Übertragungen vgl. Hogan: Televising the Space Age, v.a. S. 106ff.

29 | Zur Funktion des Kommentators, der sich dem Ereignis gegenüber loyal verhält und Bedeutungsidentifizierung wie -zuweisungen vornimmt, siehe ausführlich: Katz/Dayan: Medienereignisse.

30 | Ein Beispiel unter unzähligen findet sich in *100 Jahre – Der Countdown*, Episode: »1969 – Aufbruch zum Mond«, http://www.youtube.com/watch?v=hsKODgZdxvY (2.8.13).

wird. Denn: Auch wenn inzwischen der Satz im Gesamten zu verstehen ist, so gibt es doch innerhalb des Satzes eine bestimmte Passage, die immer noch genug für Zweifel zu sorgen scheint, um Anlass zu Spekulationen zu geben. Bis zu den Nachrufen auf Neil Armstrong im Jahr 2012 ist dies zu verfolgen. In so gut wie keinem Nachruf fehlt der Bezug auf den Satz – und zwar in einer bestimmten Wendung: Zum einen wird »That's one small step for [a] man, one giant leap for mankind« zum Gedenk- und Feieranlass.[31] Zum anderen – und in diesem Zusammenhang noch weit wichtiger – wird so gut wie immer, wenngleich ironisch distanziert, auch auf die Debatte rekurriert, die darum entbrannt war, ob Armstrong das ›a‹ tatsächlich gesagt hatte und es nur deswegen nicht zu hören war, weil es im Rauschen des Funkverkehrs untergegangen ist?[32]

Strategie 2: Rauschen durch Überlagerung von Signalen als Anlass zur Spekulation

Rauschen wird, folgt man noch einmal Shannon und Weaver, unter anderem durch Überlagerung von Signalen erzeugt, die sich dadurch gegenseitig stören und dabei Interferenzen entstehen lassen.[33] Deutlich lässt sich das anhand der ARD-Live-Berichterstattung des ersten Schrittes eines Menschen auf dem Mond verfolgen.[34] Im Fall der ARD spricht der Kommentator, im Gegensatz zur Übertragung auf CBS, über Armstrongs Satz einfach hinweg. Einer der bis dato am häufigsten zitierten Sätze der Menschheit wurde also in der ARD-Live-Berichterstattung überhaupt nicht registriert. Dadurch, dass der Satz durch andere Sätze überlagert wird, werden Interferenzen und Störungen erzeugt. Armstrongs Äußerung wird so zum bloßen Geräusch. Wenig später wird der Satz vom Korrespondenten der ARD vor Ort in Huston,

---

31 | Um nur ein Beispiel zu nennen: So wird etwa der CDU-Abgeordnete Peter Hintze, seines Zeichens Koordinator der Bundesregierung für die Luft- und Raumfahrt, in der deutschsprachigen Presse zitiert mit den Worten: Dieser Satz werde »ewig im Gedächtnis der Menschheit bleiben.« Siehe z. B.: o. A.: Neil Armstrong gestorben.

32 | Zwei Beispiele aus den Nachrufen seien nur kurz angeführt: Seidler: Zum Tod von Neil Armstrong: »Ob Armstrong den entscheidenden Artikel ›a‹ im Eifer des Gefechts verschluckt oder ob er den Tücken der Übertragungstechnik zum Opfer fällt, wird sich nie abschließend klären lassen.« o. A.: Neil Armstrong: »›That's one small step for man, one giant leap for mankind.‹ Whether he had meant to say ›a man‹ would divert pedants for decades to come.«

33 | Siehe: Weaver: Ein aktueller Beitrag, S. 196f.

34 | Ein Zusammenschnitt dieser Berichterstattung wurde vom Bayerischen Rundfunk am 21. Juli 2009 unter dem Titel *Die lange Nacht der Mondlandung. Die Live-Sendung der ARD vor 40 Jahren* ausgestrahlt.

Werner Brüderle, auf Deutsch formuliert. Der Korrespondent verliert dabei aber kein Wort darüber, dass seine Aussage die Übersetzung der Äußerung Armstrongs ist.

Für einige Verschwörungstheoretiker wurden diese Interferenzen zu einem Indiz dafür, dass nie ein Mensch auf dem Mond gelandet war. In einer vom WDR produzierten und seither unzählige Male ausgestrahlten, aber auch auf *YouTube* häufig angeklickten Sendung mit dem Titel *Die Akte Apollo* wird das besonders deutlich markiert. Gernot L. Geise, ein Autor, der unter Fans als »Pionier der Mondlügenforschung«[35] gilt und etliche Bücher über Verschwörungstheorien geschrieben hat, nimmt darin direkt Bezug auf die geschilderte ARD-Live-Berichterstattung.[36] Da Armstrongs Satz von den Worten des Moderators überlagert und der Satz in deutscher Übersetzung erst zeitverzögert vom ARD-Korrespondenten ausgesprochen worden war, wird messerscharf gefolgert: Armstrong habe den Satz überhaupt nicht formuliert, und der Korrespondent habe einfach aus einem Skript der NASA vorgelesen. Daraus wird dann die Schlussfolgerung gezogen, die bemannte Mondlandung sei eine Lüge. Anschlusskommunikation wird hier durch medientechnisch bedingte Unschärfe erzeugt. Störung ist also in diesem Falle ganz konkret *produktiv* gemacht für massenmediale Berichterstattung: Die durch Störungen erzeugten Unschärfen werden zu wilden Spekulationen und weitreichenden Schlussfolgerungen verwendet.[37]

Strategie 3: Herstellung von Hintergrundrauschen aus Signalen

Eine ganz andere Form, wie sich Rauschen produktiv machen lässt, ist ebenfalls an der ARD-Live-Übertagung der ersten bemannten Mondlandung ausfindig zu machen. In weiten Teilen der knapp siebenstündigen

---

35 | Siehe dazu bspw. einen Kommentar zu Geises Buch *Der Mond ist anders!*, http://www.amazon.de/Der-Mond-ist-ganz-anders/dp/3895396109/ref=pd_sim_b_4 (2.8.12).

36 | Vgl. dazu: »Die Akte Apollo: Mondlandung 2/5«, http://www.youtube.com/watch?v=wRf-R_Do2CY (2.9.13), 0:00-1:30.

37 | Die Verschwörungstheorie funktioniert aber auch dann noch, wenn die Unschärfe beseitigt wird – etwa indem der Satz vom kleinen Schritt aus dem ihn umgebenden Rauschen herausgefiltert wird. Gerade dieses Herausfiltern gibt Anlass zum Zweifeln, erzeugt Verdacht und produziert weitere Spekulationen. Verschwörungstheorien sehen also sowohl im Fall der Störung als auch im Fall der Beseitigung von Störung Anlass zur Anschlusskommunikation. Der Zweifel ist endlos und wird in jedem Fall nur noch bestärkt. Das dürfte auch ein Grund sein, warum Verschwörungstheorien so attraktiv für die massenmediale Berichterstattung und dort allerorten virulent sind. Anschlusskommunikation ist garantiert, denn ›alte‹ Informationen werden permanent in neue, überraschende Wendungen überführt.

Live-Berichterstattung aus dem ARD-Sendezentrum fungiert die Kommunikation zwischen Houston und Mondmission Apollo 11 als bloßes Hintergrundrauschen. Der kommunikative Austausch, der zumeist ohnehin nur Angaben von technischen Details und fachspezifische Akronyme beinhaltete, war semantisch nur bedingt relevant.[38] Weit mehr geht es erstens darum zu vermitteln, dass das Fernsehen unmittelbar beteiligt ist und dass die Kommunikation zwischen Astronauten und *ground control* permanent abgehört wird. Falls es tatsächlich etwas Relevantes geben sollte, wenn also das Rauschen Signalwert erhalten sollte, könnte das Fernsehen sofort darauf eingehen. Zweitens entsteht während der beständigen Kommunikation zwischen der Bodenstation und den Astronauten sowie durch die sogenannten Quindar-Töne, die den Anfang und das Ende einer Durchsage bei dem Funkverkehr begleiteten, ein bestimmtes *atmosphärisches* Signum und ein bestimmter *(Space-)Sound.*[39] Drittens wird damit das mangelhafte Bilderprogramm kompensiert. Denn Bilder vor Ort (vom Mond) gab es erst, als Armstrong aus seiner Kapsel ausgestiegen war. Vor diesem Moment war die Mission im Weltraum mit der Ausnahme von kurzen Live-Schaltungen auf dem Weg zum Mond bilderlos.[40] Relevant ist in unserem Zusammenhang vor allem: Semantisch klare Signale werden in voller Absicht zum Hintergrundrauschen ›umgewandelt‹. Es geht also nicht wie bei der ersten Strategie darum, das Rauschen zu vermindern und die relevanten Signale herauszufiltern, oder, wie bei der zweiten Strategie, darum, das (vermeintliche) Rauschen zu Spekulationen über den tatsächlichen Ablauf zu nutzen. Ganz im Gegenteil soll aus Signalen ein Rauschen erzeugt werden, um es als atmosphärisches Hintergrundrauschen funktionalisieren zu können.

Bei dieser Umwandlung zeigt sich sehr deutlich, was Serres' These von der Relativität des Rauschens meint: Einmal werden die Kommunikationsakte der Astronauten als sinnvolle Signale interpretiert, ein anderes Mal als Hintergrundrauschen für die Berichterstattung genutzt; je nach Interessenlage und Funktion wechseln Rauschen und Signal die Position.[41]

---

38 | Dies funktioniert ganz analog z. B. zum Einsatz von Gesprächen in den Notaufnahmegängen der Fernsehserie *ER* (USA 1994-2009) oder den Spekulationen über mögliche Krankheiten in *House* (USA 2004-2012). Die allermeisten der ZuschauerInnen werden nicht wissen, von was hier die Rede ist (wahrscheinlich nicht einmal die Schauspieler). Das ist aber nicht entscheidend, geht es doch sehr viel eher darum, eine bestimmte Atmosphäre anhand der Gespräche zu erzeugen und einen bestimmten Sound zu kreieren.
39 | Zu den Quindar-Tönen vgl. Mehring und Woods: Quindar Tones.
40 | Vgl. dazu bspw. Allen: Live from the Moon, S. 145f.
41 | Das ist im Übrigen eine gängige Praxis der Massenmedien auch jenseits der Berichterstattung über Mondmissionen, wie sich leicht am Beispiel von Sportereignissen, Börsenaktivitäten, Trauungen oder Flutkatastrophen zeigen ließe.

Strategie 4: Entzug des Signals – Inszenierung des Wartens auf ein Signal im Rauschen

Mit ›Entzug des Signals‹ ist genau das gemeint, was in David Bowies eingangs angeführtem Lied *Space Oddity* passiert: der Verlust der Kommunikation zwischen Bodenstation und Astronaut. Damit ist die größtmögliche Störung erzeugt, eine Leerstelle: Ein *LOS*, wie die akronymbesessene NASA ein *loss of signal* bezeichnet, also der Verlust des Signals der Astronauten und die damit verbundene Unterbrechung des Funkkontakts. Übrig bleibt nur Rauschen. Solch ein Verlust des Signals ist aufgrund der komplexen Kommunikationsanordnung eine gängige Begleiterscheinung von Weltraummissionen und tritt nicht nur in Katastrophenfällen auf. Sei es, dass die Satellitenstation auf der Erde das Signal des Raumschiffes kurzfristig nicht findet,[42] sei es, dass sich das Raumschiff für knapp dreißig Minuten auf der dunklen Seite des Mondes befindet oder in die Erdatmosphäre eintritt: In all diesen Fällen haben wir es mit einer *LOS*-Situation zu tun. Die spannende Frage lautet im vorliegendem Zusammenhang, was das Fernsehen in solchen Situationen macht. Wie geht es mit diesem Verlust des Signals um? Wie füllt es die Pausen während der Live-Berichterstattung? Wie reagiert es auf diese Art Rauschen? Gewöhnlich kommen dann Animationen und Modelle zum Einsatz, die zeigen sollen, was gerade geschieht bzw. geschehen sollte.[43] Der Entzug der Hörbarkeit wird durch visuelle Informationen kompensiert. Oder aber es werden Interviews und Diskussionen geführt, die zumeist einen Zusammenhang mit der dunklen Seite des Mondes haben.[44]

Daneben wählte die BBC noch eine andere Variante, die vor allem bei der Live-Berichterstattung der Apollo 13-Mission 1970 interessant wurde. Das Besondere dieser Mission war, dass sie beinahe in einer Katastrophe endete. Geplant war nach Apollo 11 und Apollo 12 eine weitere Mondlandung. Aufgrund der Explosion in einem Tank musste die Mission jedoch frühzeitig

---

[42] | Sehr amüsant wird dieser Fall im Spielfilm *The Dish* (2000) verhandelt. Das australische Parks-Observatorium findet das Signal von Apollo 11 nicht, währenddessen kommt der US-amerikanische Botschafter zu Besuch, um sich über den Funkverkehr mit den Astronauten zu informieren, der u. a. über das Observatorium in Parks abgewickelt wird. Die Mitglieder der Satellitenstation entscheiden sich in dieser Situation dafür, dem Botschafter vorzugaukeln, man hätte Funkverkehr mit den Astronauten im All. Im Nebenraum simuliert man ein Gespräch zwischen Armstrong und *ground control* in Huston (*inklusive* Störgeräusche).

[43] | Für ein Beispiel dieser Art der Präsentation vgl. »CBS News Coverage of Apollo 11 – Moon Landing«, http://www.youtube.com/watch?v=sJv5_y2l5as (2.8.13).

[44] | All dies findet sich bei der Live-Berichterstattung zur Apollo 11-Mission, egal ob in Deutschland, USA, England oder der Schweiz.

abgebrochen werden, da der Zusammenbruch der Sauerstoff-, Strom- und Wasserversorgung im Servicemodul *Odyssey* nicht zu kompensieren war. Es wurde entschieden, dass Apollo 13 durch ein sogenanntes *Swing-By*-Manöver hinter dem Mond verschwinden solle, um dessen Gravitationsfeld zur Beschleunigung zu nutzen und so zur Erde zurück zu gelangen.[45] Da nach der erfolgreichen Apollo 11-Mission die Begeisterung für Mondmissionen deutlich nachgelassen hatte, entschieden sich viele Sender, nicht mehr live oder doch nur noch sehr eingeschränkt davon zu berichten, so auch im Fall der Apollo 13-Mission. Nachdem diese Mission aber Probleme bekam, unterbrachen nahezu alle US-amerikanischen und europäischen Fernsehsender ihr ursprünglich geplantes Programm, um darüber live zu berichten.[46]

Um wieder auf die Live-Berichterstattung der BBC zurückzukommen: Während des *Swing-by*-Manövers war der britische Rundfunksender seit längerem bereist wieder live auf Sendung. Nun wird, wie beschrieben, Apollo 13 für knapp 30 Minuten aus dem Funkbereich heraus geraten. Es folgt ein *loss of signal*. Was tut nun die BBC Live-Berichterstattung in dieser Lage? Zu Beginn des *LOS* wird ein detaillierter Bericht aus dem Studio in London geliefert, mitsamt der Versicherung: »We're monitoring the situation all the time.«[47] Dann verabschiedet sich der Moderator, und es erfolgt eine Überblendung zu Archivmaterial, das bereits einige Zeit früher live über den Sender ging und nun neu montiert wird. Zu sehen sind Aufnahmen der Apollo 13-Crew in der Raumkapsel. Begleitet werden diese Aufnahmen von Bowies *Space Oddity* – also von jenem eingangs erwähnten Song, in dem der Funkkontakt eines Astronauten zur Bodenstation abbricht.

Die BBC hatte im Übrigen diesen Song als eine Art Soundtrack zur retrospektiven musikalischen Untermalung der Apollo 11-Mission eingesetzt.[48] Bei der kurzfristig interessant gewordenen Übertragung des Apollo 13-Rettungsmanövers wurde der Song erneut verwendet. Er passte nun ja auch

---

45 | Vgl. hierzu und zum Folgenden Allen: Live from the Moon, S. 165ff. Vgl. auch Hogan: Televising the Space Age, S. 109 und S. 133ff.

46 | Auch das ist ein eindrücklicher Beleg für die Affinität des Fernsehens für Störungen und mögliche Katastrophen.

47 | BBC Coverage Apollo 13, 14. April 1970. Ein Zusammenschnitt ist zugänglich unter: »BBC Coverage of Apollo 13 Re-entry«, 14. und 16. April 1970, http://www.youtube.com/watch?v=DUP5IKyOiio (2.8.13).

48 | Zwar wird hin und wieder darauf verwiesen, dass dieses Lied die Apollo-11-Mission-Übertragung der BBC permanent begleitete (vgl. bspw. Geppert: European Astrofuturism, S. 6), jedoch war es wohl tatsächlich so, dass das Lied erst nach der sicheren Landung der drei Astronauten auf der Erde in die *heavy rotation* der BBC übernommen wurde, also erst dann sehr häufig im Kontext der (Nach-)Berichterstattung gespielt wurde – siehe dazu die BBC selbst: o. A.: Bowie @ The Beeb.

inhaltlich um einiges besser. Jenseits des Eindrucks eines gewissen (nichtintendierten?) Zynismus, der dieser Kompensation des Signalverlustes wohl zugesprochen werden kann, lässt sich festhalten: Die Unterbrechung der Kommunikation wird durch (Pausen-)Musik kompensiert. Ein Lied ersetzt das Rauschen, dessen Text ein mögliches Zukunftsszenario der Crew der Apollo 13 imaginiert und diese Zukunft semantisch eindeutig besetzt.[49]

Auch beim Eintritt der Kapsel in die Erdatmosphäre lässt sich die Frage stellen: Wie geht das Fernsehen mit dieser Situation um?[50] Nach dem gelungenen *Swing-by*-Manöver wird nun noch einmal die Kommunikation – aufgrund der Hitzeeinwirkung und die daraus resultierende Umleitung der elektromagnetischen Wellen – für einige Minuten unterbrochen. Die abstrakte These, dass Medien ihre Medialität vor allem in der Störung zeigen, wird in diesem Fall ganz handfest in der televisuellen Praxis veranschaulicht und in einer bestimmten Weise konkretisiert: Das Fehlen eines Signals wird kompensiert oder dramaturgisch genutzt – und zwar dadurch, dass das Fernsehen alles ihm Mögliche aufbietet. Wir sind im Studio und im Atlantik, wo die Ankunft der Apollo 13-Crew erwartet wird; im Wechselspiel hören wir den BBC-Moderator und die NASA-Durchsagen; wir sehen in Großaufnahme die zunächst angespannten, dann glücklichen Gesichter der Moderatoren. Zudem werden grafische Elemente wie beispielsweise der »countdown« oder »splashdown in 10 seconds« eingesetzt, um klar zu machen, in welcher Situation wir uns im Moment befinden. Diese Grafiken weisen dem Ereignis eindeutige Bedeutungen zu. Sie strukturieren, was wir gerade eben hören bzw. wie wir das Gehörte verstehen sollen: »Apollo 13 Signal heard«. Oder es wird darauf verwiesen, was wir nicht hören: »Radio Blackout« oder noch nicht hören, aber höchstwahrscheinlich bald wieder hören werden, während die Kamera den Horizont nach der Kapsel absucht (vgl. Abb. 2).

Hier zeigt sich das Fernsehen – obwohl oder vielmehr gerade weil ihm bestimmte Ereignisse und Kommunikationsmöglichkeiten entzogen sind – als (nahezu) omnikompetent: Es ist live, beinahe überall (im BBC-Studio, im Atlantik auf einem Flugzeugträger, in Hustons Kontrollzentrum, später auch in der Apollo-Kapsel), es informiert, es beobachtet die Szenerie, beobachtet die Beobachter, emotionalisiert, dramatisiert und sendet polymedial.

Der Kommunikationsverlust mit den Astronauten wird hier, erstens, ganz konkret zu einem produktiven Mittel, die medialen Kompetenzen des

---

49 | Wiederum begleitet von Archivbildern der Crew, die in Form einer Abschieds- und Erinnerungszeremonie in Szene gesetzt werden.

50 | BBC Coverage Apollo 13, 16. April 1970, ausführliche Mitschnitte sind online zugänglich, u. a. (und hier besonders relevant): »Apollo 13 – all BBC's TV original reentry & splashdown footage – part 3 of 5«, http://www.youtube.com/watch?v=I2dY-sjONx0 (2.8.13).

Abbildung 2: Warten auf Apollo 13, 17. April 1970.

Quelle: Film Still aus der BBC-Fernsehübertragung der Rückkunft der Apollo 13-Crew am 17 April 1970, http://www.youtube.com/watch?v=I2dY-sjONx0 (2.8.13), 6:19.

Fernsehens in Erscheinung treten zu lassen. Mit anderen Worten, die Störung der Kommunikation wird genutzt, um Medienreflexion zu betreiben, wobei sich das Fernsehen von seiner besten medialen Seite zeigt, also werbewirksam Medienreflexion betreibt.[51] Zweitens wird der Entzug der Kommunikation auf Bild- wie auf Tonebene genutzt, um – ganz im Sinne Batesons und Serres' – die Komplexität der Kommunikationsofferte zu steigern. In schnellem Wechsel wird kommentiert, emotionalisiert, Emotion beobachtet, der Horizont nach Lebenszeichen abgesucht, Nixons Absuchen des Horizonts beobachtet. All dies geschieht, drittens, nicht aufgrund der Störung der medientechnischen Operationen des Fernsehens selbst, denn das Fernsehsignal fällt ja nicht aus, sondern der Funkkontakt zwischen Astronauten und Bodenkontrolle. Vielmehr beobachtet das Fernsehen vor dem Hintergrund des Wartens auf erneuten Funkkontakt unterschiedliche Phänomene zu unterschiedlichen Zeiten und in unterschiedlichen Kontexten: mal als Signal, mal als Geräusch. Manchmal wird die Stimme des BBC-Moderators als deutliches Signal eingesetzt, dann wieder als Hintergrundrauschen für die Durchsagen aus Huston. Zunächst teilt uns der Kommentator mit: Funkrauschen bedeutet, dass wir kein Signal von Apollo 13 erhalten. Kurze Zeit später soll dasselbe Funkrauschen jedoch bedeuten, dass wir ein Signal von Apollo 13 erhalten. Was Hintergrundrauschen, was Störung, was Signal, was bedeutsam und was bedeutungslos ist, wird hier erst durch das Fernsehen

---

51 | Rainer Leschke geht davon aus, dass diese Art der Medienreflexion die gängige Art ist, wie Medien in (Massen-)Medien sich selbst reflektieren; vgl. Leschke: Medien und Formen, S. 196.

zugewiesen, also – wiederum streng nach Serres – zuallererst durch den Beobachter definiert.

»RADIO SILENCE«

Medientechnische Störungen sind, das sollten die Ausführungen zur Live-Berichterstattung zweier Weltraummissionen gezeigt haben, in der televisuellen Berichterstattung durchaus produktive Phänomene, die Anschlusskommunikation erzeugen, Kompensationen, Reflexionen und diverse Funktionalisierungen erfahren. Auch ein *loss of signal*, also der Verlust des Signals, das größtmögliche Rauschen, dient hier noch zur Multiplikation der Signale, die das Fernsehen aussendet.

Es muss freilich nicht immer faktisch eine technische Funkverkehrsstörung vorliegen, um heftige Irritationen und Spekulationen auszulösen; es reicht bereits die Vermutung, dass eine solche Störung vorliegen könnte. Als die Apollo 11-Kapsel wieder einmal hinter der erdabgewandten Seite des Mondes hervorkam, die Crew sich jedoch nicht sofort meldete, geriet die Bodenstation in Huston in Unruhe, da sie vermeintlich nur Rauschen vernahm und kein Signal von der Kapsel empfing. Auf wiederholte Nachfrage erhielt man endlich doch Antwort. Der Astronaut Michel Collins funkte von der Apollo 11-Kapsel zur Erde: »If we're late in answering you, it's because we're munching sandwiches.«[52] Das wiederum war der BBC eine Sondermeldung im Rahmen ihrer Berichterstattung über die Apollo 11-Mission wert.[53] Ob Rauschen, Stille oder das irritierende Mampfgeräusch beim Verspeisen belegter Brote – im Fernsehen ist, ganz analog zur Medientheorie, *noise* nahezu immer eine gute Sache oder doch zumindest eine attraktive Möglichkeit für vielfältige Anschlusskommunikationen.

BIBLIOGRAPHIE

Allen, Michael: Live From the Moon. Film, Television and the Space Race, London, New York 2009.
Baecker, Dirk: Kommunikation, Leipzig 2005.

---

52 | NASA (Hg.): Apollo 11: Technical Air-to-Ground Voice Transcription, S. 28.
53 | Siehe: BBC Coverage Apollo 11, 16. Juli 1969, http://www.youtube.com/watch?v=7pxeuXFqO5M&list=PLB0B339DE69C47980 (inzwischen gelöscht). Dort wird der Satz jedoch falsch wiedergegeben. In der BBC wird der Satz von Collins noch pointierter als im Original ›zitiert‹: »That wasn't radio silence, it was a sandwich in my mouth.«

Bateson, Gregory: Kybernetische Erklärung [1967], in: Ders.: Ökologie des Geistes. Anthropologische, psychologische, biologische und epistemologische Perspektiven, Frankfurt/M. 1985, S. 519-529.

Geppert, Alexander C. T.: European Astrofuturism, Cosmic Provincialism. Historicizing the Space Age, in: Ders. (Hg.): Imaging Outer Space. European Astroculture in the Twentieth Century, New York 2012, S. 3-24.

Grampp, Sven: Marshall McLuhan. Eine Einführung, Konstanz 2011.

Griesemer, John: Rausch [original: Signal & Noise], Hamburg 2003.

Grinsted, Daniel: Die Reise zum Mond. Zur Faszinationsgeschichte eines medienkulturellen Phänomens zwischen Realität und Fiktion, Berlin 2009.

Hogan, Alfred Robert: Televising the Space Age. A Descriptive Chronology of CBS News Special Coverage of Space Exploration from 1957 to 2003, Dissertation, Maryland 2005.

Katz, Elihu und Daniel Dayan: Medienereignisse, in: Ralf Adelmann u.a. (Hg.): Grundlagentexte zur Fernsehwissenschaft. Theorie – Geschichte – Analyse, Konstanz 2002, S. 413-453.

Kirchmann, Kay: Störung und ›Monitoring‹. Zur Paradoxie des Ereignishaften im Live-Fernsehen, in: Gerd Hallenberger und Helmut Schanze (Hg.): Live is life. Mediale Inszenierungen des Authentischen im Live-Fernsehen, Baden-Baden 2000, S. 91-104.

Kümmel, Albert und Erhard Schüttpelz: Medientheorien der Störung / Störungstheorien der Medien. Eine Fibel, in: Dies. (Hg.): Signale der Störung, München 2003, S. 9-13.

Kümmel, Albert: Mathematische Kommunikationstheorie, in: Daniela Kloock und Angela Spahr (Hg.): Medientheorien. Eine Einführung, 4. Aufl., München 2012, S. 205-236.

Latour, Bruno: Die Hoffnung der Pandora. Untersuchungen zur Wirklichkeit der Wissenschaft, Frankfurt/M. 2002.

Leschke, Rainer: Medien und Formen. Zu einer Morphologie der Medien, Konstanz 2010.

Luhmann, Niklas: Die Realität der Massenmedien, 2. Aufl., Opladen 1996.

McLuhan, Marshall: Understanding Media. The Extension of Man [1964]. Critical Edition, Corte Madera 2003.

Mehring, Markus und Bill Woods: Quindar Tones, in: Apollo. Lunar Surface Journal, 21. Januar 2006, http://www.hq.nasa.gov/office/pao/History/alsj/quindar.html (2.8.13).

Mersch, Dieter: Medientheorien zur Einführung, Hamburg 2006.

NASA (Hg.): Apollo 11. Technical Air-to-Ground Voice Transcription, Texas 1969. http://www.hq.nasa.gov/alsj/a11/a11transcript_tec.pdf (2.8.13).

o.A.: Bowie @ The Beeb, http://www.bbc.co.uk/worldservice/arts/highlights/010108_bowie.shtml (29.7.13).

o.A.: Neil Armstrong, in: The Telegraph, 26. August 2012, http://www.telegraph.co.uk/news/obituaries/science-obituaries/9499820/Neil-Armstrong.html (2.8.13).

o.A.: Neil Armstrong gestorben. Einer der größten US-Helden, in: taz, 26. August 2012, http://www.taz.de/!100360/ (2.8.13).

Patterson, Graeme: History and Communications. Harold Innis, Marshall McLuhan, the Interpretation of History, Toronto u.a. 1990.

Schmidt, Siegfried J. und Guido Zurstiege: Orientierung Kommunikationswissenschaft. Was sie kann, was sie will, Reinbek b. Hamburg 2000.

Seidler, Christoph: Zum Tod von Neil Armstrong. Der stille Überirdische, in: Spiegel Online, 26. August 2012, http://www.spiegel.de/wissenschaft/weltall/zum-tod-von-nasa-astronaut-und-erstem-mann-auf-mond-neil-armstrong-a-852123.html (2.8.13).

Serres, Michel: Der Parasit [1980], Frankfurt/M. 1987.

Shannon, Claude E.: A Mathematical Theory of Communication, in: The Bell System Technical Journal 27.3/4 (1948), S. 379-423, 623-656.

Weaver, Warren: Ein aktueller Beitrag zur mathematischen Theorie der Kommunikation [1949], in: Günter Helmes (Hg.): Texte zur Medientheorie, Stuttgart 2002, S. 196-198.

Wissenschaftsrat: Empfehlungen zur Weiterentwicklung der Kommunikations- und Medienwissenschaften in Deutschland. Drucksache 7901-07, Oldenburg, 25. Mai 2007, www.wissenschaftsrat.de/download/archiv/7901-07.pdf (2.12.12).

FILMOGRAPHIE UND DISCOGRAPHIE

100 Jahre – Der Countdown (1999), Konzept: Guido Knopp, D, Farbe.
2001: A Space Odyssey (1968), Regie: Stanley Kubrick, GB/USA, Farbe.
Alien (1979), Regie: Ridley Scott, GB/USA, Farbe.
Bowie, David: *Space Oddity* (Single 1969).
Die Akte Apollo (2002), Regie: Willy Brunner, D, Farbe.
The Dish (2000), Regie: Rob Sitch, AUS, Farbe.

»Der Mund entsteht mit dem Schrei.«
Zur Inszenierung der Stimme in Heiner Goebbels' Hörstücken nach Texten von Heiner Müller

Matthias Warstat

In dem Versuch, Anhaltspunkte für die Inszenierung eines Textes von Heiner Müller zu gewinnen, beziehen sich auffallend viele Regisseure und Theoretiker auf dessen Stimme. Die Stimme von Müller ist in den auf sein Werk bezogenen Diskursen bis heute präsent – und zwar nicht im übertragenen Sinn seine Gedanken und Meinungen, sondern tatsächlich die ›physische‹ Stimme, die Lautlichkeit seiner Rede, die Art, wie er intonierte, sich artikulierte, Texte vorlas oder sich in Interviews stimmlich inszenierte. Von Müllers Stimme sind zahlreiche Ton- und Videodokumente überliefert – von frühen Radioaufzeichnungen über diverse Lesungen bis hin zu den legendären Interviews, die Alexander Kluge für seine Fernsehsendungen und Essayfilme mit ihm geführt hat.[1] Der Reiz der Gespräche zwischen Müller und Kluge besteht nicht zuletzt in der Gegensätzlichkeit dieser beiden charakteristischen Stimmen. Kluges Stimme ist leise, sanft, dabei aber außerordentlich beharrlich im Fragen und temperamentvoll in der Modulation. Kluge will seine Gesprächspartner zu Thesen und Gedankensprüngen verführen, liefert immer wieder neue Denkanstöße und Interpretationen, kann im zurückhaltenden Sprechen übergangslos pathetisch werden und wechselt in den Flüsterton, wenn es darum geht, die Dramatik des Gedankengangs zu steigern. Müller passte als Gesprächspartner nicht nur thematisch kongenial zu Kluge, sondern auch ästhetisch, weil seine Stimme zu Kluges Stimme einen direkten klanglichen Widerpart bildete.

---

1 | Abdrucke der Gespräche finden sich u.a. in: Kluge und Müller: »Ich bin ein Landvermesser«. Müller-Interviews von Kluge stehen auch auf *YouTube* zu Verfügung, u.a. das bekannte Gespräch aus dem Jahr 1989: http://www.youtube.com/watch?v=AFSQkFb P9eo (2.12.13).

Müller redete in Interviews, es ist oft beschrieben worden, spröde, langsam, fast monoton, dabei dem Gesprächspartner nicht unbedingt zugewandt. Er öffnete seine Lippen beim Sprechen nicht weit, was für manche Ohren wie ein leichtes Nuscheln klingen mochte. Er redete weder laut noch schnell und streute, gerade in seinen letzten Lebensjahren, immer wieder Pausen ein, in denen er entweder einfach Luft einsog oder den jeweils vorangegangenen Satz mit einem knappen Kopfnicken oder einem kurzen »mhm«-Laut selbst bestätigte. Die Zigarre und der Schnaps, Accessoires vieler Interviews mit Kluge und anderen, sind ein Thema für sich, dem hier nicht weiter nachgegangen werden kann. Wenn Müller aus seinen Stücken oder Prosawerken vorlas, saß er krumm, den Kopf dicht am Papier und schaute kaum je vom Text auf. Er bediente sich gerne eines Mikrofons, das er nah an den Mund hielt, so dass er noch leiser sprechen konnte. Es war dezidiert ein Lesen, kein Vortrag: Müller raschelte gern mit Papier und las eigene Texte so, als seien sie ihm fremd und als müsse er sich lesend zum ersten Mal in ihnen zurechtfinden.

Zu einem gewissen Teil lebten diese stimmlichen Inszenierungen von einem wohl bewusst gesetzten Kontrast zwischen Form und Inhalt. Es geht in Müllers Texten um große menschheitsgeschichtliche Fragen, die Vergeblichkeit historischer Entwicklung, die Gewaltsamkeit menschlicher Existenz und die Notwendigkeit von Revolutionen, die nicht stattfinden werden. In Müllers apokalyptischem Kosmos passiert im Grunde viel, wenn auch selten in traditionellen dramatischen Konstellationen, aber es wimmelt von Tätern und Opfern, gemeinschaftlicher Gewalt und individuellem Leid, von weitreichenden Entscheidungen und Handlungen, die am Ende ihre Verheißung nicht einlösen können. Von all dem las Müller ohne hörbare Emotion, ohne stimmliche Dramatisierung oder lautliche Emphase. Wenn diese Stimme etwas unterstrich, dann allenfalls die Faktizität des Gesagten, den unhintergehbaren Zwang, der für Müller in der Dialektik der vorgeführten Geschichte erkennbar war.

Es hat bereits eine gewisse Tradition zu überlegen, ob Müllers Stimme nicht auch Hinweise für die Inszenierung seiner Texte liefern kann. Dabei geht es nicht allein um deren klangliche Dimension, sondern um eine komplexe Relation aus Gesagtem und Arten des Sagens, um eine Verbindung auch aus Stimme, Geräuschen und anderen akustischen Phänomenen. Ich möchte zu dieser Verbindung drei zeitgenössische Positionen aus der Müller-Forschung vorstellen und daran eigene Überlegungen zu Heiner Goebbels' Radiostück *Die Befreiung des Prometheus* (HR, SWF 1985) nach einem Prosatext von Heiner Müller anschließen.[2] Es soll die These vertreten

---

2 | Heiner Goebbels: Die Befreiung des Prometheus. Hörstück in 9 Bildern nach Texten von Heiner Müller aus den Theaterstücken: Zement, Der Auftrag, Prometheus, Traktor.

werden, dass die klangliche Dimension der Texte für eine bestimmte Variante des Tragischen, die sich in vielen Müller-Werken findet, von konstitutiver Bedeutung ist. Als tragisch wäre hier eine Konstellation zu bezeichnen, in der ästhetische Öffnung und Brechung vergeblich gegen die Zwänge des Geschichtsverlaufs gesetzt werden.

1. Musikalisierung

Die erste theoretische Position zu Stimme *von* Müller und Klang *bei* Müller stammt von Heiner Goebbels selbst, dessen Hörstücke nach Texten von Müller im weiteren Verlauf der Argumentation genauer betrachtet werden sollen. In einem Beitrag zu dem Sammelband *Heiner Müller sprechen* (2009) zitiert Goebbels Robert Wilson mit der Behauptung, die Stimme Heiner Müllers beim Lesen seiner Texte sei mit der Musik von Bach zu vergleichen. Sie erfordere das »Aushören« einer Struktur, in der viele Bedeutungen polyphon zum Tragen kämen.[3] Goebbels versteht diese These von der Polyphonie der Müller'schen Stimme als Hinweis auf eine Enthierarchisierung von Bedeutungen beim Sprechen. Das Charakteristische des Müller'schen Sprechens sei die konsequente Reduzierung der stimmlichen Modulation. Indem Müller beim Sprechen auf Modulation weitgehend verzichte, ergebe sich auch für die möglichen Bedeutungen seiner Rede eine flache Hierarchie. Es seien keine Hervorhebungen, Akzentuierungen oder Forcierungen zu hören, die dem Hörer einen bestimmten Sinn des Gehörten nahelegen könnten. Gleichzeitig weist Goebbels aber den naheliegenden Monotonie-Vorwurf klar zurück: »Sein Sprechen ist *nicht* monoton, auch wenn es manchem so vorgekommen sein mag. Heiner Müller hat lediglich die für die Modulation charakteristischen Intervalle auf einen mikrotonalen Umfang reduziert.«[4]

Die Pointe von Goebbels' Argumentation besteht darin, Müllers Rücknahme stimmlicher Modulation in Form und Wirkung mit der Ästhetik der *minimal music* in Verbindung zu bringen. Hier wie dort gehe es um den Umschlag von »vorgeblicher Monotonie« in Polyphonie.[5] Die schwach ausgeprägte Hierarchie der Laute zwinge die Hörer dazu, den Worten »zunächst syntaktisch und weniger semantisch« zuzuhören. Es sei der Hörer oder die Hörerin selbst, der den stimmlich allesamt unbetonten Worten in der Erprobung potenzieller Bedeutungen eine bestimmte Satzstellung zuweisen

---

Produziert 1985 vom Hessischen Rundfunk und vom Südwestfunk. Veröffentlicht auf der CD: Goebbels: Hörstücke nach Texten von Heiner Müller.
3 | Vgl. Goebbels: Heiner Müller versprechen, S. 283.
4 | Ebd.
5 | Ebd.

müsse. Genau in diesem Punkt erkennt Goebbels eine direkte Verwandtschaft zur *minimal music*, denn auch in der Wahrnehmung dieser Art von Musik ist es der Hörer, der einer gleichheitlichen Konstellation von Lauten selbständig Strukturen beimessen kann oder sogar muss.

Den Vergleich von Müllers Stimme mit *minimal music* nimmt Goebbels zum Anlass, auch für die Inszenierung von Müllers Texten eine »Musikalisierung« zu fordern. Er denkt darüber nach, wie man seine Texte als musikalisches Material behandeln kann – und bezieht sich dabei auf eigene Hörstücke, allen voran auf *Die Befreiung des Prometheus*: »Die musikalischen, klanglichen Verbindungen zwischen Text, Laut, Geräusch und Musik«, so Goebbels, seien »hier eng geknüpft, um den Übergang von Semantik in Musik möglich zu machen und dadurch einen anderen auditiven Modus zu signalisieren, der einem musikalischen Hören stärker verpflichtet ist, bzw. dieses mit dem ›Verstehen‹ abgleicht.«[6] Sein Beispiel ist der erste Satz aus dem *Prometheus*-Hörstück:

Prometheus, der den Menschen den Blitz ausgeliefert, sie aber nicht gelehrt hatte, ihn gegen die Götter zu gebrauchen, weil er an den Mahlzeiten der Götter teilnahm, die mit den Menschen geteilt weniger reichlich ausgefallen wären, wurde wegen seiner Tat bzw. wegen seiner Unterlassung im Auftrag der Götter von Hephaistos dem Schmied an den Kaukasus befestigt, wo ein hundsköpfiger Adler täglich von seiner immerwachsenden Leber aß.[7]

Goebbels erläutert, wie ihm bei diesem Anfangssatz des Hörstücks eine Musikalisierung aus der Lautlichkeit der Müller'schen Sprache heraus gelungen ist. Er bezieht sich auf drei inszenatorische Kunstgriffe:

Erstens lässt Goebbels den einleitenden Satz des *Prometheus*-Fragments nicht einmal, sondern insgesamt dreimal sprechen. Diese wiederholten Lesungen sind auf unterschiedliche Stimmen verteilt. Den Anfang macht eine Frauenstimme (Angela Schanelec). Ein zweites Mal wird der Satz dann von Heiner Müller selbst gelesen. Zuletzt, nach einem längeren Zwischenspiel, hört man die Stimme von Goebbels' damals vierjährigem Sohn. Goebbels versteht diese mehrstimmigen Wiederholungen als Angebot an die Hörer, sich mit dem syntaktisch komplexen Satz vertraut zu machen, verschiedene Lesarten zu hören und zu einem ersten eigenen Verständnis zu gelangen.[8]

Zweitens arbeitet Goebbels an einer Dekomposition des Satzes. Die Sprecherstimmen zerlegen den Satz in Einzelteile, so dass erst allmählich, im

---

6 | Ebd., S. 285f.
7 | Goebbels: Die Befreiung des Prometheus. Vgl. Müller: Die Befreiung des Prometheus, S. 91.
8 | Goebbels: Heiner Müller versprechen, S. 285.

Wechselspiel von »ständiger Korrektur und allmählicher Erweiterung«, der grammatische Aufbau transparent wird. Dieser Versuch, syntaktische Strukturen transparent zu machen, ist für Goebbels eine plausible musikalische Alternative zu expliziteren Interpretationsversuchen: Denn was könne Musik hier anderes tun, wenn sie nicht interpretieren wolle, als mit kompositorischen Mitteln zur Transparenz beizutragen?[9] Alle musikalischen Mittel sollen deshalb der sprachlichen Syntax zuarbeiten: die harmonische Struktur mit einer Schließung der Kadenz in der Ausgangstonart beim Satzende, aber auch die Rhythmisierung, die sich aus einem den Stimmen zugrunde gelegten Puls und aus der metrischen Positionierung der Satzportionen ergebe.

Zur Musikalisierung gehört für Goebbels drittens ein Spiel mit Lesefehlern, Lesemöglichkeiten und rhetorischen Variationen, was auch das Ausloten von Lautähnlichkeiten einschließt. Es dauert zum Beispiel eine ganze Weile, bis die Sprecherin den »hundsköpfigen Adler« vollständig herausgebracht hat – eine schwere Geburt, die sich über eine mehrfache Selbstunterbrechung, Nachfrage bzw. Korrektur vollzieht: »Wo ein Hund? Wo ein Hundskopf? Ein Adler? Wo ein hundsköpfiger Adler? Wo ein hundsköpfiger Adler täglich von seiner Leber?« usw.[10] Unterbrochen werden diese Artikulationsversuche von dem Lautpartikel »aß«, einem vorsprachlich oder halbsprachlich anmutenden Ruf, der, teils kurz, teils gedehnt, teils zum Schrei verstärkt, unterschiedliche Bedeutungsebenen anklingen lässt. In dem schließlich entstehenden Satz meint »aß« die Vergangenheitsform des Verbs ›essen‹. Später im *Prometheus*-Text taucht »Aas« aber auch im Sinne von totem Fleisch auf, und der a-Laut wird im weiteren Verlauf des Hörstücks verschiedentlich für Schmerzensschreie verwendet. Insofern lädt die Musikalisierung des Textmaterials zur Erprobung verschiedener Assoziationsmöglichkeiten ein.

2. Historisierung

Auch der Musikhistoriker Martin Zenck bescheinigt Heiner Müllers Stimme außergewöhnliche Anziehungskraft:

> Von dieser Stimme ging eine besondere Faszination aus, obwohl sie eher abweisend, weil schroff, ungebärdig, ruhig bis zur Kälte und keineswegs die Person preisgebend war. Gar nichts hatte sie vom professionellen Sprecher, gar einem Schauspieler [...]. Müllers Stimme war eine ganz andere, vergleichbar eher den inneren Stimmen von Paul Celan und Ingeborg Bachmann, die – wie Victor Hugo in seinen *Voix intérieurs* –

---

9 | Ebd.
10 | Goebbels: Die Befreiung des Prometheus.

Schwierigkeiten damit hatten, die Sprache über die Lippen, das Innere des Körpers über seine äußeren Grenzen, den weichen und zugleich schmerzenden Mund zu bringen.[11]

In der Stimme wird, so die Wahrnehmung von Martin Zenck, die Schwierigkeit des Sprechens, die Unmöglichkeit von Kommunikation hörbar. Zenck verbindet diesen Höreindruck mit einem kurzen Text, den Müller 1979 unter dem Titel *Bruchstück für Luigi Nono* an den befreundeten Komponisten richtete. Der Text reflektiert die von Adorno aufgeworfene Frage, wie nach Auschwitz noch glaubwürdig Gedichte geschrieben und Kunstwerke produziert werden könnten. Man stößt hier auf das Bild der zerschnittenen Stimmbänder: Von woher könnte eine Stimme kommen, wen könnte eine Stimme erreichen, die von den Erfahrungen der Shoa künden würde – und wie würde sie klingen? Für Zenck korrespondiert diese, dem *Bruchstück* implizite Frage mit einer Frauenstimme aus Müllers Stück *Der Auftrag* (1979). »Ich bin der Engel der Verzweiflung. Mit meinen Händen teile ich den Rausch aus, die Betäubung, das Vergessen, Lust und Qual der Leiber. Meine Rede ist das Schweigen, mein Gesang der Schrei.«[12]

Aus Walter Benjamins ›Engel der Geschichte‹ ist hier ein (sprechender und singender) Engel der Verzweiflung geworden. Zenck postuliert auch eine Verbindung zu Antonin Artauds theaterästhetischem Programm, das die konventionalisierte Sprache als Gefängnis brandmarkt und für eine Überwindung, wenn nicht gar Aufsprengung des Logos auf dem Theater eintritt. Auch auf diesem Weg lässt sich aus dem Eindruck von Müllers Stimme eine Konzeption für die Gestaltung theatraler Klangräume entwickeln. Es wären, vereinfacht gesagt, Übergangsräume zwischen Schreien und Schweigen. Angesichts der Unaussprechlichkeit der traumatischen Erinnerung bleibt dem Theater nach Auschwitz nur der Weg, die Sprache im Schweigen oder im Schreien zu überwinden. In beiden Fällen bleibt eine Leere zurück, in die der Schmerz oder die Trauer eintreten können.

Zencks Lesart unterscheidet sich von derjenigen Heiner Goebbels' in der Bereitschaft, den Klangraum nicht allein als ästhetische, sondern als historische Erfahrung zu begreifen. Dafür spricht die obsessive Beschäftigung Müllers mit den Gewalterfahrungen von Krieg, Revolution und Faschismus. Der Lärm, der in Müllers Stücken wie auch in seinen Inszenierungen immer wieder aufkommt, ist nur allzu oft Schlachtenlärm, Geschützdonner oder Bombenhagel. Wenn man diese Dimension berücksichtigt, wirkt das Ideal einer Musikalisierung der Sprache auf einmal unzulänglich, beliebig und nachgerade harmlos.

---

11 | Zenck: Stimme/Musik, S. 351.
12 | Müller: Der Auftrag, S. 16.

»Der Mund entsteht mit dem Schrei.«[13] Mit dieser Regieanweisung aus dem »Nachtstück«, einer Szene aus *Germania Tod in Berlin* (1956/71), in der sich eine Figur nach und nach ihre Beine, Arme und Augen amputiert, formuliert Müller in aphoristischer Kürze, welche Art der Figuration, der Hervorbringung von Theaterfiguren, seine Texte erfordern oder zumindest nahelegen: Es geht um die Idee, dass sich der Mund, die eigene Stimme, die Subjektivität einer Figur, wenn überhaupt, dann nur aus Schmerzerfahrungen, leidvoller Subtraktion oder Selbstverstümmelung konstituieren können.

3. Spaltung

An dieses negative Konzept von Subjektivität knüpft Patrick Primavesis Verständnis der Müller'schen Stimme an. Entscheidend ist für ihn an Müllers Texten die Hörbarkeit einer Stimme, die »nicht mehr individueller Ausdruck und Ausdruck des Individuellen ist, sondern von einem anderen Ort her zu kommen scheint, jenseits des Subjekts und jenseits des Todes«.[14] Werde die Stimme in der Tradition des bürgerlichen Einfühlungstheaters als »Medium von Seele und Gefühl« wahrgenommen, so manifestiere sich in Müllers Stimmen – geradezu umgekehrt – eine »Entstellung von Gegenwart« bzw. eine »Wiederkehr des Verdrängten«.[15] Die Stimme drückt in diesem Sinne nichts aus, was aus einem individuellen Empfinden oder aus der Psyche eines einzelnen Protagonisten stammen könnte. Sie ist nach Primavesi überhaupt nicht in Kategorien des Ausdrucks zu fassen. Vielmehr erfährt der Hörende in der Wahrnehmung solcher Stimmen selbst eine Art Ent-Stellung, er wird seiner scheinbar sicheren Hörerposition beraubt, indem er etwas hört, das sich zur eigenen Identität, dem mühsam erworbenen Selbstgefühl, vollkommen heteronom verhält. Was sich hier Gehör verschafft, sind keine Gesänge von Glück, Trauer, Liebe oder Hass, sondern »Blockaden und Störungen, stumme Schreie und Geräusche des Erstickens«.[16] Eine solche Hörerfahrung öffnet die Wahrnehmung hin auf das ganz Andere, ist damit aber zugleich an einen Verlust des ›Eigenen‹ gekoppelt. Die Öffnung des Subjekts kann ebenso als Ausbruch wie als Spaltung beschrieben werden. In seinem Beitrag zu dem Sammelband *Heiner Müller sprechen* versucht Primavesi das im Hören zu gewinnende Andere gleich dreifach, nämlich in geschichtsphilosophischen, theaterästhetischen und psychoanalytischen Kategorien zu bestimmen.

---

13 | Müller: Germania Tod in Berlin, S. 373.
14 | Primavesi: »Stimme(n) aus dem Sarg«, S. 267.
15 | Ebd.
16 | Ebd.

Geschichtsphilosophisch liegt seine Interpretation auf der Linie der schon referierten Überlegungen von Martin Zenck. Primavesi greift aus dem Stück *Die Hamletmaschine* (1977) Müllers Idee einer »Universität der Toten« auf, die ein ständiges »Gewisper und Gemurmel« absondern.[17] Öfters beschreibe Müller Geräusche aus Körpern, die sich in einem Zustand jenseits des Todes der Person befänden. Als Beispiel zitiert Primavesi folgende Passage aus dem vierten Teil der *Hamletmaschine*:

Die erniedrigten Leiber der Frauen
Hoffnung der Generationen
In Blut Feigheit Dummheit erstickt
Gelächter aus toten Bäuchen[18]

Zeilen wie diese knüpfen an die alte Idee vom Theater als Ort eines Dialogs mit den Toten an: Die Verlierer der Geschichte, die Verstorbenen und Verdrängten, können im Theater eine Stimme zurückerhalten. In dieser Möglichkeit liegt eine Kritik an linearen, fortschrittstrunkenen Geschichtsmodellen, die über die Toten hinweggehen und mit einer Wiederkehr des Vergangenen nicht rechnen wollen.

Man darf aber nicht unterschlagen, dass die Stimmen aus der Vergangenheit nicht von intakten Subjekten oder gar handlungsfähigen Akteuren herkommen. Es sind Stimmen aus toten Körpern, leblosem Fleisch – einem materiellen Substrat, dem eigentlich keine subjektive Artikulation, keine personale Kontur und schon gar keine bürgerliche ›Seele‹ mehr zuzutrauen ist. In diesen Stimmen löst sich neben der Idee eines linearen Geschichtsverlaufs demnach auch die Vorstellung von einem individuellen Subjekt als Ursprung der Stimme auf. An dessen Stelle tritt eine Form von Kollektivität, die nicht als Gemeinschaft missverstanden werden darf.

Theaterästhetisch erkennt Primavesi bei Müller gerade keine homogene Einheit, sondern eine Aufspaltung und Vervielfältigung von Stimmen, durch die der Theaterraum zu einer »Klanglandschaft« und die Schauspieler zu »musikalischen Körpern« transformiert würden.[19] Im Sinne von Roland Barthes' Beschreibung der Geräuschhaftigkeit (»bruissement«) und Rauheit bzw. Körnigkeit der Stimme (»grain de la voix«) mache das theatrale Arrangement der Körper etwas erfahrbar, das noch nicht (oder nicht mehr) in einem System oder Code fixiert sei. Es schließe die Position des Hörers mit ein,

---

17 | Primavesi: »Stimme(n) aus dem Sarg«, S. 269f. Vgl. Müller: Die Hamletmaschine, S. 548.
18 | Müller: Die Hamletmaschine, S. 552. Vgl. Primavesi: »Stimme(n) aus dem Sarg«, S. 271.
19 | Primavesi: »Stimme(n) aus dem Sarg«, S. 272.

für den sich das Genießen der Stimme mit der Erfahrung eines spezifischen Mangels verbinde: »Weder im Sprechenden oder Singenden noch im Hörenden kommt die Stimme ›zu sich‹, ist sie doch in einem Bereich des Zwischen situiert, nicht nur zwischen Körper und Sprache, sondern ebenso zwischen Artikulation und Rezeption.«[20] Die von Primavesi beschriebene Hörerfahrung der Spaltung ergibt sich also (auch) daraus, dass die Stimme selbst bereits jene Multipolarität transportiert, die für den Theaterraum kennzeichnend ist. Stimme funktioniert hier nicht als singuläre oder unabhängige Instanz, sie bedarf notwendig der Resonanz, des Widerhalls, so dass sie die für das Theater charakteristische Aufführungssituation bewusst macht. Und dies, so möchte man hinzufügen, in einer spezifischen Weise: Denn die Aufführung kann sowohl als Präsenzerfahrung als auch als Erfahrung des Mangels beschrieben werden. Müllers Aufführungsmodell privilegiert zweifellos die Mangelerfahrung. Bei ihm ist das Verhältnis von Akteuren und Zuschauern bzw. Zuhörern keines der gegenseitigen Durchdringung oder der geteilten Fülle, sondern eines der uneinholbaren Distanz und der Spaltung.

Der Hinweis auf diese Spaltung führt zur psychoanalytischen Dimension der Stimme bei Müller, die in Primavesis Lesart ebenfalls anklingt. Neben der Aufführungssituation und ihrem notwendigen Schisma von Akteur- und Zuschauerposition gibt es eine zweite Spaltung, die gleichsam innerhalb der Stimme operiert, nämlich eine Spaltung zwischen Trieb und Sprache. Das Begehren ist auf die Sprache angewiesen, vollzieht sich innerhalb einer symbolischen Ordnung, muss entsprechend aber auch, bezogen auf seinen Ausgangspunkt, einen Verlust des ›Eigenen‹ in Kauf nehmen. Dies ist gemeint, wenn Artaud in seinen für Müller inspirierenden Schriften von einer »entwendeten« Stimme spricht.[21] In der stimmlichen Artikulation trifft ein Begehren auf Sprache, auf Intersubjektivität, auf den Anderen – eine Begegnung, aus der es nicht unversehrt hervorgeht. Die Stimme ist artikuliertes Begehren, kann sich an einen Adressaten richten, trifft dadurch aber auch auf eine Sprache und auf eine symbolische Ordnung, die das Begehren in der Artikulation entstellen. In verwandten, an Derridas Artaud-Aufsätze angelehnten Begriffen spricht Primavesi von der Stimme als einer »*Gabe*, die nur vom anderen her das Ich setzen kann«.[22]

---

20 | Ebd.
21 | Vgl. zur Idee der entwendeten Stimme insbesondere Artauds Radiostück *Pour en finir avec le jugement de dieu* (dt. Schluss mit dem Gottesgericht, 1948). Kommentierend dazu: Artaud: Letzte Schriften zum Theater, S. 51 u. 59. Siehe auch Finter: Das Reale, der Körper und die soufflierten Stimmen.
22 | Primavesi: »Stimme(n) aus dem Sarg«, S. 273. Vgl. Derrida: Die soufflierte Rede; und Ders.: Das Theater der Grausamkeit und die Geschlossenheit der Repräsentation.

Insofern sich die Stimme in die Trias von Geräusch, Spur und Schrift spaltet, kann sie niemals als ungebrochener Ausdruck einer Identität fungieren, weder einer individuellen noch einer kollektiven. Als Geräusch verbleibt die Stimme jenseits der symbolischen Ordnung und entzieht sich der Definitionsmacht einer Identität. Als Spur zeugt die Stimme von einem Körper, der als ihre Quelle gelten darf, in ihr selbst allerdings nicht mehr enthalten ist. Als Schrift wird die Stimme von Sprache durchformt und ist dadurch auf den Anderen bezogen, entfernt sich vom Eigenen, sei es, dass sie sich in etwas einschreibt, sei es, dass sie von äußeren Mächten beschriftet wird.

4. Der Klang des Tragischen

Das Hörstück *Prometheus* ist, wie auch andere auf Müllers Texte bezogene Hörstücke von Heiner Goebbels, durch das Prinzip der Unterbrechung geprägt. An der von Primavesi herausgearbeiteten Trias von Geräusch, Spur und Stimme lässt sich das zeigen. Denn diese drei Aspekte des Klanglichen greifen nicht harmonisch ineinander, sondern sind vom Komponisten mehr oder minder schroff gegeneinander gesetzt. Eine ruhige, personal definierte Sprechstimme, etwa diejenige des lesenden Autors, wird jäh unterbrochen von den wild mäandernden Schreien des Sängers David Moss, deren unbändige Eruptionen jegliche sprachliche Ordnung aufsprengen, so dass sie als Spuren eines unaussprechlichen Schmerzes wahrgenommen werden können. Eine ähnliche Unterbrechung erfährt zu Beginn die neutral gehaltene Erzählstimme von Angela Schanelec, wenn sich der a-Laut aus der Verbform »aß« plötzlich verselbständigt und zu einem Schmerzensschrei, schließlich aber auch zu einem nicht mehr klar kategorisierbaren Geräusch mutiert. Auch die Kinderstimme von Heiner Goebbels' vierjährigem Sohn erfährt mehrfache Brüche, unterbricht sich gewissermaßen selbst, wenn sie mal in kleinkindhaften, elliptischen Wiederholungsschleifen befangen bleibt, dann jedoch wieder den Erzählfaden der Erwachsenenstimmen aufnimmt und mit erstaunlicher Souveränität den kompliziertesten Teil des Anfangssatzes zum Besten gibt. In Relation zu Müllers Text erscheinen solche Brüche nicht als willkürliche Interpretationen des Komponisten Goebbels, vielmehr unterstreichen sie klanglich jene Brüche, Spalten und Verkantungen, die auch auf textueller Ebene für Müllers Montageästhetik kennzeichnend sind.

Der naheliegende Begriff der Montage, der auf Müllers literarische Vorbilder aus der ersten Jahrhunderthälfte zurückverweist, trifft den Höreindruck allerdings nur ungenau. Jedenfalls scheint die antithetische Struktur der Stücke, gerade wenn man die klangliche Ebene mit berücksichtigt, nicht einfach als dramaturgisches Prinzip, erkenntnisstiftender Effekt oder rhetorischer Appell zur Synthese zu fungieren. Sie ist vielmehr konstitutiv für ein spezifisches Moment des Tragischen, das bei Müller klangliche und narrative Aspekte zusammenführt.

Im klassischen Sinne würde ein Konfliktmodell des Tragischen ein Subjekt voraussetzen, das in seinem Handeln zwischen gegenläufigen normativen Ordnungen bzw. zwischen einander widersprechenden, aber gleichermaßen gültigen Werten zerrissen wird. Was aber, wenn es ein solches handlungs- und zurechnungsfähiges Subjekt gar nicht mehr gibt? Wenn Subjektivität sich auflöst in eine Vielstimmigkeit, die keine klare Zuordnung von Handlungen und Erfahrungen mehr erlaubt? Man könnte dann von einer postdramatischen Aufhebung des Tragischen sprechen, und tatsächlich gehört zu den Gemeinplätzen des Diskurses über postdramatisches Theater die Behauptung, dieses kenne keine tragischen Konflikte mehr. Die Statik, die weniger den Stücken als den Inszenierungen Heiner Müllers bisweilen zugeschrieben wurde, ließe sich in diesem Sinne darauf zurückführen, dass Subjekte, Handlungen und Konflikte fehlen, die dem Bühnengeschehen ein Moment des Tragischen oder zumindest eine zwingende Dynamik verleihen könnten.

Heiner Goebbels' Hörstücke zu Texten von Heiner Müller stellen eine solche These allerdings in Frage. Zunächst ist festzustellen, dass die Vielstimmigkeit mit ihren Gegensätzen und Unterbrechungen bei Goebbels vorderhand der Theatralisierung von Texten dient, die ihm als Prosatexte entgegentreten. Zwar vertont Goebbels später mit *Wolokolamsker Chaussee* I-V (SWF, HR, BR 1989/90)[23] auch eines der bekanntesten Theaterstücke bzw. einen Stück-Zyklus von Heiner Müller, aber die meisten seiner Arbeiten sind auf Prosatexte bezogen – so auch *Die Befreiung des Prometheus*. Goebbels' Kompositionen zielen darauf ab, eine innere Polyphonie dieser beim ersten Lesen oft monolithisch wirkenden Texte transparent zu machen. Im Falle des *Prometheus* richtet sich diese Vervielfältigung auf die Erzählerposition. Der erste Satz des Erzählers wird zwischen drei gegensätzlichen Stimmen aufgeteilt: einer Frauenstimme, der Stimme des Autors und der Stimme eines Kleinkinds. Es interveniert überdies eine vierte Stimme, die Singstimme von David Moss, die zwischen opernhaftem Klanggemälde und geräuschhaften, dezentrierenden Schmerzensschreien changiert. Jede dieser Stimmen weckt je eigene Assoziationen, aber auch in der Gesamtkonstellation manifestiert sich eine Haltung zum Text: Es gibt keine hörbare konsistente, einheitliche Erzählerposition. Das Schicksal von Prometheus wird aus verschiedenen Perspektiven erzählt. Die scheinbar so stringente, linear erzählte Fabel wird in ein Prisma gegensätzlicher Stimmen aufgefächert. Deutlich wird auf diese Weise, dass das Geschehen ganz verschieden wahrgenommen und

---

23 | Ebenfalls veröffentlicht auf der CD: Goebbels: Hörstücke nach Texten von Heiner Müller.

erzählt werden kann, dass die Beobachterposition selbst brüchig und instabil ist, wodurch zugleich ein möglicher Reflexionsabstand zum Geschehen markiert wird. Alles in allem weist ein solches Verfahren zurück auf die für Müller so prägende Bertolt Brechtsche Lehrstückästhetik: In der performativen Umsetzung des Textes können und sollen verschiedene Stimmen und Haltungen ausprobiert werden. Die Geschichte, so zwingend sie in ihrem Verlauf auch wirken mag, erlaubt unterschiedlichste Bezugnahmen und Haltungen; insofern wirkt sie nicht identitätsstiftend und weist keine festen Subjektpositionen zu.

Offenheit, Kontingenz und Potenzialität sind jedoch nur die eine Seite der Medaille. Auf der anderen Seite steht Prometheus, der Unterworfene, der – bei aller Dramatik des nachfolgenden Geschehens – in einem grausamen Tableau gefangen bleibt. Die bekannte Situation ist, in Müllers Bearbeitung, folgende: Prometheus muss, an einen Felsen befestigt, ertragen, dass der hundsköpfige Adler fortwährend von seiner Leber frisst. Gleichzeitig ernährt sich Prometheus vom Kot eben dieses Adlers. Er lebt buchstäblich von den Ausscheidungen seines Peinigers. An seinem Geschlechtsteil ist er wiederum mit der Kette verwachsen, die ihn an den Felsen bindet. Angesichts dieser doppelten Symbiose mit dem eigenen Gefängnis ist die von Herakles – wohlgemerkt nicht von Prometheus – intendierte Befreiung nur durch eine veritable Kastration möglich, wie Müller eindringlich verdeutlicht: »Nur am Geschlecht war die Kette mit dem Fleisch verwachsen, weil Prometheus, wenigstens in seinen ersten zweitausend Jahren am Stein, gelegentlich masturbiert hatte. Später hatte er dann wohl auch sein Geschlecht vergessen. Von der Befreiung blieb eine Narbe.«[24]

Der Akt der Befreiung dient nur dazu, die Ausweglosigkeit des prometheischen Gefängnisses zu beweisen, genauso wie der Körper in dem Versuch, einem Begehren zu folgen, nur noch fester in die eigenen Ketten hineingewachsen ist. Prometheus kann sich aus seiner doppelten Verkettung mit dem Felsen und mit dem Adler nicht lösen. Sobald die Verbindung gewaltsam gekappt wird, ist die Lebensader zerschnitten und klammert sich Prometheus umso heftiger und ängstlicher in unverhohlen kleinkindhafter Regression an den Rücken des zu seiner Befreiung eingetroffenen Herakles. Prometheus hat eine Identität, er ist in einer Identität gefangen; der Akt der scheinbaren Befreiung unterstreicht diese Gefangenschaft nur – aber diese Identität ist von Anfang an keine humane, sondern die eines Mensch-Tier-Materie-Hybrids: Prometheus, Fels und Adler bilden längst eine Einheit, einen autarken Nährstoffkreislauf, ein schmerzendes, sich selbst verzehrendes Subjekt, das Goebbels in seinem Hörstück zum Klingen bringt.

---

24 | Müller: Die Befreiung des Prometheus, S. 92.

Diese hybride und zugleich zutiefst statische Figur steht in ihrer Hermetik und Autarkie in krassem Gegensatz zur Polyphonie und Offenheit der Gestaltung. Der tragische Konflikt besteht darin, dass die Offenheit der theatralen Gestaltung gegen die Geschlossenheit der Figur und ihres Schicksals letztlich nichts ausrichten kann: Prometheus' Identität bleibt ein Gefängnis; weder die dramatische Befreiung (der Schnitt ins Fleisch) noch die ästhetische Öffnung (die Polyphonie der Stimmen) können daran etwas ändern.

Polyphonie und Tragik stehen bei Müller nebeneinander, sie koexistieren, ohne gegeneinander etwas ausrichten zu können. Dies macht die besondere Düsternis und Schwere der Müller'schen Klangwelt aus. Zwar gibt es Vielstimmigkeit, Maskerade, Rhythmisierung und eine besondere Körperlichkeit, Geräuschhaftigkeit des Klangs, aber diese Kräfte einer Öffnung fest umrissener Figuren und klar zugewiesener Erzählpositionen können der tragischen Erfahrung einer Gefangenschaft in der eigenen Identität nichts anhaben. Darin zeigt sich die – bei Müller früh durchschlagende – negative Haltung zu idealistischen Kunstbegriffen und zu der Idee ästhetischer Freiheit. Alle formalen Freiheiten, alle Bemühungen um eine ästhetische Brechung, Vervielfältigung und Prismatisierung von Erfahrungen, kommen gegen das Eingeschlossensein in den eigenen situativen Verhaftungen und in den Erfordernissen des historischen Moments letztlich nicht an. Dass ästhetische Differenzierung und historisch-situative Fixierung auf diese Weise Hand in Hand gehen, wirft auf ein spezifisches Erbe der Avantgarde, die Hoffnung auf eine Befreiung der Lebenspraxis des Menschen durch die Künste, kein besonders günstiges Licht.

BIBLIOGRAPHIE

Artaud, Antonin: Letzte Schriften zum Theater. Aus dem Französischen von Elena Kapralik, München 1988.

Derrida, Jacques: Die soufflierte Rede, in: Ders.: Die Schrift und die Differenz, Frankfurt/M. 1976, S. 259-301.

Derrida, Jacques: Das Theater der Grausamkeit und die Geschlossenheit der Repräsentation, in: Ders.: Die Schrift und die Differenz, Frankfurt/M. 1975, S. 351-379.

Finter, Helga: Das Reale, der Körper und die soufflierten Stimmen: Artaud heute, in: Forum Modernes Theater 13.1 (1998), S. 3-17.

Goebbels, Heiner: Müller versprechen, in: Ders. und Nikolaus Müller-Schöll (Hg.): Heiner Müller sprechen, Berlin 2009, S. 282-287.

Kluge, Alexander und Heiner Müller: »Ich bin ein Landvermesser«. Gespräche mit Heiner Müller, Berlin 1996.

Müller, Heiner: Der Auftrag. Erinnerung an eine Revolution, in: Ders.: Werke 5. Die Stücke 3, hg. von Frank Hörnigk. Frankfurt/M. 2002, S. 11-42.
Müller, Heiner: Die Befreiung des Prometheus, in: Ders.: Werke 2. Die Prosa, hg. von Frank Hörnigk, Frankfurt/M. 1999, S. 91-93.
Müller, Heiner: Germania Tod in Berlin, in: Ders.: Werke 4. Die Stücke 2, hg. von Frank Hörnigk. Frankfurt/M. 2001, S. 325-377.
Müller, Heiner: Die Hamletmaschine, in: Ders.: Werke 4. Die Stücke 2, hg. von Frank Hörnigk. Frankfurt/M. 2001, S. 543-554.
Primavesi, Patrick: »Stimme(n) aus dem Sarg«. Theaterarbeit mit Heiner Müllers Hamletmaschine, in: Heiner Goebbels und Nikolaus Müller-Schöll (Hg.): Heiner Müller sprechen. Berlin 2009, S. 267-281.
Zenck, Martin: Stimme/Musik, in: Hans-Thies Lehmann und Patrick Primavesi (Hg.): Heiner Müller Handbuch. Leben – Werk – Wirkung, Stuttgart u.a. 2003, S. 351-353.

FILMOGRAPHIE UND DISKOGRAPHIE

Früchte des Vertrauens (2009), Regie: Alexander Kluge, D. (4 DVDs, filmedition suhrkamp)
Goebbels, Heiner: *Hörstücke nach Texten von Heiner Müller* (1994), München: ECM.

Das Getöse der Wall Street
Die Inszenierung des Börsenhandels als *noise*[1]

Sabine Friedrich

Anhänger der Bewegung Occupy Wall Street hielten am 18. Oktober 2011 eine mehrstündige *drummer session* unweit der Börse in New York ab.[2] Die politische Protestaktion wurde durch die rasche Verbreitung unterschiedlicher Mitschnitte auf *YouTube* binnen kürzester Zeit weltweit zur Kenntnis genommen. Auf den Mitschnitten ist meist der Schauplatz der Protestaktion nicht sofort zu erkennen, da kein berühmtes New Yorker Gebäude zu sehen ist, sondern lediglich eine Straßenkreuzung, die sich in jeder beliebigen nordamerikanischen Großstadt befinden könnte.[3] Durch die begleitenden Kommentare auf *YouTube* ist jedoch deutlich ersichtlich, dass die Protestaktionen im Zuccotti Park, in der Nähe von Wall Street stattfanden. Die Mitschnitte zeigen eine Menschenmenge, die sich auf einem Platz befindet. Zahlreiche dieser Personen spielen auf unterschiedlichen Schlaginstrumenten oder erzeugen mit anderen Gegenständen, wie z.B. Kuhglocken und Pfeifen, laute Geräusche. Alle Instrumente und Gegenstände ertönen gleichzeitig, ohne dass ein bewusstes Zusammenspiel deutlich erkennbar wäre, so dass aus der Vielfalt der Geräusche und Klänge ein dissonanter Lärm entsteht. Teilweise ergibt sich ein gemeinsamer Rhythmus, der sich jedoch nicht zu

---

[1] | Wesentliche Impulse zu diesem Aufsatz stammen aus Diskussionen mit Harald Stücker, dem ich hiermit für die zahlreichen Anregungen herzlich danken möchte.
[2] | Informationen zu den Zielsetzungen und den bisherigen Aktionen der Protestbewegung finden sich auf zahlreichen Webseiten; vgl. besonders die offizielle Webseite http://occupywallst.org/ sowie die *Facebook*-Seite und https://www.adbusters.org/campaigns/occupywallstreet (alle 1.2.16).
[3] | Vgl. folgendes Video: http://www.youtube.com/watch?feature=player_embedded&v=Er7ZLcXnT7Y#! (1.2.16). Auf dieser Seite finden sich zahlreiche Verweise auf ähnliche Kurzvideos der Protestereignisse seit dem Herbst 2011. Vergleichbare Videos finden sich ebenfalls im Archiv der offiziellen Homepage und der *Facebook*-Seite von Occupy Wall Street.

einem strukturierten Klangereignis weiterentwickelt; vielmehr handelt es sich um repetitive, monoton wirkende Klänge. Einige Menschen tanzen zu den Rhythmen, andere betrachten das Spektakel. In den Videos werden jedoch vor allem die Personen gezeigt, welche die Geräusche erzeugen. Unabhängig von der Wahrnehmung der Geräusche als dissonanter Lärm oder als strukturierte Rhythmen steht außer Frage, dass die Musiker nicht primär ein Straßenkonzert geben wollten, sondern mit möglichst lautem *noise* an einem symbolisch hochgradig besetzten Ort – der New Yorker Börse an der Wall Street – gegen die Macht der Finanzwelt protestierten.[4] Die Tatsache, dass es der Bewegung tatsächlich um die Erzeugung von Lärm geht, ist auch daran zu erkennen, dass ein Jahr später im Internet – anlässlich des ersten Jahrestages der Protestbewegung – weltweit zu einem »globalNOISE« am 13. Oktober 2012 aufgerufen wurde.[5] In den Demonstrationen sollte mit Töpfen und Pfannen politisch motivierter Krach erzeugt werden, um gegen die gängigen Praktiken der Großbanken zu protestieren.

Zweifelsohne sind vergleichbare Geräusche seit Langem fester Bestandteil politischer Demonstrationen. Gerade im Kontext des Börsenhandels enthält der von Occupy Wall Street produzierte *noise* jedoch aufschlussreiche kulturanthropologische Implikationen.[6] Nicht nur die Protestbewegung Occupy Wall Street erzeugt *noise*. Auch an der Börse selbst war es lange Zeit sehr laut. Uns allen ist das prototypische *setting* des Börsenhandels, das seit dem 20. Jahrhundert durch Film und Fernsehen vermittelt wird, wohlvertraut. Wir sehen für gewöhnlich einen großen Handelsraum. Darin befinden sich zahlreiche Personen, überwiegend männlich, relativ uniform in dunklem Anzug, hellem Hemd und Krawatte gekleidet, die sich hektisch im Raum bewegen oder auf engstem Raum zusammenstehen. Überall im Handelsraum – auf Schreibtischen und Wänden – befinden sich Bildschirme unterschiedlicher Größe, welche die jeweiligen *charts* anzeigen.

---

4 | Vgl. hierzu die zahlreichen Äußerungen, Kurzkommentare und Artikel, die auf den entsprechenden Webseiten (vgl. Fußnote 2) veröffentlicht sind.

5 | Vgl. http://occupywallst.org/tag/global%20noise und https://www.facebook.com/globalNOISE (1.2.16).

6 | Holger Schulze betont, »dass Klanggestalten erst in Abhängigkeit von Bedingungen wie Räumlichkeit, Kultur und individueller Erfahrungen verständlich werden.« Vgl. insbesondere die programmatische Einleitung in: Schulze (Hg.): Sound studies, S. 9-15; vgl. ebenfalls Schulzes Beitrag »Bewegung Berührung Übertragung. Einführung in eine historische Anthropologie des Klangs«, in: Schulze: Sound studies, S. 143-165, sowie Schulze (Hg.): Gespür – Empfindung – Kleine Wahrnehmungen und Schulze und Wulf (Hg.): Klanganthropologie: Performativität – Imagination – Narration. Zum Begriff *soundscape* vgl. Schafer: The Tuning of the World. Zu einem Überblick über die vielseitigen Erforschungsmöglichkeiten von *soundscapes* vgl. Sterne (Hg.): The Sound Studies Reader.

Die visuellen Eindrücke vom Börsenhandel werden jedoch dominiert von den akustischen. In unserer medial vermittelten Vorstellung von der Börse prägt sich vor allem der Lärm ein. Unzählige Stimmen versuchen, sich gegenseitig zu übertönen. Es ist ein akustischer Wettbewerb. Der *broker* mit der lautesten Stimme kann seine *trades* am schnellsten platzieren in einem Geschäft, in dem, wie in keinem anderen, Zeit gleich Geld ist. Wir – als BeobachterInnen – sind jedoch nicht imstande, einzelne Informationen zu identifizieren und nehmen lediglich einen ohrenbetäubenden, undifferenzierten Stimmenlärm wahr.

Der Börsenlärm ist jedoch sehr vielschichtig, da er als akustisches Phänomen nicht allein Rauschen ist, sondern zugleich eine informative Dimension besitzt.[7] Der *noise* der Börse entsteht aus einer Vielzahl diskreter Zeichen, die dem Händler zeitgleich aus unterschiedlichen Quellen vermittelt werden.[8] Der *trader* verwandelt den für außenstehende BeobachterInnen nicht dechiffrierbaren, un-sinnigen Börsen-*noise* in aussagekräftige – und vor allem gewinnbringende – Daten. Es wird demzufolge eine deutliche Grenze markiert zwischen den Börseninsidern, die das Rauschen in einen strukturierten, sinnvollen Code überführen können, und den Außenstehenden, die keinen Zugang zu dem ihnen fremden System haben, als Unwissende lediglich ungeordneten Lärm wahrnehmen und somit von der Kommunikation ausgegrenzt werden.[9]

Auf einer übergeordneten Ebene erhält der chaotisch wirkende Börsen-*noise* jedoch auch für die ausgegrenzten ZuschauerInnen eine symbolische Bedeutung. Es ist gerade der unverständliche Lärm im Handelsraum, der zum sonischen Symbol für den Börsenhandel und damit zugleich für das westliche Finanz- und Wirtschaftssystem geworden ist. Als Machtzentrum dieses Finanzsystems wird die *New York Stock Exchange* an der Wall Street angesehen, die weltweit bekannteste Börse. Das heutige Gebäude der Börse wurde 1903 in der Wall Street Nummer 11 eröffnet.[10] Zunächst begründet durch die führende Kraft der nordamerikanischen Wirtschaft wurde die Wall Street

---

7 | Nicholas Knouf geht in seinem Blogeintrag »The Noises of Finance«, der das erste Kapitel seiner bislang unveröffentlichten Dissertation zu diesem Thema darstellt, ebenfalls auf die unterschiedlichen Dimensionen des Börsen-noise ein, vgl. Knouf: The Noises of Finance.
8 | Vgl. Tharp: Trade your way to financial freedom, S. 237f.
9 | In dieser Hinsicht lässt sich die akustische Ausgrenzung der BeobachterInnen auch an neuere Forschungsperspektiven der *sound studies* anschließen, denen es gerade um die Verbindung von Hören, Erleben und Empfinden geht; vgl. hierzu Schulze (Hg.): Sound studies, insbesondere die Einleitung.
10 | Zur Geschichte und kulturhistorischen Entwicklung der New Yorker Börse vgl. Geisst: Die Geschichte der Wall Street; Ho: Liquidated. An Ethnography of Wall Street.

im Verlauf des 20. Jahrhunderts rasch zum architektonischen Topos für die Macht des westlichen Finanzsystems. Das klassizistische Eingangsportal und der Handelsraum der Wall Street sind außerordentlich populäre Motive, wenn es um die Darstellung der Finanzwirtschaft in den Film- und Fernsehmedien geht. Daher ist es nicht weiter verwunderlich, dass der Börsen-*noise* der Wall Street für die Gegner des kapitalistischen Finanzsystems zur konkreten Materialisierung des Feindbildes diente und in dieser Form auch in fiktionale Verarbeitungen in Literatur und Film eingeht. Im Folgenden werden ausgehend von Film- und Textbeispielen die Spannungsrelationen, die zwischen den verschiedenen Dimensionen des Börsen-*noise* bestehen, näher untersucht. Es soll aufgezeigt werden, inwiefern vom Beginn des 20. Jahrhunderts bis heute eine mediale Verschiebung des Rauschens der Börse stattfand und welche kulturanthropologischen Implikationen dabei zu erkennen sind.

PROTOTYPISCHE FILMISCHE INSZENIERUNGEN EINES SONISCHEN TOPOS

Eine der populärsten Filmdarstellungen der New Yorker Börse ist sicherlich der 1987 unter der Regie von Oliver Stone entstandene Spielfilm *Wall Street*, der die moralische Verkommenheit skrupelloser Spekulanten anprangert. In Anlehnung an prominente Wall-Street-Millionäre, die wegen Insidergeschäften verhaftet wurden, entstand die Figur Gordon Gekko, ein prototypischer rücksichtsloser Börsenhändler, gespielt von Michael Douglas. Gerade weil es sich um eine typische Hollywood-*mainstream*-Produktion handelt, die mit dem üblichen plakativen Gut-Böse-Schema arbeitet, sind die Szenen im Handelsraum sehr aussagekräftig im Hinblick auf die stereotype Darstellung des Börsenlärms, so wie er jahrzehntelang existierte, in unzähligen Fernsehbildern weltweit übermittelt wurde und sich bis heute als sonischer Topos des Börsenhandels im kollektiven Gedächtnis verankert hat.

Zahlreiche Szenen des Films stellen den Börsenlärm exemplarisch dar. So zeigt eine Szene zu Beginn des Films den Arbeitsalltag eines jungen, unbekannten Börsenmaklers namens Bud Fox, der durch die spätere Beziehung zu Gordon Gekko aufsteigen wird.[11] Bud Fox verbringt seinen Tag damit, Kunden für Börsengeschäfte am Telefon zu akquirieren. Gezeigt wird daher zunächst nicht der Handelsraum, sondern die Situation in einem Großraumbüro, in dem sich zahlreiche Makler befinden, unmittelbar vor Beginn des Handelstags. Danach schwenkt die Kameraeinstellung auf eine große

---

11 | *Wall Street* (1987), 00:10:40-00:37:50.

digitale Wanduhr, die 9:29:59 anzeigt. In einer Großaufnahme ist sodann zu sehen, wie die digitale Anzeige auf exakt 9.30 wechselt; gleich darauf ist der blecherne Klang der Börsenglocke zu vernehmen, der den Beginn des Handels signalisiert.

Dieses Eröffnungssignal wurde an der Wall Street Ende des 19. Jahrhunderts eingeführt.[12] Zunächst wurde ein chinesischer Gong benutzt; seitdem sich die New Yorker Börse im heutigen Gebäude in der Wall Street befindet, wurde der Gong durch eine Messingglocke ersetzt. Die Glocke, die bis in die Gegenwart benutzt wird, befindet sich auf einer Empore, von der aus sämtliche Abläufe im Handelsraum überblickt werden können. Ungeachtet aller Veränderungen, die sich durch die Digitalisierung im Börsenhandel in den letzten Jahrzehnten ergeben haben, wird die Glocke an der Wall Street noch heute manuell von einer Person betätigt, teilweise von bekannten Persönlichkeiten, und als feierlicher Akt zelebriert, insbesondere bei wichtigen Börsengängen.[13] In allen drei Filmen über die New Yorker Börse, die im Folgenden behandelt werden, wird die Glocke sehr deutlich inszeniert, was auf die hochgradig ritualisierte Bedeutung dieser mechanischen Tonquelle innerhalb der Börsenwelt verweist.

Unmittelbar im Anschluss an den Glockenklang setzt im Film *Wall Street* der Börsen-*noise* ein. Gezeigt wird zunächst der große Handelsraum (vgl. Abb. 1).

---

12 | Vgl. http://www.investopedia.com/ask/answers/06/openingclosingbell.asp (1.2.16). Die Funktion solcher »funktionalen Klänge« und deren Weiterentwicklung entsprechend der jeweiligen gesellschaftlichen Veränderungsprozesse analysiert Speer: Funktionale Klänge. Auch mit dem Begriff der »Sonifikation« – verstanden als »Verfahren, Informationen auf akustischem Wege auszudrücken« (Schoon und Volmar: Informierte Klänge und geschulte Ohren, S. 10) – lässt sich die Funktionsweise der Eröffnungsglocke gewinnbringend analysieren. Einen guten Überblick über die Entwicklung unterschiedlichster Alltagsklänge aus kulturhistorischer Perspektive geben Bull und Back: The Auditory Culture Reader.

13 | So besitzt die Eröffnungsglocke auf der Einstiegsseite der offiziellen Homepage der New Yorker Börse sogar an hervorgehobener Stelle einen eigenen *link*, um auf Tage zu verweisen, an denen prominente Persönlichkeiten die Eröffnungsglocke betätigen; vgl. https://nyse.nyx.com/the-bell (1.2.16). Auch die Videos mit dem Ertönen der Eröffnungsglocke sind online.

Abbildung 1: Wall Street *(1987), 00:17:40.*

Aus einer übergeordneten Vertikalperspektive der Kamera ist von oben das chaotische Geschehen auf dem Börsenparkett zu sehen: Eine Menge hektisch agierender Menschen befindet sich dort auf engstem Raum. Einige blicken auf die zahlreichen großen Computerbilderschirme und überschreien sich gegenseitig; andere sind dabei, Papiere auszufüllen. Mit einer Horizontalperspektive bewegt sich die Kamera sodann durch die Menschenmenge, um aus der Nähe Einzelimpressionen des lärmenden Börsengeschehens zu vermitteln. Danach erfolgt ein deutlicher Schnitt. Zu sehen ist wieder das Großraumbüro. Dort versuchen die Broker, gleichzeitig zu telefonieren und untereinander zu kommunizieren. Teilweise muss die Körpergestik die verbale Kommunikation ersetzen, da ansonsten keine Verständigung zwischen den Brokern mehr möglich scheint. Die Kamera fokussiert unterschiedliche Personen von Nahem, die offenbar am Telefon ihren Börsengeschäften nachgehen. Die ZuschauerInnen können einzelne Satzfragmente identifizieren; aufgrund der schnellen Schnitttechnik vermögen sie jedoch nicht, die verschiedenen Äußerungen tatsächlich zu verstehen bzw. zwischen ihnen einen Sinnzusammenhang zu erstellen. Die schnelle Schnittfolge inszeniert und symbolisiert die Hektik des Börsengeschehens. An jedem Arbeitsplatz befinden sich einige Computerbildschirme, die eine Fülle an Informationen anzeigen; verstärkt wird die Informationsflut durch die digitalen Laufbänder an den Wänden, welche die aktuellen Börsenkurse anzeigen. Auf den Schreibtischen stapeln sich Papiere mit weiteren Börseninformationen. Aus heutiger Perspektive fällt auf, wie viel Informationen noch in Papierform übermittelt werden, die später als unnütze Fetzen auf dem Boden zu sehen sind.

Die Filmsequenz, die den Börsenbeginn zeigt, führt den konkreten fiktionalen Handlungsverlauf nicht weiter, sondern dient vor allem dazu, die Hektik, die multimediale Informationsflut und den *noise* des Börsenalltags für die außenstehenden ZuschauerInnen atmosphärisch so intensiv wie möglich zu vermitteln. Das, was für die *trader* als funktionales Signalsystem eine ziel- und profitorientierte Kommunikation ermöglicht, erscheint den FilmzuschauerInnen als ein kommunikationsstörender Lärm, der lediglich die Medialität der involvierten Kommunikationsmedien hervorhebt.

Auch eine spätere Schlüsselszene des Films spielt überwiegend im Handelsraum der Börse.[14] Das moralische Gewissen des mittlerweile erfolgreichen Bud Fox ist erwacht, und er möchte den skrupellosen Machenschaften von Gekko Einhalt gebieten, indem er ihm eine Falle stellt. In der prototypischen Börsenszene schreien die einzelnen *trader* gegeneinander an, um sich zu überbieten; vergleichbar mit Marktschreiern auf dem Obst- und Gemüsemarkt werden die Kauf- und Verkaufsaufträge durch gegenseitige Zurufe getätigt (vgl. Abb. 2).

Abbildung 2: Wall Street *(1987)*, 01:47:46.

Für die ZuschauerInnen ist in der Filmszene im allgemeinen Tumult keine einzelne Information mehr identifizierbar. Die Kamera fokussiert aus nächster Nähe die aufgewühlte Menschenmenge im Handelsraum. Erkennbar sind in kurzen Einstellungen einzelne Personen, die lauthals etwas schreien, das die ZuschauerInnen aufgrund des außerordentlichen Geräuschpegels jedoch nicht verstehen können.

So unterschiedlich die narrative Einbettung der erwähnten Szenen innerhalb der fiktionalen Handlungsverlaufs auch sein mögen; im Hinblick auf die intendierte Wirkung entsprechen sie sich. Beide Male geht es um die atmosphärische Vermittlung eines ungeordneten Lärms, den die ZuschauerInnen mit der Wall Street verbinden.[15] Stones Film inszeniert den sonischen Topos der Börse auf prototypische Weise.

---

14 | *Wall Street* (1987), 00:10:44-00:28:47.
15 | Es geht daher weniger um das Klangphänomen des *noise* als um die Empfindungen, die dadurch bei den ZuschauerInnen ausgelöst werden; vgl. hierzu die Ansätze innerhalb

INFORMATIONSTHEORETISCHE DIMENSIONEN DES BÖRSEN-*NOISE*

Wie bereits eingangs erwähnt, hat *noise* an der Börse nicht nur eine akustische, sondern auch eine informationstheoretische Bedeutung. Der Lärm kann jenseits einer negativen oder positiven Bewertung als ein Rauschen verstanden werden – gleichzusetzen mit dem Ungeordneten und Unstrukturierten.[16] Im Unterschied zu dem außenstehenden Betrachter ist es für den *trader* überlebenswichtig, aus diesem Börsen-*noise* sinnhafte Zeichen zu destillieren. Die Leistung des *trader* liegt darin, das Rauschen der unüberschaubaren Vielzahl unstrukturierter Daten, die ihn durch die Rufe der anderen Händler, aber auch durch jegliche andere mediale – analoge oder digitale – Übermittlungsformen erreichen, zu ordnen, um die ungeordneten Daten in für ihn sinnvolle Informationen zu überführen.

Im Gegensatz zu langfristig orientierten Investoren, die Aktien nach fundamentalen Gesichtspunkten der Werthaltigkeit kaufen, handeln die meisten *trader* in einem kurzfristigen Zeitrahmen, sie reagieren auf kleine bis kleinste Kursschwankungen. Solche kurzfristigen Kursausschläge, verursacht durch Nachrichten und Gerüchte, die sich auf den langfristigen Kursverlauf nicht auswirken, werden auch als *noise* bezeichnet.[17] Ein *noise trader* ist in diesem Sinne ein kurzfristig orientierter *trader*, der seine Handelsentscheidungen auf nichtfundamentale Informationen basiert. *Noise trader* wollen also alle möglichen Informationen, die aktuell auf irgendeine Art und Weise auftreten bzw. ihnen bekannt werden, ausnutzen und versuchen, daraus Gewinn zu erzielen. Da die Daten aber häufig nur Gerüchte sind und keine feste Basis aufweisen, müssen *noise trader* schnell sein und aufpassen, nicht in die Verlustfalle zu geraten.

Während der *noise* für einen langfristigen Investor irrelevant ist, muss ein kurzfristiger *trader* über Techniken verfügen, um aus dem Rauschen, das vor allem die Gefahr von Fehlsignalen birgt, Informationen herauszufiltern. An der Börse haben schon viele *trader* mit ihrem Vermögen dafür bezahlt, Muster in Kursverläufen gesehen zu haben, die sich im Nachhinein als irrelevante Zeichen, herausgestellt haben. Aufgrund der heutigen technischen

---

der *sound studies*, welche den Akzent der Untersuchung verlagern vom Senden der Klänge hin zum Empfangen der Klänge und das Gefüge von Hören, Empfindungen und (Selbst-)Wahrnehmungen herausarbeiten; vgl. Schulze (Hg.): Gespür – Empfindung – Kleine Wahrnehmungen.

16 | Zu den Übergängen zwischen Laut und Bedeutung aus kulturhistorischer Perspektive vgl. die verschiedenen Aufsätze in Teil 1 in: Kittler, Macho und Weigel (Hg.): Zwischen Rauschen und Offenbarung.

17 | Zum Begriff des *noise* im Börsenhandel vgl. Tharp: Trade your way to financial freedom, besonders S. 237f.

Möglichkeiten hat sich in jüngerer Zeit die Flut der medial übermittelten, unstrukturierten Daten, d.h. des Börsen-*noise* im informationstechnischen Sinn, in unglaublicher Weise potenziert, so dass die Strukturierung des *noise* für den *trader* ungleich komplexer geworden ist.

Demgegenüber ist der akustische Lärm nur noch Nostalgie. An den heutigen Börsen ist das hektische Parkett vor allem eine Kulisse für Touristen. Längst haben sich die Weltbörsen akustisch beruhigt. Früher ging es darum, dass sich die *trader* so laut wie möglich durch den Lärm hindurch bemerkbar machten, um ihren *trade* so schnell wie möglich zu platzieren und so einen vermeintlich günstigen Kurs fixieren zu können. Es ging um Sekunden. Heute hat sich die Situation scheinbar entspannt, denn in den modernen Handelsräumen geht es nicht lauter zu als in anderen Büros. Aber heute sind nicht mehr Sekunden, sondern Millisekunden entscheidend. Die *trader* sitzen vor einer Bildschirmwand und orchestrieren hochentwickelte Handelssysteme. Das sind in der Regel äußerst komplexe Algorithmen, die versuchen, aus den Fieberkurven der Märkte genau diejenigen Informationen zu destillieren, die sie zu Geld machen können. Der Präsenzhandel, der die persönliche Anwesenheit der handelnden Personen voraussetzt, wurde von computergestützten Handelssystemen verdrängt. Diese mediale Veränderung hat offensichtlich zu einer starken Reduktion des akustischen Börsenlärms und zugleich zu einer Potenzierung des Daten-*noise* geführt. Mit anderen Worten: Der Lärm hat sich gleichsam in die Glasfaserleitungen verlagert.

MEDIALE VERSCHIEBUNGEN DES BÖRSEN-*NOISE*

23 Jahre nach Oliver Stones erstem *Wall-Street*-Film, 2010, kam die Fortsetzung ins Kino mit dem Titel *Wall Street: Money never sleeps*. Der Film wurde überwiegend negativ besprochen.[18] Doch auch wenn Stones Sequel stark vereinfachend und naiv moralisierend auf die Finanzkrise blickt, kommt die mediale Veränderung des Börsen-*noise* darin doch sehr treffend zum Ausdruck. Zudem wird der Börsenhandel nicht mehr ausgehend von dem einen, konkret lokalisierbaren Handelsraum in der *Wall Street* gezeigt. Stattdessen werden, entsprechend der zunehmenden Vernetzung eines globalisierten Börsenhandels, gleichzeitig mehrere Standorte einbezogen. Analog zu der mittlerweile üblichen Konvention des gesplitteten Bildschirms bei Nachrichtenfernsehsendern ist auch in diesem Film die Kadrage mehrfach unterteilt, um zeitgleich die verschiedenen Handelsreaktionen weltweit und die Beschleunigung des Börsengeschehens darzustellen (vgl. Abb. 3).

---

18 | Vgl. exemplarisch Alten: Haifisch ohne Zähne; Buß: »Wall Street«-Fortsetzung.

Abbildung 3: Wall Street: Money Never Sleeps *(2010), 00:42:43.*

Die verschiedenen Einstellungen auf dem mehrfach unterteilten *screen* sind unterschiedlich lange sichtbar, so dass durch die verschobene Frequenz der Teilbilder eine zusätzliche Dynamisierung erzeugt wird. Die Personen, die in einem solchen *split screen* gezeigt werden, betreiben ihren Handel nicht mehr in Konkurrenz mit unmittelbar physisch präsenten Partnern, sondern agieren, vor allem mittels Telefon und Computer, weltweit. Der Börsenhandel verliert seine unmittelbare, physisch wahrnehmbare, konkrete Dimension – und damit zugleich seinen akustischen Lärm. Symptomatisch für die Veränderung des Börsenhandels sind diejenigen Szenen in Money Never Sleeps, welche die veränderten Kommunikationsformen zeigen.[19] Anstelle des akustischen Börsenlärms werden digitale Datenflüsse dargestellt. Farbige, flimmernde Buchstaben- und Zahlenströme verbreiten sich ausgehend von einem Rechenzentrum diagonal durch den Raum, wodurch offensichtlich die weltweite Datenübertragung im Internet versinnbildlicht werden soll (vgl. Abb. 4). Das Rechenzentrum ersetzt den Handelsraum.

Abbildung 4: Wall Street: Money Never Sleeps *(2010), 00:24:44.*

Es steht außer Frage, dass die Szene im Vergleich zum ersten *Wall-Street*-Film von 1987 auf einer veränderten Filmästhetik beruht; gleichwohl entspricht es der medialen Verlagerung des Börsen-*noise*, wenn Stone die Flut der Datenströme nun mit Musik unterlegt: Die digitale Übertragung der

---

19 | *Wall Street: Money Never Sleeps* (2010), 00:42:00-00:45:00.

Datenströme kommt ohne mündliche Kommunikation aus. Wer das Börsengeschehen beobachtet, nimmt die veränderte mediale Struktur des *noise* wahr, ist jedoch weiterhin außerstande, die Datenflüsse zu dechiffrieren und in eine sinnhafte Ordnung zu übersetzen.

NOSTALGISCHE REMINISZENZEN DES BÖRSEN-*NOISE*

Welche Gefahren der undurchsichtige Daten-*noise* in sich birgt, zeigt auf eindrucksvolle Weise der von Jeffrey C. Chandor 2011 realisierte Film *Margin Call*. Das Finanzdrama, das ebenfalls an der *Wall Street* spielt, wurde von der Insolvenz der Lehman-Brothers Bank inspiriert. Der außerordentlich düstere Film arbeitet mit den Mitteln des Kammerspiels und stellt die dramatischen Geschehnisse in einer Investmentbank innerhalb eines Zeitraums von 24 Stunden dar. Um eine riesige Investmentblase zu vertuschen, die bei Kursverlust das Unternehmen zu ruinieren droht, wird in einer nächtlichen Aktion eine Rettung initiiert, ohne Rücksicht auf deren fatale weltweite Auswirkungen auf die Finanzmärkte. Der Film zeigt die Börsenmakler nicht, wie bei Oliver Stone, als habgierige Schurken, sondern als mittelmäßige Menschen jenseits des Gut-Böse Schemas, die beim Blick auf den Daten-*noise* im Computerbildschirm zugeben, dass sie nicht mehr genau verstehen, was dort eigentlich zu sehen ist. Aufgrund der diffusen Datenströme auf dem Finanzmarkt ist auch für den Chef der Investmentbank der drohende Zusammenbruch des eigenen Unternehmens nicht mehr unmittelbar zu erkennen.

Die Schlüsselszene von *Margin Call* erzählt von einem manipulierten Börsenhandel, mit der die Bank vor dem Ruin gerettet werden soll.[20] Bei völlig schwarzem Bildschirm ist der metallische Klang der Glocke zu hören, der den wichtigen Handelstag, der über den Fortgang der Bank entscheiden wird, eröffnet. Gleich nach der Eröffnungsglocke klingelt ein Telefon. Die weltweiten Rettungsaktionen mit dem fingierten Handel beginnen. Es gibt überhaupt keine Einstellung mehr, die unmittelbar den Handelsraum der Börse zeigt, weil das Börsenparkett der Wall Street seine Funktion als Ort der Handlung verloren hat. Auch der akustische Börsen-*noise* gehört damit eindeutig vergangenen Zeiten an. Man sieht lediglich ein Großraumbüro, in dem einzelne Menschen telefonieren (vgl. Abb. 5). Die Telefonstimmen kommen allesamt aus dem *Off*. Zwischen den anwesenden Menschen findet kaum noch Kommunikation statt. Angesichts der bedrohlichen Situation erstaunt die Ruhe, die in dem Büro herrscht.

---

20 | *Margin Call* (2011), 00:28:26-00:32:10.

Abbildung 5: Margin Call *(2011), 00:23:30.*

Obwohl das Ausmaß der drohenden Finanzkrise ungleich größer ist als in Stones erstem *Wall-Street*-Film, gibt es keine sichtbaren hektischen Situationen. Die Szene endet wiederum mit einem schwarzen Bildschirm und der Glocke, die das Ende des Handelstages markiert. Insbesondere aufgrund der kompletten Verlagerung des Handelsgeschehens in die digitalen Datenströme, fällt die nun völlig anachronistisch wirkende Glocke umso deutlicher auf.

Zweifelsohne liegen den Darstellungen der Wall Street bei Stone und Chandor unterschiedliche ideologische und filmästhetische Ansätze zugrunde. Trotz aller Differenzen erscheinen jedoch zwei gemeinsame Aspekte aufschlussreich. Zum einen zeigt sich in der Zusammenschau aller drei Filme das zunehmende Verschwinden des für uns so vertrauten akustischen Börsen-*noise* sowie dessen Verlagerung in digitale Datenströme. Zum anderen bleiben aber sowohl in der filmästhetischen Darstellung als auch in der Realität des Börsenhandels trotz völlig veränderter Handelsbedingungen symbolische Versatzstücke erhalten, welche die Bewahrung vertrauter Rituale sichern sollen, wie insbesondere der Fortbestand der Eröffnungsglocke zeigt.[21] Gerade weil sich in Zeiten der Globalisierung die festen Handelszeiten aufgelöst haben, ist die zeitliche Strukturierung von einem vermeintlichen Handelsbeginn und -ende durch einen akustisch präsenten mechanischen Glockenklang offensichtlich von nostalgischem Reiz. Man könnte hier zudem im Hinblick auf die filmische Inszenierung eine dramaturgische bzw. narratologische Notwendigkeit erkennen: Endlose Daten- und Soundströme haben keine Struktur, die sich erzählen lässt. Sie widerstreben ihrer

---

21 | Zur kulturanthropologischen Bedeutung von Klängen, insbesondere im Hinblick auf die identitätsstiftende Bedeutung der Evokation von Vergangenem, vgl. Augoyard und Torgue (Hg.): Sonic Experience, S. 21-23.

eigenen Narrativierung. Daher greift der Film, der eine Geschichte erzählen möchte, mit dem Glockensignal auf tradierte Formen von Anfang/Ende zurück.

Sowohl Stones zweiter *Wall-Street*-Film als auch Chandors *Margin Call* zeigen die Auswirkungen der Globalisierung auf den Finanzmarkt und damit zugleich die reduzierte Bedeutung von konkret lokalisierbaren Handelsräumen, wie z.B. die Wall Street. Ebenso wie die Börsenglocke jedoch weiterhin ein wichtiges symbolisches Potential besitzt, besteht offenbar ein Bedürfnis nach konkreten Räumen, an denen das Börsengeschehen verortet werden soll. Dies zeigt sich gerade bei den Protestbewegungen, die sich gegen die Wall Street als architektonischer Topos des westlichen Finanzsystems richten.

ÄSTHETISCH VERFREMDETER PROTEST-*NOISE*

Die Aktionen der Bewegung Occupy Wall Street wurden durch die jüngste Finanz- und Bankenkrise ausgelöst. Proteste gegen das Zentrum der westlichen Finanzmacht sind jedoch keineswegs neue Phänomene; insbesondere in wirtschaftlichen Krisensituationen wurden sie im Verlauf des 20. Jahrhunderts immer wieder virulent. Der Börsencrash im Oktober 1929 ist hierfür ein prominentes Beispiel. Die Protestbewegungen beschränken sich dabei nicht auf Demonstrationen vor Ort, sondern sie reichen ebenfalls in Bereiche der künstlerischen Verarbeitung. Die Literatur wird zum Medium, in dem die Wall Street nicht nur explizit kritisiert, sondern darüber hinaus auf ästhetisch verfremdete Weise – verbal – angegriffen wird, so z.B. in Federico García Lorcas Gedicht »Danza de la muerte« (Todestanz) aus der Sammlung *Poeta en Nueva York* (veröffentlicht postum 1940).[22]

Der spanische Avantgardedichter hielt sich in New York von Juni 1929 bis März 1930 auf und erlebte den Börsenkrach aus unmittelbarer Nähe. Aufgrund der politischen und wirtschaftlichen Ereignisse jener Zeit war García Lorca sehr ablehnend gegenüber der nordamerikanischen Gesellschaft eingestellt, wie aus verschiedenen Briefen, Essays und Vorträgen deutlich hervorgeht.[23] Insbesondere die Wall Street verkörperte für ihn das Symbol einer ungerechten Gesellschaftsordnung, die ausschließlich auf wirtschaftliche

---

22 | García Lorca: Totentanz.
23 | Vgl. hierzu Flint: Flesh of the poet; Crispin: La Voz poética en Federico García Lorca; Menarini: ›La Danza de la muerte‹; Cañas: The Poet and the city.

Dominanz ausgerichtet ist und zu entfremdeten technisierten Lebensweisen führt, welche die Natur zerstören und Randgruppen rigoros unterdrücken.[24]

In dem Gedichtband *Poeta en Nueva York* verarbeitete García Lorca die Eindrücke seines Aufenthalts in Nordamerika. In einigen Gedichten, wie z. B. in »Nueva York (Oficina y denuncia)«, wird die Kritik an der kapitalistischen Zivilisation explizit formuliert.[25] Die meisten Gedichte sind jedoch in einer hermetischen, surrealistischen Schreibweise verfasst, so dass die Sozial- und Gesellschaftskritik in stark ästhetisch verfremdeter Weise in die Texte eingeht. Das Gedicht »Danza de la muerte« knüpft an die mittelalterliche Tradition des Totentanzes an und beschreibt die fantasmatische Zerstörung der Wall Street durch eine afrikanische Totenmaske.[26]

García Lorca war ein ausgezeichneter Musiker und hat sich eingehend mit verschiedenen traditionellen sowie avantgardistischen Musikstilen auseinandergesetzt; die intensive Beschäftigung mit der Musik prägt ebenfalls die Strukturen seiner eigenen literarischen Texte, die sich durch eine starke rhythmische Strukturierung auszeichnen.[27] Gerade im Kontext der Untersuchung der vielschichtigen Dimensionen des Börsen-*noise* zeigt sich in García Lorcas literarischem Unterfangen eine neue Facette des Protestlärms. In »Danza de la muerte« erschafft García Lorca einen ästhetischen Textraum, in dem mit dem rhythmischen Zerstörungstanz der Totenmaske eine akustische Gegenkraft eingeführt wird, welche die Wall Street auf surreale Weise auslöschen soll.[28]

---

24 | Vgl. folgenden Passus in García Lorca: Conferencia-recital de Federico García Lorca sobre Poeta en *Nueva York*, S. 172: »Lo impresionante por frío y por cruel es Wall Street. Llega el oro en ríos de todas las partes de la tierra y la muerte llega con él. En ningún sitio del mundo se siente como allí la ausencia total del espíritu; manadas de hombres que no pueden pasar del tres y manadas de hombres que no pueden pasar del seis, desprecio de la ciencia pura y valor demoníaco del presente.«

25 | Vgl. hierzu Friedrich: Transformationen der Sinne, S. 243-254.

26 | Zur Bedeutung der Totenmaske im Hinblick auf den Börsenkrach vgl. García Lorca: Conferencia-recital de Federico García Lorca sobre *Poeta en Nueva York*, S. 173 : »[...] he sentido la impresión de la muerte real, la muerte sin esperanza, la muerte que es podredumbre y nada más, como en aquel instante, porque era un espectáculo terrible pero sin grandeza. [...] Por eso yo puse allí esta danza de la muerte. El mascarón típico africano, muerte verdaderamente muerta, sin ángeles ni *resurrexit*, muerte alejada de todo espíritu, bárbara y primitiva como los Estados Unidos que no han luchado ni lucharán por el cielo.«

27 | Zur Beschäftigung García Lorcas mit Musik vgl. Friedrich: Transformationen der Sinne, S. 269-283.

28 | Ich greife folgend eine Argumentation wieder auf, die ich in einem anderen Kontext bereits entwickelt hatte; vgl. hierzu Friedrich: Transformationen der Sinne, S. 283-293.

Federico García Lorca

Danza de la muerte

El mascarón. Mirad el mascarón
cómo viene del África a New York.
[...]
El mascarón. ¡Mirad el mascarón!
20 *Arena, caimán y miedo sobre Nueva York.*

Desfiladeros de cal aprisionaban un cielo vacío
donde sonaban las voces de los que mueren bajo el guano.
Un cielo mondado y puro, idéntico a sí mismo,
con el bozo y lirio agudo de sus montañas invisibles.
25 Acabó con los más leves tallitos del canto
y se fue al diluvio empaquetado de la savia,
a través del descanso de los últimos perfiles
levantando con el rabo pedazos de espejo.

Cuando el chino lloraba en el tejado
30 sin encontrar el desnudo de su mujer,
y el director del banco observaba el manómetro
que mide el cruel silencio de la moneda,
el mascarón llegaba a Wall Street.
[...]
70 ¡Que no baile el Papa!
¡No, que no baile el Papa!
Ni el Rey;
ni el millonario de dientes azules,
ni las bailarinas secas de las catedrales,
75 ni constructores, ni esmeraldas, ni locos, ni sodomitas.
Sólo este mascarón.
Este mascarón de vieja escarlatina.
¡Sólo este mascarón!

Que ya las cobras silbarán por los últimos pisos.
80 Que ya los ortigas estremecerán patios y terrazas.
Que ya la Bolsa será una pirámide de musgo.
Que ya vendrán lianas después de los fusiles
y muy pronto, muy pronto, muy pronto.
¡Ay, Wall Street!

85 *El mascarón, ¡Mirad el mascarón!*
    ¡Cómo escupe veneno de bosque
    por la angustia imperfecta de Nueva York!

Totentanz

Die Maske, Seht nur, wie die Maske kommt –
Von Afrika nach New York.
[...]
Die Maske. Seht nur, die Maske!
20 *Sand, Kaiman und Furcht kommen über New York.*

Enge Schluchten aus Kalk waren Kerker eines leeren Himmels,
wo die Rufe der Leute hallten, die im Guano ersticken.
Es war ein geputzter, reiner, mit sich identischer Himmel
mit Flaum und spitzer Lilie auf unsichtbaren Bergen,
25 er machte Schluß mit den feinsten Stengeln des Gesanges
und verschwand in der wohlverpackten Sintflut der Säfte,
er ging durch die Pause der letzten Paraden,
sein Schweif aber wirbelte Spiegelscherben auf.

Als der Chinese auf dem Flachdach weinte
30 und doch den nackten Körper seiner Frau nicht fand,
und der Bankdirektor auf dem Manometer ablas,
wie hoch das grausame Schweigen des Geldes stand,
da brach die Maske in die Wall Street ein.
[...]
70 Laßt den Papst nicht tanzen!
Nein, laßt bloß den Papst nicht tanzen!
Noch den König,
noch den Millionär mit seinen blauen Zähnen,
noch die dürren Kathedraltänzerinnen,
75 noch Konstrukteure, Edelsteine, Irre, Sodomiten.
Nur diese Maske.
Diese Maske aus altem Scharlach.
Nur diese Maske!

Denn auf den höchsten Etagen werden die Kobras zischen.
80 Denn die Brennesseln werden Terrassen und Höfe erschüttern.
Denn die Börse wird eine Moospyramide sein.

Denn nach den Gewehren werden Lianen kommen
Und zwar bald, sehr bald, sehr bald.
Arme Wall Street!

85 Die Maske. Seht nur, die Maske!
Wie sie ihr Waldgift speit
Über die unzureichende Angst von New York![29]

Der Bezug zur Tradition des mittelalterlichen Totentanzes, der bereits im Titel des Gedichts deutlich erkennbar ist, erfolgt auf unterschiedlichen Ebenen.[30] Zum einen greift García Lorca auf wesentliche Strukturmerkmale des Totentanzes zurück, wie z.B. die plötzliche Ankunft des Todes, die Einberufung derjenigen, die daran teilnehmen werden, das Defilé usw. Er nimmt jedoch zugleich fundamentale Veränderungen vor, die sich vor allem auf die Negierung der christlichen Eschatologie beziehen. Während dem mittelalterlichen Totentanz die Heilsgewissheit zugrunde liegt und der irdischen Vergänglichkeit das Konzept ewiger Glückseligkeit gegenüberstellt, erweist sich in »Danza de la muerte« die christliche Glaubensgewissheit als obsolet. Zudem wird der Tanz bei García Lorca nicht mehr innerhalb eines abstrakten oder allegorischen Rahmens situiert, sondern ist konkret im Hier und Jetzt des Sprechers verankert; er findet in der New Yorker Wall Street während des Börsenkrachs statt.

Zum anderen erscheint der Tod bei García Lorca in Gestalt einer tanzenden Maske, in der die mittelalterliche Tradition des Spielmanns erkennbar ist. Die mittelalterliche Tradition des Totentanzes hat sich im Spannungsfeld unterschiedlicher medialer Inszenierungen und Aufführungspraktiken entwickelt; alle künstlerischen Realisierungen zeichnen sich jedoch dadurch aus, dass sie Tanz, Musik und Rhythmik konnotieren.[31] García Lorca knüpft

---

29 | García Lorca: Totentanz.

30 | Zu den Vorstufen des Totentanzes und den wichtigsten Merkmalen der mittelalterlichen Tradition vgl. Rosenfeld: Der mittelalterliche Totentanz, S. 1-79; zur Verarbeitung des Totentanzes vom Mittelalter bis zum 19. Jahrhundert vgl. Gassen: Pest, Endzeit und Revolution; zu Totentanzversionen im 19. und 20. Jahrhundert vgl. Kasten: Gründerzeit, Kaiserreich und Weimarer Republik. Einen guten Überblick über die Totentanzverarbeitungen in der Literatur, Malerei und Musik des 19. und 20. Jahrhunderts geben die Aufsätze des Sammelbandes von Franz Link, insbesondere der Einleitungsartikel des Herausgebers; vgl. Link (Hg.): Tanz und Tod in Kunst und Literatur.

31 | Vgl. Rosenfeld: Der mittelalterliche Totentanz, S. 18-23; ebenso Gassen: Pest, Endzeit und Revolution, S. 19f. Darüber hinaus konkretisiert sich die Verknüpfung mit der Musik durch die zahlreichen musikalischen Kompositionen, die seit dem 19. Jahrhundert dem Totentanz gewidmet sind, z.B. Franz Liszts *Totentanz* für Klavier und

an die rhythmischen Strukturen dieser Tradition an, um einen dynamischen urbanen Textraum ästhetisch zu erschaffen.

Die Totenmaske wird mit transgressiven, zerstörerischen Elementen assoziiert, wie insbesondere in den Refrains deutlich wird: »Arena, caimán y miedo sobre Nueva York« (V. 20); »¡Cómo escupe veneno de bosque« (V. 86). Ebenso wie der mittelalterliche Tod besitzt die Maske eine Fidel (»vihuela«, V. 64). Die Totenmaske erscheint zwar nicht als Tanzpartner einzelner Menschen bzw. Toten, wird jedoch ebenfalls ausdrücklich mit Tanz in Verbindung gebracht: »El mascarón bailará entre columnas de sangre« (V. 45, »Die Maske wird tanzen durch Blut- und Zahlenkolonnen«). Die rhythmische Bewegung wird jedoch nicht nur auf der Ebene des Dargestellten explizit vom Sprecher benannt, sie drückt sich ebenfalls in der Struktur des gesamten Textes aus.

Der Refrain, der aus zwei bzw. drei Versen besteht und die jeweilige Aktivität der Maske benennt, erscheint viermal; am Anfang und Ende sowie zweimal im Verlauf des Textes. Durch die isolierte Stellung – sowie den Kursivdruck – hebt sich der Refrain von den übrigen Versen ab und unterteilt den Text in verschiedene Abschnitte. Auf den ersten relativ kurzen Teil (V. 3-18) folgen zwei längere (V. 21-49 und V. 52-84). Trotz der ungleichmäßigen Verteilung entsteht bereits aus der Wiederholungsstruktur ein rhythmischer Effekt, der dem Gedicht einen gewissen musikalischen Charakter verleiht. Die Musikalität des Textes wird gleich zu Beginn durch die lautliche Gestaltung noch unterstrichen: »El mascarón. Mirad el mascarón« (V. 1). Die auffallende M-Alliteration geht einher mit der gehäuften Verwendung der dunklen Vokale a und o. Diese Lautphänomene, die im Verlauf des Textes immer wieder auftreten, erzeugen einen musikalischen Klang der Signifikanten.

Nach der Wiederholung des Refrains ist die Maske in New York angekommen: »El mascarón. ¡Mirad el mascarón! / Arena, caimán y miedo sobre Nueva York.« (V. 19-20) Da das Ich die Ankunft der Maske in der Jetztzeit des Sprechens ankündigt, vermutet der Leser, dass im Folgenden aus einer präsentischen Wahrnehmungssituation heraus New York im Zeichen der Todesmaske beschrieben wird. Es folgt aber wiederum eine rückblickende Betrachtung. Der Sprecher erwähnt einzelne Elemente, wie z.B. »Desfiladeros de cal« (V. 21), »cielo vacío« (V. 21), »guano« (V. 22), »montañas invisibles« (V. 24), die sich vermutlich auf die New Yorker Straßenlandschaft beziehen. Wenn in den anschließenden Versen von einem weinenden Chinesen, dem Bankdirektor, dem »cruel silencio de la moneda« (V. 32) und der »Wall

---

Orchester (1849), Johann Georg Kastners *Les Danses des Morts* (1852), Camille Saint-Saëns' *Danse macabre* (1874), Hermann Reutters *Lübecker Totentanz* (1929); vgl. hierzu Massenkeil: Der Totentanz in der Musik des 19. und 20. Jahrhunderts; Fink: Der Totentanz in Bild und Klang.

Street« (V. 33) die Rede ist, wird der Bezug zum New Yorker Börsenkrach eindeutig. Vor dem Hintergrund des bereits erwähnten Refrains (vgl. V. 20) bleibt aber unklar, weshalb die Ankunft der Maske in der Wall Street nun aus der Retrospektive angekündigt wird: »el mascarón llegaba a Wall Street« (V. 33). Während der Sprecher im Refrain die momentane Wahrnehmungssituation beschreibt, die unter dem Eindruck der Totenmaske steht, gibt er in den Versen 21-33 offensichtlich den desolaten Zustand im New Yorker Börsenviertel unmittelbar vor ihrer Ankunft wieder.

Nach dem Eintreffen der Maske geht der Sprecher zunächst nicht weiter auf die konkrete Situation ein, sondern stellt Reflektionen allgemeiner Natur über die Maske an und betont dabei zweimal, dass die Wall Street kein ungewöhnlicher Ort für den Tanz sei, der nun bald stattfinden werde. Die Überlegungen des Sprechers, die im Präsens formuliert sind, werden damit in der Jetztzeit des Börsenkrachs verankert. Aus der momentanen Lage des Erlebens erwartet er die kommenden Zerstörungen. Der dritte Refrain deutet erneut die unmittelbar bevorstehende Katastrophe an. In den folgenden Versen wird jedoch wieder im Modus der Nachzeitigkeit der Zustand des Sprechers in der Stadt mit hermetischen Bildern umrissen (V. 52-60). Ab Vers 61 geht er konkreter auf den Totentanz ein und benennt diejenigen Gruppen, die an dem Tanz teilnehmen bzw. nicht teilnehmen dürfen. Bis zum Ende des Textes spricht das Ich dann im Präsens aus der unmittelbaren Situation des Erlebens heraus. Das Gedicht schließt mit der Ankündigung, dass der Tanz nun unmittelbar bevorstehe. Die viermalige Verwendung des Futurs gibt dabei deutlich zu erkennen, dass der eigentliche Tanz bis zum Ende des Gedichts noch nicht begonnen hat. Allerdings suggeriert der abschließende Refrain, dass die zerstörerische Kraft der Maske bereits einzusetzen scheint: »El mascarón, ¡Mirad el mascarón! / ¡Cómo escupe veneno de bosque / por la angustia imperfecta de Nueva York!« (V. 85-87)

Untersucht man zusammenfassend das gesamte Gedicht im Hinblick auf die Relation zwischen der Ebene des Dargestellten und der rhythmischen Gestaltung, lassen sich vier verschiedene Tempi erkennen. Zunächst wird durch die parallele Satz- und Versstruktur eine gleichmäßige Bewegung erzeugt, die im Zeichen des sukzessiven Erscheinens und Verschwindens einzelner visueller Eindrücke steht. Im zweiten Teil, in dem das Ich die Situation im Börsenviertel vor Ankunft der Maske beschreibt und danach allgemeine Überlegungen über den Tanz anstellt, sind die syntaktischen und metrischen Wiederholungsstrukturen weitaus weniger stark ausgeprägt. Die Verse sind im Vergleich zum vorausgehenden Abschnitt länger. Insgesamt hat sich die Geschwindigkeit verringert, was zugleich die reflexive Haltung des Sprechers widerspiegelt. Der verlangsamte Rhythmus wird ebenfalls nach dem nächsten Refrain beibehalten.

Erst wenn der Sprecher konkret auf den Tanz eingeht, nehmen die parallelen Strukturen und die Wiederholungen wieder zu, wodurch sich zugleich die Rhythmisierung des Textes wieder verstärkt. Die Verse bestehen ausschließlich aus der Aneinanderreihung analoger Satzfragmente, wodurch das Tempo unweigerlich gesteigert wird. Ab Vers 70 erfolgt nochmals eine Beschleunigung. Die Verse sind im Vergleich zu den vorausgehenden Teilen auffallend kurz: »¡Que no baile el Papa! / ¡No, que no baile el Papa!« (V. 70-71) Aus den Wortwiederholungen, den Alliterationen sowie der Häufung der Ausrufe entsteht ein musikalischer Rhythmus, der den Tanz bereits einzuleiten scheint; durch die sprachlichen Strukturen werden die unmittelbar bevorstehenden Tanzbewegungen vergegenwärtigt. Dies zeigt sich ebenfalls in dem abschließenden melodiösen Ausruf vor dem letzten Refrain »¡Ay, Wall Street!« (V. 84) Betrachtet man die Gesamtbewegung des Textes, so stellt man eine enge Verflechtung der semantischen, rhetorischen, syntaktischen, metrischen sowie lautlichen Ebene fest. Erst aus dem Zusammenwirken der verschiedenen Ebenen entsteht der jeweilige Rhythmus.

Innerhalb des Textraums entstehen demzufolge tänzerische Rhythmen einer Todesmaske, die auf die Zerstörung der Wall Street ausgerichtet sind. Die ästhetischen Rhythmen sind einerseits – im Sinne von García Lorcas Ablehnung der kapitalistischen Wirtschaftsordnung – als destruktive Gegenkraft zum Börsenlärm angelegt. Andererseits besitzen sie zugleich eine ästhetische Eigenständigkeit, die sich einer vollständigen Vereinnahmung für eine ideologische Lesart entzieht.

Zu der Entstehungszeit von »La Danza de la muerte« war die Wall Street tatsächlich noch das Zentrum des westlichen Börsenhandels, und der Börsenlärm entsprach dem konkreten Handelsalltag. Wenn die Bewegung Occupy Wall Street jedoch im Jahre 2011 – und erneut 2012 – bei der New Yorker Börse demonstriert, wird – entgegen der weltweiten Dezentrierung und Vernetzung der Finanzwelt – ein vertrauter architektonischer Topos wieder aktiviert. Über den akustischen Protest wird eine unmittelbare physisch-materielle Präsenz erzeugt, die innerhalb der Demonstrierenden eine Gemeinschaft entstehen lässt. Darüber hinaus stellt der Protestlärm eine akustische Gegenkraft zu einem Börsen-*noise* dar, der nur noch in unserem kollektiven Gedächtnis als nostalgisches Relikt besteht. Lärm ist eine Form des Protests, weil er Informations- und Kommunikationsprozesse stört. Er ist ein Störsignal und vermittelt nicht unmittelbar bedeutungstragende Zeichen. Aber auch Occupy weiß, dass dieser Protest nur mehr symbolisch funktioniert, weil die mediale Kommunikationsform der Börse schon längst nicht mehr die akustische ist und der sonische Topos in der Realität des aktuellen Börsenhandels keine Entsprechung mehr findet. Gegenüber der Wall Street, die García Lorca 1929 erlebte, lässt sich also eine eigentümliche Umkehrung feststellen. Während bei ihm der geisterhafte Tod in Form der Totenmaske den konkreten Schauplatz der Finanzspekulation heimsucht, ist es jetzt die Beschwörung durch ein konkret inszeniertes Lärmspektakel an dem Ort Wall Street, der inzwischen längst nur noch mythisch-symbolische Kulisse ist. Offenbar wird jedoch über den Lärm eine materielle Konkretisierung erzeugt, welche die Illusion entstehen lässt, dass damit auch der Feind – die Finanzspekulanten – konkret lokalisierbar, präsent und damit greifbar wird. Der Feind braucht ein Gesicht und einen Ort. Die globalisierte Finanzwirtschaft aber ist gesichtslos, überall und nirgends. Das Verstummen des Börsenlärms ist dafür das Symbol.

Bibliographie

Alten, Michael: Haifisch ohne Zähne: Stones »Wall Street«, in: Frankfurter Allgemeine Zeitung, 21. Oktober 2010, http://www.faz.net/aktuell/feuilleton/kino/video-filmkritiken/video-filmkritik-haifisch-ohne-zaehne-stones-wall-street-1105187.html (6.3.16).
Augoyard, Jean-François und Henry Torgue (Hg.): Sonic Experience – A Guide to Everyday Sound, Montreal 2005.
Bull, Michael und Les Back (Hg.): The Auditory Culture Reader. Oxford, New York 2003.
Buß, Christian: »Wall Street«-Fortsetzung: Ach Papa, sei doch nicht so geldgeil, in: Spiegel Online, 19. Oktober 2010, http://www.spiegel.de/kultur/kino/wall-street-fortsetzung-ach-papa-sei-doch-nicht-so-geldgeil-a-723909.html (6.3.16).
Cañas, Dionisio: The Poet and the city: Lorca in New York, in: Manuel Durán und Francesca Colecchia (Hg.): Lorca's legacy. Essays on Lorca's life, poetry, and theatre, New York 1991, S. 159-169.
Crispin, John: La Voz poética en Federico García Lorca: Del yo íntimo al yo profético, in: Nora de Marval-McNair (Hg.): Selected proceedings of the Singularidad y trascendencia conference, Colorado 1990, S. 243-250.
Fink, Monika: Der Totentanz in Bild und Klang – am Beispiel der Werke von Franz Liszt, Cesar Bresgen und Gerhard Schedl, in: Franz Link (Hg.): Tanz und Tod in Kunst und Literatur, Berlin 1993, S. 531-540.
Flint, Christopher: Flesh of the poet: Representations of the body in *Romancero gitano* and *Poeta en Nueva York*, in: Papers on Language and Literature 24 (1988), S. 177-211.
Friedrich, Sabine: Transformationen der Sinne. Formen dynamischer Wahrnehmung in der modernen spanischen Großstadtlyrik, München 2007.
García Lorca, Federico: Poeta en Nueva York, hg. v. Piero Menarini, 8. Aufl.,- Madrid 1990.

García Lorca, Federico: Conferencia-recital de Federico García Lorca sobre *Poeta en Nueva York*, in: Ders.: Poeta en Nueva York, hg. v. Piero Menarini, 8. Aufl., Madrid 1990, S. 167-178.

García Lorca, Federico: Totentanz, in: Ders.: Dichter in New York. Gedichte. Spanisch und deutsch. Übertragung von Martin von Koppenfels, Frankfurt/M. 2000, S. 45-49.

Gassen, Richard W.: Pest, Endzeit und Revolution. Totentanzdarstellungen zwischen 1348 und 1848, in: Friedrich W. Kasten (Hg.): Totentanz. Kontinuität und Wandel eines Bildthemas vom Mittelalter bis heute, Mannheim 1986, S. 11-26.

Geisst, Charles R.: Die Geschichte der Wall Street. Von den Anfängen bis zum Untergang Enrons, München 2007.

Ho, Karen Zouwen: Liquidated. An Ethnography of Wall Street, Durham 2009.

Kasten, Friedrich W. (Hg.): Totentanz. Kontinuität und Wandel eines Bildthemas vom Mittelalter bis heute, Mannheim 1986.

Kasten, Friedrich W.: Gründerzeit, Kaiserreich und Weimarer Republik – Totentanzdarstellungen zwischen 1871 und 1933, in: Ders.: (Hg.) Totentanz. Kontinuität und Wandel eines Bildthemas vom Mittelalter bis heute, Mannheim 1986, S. 43-229.

Kittler, Friedrich A., Thomas Macho und Sigrid Weigel (Hg.): Zwischen Rauschen und Offenbarung. Zur Kultur- und Mediengeschichte der Stimme, Berlin 2002.

Knouf, Nicholas: The Noises of Finance, in: Sounding Out!, 22. April 2013, http://soundstudiesblog.com/author/nknouf/ (6.3.16).

Link, Franz (Hg.): Tanz und Tod in Kunst und Literatur, Berlin 1993.

Link, Franz: Tanz und Tod in Kunst und Literatur: Beispiele, in: Ders. (Hg.): Tanz und Tod in Kunst und Literatur, Berlin 1993, S. 11-68.

Massenkeil, Günther: Der Totentanz in der Musik des 19. und 20. Jahrhunderts, in: Franz Link (Hg.): Tanz und Tod in Kunst und Literatur, Berlin 1993, S. 265-276.

Menarini, Piero: ›La Danza de la muerte‹ en *Poeta en Nueva York*, in: Boletín de la Fundación Federico García Lorca 10-11 (1992), S. 147-159.

Murphy, John J.: Technische Analyse der Finanzmärkte. Grundlagen, Methoden, Strategien, Anwendungen, München 2000.

Rosenfeld, Hellmut: Der mittelalterliche Totentanz. Entstehung – Entwicklung – Bedeutung (Beihefte zum Archiv für Kulturgeschichte, Heft 3), Köln 1954.

Schafer, Raymond Murray: The Tuning of the World, New York 1977.

Schoon, Andi und Alex Volmar: Informierte Klänge und geschulte Ohren. Zur Kulturgeschichte der Sonifikation, in: Dies. (Hg.): Das geschulte Ohr, Eine Kulturgeschichte der Sonifikation, Bielefeld 2012, S. 9-26.

Schulze, Holger (Hg.): Sound studies. Traditionen, Methoden, Desiderate, Bielefeld 2008.
Schulze, Holger (Hg.): Gespür – Empfindung – Kleine Wahrnehmungen, Klanganthropologische Studien, Bielefeld 2012.
Schulze, Holger und Christoph Wulf (Hg.): Klanganthropologie: Performativität – Imagination – Narration (Paragrana. Internationale Zeitschrift für Historische Anthropologie. Band 16, Heft 2), Berlin 2007.
Spehr, Georg: Funktionale Klänge, in: Ders. (Hg.): Funktionale Klänge. Hörbare Daten, klingende Geräte und gestaltete Hörerfahrungen, Bielefeld 2009, S. 9-15.
Sterne, Jonathan (Hg.): The Sound Studies Reader, London 2012.
Tharp, Van K.: Trade your way to financial freedom, New York u.a. 1999.

FILMOGRAPHIE

Margin Call (2011), Regie: Jeffrey C. Chandor, USA.
Wall Street (1987), Regie: Oliver Stone, USA.
Wall Street: Money Never Sleeps (2010), Regie: Oliver Stone, USA.

Environmental Audio Programming
Geräusch und Klang in virtuellen Welten

Bettina Schlüter

Friedrich Kittlers pointierte Bemerkung, »der Nebel im Feld der Dichtung« um 1800 erwecke den Anschein, »Texte seien hermeneutisch verstehbar und nicht programmiert-programmierend«,[1] ruft eindrücklich einen Diskurs in Erinnerung, der ästhetische Kommunikation als Interaktion ›reiner‹ Medien denkt. Störungs- und rauschfrei »spreche« der »Geist« zum »Geiste«,[2] um zugleich auf ein Dahinterliegendes, einen ›eigentlichen‹ Sinn, eine ›tiefere Wahrheit‹ zu verweisen. Es mag an diesen sehr fundamentalen Annahmen liegen, dass ein spezifisches ästhetisches Programm – zumindest im Bereich der Musik – so machtvoll fortgeschrieben werden konnte, dass die mit ihm verbundenen, autonomiemusikalischen Präferenzen als implizite Limitierungen oder gar Präskriptionen auch in den musikwissenschaftlichen Bereich bis weit in das 20. Jahrhundert hinein wirken konnten. Konkreter auf die Thematik dieses Bandes bezogen, heißt dies: Die Appräsentation eines »transzendentalen Signifikats«[3] (eines ›geistigen Gehalts‹ etc.) degradiert die strukturierende Eigenlogik von Signifikanten zu Störungen – und dies sowohl in Hinsicht auf die ›Autonomie‹, ›Originalität‹ und damit ›Authentizität‹ eines einzelnen Kunstwerkes, das sich nicht auf einen Stil, eine konventionalisierte musikalische Sprache verrechnen lassen darf, als auch in Hinsicht auf den Parameter des Klangs, der materiellen Dimension des Signifikanten, der ›reiner‹ Ton werden muss:

Der blosse Schall muss zum Klange, der Klang zum Tone, die Töne müssen zur Melodie, die Melodie muss zur Harmonie gleichsam organisirt werden, wenn Tonkunst oder Musik entstehen soll. Das Geistige der Musik aber ist eben ihr belebendes, beseelendes Prin-

---

1 | Kittler: Aufschreibesysteme 1800/1900, S. 31.
2 | Hoffmann: Recension Sinfonie par Louis van Beethoven. No. 5 des Sinfonies, Sp. 658.
3 | Kittler: Aufschreibesysteme 1800/1900, S. 18.

zip, durch welches eine blose [sic] Masse von Schall und Klang, Maas und Bestimmung, Wechselbeziehung, Ordnung und Einheit erhält.[4]

In der organischen Stufenfolge Schall, Klang, Ton, Komposition (d.h. Tonkunst) wird eine in sich bereits zum Klang hin geformte Natur Ursprung (und Legitimation) von Kunst und Kultur. Die gesamte Klangästhetik um 1800 richtet sich an dieser neuen Konstellation aus und durchbricht damit die bis dato durchaus gegebene Möglichkeit, musikalische Komposition und akustische Experimente im Rahmen eines theologisch überformten pythagoräischen Musikverständnisses oder einer Vorliebe für mechanische Klangerzeugung und musikalische Apparaturen in einen gemeinsamen Deutungshorizont einzubinden.

Die folgenden Ausführungen möchten sich jedoch nicht der lang währenden Allianz zwischen autonomieästhetischer Programmatik, kompositorischer Praxis und einer Präferenz für ›reine Medien‹ zuwenden, sondern in aller Kürze vier Konstellationen umreißen, die diese um 1800 entwickelte Tendenz, Musik von Geräusch, Sound und Rauschen möglichst trennscharf zu separieren, im Kontext anderer Argumentationslinien überschreiben, nivellieren oder gar umkehren. Diese vier Beispiele stellen allesamt Wege durch einen künstlich gezeugten akustischen Raum dar und verweisen auf unterschiedliche Modi seiner auditiven Aneignung – pointierter formuliert: seiner medienanthropologischen, psychotechnischen, kulturellen und schließlich auch digitalen ›Programmierung‹; sie sollen exemplarisch Wissensformationen zu erkennen geben, in denen allesamt – obgleich aus jeweils anderen Gründen – Geräusch und Musik (wieder) in einem gemeinsamen Sinnhorizont erscheinen.

1. Der Weg der Statue

In seiner 1754 erstmals publizierten »Abhandlung über die Empfindungen«[5] diskutiert Étienne Bonnot de Condillac in der Form eines Gedankenexperiments, d.h. am Beispiel einer Statue, die Schritt für Schritt und in verschiedenen Kombinationen ihre Sinneswahrnehmungen erweitert, auf welche Weise sich menschliche Vorstellungskraft, Erkenntnis- und Reflexionsvermögen entwickeln. In jedem einzelnen der fünf Sinne sei, so schlussfolgert Condillac, das Potential zur Entfaltung aller »Seelenvermögen«[6] enthalten. Wie der Geruchssinn, der Gesichtssinn und der Geschmack ermöglicht es

---

4 | Michaelis: Über den Geist der Tonkunst und andere Schriften, S. 200.
5 | Condillac: Abhandlung über die Empfindungen.
6 | Ebd., S. 38ff.

auch der Hörsinn der Statue, zu »erinnern, zu vergleichen, zu urteilen, zu unterscheiden«, »abstrakte Begriffe, Vorstellungen von Zahl und Dauer« zu entwickeln.[7] Die Unterscheidung zwischen Ton und Geräusch, die Condillac in einer Fußnote zugleich auf der Grundlage akustischer Forschungen seiner Zeit als unterschiedlich ausgeprägtes Verhältnis zwischen Grundton und »Nebentönen«[8] definiert, besetzt im Kontext seines Argumentationsaufbaus die Unterscheidung zwischen »Lust und Unlust«, eine Unterscheidung, die als Differenz, d.h. im Modus des Vergleichs, die Antriebskraft der Statue verstärkt, Wünsche und Vorstellungen sowie das Wissen um das Mögliche zu entwickeln. Dieser differenztheoretische Zugang prägt die gesamte Abhandlung und findet seinen eigentlichen Kern in der Herleitung der Unterscheidungsfähigkeit, die die Statue zwischen sich selbst und ihrer Umwelt zu ziehen vermag; denn zunächst einmal verfügt diese über keinerlei Vorstellung eines ›Außen‹: »Wenn ihr Ohr getroffen wird, so wird sie die Empfindung werden, die sie erfährt. [...] Es ist der Schall, der in ihr lebt. Demnach werden wir sie beliebig in ein Geräusch, einen Schall, eine Symphonie verwandeln, denn sie vermutet nicht, dass es etwas anderes als sie gebe.«[9]

Es ist bekanntermaßen der Tastsinn, dem Condillac die Möglichkeit zuspricht, in der Differenzerfahrung zwischen der Berührung des eigenen und eines fremden Körpers eine erste Grenze zwischen Selbst und Außenwelt zu ziehen, Vorstellungen über räumliche Ausdehnung zu gewinnen und sich letztlich auch in Bewegung zu setzen. Die Etablierung dieser neuen Dimension, der Bewegung im Raum, ermöglicht es dem Tastsinn, die anderen Sinne – wie Condillac es nennt – zu »unterweisen«.[10] Interessant im Rahmen der Thematik des Bandes erscheint mir, dass an dieser entscheidenden Stelle, an der die Statue in der Unterscheidung zwischen Innen und Außen das Bewusstsein eines Selbst entwickelt, Condillac allein Geräusche anführt, die – in Kombination mit dem Tastsinn – die erforderlichen Erkenntnisimpulse vermitteln:

Sie findet, was sie nicht suchte; denn nachdem sie einen tönenden Körper ergriffen hat, bewegt sie ihn absichtslos hin und her, und wenn sie ihn durch Zufall bald näher ans Ohr, bald weiter davon weg gehalten hat, so reicht das hin, sie zu wiederholtem Annähern und Entfernen zu veranlassen. [...] Jedoch beobachtet sie, daß ihr Ohr nur auf Veranlassung dieses Körpers modifiziert wird. Sie vernimmt Töne, wenn sie ihn hin und her bewegt, vernimmt aber nichts mehr, wenn sie es sein lässt. Mithin urteilt sie, dass diese Töne von ihm kommen. [...] Anstatt sie also als Daseinsweisen ihrer selbst

---

7 | Ebd., S. 38f.
8 | Ebd., S. 41.
9 | Ebd., S. 40.
10 | Ebd., ab S. 120.

wahrzunehmen, nimmt sie sie als Daseinsweisen des tönenden Körpers wahr. [...] Die Statue beginnt ihre Versuche mit den Dingen, die sie mit der Hand erreichen kann. Demzufolge meint sie anfänglich bei jedem Geräusch, das ihr Ohr trifft, sie brauche, wenn sie den Körper erreichen wolle, der es von sich gibt, nur den Arm auszustrecken; denn sie hat noch nicht gelernt, ihn für weiter entfernt zu halten. Aber da sie darin irrt, macht sei einen Schritt, macht noch einen und beobachtet, daß in dem Maße, wie sie vorwärts geht, das Geräusch zunimmt, bis zu dem Augenblick, wo der Körper, der es erzeugt, ihr so nahe ist, wie er nur sein kann.[11]

Auf diese Weise lernt die Statue, Entfernungen und Richtungen zu unterscheiden und den »Gesang der Vögel, dort das Geräusch des Wasserfalls, weiter entfernt das Rauschen der Bäume, einen Augenblick später das Getöse des Donners oder eines furchtbaren Sturmes«[12] wahrzunehmen. Ein durch den Tastsinn ›unterwiesener‹ Hörsinn externalisiert die Höreindrücke, schreibt sie somit einer akustischen Umwelt zu und vermittelt zugleich der Statue ein Bewusstsein davon, dass sie überhaupt über so etwas wie einen Hörsinn verfügt. In der Selbstprogrammierung der Wahrnehmung auf eine Innen/Außen-Differenz hin spielen mithin die Koordination der Sinne, die Materialität des eigenen und des fremden Körpers, Kollisionen, Bewegungen, Abstände, Richtungen und Raumeigenschaften eine zentrale Rolle, nicht jedoch Differenzen zwischen »Geräusch«, »Schall« oder »Symphonie«.[13]

Im Verlauf des 19. Jahrhunderts leiten Forschungen zur Struktur und Eigenlogik des ›Hörsinns‹, zum Zusammenspiel von akustischen und physiologischen Parametern, zur Vermessung von Schall und Nervenlaufzeiten dann jene technischen Innovationen ein, die die medienanthropologische Grundkonstellation einer prozessualen Selbstexternalisierung von auditiver Wahrnehmung, wie sie Condillac beschreibt, in eine komplexere Relation von akustischen Ereignissen und Informationsverarbeitung überführen. Die auf diesen Forschungen basierenden technischen Erfindungen, insbesondere der Phonograph, initiieren in der nun anders definierten Grenzziehung zwischen einem Selbst und seiner Umwelt dann jene Rückkopplungen, die unter dem Begriff der Psychotechnik um 1900 die neuen Wissensfelder aus Hirnforschung, Psychoanalyse, Technik und Kulturforschung zusammenschließen und den Interferenzen, den Störungen, dem Rauschen (sowohl literal als auch metaphorisch verwendet) eine eigene, systematisch nicht mehr wegzudenkende Position zuweisen. Die Situierung medialer Apparaturen an der Grenze zwischen Selbst und Umwelt, die dadurch neuerlich exponierte Fragilität der Grenze zwischen Innen und Außen, begründet im

---
11 | Ebd., S. 126, 128.
12 | Ebd., S. 126.
13 | Ebd., S. 43.

Verlauf des 20. Jahrhundert dann gerade im Kino eine eigene Tradition der selbstreflexiven Auseinandersetzung mit der Bild- und Tonspur – eine Entwicklung, die in avancierter Form bis zu David Lynchs Filmexperimenten[14] führt. Ich möchte an dieser Stelle als zweites der angekündigten Beispiele deshalb auf eine Filmproduktion von 1974 eingehen – *The Conversation* –, die sich in der Tradition des New Hollywood auf selbstreferentielle und medienreflexive Weise mit dem Soundtrack im Spannungsfeld von Musik, Geräusch und Sprache auseinandersetzt. Regie führte Francis Ford Coppola, für die Tonspur war Walter Murch verantwortlich, der wenige Jahre später in den Credits für *Apocalypse Now* als erster ›Sound Designer‹ in der Geschichte des Films gelistet wurde.

2. DER WEG DES ABHÖRSPEZIALISTEN

Die in der ersten Szene des Films exponierte urbane *soundscape* des Union Square in San Francisco bildet – wie dem Kinopublikum nach einiger Zeit durch das Auftreten akustischer Interferenzen zu verstehen gegeben wird – einen bereits durch Aufzeichnungsverfahren und Richtmikrophone gefilterten Klang. Diese Filter schalten sich somit zwischen Sinneswahrnehmung und Umgebungsklänge. Im Rahmen der weiteren Filmhandlung besteht die Herausforderung für den Protagonisten des Films, den Abhörspezialisten Harry Caul, zunächst darin, eine entscheidende Passage des aufgezeichneten Dialogs unter den komplexen Überlagerungen von Musik und Umgebungsgeräuschen klanglich zu isolieren.[15] Durch den Einsatz von technischen Apparaturen, die den Abstand zwischen Signal und Rauschen, d.h. die Differenz zwischen Sprache und den anderen akustischen Ereignissen, erhöhen, tritt die entscheidende Dialogpassage schließlich als intelligible Struktur hervor.[16] Sie konfrontiert Caul mit einer traumatischen Erfahrung aus seiner Vergangenheit: den durch seine Arbeit für einen früheren Auftraggeber indirekt verursachten Tod mehrerer Menschen. Die daraus resultierende innere Affizierung des Protagonisten inszeniert *The Conversation* als Rückkopplungsschleife zwischen psychischer und medialer Apparatur; die Herkunft der auditiven Eindrücke – ob aus der akustischen Umwelt stammend oder als

---

14 | Vgl. *Eraserhead* (1977), *Lost Highway* (1997), *Mulholland Drive* (2001) und insbesondere *Inland Empire* (2006).
15 | *The Conversation* (1974), DVD-Edition, Track 3.
16 | Mit der Exposition der Sprachverständlichkeit als Handlungsmotiv zitiert *The Conversation* zugleich ein Dogma des traditionellen Hollywood-Films, von dem sich New Hollywood im Anschluss an Vorbilder der Nouvelle Vague filmästhetisch abgrenzt. Vgl. dazu auch den Beitrag von Kay Kirchmann in diesem Band.

Effekt eigener Projektionen – wird zunehmend diffus. In der auditiven Wahrnehmung kollabiert Stück für Stück die Unterscheidungsfähigkeit zwischen Information und Rauschen, zwischen Außen und Innen – eine Unterscheidungsfähigkeit, die Condillacs Statue sich mit umgekehrtem Richtungsimpuls schrittweise als Erkenntnisprozess erarbeitet hat. Der sich dann erneut ereignende Mord wird auf der Tonspur als point of hearing des Protagonisten inszeniert, der in den Interferenzen zwischen psychischen Obsessionen und Aufzeichnungsmedien den panischen Schrei des vermeintlichen Opfers nurmehr in medial-technischer Verzerrung als klanglich bearbeiteten Loop wahrnehmen kann.[17]

Die letzte Wendung, die der Film bereit hält, liegt schließlich in der sowohl dem Kinopublikum als auch dem Protagonisten vermittelten Einsicht, dass das Rauschen und die psychischen Projektionen die Eindeutigkeit, die Strukturiertheit, die Intelligibilität der Sprache selbst unterlaufen, dass Sinn nicht durch das Medium der Sprache vermittelt, sondern durch vorgelagerte Strukturen (die semantischen Kontexte, die Erinnerung, die diskursiven Rahmungen) ›programmiert‹ wird. Den Versuch, Sinn aus den Medien bzw. Sprechakten selbst herauszufiltern, indem Signale vom Rauschen separiert werden, charakterisiert der Film letztlich als pathologischen Akt, der in ein Desaster mündet.

Abbildung 1: The Conversation, *1:58:00, Schlussframe.*

Während der medienanthropologische Zugang einer Differenzierung zwischen Geräusch, Schall und Musik im Kontext des Erkenntnisprozesses nur eine untergeordnete Funktion zuschreibt, verweist die hier mit dem Begriff der Psychotechnik gekennzeichnete Allianz verschiedener Wissensgebiete auf eine bereits fest etablierte Unterscheidung zwischen Information und

---

17 | *The Conversation*, Track 11.

Rauschen, zwischen strukturierten und unstrukturierten Lauten. Das Kollabieren dieser Unterscheidung wird dann als Prozess inszeniert, der die Affizierung des Intelligiblen mit dem Unwillkürlichen, dem Unbewussten selbst- und medienreflexiv in Szene setzt. Ausgespart bleiben in beiden vorausgehenden Fallbeispielen Facetten einer kulturellen ›Programmierung‹, die – wie das nächste Beispiel zeigt – eine eigene Systematisierungslogik von Lärm und Störung jenseits aller bislang thematisierten Differenzierungen zwischen Musik, Klang und Geräusch entwickelt.

3. DER WEG DES »CHAUVINISTISCHEN OHRES«

In diesem dritten Beispiel wird der Weg eines Ohres durch einen öffentlichen Raum thematisiert – eines Ohres, das vor dem Hintergrund des Jugoslawienkonfliktes ethnische und religiöse Differenzen verschärft wahrnimmt und zum Entsetzen seiner eigenen Trägerin, der kroatischen Schriftstellerin Dubravka Ugresic, diese Differenzen jenseits aller Normen einer *political correctness* als Lärm codiert. Im Abschnitt »Alle Fremden piepsen«[18] verdeutlicht Ugresic am Beispiel einiger Alltagsszenen ihr ›gespaltenes‹ Verhältnis zu ihrem eigenmächtig agierenden Ohr:

> Er marschiert auf mich zu wie ein Soldat in voller Kriegsausrüstung, schreitet entschlossen auf einer imaginären Geraden, die Ohren mit iPod-Stöpseln verstopft. [...] Seinen Körper benutzt er als einen unsichtbaren Pflug, alles wie Schnee vor sich wegräumend. Ich trete unterwürfig zur Seite. Immer mehr Leute benutzen im öffentlichen Raum ihren Körper als Schneepflug. [...] Während ich an der Kasse eines Lebensmittelgeschäfts in der Schlange stehe, bohrt sich wie ein plötzlicher Schmerz der laute Ruf eines Muezzins in mein Ohr. Ich drehe mich um und erblicke eine zierliche junge Frau in einem langen Jeansrock, an den Füßen mit glitzernden hellblauen Pailletten besetzte Flip-Flops, auf dem Kopf ein Tuch. Sie nimmt ihr Mobiltelefon aus der Handtasche und drückt darauf herum. Vielleicht mahnt das Handy sie, dass es Zeit ist fürs Gebet, denke ich versöhnlich. Inzwischen ist auch mein Ohr versöhnt. Dann aber wird es von einem neuen Geräusch durchbohrt: Eine junge Chinesin in der Schlange kreischt etwas Unverständliches in ihr Handy. Die Stimmen junger Chinesinnen und die junger Marokkaner sind ähnlich durchdringend, denke ich. Dann schiebe ich verschämt diesen Gedanken beiseite. Ich schwöre, das war nicht ich, das war mein Ohr, geschult in einer Gegend, in der das hohe C nie besonders geschätzt wurde. Ein chauvinistisches Ohr! [...] Mein Ohr ist gereizt, an so etwas nicht gewöhnt, intolerant. Mein Ohr ist ein widerlicher controlfreak.[19]

---

18 | Ugresic: Karaokekultur.
19 | Ebd., S. 177f.

Ob Handyklingelton, Gesang, Musik, Geräusch, Sprache: Alles ist Lärm. Die Egalisierung dieser verschiedenen Phänomene vollzieht sich vor dem Hintergrund eines Wissens um kulturelle und religiöse Konfliktlinien im Kontext einer vielfältig ausdifferenzierten urbanen Klanglandschaft, deren akustische Interferenzen nicht länger als positive Varianten von Transkulturalität oder kultureller Hybridität wahrgenommen werden (wie dies beispielshalber Fatih Akin in *Crossing the Bridge – The Sound of Istanbul* nahelegt), sondern als Friktionen in einem Hörraum, der die wechselseitige Koordination individueller Artikulations- und Bewegungsformen preisgibt zugunsten von Macht- und Kontrollgesten. Der öffentliche Raum als einstmals auch gemeinsam verwaltete akustische Umwelt zerfällt auf diese Weise in territoriale Einheiten. Das »chauvinistische Ohr« löst aus der akustischen Umgebung Musik, Geräusche, Stimmen, Klänge als akustische Signale und als Markierung von Dominanzansprüchen heraus, rechnet sie auf ethnische und religiöse Gruppen hoch und lässt sich in diesem Wahrnehmungsprozess von keiner selbstreflexiven Instanz, einem distanzierten Ich, auf tolerantere Wahrnehmungsformen umprogrammieren. Das kulturell sozialisierte und kulturhistorisch kundige Ohr definiert die Grenze zwischen »Lust und Unlust« (um noch einmal Condillacs Begriffe zu bemühen) auf ganz eigene Weise, und zwar nicht primär auf der Grundlage von (psycho-)akustischen Parametern, sondern aufgrund von kultureller Signifikanz. Das ›Ich‹ ist bei diesem Vorgang ähnlich ohnmächtig der kulturell-diskursiven Programmierung seiner eigenen auditiven Wahrnehmung ausgeliefert wie der Protagonist von *The Conversation* den Rückkopplungen zwischen psychischen Prozessen und medialen Aufzeichnungs-, Bearbeitungs- und Wiedergabeverfahren.

Strukturiert und klassifiziert in diesem Beispiel somit ein kulturell ›vorprogrammiertes‹ Ohr ein akustisches Umfeld (samt der dadurch allererst erzeugten Unterscheidungen zwischen Klang, Geräusch, Lärm), so kann umgekehrt auch das akustische Umfeld (oder zumindest dessen Raumparameter) ganz in das Ohr des Hörers selbst verlagert – oder präziser formuliert: einem *listener object* zugewiesen – werden. Diese vierte Variante eines *Environmental Audio Programming* führt in den Bereich digitaler Informations- und Datenverarbeitung.

4. DER WEG DES AVATARS

In *Doom 3*, einem Computerspiel aus dem Jahre 2004, steuern die Spielerinnen und Spieler einen Avatar (einen *Marine*) durch eine Umwelt (eine von feindlichen Kreaturen übernommene Raumstation auf dem Mars). Die akustische Umgebung wird – abgestimmt auf die Bewegungen des Avatars im Raum – per Lautsprecherausgabe an die Wahrnehmung der Spielerinnen und Spieler vor den Computern zurückgeleitet. Anders als im Film muss in einem Computerspiel die Korrelation von Bild, Ton und Raumbewegung in ein offenes, vom Verhalten der Spielerinnen und Spieler abhängiges Möglichkeitsfeld überführt werden. Sowohl die kompositorischen Verfahren als auch die technische Implementierung der Soundschicht haben diese Variabilität auf der Zeitachse zu berücksichtigen und somit auf einer anderen Ebene der Strukturabstraktion anzusetzen: Pre- und Endmix müssen in ›Echtzeit‹, d.h. in unmittelbarer Synchronisation mit der spielerischen Interaktion, berechnet werden. Diese Notwendigkeit, musikalisch-klangliche Syntax und spielerische Interaktion in ihren jeweiligen Rhythmen aufeinander abzustimmen, stellt eine spezielle Herausforderung innerhalb der Audioproduktion dar.[20] Eine praktikable Möglichkeit besteht darin, dramaturgische Intensitäten über eine Staffelung mehr oder weniger verdichteter Klangschichten auf- und abzubauen, also in flexibler Abstimmung mit dem jeweiligen Gameplay Änderungen der klanglichen Textur herbeizuführen, ohne syntaktische Brüche zu erzeugen. Diese Layertechnik, die auch *Doom 3* nutzt, löst dann – gleichsam als Konsequenz aus den Synchronisationsbemühungen zwischen Audio-Engine und Spiele-Engine – die Differenzen zwischen Musik und Geräusch sowie, eng hiermit verbunden, die Unterscheidung zwischen extra- und intradiegetischen Klängen weitgehend auf.

Abbildung 2: Screenshot aus Doom 3.

---

20 | Vgl. hierzu im Detail Boer: Game Audio Programming.

Die einzelnen Layer setzen sich in *Doom 3* ihrerseits aus zwei Typen von Klängen zusammen: Zum einen prägt das Spiel eine durchgehende, zwischen Musik und Geräusch changierende Klangschicht, eine Art Grundrauschen, aus dem sich einzelne distinkte Elemente herauslösen; zum anderen sind in der virtuellen Welt eine Vielzahl so genannter *soundemitter* platziert, die die Umgebungsgeräusche der Raumstation (z.B. den Lärm von Maschinen, das Surren der Ventilatoren etc.) erzeugen. Die von ihnen ausgehenden Klänge und Geräusche werden aktiviert, wenn sie in den Hörradius des Avatars gelangen; ihre Abstands- und Richtungskoordinaten werden mit denen des Avatars (bzw. seiner Kameraposition) bis zu dreißigmal in der Sekunde abgeglichen.

Der Audiotreiber, der für diesen Abgleich zuständig ist, ›bemerkt‹ gleichsam, was in der virtuellen Welt passiert; er lädt die entsprechenden Audiodateien und eruiert, auf welche Weise sie – angepasst an die jeweils aktuelle Koordinatenrelationen sowie die Umgebungsakustik – abzumischen sind. In diesem Prozess werden Abstrahlwinkel und die relative Geschwindigkeit beider Instanzen zueinander bestimmt und über die Modifikation des Frequenzgangs (bis hin zur Berechnung des Dopplereffekts) simuliert. Klangliche Maskierungseffekte werden auf der Grundlage psychoakustischer Daten kalkuliert, während auch Anteile von direktem und indirektem Schall, von Verzögerungen, Ausschwingvorgang, Hall und Echo auf der Basis der virtuellen topographischen Gegebenheiten und Materialeigenschaften jeweils in Echtzeit berechnet werden. Die akustischen Raumparameter – samt komplexer Überlagerungen mehrerer Raumakustiken respektive ihrer wechselseitigen Interpolation über Schallhindernisse hinweg – werden als so genannte *Potentially Audible Sets*[21] dem Avatar respektive der Kamera als *listener object* zugewiesen. Die Raumakustik als Kombination prädefinierter Parameter wird auf diese Weise, wie oben bereits erwähnt, in das virtuelle ›Ohr‹ des Avatars verlagert. Die akustische Simulation beginnt daher im Spiel – dies zeigen all diese Details – als virtuelle Rekonstruktion des Hörsinns zu wirken, die auf dem Zusammenspiel zwischen dem algorithmisch generierten Ohr des *listener objects* und den Ohren der Spielerinnen und Spieler beruht, die über Kopfhörer oder Lautsprecher an dieser auditiven Wahrnehmung partizipieren.

Die zentrale Rolle, die Geräusche gerade auch in der Auflösung der Unterscheidung gegenüber musikalischen Klängen in Computerspielen gewinnen, gründet sich jedoch nicht nur auf der Notwendigkeit einer flexiblen Synchronisation von Klangdramaturgie und Gameplay, sondern basiert darüber hinaus auf Momenten, die uns zum Teil in ähnlicher Weise schon in den

---

21 | Vgl. ebd., S. 544ff.

vorausgegangenen Beispielen begegnet sind und die hier gleichsam auf der Ebene des Virtuellen noch einmal verdoppelt werden.

Dies betrifft zum einen – und ganz offensichtlich – die Relevanz, die diegetische Klänge, d.h. vornehmlich Geräusche, in interaktiven Medien gewinnen, da sie Optionen einer Orientierung im Raum ermöglichen (ein Aspekt, der schon für Condillacs Statue zentral war). Auf der Grundlage eines über den Avatar an den Spieler weitervermittelten ›Hörsinns‹ können Informationen über Objekte, Distanzen und Richtungswinkel gewonnen werden, die für die spielerische Interaktion essentiell sind.

Zum anderen gewinnt eine solche virtuelle Rekonstruktion des Hörsinns eine neue Dimension, wenn sie an die Programmierung einer künstlichen Intelligenz rückgebunden wird. In diesem Fall verfügt nicht nur der eigene Avatar über ein entsprechendes Abbild der akustischen Ereignisse und Strukturen, sondern auch die anderen Figuren des Spiels, die Non-Player-Characters (NPCs), werden in die Lage versetzt, Klänge und Geräusche gemäß menschlicher Perzeption ›wahrzunehmen‹ und sich entsprechend zu ›verhalten‹. In solch einem Fall nimmt auch die Interaktion zwischen Spieler und NPCs den Charakter einer Simulation an. Geräusche sind als zentrale Konstituente einer akustischen Umwelt somit Katalysatoren der spezifischen Potentiale, die in Computerspielen als interaktiven Medien liegen.

Zum dritten zeigt das Beispiel *Doom 3*, dass die Akzentuierung des Hörsinns in Relation zu einer komplexen klanglichen Umwelt zugleich ein intensiviertes Zusammenspiel mit anderen Sinneswahrnehmungen initiiert. Die Profilierung der Hörperspektive des Avatars wird auch als Ort der Wahrnehmung physiologischer Reaktionen des eigenen Körpers markiert (beispielshalber in Form von Herzschlag- und Atemgeräuschen). Somatische Geräusche fungieren als Indikatoren der Materialität von virtuellen Objekten, denn sie verleihen ihnen im Zusammenspiel mit Oberflächentexturen, mit speziellen Techniken der Computergraphik und der Physik-Engine einen starken Eindruck von physischer Solidität.

Wenn Kittler in Anlehnung an Lacan diagnostiziert, dass Sound das »Unaufschreibbare, das Reale, an der Musik und unmittelbar ihre Technik« sei,[22] dann gewinnt diese materielle Dimension von Schall nicht nur Signifikanz in Differenz zu einer symbolisch fixierten Notenschrift, hinter der im Aufschreibesystem um 1800 geistige Operationen oder die Stimme des Komponisten als Instanzen des Imaginären aufscheinen, sondern es bildet im Virtuellen das Reale als Modus einer digital simulierten analogen Dimension des Materiellen und Taktilen ab. Und umgekehrt gewinnt ›Musik‹ um noch einmal auf die ersten beiden Beispiele einzugehen, nur in spezifischen (allerdings sehr machtvollen und einflussreichen) Kontexten, d.h. vornehmlich

---

22 | Kittler: Draculas Vermächtnis, S. 133.

in den ästhetischen Diskursen des 19. Jahrhunderts und ihren Ablegern im 20. Jahrhundert, eine dem Geräusch diametral gegenübergestellte Differenzfunktion – eine Unterscheidung, die im Horizont der hier exemplarisch angerissenen medienanthropologischen, psychotechnischen, kulturhistorischen und digital-virtuellen Selbst- und Fremdprogrammierungen schon längst auf vielfältige Weise unterlaufen und durch andere Bezugssysteme und Allianzen ersetzt worden ist.

BIBLIOGRAPHIE

Boer, James: Game Audio Programming, Hingham/MA 2002.
Condillac, Étienne Bonnot de: Abhandlung über die Empfindungen, Hamburg 1983.
Hoffmann, Ernst Theodor Amadeus: Recension Sinfonie par Louis van Beethoven. No. 5 des Sinfonies, in: *Allgemeine musikalische Zeitung*, Jg. 12, 11. Juli 1810, Sp. 630-642; 18. Juli 1810, Sp. 652-659.
Kittler, Friedrich A.: Draculas Vermächtnis. Technische Schriften, Leipzig 1993.
Kittler, Friedrich A.: Aufschreibesysteme 1800/1900. 3., vollständig überarbeitete Neuauflage, München 1995.
Michaelis, Christian Friedrich: Über den Geist der Tonkunst und andere Schriften, hg. von Lothar Schmidt, Chemnitz 1997.
Ugresic, Dubravka: Karaokekultur, Berlin 2012.

FILME UND SPIELE

Apocalypse Now (1979), Regie: Francis Ford Coppola, USA.
Crossing the Bridge – The Sound of Istanbul (2005), Regie: Fatih Akin, D.
Doom 3 (2004), id Software, Activision.
Eraserhead (1977), Regie: David Lynch, USA.
Inland Empire (2006), Regie: David Lynch, USA.
Lost Highway (1997), Regie: David Lynch, USA.
Mulholland Drive (2001), Regie: David Lynch, USA.
The Conversation (1974), Regie: Francis Ford Coppola, USA.

Autorinnen und Autoren

George Brock-Nannestad, Dipl.-Ing., ist seit langen Jahren auf dem Feld der Medienbewahrung tätig, u.a. an der Konservatorenschule der Kunstakademie in Kopenhagen. Im Rahmen von Patent Tactics forscht er quellenkritisch zu Schallaufnahmen und zur Geschichte der Schallaufnahmetechnik. Jüngste Publikation: »The mechanization of performance studies«, in: *Early Music* XLII/4 (2014), S. 623-630.

Ben Byrne is an academic, musician, artist and organizer interested in sonic philosophy, art and culture. He is currently teaching in Media & Communication at RMIT University in Melbourne, Australia. He runs the Avantwhatever contemporary experimental music label (www.avantwhatever.com). Academic Audio on »Place Time (Sounds): Hearing Manfred Werder's 2005«, produced and presented at the Fluid Sound 2015 Conference in Copenhagen, now on http://seismograf.org/fokus/fluid-sounds/place-time-sounds

Sabine Friedrich, Prof. Dr. phil., seit 2005 Inhaberin des Lehrstuhls für Romanistik, insbesondere Literatur- und Kulturwissenschaft an der Friedrich-Alexander-Universität Erlangen-Nürnberg; seit 2015 Sprecherin des Interdisziplinären Zentrums für Literatur und Kultur der Gegenwart; Forschungsschwerpunkte: Narratologie, Inter-/Transmedialität, Theatralität und Performanz aus medienhistorischer Perspektive, Beziehungen zwischen Mediensystemen und Wahrnehmungsstrukturen. Jüngste Publikation: »La performance teatral de las máquinas maravillosas: Configuraciones ambivalentes de la técnica y el teatro en los siglos XVI y XVII (En línea)«, in: *Olivar* 16(23), http://www.memoria.fahce.unlp.edu.ar/art_revistas/pr.7063/pr.7063.pdf.

Christine Ganslmayer, Dr. phil., Akademische Rätin am Lehrstuhl für Germanistische Sprachwissenschaft an der Friedrich-Alexander-Universität Erlangen-Nürnberg. Hauptarbeitsgebiete: Historische deutsche Sprachwissenschaft (Mittelhochdeutsch, Frühneuhochdeutsch), Wortbildung,

Lexikologie, Syntax, Textlinguistik, Sprachkontaktforschung. Jüngste Publikation: »Sprachkombination und Sprachmischung in deutsch-lateinischen Mischtexten. Überlegungen zu Analyse, Formen und Funktionen«, in: Claudia Wich-Reif (Hg.): *Historische Sprachkontaktforschung*. Berlin, Boston 2016 S. 76-115.

Sven Grampp, PD Dr. Phil., Akademischer Rat am Institut für Theater- und Medienwissenschaft der Friedrich-Alexander-Universität Erlangen-Nürnberg. Arbeitsschwerpunkte: Space Race, Fernsehserien. Jüngste Publikation: *Medienwissenschaft*, Konstanz: utb 2016.

Uta von Kameke-Frischling, Dozentin für Gesang an der Musikschule Friedrichshain-Kreuzberg und für Stimmbildung an der Lehranstalt für Logopädie, CharitéCampus (Berlin); Sängerin (Schwerpunkt im französischen Lied um 1900). Künstlerische Leiterin der Ribbecker Sommernacht 2006, 2008, 2009, 2012 und 2016, Mutter von vier Kindern. Abschlussarbeit »Zur Dialektik von Klang und Geräusch« an der Hochschule für Künste Bremen 1991. Veröffentlichung: »Prozessorientiertes Lernen als missing link zwischen Körpertechnik und Gesang«, in: *Zeitschrift der Deutschen Gesellschaft für Musikphysiologie und Musikmedizin* 21/1 (2014), S. 23-29.

Kay Kirchmann, Prof. Dr. phil., leitet den Lehrstuhl für Medienwissenschaft an der Friedrich-Alexander-Universität Erlangen-Nürnberg. Arbeitsschwerpunkte: Mediengeschichte und -theorie, Medialität und Temporalität, Medien und Historiographie. Jüngste Buchpublikation: *Medienreflexion im Film. Ein Handbuch*, hg. mit Jens Ruchatz, Bielefeld 2014.

Brandon LaBelle, PhD, Prof. an der Bergen Academy of Art and Design (Norwegen). Arbeitsschwerpunkte: Klangkultur, Stimme und die Politik des Zu/Hörens. Jüngste Publikationen: *Background Noise: Perspectives on Sound Art*, London 2015, *Room Tone*, Berlin, 2016. http://www.brandonlabelle.net/

Thomas Martinec, PD Dr. phil., ist Akademischer Rat am Institut für Germanistik der Universität Regensburg. Arbeitsschwerpunkte: Musikalische Poetik, Literatur der Aufklärung, Tragödientheorie. In Vorbereitung: *Musikalische Poetologien um 1900. George, Hofmannsthal, Rilke*.

Sylvia Mieszkowski, PD Dr. phil., derzeit Gastprofessorin an der Universität Wien, ist Anglistin. Arbeitsschwerpunkte: Viktorianische und Neo-Viktorianische Literatur, Kulturanalyse, Gender Studies und Queer Theory, Sound Studies, zeitgenössische Kurzgeschichtenforschung. Jüngste

Buchpublikation: *Sound Effects: The Object Voice in English Fiction*, hg. mit Jorge Sacido-Romero, Leiden 2015.

Anthony Moore, Prof. für Medien an der Kunsthochschule Köln. Arbeitsschwerpunkte: Recording and Live performances of experimental electronics, analogue deconstruction of the voice and performed text. Recent works: Concerts in Berlin, Cologne and the ZKM Karlsruhe 2015/16.

Daniel Morat, Dr. phil., ist Dilthey-Fellow der Fritz Thyssen-Stiftung am Friedrich-Meinecke-Institut der Freien Universität Berlin. Arbeitsschwerpunkte: Sound History, Stadtgeschichte, Mediengeschichte, Ideen- und Intellektuellengeschichte. Jüngste Publikation: *Weltstadtvergnügen. Berlin 1880-1930*, zus. mit Tobias Becker et al., Göttingen 2016; als Herausgeber: *Sound of Modern History: Auditory Cultures in 19th- and 20th-Century Europe*. New York und Oxford 2014.

Sigrid Nieberle, Prof. Dr. phil., lehrt Neuere deutsche Literaturwissenschaft an der Kulturwissenschaftlichen Fakultät der TU Dortmund. Forschungsschwerpunkte: Intermedialität der Literatur, insbesondere Musik und Film, Gender Studies, Biographik und Autorschaft. Letzte Publikationen: »Das insulare Genre: Melodrama«, in: *Gattung und Geschlecht*, hg. v. Christoph Ehland u.a. (im Druck); Herausgabe des Handbuchs *Musik und Literatur* (in Vorbereitung).

Ina Schabert, Prof. Dr. phil., emeritierte Anglistin an der Universität München. 1987-1989 Vizepräsidentin der Ludwig-Maximilians-Universität München, 1992-2001 Mitglied und Sprecherin des Graduiertenkollegs »Geschlechterdifferenz & Literatur«. Derzeitiges Forschungsinteresse: französische Autorinnen des 18. und 19. Jahrhunderts, insbesondere deren Shakespeare-Rezeption. Neuere Buchveröffentlichung: *SHAKESPEAREs: die unendliche Vielfalt der Bilder*, Stuttgart 2013.

Bettina Schlüter, Prof. Dr. phil., seit 2008 Professorin für Musikwissenschaft an der Universität Bonn, seit 2013 Leiterin der Abteilung Digitale Gesellschaft am Forum Internationale Wissenschaft der Universität Bonn. Forschungsschwerpunkte: Kulturwissenschaftliche Fragestellungen zu musikalischen Phänomenen des 18. bis 20. Jahrhunderts; Digitale Kultur und Ästhetik. Jüngste Publikationen: »Eigenzeiten der musikalischen Form. Musik-Wissen im Gefüge der Disziplinen des 19. Jahrhunderts«, in: *Zeiten der Form, Formen der Zeit*, hg. v. Michael Gamper u.a., Hannover 2016; »›Wellenformen‹ – Die Leistung mathematischer Modellbildung für Akustik,

Physiologie und Musiktheorie«, in: *Forum Interdisziplinäre Begriffsgeschichte* 5.1 (2016), S. 31-42.

Marion Schmaus, Prof. Dr. phil., seit 2012 Professorin für Neuere deutsche Literatur an der Universität Marburg. Arbeitsschwerpunkte: Literarische Ethik, Literatur und Philosophie / Wissen, Intermedialität. Letzte Buchveröffentlichung: *Melodrama – Zwischen Populärkultur und Moralisch-Okkultem. Komparatistische und intermediale Perspektiven*, hg. v. Marion Schmaus, Heidelberg 2015.

Barbara Straumann, Prof. Dr. phil., ist Assistenzprofessorin mit Tenure Track für Englische Literatur seit 1800 an der Universität Zürich. Arbeitsschwerpunkte: Literatur- und Kulturtheorie, Psychoanalyse, Gender, Visualität, Celebrity Culture, Literatur und Ökonomie. In Vorbereitung: *Corinne's Sisters: Female Performers in the Long Nineteenth Century* (Publikation der Habilitationsschrift).

Matthias Warstat, Prof. Dr. phil., lehrt Theaterwissenschaft an der Freien Universität Berlin. 2011 ERC-Advanced Grant für das Projekt *The Aesthetics of Applied Theatre*. Arbeitsschwerpunkte: Theater und Gesellschaft, Theatralität der Politik, Performance und Ritualität, Theorien des Ästhetischen. Jüngste Buchpublikation: *Theater als Intervention. Politiken ästhetischer Praxis*, hg. mit Julius Heinicke et al., Berlin 2015.

Musikwissenschaft

Michael Rauhut
Ein Klang – zwei Welten
Blues im geteilten Deutschland, 1945 bis 1990

Juni 2016, 368 S., kart., zahlr. Abb., 29,99 € (DE),
ISBN 978-3-8376-3387-0
E-Book: 26,99 € (DE), ISBN 978-3-8394-3387-4

*Sebastian Bolz, Moritz Kelber,
Ina Knoth, Anna Langenbruch (Hg.)*
Wissenskulturen der Musikwissenschaft
Generationen – Netzwerke – Denkstrukturen

Juli 2016, 318 S., kart., 34,99 € (DE),
ISBN 978-3-8376-3257-6
E-Book: 34,99 € (DE), ISBN 978-3-8394-3257-0

Mark Nowakowski
Straßenmusik in Berlin
Zwischen Lebenskunst und Lebenskampf.
Eine musikethnologische Feldstudie

April 2016, 450 S., kart., zahlr. Abb., 34,99 € (DE),
ISBN 978-3-8376-3385-6
E-Book: 34,99 € (DE), ISBN 978-3-8394-3385-0

Leseproben, weitere Informationen und Bestellmöglichkeiten
finden Sie unter www.transcript-verlag.de

Musikwissenschaft

Frédéric Döhl, Daniel Martin Feige (Hg.)
Musik und Narration
Philosophische und
musikästhetische Perspektiven

2015, 350 S., kart., 34,99 € (DE),
ISBN 978-3-8376-2730-5
E-Book: 34,99 € (DE), ISBN 978-3-8394-2730-9

Dietrich Helms, Thomas Phleps (Hg.)
Speaking in Tongues
Pop lokal global

2015, 218 S., kart., 22,99 € (DE),
ISBN 978-3-8376-3224-8
E-Book: 20,99 € (DE), ISBN 978-3-8394-3224-2

Philipp Hannes Marquardt
Raplightenment
Aufklärung und HipHop im Dialog

2015, 314 S., kart., 34,99 € (DE),
ISBN 978-3-8376-3253-8
E-Book: 34,99 € (DE), ISBN 978-3-8394-3253-2

Leseproben, weitere Informationen und Bestellmöglichkeiten
finden Sie unter www.transcript-verlag.de